WOMEN IN HIGHER EDUCATION

Advisory Board

WOMEN IN HIGHER EDUCATION

An Encyclopedia

Ana M. Martínez Alemán
and Kristen A. Renn, Editors

A B C CLIO

Santa Barbara, California
Denver, Colorado
Oxford, England

Library of Congress Cataloging-in-Publication Data
Women in higher education : an encyclopedia / Ana M. Martínez Alemán and Kristen A. Renn, editors.
p. cm.
Includes bibliographical references and index.
ISBN 1-57607-614-8 (alk. paper)
1. Women in higher education—United States—Encyclopedia. I. Martínez Alemán, Ana M. II. Renn, Kristen A.
LC1569 .W66 2002
78.1'982'03—dc21
2002011570

07 06 05 04 03 02 10 9 8 7 6 5 4 3 2 1 (cloth)

ABC-CLIO, Inc.
130 Cremona Drive, P.O. Box 1911
Santa Barbara, California 93116-1911

This book is also available on the World Wide Web as an e-book. Visit www.abc-clio.com for details.

This book is printed on acid-free paper
Manufactured in the United States of America

CONTENTS

Contributors

Vivyan C. Adair
Hamilton College
Hamilton, New York

Elizabeth J. Allan
University of Maine
Orono, Maine

Marilyn J. Amey
Michigan State University
Lansing, Michigan

Janni L. Aragon
University of California, Riverside
Riverside, California

Karen D. Arnold
Boston College
Boston, Massachusetts

Helen S. Astin
University of California, Los Angeles
Los Angeles, California

Benjamin Baez
Georgia State University
Atlanta, Georgia

Roberta Malee Bassett
Boston College
Boston, Massachusetts

Marcia B. Baxter Magolda
Miami University
Miami, Ohio

Kay Beaver
Kent State University
Kent, Ohio

Elizabeth María Béjar
Boston College
Boston, Massachusetts

Estela M. Bensimón
University of Southern California
Los Angeles, California

Debra J. Blanke
Ohio State University
Columbus, Ohio

Kalina M. Brabeck
University of Texas, Austin
Austin, Texas

Mary M. Brabeck
Boston College
Boston, Massachusetts

Felecia M. Briscoe
University of Texas, San Antonio
San Antonio, Texas

Ellen M. Broido
Bowling Green State University
Bowling Green, Ohio

Alyssa N. Bryant
University of California, Los Angeles
Los Angeles, California

Sandra S. Butler
University of Maine
Orono, Maine

Toni Calasanti
Virginia Tech
Richmond, Virginia

Katy Campbell
University of Alberta
Calgary, Alberta, Canada

Tiffany Gayle Chenault
Virginia Tech
Richmond, Virginia

Pamela Merchant Christian
Azusa Pacific University
Azusa, California

Dana E. Christman
Northwest Missouri State University
Maryville, Missouri

Joanne E. Cooper
University of Hawaii, Manoa
Honolulu, Hawaii

Elizabeth G. Creamer
Virginia Tech
Richmond, Virginia

Christine M. Cress
Portland State University
Portland, Oregon

Gypsy M. Denzine
Northern Arizona University
Flagstaff, Arizona

Luisa S. Deprez
University of Southern Maine
Portland, Maine

Myrna Cherkoss Donahoe
California State University, Long Beach
Long Beach, California

Pamela L. Eddy
Central Michigan University
Mount Pleasant, Michigan

Cassandra P. Evans
Fort Valley State University
Fort Valley, Georgia

Jane Fried
Central Connecticut State University
New Britain, Connecticut

Shannon K. Gilmartin
University of California, Los Angeles
Los Angeles, California

Betty J. Glass
University of Nevada, Reno
Reno, Nevada

Judith Glazer-Raymo
Long Island University
Long Island, New York

Roger Geertz González
Pennsylvania State University
University Park, Pennsylvania

Marilyn L. Grady
University of Nebraska, Lincoln
Lincoln, Nebraska

Florence Guido-DiBrito
University of Northern Colorado
Greeley, Colorado

Linda Serra Hagedorn
University of Southern California
Los Angeles, California

Lee Scherer Hawthorne
University of Maryland, Baltimore County
Baltimore, Maryland

Patricia Helland
Vanderbilt University
Nashville, Tennessee

LuAnn Hiniker
Southern Illinois University
Carbondale, Illinois

Carol L. Hodes
Pennsylvania State University
University Park, Pennsylvania

Janet M. Holdsworth
University of Minnesota
Minneapolis, Minnesota

Lori M. Ideta
University of Hawaii, Manoa
Honolulu, Hawaii

Lynn T. Inoshita
University of Hawaii, Manoa
Honolulu, Hawaii

Mary Lou Jackson
Boston College
Boston, Massachusetts

Stacy A. Jacob
Indiana University
Bloomington, Indiana

Laurel Jeris
Northern Illinois University
DeKalb, Illinois

Christine L. Jocoy
Pennsylvania State University
University Park, Pennsylvania

Barbara J. Johnson
University of New Orleans
New Orleans, Louisiana

Linda K. Johnsrud
University of Hawaii, Manoa
Honolulu, Hawaii

Jean V. Kartje
Loyola University
Chicago, Illinois

Jeffrey Kealing
University of Southern California
Los Angeles, California

Kimberly Lenease King
Auburn University
Auburn, Alabama

Shawn Ladda
Manhattan College
New York, New York

Berta Vigil Laden
OISE/University of Toronto
Toronto, Ontario, Canada

Emily Langdon
Chatham College
Chatham, North Carolina

Steven J. Leider
University of California, Los Angeles
Los Angeles, California

Jennifer Lindholm
University of California, Los Angeles
Los Angeles, California

Courtney A. Little
Carnegie Mellon University
Pittsburgh, Pennsylvania

John Wesley Lowery
University of South Carolina
Columbia, South Carolina

Reitumetse Obakeng Mabokela
Michigan State University
East Lansing, Michigan

Eleanor MacDonald
Queens University
Kingston, Ontario, Canada

Frances A. Maher
Wheaton College
Norton, Massachusetts

Kerry Brian Melear
Council for Education Policy Research, Florida Legislature
Tallahassee, Florida

Laura Marie Micheletti
University of North Carolina
Raleigh-Durham, North Carolina

Estelle Miller
Kingsboro Community College, City University of New York
Brooklyn, New York

Thalia M. Mulvihill
Ball State University
Muncie, Indiana

Jana Nidiffer
University of Michigan
Ann Arbor, Michigan

Samantha J. Ortiz
University of Richmond
Richmond, Virginia

Linda C. Pacifici
Appalachian State University
Boone, North Carolina

Laura Perna
University of Maryland
College Park, Maryland

Tess Pierce
University of Denver
Denver, Colorado

Susan M. Pliner
Mount Holyoke College
South Hadley, Massachusetts

Francesca B. Purcell
Boston College
Boston, Massachusetts

Shaireen Rasheed
Long Island University
Long Island, New York

Jeanette Reichmoth
Harvard University
Cambridge, Massachusetts

Anita Tijerina Revilla
University of California, Los Angeles
Los Angeles, California

Rebecca Ropers-Huilman
Louisiana State University
Baton Rouge, Louisiana

Vicki J. Rosser
University of Missouri
Columbia, Missouri

AnnMarie Rousey
University of California, Riverside
Riverside, California

Melissa A. Rychener
Ohio State University
Columbus, Ohio

Lynn Safarik
University of Colorado
Boulder, Colorado

Mary Ann Danowitz Sagaria
Ohio State University
Columbus, Ohio

Katya Salkever
Boston College
Boston, Massachusetts

Ronni L. Sanlo
University of California, Los Angeles
Los Angeles, California

Linda J. Sax
University of California, Los Angeles
Los Angeles, California

T. Laine Scales
Baylor University
Houston, Texas

Tracy Schier
Boston College
Boston, Massachusetts

Ann K. Schonberger
University of Maine, Orono
Orono, Maine

Susan L. Schramm
University of South Carolina
Cumberland, South Carolina

Shilpi Sinha
Columbia University
New York, New York

Laura M. Sinnett
Grinnell College
Grinnell, Iowa

Janice Witt Smith
Winston-Salem University
Winston-Salem, South Carolina

Verity Smith
University of California, San Diego
San Diego, California

Patricia Somers
University of Missouri, St. Louis
St. Louis, Missouri

Marta Soto
University of Southern California
Los Angeles, California

Dafina Lazarus Stewart
Ohio State University
Athens, Ohio

Susan Talburt
Georgia State University
Atlanta, Georgia

Mary Kay Tetreault
Portland State University
Portland, Oregon

M. Elizabeth Tidball
George Washington University Medical Center
Washington, D.C.

Sarah M. Tillery
University of Maryland
College Park, Maryland

Rebecca Tolley-Stokes
East Tennessee State University
Johnson City, Tennessee

Diana B. Turk
New York University
New York, New York

Susan B. Twombly
University of Kansas
Lawrence, Kansas

Vernicka K. Tyson
Michigan State University
East Lansing, Michigan

Kim VanDerLinden
Michigan State University
East Lansing, Michigan

Virginia B. Vincenti
University of Wyoming
Laramie, Wyoming

Christina Vogt
University of Southern California
Los Angeles, California

MaryBeth Walpole
Rowan State University
Glassboro, New Jersey

Kelly Ward
Oklahoma State University
Stillwater, Oklahoma

Jennifer Weisman
Columbia University (Barnard)
New York, New York

Amy E. Wells
University of New Orleans
New Orleans, Louisiana

Shelly Westebbe
University of Southern California
Los Angeles, California

Evangeline Wheeler
Towson State University
Towson, Maryland

Lisa E. Wolf-Wendel
University of Kansas
Lawrence, Kansas

Faith I. Womack
University of Southern California
Los Angeles, California

Rochelle L. Woods
University of Michigan
Ann Arbor, Michigan

Tara J. Yosso
University of California, Santa Barbara
Santa Barbara, California

Foreword

New ground for women was broken in 1989 by *Educating the Majority: Women Challenge Tradition in Higher Education,* a publication of the American Council on Education's Higher Education Series. Here appeared for the first time attempts on a comprehensive and coherent scale to study academic women in context. From the included writings and analyses, the authors concluded that assessing the dynamic interactions between various campus constituencies requires more than studying only those conditions particular to student or faculy. A follow-up volume, also from the American Council on Education's Higher Education Series, titled *Taking Women Seriously: Lessons and Legacies for Educating the Majority,* appeared in 1999. It reinforced a similar though updated conclusion: "In order to understand what is happening with respect to institutions that take women seriously, one must not imagine that there is any one way to meet the challenge. Rather, one must consider the *whole,* the totality or the interrelated functions and groups of individuals whose actions, beliefs, and energies are combined and interwoven in a multicolored tapestry that is incontrovertibly committed to taking women seriously" (1999, 139).

Now comes *Women in Higher Education: An Encyclopedia,* yet another and more recent effort to bring together in one place many of the disparate aspects of collegiate education as they pertain to women. At the outset, therefore, one might well ask why such a compendium continues to be necessary. The answer may readily be found simply by reading the contents. Women in academe still live and work in a male-dominated world and institutional environment, where access may have indeed improved, but the *quality* of that access remains a critical issue. Further, the included selections make it apparent that there is no single definition of student, college, or faculty; nor is there any uniformity with respect to what constitutes "the" route to the presidency, "the best type" of undergraduate institution for women, or "the most desirable" curricular form and content. The diversity of definitions, intentions, and agendas, now obvious for women, has become so great that it is increasingly difficult to make generalizations that can bring insight to those who are not seeking it or to convince those whose minds are closed. Yet the attempt must be made, lest we miss the interrelated totality, the integrated whole that we know to be the essence, the sine qua non, of what works for women. We do this, being thoroughly aware that the knowledge gained from a half-century of intensive research relating to women in higher education and recorded in this encyclopedia is at best, a work in progress. These, then, are more than sufficient reasons to pause, collect, take stock, and offer this latest snapshot of where we are—of where we have come from and where we would go.

To facilitate the usefulness of this book, the editors have chosen nine major categories for organizing the contents, each preceded by an overview of generous length. Within each category are as few as one to as many as thirty related entries of varying length and substance. Categories that generate no surprise include Historical and Cultural Contexts, Students, Faculty, Administrators, and Employees. Less apparent and less standard are sections on Gender Theory and the Academy, Feminism in the Academy, Women in the Curriculum, and Women and Higher Education Policy. It is instructive to realize that when many of these areas are discussed in higher education writings, they are generally subsumed under headings that bear no gender assignation, yet their expression is surely gender-related. One of the significant values of the present work is the fact that issues that have gender salience have been sex-disaggregated for discussion, a reminder that we have surpassed an earlier time when women and men were simply listed together under unitary categories such as "student" or "faculty."

Many variously categorized entries attempt to provide a look at women with regard to their race, ethnicity, national origin, and sexual orientation, that is, women about whom little research is available but who nonetheless are participants in American higher education. It must be acknowledged that large national databases have only recently disaggregated their data in ways that make such research possible. Indeed, it is important to recall that it was not until 1977 that the *AAUP Bulletin* provided sex-disaggregated data for faculty (number, rank, and salary), thereby making possible the first research dealing with women faculty as distinct from men on a national scale. Thus, although the present volume provides an ongoing if sometimes sketchy look at women in American higher education who identify themselves as black, Native American, biracial/biethnic, Latina, African American, Asian American, and lesbian, at some time in the future what has been included here will serve as important benchmarks for subsequent research and understanding, even as *Educating the Majority* has served for the present volume.

The "Historical and Cultural Contexts Overview" presents well the reality that American higher education is still a male-dominated institution with respect to rewards and renown. Many research reports document this fact of male domination, even as current commentators regularly opine that because women's access has improved, there is no longer a "problem." Yet as the overview reinforces, the critical issue is the *quality* of that access. Subtopics are primarily concerned with students and include more modest discussions of women in other constituencies of the academy, such as faculty, administrators, trustees, and alumnae. However, there is a richness of collegiate types presented that includes not only traditionally coeducational institutions but also "change colleges"—colleges originally admitting one sex only but now admitting students of the other sex as well; black female colleges and historically black colleges and universities; Hispanic-serving institutions; an exemplar of a church-related college; community colleges; military colleges, including the federal service academies;

tribal colleges; and women's colleges. How vast are the ways we now type our institutions! All of which should make it obvious that "*the* form of schooling . . . *most* beneficial to college women" is irrelevant (italics added for emphasis), for it assumes a common identity for all women. Although this section moves us forward another increment, we shall have to wait for the next compilation to learn more about the importance of woman-affirming mission statements, progress of women into the ranks of trustees and regents, and institutional responses to part-time women, both in terms of policies and services.

The overview on women students tacitly includes principally undergraduate women of traditional age. Most of the entries in this section relate to institutional services, curricular and developmental issues, and athletics for what once was the typical undergraduate woman. Clearly, it is important to consider the *whole* and the ways in which the several constituencies interact with one another, eventually affecting all members of the community.

Several entries deserve special kudos. In the section "Women and Higher Education Policy," "Affirmative Action and Employment," though brief, is helpful by virtue of the factual material presented as well as its insight that the debate has not and may never come to an end. This perspective is well worth contemplating as energies are gathered for those efforts that have greater chance of producing measurable results for women. Similarly, "Gender Inequality" lists numbers and percentages of women students by race and ethnicity, women in the professoriat (including tenure and salaries), and women in academic leadership (deans, presidents, and trustees). The numbers speak for themselves, with explicit conclusions left to the reader. A major work on Title IX may be found here as well, possibly the most thorough and articulate review of this topic to be so readily accessible. It reminds us that although controversy over Title IX may never cease, it will nonetheless "continue to promote small, incremental changes for women for decades to come."

In the section "Women in the Curriculum," "Medical Education," is thoughtful and on target. Among the entries in the section "Women Administrators," "Leadership in Roman Catholic Institutions" brings forward information frequently overlooked. An entry titled "Feminist Pedagogy" in the section on "Feminism in the Academy" is thoughtful, challenging, and substantive. The entry "Salaries" in the section on "Women Faculty" is refreshing in that it presents some data graphically, a pleasing change from standard verbal formats. The inclusion of "Sexuality" in the "Women Students" section provides a thoughtful and open presentation of material not otherwise readily available in this context.

Thus *Women in Higher Education* provides a new and fresh look at women in the academy. Those aspects of women's participation that emerge as of greatest importance by virtue of the extent of their inclusion relate to (1) negative influences of continued male domination, (2) diversity related to personal histories, and (3) legal considerations. The pervasiveness of male domination is reconfirmed and reflected in all areas, reinforcing the explicitly feminist approach that emanates from the book as a whole. Women of many backgrounds, both students and faculty, have here a voice that makes the individual, rather than the community, role, responsibilities, the important identifier. Formal legal decisions and actions relative to women's issues are presented and thoroughly documented. The many entries that report some aspect of these three areas of concern are important contributions to our understanding of women in American higher education. In sum, the entries in this compendium gather together in one place the record of the present while also permitting us to reflect on those areas and concerns we wish to emphasize tomorrow, as we continue our efforts to contribute to the development of an equitable and humane society.

M. Elizabeth Tidball

References and further reading

Pearson, Carol S., Donna L. Shavlik, and Judith G. Touchton. 1989. *Educating the Majority: Women Challenge Tradition in Higher Education.* American Council on Education Higher Education Series. New York: Macmillan.

Tidball, M. Elizabeth, Daryl G. Smith, Charles S. Tidball, and Lisa E. Wolf-Wendel. 1999. *Taking Women Seriously: Lessons and Legacies for Educating the Majority.* Higher Education Series. Phoenix: American Council on Education/Oryx.

Introduction

To describe the experience of women in higher education in the United States requires discussion of their history, their impact on the academy, and their current roles and status as students, faculty, administrators, and staff. Since 1837, when Mary Lyon founded Mount Holyoke Female Seminary and Oberlin College opened its doors to men and women, the number of women involved in higher education has increased steadily. With this increase have come changes in the curriculum and extracurriculum, and, most important, an expansion of the possibilities for postcollege life and work for female graduates. No longer constrained only to the roles of daughter, wife, and mother, white middle- and upper-class women have gained a measure of economic and social independence. Women of color—including black women descended from slaves, American Indians confined to reservations, and Asian and Latina immigrants—also have increased their life options through higher education, though they have remained limited by prejudiced attitudes and discriminatory admissions policies, laws, and employment practices.

Women's Participation in Higher Education as Students, Faculty, and Administrators

The alleged democratization of higher education in the United States, facilitated by such landmark legislation as the Morrill Acts of 1862 and 1890 and the 1944 Servicemen's Readjustment Act (also known as the G. I. Bill), opened university doors to millions of Americans who would otherwise have been unable to participate in postsecondary study. Though men originally were the primary beneficiaries of the federal land grants to the states, the Morrill Acts did not specifically exclude women's participation, and public higher education became an option for a growing number of female students. Millions of American men took up federal assistance through the G. I. Bill and flooded higher education in the middle of the twentieth century. Female veterans benefited as well but were such a small minority of the military that this legislation had very little to do with increasing women's access to postsecondary education. In fact, the gains that women had made as a percentage of the college population in the 1930s were reversed in the 1950s.

In the late twentieth century, women overtook men in their participation as students in higher education. In 1999, 56 percent of students enrolled in all sectors of postsecondary education were women. Two main factors account for this phenomenon. First, the majority of high school graduates are female. Second, the majority of individuals who enter or return to higher education later in life are women who have taken time away from education to work, care for family members, or do both. Together, these two groups constitute a majority of undergraduates.

The story of women in higher education does not fit some grand narrative of unfettered progress from no access to majority participation. Female students currently constitute a majority of undergraduates, but they are not represented equally across all disciplines or in graduate and professional programs. And although the absolute number of female students has increased unceasingly since 1837, the percentage of women among undergraduates dropped precipitously from 1930 (44 percent) to 1950 (30 percent), only rising again to 35 percent in 1958. Although the G. I. Bill is often heralded as a critical moment in expanding access to higher education, the effects of the influx of millions of male veterans combined with a national attitude of conservatism and compulsory heterosexuality to depress the participation of women in postsecondary education.

Furthermore, although women have made extraordinary progress as students, among the faculty and administration, progress has been much slower in coming. Among full-time faculty at research universities in 1998, women comprised 29 percent; at community colleges, they were 50 percent. In some academic fields (education, nursing, social work, humanities), women are better represented than in others (science, medicine, engineering, law). Women in postsecondary administration have made similarly spotty progress, dominating some fields (e.g., student affairs) but making slow inroads in others (e.g., provost, presidency). Some scholars believe that the upcoming retirement of the very large cohort of (predominantly white male) faculty and administrators brought in to cope with the influx of war veterans in the mid-1900s will provide an excellent opportunity for women finally to break the "glass ceiling" that has been holding them in mid-level positions; other scholars point to institutions' increased reliance on part-time faculty and administrators brought from outside academe as reasons to withhold optimism. It is indisputable, however, that opportunities for women's scholarship, teaching, and administrative leadership are far greater than they once were.

Women's Influence on Higher Education through Curricula, Theory, Research, and Teaching

Women have changed not only the demography of college campuses but also what goes on there. Once relegated to designated "women's courses" or "female curricula," women now participate in the full range of curricular offerings, albeit not always in proportions equal to their presence on campus. In addition to participating in established courses and curricula, women have generated new ways of looking at theory, research, and teaching through women's studies and gender studies programs, as well as feminist theory, research, and pedagogy. With epistemological roots parallel to the political roots of "second-wave" feminism, feminist approaches to faculty work have changed more than those courses taught by adherents to feminist theory. Faculty with a range of philosophical and political orientations have adopted collaborative learning exercises, learner-centered classrooms, and nonhierarchical approaches to teaching and learning, all with roots in feminism and feminist method.

The ongoing debate about the efficacy of separate women's studies courses and programs has kept important ideas at the forefront of academic planning. Should content and method relevant to women and women's experience as learners be integrated into every classroom? Or are the needs of students—female and male—better met in separate women's or gender studies courses? What is considered "core" knowledge, and what is placed at the margins? How can material historically excluded from the curriculum (related to women; people of color; poor people; people with disabilities; lesbians, gays, and bisexuals, etc.) be included while also covering knowledge considered essential for successful participation in a society still dominated by the history and cultures of white Western men?

We anticipate that these questions will persist, as will masculinist academic culture, which emphasizes individual achievement over cooperation and hierarchical decisionmaking over consensus. Although women's and gender studies have influenced curricular content, teaching methods, and research paradigms, they have not had a commensurate impact on the structures and reward systems of higher education and remain marginal in all but a few institutions.

Organization of the Encyclopedia

The decision to compile an encyclopedic resource on women and gender in higher education stems in part from our recognition of the progress and contributions of women in the academy as well as the continued marginality of women, women's studies, and feminist thought. Although other reference texts, such as *Higher Education in the United States: An Encyclopedia* (Forest and Kinser 2002), include the experiences of women, they must sacrifice some depth in coverage of important topics to include the breadth of information relevant to the study of higher education as a whole. We realize that an encyclopedia, by its authoritative nature, risks further reifying those topics it includes and further marginalizes those left out. We undertook this risk in order to create a resource that might serve as an entry point for individuals seeking information on women and gender in higher education. This text is not the final word on what is considered important knowledge; it is instead a selective compilation of topics that have been, are, and will be important issues in the study of women and gender in postsecondary settings in the United States.

We have organized the encyclopedia in nine major content sections: Historical and Cultural Contexts, Gender Theory and the Academy, Feminism in the Academy, Women in the Curriculum, Women and Higher Education Policy, Women Students, Women Faculty, Women Administrators, and Women Employees. Each section begins with a topical overview that is designed to provide a broad introduction to the area. Following the overview are individual entries of varying lengths, arranged alphabetically by subject heading. Each entry contains a bibliography of print and electronic resources for further information, and most entries include cross-references to other entries that may be of interest to the reader. Following the nine content sections are an appendix of Women's Studies Research Resources and a bibliography of all sources noted in individual entries. To orient the reader, we include here an introduction to the nine sections.

"Historical and Cultural Contexts" is intended to provide an introduction to the historical and sociological study of women and gender issues in higher education in the United States. Jana Nidiffer's overview traces women's participation in U.S. higher education from its beginnings. Individual entries describe the unique histories of several categories of postsecondary institutions (e.g., historically black women's colleges, community colleges, military colleges, tribal colleges, women's colleges), important developments in women's participation in higher education (e.g., coeducation), and gender-related cultural contexts (e.g., lesbian, gay, bisexual, and transgender issues).

The section "Gender Theory and the Academy" addresses several key issues in the areas of philosophy, psychology, sociology, and pedagogy. In her overview, Eleanor MacDonald frames the theoretical perspectives presented in the entries. Entries on gender and assessment and the psychological research on sex differences complement entries on gender and race, sexism, and sexual harassment to provide a broad information base for understanding gender theory in the context of higher education.

"Feminism in the Academy" includes entries that relate important areas of feminist theory and philosophy to functions and approaches prevalent in postsecondary settings. The epistemological challenges to the academic enterprise brought by feminist research and pedagogy are discussed. Rebecca Ropers-Huilman commences the section with an overview in which the key issues are identified.

The section "Women in the Curriculum" begins with Ann Schonberger's overview of how women have influenced and been influenced by higher education curricula. The section includes entries on individual fields of study (e.g., family and consumer sciences, physical education, teacher education), women's studies, and the influence of new technologies for teaching and learning (e.g., Internet education). The development of women's or gender studies caucuses in scholarly associations and the transformation of the curriculum are treated in individual entries as well.

Policy has had a significant influence on women's participation in higher education. "Women and Higher Education Policy" addresses important policy developments (e.g., Title IX, affirmative action, welfare-related education policies), legal issues, students' rights, and gender inequality. Vivyan Adair's overview takes a historical approach and analyzes the impact of policy on women in postsecondary settings. Women participate in higher education as students, faculty, administrators, and other institutional employees (e.g., clerical and technical workers). Several important issues cut across these roles (e.g., the influence of race and ethnicity, campus climate) but tend to affect women differently, depending on their institutional role. There are also unique gender-related issues relevant to each role. We have therefore divided the four groups (students, faculty, administrators, other employees) into separate sections.

Florence Guido-DiBrito provides the overview to the section "Women Students," addressing their participation and status in higher education, developmental issues, and diversity. The section includes entries related to what women do as students (e.g., activism, athletics, black sororities, co-curricular activities), their academic experiences (e.g., classroom climate, graduate and professional education, persistence, women students in the sciences), development (e.g., identity, sociocultural, or cognitive and epistemological development), and the unique experiences of women from different backgrounds (e.g., African American, American Indian, Asian American, Latina, Jewish). This section also includes entries on issues important though not unique to women, such as curricular and professional choices, sexual assault, and service learning.

The section "Women Faculty" similarly addresses topics that are specifically gendered (e.g., campus climate, sex discrimination, women of color at predominantly white institutions) and those that are common to faculty life yet are experienced in gendered terms (e.g., disciplinary socialization, evaluation, hiring, research, teaching, tenure and promotion, unionization). Entries include a discussion of racial and ethnic diversity among women faculty, as well as the history and status of lesbian and bisexual faculty. In her overview to this section, Joanne Cooper reviews the key issues and concerns.

Susan Twombly and Vicki J. Rosser's overview for "Women Administrators" introduces several important topics, including women's leadership. Entries in the section describe the experiences and status of racially and ethnically diverse women administrators, as well as critical issues in postsecondary administration as viewed through the lens of women and gender (e.g., administrative ethics, career mobility, leadership, the presidency).

The section "Women Employees" is the shortest in the encyclopedia. We include in the category "employees" those individuals who work in support positions on campus; they are the clerical, technical, police and security, maintenance, and other workers who facilitate the work of faculty and administrators. Often though not always unionized, these employees have received little attention by higher education researchers, and issues related to gender or women in this category have received even less. In their overview, Linda Johnsrud and Lynn T. Inoshita summarize what is known about women's experience and status as employees in postsecondary education. An entry on unionization of higher education employees (other than faculty) completes this section of the book.

Following the nine major sections, we have included data relating to women's experience in higher education, a comprehensive appendix of women's studies resources, and a bibliography of print and electronic sources for further reading.

Conclusion

An encyclopedia is meant to convey essential information about an area of interest to a broad audience, including experienced scholars, students, and first-time inquirers. An encyclopedia should be broad enough to provide entry to a subject through a wide variety of topics yet deep enough to provide detailed information on those topics. An encyclopedia also provides users with resources for further exploration of topics of interest. In planning and editing this volume, we have attempted to meet each of these standards by creating a comprehensive source of information and resources related to women in higher education in the United States.

To be sure, any edited book betrays the knowledge, biases, and epistemological preferences of its editors. This encyclopedia is no different in that respect. Although we have consulted many colleagues from a wide range of specializations, viewpoints, and backgrounds to develop an entry list that covers the landscape of research and knowledge in the area of women in U.S. higher education, we know that there are important topics that are not accounted for in this encyclopedia. We also know that our decision to organize the contents into the nine sections described above constructs artificial divisions of knowledge that reify the rigid disciplinary boundaries that many women's studies scholars, among others, advocate abandoning. Nevertheless, in an effort to assist the reader in locating information and to provide depth as well as breadth in content, we have organized the book into what we believe are meaningful, if constructed, categories.

Where we have left gaps in information or topics not addressed, we encourage readers to consult other reference sources related to women, higher education, or both. As women students, staff, faculty, and administrators continue to take and make their place in American higher education, so changes the academy. New data will continue to emerge as a consequence of women's participation in higher education, and as such, this encyclopedia endeavors to serve as both a historical marker and foundation for future study.

Acknowledgments

We are grateful for the support and contributions of the many women scholars who have authored entries and overviews. Our thanks also go to James J. F. Forest, Kevin Kinser, and Matthew Prentice. Most importantly, we are especially appreciative of Francesca B. Purcell, our research assistant, whose dedication to the quality of the project was admirable and complete.

Ana M. Martínez Alemán
and Kristen A. Renn

Part 1

HISTORICAL AND CULTURAL CONTEXTS

Overview

Today women of all ages and backgrounds are part of every aspect of higher education. They comprise the majority of undergraduate students and represent significant numbers of graduate students, faculty members, and administrators. Women are found in every discipline, even those historically reserved for men, such as engineering and medicine. Women are part of every type of institution, including elite public and private research universities, four-year colleges, community colleges, and specialized institutions such as military academies, tribal colleges, and historically black colleges and universities (HBCUs). Women are educated in and leaders of both secular and religious institutions. There is no doubt that the contemporary status of women is better than it has been in the almost 400 years of American higher education. Yet only a cautious optimism is called for.

There are several "prestige hierarchies" that exist within higher education, and within them women are better represented at the lower levels of the hierarchy than at the top. For example, one prestige hierarchy exists among institutional types, in which elite research universities are generally more prestigious than baccalaureate (four-year) and community colleges. Thus, women are better represented among the faculty and leadership of the four- and two-year institutions than the research universities. Similarly, women hold fewer full professor positions than assistant professor and lecturer slots; are more likely to be deans of schools of education or nursing than medicine or law; and are underrepresented in all levels of basic science, technology, business, and engineering departments. It was not until 2001 that an African American woman, Ruth Simmons, became the president of a former colonial college and Ivy League institution—Brown University. White women still do have not parity with white men, and women of color are not as well represented as white women. This situation, known as "the higher, the fewer," is the direct legacy of America's historical antagonism toward women's higher learning. Thus, a brief description of the social and institutional constraints placed on women's education during the formative years of the nineteenth century provides the context for understanding today's realities.

American higher education began with the founding of Harvard College in Massachusetts Bay Colony in 1636. The founders were men educated in Britain's Oxford and Cambridge Universities and were deeply religious. Their primary need for a college was to train young men for the ministry and for future leadership positions within colonial government.

Because young women were never even considered for positions of clerical or civil leadership, college attendance for women was also never considered. The eight other colonial colleges were founded for similar purposes, and therefore girls' education was confined to basic literacy or perhaps the equivalent of today's grammar school. The intellectual foment of the American Revolutionary era (approximately 1770–1789), introduced new ideas into the minds of educational reformers. A few men, including Thomas Jefferson and Benjamin Rush, argued to expand the missions and purposes of American colleges. They wanted the classically oriented curriculum to make room for more "modern" subjects inspired by the European Enlightenment, such as courses in democratic government and capitalist economics, and for the entire curriculum to be taught in English rather than Latin. Women such as Abigail Adams and Lucy Otis Warren wanted higher education for women, grounding their arguments in Enlightenment ideas of inherent rationality in all *humans,* not just males. Radicals such as Mary Wollstonecraft called for greater political participation and recognition; a cry that fell mostly on deaf ears. In general, however, it was not until the 1820s and 1830s that colleges began slowly changing their curricula, experimenting with teaching in English, and adding any "practical" subjects. For the most part, they remained for men only. Only a small handful of institutions taught women before the Civil War (1861–1865).

Educating women took two forms in the early nineteenth century—single-sex or women's colleges and coeducation. The first institutions were single-sex and were started by reformers in New England. One of the earliest was Sarah Pierce's Respectable Academy in Litchfield, Connecticut, founded in 1791. Emma Willard began her seminary in Troy, New York, in 1821. Catharine Beecher started the Hartford Female Seminary in 1823, and Mary Lyon opened Mount Holyoke Female Seminary in 1837. In the South, Georgia Female College opened in 1836, and Mary Sharp College in Tennessee was founded in 1853. At first, many women's colleges were actually more like high schools in terms of academic rigor, even if they were modeled after the better men's colleges. Eventually, as the level of common schooling improved, the women's colleges resembled men's in curricula and level, that is, some were collegiate-level, and some were not.

Coeducation began cautiously at Oberlin College in 1837 and was followed by Antioch College in 1852. Although these early efforts were quite important, they were struggling against powerful social norms that resisted accepting highly educated women. The religious, intellectual, biological, and social arguments against women's higher education reveal a great deal about the attitudes and beliefs of America's dominant white middle class, as well as the growing importance of higher education to the social and economic welfare of the nation.

The Separate Spheres

The Judeo-Christian heritage on which the country was founded was the cornerstone of resistance to women's higher education. Laws, social practice, and common custom, especially among middle- and upper-class white citizens, were informed by the dominance of Protestantism in early America. Included among Protestant beliefs was the conviction that women were to be subservient, first to a father, then to a husband, and at all times to God. Subscribing to a divinely ordained world order, most people believed God meant things to be exactly as they were. Therefore, dramatic change in social custom was against God's will. Within American society, women were confined to one sphere of life, the domestic, and only men were part of the public—political, economic, and social—sphere of the larger communities. White women were expected to conform to a "cult of true womanhood" that demanded piety, obedience, purity, and domesticity.

As the young country grew and midwestern territories became states, the new infrastructure and increased mercantile opportunities created numerous nonagricultural jobs for men and a small but important middle class. On the East Coast, a greater percentage of the population lived near or in cities. These factors meant a smaller percentage of the labor force were farmers. With fewer people working on family farms, where the work of women and children often meant the difference between starvation and survival, the gender spheres grew even more immutable. More men left the home to work, and the economic contribution of "women's work" became less obvious. The 1830s and 1840s brought an increased demand in common schooling for both sons and daughters. The religious fervor of the Second Great Awakening also spurred literacy rates because many Protestant sects wanted all children to have at least the ability to read the Bible. Even higher education began to change, albeit slowly at first, as young colleges sprang up like weeds across the East and Midwest. Even in the South, where the number of colleges was fewer, it was still a time of precipitous growth.

This poster by Emily Harding Andrews, published by the Artists' Suffrage League c. 1908, shows the link between advocacy of education for women and votes for women (Library of Congress)

The growth in common schooling, combined with increased economic opportunities in business for men, created a demand for teachers; women filled this demand. The revivalist spirit of the era also stimulated a need for missionaries. The early champions of women's higher education at Troy Mount Holyoke Seminaries and Oberlin and Antioch Colleges seized the chance to educate women to fill these two new roles. Middle-class society and the new colleges agreed upon a new social contract. Women could continue their education and find intellectual and professional fulfillment in work that was genuinely needed. Yet their two roles, teachers and missionaries, only

Education for women was one of the planks of the Declaration of Sentiments *signed at the Seneca Falls Convention of 1848 (Bettmann/Corbis)*

minimally expanded the edges of the female sphere because educated women still remained obedient Christian women and nurturers of children.

Grudgingly, male educators accepted the idea of women's higher education as long as it was designed to fulfill specific, pragmatic needs. However, most such educators also assumed that women did not have the intellectual capacity to study the same subjects as men. The revered classical education designed to train the logical minds of men was thought beyond most women. If they studied at all, it should be the domestic arts; "finishing" subjects such as sewing, drawing, or French; or disciplines of minimal rigor and importance at the time, such as science. Only later in the nineteenth century, when science was considered both rigorous and economically viable, were women deemed incapable of scientific and mathematical study.

An expanded opportunity for higher education for women was one of the gains reformers sought in the so-called first wave of feminism. Susan B. Anthony, Elizabeth Cady Stanton, and other women's rights advocates included women's education in the *Declaration of Sentiments* at the first women's rights convention in Seneca Falls, New York, in 1848. In the United States of the 1840s, social and political progressives were likely to support two causes—women's suffrage and education and the abolition of slavery. Most male progressives argued that abolition was the more urgent societal problem and asked women's suffrage supporters essentially to place their agenda on hold. After the Civil War, many feminists were disappointed that women's suffrage was not added to the U.S. Constitution at the same time as the Fifteenth Amendment, which gave African American men the vote. Although suffrage remained a goal, most political energy on behalf of women from the late 1860s to the turn of the century was focused on winning the chance to go to college.

The passage of the Morrill Act in 1862 brought several changes to American higher education, but no single change was more important than the development of a significant sector of public higher education. Prior to 1860, the majority of institutions were private—at least in the contemporary understanding of the term. Although the distinction between public and private was never as cleanly delineated as might be believed, the two sectors increasingly assumed distinguishing characteristics after the Civil War. For women, the private sector of previously all-male colleges remained largely closed for decades, well into the twentieth century. However, a significant sector of private women's higher education, including the seven sisters colleges of Mount Holyoke, Smith, Wellesley, Radcliffe, Barnard, Vassar, and Bryn Mawr, was established in the 1870s. Other women's colleges in the South and Midwest were also founded after 1870, but the growth of women's higher education was actually greater in the public sector, either at the smaller normal schools or the state universities, which were mostly coeducational. As more and more public institutions admitted women, the debate regarding coeducation grew. This debate was acrimonious and long-lasting.

The title of the first novel written by a woman graduate of a coeducational university, *An American Girl and Her Four Years in a Boy's College,* is revealing. The author, Olive San Louis Anderson (publishing under an anagram of her name, SOLA) located her story at the fictitious University of Ortonville, but she was actually writing about the University of Michigan. She spoke of her isolation and lack of integration into full university life: "The girls are not expected to have much class spirit yet, but are supposed to sit meekly by and say 'Thank you' for the crumbs that fall from the boys table." Yet at the same time, Anderson felt her "bosom swell with pride" to be included in such a great institution and knew she was given an opportunity that very few women before her had ever experienced. Such was the dilemma of coeducation. The climate was hostile and the social cost was enormous, but the opportunities were unparalleled.

Biological Determinism and Race Suicide

Americans became increasingly fascinated by science and in 1859 were captivated by Charles Darwin's *Origin of Species.* Another Englishman, Herbert Spencer, became famous applying the concept of evolution to the full range of human activities. Spencer believed that "specialization of function" was critical to both social and biological evolution, including specialization between men and women, each of whom had their prescribed roles. Thus, the separate spheres were not only as God ordained but also were dictated by science. Antagonists to women's higher education, especially coeducation, added a new argument in the latter part of the nineteenth century. In addition to concerns about violating the separate spheres of men and women, opponents used science, specifically biology, as evidence of women's physical and intellectual limitations.

Scientists generally described the body as a closed biological system, where the expenditure of energy in one part necessarily deprived another part. One of the first widely read attacks on coeducation emerged from the medical community. In 1873 a former member of the Harvard Medical School faculty, Dr. Edward H. Clarke, published his views on women's education in a small book entitled *Sex in Education; or, a Fair Chance for the Girls.* Clarke based his views on the proposition that biology was destiny. He argued that women's brains were less developed and could not tolerate the same level of mental stimulation (meaning higher education) as men, so they should not be taught in the same manner as men. More important, however, Clarke linked intense brain activity with the potential malfunction of the reproductive "apparatus," especially if women were overtaxed during the "catamenial function" (menstruation).

Clarke's book was extremely popular, had a tremendous impact, and was used extensively by opponents of women's education. Response on campuses and in college towns, women's clubs, medical schools, reading circles, and anywhere that people were debating women's education was overwhelming. Although the University of Michigan had been coeducational for three years by 1873, on one occasion 200 copies were sold in Ann Arbor in one day. At the University of Wisconsin, the regents of the university used Clarke's findings to justify withdrawing support for women's education.

Proponents of women's education were shocked and angered by Clarke's wrongheaded but unfortunately persuasive theories. M. Carey Thomas, the future president of Bryn Mawr College, recalled, "We did not know when we began whether women's health could stand the strain of education. We were haunted in those days by the clanging chains of the gloomy specter, Dr. Edward Clarke's *Sex in Education.*" Feminists denounced Clarke, but the need to prove that higher education was not harmful to women's health loomed over women educators for decades.

Although many opponents embraced the "ruined health" thesis of Dr. Clarke, others opposed women's education because it was "socially undesirable." Throughout the 1870s and 1880s, the anxiety surrounding changing gender roles was often expressed as a fear of "masculating" or "unsexing" women, thereby making them unfit for marriage. Annie Nathan Meyer, founder of Barnard College, recalled with sadness what her father said when she announced her intention to seek higher education. "You will never be married," he said. "Men hate intelligent wives" (Kendall 1976, 76).

Critics in the 1890s moved beyond the fear of masculinization and "ruined health" of women students. As the nineteenth century came to a close, coeducation was deemed to be causing grievous harm to the larger society. The academic success and low birth rates of college women caused the arguments against coeducation to shift to the slightly different yet integrally related notion of "race suicide." Anxiety regarding acceptable sex roles combined with increasing xenophobia and anti-immigration sentiments. This wave of attacks upon women's education focused on the fact that college-educated women married later, if at all, and had fewer children than their less-educated contemporaries. Critics held that a college education was responsible for falling marriage and birth rates and the increasing divorce rates among white, native-born Americans.

The critics were numerous and prominent, including President Charles Eliot of Harvard College and U.S. president Theodore Roosevelt, who warned Americans that the "best classes" were not reproducing themselves. Throughout the Progressive era, scholars and commentators published articles on the issue. The critics enjoyed the advantage of statistics. Approximately one-half of the first generation of college-educated women married, in contrast to marriage rates of 90 percent for women with no college education. Women who went to college after 1890 had higher marriage and birth rates than the first generation, although they were still lower than the rest of the population. However, in reality, racism and xenophobia lay at the heart of the criticism, not demographics.

In addition to race suicide, coeducation was accused of feminizing both male students and the institutions themselves. It was commonly held that increasing industrialization and urbanization were rendering men too soft. But some critics considered higher education to be the real culprit. They charged that coeducation was responsible for the loss of manly verve. Even the popular press encouraged American men to be more manly, athletic, and aggressive. One response on college campuses was to embrace athletics, especially football, with unrestrained fervor.

At colleges and universities, antagonism toward women became disdain for anything feminine. The movement toward departmentalization as an organizational structure and specialization among faculty members began in the 1880s. As faculty interests became narrower, clear gender distinctions emerged. One common division was the separation of the theoretical (considered masculine) from the practical (feminine). For example, psychology divided into experimental and clinical departments. Theoretical sociology was made distinct from professional social work. The professional schools of law, medicine, business, and divinity were dominated by male students and maintained a social ethos that women did not belong. Only social work graduate programs, newly forming in the Progressive era, had significant female enrollments. Therefore, it was reasoned that establishing more male-oriented professional schools would increase the number of men on campus, and the new universities established such schools at an accelerated rate.

Women did have their champions, however. Supporters of women's higher education included women's rights activists and numerous grassroots organizations. Strong pockets of local support existed, and women's clubs of the era were active campaigners for coeducation. Comprising primarily older women denied the opportunity to get a college education, these clubs worked diligently on behalf of their daughters and younger sisters, lobbing university administrations and state legislatures and convincing husbands and brothers to support legislation that would open public colleges to women.

They Came Anyway

The new colleges funded by the Morrill Act and their sister state institutions were notorious for experiencing serious financial pressures in their early years, from the 1860s through to the 1880s. Most institutions decided unenthusiastically to admit women for a variety of economically oriented reasons; their leaders were not moved by a spirit of egalitarianism. Substantial Civil War causalities caused a drop in male enrollments, and colleges needed tuition revenue. The growing number of students in public elementary schools prompted states to seek a cheap supply of teachers. Women students paid tuition, so they were revenue; women teachers were often paid only half of what men earned, so they were cheap labor.

One manifestation of the antagonism was the inequitable distribution of resources that universities bestowed on women. In general, the midwestern universities did not provide women with housing, medical care, or physical education facilities, despite the fact that such facilities existed for men by the 1870s. Access to a gymnasium was quite important because of the concerns regarding the health and fitness of women students, but universities barred women from the gyms at first. When access was granted, it was usually at times deemed less desirable by men, for example, during the dinner hour. Of equal concern was the paucity of scholarship money available to women. Universities gave little, if any, of their available funds to female students.

Male students made it difficult for women to enter their preserve. Photographs of lecture halls of the era revealed a pattern of strict segregation. Women were explicitly ridiculed under the guise of humor as misogynistic cartoons and stories filled campus newspapers, literary magazines, and yearbooks. "Coeds," as they came to be called, were excluded from clubs, eating halls, music groups, honorary societies, and most activities associated with campus prestige. Unfortunately, it was not only the young students who exhibited their hostility. Faculty members sometimes ignored women in the classroom, refused to answer questions, or prohibited discussion. Occasionally, even official university policy ignored or excluded women.

In response, college women established a separate student culture in much the same manner as adult women in the larger society. They had women's literary and debating clubs, women's magazines, and newspapers or special "women's pages" inside the dominant campus publications, and they formed sororities. Depicted in the diaries and letters of women students as well as in the fiction written by them and about them, these special, all-female worlds were cozy and valuable assets in coping with the daily indignities of life. Despite their obvious drawbacks, alumnae remembered their female worlds fondly.

As time passed, the women found that some men were increasingly receptive to the idea of female friends and classmates. Correspondingly, several women savored friendships and working relationships with men, which again was not a typical nineteenth-century female experience. Occasionally, friendship led to romance for college women, and among those who married, several married classmates. Most women, however, viewed an intellectual and professional career as one life choice and marriage and motherhood as another.

Despite the challenges, women entered higher education in droves and were successful in numerous ways. Women entering college between 1870 and 1910 represented approximately 2.2 percent of their age cohort (eighteen- to twenty-one-year-old women), but they represented 35 percent of all college students. Slightly over 70 percent of these students were in coeducational institutions. By example, they illustrated that women could withstand the intellectual rigors of college and remain healthy. They performed well academically. For example, at the University of Chicago between 1892 and 1902, women earned 46 percent of the baccalaureate degrees but 56.3 percent of the Phi Beta Kappa keys. Similar levels of accomplishment occurred elsewhere, and it prompted some universities to impose limits on the number of honors women were eligible to earn. Women graduated in significant numbers, and several pursued careers in medicine, science, teaching, and social work. Others entered higher education as professors and the first professional women administrators—deans of women, physicians, or health and physical education supervisors. By 1920, women represented almost half of all higher education enrollments, and 80 percent of them were in coeducational institutions.

In summary, the nineteenth century saw the initial entry of women in higher education as undergraduate students. By 1900, women were also entering graduate and professional schools and challenging the strict gender segregation of the labor market. As women earned Ph.D.'s, they also desired to enter the professoriat. But with each step, each challenge to the status quo or each threat to male economic advantage, criticisms emerged. Women were thought intellectually incapable of the most prestigious or most economically viable courses of study and physiologically or temperamentally unsuited to certain pursuits; they were accused of violating either the divine order or social custom, ruining their health, becoming masculinized, harming the Anglo-Saxon race, or feminizing men. Vestiges of these attitudes remain and undergird the infamous "chilly climate" in today's higher education for women. Sadly, racist and xenophobic attitudes brought a different but analogous legacy into twentieth-century higher education, obligating women of color to struggle against the combined burden of racism and sexism.

The Twentieth Century and Beyond

The entries in the Historical and Cultural Contexts section build on the events of the nineteenth century and primarily deal with women's higher education as it evolved over the twentieth century and entered the new millennium. The entries cover the two modes of educating women in the twentieth century, single-sex women's colleges and coeducation; the often overlooked contributions of religiously affiliated colleges; and women's roles in specialized institutions such as community colleges, historically black colleges and universities, tribal colleges, and the military academies. Highlighting key points from the entries that follow, this section illustrates the diversity of women's experience in higher education in the twentieth century.

At the turn of the twentieth century, enrollment in women's colleges increased by 348 percent, and the gain of female students at coeducational colleges was even larger, at 438 percent. By the 1920s, a high point for women's education, female students represented 47 percent of the student body in colleges and universities. The 1930s through 1950s saw the percentage of women in higher education drop to a low of 30 percent, and enrollment at many women's colleges began to decline precariously. In the 1960s and 1970s, there was a dramatic shift away from single-sex institutions toward coeducation, including very prestigious and previously all-male institutions. As a result, the number of women's colleges today has declined to fewer than 75 institutions, down from the more than 200 institutions that were in existence in 1960. Women's colleges are almost all private, and a third of them are Catholic institutions. They also tend to be small, educating less than 1 percent of all women attending postsecondary institutions and awarding 1 percent of all degrees conferred. In terms of geographic location, almost half the women's colleges are located in the northeastern United States, and 33 percent are located in the South. There are three women's colleges in California, and the rest are scattered around the country.

What is of greater interest, however, are the unique contributions and challenges of single-sex higher education. Although less than 5 percent of all high school students apply to women's colleges, the colleges serve women of color and nontraditional-age women in higher proportions than comparable coeducational institutions. Women's colleges are also more likely than their coeducational counterparts to grant undergraduate degrees to women in typically male-dominated fields. Women's colleges are among the most accessible in promoting environments wherein women are taken seriously. The entry on women's colleges analyses and evaluates the research that suggests that women's colleges have a direct, positive impact on their students and points to several characteristics of women's colleges that could be used as a model by coeducational institutions interested in improving educational outcomes for women. Any of the characteristics inherent to women's colleges parallel traits associated with successful academic institutions for men and women students. What sets women's colleges apart from most coeducational institutions, however, is the purposefulness with which the former respond to the needs of their women students.

Most colleges and universities today are coeducational (94 percent), but different types of institutions came to coeducation at different times. HBCUs generally adopted coeducation relatively early in the course of their histories, but Catholic colleges were the most resistant, and many remain single-sex. Ironically, some prestigious graduate schools actually became coeducational prior to allowing women into the undergraduate colleges at the same institution.

Coeducation was spurred by the massive influx of students subsequent to World War II. The Serviceman's Readjustment Act of 1944, better known as the G. I. Bill, actually caused some women's colleges to change to coeducation. In the 1970s, feminist activism and the passage of Title IX Education Amendments of 1972 encouraged coeducation and sought to guarantee equal treatment for the women students at these institutions. The growing prevalence of coeducation did not stop the debate about which mode of education was best for young women. Ardent supporters of single-sex colleges argue that the chilly climate at most coeducational school does a disservice to women, but as the essay on women's colleges reveals, the research has not yet definitely resolved the debate.

Within the history of American higher education, it is generally acknowledged that several Protestant sects founded colleges and that American Christianity played a vital role in the shaping the structure, curriculum, faculty, and student body of early higher education. Members of non-Protestant denominations, most notably Catholics, responded to being excluded from Protestant colleges by founding separate institutions consistent with their religious beliefs. Literally hundreds, if not thousands of colleges in the United States owe their founding to a particular church, but for the great majority, their denominational beginnings are merely historical artifacts. There are, however, a small percentage of colleges still closely aligned with their founding denominations, and as such, they are considered parochial institutions.

Prior to the establishment of the first virtual university, community colleges were the most recent institutional type in American higher education. The first "junior" college, as these colleges were called in the beginning, opened in 1901 in Joliet, Illinois, at the instigation of the president of the University of Chicago, William Rainey Harper. He was interested in turning the very young University of Chicago (founded in 1892) into a powerful research university very quickly. He believed that if universities could educate only upper-division undergraduates (juniors and seniors), then the faculty could focus more energy on research and graduate education. He wanted smaller colleges and a new type of institution to assume the burden of lower-division undergraduate education. Harper also hoped that students "unsuited" to advanced education would take their associate's degree for two years of work and leave higher education. To many on Chicago's campus, including Professor John Dewey and Dean of Women Marion Talbot, it was clear that Harper included almost all women in the "unsuited" category. Harper's attempts to rid Chicago of freshman and sophomore students failed, but his ideas of creating a new junior college caught on.

Junior colleges grew slowly at first, and most concentrated on the transfer function; that is, they focused on preparing students to transfer to a four-year institution after completion of junior college coursework. It was not until the middle of the twentieth century that community colleges began to take on their current form. The passage of the G. I. Bill after World War II created the need for more higher education options. In 1947, the President's Commission on Education and Democracy, also known as the Truman Commission, gave junior colleges a more community-oriented mission and coined the term "community colleges." During the decade of the 1960s, over 450 public community colleges opened, doubling the number of existing institutions.

Although women were one of the intended audiences of the first community colleges, they figure little into the early history of these institutions, which demonstrated no particular interest in women's issues for almost three-quarters of a century. It was not until the 1970s and 1980s, when women students became a majority, that women's experiences as students, faculty, and administrators began to be noted. Community colleges are commonly referred to as "the people's college," "democracy's college," and the "open-door college." Thus it is not surprising that with its commitment to access and opportunity, the community college is thought to be a more welcoming sector of higher education to women and people of color.

Today, community colleges educate nearly half the nation's undergraduates, and more than half of those students are women. More so than four-year institutions, community colleges serve a diverse set of learners with differing goals, needs, backgrounds, and life circumstances. Women now attend community colleges for a variety of reasons: to prepare for careers in vocational and technical areas, to prepare for transfer to a four-year institution, to upgrade current skills, or to pursue remedial or developmental education. Only recently have community colleges added services directly targeted at women students.

In keeping with the unfortunate, "the higher, the fewer" dilemma for women in higher education, community colleges faculties are more diverse than the faculties of four-year institutions. Today, approximately one-half of community college faculty are women, as compared to only 34 percent at four-year institutions. Sadly, it was pragmatism, rather than idealism or a sense of equity, that led community colleges to hire more women professionals. Women are also better represented among the senior ranks of administrators at community colleges. In fact, 22 percent of the presidencies are held by women, but still more women than men languish at middle levels of administration. And women administrators still earn less than their male counterparts. However, women in community colleges gain support through such organizations as the American Association for Women in Community Colleges (AAWCC).

Most historically black colleges and universities (HBCUs) are coeducational, but Bennett College of Greensboro, North Carolina, and Spelman College of Atlanta, Georgia, enroll women only. During much of the twentieth century, higher education was either legally or de facto segregated. African American students, especially in the South, comprised only miniscule numbers of the student body at predominantly white institutions (PWIs). In addition to HBCUs, tribal colleges and universities (TCUs) were established to provide opportunities for students of color in higher education. There are thirty-two such institutions in the United States, concentrated in the upper Midwest and Southwest near population centers of Native Americans. Most grant associates degrees, but there are four-year programs as well. TCUs enroll over 30,000 students, 64 percent of whom are women. Faculty at TCUs are 30 percent American Indian and Alaska Native, which is in sharp contrast to the rest of higher education, where these two groups represent less than 1 percent of the faculty. Women are the majority of faculty at all levels but comprise only 39 percent of TCU presidents.

The last institutions in the U.S. to accept women students were the military academies, and it took congressional debate, litigation, and a Supreme Court ruling to make it possible. Coeducation enabled women to take advantage of the elite training and privileged alumni networks that are hallmarks of the academies. Like the earliest debates on coeducation, the question of women in the military academies once again asked: What is the purpose of higher education for women? Is it a different purpose than education for men?

Collectively, the entries in this section illustrate the history of women in higher education, from the establishment of "female seminaries" to the coeducational public land grant institutions to the admission of women to the elite private men's colleges and military academies. Furthermore, these entries provide examples of the myriad forms of women's higher education today (HBCUs and Hispanic-serving institutions, religious colleges, community colleges, women's colleges, etc.). The challenges and benefits are illustrated not only for women students but for women faculty and administrators as well.

Jana Nidiffer

References and further reading

Clifford, Geraldine J. 1989. *Lone Voyagers: Academic Women in Coeducational Universities, 1870–1937.* New York: Feminist Press at the City University of New York.
Harwarth, Irene, Mindi Maline, and Elizabeth DeBra. 1997. *Women's Colleges in the United States: History, Issues, and Challenges.* Washington DC: U.S. Government Printing Office.
Horowitz, Helen L. 1984. *Alma Mater: Design and Experience in the Women's Colleges from their Nineteenth Century Beginnings to the 1950s.* New York: Alfred A. Knopf.
Kendall, Elaine. 1976. *Peculiar Institutions: An Informal History of the Seven Sister Colleges.* New York: G. P. Putnam's Sons.
McCandless, Amy T. 1999. *The Past in the Present: Women's Higher Education in the Twentieth-Century American South.* Tuscaloosa: University of Alabama Press.
Newcomer, Mabel. 1959. *A Century of Higher Education for American Women.* New York: Harper and Row.
Nidiffer, Jana, and Carolyn T. Bashaw, eds. 2001. *Women Administrators in Higher Education: Historical and Contemporary Perspectives.* Albany: State University of New York Press.
Rosenberg, Rosalyn. 1982. *Beyond Separate Spheres: The Intellectual Roots of Modern Feminism.* New Haven, CT: Yale University Press.
Solomon, Barbara M. 1985. *In the Company of Educated Women: A History of Women and Higher Education in America.* New Haven, CT: Yale University Press.
Woody, Thomas. 1929. *A History of Women's Education in the United States.* New York: Science Press.

Black Women's Colleges

Two postsecondary institutions have the specific mission of educating African American women: Bennett and Spelman Colleges. Considered among the nation's historically black colleges and universities (HBCUs), Bennett and Spelman have long, distinguished histories of educating black women who have become leaders in politics, science, religion, and education.

Bennett College

Bennett College, located in Greensboro, North Carolina, is a small, residential, four-year liberal college affiliated with the United Methodist Church. The school was established in 1873 as a coeducational institution for emancipated slaves and was named Bennett Seminary after New York businessman Lyman Bennett donated $10,000 for the purchase of land and the erection of a large building for a classroom and dorm. Before the school was built, lessons were held in the basement of Warnersville Methodist Episcopal Church North.

By 1879, Bennett was offering instruction at the postsecondary level. The institution had grown so much that it had four departments: college, normal, music, and English courses. Ten years later, Bennett Seminary was renamed Bennett College. In 1926 the college reorganized again and became a college for women.

Bennett offers thirty areas of undergraduate studies in education, the humanities, the natural sciences, and social science. In 2000–2001, there were over 600 enrolled students from twenty-nine states and eleven foreign countries. The majority of women who attend the college are of African American descent. *Money* magazine ranked Bennett College in the top five best buys among historically black colleges and universities in 1996 and 1997.

First graduating class of Spelman College, 1887 (Courtesy of Spelman College)

Since 1930, Bennett has graduated over 5,000 women. Some distinguished Bennett alumnae include Dr. Glendora M. Putman, the first African American woman to become president of the national Young Women's Christian Association; Barbara Hamm, the first African American female television news director in the United States; and Faye Robinson, internationally acclaimed opera singer.

Spelman College

Spelman is a four-year, private, liberal arts college in Atlanta, Georgia. Two members of the Woman's American Baptist Mission Society of New England, Sophia Packard and Harriet Giles, founded the institution in 1881. The women started teaching eleven black female former slaves in the basement of the Friendship Baptist Church. At that time, the institution was called Atlanta Baptist Female Seminary. Two years after its founding, the institution purchased Fort McPherson, which was a former Union training site, for $15,000. The black community of Atlanta raised $7,000 to pay for the school, and John D. Rockefeller paid the balance. In 1884 the school was named Spelman Seminary after the mother-in-law of John D. Rockefeller (Laura Spelman). In 1901 Spelman Seminary awarded two college degrees to black women, and in 1924 the name was officially changed to Spelman College.

The college offers bachelors degrees in more than twenty fields. The 2000–2001 enrollment was approximately 2,000 students. Spelman is also a part of the Atlanta University Center, a group of six HBCUs that work together in a cooperative cluster of knowledge and resources.

In February 1998, Spelman College was awarded the oldest and most prestigious honor society in the nation, Phi Beta Kappa. Spelman was among the top five best college buys in *Money* magazine and was also ranked first among historically black colleges and universities, first among women colleges, and second in the southeastern region.

Some distinguished alumnae of Spelman include Marian Wright Edelman, founder of the Children's Defense Fund; Alice Walker, writer and Pulitzer Prize recipient; and Marcelite J. Harris, first black woman Air Force brigadier general.

Tiffany Gayle Chenault

See also Part 1: Hispanic-Serving Institutions; Historically Black Colleges and Universities; Women's Colleges; Part 6: African American Students; Black Sororities; Part 7: African American Faculty; Part 8: African American Administrators

References and further reading

Bennett College. http://www.Bennett.edu.

Roebuck, Julian R., and Komanduri S. Murty. 1993. *Historically Black Colleges and Universities and Their Place in American Higher Education.* Westport, CT: Praeger.

Spelman College. http://www.Spelman.edu.

Catholic Women's Colleges

Since the end of the nineteenth century, over 150 Catholic colleges for women have been founded in the United States by congregations of nuns. More than 100 of these institutions remain, although many have changed considerably from their original mission of exclusively serving women in baccalaureate programs. Many have developed graduate programs, become coeducational, or formed merger or other consolidation arrangements with other institutions. Their original intent, however, was to provide higher education for Catholic women when such opportunities were limited. Hundreds of thousands of graduates benefited from these colleges.

The development of these institutions needs to be seen in light of the entire American higher educational landscape in the nineteenth century. Until the middle of that century, a college education was available solely to males. Only when such institutions as Mount Holyoke Seminary opened in Massachusetts in 1837 do we see the beginnings of advanced learning opportunities for women. By the 1870s, female seminaries and academies dotted the land, but they did not exist without a certain amount of controversy. Popular sentiment dictated that women remain within the confines of their homes. Several forces converged, however, in the nineteenth century that helped to crumble the taboo against women's participation in the larger society. One was the Industrial Revolution, which brought large numbers of women into the workforce. Another was the suffrage movement, which mobilized women to become aware of their rights. A third was the development of mandatory education for youth that provided opportunities for women to become teachers.

The development of the Catholic educational system in the United States is also an important part of this early picture. Catholics experienced legal and social discrimination in the American colonial period, and as the centuries progressed, integration into the American mainstream became important to Catholics as they struggled to preserve and enhance their faith in a largely Protestant environment. In 1829 the American bishops, at their First Provincial Council of Baltimore, decreed the establishment of elementary schools in which children would learn both secular subjects and the elements of their faith. By 1884, the bishops had determined that within two years, every parish in the nation should have a parochial school with scholastic standards on a par with those of public schools. To accomplish this goal, the bishops recruited priests and congregations of religious brothers and sisters from Europe to establish and teach in the new schools.

Hundreds of groups of nuns were a part of this migration to the United States, bringing with them a tradition of teaching and studying that was unique to a few privileged women but was an established part of the monastic tradition from the Middle Ages. Although many of these groups of nuns came to teach in the parish schools in the latter half of the nineteenth century, they were preceded by numerous communities that arrived on American shores as early as the sixteenth century to establish academies for girls. The earliest was founded in 1727 in New Orleans by Ursuline sisters from France. In 1801 the Poor Clares founded an academy in Georgetown, and in 1808 Elizabeth Seton, founder of the Sisters of Charity, established a boarding school for girls. By 1840, the academy of Saint Mary-of-the-Woods was founded in Indiana by Sisters of Providence from France, evidencing the westward move of these institutions that by the year 1900 would number 662. The successive waves of Catholic immigration, including large numbers from Germany, Italy, Ireland, and the Slavic countries, were predisposing the country to this educational option. Interestingly, many of these academies educated Protestant students in part because of location and in part because of the reputation that sisters had for providing a genteel education for the middle and upper classes.

Georgetown, begun in 1789, was the first Catholic college in the United States, arriving on the scene some 150 years after the founding of Harvard University. Georgetown, like the early colleges of the colonial period that were established under the influence of evangelical Protestantism, followed a classical curriculum and was for male students only. By 1900, there were 152 Catholic colleges for men and only the beginnings of an effort to provide a higher education for Catholic women. As American Catholics struggled to emerge from their immigrant status, they began to worry about the inability of the American Catholic Church to offer higher education for women. The more liberal Catholics at the time were concerned that the lack of such opportunity for women would make the church appear to be against the progressive, expanding vision of women in society. Among conservative Catholics, there was the worry that Catholic women would attend non-Catholic colleges, something that they feared would jeopardize their faith.

The academies sponsored by communities of nuns became the starting point for higher education for women. As college attendance became more conventional across the United States, these religious women saw that they had an opportunity to expand their academies' curricular offerings and increase and upgrade their faculties and facilities in order to become chartered as colleges. The first state-chartered institution for Catholic women was the College of Notre Dame in Baltimore, chartered in 1895 and sponsored by the School Sisters of Notre Dame. Following close are Saint Mary-of-the-Woods College (near Terre Haute, Indiana), founded by the Sisters of Providence, Saint Mary's College (South Bend, Indiana), founded by the Sisters of the Holy Cross, and the College of St. Elizabeth (Convent Station, New Jersey), founded by the Sisters of Charity. Other early colleges were the College of New Rochelle (New Rochelle, New York), founded by Ursuline Sisters, and Trinity College (Washington, D.C.), founded by the Sisters of Notre Dame de Namur and the first of these institutions not to evolve from an academy. By 1930, there were seventy-four Catholic women's colleges in the United States, and that number would peak in 1968 at some 170 four-year institutions, plus a number of two-year colleges, sister formation colleges that were specifically founded to educate nuns for the parochial schools, and professional schools and graduate-level programs. In the middle of the twentieth century, there were more students in Catholic women's colleges than in non-Catholic women's colleges. That these institutions took their educational responsibilities seriously can be evidenced by the fact that as early as the 1930s, forty-five Catholic women's colleges were accredited by the National Catholic Education Association, forty-four by regional accrediting agencies, and eleven by the Association of American Colleges and Universities.

In the 1920s it became evident that there were growing numbers of working- and middle-class young women who could afford neither the tuition nor the travel expenses of the earliest colleges. Thus colleges such as Emmanuel in Boston and Mundelein in Chicago opened their doors to serve commuter students. Rivier College in New Hampshire opened in 1933 to educate the daughters of French-Canadian textile mill workers who had emigrated from Canada. Because students from blue-collar families were likely to seek employment after graduation, these institutions, in addition to their core of liberal arts courses, offered such professional programs as home economics, nursing, education, and library science. A number of the institutions initiated master's degree programs by the 1950s, especially in education, and they typically served both men and women. It was, in fact, such programs that prompted the gradual progression of many of the colleges into coeducation. This trend to serve both men and women picked up momentum in the 1970s, and by 2000, only 14 of the 110 existing colleges founded by nuns remained single-sex in their full-time baccalaureate programs.

In the early years of the Catholic women's colleges, daily life was highly regulated. Frequent Mass attendance, dress regulations, quiet hours, and proscribed study and recreation times were all taken for granted. These colleges also discouraged the establishment of such organizations as sororities, which were considered exclusive and social. However, other organizations with a religious purpose, such as sodalities and Catholic Action organizations, were encouraged, along with groups that supported the academic culture: literary associations, newspapers and magazines, language clubs, debate societies, and dramatic and music clubs were amply visible on the campuses.

The nuns who operated the colleges served as administrators and faculty members as well as monitors of student behavior and dress. The sisters typically lived in the dormitories, serving as housemothers and hall monitors. The boards of these institutions, until the 1960s, were usually composed of the sisters as well, and the superior of the community would serve as board chair or college president (or both). By the 1960s, lay members began to be invited onto the boards because of their business acumen and contacts for purposes of fund-raising. Contrary to popular belief, these colleges (as well as those founded for men by men's religious communities) were never financially supported by the church. Some colleges might receive token support from their dioceses, but on the whole they depended on the contributed services of the sisters (or priests and brothers in the case of the men's colleges) and upon the generosity of alumni and friends to supplement tuition income. Thus the development of lay boards and the cultivation of prospective donors became an imperative as schools began to expand their campuses, improve programs, and hire increasing numbers of lay faculty.

The Catholic women's colleges were not immune to the challenges of the 1960s. The Second Vatican Council (1962–1965) and the decline in numbers of nuns during that decade prompted a reliance on laypersons, not only to serve on boards but to fill faculty and administrative positions as well. This transition has prompted intentional and ongoing debates and conversations about what "sponsorship" of a college by a religious congregation really means. And, as the colleges began to incorporate separately from the religious congregations, they found that they were in a better position to apply for government, corporate, and foundation grants and to participate in federally funded programs. By the year 2000, boards of trustees typically retained a certain number of seats for sister-members, but even that is changing as the median age of sisters rises into the seventies. In most institutions at the beginning of the twenty-first century, the religious congregations retain certain "reserved powers" that include such things as hiring the president, altering the college mission, changing by-laws, and buying or selling college property, among other significant activities. At the turn of the century, many of the colleges developed special offices, often headed by a vice president for mission and ministry, to further the understanding of the relationship between the religious congregation and the college.

Many of these colleges, as the century turned, were in the vanguard in higher education by providing programs for nontraditional-age women and by serving new populations of immigrant or underserved women (and men). Notable are Mt. St. Mary's College in Los Angeles, Trinity College in Washington, D.C., Marygrove College in Detroit, and Saint Mary-of-the-Woods College near Terre Haute, Indiana. It must be noted that not all of the colleges founded by nuns have survived: colleges such as Mt. St. Mary in New Hampshire and Dunbarton in Washington, D.C., rely on groups of loyal alumnae to keep the college name alive. Other colleges, such as Mundelein in Chicago and Mercy in Detroit, have merged with neighboring Jesuit institutions.

Nevertheless, the 110 colleges that remain in the year 2002 appear vigorous and adept at serving new populations, sharing resources, and cooperating in ventures that serve their educational mission. The Neylan Commission (a subgroup of the Association of Catholic Colleges and Universities) operates as an umbrella organization to further the collective interests of all of the colleges founded by nuns. As these institutions continue into the future, they carry with them their long histories of service to underserved populations as well as a dedication to fostering the idea that the life of the spirit is not distinct from the life of the mind.

Tracy Schier

See also Part 8: Leadership in Catholic Institutions

References and further reading

Gleason, Philip. 1995. *Contending with Modernity: Catholic Higher Education in the Twentieth Century.* New York: Oxford University Press.

O'Brien, David J. 1994. *From the Heart of the American Church: Catholic Higher Education and American Culture.* Maryknoll, NY: Orbis Books.

Schier, Tracy, and Cynthia Russett, eds. 2002. *Catholic Colleges for Women in America.* Baltimore: Johns Hopkins University Press.

Coeducation

Coeducation, also known as joint education, refers to the schooling of males and females at a single institution. Although the term originated in the 1850s, the practice of coeducation had existed in the United States since the colonial period, albeit initially concentrated in primary and secondary facilities. The founding of Oberlin College in 1833 represents the beginning of formal coeducational higher education in the United States. Although the first female students enrolled only in preparatory courses, women entered the collegiate department in 1837. Four years later, in 1841, Oberlin granted its first bachelor's degrees to women, marking the first time that women received college degrees on equal terms with men. Until 1870, however, the majority of women who sought postsecondary education remained in all-female institutions. Since then, coeducation in higher education has expanded rapidly, and today more than 95 percent of female students attend coeducational institutions.

The precedent set by Oberlin College in admitting and graduating students of both sexes facilitated the creation of several other coeducational colleges and universities in the United States prior to the Civil War. Small schools such as Hillsdale (1844) and Antioch (1853) soon sprouted, especially in the Midwest. At this time, two state universities also admitted women. The University of Deseret (1850), now known as the University of Utah, enrolled women in 1851 but within a year was forced to suspend instruction until after the Civil War because of a lack of funds. The University of Iowa (1855), however, has continuously admitted women since its inception. Other antebellum public universities had pledged to admit women but failed to carry though with their plans.

With the Civil War came a number of important developments in higher education. Because of the scarcity of college-aged men during the war years, several previously all-male institutions admitted women for the first time in their histories. Despite the fact that some schools rescinded their coeducational policies after the war's end, the trend of coeducation in American institutions of higher education continued to spread. By the turn of the twentieth century, institutions as diverse as Cornell, Boston, Howard, and Stanford Universities, the Universities of Michigan and California, and Swarthmore College had adopted coeducation.

The coeducation explosion that occurred after 1870 can be attributed to a number of factors. First, the rapid growth of the public school system in the years following the Civil War created a dire need for teachers that could not be met by men alone. At the same time, larger numbers of women, widowed by war, faced the reality that they would have to support themselves financially and turned to teaching as a way to do so. As a result, more and more colleges and universities began opening their doors to women in order to provide teacher training. Second, the Morrill Land Grant Act of 1862 further stimulated the expansion of coeducation by subsidizing the establishment of state colleges and universities. Although the congressmen who authored the legislation did not call explicitly for the education of women, neither did they impose any gender-based admission restrictions. Consequently, taxpayers soon demanded that their daughters as well as their sons have the right to be educated at the new state-supported schools.

Third, the nineteenth-century campaign for women's rights contributed to the development of coeducation. Early feminist leaders believed that all-female schools relegated women to a separate, subordinate sphere and, accordingly, that coeducation was a necessary precondition for equality between the sexes. Drawing from their own experience in the abolitionist movement, many of these feminists sought to advance their cause by comparing the status of women to the status of slaves. This approach gained new currency in the years immediately following the Civil War, as debates concerning the legal and political rights of citizens proliferated. The appropriation of abolitionist rhetoric strengthened feminist demands that women be able to receive an education equal to that of their male counterparts. Such continued pressure from women's rights advocates eventually helped to convince scores of university and college officials to admit women to their respective institutions.

A fourth, often interrelated, reason for the expansion of coeducational higher education in the nineteenth-century United States was that of finances. For many schools, the exclusion of women—and their tuition—was not an option. This circumstance particularly applied to newly founded schools struggling to obtain students and funding. Financial concerns combined with tradition to produce a distinctive pattern of coeducational development: more established schools, such as those in the North and white southern schools, were more likely to deny admission to women, whereas newer schools in the Midwest and the West, as well as black schools, tended to admit students of both sexes.

The history of coeducation actually followed a number of trajectories. Historically black colleges and universities (HBCUs) generally adopted coeducation relatively early in the course of their histories. Faced with a lack of funding that stemmed from both race-based discrimination and the accompanying low priority given to black schooling, the majority of HBCUs could not afford to exclude female students and, as a result, admitted women alongside men. Fisk University, for example, which was founded in 1866, admitted students ranging from ages sev-

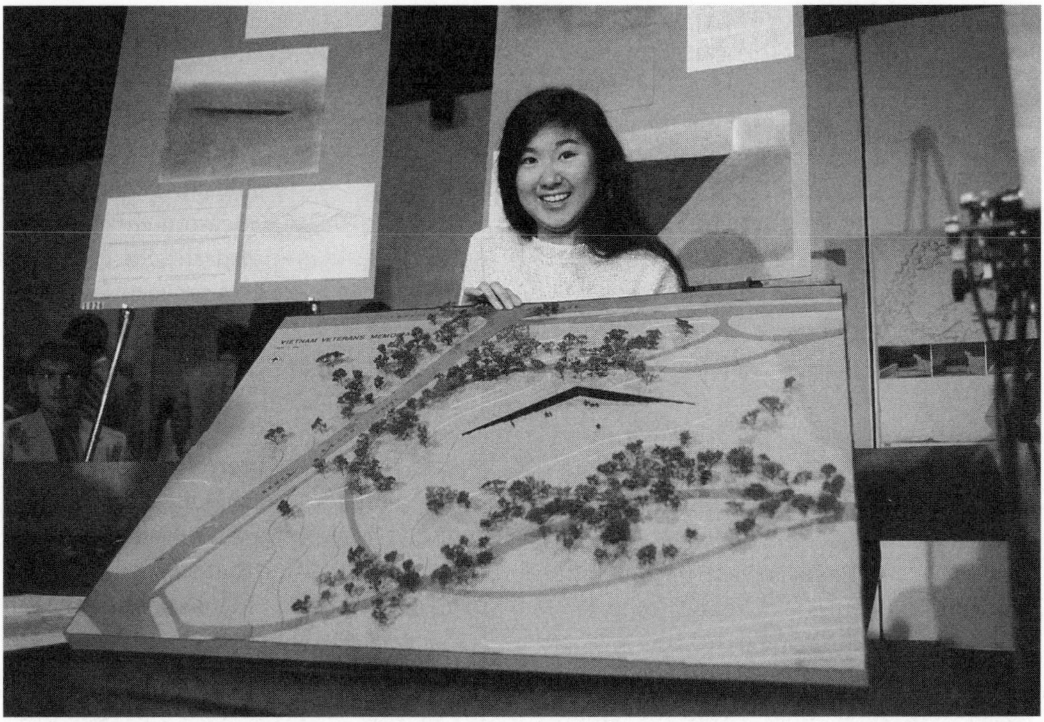

Maya Lin, the architect who designed the Vietnam War Memorial (shown here) also designed the Women's Table, which lists all women who attended Yale University from 1901 to 1990 (Corbis/Bettmann/UPI)

enteen to seventy. For Fisk, as well as for countless other HBCUs, separation of the sexes was neither economically feasible nor necessarily desirable. Although a small number of all-female schools for black women did exist, they were the exception. In fact, the first woman to receive a bachelor's degree from any southern liberal arts college was a Fisk graduate.

Graduate schools also tended to accept women more readily than undergraduate programs, even those within the same institution. This phenomenon can be partially attributed to the relatively late establishment of American graduate schools in general: although various universities had been granting graduate degrees since the mid–nineteenth century, the founding of Johns Hopkins University in 1876 marked the beginning of genuine graduate education in the United States. By this point, the concept of women's higher education was no longer uncommon. Moreover, the success of women's higher education at both all-female and coeducational institutions resulted in a pool of qualified female applicants eager to pursue graduate study. Graduate schools could also accept female students with a certain confidence since the applicants had already proven themselves at the undergraduate level. Finally, the expansion of graduate education during the last quarter of the nineteenth century further fueled the movement to admit women to graduate schools, particularly those schools that were intent on increasing enrollments and numbers of academic program offerings. Yale University, for example, admitted female graduate students in 1892, even though administrators refused to accept female undergraduates until 1969.

Catholic colleges and universities were arguably the most resistant to the idea of educating women, especially on equal terms with men. In fact, no Catholic institution of higher education admitted women until 1895, when the School Sisters of Notre Dame established the single-sex College of Notre Dame of Maryland in response to the Catholic University of America's refusal to accept female students. Women seeking higher learning in Catholic schools would have no option other than these all-female institutions for nearly another two decades. Opposition to coeducation in Catholic colleges and universities, as in other religious schools, was partially based on the assumption that joint schooling of men and women would foster sexual immorality. Moreover, the Catholic tradition of training priests and the religious in sex-segregated convents and monasteries helped to set precedent for other Catholic institutions. The eventual decision to admit women to what were formerly men's colleges and universities grew out of the general concern with maintaining enrollment and tuition figures, as well as the more specific concern among Catholic officials that Catholic women, who were needed as teachers in parochial schools, were increasingly enrolling in secular institutions of higher education. Although Catholic colleges and universities for men began admitting women on a limited basis between 1910 and 1920, only ten of these seventy-four schools had adopted full coeducation by 1940.

With the exception of Catholic colleges and universities, coeducation had become the norm by 1900, at which time approximately 71 percent of American colleges and universities were coeducational. The widespread growth of coeducation, however, did not occur without considerable resistance or reaction. During the latter part of the nineteenth century, anxiety mounted over the effects of education on women. Dr. Edward H. Clarke, a Harvard Medical School professor, was one of the most outspoken opponents of women's education. In his widely read *Sex in Education* (1873), Clarke argued that women endangered their reproductive health when using their limited energies to study; according to Clarke, women were not equipped physically for strenuous coursework. Other prominent educators and physicians of this period articulated arguments against schooling women on the grounds that education, particularly coeducation, would remove women from their "proper" spheres and unfit them for lives as mothers and wives.

As female students proved themselves to skeptics and entered institutions of higher education in ever increasing numbers, new concerns arose as college and university officials became less concerned with the well-being of women and more concerned with the well-being of coeducational institutions. Some campus leaders believed that women would take over the very schools that had formerly been the sole territory of men. Others feared that female students would distract men from their studies and, in effect, harm men's scholarly pursuits. Another concern was that women's presence would feminize the institution itself, thereby devaluing earned degrees, and lead to decreased male enrollment. Consequently, many schools sought to safeguard themselves from such threats by segregating men and women within the institution, establishing quotas restricting female enrollment, or creating separate colleges for female students. In 1899, for example, Stanford University limited female enrollment to 500 students, and three years later, in 1902, the coeducational University of Chicago required that first- and second-year female students attend its new junior college. Wesleyan College (Connecticut) went so far as to reverse its coeducational policy in 1909, refusing to readmit women until 1970, when it readopted coeducation.

In spite of such resistance, coeducation continued to grow throughout the twentieth century. World War II was accompanied by several significant changes in the pattern of coeducational development. Not only did men's colleges open their doors to women to maintain enrollment, but in the immediate postwar period, a substantial number of women's colleges also admitted men in order to accommodate the influx of veterans using the G. I. Bill to attend American colleges and universities. For many of these schools, coeducation became a permanent policy, persisting even after immediate war-related needs had subsided.

The general expansion of higher education during the mid–twentieth century resulted in further acceptance of coeducation. The increase in the number of colleges and universities compelled many men's and women's colleges to admit students of both sexes to counter declining enrollment caused by greater competition. Growing student preference for schools close to home especially influenced colleges and universities to adopt coeducation. Moreover, the second-wave feminist movement once again brought to the forefront questions of educational equity, culminating in the passage of Title IX (1972) and other affirmative action measures that legally banned sex-based discrimination in education. Although this legislation provided exceptions for certain schools that had been traditionally single-sex since their inception, the majority of them converted to coeducation throughout the next several decades. The last single–sex Ivy League university, Columbia, became coeducational in 1983. Today, fewer than 6 percent of all colleges and universities are single-sex, and the vast majority of them are women's schools. In recent years, however, feminists have reassessed earlier claims that coeducation would result in equality between the sexes. Evidence pointing to discriminatory practices within coeducational facilities, coupled with studies showing that women's colleges provide female students with a more supportive learning environment and greater leadership opportunities, have forced advocates and critics alike to reevaluate women's higher education. The resulting debate over which form of schooling is most beneficial to college women has yet to be resolved.

Laura Marie Micheletti

See also Part 1: Military Colleges; Part 5: Title IX; Part 6: Classroom Climate; Graduate and Professional Education

References and further reading

Faragher, John Mack, and Florence Howe, eds. 1988. *Women and Higher Education in American History.* New York: W. W. Norton.

Graham, Patricia Albjerg. 1993. "Expansion and Exclusion: A History of Women in American Higher

Education." Pp. 218–232 in *History of Women in the United States.* Vol. 12, *Education,* ed. Nancy F. Cott. Munich: K. G. Saur.

Lasser, Carol, ed. 1987. *Educating Men and Women Together: Coeducation in a Changing World.* Urbana: University of Illinois Press.

McCandless, Amy Thompson. 1999. *The Past in the Present: Women's Higher Education in the Twentieth-Century American South.* Tuscaloosa: University of Alabama Press.

Newcomer, Mabel. 1959. *A Century of Higher Education for American Women.* New York: Harper and Brothers.

Rossiter, Margaret W. 1982. "Doctorates for American Women, 1868–1907." *History of Education Quarterly* 22, no. 2 (Summer): 159–183.

Solomon, Barbara Miller. 1985. *In the Company of Educated Women.* New Haven, CT: Yale University Press.

Woody, Thomas. 1929. *A History of Women's Education in the United States.* New York: Science Press.

Community Colleges

Community colleges are those public and private institutions that grant associate's degrees, prepare individuals through workforce training and certificate programs, offer continuing education to adults in nondegree programs, and prepare students for transfer to bachelor's degree programs at four-year institutions. Although the first community colleges, initially known as junior colleges, emerged at the turn of the twentieth century, they did not begin to take on their current form until the middle of that century. The passage of the G. I. Bill after World War II created the need for more higher education options. And with the suggestions of the Truman Commission in 1947, the development of community-based colleges to serve local needs became a national priority. During the 1960s, over 450 public community colleges opened, which was double the number of institutions that had existed prior to that decade.

The history of women in community colleges is limited. Because the majority of community colleges were founded in the 1960s, this sector has significantly less history to tell as compared to its four-year counterparts. Even though women play an integral role as students, faculty, and administrators in today's community colleges, their stories are relatively absent from the historical writings on the sector's founding and development. In fact, it was not until the 1970s and 1980s, when women students became a majority at the community colleges, that women's experiences as students, faculty, and administrators began to be noted.

Community colleges are commonly referred to as "the people's colleges," "democracy's colleges," and "open-door colleges." Thus it is not surprising that with its commitment to access and opportunity, the community college is thought to be a more welcoming sector of higher education to women and also to people of color. The sector's historical roots, however, are dominated by male and elite imagery, as well as by a profound and fundamental indifference to women's issues.

Women Students

A distinctive feature of the early junior college at the turn of the century was its accessibility to women students. Junior colleges played a significant role in preparing grammar school teachers during this era. The American Association of Community Colleges (AACC) reports that during the first part of the twentieth century in a state like Missouri, which did not require a bachelor's degree to teach K–8, it was likely that women accounted for 60 percent of the student body—with almost all the women preparing to be teachers.

Today, community colleges educate nearly half the nation's undergraduates. More so than four-year institutions, community colleges serve a diverse set of learners with differing goals, needs, backgrounds, and life circumstances. Unlike in its earliest history, women attend the community college for a variety of reasons, including preparation for careers in vocational and technical areas, preparation for transfer to a four-year institution, to upgrade current skills, or for remedial or development education. The community college, which has been accused of trying to "be all things to all people," has different measures of student success that must take into account these varied reasons for attending.

Throughout the 1990s, women accounted for 58 percent of the students attending community colleges, and the majority of these women attended college less than full-time. Historically, the number of women attending college in the United States did not equal or exceed the number of men until 1978. In each year since 1978, women have outnumbered men in the number of earned associate degrees. Traditional gender-differentiated fields persist at the community college. For example, in 1990 women earned 92 percent of the associate degrees in nursing, 95 percent of the dental assisting degrees, 98 percent of the medical assisting degrees, and 98 percent of the secretarial-related degrees.

Although women accounted for a significant portion of the student body at community colleges, it was not until recent decades that programs and services emerged to assist women students. In the 1970s, some campuses established women's centers, counseling services, and child care centers. A 1974 survey found that nearly 51 percent of junior colleges operated a specific women's program or service. Recent criticisms voice the concern that services for women are seen to be outside the traditional student services structure and thus are devalued by the institution.

Of particular note, though, are the new populations of women since the 1970s who would have had few other educational options than community colleges. Women students who could not afford other educational settings, many nontraditional-age women who had never gone to college or who had dropped out to marry and have children, and first-generation college students were provided with a major gateway to enter higher education.

Women Faculty

Much like the students, faculty at community colleges are more diverse than faculty at four-year institutions. Community college faculty are more likely than faculty at four-year colleges to be women. Today, approximately one-half of community college faculty are women, as compared to only 34 percent at four-year institutions. Those who study faculty view the high percentage of women in community colleges, however, as evidence of the marginalization of women in a sector that has low institutional status.

Most likely, women were hired by community colleges for pragmatic reasons rather than ideological or altruistic ones. With the vast expansion of higher education during the 1960s, institutions needed large numbers of faculty. Although four-year institutions usually hired men, community colleges turned to secondary schools to fill their faculty ranks, with the result that many women were hired. Teaching in community colleges provided women with more status than teaching in K–12 education, and although a community college job was not as prestigious as one at a four-year institution, during this period, it was a major career opportunity for women.

Requirements for employment, faculty roles and reward structures, and the hierarchy of ranks are quite different for faculty at community colleges. Because doctorates are not required for employment, fewer community college faculty, as compared to four-year college faculty, have doctorates. The faculty's primary responsibility is to teach and transmit knowledge rather than to advance knowledge via research. Tenure and promotion are more easily attained at community colleges and are usually based on years of full-time employment. These conditions may create a more equitable environment for women, as movement up the professional hierarchy is less reliant on measures that may be subject to gender bias. Even though much has been written about women faculty being concentrated in part-time and lower-paying appointments, differences in employment status and salary differences among men and women community college faculty may be eliminated when differences in educational attainment and years of experience are taken into account.

Another striking difference on community college campuses is the prevalence of unions, which may create a more equitable environment for women. Ninety-four percent of public community college faculty are represented by bargaining agents. Little is known, however, about the role of women or gender relations in these unions.

Women Administrators

Before 1970, female leaders in the community college movement were virtually nonexistent. Early women presidents of two-year colleges appear to have been marginal figures nationally, and male domination of administrative positions was taken for granted. As one example, the 1960 profile of junior college presidents did not even mention gender. Nevertheless, women were not necessarily powerless or lacking in influence over the evolution of the community college, and some evidence indicates that early women deans and counselors may have had a cumulative and incremental effect in advancing women in this sector.

Numerically, women do appear to be making some gains in senior administration. In 1986, 8 percent of community college presidents were women. This number increased significantly to 22 percent in 1998, putting the community college sector at the forefront in placing women into presidencies. Again, though, as was the case with women in faculty positions, some question whether these advances are simply the result of the institution's lower status in academe.

Women appear to fare better at gaining employment in community college administration than in other types of institutions, but they may begin their careers on the organizational periphery, in temporary positions, or in middle-level rather than senior-level administrative positions. In addition, the American Association of Community Colleges reports discrepancies in the median salaries of top men and women administrators. For example, in the late 1990s, the reported median salary of women chief executive officers was $80,000, whereas men's median salary was $96,000.

As in other organizational settings, women aspiring to senior-level leadership positions in community colleges may face certain barriers. Women's entry into the organization and access to certain jobs may be limited, and upward mobility may be restricted by what some term a "glass ceiling." Women's career advancement in this sector may be particularly important, given the current "leadership crisis" of the twenty-first century. Pending administrative retirements coupled with the concern over the possible lack of qualified individuals in the leadership pipeline may create new leadership opportunities for women. The historical imagery of the so-called great men who founded community colleges may be replaced by inclusive imagery that better fits the seemingly inclusive nature of the community college.

Women Trustees

Community college boards of trustees remain largely male, and little is known about the women who serve as trustees. In 1987, 29 percent of community college trustees were women; by 1997, the percentage had increased to 33 percent.

Professional Organizations for Women in Community Colleges

Women in community colleges gain support through such organizations as the American Association for Women in Community Colleges (AAWCC). It formed in 1973 and is currently organized on both a state and regional basis, offering a variety of professional development activities for women. The main purposes of AAWCC include developing leadership at all levels of the organization, providing information and assistance to educators as they provide services that are sensitive to the needs of women students, supporting the professional development of all women employed and enrolled in community colleges, collecting and disseminating data and research related to women in community colleges, and monitoring and acting on legislation related to women in community colleges.

Women's Two-Year Colleges

Although the bulk of the writing on community colleges refers to public institutions, a small number of private women's two-year colleges exist today. In the 1920s, some sixty two-year women's colleges were in existence; most were private, and many were church-affiliated. During this period, these colleges served as feeder schools for four-year institutions or as finishing schools for middle-class women. As of 1997, only five two-year women's colleges remained in the United States, and they may well face extinction if the patterns of the 1990s—converting two-year to four-year colleges and admitting men—continue.

Kim VanDerLinden

See also Part 7: Hiring; Teachers; Part 8: Leadership; Mobility; Presidency

References and further reading

Amey, Marilyn J., and Susan B. Twombly. 1992. "Re-visioning Leadership in Community Colleges." *Review of Higher Education* 15, no. 2: 125–150.

Cohen, Arthur M., and Florence B. Brawer. 1996. *The American Community College.* San Francisco: Jossey-Bass.

Frye, John H. 1995. "Women in the Two-Year College, 1900 to 1970." Pp. 5–14 in *Gender and Power in the Community College,* ed. Barbara K. Townsend. New Directions for Community Colleges no. 89. San Francisco: Jossey-Bass.

Phillippe, Kent A., ed. 2000. *National Profile of Community Colleges: Trends*

and Statistics. 3rd ed. Washington, DC: Community College Press.
Townsend, Barbara K. 1995. "Women Community College Faculty: On the Margins or in the Mainstream?" Pp. 39–46 in *Gender and Power in the Community College,* ed. Barbara K. Townsend. New Directions for Community Colleges no. 89. San Francisco: Jossey-Bass.
Twombly, Susan B. 1993. "What We Know about Women in Community Colleges." *Journal of Higher Education* 64, no. 2: 186–210.
Wolf-Wendel, Lisa, and Sheila Pedigo. 1999. "Two-year Women's Colleges: Silenced, Fading, and Almost Forgotten." Pp. 43–112 in Barbara K. Townsend, ed., *Two-year Colleges for Women and Minorities.* New York: Falmer Press.

Hispanic-Serving Institutions

The term "Hispanic-serving institutions" (HSIs) is somewhat new in the educational and political arena. Informally, HSI refers to institutions that are serving a large percentage of Hispanic students; the generally accepted figure is at least 25 percent. The legal definition of the term HSI was written into Title III of the Higher Education Act of 1965, as amended in 1992. To be eligible under the Title III criteria, an HSI must meet all the following criteria: It must (1) be a not-for-profit organization; (2) offer at least two-year academic programs that lead to a degree; (3) be accredited by an accrediting agency or association that is recognized by the secretary of education; (4) have high enrollment of needy students; (5) have low to average education expenditures; (6) have at least 25 percent Hispanic undergraduate full-time enrollment; (7) provide assurances that no less than 50 percent of its Hispanic students are low-income and first-generation students; and (8) provide assurances that an additional 25 percent of its Hispanic students are low-income or first-generation college students.

The federal definition of HSI is quite cumbersome and, generally speaking, is only used in the context of determining eligibility for grant status. Once eligible under the federal guidelines, Hispanic-serving institutions are able to compete for grants specifically designated to help the institutions to plan, develop, undertake, and carry out programs to improve and expand the institutions' capacity to serve Hispanic students.

Currently, Hispanic-serving institutions account for approximately 6 percent of all not-for-profit postsecondary institutions and 46 percent of all Hispanic students enrolled in college. That percentage currently amounts to 1.4 million students being served by approximately 200 institutions. These institutions, as one might expect from the previous data, award more associate and bachelor degrees to Hispanic students than all other colleges and universities in the United States. The failure of organizations and researchers to disaggregate data for race *and* gender makes it difficult to know the direct impact HSIs have on women. With the knowledge we do have about postsecondary attendance rates and gender, it is safe to presume that at least 50 percent of the enrollment at HSIs can be attributed to women; thus at least 650,000 women are being served by Hispanic-serving institutions.

Unlike other institutions chartered for the specific mission of serving a minority population, such as HBCUs or tribal colleges, HSIs evolved into their new role. This progression came about largely because of increased migration patterns within and immigration patterns to the United States.

Similar to other minorities, such as black Americans and Native Americans, the increasing number of Hispanic Americans were experiencing limited access to higher education. A lack of opportunity, limited understanding of the tacit knowledge required to attend postsecondary education (common among immigrants), discrimination from both the majority and other minority populations, de facto segregation in many communities, and ethnic and cultural customs each played a significant role in hindering their access.

After decades of limited access to higher education by an ever-increasing number of Hispanic Americans, advocacy by and for Hispanics was limited and sporadic. During the twenty-year period from the mid-1970s to the mid-1990s, while the population of Hispanics was increasing, enrollment of white students at four-year institutions increased at a rate two times higher than that of Hispanic students.

In 1986, an advocacy group was formed by a group of postsecondary educators and educational policymakers who decided that something had to be done to begin to close the gap between Hispanics and white students. The Hispanic Association of Colleges and Universities (HACU) was formed to foster awareness and create a professional association that would have national recognition and a collective voice for strength and representation.

HACU created the term "Hispanic-serving institutions" and through concerted efforts was able to promote the inclusion of HSIs by the federal government into the reauthorization of the Higher Education Act in 1998. They were originally included under Title III and thus became eligible for funding. A few short years later, HACU successfully lobbied for the inclusion of HSIs under Title V, which is where they reside today. HACU was also instrumental in coordinating the creation of the President's Advisory Commission on Educational Excellence for Hispanic Americans.

At its inception, HACU originally identified 78 institutions with at least 25 percent Hispanic full-time enrollment. By 1994, that number had increased to 125. The enrollment of Hispanics at HSIs, both colleges and universities, more than doubled during this time as well. In 1986 enrollment stood at approximately 197,000, and by 1994, it had reached over 435,000. By 1997, it had doubled yet again, as enrollment reached over 1 million students. Not even ten years after HACU began, HSIs enrolled 42 percent of all Hispanic students in the country. Despite these impressive numbers, the disparity in the overall number of degrees conferred on Hispanic students and white students is alarming. Hispanic degree attainment rates of 6 percent at the associate level, 4 percent at the baccalaureate level, and 3 percent at the master's level have barely changed since the early 1980s.

As we enter into the twenty-first century, representation of Hispanics at the postsecondary level is still limited. As a consequence of demographic patterns, cultural and familial cohorts, and immigration routes, the majority of HSIs exists in a relatively few number of states. Most of them are located in the ten states with the highest concentration of Hispanics. The 2000 U.S. Census estimated that there are almost 35 million Hispanics living in the United States—approximately 4 million of whom live in Puerto Rico.

HSIs currently represent 4 percent of all American colleges and universities but form the foundation of Hispanic higher education in the United States by serving

42 percent of all Hispanic students. The most typical HSI is a public two-year community college that is severely reliant on funding from the state and federal government, is usually on a limited budget, and has almost no endowment.

Currently, there is no specific information with respect to the education of Hispanic females at HSIs, but the data do indicate that HSIs appear to do better than any other type of institution when it comes to educating Hispanics in general. At HSIs, Hispanics earn 46 percent of all associate's degrees, 23 percent of all bachelor's degrees, almost 20 percent of all master degrees, and 6 percent of all doctorates. There is a dire need to begin collecting data by institutional type, race, and gender to more effectively understand the role institutions such as these play in educating not only Hispanics but also women and all other minorities. To more effectively assess the role of HSIs, more information with respect to gender is greatly needed.

Elizabeth María Béjar

See also Part 6: Latina Students; Part 7: Latina Faculty; Part 8: Latina Administrators

References and further reading

Bush, George W. 2001. *President's Advisory Commission on Educational Excellence for Hispanic Americans: Executive Order.* Office of the Press Secretary. Washington, DC: Government Printing Office.

Higher Education Act of 1965. 1998 "Amendments" (P. L. 105–244). www.ed.gov/legislation/HE/sec501.html. Cited August 8, 2001.

Hispanic Association of Colleges and Universities. 2001. www.hacu.org. Cited February 27, 2001.

Merisotis, Jamie P., and Colleen T. O'Brien, eds. 1998. *Minority-Serving Institutions: Distinct Purposes, Common Goals.* New Directions for Higher Education 102. San Francisco: Jossey-Bass.

National Center for Education Statistics. 2001. *2000 Digest of Education Statistics.* Washington, DC: U.S. Department of Education.

Vigil-Laden, Berta. 2001. *Deconstructing Hispanic-Serving Institutions: Is Their Role and Function Unique within Higher Education?* Paper presented at the Annual Meeting of the Association for the Study of Higher Education. Richmond, VA, November.

Wilds, D. J. 2000. *Minorities in Higher Education, 1999–2000. Seventeenth Annual Status Report.* Washington, DC: American Council on Education.

Historical Documents

The key documents in the Western history of women's attempts to combat their subordination were largely generated in periods of broader revolution or social upheaval in France, Great Britain, and the United States in the late eighteenth through the mid–nineteenth centuries. In the wake of the American (1776–1783) and French Revolutions (1789–1795) and the revolutions throughout Europe in 1848, women's rights advocates in each country issued their own declarations, rewriting the key documents of these revolutions so as to highlight and contest their exclusion from the rights of citizenship, which ostensibly had natural and universal bases. In so doing, early feminists put special emphasis on the importance of equal educational opportunity, both as an end in itself and as a means to access the other "rights of man," such as property rights and suffrage. Although 1791–1848 is the critical period in which the *Declaration of the Rights of Woman and Citizen* (1791), the *Vindication of the Rights of Woman* (1792), and the Seneca Falls *Declaration of Sentiments* (1848) were written and disseminated, the foundation for the claims made in these exemplary documents predates the birth of the women's movement. Moreover, the legacy of these texts continues into the contemporary era, as documents such as the National Organization for Women Bill of Rights for Women (1967); the United Nations Declaration of Women's Rights (1967); and the Beijing Declaration and Platform for Action (1995) draw on and reformulate key revolutionary and constitutional documents, as well as early feminist documents, in both form and content.

Christine de Pisan, the French courtier who wrote *The Book of the City of Ladies* (1405), is credited with having been the first woman to have participated in the philosophical and literary debate about women's value, known as the *querelles des femmes.* This debate, which took place from the early fifteenth century until the eighteenth century, raised questions as to women's nature, their humanity, and whether they could and should be educated. Following the landmark arguments made by Christine de Pisan, women increasingly championed gender equality (Anderson and Zinsser 1988b, 341–343). Christine de Pisan refused the traditional description of women as subordinate and decided to trust herself, rather than male authorities. *The Book of the City of Ladies* was especially important in that it argued that women's disadvantages in education and training relative to men produced inequality, *not* inherent inferiority.

Early English feminist Mary Astell continued this vein of argument in *A Serious Proposal to the Ladies* (1694) and *Some Reflections upon Marriage* (1694). In the former treatise, she maintained that men keep women from having the advantages they do and then blame them for the resulting "vices." She contested the ostensibly natural inferiority of women and contended that education would improve rather than corrupt women's morality, proposing that women should be able to study in conventlike retreats. She dedicated a proposal for a women's college, which she thought justified by women's reasonableness and necessary for their moral development, to the future Queen Anne of England, later arguing that her presence on the throne set an example for women and made belief in women's inferiority seditious and perhaps treasonous (Anderson and Zinsser 1988b, 345; Ferguson 1985, 191). In the latter treatise, Astell explicitly connected her arguments

Olympe de Gouges, French revolutionary, penned the Declaration of the Rights of Woman and Citizen *in 1791 (Giraudon/Art Resource)*

Mary Wollstonecraft wrote A Vindication of the Rights of Women *in 1792 (Library of Congress)*

against women's subordination to arguments against governmental tyranny that had been made in the context of the recent "Glorious Revolution" of 1689, which limited royal power in England, asking: "If all Men are born Free, how is it that all Women are born Slaves?" (quoted in Ferguson 1985, 192–193). This strategy of claiming inalienable rights or civil liberties on the same basis as men would later become known as arguments for "equal rights."

French revolutionary and women's rights advocate Olympe de Gouges took this strategy a step further in the landmark *Declaration of the Rights of Woman and Citizen* (1791). In this infamous treatise, de Gouges revised the *Declaration of the Rights of Man and Citizen,* which was passed in the summer of 1789, at the start of the French Revolution, so that it included women. De Gouges wrote and disseminated her revisionist *Declaration* in the midst of debates in the French Assembly as to the precise form the constitution should take in implementing the abstract and universalistic pronouncements of the *Declaration of the Rights of Man and Citizen.* She proposed that the *Declaration of the Rights of Woman and Citizen* be adopted as a supplement to the new constitution and dedicated the treatise to Queen Marie Antoinette, an act for which she was later guillotined as a royalist (Scott 1996, 36; Anderson 2000, 70). Though her proposal was vehemently rejected by the French Assembly, her *Declaration* was widely reproduced and read throughout Europe and America and influenced the writing and work of countless women's rights advocates.

Acting as "a self-appointed legislator" (Scott 1996, 36) at a time when women were not thought capable of self-representation, de Gouges challenged the universality of the term "Man" in the original *Declaration* by pluralizing the reference and replacing the singular "Man" with "Woman and Man" in each of her *Declaration*'s seventeen articles, which exactly paralleled those of the original document (Scott 1996, 42). In restating the revolution's guaranteed freedoms as available to women, de Gouges not only included women where they had been excluded but added explicit reasons for acknowledging that women as well as men possessed these rights, making a particularly strong case for freedom of expression and speech: "Woman has the right to mount to the scaffold; she ought equally to have the right to mount to the tribune" (quoted in Scott 1996, 42).

De Gouges claimed for women all the rights men had established for themselves in the *Declaration of the Rights of Man and Citizen* and added a sample "Social [Marriage] Contract between Man and Woman" in a postscript, thus recognizing women's particularity and specific needs as women while simultaneously arguing that they were entitled to all the same constitutional and political rights as men on the basis of their status as individuals (Levy, Applewhite, and Johnson 1979, 87–96). This strategy of making arguments on the basis of both sameness *and* difference is one that contemporary feminists deploy to this day, as the tension between the aspiration to universalistic bases of citizenship and the particularities of contexts and persons is an inherited feature of liberal constitutional regimes.

Just one year after de Gouges wrote her revisionist *Declaration,* the English radical Mary Wollstonecraft penned her *Vindication of the Rights of Woman* (1792). She dedicated this to Talleyrand, who had just written the education report for the French revolutionary government, and urged him to include women in the new French constitution (Anderson 2000, 69). She further proposed that the French establish a national system of universal, publicly funded primary education for both sexes, with additional education according to social class (vocational for the working classes and higher education for the aristocracy and meritocracy) but equal with respect to gender. Wollstonecraft urged Talleyrand to revise that part of his educational plan in which he had suggested that French girls and their brothers be educated together in public schools only until age eight, after which time girls would remain at home (Rossi 1988, 29).

The previous year, in 1791, Wollstonecraft had responded to Edmund Burke's *Reflections on the Revolution in France* with a defense of the principles of the Enlightenment in general and the French Revolution in particular, publishing a pamphlet that brought her instant public recognition, *A Vindication of the Rights of Man* (Rossi 1988, 28). Now she went further by extending these ideas to women. Her primary claim was that with education, women's equality to men would be impossible to deny. Women, she claimed, are born human but *made* "feminine" or inferior to men through poor education. Given equal education, women would be men's equals morally, rationally, and otherwise. Her argument thus prefigured those made by later feminists regarding what they would call the "social construction of gender roles."

Building on the foundation laid by early feminists like Christine de Pisan and Astell, Wollstonecraft repudiated the claims of not only Talleyrand but also Jean-Jacques Rousseau. Rousseau's writings on education were popular with progressive reformers of the day, but Wollstonecraft abhorred his claims for distinction and segregation on the basis of sex (Anderson and Zinsser 1988b, 347). Rousseau contended that men needed education in order to be citizens capable of electing and participating in government; whereas women's role was to support men, please them, and have a morally edifying effect on them. Women, for Rousseau, were emotional and sentimental, whereas men were rational. Wollstonecraft responded to these claims by contending that the apparent differences in women's nature, such as emotionality and physical weakness, which seemed to better suit them to the home than the public sphere, were the *result* of and ought not to be the *justification* for being confined to the home (Wollstonecraft 1988, 40–85). Drawing heavily on the arguments of Catharine Macaulay's *Letters on Education,* published in the late 1780s, Wollstonecraft denied a fundamental difference in nature or character between the sexes and urged that girls should receive the same education as boys—including physical education (Rossi 1988, 29).

In addition to advancing important and vastly influential arguments for equal education, Wollstonecraft's *Vindication* made strong claims for women's rights to property and inheritance, drawing on the Enlightenment and French revolutionary arguments in the *Declaration of the Rights of Man and Citizen* and extending them to women. Just as the assertion of the rights of man was a rejection of the divine right of kings, Wollstonecraft opposed the rights of husbands to control their wives and thus provided an important "liberationist" model of feminist writing, laying the foundation for further opposition to the common law doctrine of "coverture," by which a married woman had no truly separate legal identity and could not inherit or own property in her own right except in the most limited ways (Kerber 1998, 28–30). Harriet Taylor and John Stuart Mill would later build on and extend Wollstonecraft's arguments for suffrage, education, and property rights in Taylor's 1851 "Enfranchisement of Women" and especially Mill's 1869 book, *The Subjection of Women,* which would become one of the most influential arguments for women's rights in the history of the suffrage movement.

In the years following the production of de Gouges's *Declaration* (1791) and Wollestonecraft's *Vindication* (1792), both documents were widely disseminated and reproduced and served as inspirational founding documents for early feminists who came together from other forms of activism, such as antislavery, radical socialism, and religious movements, to form the beginnings of an international women's movement (Anderson 2000, 66). In 1832 the French newspaper produced by female socialists calling themselves the "new women" (*femmes nouvelles*) published "The Call to Women." It was reprinted in the English socialist journal published by Robert Owen, the *Crisis,* in 1833, at the initiative of his colleague, Irish feminist Anna Wheeler, who translated it and appended her own commentary (Anderson 2000, 67).

The "Call" insisted that demands for economic justice and political equality must include women; urged women not to marry unless their husbands supported equal rights; and exhorted women to unite to obtain the common ends of equality, liberty, and the chance to develop all their faculties (Anderson 2000, 67; Moses and Rabine 1993, 282–284; Pankhurst 1957, 109–111). The English version of the "Call" was read by prominent radicals in London, including John Stuart Mill, Ernestine Rose, and Harriet Martineau, and it was subsequently read, circulated, and discussed on both sides of the Atlantic, consolidating the birth of the nascent international women's movement (Anderson 2000, 68).

In Europe, women's rights advocates often came to the struggle from socialist activism, but in the United States the suffrage movement was more closely tied to the movement to end slavery. The arguments women made on behalf of emancipation and suffrage for slaves were logically extended to themselves. Two women at the forefront of these linked reform movements were the Grimké sisters, Angelina and Sarah, who were born into a slave-owning upper-class family in the South and left their home for the North to become Quakers and leaders of these radically egalitarian causes. The sisters were among the earliest American writers on sex equality (Rossi 1988, 282). In 1838, Sarah Grimké wrote her *Letters on the Equality of the Sexes and the Condition of Women,* which was distributed widely in Great Britain as well as the United States (Grimké 1988, 306–318). In this seminal document, which draws heavily on the Bible, Grimké argued for full emancipation from the "bonds of womanhood," or the system of male domination that reduced all but a few female rulers to the status of "slaves." She then invoked well-known female rulers, such as Catherine of Russia and Elizabeth I of England to demonstrate that "the intellect is not sexed" (quoted in Anderson 2000, 123).

By 1848, radical movements had inspired democratic revolutions in France, Austria, and the German and Italian states. The United States was the first nation to recognize the newly constituted French Republic, and revolutionary events abroad fired the imaginations of abolitionists, women's rights advocates, and reformers of all stripes. They particularly energized American abolitionist and women's rights advocate Lucretia Mott, who contended that the cause of freedom was universal and urged the American Anti-Slavery Society and women's groups alike to "take courage" (Anderson 2000, 16, 168). When she decided to visit fellow women's rights activist Elizabeth Cady Stanton in Seneca Falls, the impetus for the first women's rights convention in the United States was born.

On Thursday, 13 July 1848, Elizabeth Cady Stanton, Lucretia Mott, and three other women's rights advocates spent the day together and decided to call a convention. They placed an advertisement in the *Seneca County Courier* and in Frederick Douglass's antislavery paper, the *North Star.* On Sunday, 16 July, they met again to compose the now legendary Seneca Falls *Declaration of Sentiments,* which paralleled the structure of the 1776 American Declaration of Independence to draw an analogy between the tyranny of King George III and that of men who would refuse rights to womankind, thus comparing the American colonists and the women's rights advocates. The declaration was delivered and adopted at the Women's Rights Convention at Seneca Falls on 19–20 July 1848, which attracted about 300 participants. One hundred people signed the declaration.

Expanding on the powerful theoretical strategies deployed by de Gouges before them, the authors of the *Declaration of Sentiments* creatively paraphrased the original text of the Declaration of Independence to survey a vast array of female grievances and demonstrate the irrationality and injustice of excluding the female half of humanity from ostensibly universal rights. Thus, the declaration transformed the original list of eighteenth-century colonial grievances against King George III into a nineteenth-century catalog of women's grievances and claims. It asserted that women should have, as men did, access to higher education, property rights, legal standing in court, the ability to initiate divorce, access to well-paid jobs and the professions, representation in government, and the right to serve as ministers. The declaration also supported a single standard of sexual morality for men and women and made charges regarding the strategies man employed to keep woman from determining her own course, such as rendering her dependent and undermining her self-respect (Stanton 1988, 415–421).

Perhaps most famously, the list of demands included the right to vote, though this provision was quite controversial and was adopted by an extremely narrow margin. Those at Seneca Falls were in greater accord on other demands, such as educational reform and property rights. But although suffrage may have been one demand among many in the context of the Seneca Falls *Declaration of Sentiments,* by the early 1850s, it had become the key demand on the agenda of a growing women's movement, for which the declaration had paved the way. Moreover, the attacks made in the declaration on the assumptions of coverture eventually led to married women's property acts in many states (Keyssar 2000, 38) and triggered a whole host of later women's rights conventions.

The "first wave" of the women's movement in the United States is widely held to have drawn to a close with the hard-won ratification of the Nineteenth Amendment to the U.S. Constitution in 1920. Its text was simply and straightforwardly modeled on that of the Fifteenth Amendment, which extended the suffrage to African American men in 1869. The many early women's rights advocates who had also worked as abolitionists had hoped that the suffrage would be extended to both groups at once. Thus, the parallel wording, though it came many years later for women than it did for African American men, was for some a fitting close to this chapter of the movement's struggle. The Nineteenth Amendment stated: "The right of citizens of the United States to vote shall not be denied or abridged by the United States or any State on account of sex" and authorized Congress to enact enforcing legislation, thus granting women the right to vote after more than seventy years of struggle.

Insofar as many aspects of women's subordination remained unchanged by their enfranchisement in the decades subsequent to the ratification of the Nineteenth Amendment, however, a "second wave" of feminist activity soon brought with it a new wave of feminist writing, this time in the context of the civil rights movement. The legacy of early feminists like de Gouges, Wollstonecraft, and Stanton, who revised and redeployed revolutionary and foundational documents to include women while simultaneously setting agendas for reform, was inherited by these later feminists and is in fact alive and well in the contemporary era.

One such second-wave document was the National Organization for Women (NOW) Bill of Rights for Women (1967), the founding charter of that group, which was formed in 1966. The basic aim of NOW's bill of rights was to secure for women the same rights that men enjoy. Its eight original demands were immediate passage of the Equal Rights Amendment; enforcement of antidiscrimination laws; (paid) maternity leave; tax deductions for home and child care expenses of working parents; publicly funded community child care centers; equal and desegregated education; equal job training and allowances for women in poverty; and the right of women to control their own reproductive lives, including the right to legalized abortion (Chafetz and Dworkin 1986, 168; Tong 1998, 24–25).

The proposed Equal Rights Amendment (1972–1982), which failed to achieve ratification in 1982, is itself an important document in the history of women's subordination. Providing that "equality of rights under the law shall not be denied or abridged by the United States or by any State on account of sex" and authorizing Congress to enact enforcing legislation, the amendment was sent to the states by Congress in early 1972. Although about half of the states ratified it within a few months, opposition groups began to lobby soon thereafter. Only thirty-five states had approved the ERA before the ratification deadline, rendering it three states short of the number required for it to become law (Urofsky and Finkerman 2002, 911).

One of the most important legacies of the writings of early women's rights advocates in the contemporary era has been the appropriation of the form and language of early revolutionary documents and of the women's rights agenda by international human rights advocates. In the Preamble to the United Nations Charter (1945), its members declared their commitment to the equal rights of men and women as part of a faith in fundamental human rights and the dignity of personhood. The UN Declaration of Women's Rights (1967), which was unanimously adopted by its member nations, asserted the principle of nondiscrimination and proclaimed that all humans are born free and possess equal rights and dignity without distinction as to sex. It enumerates areas in which measures are to be taken to enforce this principle, including provisions to ensure that girls and women receive equal rights to education at all levels, equal rights to vote, and equal economic rights (UN General Assembly 1977).

In September 1995, the year of the fiftieth anniversary of its founding, the United Nations held a major international conference on women's rights, the Fourth World Conference on Women, from which issued the Beijing Declaration and Platform for Action. The Beijing Declaration affirmed the commitment of the governments participating in the UN to the goals of equality, peace, and development for all women in the interest of all humanity. It recognized that the status of women has advanced in an uneven manner and that inequalities between men and women persist. It stressed the role of poverty in exacerbating inequality for women and children. It reaffirmed the right of women to control all aspects of their health and their fertility and declared the necessity for women to have a greater role in decisionmaking and access to power in all spheres of society. The Platform for Action stressed the importance of the right to inherit and called education a "human right" while setting forth a detailed set of strategies to improve access to education and training for girls (UN General Assembly 1997). Both the form and content of the declaration are reminiscent of earlier feminist declarations, though there is now a greater focus on the effects of economic development and globalization. But the basic strategies and agenda are familiar ones, and the overriding message of the conference, which was that these issues are global and universal, could have come from the 1832 "Call to Women."

Verity Smith

References and further reading

Anderson, Bonnie S. 2000. *Joyous Greetings: The First International Women's Movement, 1830–1860.* New York: Oxford University Press.

Anderson, Bonnie S., and Judith P. Zinsser. 1988a. *A History of Their Own: Women in Europe from*

Prehistory to the Present. Vol. 1. New York: Harper and Row.

———. 1988b. *A History of Their Own: Women in Europe from Prehistory to the Present.* Vol. 2. New York: Harper and Row.

———. 2000a. *A History of Their Own: Women in Europe from Prehistory to the Present.* Vol. 1. New York: Oxford University Press.

———. 2000b. *A History of Their Own: Women in Europe from Prehistory to the Present.* Vol. 2. New York: Oxford University Press.

Chafetz, Janet Saltzman, and Anthony Gary Dworkin. 1986. *Female Revolt: Women's Movements in World Historical Perspective.* Totowa, NJ: Rowman and Allanheld.

Davis, Angela Y. 1981. *Women, Race and Class.* New York: Random House.

Ferguson, Moira. 1985. *First Feminists: British Women Writers, 1578–1799.* Bloomington: Indiana University Press.

Flexner, Eleanor. 1975. *Century of Struggle: The Woman's Rights Movement in the United States.* Rev. ed. Cambridge, MA: Harvard University Press.

Grimké, Sarah. 1988 *Letters on the Equality of the Sexes and the Condition of Women.* Pp. 306–318 in *The Feminist Papers: From Adams to de Beauvoir,* ed. Alice S. Rossi. Boston: Northeastern University Press.

Kerber, Linda K. 1998. *No Constitutional Right to Be Ladies: Women and the Obligations of Citizenship.* New York: Hill and Wang.

Keyssar, Alexander. 2000. *The Right to Vote: The Contested History of Democracy in the United States.* New York: Basic Books.

Levy, Darline Gay, Harriet Branson Applewhite, and Mary Durham Johnson. 1979. *Women in Revolutionary Paris: 1789–1795.* Urbana: University of Illinois Press.

Moses, Clair Goldberg, and Leslie Wahl Rabine. 1993. *Feminism, Socialism, and French Romanticism.* Bloomington: Indiana University Press.

Pankhurst, Richard K. P. 1957. *The Saint Simonians: Mill and Carlyle: A Preface to Modern Thought.* London: Sidgwick and Jackson.

Pisan, Christine de. 1982. *The Book of the City of Ladies.* Trans. Earl Jeffrey Richards. New York: Persea Books.

Rossi, Alice S., ed. 1988. *The Feminist Papers: From Adams to de Beauvoir.* Boston: Northeastern University Press.

Scott, Joan Wallach. 1996. *Only Paradoxes to Offer: French Feminists and the Rights of Man.* Cambridge, MA: Harvard University Press.

Stanton, Cady Elizabeth. 1988. *Selections from* The History of Woman Suffrage. Pp. 415–421 in *The Feminist Papers: From Adams to de Beauvoir,* ed. Alice S. Rossi. Boston: Northeastern University Press.

Tong, Rosemarie Putman. 1998. *Feminist Thought: A More Comprehensive Introduction.* 2nd ed. Boulder, CO: Westview Press.

United Nations. 1997. *The World Conferences: Developing Priorities for the Twenty-First Century.* UN Briefing Papers series. New York: United Nations.

United Nations General Assembly. 1977. *United Nations Declaration of Women's Rights,* Resolution 2263 (XXII), 7 November 1967. In *History of Ideas on Women: A Source Book,* ed. Rosemary Agonito. New York: G. P. Putnam's Sons.

Urofsky, Melvin I., and Paul Finkerman. 2002. *A March of Liberty: A Constitutional History of the United States.* Vol. 2, *From 1877 to the Present.* 2nd ed. New York: Oxford University Press.

Wollstonecraft, Mary. 1988. *A Vindication of the Rights of Women.* Pp. 40–85 in *The Feminist Papers: From Adams to de Beauvoir,* ed. Alice S. Rossi. Boston: Northeastern University Press.

Historically Black Colleges and Universities

Historically black colleges and universities, commonly referred to as HBCUs, have been established throughout U.S. history to serve the principal mission of the education of black Americans. HBCUs have existed since the 1830s, although their history and existence has often been considered tenuous. Regardless, it is undisputable that HBCUs have succeeded in educating black Americans and contributing to the U.S. effort to achieve equal opportunity. Today's just over 100 institutions continue to serve their central purpose—awarding almost one-third of all baccalaureate degrees awarded to black Americans. In 1998, total enrollment for HBCUs was approximately 300,000 students, of which 55 percent were women (Brown and Freeman, 2002).

Harriet E. Giles and Sophia B. Packard founded Spelman College in 1881 (Courtesy of Spelman College)

Historically black colleges and universities were not founded as a group. They were set up one by one through the work of private, philanthropic, and religious organizations attempting to overcome the effects of a divided nation. In 1837, the Institute for Colored Youth was created in Pennsylvania (present-day Cheyney State University). Between this historic event and the Civil War, a few sporadic institutions were founded throughout the northern states. It was not until after the Civil War, when almost 4 million slaves were freed, that the establishment of HBCUs became more prevalent.

One prominent organization in establishing institutions to educate these newly freed slaves in the southern and border states was the Freedman's Bureau. It first established institutions in Georgia, North Carolina, Tennessee, and Washington, D.C. These first HBCUs were all private, nonprofit institutions, funded without any government support. The most notable was Howard University, founded in 1867 in Washington, D.C. Black women also received support early on from private foundations. Spelman College, established in 1881, was the first HBCU dedicated solely to the education of women. Spelman College, as well as Bennett College, which was originally coeduational, continue to serve their original mission of educating black women. In 1871, the first publicly supported black land grant college, Alcorn College, was established in Mississippi. The Morrill Acts of 1862 and 1890 supported the creation of land grant colleges across the country. In the southern and border states, where the newly freed slaves were not truly embraced, a dual system of higher education was created. A total of nineteen states created separate schools under the auspices of the "separate but equal" doctrine, rather than accept blacks into their flagship institutions. Their creation was the beginning of the educational cohort now known as historically black colleges and universities.

State support for HBCUs was as limited as the states could get away with. The majority of states never did comply with the true spirit of the provisions of the Morrill Act. As such, HBCUs from their inception were severely underfunded, were discriminated against, and lacked support from the public. This scenario continued well through the mid–twentieth century. The same can be said of almost every HBCU—public and private—with the exception of one: Howard University.

As stated previously, Howard University was privately established by the Freedman's Bureau in 1867. After years of supporting Howard University, the Freedman's Bureau was abolished in 1873. Without financial support, the university began struggling financially. Six years later, Congress intervened and presented the institution with a financial gift to educate the slaves it had freed and ensure their endurance as free citizens. The government felt it was fulfilling a responsibility. Support in the form of annual gifts from Congress continued until 1928, when Congress decided to amend the Howard University charter and officially recognize an annual appropriation to the institution. Federal support for Howard University continues to this day. Howard currently enrolls over 10,000 students, both undergraduate and graduate. Women comprise over 6,100 of the current student body, or approximately 60 percent.

The situation for HBCUs remained relatively stable through the first half of the twentieth century. Inadequate funding and little political clout were common among most institutions. Yet HBCUs continued to grow in number. By the end of World War II, there were about 100 institutions, their growth spurred on by the G. I. Bill and the early stages of the civil rights movement, such as the 1954 U.S. Supreme Court decision desegregating education, *Brown v. Board of Education of Topeka, Kansas.*

The Civil Rights Act of 1964 changed things dramatically for these institutions. Federal and state policy could no longer continue to neglect these institutions, which were understood to fulfill a priceless goal. As a result, Title III of the Higher Education Act of 1965 thereby provided direct support to "developing institutions," a category in which HBCUs were included. At this historic moment, the government de facto created the group known as historically black colleges and universities, all accredited universities, both public and private, established prior to 1964 whose principal mission was the education of black Americans.

At the time of this legislation, almost 70 percent of all black Americans attended HBCUs. With the onset of governmental support, one would have expected that enrollment would continue to grow. That was not the case. External factors such as legal cases, the increased availability of student aid, and increased minority recruitment from majority institutions all succeeded in actually reducing the rate at which black Americans enrolled in HBCUs. The period from the late 1960s through the early 1980s witnessed an overall decline in enrollment of 5 percent.

Witnessing this decline in what many considered to be a "national treasure," the federal government established a new policy toward HBCUs. In 1980, President Jimmy Carter issued Executive Order 12232. Its purpose was "to overcome the effects of discriminatory treatment and to strengthen and expand the capacity of historically Black colleges and universities to provide quality education" (White House Initiative on HBCUs 2002).

The aim of President Carter's original order was to provide a base on which the federal government and each agency would erect various programs to support HBCUs. Since President Carter's original proposal, each subsequent president has revoked the previous and reinstated his own order, always with a few changes. Since 1980, each order has become a bit stronger, each time requiring a bit more action and accountability from the various federal agencies.

There can be no doubt that the executive orders succeeded in supporting the cause of HBCUs. Although black Americans continue to attend majority institutions in record numbers, enrollment at HBCUs has grown steadily since 1980. In 1980 total enrollment at HBCUs was 233,557 and in 1998 was 273,472. For women students, enrollment has increased by almost 37,000, from the 1980 enrollment rate of 127,170 to a little over 164,000 in the fall of 1998 (National Center for Education Statistics 2001, table 223).

Historically black colleges and universities continue to serve their population and the United States. In 1994 these institutions, public and private, two- and four-year, together enrolled almost 16 percent of black Americans in all postsecondary education and awarded almost 30 percent of the bachelor's degrees awarded to them. In fiscal year 1997, $120 million was appropriated for HBCUs—$109 million for the formula grants awarded to institutions and $20 million for the specific support of historically black graduate institutions. In 1998, historically black colleges and universities conferred over 19,000 bachelor's degrees to women alone (National Center for Education Statistics 2001, table 222).

Their future is once again at a crossroads. Institutions continue to operate with large deficits, and majority institutions under the scrutiny of the public eye continue to heavily recruit minorities. The very public discourse that has occurred recently with respect to admissions criteria will in no uncertain terms affect the future of HBCUs. In its *United States v. Fordice* decision (1992), the U.S. Supreme Court made arguments for closing institutions such as HBCUs in states where the educational system is duplicative. The effects of this hoopla and other pending cases are still not clear.

Regardless, those who believe in the mission of the historically black colleges and universities continue to serve them diligently. Interestingly, more than 75 percent of black lawyers, military officers, physicians, and federal judges have graduated from an HBCU at some level. The opportunities that HBCUs have provided for black women in American higher education have been unprecedented. At times when higher education was barely accessible to women, historically black colleges and universities, some established solely for women, remained open and accessible to a minority group within a minority: female black Americans.

Elizabeth María Béjar

See also Part 1: Black Women's Colleges; Part 6: African American Students; Part 7: African American Faculty; Part 8: African American Administrators

References and further reading

American Association of State Colleges and Universities. 1988. *Minorities in Public Higher Education: At a Turning Point.* Washington, DC: American Association of State Colleges and Universities.

Brown, M. Christopher, and Kassie Freeman. 2002. "Introudction." *Review of Higher Education* 25, no. 3: 237–240.

Brown v. Board of Education of Topeka, Kansas, 347 U.S. 483 (1954).

Harvey, William B., and Lea E. Williams. 1989. "Historically Black Colleges: Models for Increasing Minority Representation." Pp. 233–241 in *Racial and Ethnic Diversity in Higher Education,* ed. Mildred C. G. Turner, Amaury Nora, and Laura Rendon. Boston: Pearson Custom Publishing.

Merisotis, Jamie P., and Colleen T. O'Brien, eds. 1998. *Minority-Serving Institutions: Distinct Purposes, Common Goals.* New Directions for Higher Education 102. San Francisco: Jossey-Bass.

National Center for Education Statistics. 2001. *2000 Digest of Education Statistics.* Washington, DC: U.S. Department of Education.

Selingo, J. 2002. "Bush Budget Will Seek Increases for Historically Black Colleges and Institutions with Many Hispanic Students." *Chronicle of Higher Education,* January 22. http://www.chronicle.com/daily/2002/01/2002012202n.htm. Cited June 20, 2002.

United States v. Fordice, 1125 S. Ct. 2727 (1992).

White House Initiative on Historically Black Colleges and Universities. 2002. http://www.ed.gov/OPE/hbcu. Cited June 13, 2002.

Lesbian, Gay, Bisexual, and Transgender Issues on Campuses

Lesbian, gay, bisexual, and transgender (LGBT) issues in higher education are those concerning campus climate, policy, and programs that differentially affect individuals who are not heterosexual (i.e., lesbian, gay, bisexual) or whose gender identity is not the same as the biological sex assigned to them at birth (i.e., transgender) or both. Issues of sexuality and gender are inextricably linked in higher education, not only because women constitute half of the LGBT population but also because societal definitions of gender and sexuality are based on a heterosexual gender binary.

Beginning with the Stonewall riots in New York in 1969 and the birth of the Gay Liberation Front, LGBT people have become visible on college and university campuses around the United States. Campus movements for gay rights paralleled those for women's rights, and the lesbian feminist movement in particular connected the two ideologies.

One of the major issues that continues to elude researchers is the number of LGBT people on campuses. There are no accurate statistics of the sexual orientation of students, faculty, or administrators in higher education. Higher education institutions do not ask the question on admissions forms or job applications, and LGBT students and job candidates would not be likely to offer the data if they were asked. This failure to ask means that campus programs, policies, and services are often based on anecdotal data.

When they are available, programs and services for LGBT people are generally provided in one of two ways. More commonly, volunteer students, faculty, and staff form formal or informal membership organizations. Examples of this type are registered student organizations and faculty associations. Except at some religiously controlled institutions, courts have provided that these organizations are protected by the First Amendment and must be permitted on campus. Less common than student or faculty groups are LGBT campus resource centers. These centers are institutionally funded campus units, usually with a full- or part-time paid staff member as coordinator or director. This is a growing area in higher education administration, with nearly 100 postsecondary institutions funding resource centers. The administrative directors of these centers formed a national consortium (www.lgbtcampus.org) to support new center directors and provide professional development opportunities for established directors.

Institutional Nondiscrimination Policies

To comply with relevant state and federal law, postsecondary institutions state that they do not discriminate in educational programs and hiring on the basis of a number of factors (sex, race, nationality, status as a Vietnam-era veteran, disability, etc.). Because there are no federal laws prohibiting discrimination based on sexual orientation or gender identity and because only 20 percent of states have such laws, it is incumbent on individual institutions voluntarily to include these categories in their nondiscrimination policies. Although the inclusion of sexual orientation and gender identity in a nondiscrimination policy does not guarantee a campus free from individual acts of prejudice and intolerance, it provides an institutional mechanism to address violations. Occasionally institutional nondiscrimination policies run afoul of federally sponsored activities on campus (such as Reserve Officer Training Corps programs or military recruiting, in which openly LGBT people may not participate); to avoid losing access to federal funds, most institutions make an exception for such activities.

Housing and Facilities

At many institutions, same-sex couples are not permitted to live in family housing. When campuses do offer housing for same-sex couples, they frequently require additional levels of paperwork, such as producing a domestic partner certificate in a state that does not recognize domestic partnerships. Same-sex domestic partners with children are required to produce copies of birth certificates for their offspring, whereas many opposite sex couples are not required to produce such documentation. Policies, however, are slowly beginning to change to be more inclusive of same-sex families, with some institutions declaring that single parents with children and then couples with children, regardless of the couple's sexual or gender identity, have housing priority. Mortgage origination programs that are intended to help recruit and retain valued faculty and high-level administrators usually do not include same-sex partners. When the valued employee dies, the same-sex spouse must sell the house or buy out the mortgage. A remaining heterosexual spouse may simply continue to live in the house and pay on the mortgage forever. There is also a need for transgender-friendly gyms and recreational facilities that include showers, locker rooms, toilet stalls, and bathrooms appropriate for any individual, regardless of gender status. Failure to accommodate transgender campus members puts them at risk for taunting at best and, more often, places them in physical jeopardy.

Domestic Partner Benefits

An increasing number of postsecondary institutions offer the same employee benefits to same-sex domestic partners as they do to the spouses of heterosexual employees. Benefits may include some that cost the institution nothing (library privileges, recreation center passes, university identification cards), as well as those that have a direct financial cost to the institution (course fees, health and life insurance policies). When health insurance benefits are offered to same-sex partners of employees, employees who provide their same-sex partners with health insurance are required by federal law to pay taxes on health benefits, whereas heterosexual couples do not have such a requirement. For example, if a female employee adds her female partner to her health insurance policy, the institution adds its contribution to its report of the employee's salary, which is then taxed as additional income. Heterosexual couples who are legally married do not have to pay this unrecoverable tax.

Campus Climate
Based on the original studies of the "chilly climate" for women on campus, more than 100 institutions have conducted studies of their campus climate vis-à-vis LGBT issues (see www.lgbtcampus.org for links to several of the studies online). Through interviews, surveys, and public testimonials, the studies collected data about antigay language and violence on campus, in and out of the classroom. LGBT flyers, posters, and other materials are often torn down, stolen, or defaced with antigay graffiti. Antigay language is ubiquitous on American college campuses; for example, the popular phrase "that's so gay" is meant to be an all-purpose insult and putdown, and students commonly insult one another or rival student organizations by branding them "fags." Antigay language among student athletes, especially if they are elite athletes, is often ignored and goes unpunished. The result of this pervasive antigay rhetoric is that students may be afraid to go to LGBT resource centers or to other LGBT-specific spaces on campus for fear of being targeted.

Faculty who use language that demeans LGBT people frequently go unchallenged by students who fear lowered grades or targeting by the professor or by other faculty or staff who, ironically, fear accusations that they themselves are LGBT. Students are often overtly and covertly discouraged at both the undergraduate and graduate levels from studying LGBT issues and topics.

Finally, institutional forms are ubiquitous and unavoidable on campus. Nearly all, regardless of venue, contain sexist and heterocentric language regarding gender, marital status, sexual activity, or relationship partners. Consistently inclusive language on forms demonstrates to students that they and their issues are important to the university. For example, student health center forms should ask first if students are sexually active and then with men, women, or both.

Financial Aid
A major issue for many LGBT students is the difficulty they experience in establishing emancipated student status when they have been cut off by their family as a result of coming out. Federal financial aid policy dictates that students must be twenty-four years old or off their parents' income tax forms for at least one year before they can qualify on their own for financial aid. Delays in student financial aid can lead to temporary homelessness for students without family support. Transgender females-to-males experience problems with financial aid offices regarding their failure to register for the draft at the age of eighteen; most of these transgender students had not transitioned at the age of eighteen and therefore did not think about Selective Service issues. However, when a student does transition from female to male, he must be counseled to register for Selective Service regardless of his age.

LGBT Issues in the Curriculum
Some campuses offer diversity training or require diversity courses in the first-year curriculum; few, however, include LGBT issues as part of such training or curricula. LGBT studies (also called "queer studies") programs are sometimes not taken seriously by academics, or they compete with other relative newcomers to intellectual life (ethnic studies, women's studies, interdisciplinary studies, etc.) and thus suffer from insufficient resources, selected classes, and very few endowed chairs. There are no undergraduate or graduate degrees specifically available in LGBT studies. The first LGBT studies program, founded by Jonathon Katz at the City College of San Francisco, is the only degree-granting (associate of arts) program in the United States, although other institutions offer minors in LGBT studies. Some institutions have taken a broader approach by placing LGBT studies in larger cultural contexts; for example, Brown University offers an undergraduate concentration (major) in sexuality and society.

Student Health Services
LGBT-friendly programs in student health and student psychological services have improved and are an important element of campus life. An LGBT-friendly program would be one in which the men's and women's sexual health or health education departments are demonstrably inclusive of LGBT issues, including appropriate and culturally sensitive sexually transmitted diseases testing as well as anonymous human immunodeficiency virus testing. To improve health services for LGBT clients and patients, staff at student health programs on campus could receive sensitivity training regarding LGBT issues, and LGBT students could be specifically recruited for peer student health counselor teams.

Faculty and Staff
According to campus climate surveys, sizable portions of the LGBT faculty and staff remain in the closet, citing their fear that they will be targeted by hostile department chairs or colleagues or that they will be denied tenure based on their sexual orientation or gender identity. Some also fear that coming out to students may result in accusations of sexual harassment or blackmail. Many faculty are also concerned about the opportunity to conduct LGBT-related research because such research tends not to be valued by departments and because it is difficult to obtain extramural funding for such studies. The funding challenge is increased because much research in LGBT studies occurs outside the academic disciplines (i.e., in medicine, basic science, defense) where most funding is available. These challenges may be particularly keen for lesbian or bisexual women faculty, who are already marginalized by their gender and further risk intellectual marginalization if they choose to study topics outside the mainstream of their academic departments.

Alumni
A recent surge of LGBT-specific donations to colleges and universities by LGBT alumni has resulted in some programs, services, and LGBT resource offices becoming permanently endowed. A number of institutions now have LGBT alumni associations, many of which are directly connected to the institution's alumni association.

Ronni L. Sanlo and
Steven J. Leider

See also Part 5: Students' Rights; Part 6: Romantic Relationships; Sexuality

References and further reading

McNaron, Toni A. H. 1997. *Poisoned Ivy: Lesbian and Gay Academics Confronting Homophobia.* Philadelphia: Temple University Press.

National Consortium of Directors of Lesbian, Gay, Bisexual, and Transgender Resources in Higher Education. www.lgbtcampus.org. Cited June 3, 2002.

Sanlo, Ronni L. 1998. *Working with Lesbian, Gay, Bisexual, and Transgender College Students: A Handbook for Faculty and Administrators.* Westport, CT: Greenwood Press.

Sanlo, Ronni L., Susan R. Rankin, and Robert Schoenberg. 2002. *Our Place on Campus: LGBT Services and Programs in Higher Education.* Westport, CT: Greenwood Press.

Talburt, Susan. 2000. *Subject to Identity: Knowledge, Sexuality, and Academic Practices in Higher Education.* Albany: State University of New York Press.

Tierney, William G. 1997. *Academic Outlaws: Queer Theory and Cultural Studies in the Academy.* Thousand Oaks, CA: Sage.

Military Colleges

Women's entrance into American military colleges resulted from more than two decades of congressional debate and litigation that ended with a Supreme Court ruling. This right of entry is an important achievement in women's fight for equality, as it provides them the opportunity for elite training that can accelerate achievement and lead to high military rank. Military college attendance also gives women membership in privileged alumni networks, particularly in states with historically strong military colleges, such as South Carolina and Virginia. To what extent women are accepted as peers within this training and are later treated as members of the alumni networks could vary greatly, depending on the individuals with whom the women come into contact. In the United States, there are three types of military colleges and therefore three separate paths to coeducation. First, the Department of Defense (DOD) Service Academies (the Merchant Marine Academy, the U.S. Military Academy at West Point, the U.S. Naval Academy in Annapolis, the U.S. Air Force Academy in Colorado Springs, and the U.S. Coast Guard Academy in New London, Connecticut) became coeducational in 1976 by law. Second, the state-supported military institutions (Virginia Military Institute and the Citadel) went coed in 1996 in accordance with a Supreme Court ruling. Third, one institution (Norwich University) became coeducational by choice.

The effort to establish coeducation at the DOD Service Academies began in the 1960s, when Representative Robert B. Duncan nominated a woman to the U.S. Military Academy. In 1972, Senator Jacob Javits nominated Barbra J. Brimmer to the U.S. Naval Academy. When the Naval Academy refused to consider Brimmer for admission, Javits brought the issue to the public's attention. Debates on women's entrance into the service academies began to surface among members of Congress and members of the service academies. In September 1973, two women and four members of Congress brought lawsuits against the U.S. Naval Academy and the U.S. Air Force Academy. In October of that same year, Representative Pierre du Pont introduced a bill in the House that called for the admittance of women into the service academies. In December, the Senate accepted by a voice vote an amendment that allowed women entry into the service academies.

Based on a dispute over whether the aforementioned amendment could be considered with a bill on bonus pay in the military, the House struck the amendment, saying that women's admission into the service academies should be considered separately. In 1974, the House began hearings on admitting women into the service academies. In the meantime, the 1973 lawsuit began making its way through the court system. When the House hearing ended, the issue was still undecided. In July 1974, Senators William Hathaway, Strom Thurmond, Mike Mansfield, and Javits reintroduced legislation in the Senate. In May 1975, the House passed legislation commanding women's entrance into the service academies, and in June 1975 the Senate passed equivalent legislation. In October of that same year, President Gerald Ford signed Public Law 94-106, which states that the service academies "shall take such action as may be necessary and appropriate to insure that . . . female individuals shall be eligible for appointment and admission to the service academy concerned" (Title VIII). Public Law 94-106 was signed before the 1973 litigation made its way through the court system and therefore made it unnecessary. In the summer of 1976, women entered all the national service academies.

Women's entrance into the state-supported military institutions was achieved through a series of court battles. On 1 March 1990, the Justice Department filed suit against the State of Virginia, based on a complaint from a high school student that Virginia Military Institute (VMI) would not admit women. The Justice Department alleged that VMI's failure to admit women constituted discrimination on the basis of sex and violated the Fourteenth Amendment's equal protection clause. VMI responded that the equal protection clause was not violated because the exclusion of women helps preserve VMI's adversative model of education. VMI also argued that the exclusion of women ensured educational diversity within the State of Virginia, even though it did not promote gender diversity within VMI itself.

After losing this case, the Justice Department appealed. The Fourth Circuit Court of Appeals heard the case and agreed with the District Court's finding that single-sex education is justifiable because of the differences between a single-sex student body and coeducational student body. The court also agreed that VMI's method of education would be altered if women were to be integrated into the institution. However, the court also found that since the women of Virginia were not afforded the educational opportunities of a VMI education, the single-sex military program violated the equal protection clause. The court offered the following three solutions to this dilemma: (1) admit women, (2) become a private institution, or (3) establish a similar program for woman. VMI decided to establish a similar program for women. The evaluation of the proposed plan was argued before the District Court on 29 April 1994.

While the VMI case was being litigated, Shannon Faulkner, a female high school senior, applied and was admitted to the Citadel in January 1993. However, once the Citadel discovered Faulkner's gender, the institution revoked her admission. Faulkner claimed a violation of her equal protection rights and brought suit against the Citadel. In April 1994, Faulkner's case went to trial. The Citadel contended that single-sex military education for women was unnecessary because

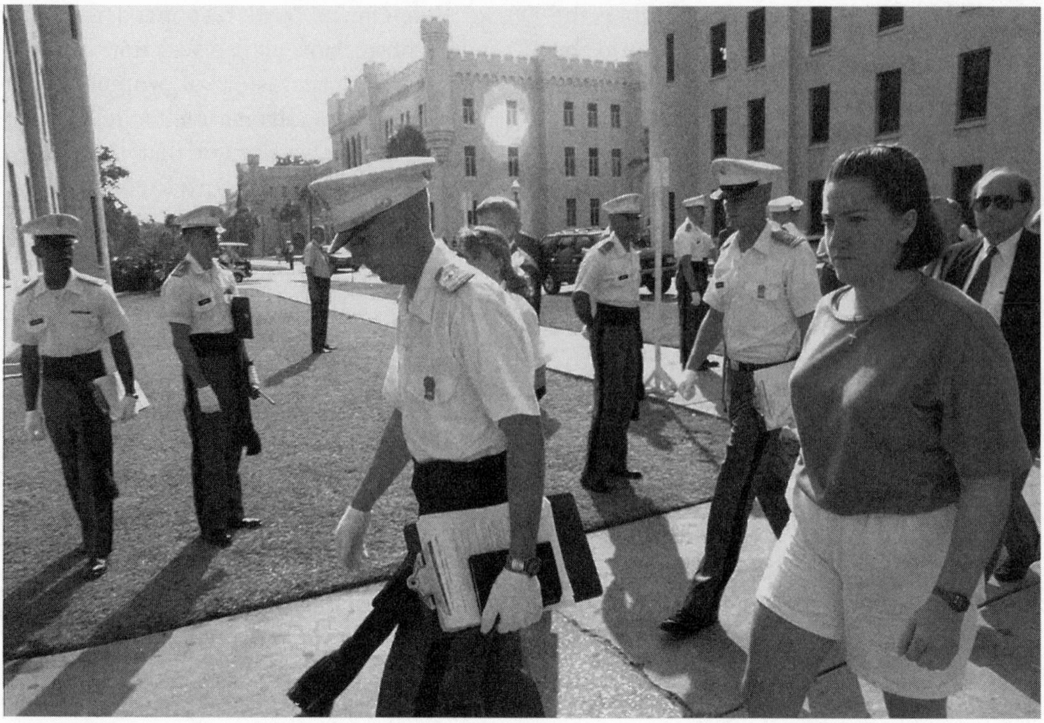

Shannon Faulkner was the first woman to enter the Citadel, a traditional military college (AP Photo/Post and Courier, Gabriel B. Tait, Pool)

there was insufficient demand for it. They further reasoned that the state's private women's colleges met demand among South Carolina's women for single-sex education. However, this rationale did not address the fact that some of South Carolina's women might desire a military education. The court rejected South Carolina's position, saying that the state failed to articulate the unique benefits of the Citadel education to men only and why women could not be included. The court further found that the Citadel failed to propose a remedy. In evaluating the three remedies proposed to VMI, the judge reasoned that since time was of the essence (Faulkner was about to enter her junior year of college), the Citadel must immediately admit Faulkner into the corps of cadets. The court also ordered that the Citadel should be prepared to implement a remedy that was in accordance with the VMI case ruling by August 1995.

In the meantime, VMI created a parallel leadership-training program as a remedy for the aforementioned constitutional violation. The new program was called the Virginia Women's Institute for Leadership (VWIL). Mary Baldwin College agreed to house the VWIL, and the Virginia legislature passed a budget bill funding VWIL at the same level of funding per student as VMI. The VMI Alumni Association also agreed to extend its career placement services to VWIL, offer assistance in recruiting prospective students, and develop a networking program with Mary Baldwin College. In addition, the VMI Foundation pledged $5.6 million for the endowment of VWIL. The designers of the VWIL program decided to deemphasize the adversative model and to create an environment emphasizing leadership training. It was also decided that although the women of VWIL would pursue the same five pedagogical themes as the men of VMI, VWIL was not intended to mirror VMI's model. After submitting this plan, the court ruled that the VWIL program would remedy the constitutional violation and ordered an immediate implementation. However, this decision was appealed and reached the Supreme Court. In 1996, the Supreme Court ruled that VMI's admissions policy was unconstitutional and insisted that women be admitted, thus ending male-only admissions policies at state-supported military institutions.

Women's entrance into private military colleges has been based on decisions that individual institutions have made. It is important to note that had these institutions remained single-sex, this status may have been protected under the law based upon the Dartmouth College Case, which established the legal difference between private and public institutions. However, since there are currently no private, single-sex military institutions in the United States, this issue has not been challenged within the courts. As of this writing, there are fund-raising efforts by VMI and Citadel alumni and friends to establish a private, all-male military college to be called the Southern Military Institute.

It is important to note that women have also gained entry to other types of military college experiences based on institutional choice. Two examples of this phenomenon are the Texas A&M corps of cadets and the Virginia Tech corps of cadets. Both schools, like Norwich, offer a military experience similar to the service academies or the state-supported military institutions. However, not all students are members of the corps of cadets. In addition, New Mexico Military Institute, which is state-supported, offers a two-year military college experience. There are a variety of reasons that an institution or corps of cadets may have decided to become coeducational, which could include external governmental or military pressure, the need to maintain enrollments, or a belief in social justice (although the latter is least likely).

There have been several paths leading to coeducation at American military colleges, but three consistent themes emerge. First, almost all the institutions took a great deal of time to research coeducation and plan for it on their campuses. Second, the overarching sentiment of these institutions was that although coeducation was unwanted, the schools would "follow orders" to the best of their ability. Third, the military institutions believed that the admittance of women would irrevocably change military institutions and therefore women could never have the very education that they sought. In addition, it is interesting to note that many of the questions raised about the coeducation of military colleges in both the 1970s and the 1990s were the very questions that women tried to answer in the 1800s as they sought admission to educational institutions. Although the context of these questions may be different (e.g., "What is the purpose of educating women as scientists?" versus "What is the purpose of educating women as fighter pilots?"), the basis remains the same. The questions include the following: Do women need this education? What is the purpose of educating women for a career they will never have? Are women's minds and bodies fit for this education?

Stacy A. Jacob

See also Part 1: Coeducation; Part 5: Legal Issues

References and further reading

Holm, Jeanne. 1982. *Women in the Military: An Unfinished Revolution.* Novato, CA: Presidio Press.

Jungreis, Jeremy N. 1996. "Holding the Line at VMI: The Preservation of a State's Right to Offer a Single-Gender Military Education." *Florida State University Law Review* 23, no. 3: 795–839.

Lederman, Douglas. 1996. "Supreme Court Rejects VMI's Exclusion of Women." *Chronicle of Higher Education,* July 5, A21.

Stiehm, Judith Hicks. 1981. *Bring Me Men and Women: Mandated Change in the U. S. Airforce Academy.* Berkeley: University of California Press.

Title VIII: Department of Defense Appropriation Authorization Act, P.L. 94-106, 1975.

Zook, Jim. 1992. "Court Defines How VMI Could Remain All Male." *Chronicle of Higher Education,* October 14, A22.

Southern Baptist Colleges

The Southern Baptist Convention (SBC) began opening higher education to women in the mid–nineteenth century. By creating separate schools for women, Southern Baptists avoided coeducation and prepared women for vocations considered appropriate for their gender. Although a few Southern Baptist colleges experimented with coeducation in the nineteenth century, most colleges were single-sex. Some women's colleges coordinated with nearby Southern Baptist colleges for men, often sharing faculty or operating coeducational classes in particular subjects. Southern Baptist colleges excluded African Americans until the mid–twentieth century. Women pursuing careers in Christian service attended single-sex training schools for missionaries and social workers until the 1950s, when the all-male seminaries opened their doors to women. Coeducation became the most popular option for young Southern Baptist men and women in the mid–twentieth century as men's colleges began enrolling women, and many coordinating men's and women's colleges merged. In the late twentieth century, as fundamentalists took control of the SBC, opportunities for Southern Baptist women to train as ministers were eliminated, and alternative Baptist seminaries from outside the SBC emerged to educate women ministers.

Baptists emerged in seventeenth-century England. They migrated to New England seeking religious freedom and eventually migrated to the southern colonies. In 1845, after controversy between Baptist abolitionists and southern Baptist slaveholders, Baptists in the South broke away to form their own Southern Baptist Convention. Women played a very active role in early Baptist churches in England, serving as deacons and sometimes preachers. However, the public role of Baptist women declined over the years. Women of the mid–nineteenth and twentieth centuries found churches questioning their right to serve as church leaders. The Trienniel convention and the early SBC were for men only, and therefore women's mission societies sent male representatives.

Some early Baptists supported higher education to train missionaries, pastors, and laymen to improve church leadership. However, other Baptists were strongly opposed to education, especially theological education. Many associated education with their persecutors in England, and others on the frontier feared that education would lead to spiritual pride or undermine faith. However, antieducation sentiment began to moderate during the nineteenth century, and enthusiasm for missions spurred the creation of Southern Baptist colleges to train male ministers and missionaries. The earliest of these, Georgetown College in Kentucky (1829), Richmond College in Virginia (1832), Mercer University in Georgia (1833), and Wake Forest in North Carolina (1834) would not open their doors to women students for about 100 years. The majority of Southern Baptists were opposed to coeducation. Even those who supported women's education expected that women would be educated for "women's work" and did not see the need for offering women the same curriculum as men. This opposition to coeducation led Southern Baptists to create colleges for women, which sometimes coordinated their programs with colleges for men.

Judson Female Institute, created in 1838, was the first Southern Baptist College for women and set the pattern for others such as the Johnson Female Seminary in South Carolina (1847), Forsyth College in Georgia (1847), and Meredith College in North Carolina (1899). Meredith's curriculum was typical for Southern Baptist women's schools at the turn of the twentieth century: a student who earned a B.A. degree from Meredith College in 1904 studied Latin, English, mathematics, history, and physiology; she may have elected to study other courses in the sciences, languages, logic, ethics, art, music, or pedagogy. She had an opportunity to study Greek or perhaps take the Bible course introduced in 1902.

Historians of women's higher education observe that coordinate colleges provided a means for institutions to avoid coeducation while still sharing resources. The story of Greenville Baptist Female College, established in 1855 in South Carolina, illustrates a typical coordinate arrangement used by Southern Baptists. In 1853, the Baptist State Convention of South Carolina established a committee to explore the need for a college to educate young women. The convention voted to establish the liberal arts school but noted that it must be controlled by the board of trustees of all-male Furman University. In 1908, the Female College established a separate board of trustees and was chartered as Greenville Woman's College, remaining a single-sex college until 1933, when it merged with Furman University.

Although the majority of Southern Baptist colleges were sex-segregated well into the twentieth century, a few institutions, like Baylor University in Waco, Texas, began placing men and women in the same classrooms by the late nineteenth century. First located in Independence, Texas, Baylor experimented with a coordinate arrangement, leading to the establishment of a separate women's school in Belton in 1866 called Baylor Female College. Twenty years later, when the all-male Baylor moved from Independence to Waco, coeducation was resumed but with strict rules limiting interaction between the sexes. At first, women and men followed different curricula, but by 1891, all courses of study, including biblical studies and business courses, were open to women.

The conditions of the Civil War led to temporary closings of almost all institutions of higher education in the South. The all-male institutions sent students and faculty to the front lines, and economics and additional responsibilities prevented women from attending colleges. Charles Johnson (1955) noted that for a period of twenty years, even schools with strong prewar financial support were barely able to reestablish programs when endowments were lost.

Southern women's schools of the nineteenth and early twentieth centuries used the term "college" to designate schools with very different academic standards. Some Southern Baptist women's schools were similar to academies or finishing schools, offering training in subjects such as music, elocution, domestic skills, and etiquette. Others, like Judson College in Marion, Alabama, featured a preparatory division for young girls as well as a postsecondary department. Therefore, when student records of this period show college attendance, it is unclear whether the student was engaged in secondary or postsecondary learning.

For women pursuing careers in Christian service, Southern Baptists created single-sex training schools for missionaries and social workers. Training schools for Southern Baptist women were modeled after those established by Northern Baptist women, particularly the Baptist Missionary Training School of Chicago, founded in 1881. The Woman's Missionary Union Training School for Southern Baptists opened in 1907 in Louisville, Kentucky, and coordinated with the nearby Southern Baptist Theological Seminary, which trained male ministers. The Training School's curriculum included some theological courses at the seminary and a women's curriculum, including social work, domestic science, music, elocution, and nursing. Another school that offered missionary training for women was Southwestern Baptist Theological Seminary in Fort Worth, Texas. Originating as a theological department of Baylor University in Waco, Texas, Southwestern moved to Fort Worth in 1910 and was considered coeducational since it enrolled women as seminary students. However, Southwestern had many features of a coordinate arrangement; with women living in a separate building where they studied a women's curriculum. A nursery and kindergarten were provided so that married women could study with their husbands. Until the late twentieth century, Southwestern Seminary observed the Southern Baptist sanction against women entering professions reserved for males, including preaching.

Although the Chicago, Louisville, and Fort Worth missionary training schools were reserved for Caucasian women, African American women also received training for the mission field. The Baptist Missionary Training School of Chicago served as a model for missionary training programs established in schools for African American women. Northern Baptist women assisted in the establishment of several programs in southern schools, including those at Spelman Seminary, Shaw University, and Bishop College in the early 1890s. Spelman Seminary, a school for black women located in Atlanta, Georgia, founded a missionary training department in 1891 featuring a two-year course with five months of field experience.

In 1909, the National Training School for Women and Girls was launched under the leadership of Nannie Burroughs. She inspired members of the Woman's Convention, an auxiliary of the National Baptist Convention, to provide training for African American women in domestic service, teaching, and missionary work. In its first year, the school enrolled thirty-one students, ranging in age from twelve to forty-three. Unlike the training schools at Louisville and Fort Worth, the National Training School in Washington, D.C., offered training in vocations that were secular as well as religious.

African American studies scholar Evelyn Brooks Higgenbotham notes that the philosophy under which the school operated was influenced by Burroughs's notion of self-help for African Americans. An admirer of Booker T. Washington, Burroughs rejected the notions of northern white Baptists and black intellectuals like W. E. B. DuBois, who believed African Americans should focus on the development of a "talented tenth" to serve as African American leaders. Burroughs believed in the dignity of labor and the duty of African American Baptist women to provide training, not only for an elite group with special talent but also for those engaged in domestic service. Both Washington and Burroughs focused on the advancement of the majority of African Americans rather than the cultivation of a professional elite.

Like other schools for women of this era, the National Training School focused on developing moral character through strict behavioral codes. It was called the "School of the 3 Bs," emphasizing the Bible, bath, and broom as tools to advance the African American race. At 6:00 each morning, the neatness and personal cleanliness of each student were inspected. Those who had been untidy or careless in attire did not receive diplomas. Students provided hard labor to help control the school's expenses. Although women at other schools were involved in extracurricular recreation, the women of the National Training School cleared weeds, planted trees, and built concrete walkways. They did gardening, raised pigs, milked cows, and churned butter.

Due to the emphasis on racial self-help, no contributions from white donors were accepted until after the school was operating. However, in 1912, northern white women of the Woman's American Baptist Mission Society supplied a model home in which domestic science lessons could be taught. Higgenbotham noted an important difference between domestic science courses in the National Training School and in schools for white students. Courses in domestic science in schools for white students were designed to train women to become better wives and mothers. However, domestic science courses in schools for African American women trained women for paid domestic service.

By the mid–twentieth century, the majority of the Southern Baptist colleges originally designated as men's colleges were enrolling women students. In addition, many schools began admitting African American students. Men's and women's colleges previously having a coordinating arrangement typically merged into one coeducational college. Some women's colleges, like Meredith, continued as women's colleges until the latter twentieth century, when men were admitted as students. The 1980s and 1990s brought many political changes to the SBC, causing some colleges and universities, such as Wake Forest and Baylor, to break or modify their connections with the SBC while maintaining strong affiliations with their state conventions.

In the early twentieth century, Southern Baptists opened theological education to women but insisted that women were preparing for different vocations than male ministers. In the 1950s, half a century after women had been invited to listen quietly to lectures, the Southern Baptist seminaries began enrolling women students. Women typically pursued seminary degrees in the areas of music and religious education. By the 1960s, women were not an unusual sight in seminary classrooms. In 1964, Addie Davis became the first woman to be ordained by Southern Baptists after she completed theological training at the nearby Southeastern Baptist Theological Seminary in North Carolina. A great deal of protest was raised, but it soon subsided when Davis accepted a pastorate outside the Southern Baptist denomination. Baptist historian Leon McBeth estimates that fifty or more women were ordained between 1964 and 1977, although many were employed by non–Southern Baptist churches or served in nonpreaching roles such as a hospital chaplaincy.

The decade of the 1980s brought about a deep schism among Southern Baptists that drew a great amount of attention to the matter of women in seminaries. Throughout the 1970s, a group of Southern Baptist conservatives organized a plan to gain control of the more moderate SBC in order to make the belief in biblical inerrancy normative among Southern Baptists. Southern Baptist historian Bill Leonard points out that although fundamentalists insisted that clarification of biblical authority was the primary goal, fundamentalists were promoting doctrines that they viewed as inseparable from the inerrancy issue. These doctrines were concerned with controversial issues such as the role of women and the nature of ministry. As the SBC moved in a more conservative direction, in 1984, Southern Baptists made a public statement of protest against ordination of women, basing the resolution on selective references to Scripture, particularly the Pauline letters. In spite of this statement of opposition, 232 women were ordained to the Southern Baptist ministry by 1986.

Although Baptist women continue working to develop networks of support, opposition to women in the preaching ministry permeated the SBC at the beginning of the twenty-first century. SBC seminaries have been enjoined by the denomination to discourage women from entering the preaching ministry. Although women continue to enroll in Southern Baptist seminaries, they cluster in the areas of music, missions, and religious education and no longer study for the preaching ministry. Baptist women continue the struggle to define their places of service, with many leaving the SBC to find employment by other denominations. Others have found acceptance among alternative Baptist groups such as Alliance of Baptists or the Cooperative Baptist Fellowship, formed in the 1980s in response to changes in the SBC leadership. These organizations, composed of former and current members of the SBC, support women in all forms of church leadership, including the preaching ministry. They support seminaries such as George W. Truett Seminary in Texas, Baptist Theological Seminary in Richmond, Virginia, McAfee School of Theology in Georgia, and others educating both men and women for ministry, including preaching.

T. Laine Scales

References and further reading

Anders, Sarah Frances. 1975. "Woman's Role in the Southern Baptist Convention and Its Churches as Compared with Selected Other

Denominations." *Review and Expositor* (Winter): 31–39.
Bailey, Faith C. 1964. *Two Directions.* Rochester, NY: Baptist Missionary Training School.
Hamilton, Frances D., and Elizabeth C. Wells. 1989. *Daughters of the Dream: Judson College 1838–1988.* Marion, AL: Judson College.
Higginbotham, Evelyn B. 1993. *Righteous Discontent: The Woman's Movement in the Black Baptist Church, 1880–1920.* Cambridge, MA: Harvard University Press.
Johnson, Charles D. 1955. *Higher Education of Southern Baptists: An Institutional History, 1826–1954.* Waco, TX: Baylor University Press.
Johnson, Mary L. 1956. *A History of Meredith College.* Raleigh, NC: Meredith College.
Leonard, Bill J. 1990. *God's Last and Only Hope: Fragmentation of the Southern Baptist Convention.* Grand Rapids, MI: Eerdmans.
McBeth, Leon. 1979. *Women in Baptist Life.* Nashville, TN: Broadman Press.
Scales, T. Laine. 2000. *All That Fits a Woman: Educating Southern Baptist Women for Charity and Mission, 1907–1926.* Macon, GA: Mercer University Press.
Scarborough, Lee R. 1939. *A Modern School of the Prophets.* Nashville, TN: Broadman Press.

Tribal Colleges

Tribal colleges and universities (TCUs) provide significant opportunities for women and American Indians to receive supportive services to graduate, pursue advanced degrees, and enter at the highest levels of administration. However, their scarce financial resources place many demands on faculty and staff to fulfill multiple roles with limited monetary rewards.

There are thirty-two tribal colleges and universities (TCUs) throughout the United States. They are not distributed throughout the country but rather are concentrated in those areas that have a larger proportion of Native American residents, principally the upper Midwest and Southwest. There are seven in Montana, five in North Dakota, four in South Dakota, three each in Minnesota and New Mexico, two each in Wisconsin, Michigan, and Nebraska, and one each in Kansas, Arizona, California, and Washington.

All tribal colleges and universities share certain characteristics. All serve student bodies that are predominantly American Indian and low income. All incorporate American Indian culture in the curriculum, are open admissions institutions, and began as two-year colleges. All are relatively new institutions. The oldest tribally controlled institution of higher education is Diné College (formerly Navajo Community College), founded in 1968. Most, but not all, tribal colleges and universities are small (fewer than 1,000 students), located on reservations, and chartered by a tribe. Most grant degrees no higher than the associates level. There are, however, four colleges that grant bachelor's degrees and two that award master's degrees. Tribal colleges gained land grant status in 1994, which makes them eligible for federal funds supporting extension work in home economics and agriculture.

Women Students

Data from the Department of Education showed approximately 25,000 students enrolled at tribal colleges and universities in 1996. By 2001, the American Indian College Fund estimated that over 30,000 students were enrolled at TCUs. Compared to students at nontribal institutions, tribal college students are more likely to have an income below the poverty level, to have a GED rather than a high school diploma, to be pursuing an

Entrance sign and logo of Salish Kootenai College in Pablo, Montana. (Yolanda Matt, 2001)

associates degree, and to be female. Women make up 64 percent of the tribal college and university student population.

The modal tribal college student is a single mother in her thirties with an income below the poverty level. Not surprisingly, the two most common reasons for student dropout are difficulties in arranging child care and financial problems. In response to these demographics and concomitant problems, one-third of the colleges maintain full-time day care on-site. Some tribal institutions offer a range of child and family services that are extremely rare at nontribal schools. For example, Cankdeska Cikana Community College offers an early enrichment program for children up to age three, a Head Start program, Head Start Wrap-Around for parents who need extended day care hours, an hourly drop-in day care, and domestic violence counseling. The array of student support services, combined with the greater emphasis and value placed on American Indian culture, is generally credited with the substantially higher retention and graduation rates for Native American students at tribal institutions in comparison with mainstream schools. On the average, 30–33 percent of Native American students entering tribal colleges will graduate, compared to 15–20 percent of Native American students at mainstream institutions. The extremely high dropout rate for American Indian students was a major impetus to the founding of tribal colleges.

What is particularly impressive is that this higher retention is achieved by tribal colleges with expenditures per student that are dramatically lower than public institutions of higher education. For example, in 1999, tribal colleges and universities received an average of $2,964 per student in federal support, compared to an average of $4,743 per full-time student received by mainstream community colleges during the same period.

Although tribal colleges and universities are more likely to be attentive to the needs of women students in their provision of student support services, their curriculum rarely reflects the specific concerns of women. At all tribal colleges, coursework in Native American or tribal studies is a graduation requirement. However, few offer courses in women's studies, even as independent studies.

Currently, no tribal college offers a course on Native American women.

Women Administrators

Tribal colleges and universities have a much better track record than mainstream institutions for promotion of women to top administrative positions. Despite the fact that women are the majority of Native American college graduates, only 39 percent of tribal college presidents in 2001 were women. Still, in the United States as a whole, women made up only 18 percent of community college presidents. Women presidents of TCUs were somewhat less likely to hold doctoral degrees (42 percent) compared to male college presidents with doctorates (55 percent), a reflection of the greater proportion of males with doctorates in the American Indian population.

Women administrators are extremely active at the policy level throughout American Indian higher education. Women have always been well-represented in the American Indian Higher Education Consortium (AIHEC), the premier professional organization for tribal institutions. In its twenty-nine-year history, AIHEC has had two women as executive directors, two female board presidents, and numerous female senior administrators. Dr. Janine Pease-Pretty on Top, the founding president of Little Big Horn College on the Crow Reservation, was the first woman elected president of the governing board of AIHEC. The current editor of the *Tribal College Journal,* the major publication in the field, is a woman, Marjane Ambler. The executive director charged with implementing the executive order on tribal colleges under the Clinton administration was also a woman, Carrie Billie from the Navajo Reservation.

Women Faculty and Staff

In ways both positive and negative, working conditions for tribal college faculty and staff positions vary dramatically from those at mainstream institutions. Valuable role models exist for students at tribal colleges and universities, where 30 percent of faculty are American Indian/Alaskan Native, in contrast to less than 1 percent of the faculty at nontribal institutions. In the beginning years of the tribal colleges, most American Indian faculty members taught in the Indian studies curriculum, with general education courses taught by white faculty members with the appropriate academic credentials. Tribal elders still teach the overwhelming majority of courses in Indian culture and indigenous languages. In these areas, women are a slight majority of faculty members, possibly reflecting the greater longevity of women. As tribal institutions of higher education have been successful in graduating students in academic disciplines, the proportion of American Indian faculty in all departments has increased.

All tribal colleges and universities incorporate Native American culture in the curriculum. Turtle Mountain Community College was one of the first to make inclusion of cultural content part of its assessment process. It is becoming increasingly common for tribal institutions of higher education to require some tribal cultural content in all courses and to make this integration a part of all faculty evaluations.

In terms of credit hours, the typical tribal college faculty member has a much higher teaching load than her counterparts at mainstream institutions. Full-time faculty members generally teach four to six courses each semester. Although course load is high, class size tends to be very low, with an average of six to ten students per class. Through a combination of small class size and instruction of students in many different courses, most full-time tribal college faculty come to know their students on a much more personal basis than is typical for higher education.

The cultural and personal advantages of teaching in a tribal institution are offset by significant financial disadvantage. Average faculty salaries are low, less than $24,000 for the 1996–1997 academic year, in contrast to an average salary of more than $43,000 for full-time faculty at public two-year institutions. Tenure is generally not available to tribal college faculty. Most tribal colleges are under the auspices of the tribal government, which has the legal authority to terminate any individual's employment when, in the judgment of the tribal council, such action is in the best interests of the tribe. In addition, the notion of treating one class of employees differently, such as by granting tenure, is not culturally acceptable on most reservations.

Women are in the majority across all types of tribal college faculty, both tribal and nontribal members and both full- and part-time. Because TCUs cannot compete economically with other institutions, they must offer other, less tangible incentives to faculty. One such incentive is greater opportunities for professional development and achievement. Women in the sciences are less underrepresented at tribal institutions, and they participate in a broader range of activities. For example, at Cankdeska Cikana Community College, Melinda Martin, an instructor in animal science, is also charged with responsibility for management of the tribal bison herd. As noted above, tribal colleges also have a superior track record for promotion of women into senior administrative positions.

A combination of factors (low salary, lack of tenure, and location in isolated rural communities) makes faculty and staff recruitment and retention difficult for tribal colleges. As a result, faculty and staff with doctoral or other terminal degrees are an exception. However, tribal college faculty have benefited greatly from the Bush Foundation Faculty Development Program. These grant funds have provided many tribal college faculty members the opportunity to pursue advanced degrees. On many campuses, Bush grants have funded on-site training and travel to conferences for continuing professional development.

The issue of whether academic librarians should be accorded faculty status is the subject of much debate within the academic community. As with other academic institutions, tribal college librarians may or may not be accorded faculty status and may or may not have teaching responsibilities. To complicate the issue still further, many tribal libraries also serve as the reservation public library. Women hold 74 percent of the positions as tribal college librarians, a figure squarely in between the 68 percent of librarian positions held by women in nontribal institutions of higher education and the 79 percent of librarian positions held by women at public libraries. Although opportunities are slightly better for women desiring academic careers in tribal college libraries, the proportion of American Indian women in the field is dramatically higher. American Indians of either gender hold approximately one-half of 1 percent of academic library positions in the United States. Within tribal institutions, American Indian librarians are the majority of all librarians.

AnnMarie Rousey

See also Part 1: Community Colleges; Part 2: Demographics of Gender and Race; Part 6: Developmental Issues; Part 7: Researchers; Teachers; Tenure and Promotion; Part 8: Presidency

References and further reading

American Indian Higher Education Consortium. 1999. *Tribal Colleges: An Introduction.* Alexandria, VA: AIHEC.

Dakota Roundtable III. 1996. *Dakota Roundtable III: A Report on the Status of Young Native American Women in the Aberdeen Area.* Aberdeen, SD: Native American Women's Health Education Resource Center.

Krumm, Bernita L. 1998. "Tribal Culture Supports Women in Campus Presidencies." *Women in Higher Education* 7, no. 12: 39.

National Center for Education Statistics. 1997. *Characteristics of American Indian and Alaska Native Education.* NCES 97-451. Washington, DC: U.S. Department of Education.

Rousey, AnnMarie, and E. S. Longie. 2001. "The Tribal College as Family Support System." *American Behavioral Scientist* 44: 1492–1504.

Yellow Bird, Doreen. 1999. "Turtle Mountain Faculty Helps Build Model Assessment Tool." *Tribal College Journal* 10, no. 2: 10–15.

Women's Colleges

Women's colleges are those postsecondary institutions that admit and enroll only female undergraduates. These colleges, which numbered approximately 214 institutions at their peak in 1960 and today number fewer than 80 institutions, represent an important institutional type, in terms of their historical and contemporary contributions to higher education for women.

Catharine Beecher (Dover Pictorial Archives)

Historical Contribution

Educational options for women were limited prior to the Civil War. It was widely believed that women were intellectually inferior to men and that educating women might lead to health problems and eventually to a decreased ability to bear children. Because education in the colonial period was aimed at preparing men for the clergy and other male-only professions, there was no real impetus to provide higher education for women. Formal higher education was not an option for women during this era.

In the early 1800s, several seminaries for women only were founded to provide girls with a liberal education equivalent to a high school education. Graduates of these seminaries were prepared in the Jef-

Emma Hart Willard (Dover Pictorial Archives)

Mary Lyon (Library of Congress)

fersonian ideal to be mothers, wives, and teachers. These seminaries were not immediately classified as colleges, although schools such as that founded by Emma Willard (est. 1821) modeled their curricula, in large part, after that offered at the most prestigious men's colleges of the day. Other women-only institutions, such as those founded by Catharine Beecher (est. schools in 1824 and 1832) and Mary Lyon (est. Mount Holyoke Seminary in 1837), became prototypes for today's women's colleges and were seen by many as the best way to educate women.

There are several women-only institutions that claim to be the first women's "college." Georgia Female College was chartered by the state legislature in 1836; its curriculum, however, was more similar to that of a high school than a college. In 1853, Mary Sharp College in Tennessee was founded; its curriculum looked very similar to the four-year degree program offered at the men's colleges. Similarly, Elmira Female College in New York, chartered in 1855, offered a true collegiate course. In the early days of women's access to higher education, single-sex institutions were the norm. By 1860, there were approximately 100 women's colleges in existence, about half of which offered a collegiate level curriculum.

Also by 1860, several institutions, including Oberlin College, began experimenting with coeducation. The passage of the Morrill Land Grant Act after the Civil War led to the creation of land grant institutions, all of which were coeducational. During this period, normal schools and public high schools also began to emerge as educational alternatives for women. These factors offered women a broader array of educational options, which affected the growth and popularity of women's colleges. By 1880, more than 20,000 women were enrolled in college; this figure represented 33 percent of the college-going population. Approximately half of these students were enrolled in women-only institutions.

By 1880, there were 155 women's institutions that awarded college degrees. As they do today, these early women's colleges constituted a diverse array of institutions. Among them were religiously affiliated and independently controlled schools, including a large number of Catholic institutions. Some of these women's colleges were highly selective, and others were open admission; some were urban and others rural; and some offered a liberal arts curriculum, whereas others offered vocational training programs. Many of these women's colleges were founded in the South and Northeast. In the Midwest and West, coeducation was the norm during this era. The institutions in the South were widely perceived as "finishing schools" and were not taken seriously by many in higher education.

After the Civil War, the women's colleges of the Northeast, especially the "seven sisters" (Barnard, Bryn Mawr, Mount Holyoke, Smith, Wellesley, Vassar, and Radcliffe) wished to demonstrate that women were as capable of achieving advanced education as were men. These institutions replicated the classical curriculum of the most elite men's colleges. Indeed, compared to other educational options that women had at normal schools and coeducational institutions, the curriculum at these women's colleges focused on a liberal education rather than on preprofessional programs. These women's colleges not only replicated the curriculum of the men's colleges but also required students to meet the admission standards of the men's schools, which created enrollment problems because few women had the necessary background in Greek and Latin. Finding qualified faculty willing to teach at these women's colleges was also a significant problem in the early days. One solution to these dilemmas was the founding of coordinate colleges, institutions that shared the faculty and curriculum of men's colleges but operated as separate institutions. These institutions, including Radcliffe, Pembroke, and Barnard (coordinates of Harvard, Brown, and Columbia Universities, respectively), were considered women's colleges because the male and female students did not take classes together and because the institutions had different administrators. The seven sisters served as an enduring model of high-quality education for women.

Between 1890 and 1910, enrollment at women's colleges increased by 348 percent, but female matriculation at coeducational colleges rose 438 percent. Over a similar period, male student attendance in college increased by only 214 percent. By the turn of the twentieth century, coeducation had become the norm for women. Among the arguments in favor of coeducation were that separate education was economically wasteful, that women were equal to men and should therefore be educated with them, that single-sex institutions were unnatural, and that coeducation would be helpful in taming the spirits of young men. By 1920, women students represented 47 percent of the student body in colleges and universities. Indeed, the 1920s were a high point in women's education, and in many cases, women outnumbered men in colleges. During this era, 74 percent of the colleges and universities were coeducational, and the vast majority of female students attended these institutions. Women's colleges, however, continued to attract sufficient numbers of students to remain educationally and economically viable. The 1930s–1950s were marked by a return to more traditional views about the role of women in society. By 1950, the percentage of women in higher education dropped to a low of 30 percent, and enrollment at many women's colleges began to decline precipitously.

The 1960s and 1970s saw a more pronounced shift away from single-sex institutions and toward coeducation. During this period, the most prestigious exclusively male colleges and universities began to admit women, and many women's colleges also became coeducational. Many of the women's colleges that decided not to admit men closed due to financial exigency during this period. Indeed, many small, private, liberal arts colleges, both coeducational and single-sex, closed at this time. To many, the replacement of single-sex education with coeducation was seen as part of women's attainment of parity with men. In fact, many people believed that the shift from single-sex institutions to coeducational ones served both sexes better. Some argued that those who believed that women should attend women's colleges considered women to be different from or inferior to men. Others argued that women who attended single-sex institution did not learn to deal with men and were therefore less ready to compete and function in the "real world." As a result, the number of women's colleges today has declined to fewer than eighty institutions. The women's colleges that survived the decline in the 1970s transformed themselves from women's colleges to "colleges for women." Many of these institutions purposefully rededicated themselves and their institutional missions to serve women students. The Women's College Coalition, founded in 1972, was created to support these institutions and to increase the visibility and acceptability of women's colleges.

Contemporary Characteristics

Today, women's colleges, which number approximately seventy, educate fewer than 1 percent of all women attending postsecondary institutions and award 1 percent of all degrees conferred (25,000 degrees in 1998). Estimates are that fewer than 5 percent of college-going high school seniors will even apply to attend a women's college. Women's colleges tend to be small, ranging in size from 94 to 5,000 full-time students. Although all women's colleges are private institutions, more than half of the existing women's colleges have a religious affiliation, most often with the Catholic Church (33 percent). In terms of geographic location, almost half of the women's colleges are located in the northeastern United States, and 33 percent are located in the South. There are three women's colleges in California, and the rest are scattered around the country.

Although the most selective women's colleges, those remaining from the "seven sisters," receive the majority of attention in the media and in the research literature, women's colleges represent a diverse array of institutions. The seven sisters include the oldest, most selective, and most well endowed of the women's colleges, although two of the sisters, Vassar and Radcliffe, are no longer women's colleges. There are also two historically black four-year women's colleges, Bennett and Spelman, and a small number of two-year women's colleges. In addition, seventeen women's colleges grant master's degrees, and forty-seven grant bachelor's degrees. Women's colleges range from very selective to nonselective. From a resource perspective, the women's colleges also vary greatly—from those with healthy endowments to those institutions that are entirely dependent on tuition revenue to cover operating expenses.

Though women's colleges do not come from a single mold, they do share some common traits. For example, they serve women of color and nontraditional-age women in higher proportions than comparable coeducational institutions. The explanation for this phenomenon is twofold. First, serving women in all their diversity is a major component of the mission of many women's colleges. Second, for the existing women's colleges to survive with their original missions still intact, many had to be creative in attracting and retaining women students. Because fewer than 5 percent of high school women will even consider applying to a women's college, maintaining enrollment means that many women's colleges have had to focus their attention on attracting older women, part-time students, and transfer students. Women's colleges are also more likely than their coeducational counterparts to grant undergraduate degrees to women in the traditionally male-dominated fields (math, sciences, engineering) as compared to similar coeducational institutions.

Contemporary Importance

The contemporary importance of women's colleges outweighs their number and size. A wide array of research projects, using both quantitative and qualitative data, have demonstrated that women's colleges are among the most accessible and female-promoting environments, wherein women are taken seriously and ultimately experience success. Specifically, research suggests that women's colleges have a direct, positive impact on their students. Compared to women at coeducational institutions, for example, students at women's colleges are more satisfied with their overall college experience, are more likely to major in nontraditional fields, and express higher levels of self-esteem and leadership skills. Researchers have also found that students who have attended women's colleges are more likely than their coeducational counterparts to graduate, have high expectations of themselves, attend graduate school, and be successful in their adult lives.

There are some critics who have questioned the results of individual studies, especially those studies that measure the impact of attending a women's college on career and postgraduation outcomes. These critics focus first on those studies that use institutions rather than individuals as the unit of analysis and the fact that the studies cannot adequately control for individual student background characteristics. Second, some critics suggest that the relative success of graduates of women's colleges may be a dated phenomenon. In other words, when women students began to have access to prestigious men's colleges, did claims about women's colleges remain true? This question assumes that the success of women's colleges is due to the fact that the so-called best women students could not attend the so-called best schools in the country until the 1960s and 1970s. It also assumes that studies of women's colleges focus on the most elite of these institutions. A third critique about the research on women's colleges is that it fails to account for the self-selection of students. In other words, some suggest that women who choose to attend women's colleges are somehow predestined to be successful and that one cannot credit the institution for the outcomes produced.

The best way to address such critiques is to examine the literature on women's colleges in its totality rather than to look at one study at a time. Indeed, studies taken one at a time represent only pieces of a larger puzzle. Research is most powerful when conclusions are drawn from a wide variety of studies using different methods, sources of data, and time periods. In reviewing the literature, it is clear that the majority of studies on women's colleges, including those that control for both institutional and individual characteristics of students, come to the same conclusion. As such, although it is impossible to randomly assign students to attend either a women's college or coeducational college, the self-selection argument appears specious. Further, not only early studies make claim to the outcomes associated with women's colleges; current studies using contemporary college attendees also come to the same conclusions. An examination of the totality of scholarship on women's colleges finds that despite differences between methodologies and approach, the extent of overlap, consistency, and corroboration in research findings are so great as to warrant the conclusion that a woman attending an all-women's college, compared with her counterpart at a comparable coeducational institution, is more likely to achieve positive outcomes such as having higher educational aspirations, attaining a graduate degree, entering a sex-atypical career, and achieving prominence in her field.

Women's Colleges as Models

The positive outcomes associated with attending a women's college have led some researchers to explore the characteristics of these institutions to see how they can serve as models for coeducational institutions. Seven institutional traits stand out as descriptive of how women's colleges facilitate the success of their women students. Women's colleges (1) clarify and communicate a mission that puts women at the center; (2) believe women can achieve and hold them to high expectations; (3) make students feel like they matter; (4) provide strong, positive role models; (5) provide ample opportunities for women to engage in leadership activities; (6) include women in the curriculum; and, (7) create safe spaces where women can form a critical mass.

Many of the characteristics common to women's colleges parallel traits associated with successful academic institutions for men and women students. What sets women's colleges apart from most coeducational institutions, however, is the purposefulness with which the former respond to the needs of their women students. The success of women is central to the values held by campus constituents. This belief undergirds many of the actions of both the institutions and individual campus constituents. These are environments in which the situation for women is not only favorable but also empowering, colleges where there is a critical mass of women faculty, women are nurtured and challenged, and woman-related issues dominate campus discussions. These colleges act intentionally to take women seriously.

Women's colleges carry out these traits in different ways, exemplifying the idea that "successful" colleges are not all alike. Although separate examinations of the characteristics of each institution are illuminating, it is important to understand that the whole of these institutions is greater than the sum of their parts—one cannot look at a single element in isolation. Instead, it is the combination of characteristics, the ethos of these institutions, that makes them unique and able to facilitate the success of their students. What sets women's colleges apart from other campuses is that they are purposeful in their adoption of structures, policies, practices, and curricula that are sensitive to the needs of women.

Lisa E. Wolf-Wendel

See also Part 1: Black Women's Colleges; Catholic Women's Colleges; Coeducation; Southern Baptist Colleges

References and further reading

Harwarth, Irene, Mindi Maline, and Elizabeth DeBra. 1997. *Women's Colleges in the United States: History, Issues, and Challenges.* Washington, DC: U.S. Government Printing Office.

Lasser, Carol, ed. 1987. *Educating Men and Women Together: Coeducation in a Changing World.* Urbana: University of Illinois Press.

Riordan, Charles. 1994. "The Value of Attending a Women's College: Education, Occupation and Income Benefits." *Journal of Higher Education* 65: 486–510.

Solomon, Barbara M. 1985. *In the Company of Educated Women: A History of Women and Higher Education in America.* New Haven, CT: Yale University Press.

Tidball, Elizabeth, Daryl Smith, Charles Tidball, and Lisa Wolf-Wendel. 1999. *Taking Women Seriously: Lessons and Legacies for Higher Education from Women's Colleges.* Phoenix, AZ: ACE/Oryx Press.

Wolf-Wendel, Lisa E. 1998. "Models of Excellence: The Baccalaureate Origins of Successful African American, European American and Hispanic Women." *Journal of Higher Education* 69, no. 2: 144–172.

Part 2

GENDER THEORY AND THE ACADEMY

Overview

Gender theory in the West arose from the distinction made between biological differences between men and women, designated as "sex," and social, cultural, and psychological differences that were ascribed to sexual difference, designated as "gender." The concept of "gender" embraced a very wide spectrum of phenomena, including social roles, behaviors, appearance, experience, and identity.

Although some theorists maintained that human biological sex differences were the basis for all gender differences, for most, the sex/gender distinction affirmed the relationship between the two as "not natural," or not necessarily or fully so, and thus opened a field of study regarding the "social construction of gender." In this, Simone de Beauvoir's assertion that women are not born but rather made launched a significant critical inquiry into gender.

Several lines of inquiry developed from this beginning. First, gender theorists studied gender itself, asking about the apparent differences between men and women in respect to their attitudes, behaviors, relationships, social roles, activities, and interactions. Numerous studies delved into the nature and extent of these differences. Within higher education, for example, it became possible to argue that men and women may have different teaching and learning styles and that approaches to education that used men as the norm for both student and teacher would therefore be less effective for or even detrimental to women. Second, gender theory investigated the construction of gender—the means and mechanisms through which societies transformed biologically "sexed" beings into "gendered" ones. Again, regarding higher education, it was apparent that the structure and content of education was part of this socializing process and thus should be subject to question and critique. Finally, gender theorists also inquired as to the reasons for the existence of gender, asking whether differentiation on the basis of sex has been necessary for social survival, convenient to the division of labor, enabling of the maintenance of other social relations, and so forth.

All these lines of inquiry contained both normative and empirical dimensions. The emergence and development of these questions alongside as well as within "second-wave" (post–World War II) feminist theory dramatically heightened the critical bent of the debates within gender theory. Feminist theorists, while disagreeing about the origins of gender, the value of "femininity," and the direction that feminist politics should take in response to gender, nevertheless concurred that gender theory

Women were once thought intellectually inferior to men; here, students at the Hampton Institute learn math and science in 1899 (Library of Congress)

should be governed by an analysis of gender that saw it not just as a question of difference but as one of power. That is, gender is marked by sexual asymmetry, inequality, and male dominance. Gender theory provides a very useful way of distinguishing among the various branches of feminist theory. Each theory can be examined for its explanation of gender difference, arguments regarding the value of gender, implications, and relationship to social change.

Liberal feminism argued that gender was largely the result of childhood socialization. More liberated parenting approaches combined with the removal of gender stereotypes in education would free children to develop as individuals, unencumbered by expectations of their behavior based on their biological sex. Although some liberal feminists emphasized the importance of increased confidence, competitiveness, and achievement for girls, ensuring them greater public success, others stressed the need to allow both sexes to develop in a nongendered fashion. Within higher education, the liberal approach was two-pronged. It attempted to reduce the socialization effects that produced women as differently gendered from men and thereby to emphasize the essential similarity of women and men and their ability to compete and succeed on equal terms. In addition, the liberal feminist approach attempted at the same time to remove barriers to women's full participation, including consideration of and recognition for barriers based in differently gendered experience, such as different educational styles, familial responsibilities, career paths, and so forth.

Radical feminists were more critical of "femininity" than liberal feminists. Rather than viewing gender stereotypes as vestiges of less progressive times, radical feminists saw the imposition of "femininity" on women as one of the chief tools of patriarchal power. As long as women conformed to social expectations of passivity, submissiveness, nurturance, gentleness, and so forth, it served male domination. Consequently, radical feminists advocated the overthrow of gender and liberation of women from conventional gender roles, including motherhood, heterosexuality, and sexual monogamy. Among those institutions that radical feminists saw as historically aligned with patriarchy were institutions of higher education. Women in higher education would thus be hard-pressed to break with patriarchal, hierarchical structures within the institutions, suspicious of any benefits they might gain from the institution, and wary of reproducing asymmetrical power relations as a result of their participation.

Cultural feminists, by contrast, saw women's "femininity" as an alternative and profound source of female power, one that women themselves and society in general needed to value more greatly. Whether understood as the result of women's biology and especially women's role in reproduction or as the result of women's socialization, the capacity of women to be intimate, form connections with others, nurture, and sustain was proffered as the legitimate basis for feminism and as a model for greater societal health. The cultural feminist approach to gender extended into some models of ecofeminism, the women's spirituality movement, and the women's peace movement. In higher education, the intent of cultural feminists was often to introduce alternative learning models into the classroom—ideally even to create women's universities and colleges, which would serve as models of feminist culture and practice.

Socialist feminists examined the issue of women's oppression as imbricated with other oppressions, specifically class-based oppression. Initially divided among those who sought single-system analysis (a single explanation for the mechanisms of oppression operative in capitalism and in patriarchy) and others who developed dual-system analyses (separate, albeit integrated analyses of capitalist oppression and patriarchal oppression), this body of theory has been oriented toward finding the material, historical, and contextual bases for multiple oppressions (class, gender, race, sexuality, and so forth). The gender theory proffered in these analyses has varied widely. Among the most noteworthy was Gayle Rubin's development of the concept of "sex/gender system" in 1975, in which she theorized that social structures such as kinship "produce" women as gendered, "domesticated," and heterosexual in order to meet labor, sexual and reproductive, and societal needs. Other socialist feminists have noted the usefulness to capitalism of the gendered division of labor in the household, volunteer work, and paid labor (Barrett 1980). Socialist feminists have examined the maintenance of gender relations (subordination of women through lower pay, devaluation of women's work, sexual harassment, etc.) in the workplace, as well as the phenomenon of the double workday.

Psychoanalytic feminists focused less on gender behavior and issues of socialization and more on the acquisition of gender identity itself. Freudian theory posited that gender identity was entrenched in the Oedipal phase of child development. The sex of a child determined his or her passage through this stage and its eventual outcome. The post-Oedipal stage resulted in a child with marked gender characteristics, which would be sustained into adulthood, including both different energy levels for men and women and differently established superegos (with women having less available energy and reduced moral capacity). Feminist usages of Sigmund Freud's work, such as that of Juliet Mitchell (1974), attempted to rehabilitate psychoanalysis for feminism by adapting his analysis of gender formation into a critique of gender itself and, coinciding with it, a critique of patriarchal social relations and the nuclear family. According to Mitchell, Freud's work could be used to show how the patriarchal family was destined to reproduce male hierarchy, heterosexuality, and the devalorization of women.

Two other models of psychoanalytic theory have also had a significant effect on feminist theory. Object relations psychoanalytic theory, which stresses the child's relationship with its earliest caregiver, has been analyzed by Nancy Chodorow (1978) as a profoundly gendered relationship in which the fact that mothers do the vast majority of early child care results in differential gender identity development among male and female children. Male children develop a sense of self in distinction from their mothers, one that is thereby more role-based, individuated, and focused on achievement. Female children, by contrast, develop their identity as relational, contextual, and personal. As with Freudian analysis, gender identity is argued to be aligned with a particular ethical sensibility. In the case of object relations–based psychoanalytic feminism, boys mature morally into patterns of ethical reasoning based on notions of universal principles of justice. Girls are more likely to develop moral reasoning abilities that emphasize particularity, context, and relationships (Gilligan 1982).

Lacanian psychoanalytic theory reinterpreted Freud along structuralist and linguistic lines. According to this revision of classical psychoanalysis, the sense of ourselves as coherent, stable, unitary subjects necessitated the repression of otherness, difference, instability, and chaos. The desire to be self-mastering subjects also required internalizing the "Non/nom" of the father. That is, becoming a social subject required the necessary repression of and identification with existing social structures and linguistic representations in which masculinity and maleness dominate. Although both men and women attain subjectivity in this way, "woman" as a concept endures as the principal figure of the other, of repression. Subjectivity is thus, by definition, a masculine position. Women's assumption of subjectivity is inherently divided and problematic as a result. Theorists like Luce Irigaray, in her adaptation of Lacanian and Freudian psychoanalytic theory, attempt to use the depiction of female subjectivity as problematic, divided, multiple, and incomplete as a liberating tool for feminism.

In all the models of psychoanalytic theory, gender, although not fully biologically determined, appeared to be certainly less mutable than theories that focused more on socialization as the basis for gender differences. Their emphasis on gender identity is strongly linked to typical gender behavior and attitudes, entrenching these as corollary to the acquisition of gender identity itself. One attains a core sense of self that is either male and masculine or female and feminine. Psychoanalytic theory also stressed the connection between one's gender identity and one's reasoning, values, relational ability, and sense of self.

Postmodern feminist theory embraced the Lacanian version of the self as inherently far more fluid, multiple, and indeterminate than it is in self-presentation. French postmodern feminists sought to exploit the potential of women's ambiguous and ambivalent position in relation to the defined masculine self. Postmodern theory's critique of the subject was developed by postmodern feminism into a critique of the subject as "always-already" gendered. Truly radical politics, according to this theoretical model, required deconstructing this self; an explicit deconstruction of the categories of gender and sex was seen by postmodern feminism as necessary to this project. In Judith Butler's influential work, she suggests that gender could be usefully deployed against itself, undermining its own social power (1990). Donna Haraway, in a significant postmodern feminist tract, "The Cyborg Manifesto" (1991), argues against analyses of gender or class based on oppression and dualistic differentiation. Rather she extols the production of new categories that blur distinctions of human or animal, male or female, and human or machine, advocating the imagery of the cyborg as a means to do so. From quite a different use of postmodern feminist theory, Sandra Bartky (1990) employs Michel Foucault's theoretical development of "discourse theory" to describe the ways in which gender is played in the disciplinary practices of contemporary femininity.

Postmodern feminist theory enjoys an ambivalent relationship with higher education. The critique of reason that postmodern theory presents operates at a sophisticated theoretical level. It has, perhaps ironically, assisted in an acceptance of postmodern feminist gender theory, even with its critique of Western-based models of rationality and subjectivity, within the social sciences and humanities (usually dependent on those self-same models) at a faster rate and with more credibility than some earlier models of feminist theory.

Postmodern theory's critique of the categories of gender also converges with a critique of the category of gender arising from women of color's critique of feminism. The centrality of gender to feminist theory has served, according to this critique, to "other" all other "others." Many feminist proponents of gender theory rested their analyses on universalist presumptions about both the significance of gender identity and the specific characteristics of masculinity and femininity that were based on white Western women's experience of gender. Antiracist feminism argued against the assumptions that were made about gender and femininity, always presented as the femininity ascribed to white Western women. Sojourner Truth's compelling speech "Ain't I a Woman" has been regularly used to make this point. Truth argues that assumptions about femininity as passive and weak have never applied to her, and yet she has equal claim to the category of "woman." At the same time, many antiracist feminists also argued against the centrality of gender to feminist theory. If gender is indeed socially constructed and therefore most often applies differently to different women in different times and contexts, then positing an understanding of gender as primary within feminist theory marginalizes all those women who do not conform to the dominant pattern of socialization and experience. This set of assumptions has been further developed by its extension into Third World scholarship by Western feminists such as Chandra Talpade Mohanty (1991). Some women of color have worked directly to combat this dominance by presenting their own lives and perspectives (Hull, Scott, and Smith 1982; Moraga and Anzaldúa 1983). Many have written about the need to develop an expressly antiracist feminism to deal with issues of identity and oppression (hooks 1981; Bannerji 1993; Spelman 1988). Although there are some logical parallels between antiracist feminism and postmodern feminism, there is also some ambivalence about situating antiracist feminism or its analysis of identity within any one feminist theoretical model.

Most recently, the concept of gender has come under further scrutiny in the development of transgender and transsexual politics. Further debates within this movement separate the aspects of gender that focus on traditional gender behaviors, roles, and activities from those that focus on a sense of core gender identity (Namaste 2000). Many of those who identify as transgender dispute the binary division of gender into either male or female. Some argue there is a need for multiple gender categories beyond male and female. Others who identify as transsexual defy explanations of core gender identity, which ground it either in a simple understanding of biological sex or in a straightforward analysis of socialization processes. In either case, there are complex relationships to feminist theory, which has largely continued to presume the confluence of gender and sex, even while being critical of it.

As the editors of the summer 1987 edition of *Signs* argued, "gender is an analytic concept whose meanings we work to elucidate, and a subject matter we proceed to study as we try to define it." In the analyses of women's participation and role in higher education, gender as an analytic category serves to explain their advances and continued challenges.

Eleanor MacDonald

References and further reading

Bannerji, Himani. 1993. *Returning the Gaze: Essays on Racism, Feminism and Politics.* Toronto: Sister Vision Press.

Barrett, Michele. 1980. *Women's Oppression Today: Problems in Marxist Feminist Analysis.* London: Verso.

Bartky, Sandra Lee. 1990. "Foucault, Femininity, and the Modernization of Patriarchal Power." Pp. 63–82 in *Femininity and Domination.* New York: Routledge.

Beauvoir, Simone de. 1953. *The Second Sex.* Trans. H. M. Parshey. New York: Alfred A. Knopf.

Butler, Judith. 1990. *Gender Trouble: Feminism and the Subversion of Identity.* New York: Routledge.

Chodorow, Nancy. 1978. *The Reproduction of Mothering: Psychoanalysis and the Sociology of Gender.* Berkeley: University of California Press.

Gilligan, Carol. 1982. *In a Different Voice: Psychological Theory and Women's Development.* Cambridge, MA: Harvard University Press.

Haraway, Donna. 1991. "A Cyborg Manifesto: Science, Technology, and Socialist-Feminism in the Late

Twentieth Century." Pp. 149–181 in *Simians, Cyborgs, and Women: The Reinvention of Nature,* by Donna Haraway. New York: Routledge.

hooks, bell. 1981. *Ain't I a Woman: Black Women and Feminism.* Boston: South End Press.

Hull, Gloria R., Patricia Bell Scott, and Barbara Smith. 1982. *All the Women Are White, All the Blacks Are Men, but Some of Us Are Brave.* New York: Feminist Press.

Irigaray, Luce. 1985. *This Sex Which Is Not One.* Trans. Catherine Porter. Ithaca, NY: Cornell University Press.

Mitchell, Juliet. 1974. *Psychoanalysis and Feminism.* London: Allen Lane.

Mohanty, Chandra Talpade. 1991. "Under Western Eyes: Feminist Scholarship and Colonial Discourses." Pp. 51–80 in *Third World Women and the Politics of Feminism,* ed. Chandra Mohanty, Ann Russo, and Lourdes Torres. Bloomington: Indiana University Press.

Moraga, Cherrie, and Gloria Anzaldúa, eds. 1983. *This Bridge Called My Back: Writings by Radical Women of Color.* New York: Kitchen Table, Women of Color Press.

Namaste, Viviane Ki. 2000. *Invisible Lives: The Erasure of Transsexual and Transgendered People.* Ithaca, NY: Cornell University Press.

O'Barr, Jean F., ed. 1987. "Within and Without: Women, Gender, and Theory." *Signs* 12, no. 4 (Summer).

Rich, Adrienne. 1979. "Toward a Woman-Centered University." In *On Lies, Secrets and Silence: Selected Prose 1966–1978,* by Adrienne Rich. New York: W. W. Norton.

Rubin, Gayle. 1975. "The Traffic of Women: Notes on the Political Economy of Sex." Pp. 157–210 in *Toward an Anthropology of Women,* ed. Rayna R. Reiter. New York: Monthly Review Press.

Spelman, Elizabeth. 1988. *Inessential Woman: Problems of Exclusion in Feminist Thought.* Boston: Beacon Press.

Truth, Sojourner. 1998. "Ain't I a Woman." Pp. 520–521 in *Issues in Feminism: An Introduction to Women's Studies,* ed. Sheila Ruth. Mountain View, CA: Mayfield.

Demographics of Gender and Race

Although the twentieth century saw legal, social, political, and cultural changes that have enabled women to make much progress in their access to and success in higher education, the progress made is by no means complete. Disparities and obstacles can still be readily evidenced across and within higher educational institutions: the distribution of women and men across certain fields of study remains highly disproportional; women continue to trail men in graduating from top-tier colleges and universities; within colleges and universities, black and white students are highly segregated by major; women, specifically those of color, face barriers when compared to their male colleagues in decisions regarding faculty reappointment, tenure, promotion, and salaries.

Laws to open up higher education for women have been instituted since the 1970s. In 1972 the U.S. Congress passed Title IX of the Educational Amendments Act, which prohibited sex discrimination in federally funded education. Regulations declared under Title IX allowed for "affirmative or remedial action in instances in which members of one sex must be treated differently to overcome the specific effects of past discrimination" (NOW Legal Defense and Education Fund, Subpart A, 106.1–106.9). Also in 1972, Title VII of the Civil Rights Act of 1964, which banned employment discrimination on the basis of race, color, religion, sex, or national origin, was amended to apply to private and public educational institutions. In 1974, Congress passed the Women's Educational Equity Act, which made provisions for the technical and federal monetary support of local efforts to eliminate obstacles for females in every area of education. Finally, in 1976 the Vocational Education Act of 1963 was amended to require affirmative action by states in eliminating discrimination and sex bias in vocational education. In 1984, however, the Supreme Court, in *Grove City v. Bell,* decided that the nondiscrimination law in Title IX did not cover all programs in an educational institution, but only those that directly received federal funds. However, Title IX's provisions were restored with the Civil Rights Restoration Act of 1987.

Before 1972, the climate and policies of most colleges and universities were inhospitable to women: quotas were instituted to limit the number of women admitted; women had to meet more stringent admissions criteria than men; as doctoral program applicants, women oftentimes had to explain how they could balance a career and family; greater preference was given to men in the awarding of loans, scholarships, and fellowships; legal protection against sexual harassment within educational institutions was nonexistent; women were not granted tenure, especially at the elite universities and colleges; women earned less than and were not promoted at the same rates as their male counterparts; and finally, women's access to high-level administrative positions was severely limited.

Since the passage of Title IX, women have indeed steadily exceeded men in terms of the number of associate, bachelor's, and master's degrees earned. In 1970, 43.2 percent of the total number of undergraduate degrees awarded were given to women, but by 1994 the number had increased to 55.7 percent. Women received 59.5 percent of all associate degrees, an increase from 42.9 percent in 1970, and 54.6 percent of all bachelor degrees, an increase from 43.2 percent in 1970. By 1994, women also earned 57.3 percent of all graduate degrees. In 1994 women earned 54.5 percent of all master's degrees, an increase from 39.7 percent in 1970, and 41.2 percent of all first professional degrees, an increase from 5.2 percent in 1970. In terms of the particular professional degrees, from 1993 to 1994 women were awarded "43 percent of all J.D.s, 41 percent of all M.D.s, 38.5 percent of all D.D.S./D.M.D.s, and 46 percent of all M.B.A.s." By 1995, women were earning 39 percent of the Ph.D.s, an increase from the 11.7 percent earned between 1960 and 1970 (Glazer-Raymo 1999, 40–41).

However, women's progress in higher education cannot be measured solely by the number of degrees given. Women's participation in the physical sciences, mathematics, engineering, and computer science continues to lag behind that of white and Asian men's. At the undergraduate level, in terms of associate degrees, women were awarded 31 percent of the degrees given in science and engineering in 1996, compared to 23 percent in 1983. With reference to the racial/ethnic breakdown, however, minority women did receive a greater proportion of associate science and engineering degrees than did white women: white women received 29 percent of the associate science and engineering degrees awarded to whites, whereas Asian women received 33 percent, Hispanic women received 34 percent, black women received 38 percent, and American Indian women received 48 percent of those awarded to their respective racial/ethnic group. Black, Asian, and American Indian women received 50 percent of the associate physical science degrees and more than 50 percent of the associate computer science degrees

Fewer women, especially women of color, are found in nontraditional fields such as science and engineering (Courtesy of the Association of Women in Science)

awarded to their respective group. In terms of bachelor's degrees in science and engineering, even though women earned 47 percent of those awarded in 1996, compared to the 38–39 percent in the early to mid-1980s, women's representation in those categories is skewed toward the fields of psychology, the biological sciences, and the social sciences. In 1996 women earned 36.2 percent of bachelor's degrees in physical and earth sciences, compared to 14 percent earned in 1966. In 1984 women were awarded a high of 37 percent of all computer science bachelor's degrees, but in 1996 the proportion dropped to 28 percent. Women also earned 18 percent of the engineering bachelor's degrees, an increase of only 1 percent of the total in 1966. In terms of the racial/ethnic breakdown of science and engineering bachelor's degrees awarded, in 1996 black, Hispanic, and American Indian women earned more than 50 percent of the total science and engineering degrees given to their respective groups, whereas white and Asian women were awarded less than 50 percent. But once again, the proportional gain for black, Hispanic, and American Indian women came from an increase of degrees awarded in biological or agricultural sciences, psychology, and social sciences. Black women were the only group who received a larger proportion than men of bachelor's degrees awarded to their racial/ethnic group in the physical sciences (57 percent) and mathematics (51.6 percent).

At the graduate level, in terms of master's degrees, in 1996 women received 39 percent of the degrees awarded in science and engineering, compared with 13 percent in 1966. However, as with the bachelor's degrees, in 1996 women earned the greater percentage of the science and engineering master's degrees in the biological or agricultural sciences, the social sciences, and psychology. In 1996 women received only 17 percent of the master's degrees awarded in engineering, and approximately 30 percent of the degrees in mathematics and computer science, a proportion that has not changed much since the late 1980s. With reference to the racial/ethnic breakdown of the science and engineering master's degrees awarded, black women were the only minority group who received more than half (56 percent) of those degrees awarded to their ethnic/racial group.

Finally, in terms of doctorates, by 1997, women earned 33 percent of all those awarded in science and engineering, as compared to the 8 percent awarded in 1966. In 1994 women had received 22 percent of the doctoral degrees awarded in the physical sciences, 24.5 percent of those in mathematics, and 14.4 percent of those in engineering. By 1997, the proportion of degrees awarded to women in engineering had dropped to 12 percent. In terms of the racial/ethnic breakdown of the doctoral science and engineering degrees given, in 1975, Hispanic, Asian, American Indian, and black women received fewer than 1 percent of all those degrees awarded. By 1996 that proportion had increased to 1.5 percent for Hispanic women, 0.2 percent for American Indian women, 5 percent for Asian women, and 1.6 percent for black women. Hispanic, American Indian, Asian, and black women also received less than half the science and engineering doctorates awarded to their respective racial/ethnic group (National Science Foundation 2000; Glazer-Raymo 1999).

Educational research also points to a gender gap in terms of women's graduation from high-ranking and elite colleges and universities. Though the gap is modest, in that "only 14.5 percent of women would have to change schools to be distributed in the same manner as men" (Jacobs 1999, 172), the reasons given for the gap in the current literature raise pertinent social and cultural questions about why it exists (Glazer-Raymo 1999; Herbst 1989). The gender stratification that exists between high-ranking and lower-ranking colleges and universities is attributed to two factors. First, a disproportionate number of men are represented in engineering programs, which historically are found in colleges and universities that are highly selective or elite. In contrast, women are overrepresented in schools of education, which historically are found in low-ranking colleges and universities. Second, women constitute the majority of part-time students. Elite colleges and universities, however, usually do not accept many part-time students. With reference to the first point above, education is among one of the largest fields of study. From 1997 to 1998, the third-largest number of bachelor's degrees was given in the field of education (105,968), and the highest number of master's and doctoral degrees was also given in that field, with 114,691 and 6,729, respectively (*Digest of Education Statistics* 2000). Since women earn the majority of the large number of education degrees conferred across all levels (from 1997 to 1998, women were awarded 79,666 bachelor's, 87,621 master's, and 4,250 Ph.D./Ed.D. degrees), their overrepresentation in this field lowers the average standing of the colleges they attend (*Digest of Education Statistics* 2000). However, researchers question why schools of education are linked to low-ranking colleges and universities. Historical review of the situation indicates that although engineering schools originated in affiliation with large land grant institutions and were connected intellectually to the physical sciences and thereby to the elite universities from the nineteenth century onward, undergraduate education programs were an outgrowth of normal schools that eventually evolved into state colleges and occasionally universities and were thus viewed as lacking a distinct intellectual foundation. But pushing this reasoning one step further, some researchers (Jacobs 1999; Glazer-Raymo 1999; Herbst 1989) question whether the gender of the students and practitioners who constitute the majority in the field of education is in fact closely linked to the low-status valuation of the field and the institutions in which it is located. Since it was mainly women who taught in the schoolrooms, education has usually been associated with low-paid, low-prestige "women's work." Researchers point out that the lens through which one views and evaluates programs of education is often colored with gender presuppositions and biases. Therefore, women's attainment of parity with men in graduating from high-ranking colleges and universities may be partly dependent upon a cultural and social change in the way one perceives and evaluates the status of education programs and schools of education.

Further, although segregation by major across universities and colleges between African American and white women is low, segregation by major *within* colleges and universities between black and white women is quite high. For there to be an even apportioning of African American women and white women across fields of study, 44.3 percent of the black women students would have to change their majors (Jacobs 1996; Simpson 2001). Moreover, black students are not only segregated by major but are also clustered around a limited range of majors that differ from one college to the next. Precisely because the majors that students cluster around are different depending upon the college or university, such clustering, according to researcher Jerry A. Jacobs, cannot be attributed to students' failure rates in particular competitive fields of study. If such had been the case, then the clustering evidenced would have been in the same majors regardless of which college or university the student attended. Rather, one of the causes that Jacobs attributes for the racial segregation by major within colleges and universities is the academic and social isolation that limits black students' study and career choices, an isolation that has been well-documented by others (Johnson 1997; Aubert 1997; Williams 1996; Wilson 1993; hooks 2000). For example, black students may find that certain majors have very few minority students or are structured in a way that the material is presented from a unilateral perspective (usually a white male one) and thus may find such majors unwelcoming. Students may also gravitate to the majors in which there are women and black faculty members.

The unfortunate fact is that faculties of color are still underrepresented at the university level, and many face racial and gender-based discrimination, loneliness, and lack of mentoring and support mechanisms. Women of color are often deliberately not included in collaborative research projects with their colleagues and consequently have less access to sources for research (Justus, Freitig, and Parker 1987). In addition, they often face the serious challenge of integrating their career values with the demands of cultural traditions and family life.

According to the American Council on Education, black scholars constituted only 2.1 percent of full-time faculty and 2.4 percent of part-time faculty in 1989, compared to 2.0 percent and 2.3 percent in 1979. In 1989 only 0.7 percent of black women working in higher education were full professors; 1.6 percent associate professors; 2.7 percent assistant professors; 3.3 percent instructors, lecturers, and other faculty; and 0.2 percent administrators (U.S. Equal Opportunity Commission 1988).

This disparity is even greater in fields that have been traditionally dominated by men, namely those of science and engineering faculties. And at some institutions, even though the applicant pool of qualified young women scientists continues to expand, the percentages of women holding faculty positions are decreasing rather than increasing. At Harvard University, the percentage of women faculty members in the natural sciences dropped from 19.7 percent in 1995 to 13.7 percent in 2001. According to National Science Foundation data, after almost three decades, women still make up only 12.5 percent of senior faculty (associate and full professors) in the natural sciences and engineering at all U.S. universities and four-year colleges. In the top ninety research universities, less than 10 percent of senior faculty in those disciplines were women in 1995. And at the senior academic ranks, the numbers are particularly uneven; in 1995 less than 5 percent of Harvard University's senior faculty were female, and at Massachusetts Institute of Technology, women made up only 6.2 percent of the top ranks (Lawler 1999).

To exacerbate the inequality still further, the passage of an anti–affirmation action ballot measure called Proposition 209 has widened a gender and racial gap that already needed bridging. Proposition 209, which was initiated in 1996 in California, required that the state and its local jurisdictions "not discriminate against, or grant preferential treatment to, any individual or group on the basis of race, sex, color, ethnicity, or national origin in the operating of public employment, public education, or public contracting." As a direct result of the ballot, the numbers of women and minorities at the University of California have been decreasing (Ong 1999).

In 1998 women accounted for only 27 percent of the University of California's new hires, a year when women earned 48 percent of doctorates awarded to U.S. citizens, according to data prepared for the Senate Select Committee on Government Oversight. Although university officials have defended their position by claiming to have hired more women than any other major university for the year 1997–1998, the University of California's faculty was 23.5 percent female, compared to Harvard's total of 12.9 percent ("UC Hiring Fewer Professors after Prop. 209" 2001).

According to the U.S. Department of Education, the number of women Ph.D.'s has been progressively rising. The department projects that the percentage of doctoral degrees awarded to women will grow from 37.9 percent in 1996 to 49.00 percent by 2006, but women will still be predominantly clustered in the generally untenured ranks of assistant professors and lecturers ("The Future" 1997).

At first-tier universities nationwide, women make up only a fraction of tenured arts and sciences faculty as a whole. According to a recent survey by the American Chemistry Society of the top fifty universities, 6 percent of full professors are women. The figure escalates to only 8 percent when all Ph.D.-granting institutions are added to the mix (Schneider 2000). At Harvard University, women were among the nineteen newly tenured appointments in Harvard's faculty of arts and sciences last year. Yet women still account for only 14 percent of the tenured arts and sciences faculty as a whole (Healy 2001).

In *Unbending Gender: Why Family and Work Conflict and What to Do About It,* Joan Williams states that women are much less likely than men to receive tenure. Though women's rate of tenure was the same in 1992 as it was in 1975, men's rate of tenure rose sharply over a similar time frame, from 46 percent in 1975 to 72 percent in 1994–1995 (Williams 1999). According to panelists at a recent Association of American Law Schools meeting, the probability of female and minority professors receiving tenure was much less than that for their white male colleagues. In 1997–1998, 90 percent of tenured law faculty were white, 4.9 percent were black, 2.5 percent Latino, and 1.2 percent Asian. Of the faculty members hired in 1990 and 1991, 80.6 percent of white male professors won tenure, but only 57.1 percent of minority law professors met the same success, according to the report. And 61.3 percent of women received tenure, compared with 72.4 percent of men (Willdorf 2000).

In addition to biases in tenure and promotion, salary discrepancies between men and women have been found for every category of U.S. academic institution and for institutions with and without unions or collective bargaining agreements. S. Martha West documented the fact that female full professors were earning 89 percent of the salaries of males in 1982 and 88 percent in 1995; women assistant professors were making 93 percent of the salaries of their male colleagues at that rank (West 1995).

Segregation and discrimination by race and gender for women in higher education point to the continuing need for positive practices and policies that increase the hiring, tenure, and promotion of women and minority professors; that sensitize nonminority professors to the needs and challenges that often face minority students; and that allow for the active inclusion of minority voices in administrative decisions, be they of curriculum development or campus activities. Such policies and practices can serve to engender an inclusive and equitable climate within colleges and universities for women of all races and ethnicities.

Shaireen Rasheed and Shilpi Sinha

See also Part 2: Intersection of Gender and Race; Part 5: Gender Inequality

References and further reading

Aubert, Sandy E. 1997. "Black Students on White Campuses: Overcoming the Isolation." Pp. 141–146 in *Sailing against the Wind: African Americans and Women in U.S. Education,* ed. Kofi Lomotey. Albany: State University of New York Press.

Glazer-Raymo, Judith. 1999. *Shattering the Myths: Women in Academe.* Baltimore: Johns Hopkins University Press.

Grove City College v. Bell, 465 U.S. 555 (1984).

Healy, Patrick. 2001. "Faculty Shortage: Women in Sciences Colleges Talk Perks, New Tenure Rules." *Boston Globe,* 31 January.

Herbst, J. C. 1989. *And Sadly Teach: Teacher Education and Professionalization in American Culture.* Madison: University of Wisconsin Press.

hooks, bell. 2000. "Black and Female: Reflections on Graduate School." Pp. 386–390 in *Women in Higher Education,* ed. Judith Glazer-Raymo, Barbara K. Townsend, and Becky Ropers-Huilman. 2nd ed. Boston: Pearson Custom Publishing.

Jacobs, Jerry A. 1996. "Gender, Race, and Ethnic Segregation between and within Colleges." Philadelphia: Mellon Foundation (draft report).

———. 1999. "Gender and the Stratification of Colleges." *Journal of Higher Education* 70, no. 2 (March–April): 161–187.

Johnson, Stuart. 1997. "Ethnic/Cultural Centers on Predominantly White Campuses: Are They Necessary?" Pp. 155–162 in *Sailing against the Wind: African Americans and Women in U.S. Education,* ed. Kofi Lomotey. Albany: State University of New York Press.

Justus, Bennett J., Sandra Freitig, and Leann L. Parker. 1987. *The University of California in the Twenty-First Century: Successful Approaches to Faculty Diversity.* Berkeley: University of California Press.

Lawler, Andrew. 1999. "Tenured Women Battle to Make It Less Lonely at the Top." *Science,* November 12.

National Center for Education Statistics. 2001. *Digest of Education Statistics.* Washington, DC: U.S. Department of Ecucation.

National Science Foundation. 2000. *Women and Minorities and Persons with Disabilities in Science and Engineering.* NSF00–327. Arlington, VA: National Science Foundation.

NOW Legal Defense and Education Fund, Mid-Atlantic Equity Consortium, and The Network. *An Annotated Summary of the Regulation for Title IX, Education Amendments of 1972.* http://www.maec.org/annotate.html. Cited July 24, 2001.

Ong, Paul. 1999. "Proposition 209 and Its Implications." P. 198 in *Impacts of Affirmative Action: Policies and Consequences in California,* ed. Paul Ong. Thousand Oaks, CA: Sage.

Schneider, Alison. 2000. "Support for a Rare Breed: Tenured Women Chemists." *Chronicle of Higher Education* (November 10): A12.

Simpson, Jacqueline C. 2001. "Segregated by Subject: Racial Differences in the Factors Influencing Academic Major between European Americans, Asian Americans, and African, Hispanic, and Native Americans." *Journal of Higher Education* 72, no.1 (January–February): 63–100.

"The Future: Women Get More Degrees Than Men Except at Doctoral Level." *About Women on Campus* 6, no. 2 (Spring 1997): 7.

"UC Hiring Fewer Professors after Prop. 209." 2001. *Black Issues in Higher Education* (March).

U.S. Equal Opportunity Commission. 1988. "EEO-6 Higher Education Staff Information Surveys, 1985." Pp. 33–34 in *Minorities in Higher Education, Seventh Annual Status Report.* Washington, DC: American Council on Education.

West, S. Martha. 1995. "Frozen in Time." *Academe* 81: 26–29.

Willdorf, Nina. 2000. "Minority Law Professors Said to Need Mentors." *Chronicle of Higher Education* (January 21): A18.

Williams, Joan. 1999. *Unbending Gender: Why Family and Work Conflict and What to Do about It.* New York: Oxford University Press.

Williams, Patricia J. 1996. "Talking about Race, Talking about Gender, Talking about How We Talk." Pp. 69–94 in *Anti-Feminism in the Academy,* ed. Veve Clark, Shirley Nelson Garner, Margaret Higonnet, and Ketu H. Katrak. New York: Routledge.

Wilson, John Silvanus, Jr. 1993. "The Campus Racial Climate and the Demographic Imperative." Pp. 85–109 in *Opening the American Mind: Race, Ethnicity, and Gender in Higher Education,* ed. Geoffrey M. Sill, Miriam T. Chaplin, Jean Ritzke, and David Wilson. Newark: University of Delaware Press.

Feminist Assessment

Feminist assessment is a form of program evaluation in higher education built upon unique principles of assessment that exemplify the feminist ideals of student-centeredness, activism, and the impact of context. The foundation in all of the guidelines is the recognition of values: values of the student, values gained from the learning experience, and values of the higher education program (Lambert 1997). Although it accounts for only a minor proportion of program assessment in higher education, feminist assessment provides higher education with an alternative assessment option that focuses on student voice and makes individual and group identity central to the assessment process (Hutchings 1992). The evaluation tools used in the feminist assessment process include institutional profile data, historical document analysis, student evaluation, surveys, portfolios, interviews, focus groups, self-assessment, performance assessment, feminist classroom observation, and course syllabi analysis (Shapiro 1992). Ultimately, this assessment aims to investigate the needs of college students in their preparation for involvement in and contributions to a pluralistic society (Musil 1992).

The feminist assessment movement originated from a Fund for the Improvement of Post Secondary Education (FIPSE) grant evaluating women's studies programs. This project, *The Courage to Question,* included the assessment processes of ten women's studies programs over the span of three years. At the time of the grant (1989), women's studies was facing tremendous backlash from institutions and the public who felt that teaching women's studies was an institutional response to placate small but vocal special interest groups. Additionally, many women's studies programs faced scrutiny because of their interdisciplinary structure. At the same time, there existed a national wave of education reform, led by then President George H. W. Bush, based on the belief that education would be improved by rigorous quantitative evaluation and testing. The women's studies assessment project served as an opportunity to gather recognition for women's studies and demonstrate alternative means to quantitative large-scale assessment.

Through the assessment experiences resulting from *The Courage to Question* along with the input of assessment experts, a feminist assessment framework was established, grounded in feminist theory. This basis of feminist theory lends to feminist assessment a unique frame through which to view the process of assessment that celebrates complexity, the role of context, and point of view as they inform knowledge (Code 1991). It makes no claims of knowledge being value-free or value-neutral. It assumes that the established norms of educational values need to be examined along with all existing assessment traditions. Built on this feminist theoretical foundation and modeled after the American Association of Higher Education's *Principles of Good Practice for Assessing Student Learning,* feminist assessment is formed around a structure of nine principles.

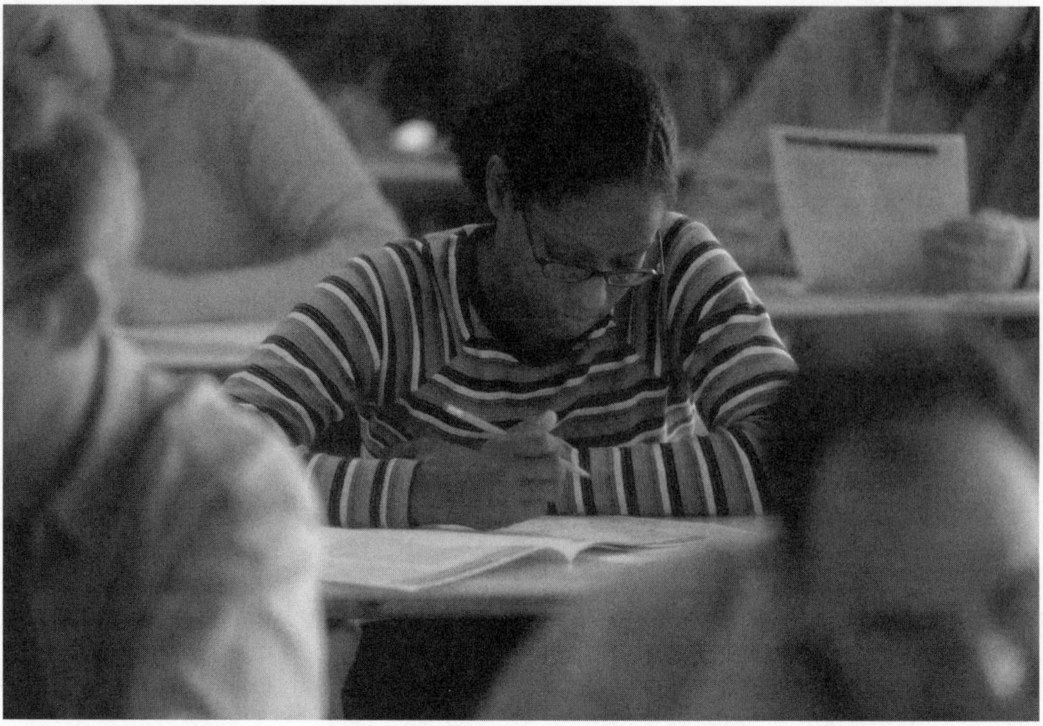

Feminist assessment includes methods that value student input, such as student surveys (Jose Luis Peleaz, Inc./Corbis)

The principles of feminist assessment serve as provisional guides to evaluation. The goal of feminist assessment is to improve the situation of teaching and learning for all individuals involved. The voices of all students, professors, administrators, and other members of the community are included through the framework. The values emphasized by the framework include social responsibility, awareness of diversity, and the importance of asking questions (Lambert 1997), as well as the idea that knowledge is subjective, contextual, complex, and value-laden. These values and assumptions are significantly different from the values and ideals of traditional assessment, and these differences create a distinct set of principles for feminist assessment.

Feminist assessment questions almost everything related to evaluation. It is student-centered, participatory, deeply affected by its context or institutional culture, and decentered. Feminist assessment approaches should be compatible with feminist activist beliefs. The process itself is heavily shaped by the power of feminist pedagogy and is based on a body of feminist scholarship and feminist research methodology that is central to this interdisciplinary area. Feminist assessment appreciates values (Shapiro 1992).

As a group, these principles attempt to approach assessment through a nontraditional lens that places students at the center. This process begins by questioning all existing assumptions about assessment. The history and traditions behind assessment are challenged, and the intentions and context of the assessment initiative are scrutinized. In feminist assessment, it is essential to consider and acknowledge the role and impact of authority and politics on the assessment effort. Unlike traditional assessment, feminist assessment makes no effort to examine data or results in the absence of the consideration of their context. Instead, the context informs the knowledge of student learning. The politics of assessment are also considered because the types and depths of assessment are limited by the culture and realities of the campus climate. What emerges from this guideline is that only with site-specific assessments can the context be fully appreciated (Shapiro 1992).

Once this frame for scrutiny is established, feminist assessment then addresses the question: is the learning serving the students? To answer this question, students are both included in the assessment and focused on as the primary reason for exploring the state of teaching and learning in higher education. When student learning is established as the central tenet for assessment, a participatory dialogue about the learning process must be initiated. It is based on feminist pedagogy that attempts to give students voice and is also grounded in feminist theory that tries to educate about oppression and silence. The participants take the lead on and contribute to deciding what the focus of the assessment should be, outlining the initiative, designing the instruments, selecting the members, analyzing the data, reporting the results, and making recommendations for change. Program directors, faculty members, students, and alumni all take responsibilities in the design and development of the assessment (Hutchings 1992).

The decentered nature of the assessment eliminates the existence of a single ideal of excellence established by a hierarchical structure (Shapiro 1992). Instead, feminist assessment allows the voices of many actors to shape the discussion of quality in education. By distributing the responsibility and broadening the sources of input on the assessment process, the center of power shifts away from a traditional expert and hierarchical leaders toward individuals who are connected with and have input and insight into the programs being assessed. This participatory process aims to broaden the frame of thought and invests all individuals in the improvement of the learning experience. Additionally, the broad participation lessens hierarchical decisionmaking and gives power to previously silenced voices.

Throughout the process of feminist assessment, feminist activist beliefs, pedagogy, scholarship, and methodology play a significant role. Feminist assessment has direct implications for the process of actively improving the student learning experience. Based on the feminist working standards of collectivity and collaboration, formal and informal means of conversation allow the learning process to be explored and changed as a result. In this exploration, it is recognized that outcomes of learning are inseparable from the pedagogy of the teacher. The relationships between the teacher and the learner inform all that can be assumed about the outcomes of the learning process and are investigated in the assessment by using a number of narrative tools that illuminate issues of power and context. These tools utilized in the assessment reflect the feminist scholarly ideals of flexibility, emphasis on improvement, and nurtured development (Shapiro 1992). Feminist assessment looks more at the journey of learning than the grade received or the degree attained. It relies not on testing scores but on the ability of students to improve, grow, and apply their knowledge in a manner that demonstrates their understanding of the material and their ability to use this knowledge in practice.

Feminist assessment brings to the dialogue of the assessment movement questions about whom the assessment is serving and whose voices are not heard. Its feminist activist and theoretical grounding question the establishment of traditional educational values and the assumptions of learning. This alternative assessment approach provides higher education with an evaluation framework option that uniquely explores and has the potential to improve the process of teaching and learning.

Katya Salkever

See also Part 3: Feminist Pedagogy; Feminist Research Methodology; Part 4: Women's Studies

References and further reading

Code, Lorraine. 1991. *What Can She Know? Feminist Theory and the Construction of Knowledge.* Ithaca, NY: Cornell University Press.

Hutchings, Pat. 1992. "The Assessment Movement and Feminism: Connection or Collision?" Pp. 17–28 in *Students at the Center: Feminist Assessment,* ed. C. M. Musil. Washington, DC: Association of American Colleges.

Lambert, J. L. 1997. "Feminist Assessment: What Does Feminist Theory Contribute to the Assessment Conversation?" Paper presented at the Annual Conference of the Association for the Study of Higher Education, Albuquerque, NM.

Musil, C. M. 1992. "Relaxing Your Neck Muscles: The History Project." Pp. 3–16 in *Students at the Center: Feminist Assessment,* ed. C. M. Musil. Washington, DC: Association of American Colleges.

Shapiro, J. P. 1992. "What Is Feminist Assessment?" Pp. 29–38 in *Students at the Center: Feminist Assessment,* ed. C. M. Musil. Washington, DC: Association of American Colleges.

Intersection of Gender and Race

There is current widespread acknowledgement among postmodern theorists that race and gender are interlocking systems in the United States, yet many people in the academy—as well as in the mainstream community and the media—still see them as separate issues. Viewing gender and race as separate issues leads many to believe that sexism can be abolished while racism remains intact. Political and representational practices connected to race and gender interrelate, and this interrelationship is relevant to higher education because the separate rhetorical strategies that characterize racist and antifeminist politics frequently intersect in ways that create new dilemmas for women and people of color.

The social relations of gender and race are produced, challenged, and transformed every day in the context of the academy. They simultaneously highlight both the powerful social forces that guide, steer, and push individuals into particular life paths based on their social location in race and gender hierarchies and the powerful personal and group forces that resist, reject, redefine, and overcome structural and psychological limits. We cannot fully understand these forces by isolating them from each other or by treating only one as primary.

Modernist discourses—marked by a celebration of the West as a universal civilization, the power of human reason, and a keen interest in science—still drive much of our thinking and promote an "either/or" competition between the oppressive systems of sexism and racism. Within modernist epistemologies, culture becomes a set of "essential" characteristics that distinguish "us" from "them" (i.e., binary opposition of sameness and difference). Cultural tensions that flow from a modernist mindset include dichotomizing not only gender (women versus men) but also race (people of color versus whites). White men are taught to think of their lives as morally neutral, normative, and ideal because they have done most of what is important or distinctive in Western civilization. Luce Irigaray (1997) argues that the "universal subject" of Enlightenment modernism is a Western, bourgeois, white, heterosexual man and therefore that feminist thought cannot be as historically contingent and exclusionary. Otherwise, the essential "woman" will just be a Western, bourgeois, white, heterosexual woman. Rather, Irigaray notes, feminist thought can embrace differences between women and accept a position of partial knowledge(s).

Postmodernism's debate with—or deconstruction of—modernism begins with examining the essentialist notion of white, privileged, heterosexual men of the industrialized West as central. In *The Second Sex* (1949), Simone de Beauvoir argued that man had assigned to himself the category of "self" and constructed woman as "other." Much feminist theory of the 1960s and early 1970s set out to expand and transform modernist discourses and existing theoretical models such as Marxism and psychoanalysis. Early feminism had as its aim women's equality through their admission to those spheres from which they had historically been excluded, which included the spheres of rational thought and intellectual discourse. Women's insights could be used to illuminate women's experiences; thus dominant theoretical discourses would be expanded and transformed. It became clear that it was not possible to simply expand such theories to include women, for the exclusion of women *and* people of color was not accidental but fundamental to white patriarchy.

In *Nomadic Subjects* (1994), Rosi Braidotti struggles with the issue of how feminist theory can hold onto a belief in "woman" and respect cultural diversity and difference. Adopting a "politics of location," Patricia Hill Collins, in *Black Feminist Thought* (1991), argues that black women's experiences are grounded in their collective resistance to economic and political oppression and are impossible to understand by those who are not black and female. African American women are a subordinate group that experiences a different world from those who are not black and female. This experience, in turn, produces a distinctive black feminist consciousness about that experience and a distinctive black feminist intellectual tradition.

However, Adrienne Rich (1986) warns that this type of thinking can become oversimplified and reductive (i.e., *this* set of experiences inevitably produces *that* mode of consciousness). For example, we cannot assume that all black women are American and that all African American women share a common position. Rich suggests that we avoid overemphasizing experiences but rather *interpret* those experiences. Nancy Hartsock (1997) urges the development of an alternative account of the world, one that treats women and people of color not—as seen from the center—as mastered or rebellious knowledges but instead as primary and as capable of constituting a different world.

Racist and sexist oppression is at the root of many forms of patriarchal domination within the academy. Postmodern discourses view this intersection as multilayered and posit circumstance and difference against various forms of essentialism. Elizabeth Minnich, Jean O'Barr, and Rachel Rosenfeld (1988) have pointed out that whites are taught to think of their lives as morally neutral, normative and average, and also ideal, so that when they work to benefit others, it is seen as work that will allow "them" to be more like "us." Male privilege and white privilege are entrenched in our society; they are protected by preventing awareness of them through institutionalized practices that both deny and enforce them.

Institutional racism and sexism broadly defined are any discursive practices that result in the stratification, exploitation, oppression, or alienation of articulated racial and gendered groups. The United States was created as both a racist nation (slavery was legal at the outset) and a sexist nation (women were denied the right to vote and own property at the outset). The racism and the sexism that helped form our cultures and ideologies are embedded in the discourses and practices of our institutions. Almost anybody in an American institution of almost any sort does, at times, reinforce racism and sexism that is institutionalized in the organization's rules, procedures, values, or goals. For this reason, nobody is immune from carrying out racist or sexist actions from time to time. The focus on who is racist and who is sexist is misdirected. The relevant issue is not whether a person is racist or sexist but rather what a person does to recognize and eliminate the racism and sexism embedded in the institutions in which she or he works or plays. To begin unlearning sexist and racist practices, people in higher education must investigate the ways in which race and gender interlock.

Domination and subordination uphold and sustain one another within the overlapping discourses of race and gender. One way that dominant groups justify their existence and privilege is by promoting beliefs that race and gender are not important in determining group location and therefore should not be taken into account when attempting to understand events or processes. This denial is represented in the popular notions of society as "gender-blind" or "race-blind." Women and people of color have a special role to play in alerting all of us to the workings and consequences of these systems of inequality. Within higher education hierarchies, for example, white men on the top of the hierarchy are more likely to impose their ways of seeing and their views upon women and people of color at the bottom.

Framing this debate in binary oppositions, which suggests that university personnel—women and persons of color—cannot be complicit in their own oppression and that domination assumes a singular and uncomplicated form, is a modernist tactic. Postmodern challenges to this ideological hegemony are well expressed by bell hooks in *Talking Back: Thinking Feminist, Thinking Black* (1989). She avoids the politics of separatism by invoking individuals committed to antisexist and antiracist work to resist the politics of domination within the systems of race and gender and to work to understand the importance of not promoting an "either/or" competition between oppressive systems. Her work in feminist theory has stressed the importance of understanding the ways in which race and class status determine the degree to which one can assert male domination and privilege and, most important, the ways racism and sexism uphold and sustain one another.

In *Modest Witness* (1997), Donna Haraway expressed the concept of "situated knowledges," in which she views the female subject not as "fixed subject" but as a "nomadic" subject—she might have all kinds of multiple experiences, and they overlap with variables such as class, race, age, lifestyle, and sexual preference. Without the consideration of the intersection of race and gender, the struggle over power becomes a form of "us" against "them" politics that works against developing community within a broad and diversified academic culture. It is important to be politically aware so as not to be complicit in perpetuating white male supremacy, which continues to be at the root of so much discrimination in the academy.

Social categories like race and gender are culturally constructed or determined by cultural and social contexts and historical circumstances. This distinction is important to those thinking about higher education because issues of difference are constantly being raised in the academy. Are women "naturally" more caring, as Nel Noddings suggests in her book, *Caring: A Feminine Approach to Ethics and Moral Education* (1984)? And if so, does that mean a different curriculum or structure should be created for or used by women in the academy? Are certain ethnic groups "naturally" smarter in math and science or the humanities, and how do we know if they are? What are the assumptions of professors regarding the categories of race and gender, and how do these assumptions organize how professors do their daily work?

Race is an articulation that groups people based on physical characteristics. It claims that group membership is heritable, implies that racial differences are scientific, and suggests that races are similar to subspecies. Not very long ago, we were taught that scientists divided the human species into three races: Caucasian, Negroid, and Mongoloid. The implication was that there is scientific justification for such a claim, but there is no scientific justification for dividing humans into any subspecies. Clearly, the concept of race developed as justification for the European colonization of the world and slavery in particular. If it could be shown that some humans (namely Europeans) descended from a superior race, then the exploitation and enslavement of non-Europeans could be justified and defended. The concept of race is still being used to justify the inequitable treatment of some people by others. In higher education, for example, some still attempt to explain the subpar academic performance of many people of color by reference to "heritability."

Race is largely a linguistic category with two different (though overlapping) meanings: *social identity* (what others think you are, based on obvious characteristics such as skin color that are assumed to be inherited from your parents) and *ethnic identity* (what you consider yourself to be, based more on your culture than physical characteristics). In the United States, there seems to be general agreement to use four racial groups; Asian (not oriental, which refers to cultural artifacts such as rugs, art, and food); black, Hispanic, and white. These categories are culturally constructed, not scientifically discovered.

Racism emerges from the discursive practices that attribute inferiority or superiority to a group based on heritability and as a sociological category located in social actions.

Gender is also a social category. Sex refers to the biological division of the species into male and female. Sex differences are differences between males and females that occur because of physiological phenomena—literally, the arrangement of chromosomes in a fertilized egg. Gender refers to social categories and characteristics that are related to but not identical with sex. Gender differences between men and women occur because of social and cultural phenomena. Thus, gender may be viewed as the interpretation of the significance of sex. Ideas about gender structure our choices and guide our behavior in ways that our particular society views as gender-appropriate. A society that views women as having natural abilities for teaching and nursing and no natural ability at scientific or quantitative work is not apt to spend valuable resources training women in science or quantitative studies. Women in such a society may learn to believe that they have little or no aptitude for science and that they are "naturally" (because of their biology) better at basic science than at chemistry and physics. In fact, in the United States this cultural construction has created a kind of self-fulfilling prophecy.

Race and gender are interrelated systems of inequality based on social relationships of power and control. Everyone is situated in race and gender hierarchies, and privilege and oppression cannot be understood in isolation from one another. The cultural constructions of gender and racial norms that are stereotypical are problematic in society because they limit the potential growth of individuals and restrict the nature of relations between people. Women and people of color are disadvantaged by the cultural construction of gender and racial norms in part because the roles leave them in positions of powerlessness and white men in positions of dominance in the culture.

Confusing intersections of race and gender are pervasive in every aspect of our culture—from the ways in which men and women are treated in the academy to the ways in which whites and people of color are treated in the academy. Colleges and universities are major social institutions in the United States that prepare people for different social locations as adults—their occupations, social classes, earnings, and political power. An inferior college education leaves people less able to compete in the marketplace. Although the consequences are felt by individual students, the process of reproducing racial and gender hierarchies by sorting people for different treatment or by blocking people from access to programs of study affects all American citizens. Thus, the ways in which the social relations of gender and race are produced, challenged, and transformed every day in the context of the academy deserves further exploration.

Susan L. Schramm

See also Part 2: Demographics of Gender and Race; Part 3: Black Feminism and Womanism; Part 6: Development of Multiple Social and Cultural Identities

References and further reading

Beauvoir, Simone de. 1949. *The Second Sex.* Trans. and ed. Howard Parshley. New York: Alfred A. Knopf.

Braidotti, Rosi. 1994. *Nomadic Subjects.* New York: Routledge.

Collins, Patricia Hill. 1991. *Black Feminist Thought: Knowledge, Consciousness, and the Politics of Empowerment.* New York: Routledge.

Haraway, Donna J. 1997. *Modest Witness: Feminism and Technoscience.* New York: Routledge.

Hartsock, Nancy. 1997. "The Feminist Standpoint: Developing the Ground for a Specifically Feminist Historical Materialism." Pp. 216–240 in *Feminist Social Thought: A Reader,* ed. Diana T. Meyers. New York: Routledge.

hooks, bell. 1989. *Talking Back: Thinking Feminist, Thinking Black.* New York: Free Press.

Irigaray, Luce. 1997. "And the One Doesn't Stir without the Other." Trans. Helene Vivienne Wenzel. *Signs* 7: 60–67.

Minnich, Elizabeth, Jean O'Barr, and Rachel Rosenfeld, eds. 1988. *Reconstructing the Academy: Women's Education and Women's Studies.* Chicago: University of Chicago Press.

Noddings, Nel. 1984. *Caring: A Feminine Approach to Ethics and Moral Education.* Berkeley: University of California Press.

Rich, Adrienne. 1986. "Compulsory Heterosexuality and Lesbian Existence." Pp. 120–141 in *Feminist Frontiers,* ed. Laurel Richardson and Verta Taylor. New York: McGraw-Hill.

Psychology of Sex Differences

Research documenting sex differences in abilities, traits, and social behaviors has been a central focus in psychology throughout the history of the discipline. Empirical work has found small to moderate sex differences in virtually all domains that have been studied. These differences vary considerably in direction and magnitude, depending on the nature of the measured variables (e.g., mathematical computation versus mathematical problem solving) and the context in which they have been studied (e.g., leadership style in the laboratory versus in actual organizations). Sex differences research has been critiqued by feminist researchers for a number of reasons, including the a priori presumption of differences between women and men and the treatment of differences as immutable. Theoretical explanations for sex differences can be distinguished according to the presumed genesis and locus of the sex differences, both of which may be conceptualized as being either individual or situational. Advances in quantitative reviewing techniques have resulted in a better understanding of the nature of and explanation for sex differences, especially as they have been studied in the standardized situations in which psychologists typically gather data.

History

Differential psychology dates back to the nineteenth century, when investigators first began to account for the presumed greater intelligence of men and greater emotionality of women on the basis of structural features of the brain. Researchers in the twentieth century continued to study sex differences in abilities but added the study of differences in personality traits and social behaviors. At the same time that the nature of the behaviors investigated expanded into the social domain, the presumptive explanatory power of biology receded. Social learning of different skills and behaviors and structural explanations of behaviors afforded by different situations gained increasing support in accounting for sex differences as findings about sex differences and more important, their contextual variation, began to accumulate (Deaux and LaFrance 1998). The literature was large enough by the 1970s to warrant a review of the findings to date. Eleanor E. Maccoby and Carol N. Jacklin completed the first major narrative review of sex differences in 1974. They reported little evidence to support large and far-reaching differences but concluded that there were small and reliable sex differences in data gathered from children in four areas: verbal, mathematical, and visual-spatial abilities and aggression.

The pace of psychological research on the topic of sex differences accelerated following Maccoby and Jacklin's review. In the 1970s, the first *Annual Review of Psychology* chapter on the psychology of women was published; the journals *Sex Roles, Signs,* and *Psychology of Women Quarterly* were founded; and the American Psychological Association established Division 35 on the psychology of women. The basic research literature on sex differences has continued to expand since this time; it is arguably one of the largest literatures within all of psychology. A keyword search of the PsycINFO database identified over 44,000 journal articles on sex or gender differences published between 1887 and June 2001. Almost 90 percent of this work occurred after 1975, and trends suggest no sign of declining interest into the twenty-first century. The ubiquity of basic research contrasts with the paucity of theoretical explanations for sex differences. A "title" search of the two major review journals in psychology (*Psychological Bulletin* and *Psychological Review*) for the same period of time indicated only nine publications in which theories or models were offered to account for sex differences; there were only seven such articles published by *Psychology of Women Quarterly.*

The size of the sex difference literature provides a challenge to reviewers. Early reviewers (e.g., Maccoby and Jacklin 1974) were forced to rely on a narrative reviewing technique in which a count of the number of studies that reported an effect in one direction was compared to the number of studies that reported either no effect or an effect in the opposite direction. Narrative reviewers were limited in their abilities to systematically account for inconsistencies in the data because of the difficulty of formulating and testing hypotheses across an often large group of heterogeneous findings. Contemporary reviewers have made use of newer quantitative review or meta-analytic techniques, which allow a reviewer to compute an effective size statistic that represents the average sex difference across the entire literature under review. However, the real power of meta-analysis lies in its ability to quantitatively account for the typically heterogeneous sex difference findings in a manner that can be used to test the assertions of one theoretical explanation for sex differences versus another. Meta-analytic reviews of sex differences form the basis for most of the findings reported below.

Abilities

There is a small overall sex difference in verbal abilities that favors women, although the size of the sex difference varies across different types of verbal ability. Women especially outperform men on measures of speech production; the difference is smallest on measures of general verbal ability. No reliable variation in the size of the effects is exhibited across different age groups. There is a trend toward more equal performances by males and females in more recent years (Hyde and Frost 1993).

The widely reported advantage that men are said to have on standardized tests of math achievement varies considerably, depending on the age group studied and the type of skill assessed. In fact, the overall average sex difference in the general population indicates that women slightly *outperform* men. Furthermore, females score higher than males on measures of computation ability; this effect is especially strong during the elementary and middle years. It is on measures of mathematical problem solving that men outscore women; this effect shows sharp increases with age, particularly during the high school and college years. The differences between males and females are particularly strong in samples preselected for mathematical giftedness. As with verbal abilities, the size of the sex difference in problem solving shows signs of significantly decreasing over time (Hyde and Frost 1993).

Sex differences in spatial abilities have been examined in an attempt to account for the greater achievement of men in math and science, with the assumption that many forms of mathematical and scientific problem solving require spatial skills. The average sex difference effect size across three different types of spatial ability indicates a male advantage in each case. The sex difference is smallest for spatial visualization and larger and considerably variable for measures of spatial perception and mental rotation. The larger sex differences in spatial perception are exhibited by adult (versus child) samples; the size of the sex differences in mental rotation depends on the particular assessment measure employed. However, even the largest of the sex differences observed on these standardized tests does not begin to approach the striking sex difference in actual math and science achievement, leading to the conclusion that it is not differences in spatial abilities per se that account for sex differences in achievement in associated domains. Furthermore, the finding that spatial ability performance is enhanced in both males and females as a result of experience suggests caution in positing these particular abilities as an essential explanatory factor for sex differences in related domains (Linn and Petersen 1986, reported in Hyde and Linn 1986).

Personality Traits and Social Behaviors

Men tend to be more instrumental (e.g., independent, assertive) than women, and women tend to be more expressive (e.g., emotionally expressive, nurturing) than men (Deaux 1985), regardless of when these constellations of traits have been measured or the particular measure on which they have been assessed. Although men and women do not differ in overall levels of self-reported well-being (Hyde and Frost 1993), the instrumental traits associated with men are predictive of well-being, self-esteem, and general psychological adjustment, whereas the expressive traits associated with women are independent of these outcomes. Men and women differ in the types of mental disorders they evidence. Depression, anxiety, and eating disorders are diagnosed in women at much higher rates than they are in men; chemical dependencies and antisocial personality disorder are more prevalent in men than women.

Comparisons of aggressive behavior displayed by males and females aged fourteen and older in situations in which participants aggress against a stranger indicate that males are more aggressive than females. The direction of this finding is consistent, although its strength varies; the sex difference is moderate for measures of physical aggression (e.g., delivering a "shock" to a another research subject) and small for psychological aggression (e.g., nonverbal behavior).

Additional variations in the features of the studies are also associated with variations in the strength of the aggression sex difference. More significant to the theoretical analysis offered below, sex differences in college students' estimates of the amount of harm aggression would inflict upon a target, their own guilt or anxiety as a result of attacking a target, and the potential for harm to themselves because of retribution by the target all significantly predict the strength of the actual behavioral sex differences in the basic research literature. For example, if women estimated that a particular aggressive act would leave them feeling guilty, then when the likelihood of that particular act was measured, men aggressed more than women (Eagly 1987).

When social psychologists have studied situations in which a subject helps a stranger, the results have paralleled those in the aggression literature. In these situations, males aged fourteen and older help others more than females do. The sex difference is moderate to large when the helping behavior is measured in off-campus or field settings (versus other types of settings), when the helping behavior is watched by others (versus anonymous), and when the appeal for assistance is a mere presentation of a need (versus a direct request). As reported above, sex differences in college students' predictions of their behavior significantly predicted the actual size of the behavioral sex differences in helping. Thus, men were more likely to help a target than were women in the sample of studies reviewed to the extent that college student men, more than women, predicted that they would be more competent to deliver the necessary assistance and that helping would entail placing themselves in less danger. In another review, Alice H. Eagly found a small sex difference indicating that women are more susceptible to influence than men, especially in group pressure conformity situations versus more private persuasion situations (Eagly 1987).

Women are moderately better than men at discerning or decoding the nonverbal behavior of others, especially facial expressions. Adult women are also much more facially expressive than men and smile more, although children show no such sex difference in social smiling. Women approach others more closely than do men and are approached more closely by others than are men. Effect sizes are largest on both approach measures when the behavior is observed under natural conditions versus when it is staged in a laboratory (Hall 1984, cited in Hyde and Frost 1993).

Performance-Related Traits and Social Behaviors

Fear of success was proposed to explain why women lagged behind men in achievement. A flurry of subsequent research activity failed to find reliable evidence for the existence of fear of success in women. This result, as well as a lack of clarity in the conceptualization of fear of success—as either a motivation to avoid success or as a possible response to perceived violations of gender roles—has resulted in a decreased emphasis on fear of success. Researchers have also devoted considerable efforts to studying achievement motivation, initially only in men and then later in women. Much of the subsequent research either failed to find sex differences in achievement motivation or employed only women participants and failed to find evidence for any achievement motivations. These latter findings were sometimes accepted as evidence that women lacked the achievement motivations of men, despite the obvious possibility that the laboratory situation and the stimuli employed may not have been sufficient to arouse achievement motivations in either women or men, had both groups been studied (Mednick and Thomas 1993).

Two analyses of sex differences in success and failure performance attributions on laboratory and natural tasks (e.g., exam scores) were performed by Bernard E. Whitley and colleagues (reported in Hyde and Linn 1986) to see if any of the proffered theories of women's attributional styles could explain sex differences in achievement patterns. They found inconsistent support for all three models: the externality model (that women make external attributions), the self-derogation model (that women make external attributions for success and internal attributions for failure), and the low expectancy model (that women's successes are attributable to unstable causes such as luck or the assistance of others, whereas their failures are due to stable causes such as a lack of ability). Men are somewhat more likely than women to attribute success to ability (an internal-stable cause), but men are also somewhat more likely than women to attribute failure to ability. Furthermore, even though women are more likely than men to attribute their success to outside factors such as luck, they are also somewhat more likely than men to attribute failure to poor luck. Gender typing of the domain of success and failure performances was not included in the analysis by Whitley and his colleagues, despite the fact that task domain has been a significant moderator in some individual studies. There is evidence that both research participants and observers derogate women (including themselves) when women complete masculine gender-typed tasks, but not when women perform neutral or feminine-typed tasks (Deaux and LaFrance 1998).

Future research that addresses the weaknesses noted in the aforementioned research areas may provide some explanation for sex differences in achievement patterns. Research into academic and career choices has found that expectancies for success and the subjective value of a particular achievement domain are both significant predictors of choices. Moreover, these expectancy and value variables are influenced by self-efficacy expectations, perceived task demands, gender and occupational stereotypes, and the beliefs of significant others. Understanding how men and women define success and achievement in different domains also holds promise for clarifying the importance of these variables (Mednick and Thomas 1993).

Eagly and her colleagues have completed a number of meta-analytic reviews of the literature on sex differences in leadership behaviors. They found that women demonstrate a more interpersonal leadership *style* than men in laboratory and assessment or rating studies, but there is no difference in interpersonal style in studies conducted using men and women leaders in actual organizations. Across all settings, men and women do not differ in their use of a task-focused leadership style (Eagly and Johnson 1990). Ratings of the overall *effectiveness* of men and women leaders also do not differ, although men are rated as moderately more effective than women in studies conducted in military settings and slightly less effective than women in studies conducted in educational, government, and social service organizations. The percentage of men represented in the leadership role in a particular setting and the percentages of male subordinates and raters of effectiveness are all positively associated with relatively greater effectiveness ratings for men (Eagly, Karau, and Makhijani 1995). *Evaluations* of leaders in laboratory experiments in which the sex of the leader varied indicate a slightly higher overall evaluation of men versus women leaders. Men and women who demonstrate a democratic leadership style are not evaluated differently, but women who employ an autocratic style are evaluated significantly more poorly than autocratic men. Other moderators of evaluations of men and women leaders include the sex of the evaluator: men evaluate female leaders slightly lower than males ones, but female raters show no gender preference (Eagly, Makhijani, and Klonsky 1992). A leadership *emergence* meta-analysis found that men are moderately more likely than women to emerge as task leaders in initially leaderless groups, whereas women are somewhat more likely to emerge as social leaders in such groups. Men emerge as leaders much more often than women on masculine-typed and neutral tasks, but there is an insignificant tendency favoring men even for feminine-typed tasks. The sex difference in leader emergence, although still favoring men, diminishes as the interaction time of the groups increases and in real or naturalistic versus laboratory settings (Eagly and Karau 1991).

Criticisms of Sex Differences Research

Research on differences in the behavior of men and women has been criticized by feminist scholars on a number of grounds. Oftentimes, the research has been atheoretical and has been conducted with the sole purpose of demonstrating a difference rather than a similarity between the behavior of men and women. Differences have also been conceptualized within a model that presumes that men provide a behavioral standard against which the deficiencies of women are judged. Furthermore, the logic of scientific hypothesis testing is ill-suited to accommodate "no difference" hypothesis testing and findings. Thus, it is impossible to *prove* a similarity between two groups because any number of validity or statistical power weaknesses provide alternative explanations for not finding a difference. The differences that have been observed have tended either to be minimized or, more often, exaggerated and then have been subsequently used to justify the differential access of men and women to educational and employment opportunities. Also at issue is the practical interpretation of the size of observed sex differences. A statistically significant effect does not necessarily translate into large differences in the average behaviors of men and women. Furthermore, the variation within each group and the overlap of the male and female distributions of the behaviors of interest are often pronounced. Nonetheless, the magnitude of the sex difference findings is consistent with the magnitude of other findings in social psychology. Sex differences are often large enough to be noticed by the average perceiver and are well predicted by social stereotypes. Finally, because men and women cannot be randomly assigned to treatment groups in which maleness and femaleness are manipulated by an experimenter, anything that co-occurs or is confounded with gender provides a tenable causal explanation for differences that are observed. For this reason, biological sex itself has been inappropriately treated as an explanation for many observed differences. Even when essentialist explanations have not been offered, there has been a tendency to assume that the mechanisms that produce observed differences reside within the person rather than within the situation in which behavior is produced ("Current Issues" 1995).

Theoretical Explanations

Biological explanations for sex differences include genetic, hormonal, and brain structure-function differences between males and females that are hypothesized to account for a wide range of behaviors, including intellectual and cognitive performance (Deaux 1985). Recent findings about the degree to which the brain is modified by experience suggest that simple unidirectional causal theories about sex differences in biological variables are insufficient to account for a practically significant proportion of the measured sex differences in behavior.

Evolutionary theory proposes that whenever differences can be found in the adaptive behaviors required of men and women, sex differences in behavior should follow. Mate selection and parental investment are two such areas. Evolutionary theory predicts that because men can never be confident of paternity and because it is to their advantage to have as many offspring as possible, men should invest relatively little in each child and be attracted to young, presumably fertile women. Women are confident of maternity but because of pregnancy and lactation are more invested in their offspring. Consequently, women can best ensure the survival of their children (and genes) by selecting a mate who can provide the necessary resources. Evolutionary accounts are consistent with sex difference data about preferences in mates and sexual strategies but have been criticized because of their distal and therefore weak relationships to contemporary social behaviors (Eagly 1987).

Sigmund Freud emphasized genital differences in the production of sex differences in social behaviors. His work has been skeptically received by many research psychologists because of the impossibility of empirically testing many of his ideas. More contemporary adaptations of the psychoanalytic model of development suggest that it is not the presence or absence of male genitalia per se that results in sex differences but the symbolic value afforded the penis in patriarchal societies.

Explanations of sex differences in abilities and social behaviors based on individual differences have not been well received by social psychologists because such explanations have at times been proposed to justify inequities in the treatment of women and men. Moreover, these explanations predict that global and invariant differences should be found in the behavior of men and women and so have difficulty accommodating both the complex array of sex differences in behaviors and the pronounced situational variations of sex differences. Although social psychologists do not deny that variables such as evolutionary pressures and hormones likely explain some proportion of sex differences, they prefer more proximal explanations for sex differences that are also predictive of the situational variations in behavior.

Socialization Explanation

Social learning theory attempts to understand the mechanisms that govern social behavior, including the process by which the biological categories of female and male have become associated with a range of variables (e.g., traits, social roles, social power) that denote "woman" and "man." Learning about behaviors and their consequences either directly through experience or vicariously by observing others is emphasized in socialization accounts of sex differences. Behavior is predictable from knowledge of these consequences, an individual's learning history, and the situational context of the behavior. A meta-analytic review of parents' socialization practices found that the only significant predictor of behavioral differences in girls and boys was mothers' and fathers' encouragement of sex-typed activities (Lytton and Romney 1991). That review, confirmations of an expectancy-value model of academic and career choice (Meece et al. 1982), and the predictive validity of sex differences in estimates of the consequences of performing aggressive and helping behaviors (Eagly 1987) all provide impressive support for the role of social learning in the production of gendered behaviors. Critics of a social learning approach contend that although behavior is produced as a result of learned associations that depend on one's environment, the resulting behavioral tendencies or habits reside within the person. As a result, social learning mechanisms alone are insufficient to account for the situational variations of observed sex differences in behavior.

Structural Explanations

Structural explanations for sex differences are wholly located within the situations in which sex differences in behavior are produced. The strength of the structural approach is that it is consistent with the situational variation in sex difference findings that is predominant in the literature. The gender-as-process model and social role theory are discussed below. There are other theories congenial to understanding sex differences and making a priori predictions that can be empirically tested, but they have not received the systematic attention they deserve. These theories include expectation states theory, which treats gender as a diffuse status characteristic with associated inferences about competence and power, and social constructionism theory.

The gender-as-process model draws heavily on the well-supported self-fulfilling prophecy or expectancy confirmation process, in which perceiver, target, and situational variables interact to produce behavior. Important roles are accorded to (1) perceivers' and targets' gender belief systems (stereotypes, attitudes, and self-definitions) responsible for their expectations for self and other behavior, (2) goals for an interaction between perceiver and target, and (3) the nature of the situation, including the proportion of women and men present and the gender typing of the situation. The gender-in-process model is theoretically consistent with a number of basic research findings regarding the expectancy confirmation process and can easily accommodate findings in more applied research literatures (Deaux and LaFrance 1998).

Social role theory relies upon the pervasive division of labor by sex to account for sex differences in social behaviors. In this process, sex differences in skills become sex-typed because of their ubiquity, beliefs about the consequences of behavior, and gender-role expectations. These differences result from the tendency of men and women to occupy segregated social roles, and they have a direct causal influence on sex differences in behaviors. Attributing the source of sex differences to any "natural" difference between females and males represents a *mis*attribution; sex differences are instead more correctly attributed to the social roles associated with women and men (Eagly 1987). Social role theory is unique among all others in its ability to account for the variation of sex differences in behaviors, not only in individual research studies but also across entire literatures. Theoretically derived predictions about sex differences in skills, sex differences in beliefs about the consequences of behavior, and the relevance of gender to a situation—based on, among other variables, the gender typing of the situation and the extent to which other nongender cues are important—account for most of the variation in sex differences in aggressive, social, and leadership behaviors.

Laura M. Sinnett

See also Part 3: Feminist Research Methodology; Part 8: Leadership

References and further reading

"Current Issues." 1995. *American Psychologist* 50, no. 3: 145–171.

Deaux, Kay. 1985. "Sex and Gender." *Annual Review of Psychology* 36: 49–81.

Deaux, Kay, and Marianne LaFrance. 1998. "Gender." Pp. 788–827 in *The Handbook of Social Psychology,* ed. Daniel T. Gilbert, Susan T. Fiske, and Gardner Lindzey. 4th ed., Vol. 1. Boston: McGraw-Hill.

Eagly, Alice H. 1987. *Sex Differences in Social Behavior: A Social Role Interpretation.* Hillsdale, NJ: Erlbaum.

Eagly, Alice H., and Blair T. Johnson. 1990. "Gender and Leadership Style: A Meta-Analysis." *Psychological Bulletin* 108, no. 2: 233–256.

Eagly, Alice H., and Steven J. Karau. 1991. "Gender and the Emergence of Leaders: A Meta-Analysis." *Journal of Personality and Social Psychology* 60, no. 5: 685–710.

Eagly, Alice H., Steven J. Karau, and Mona G. Makhijani. 1995. "Gender and the Effectiveness of Leaders: A Meta-Analysis." *Psychological Bulletin* 117, no. 1: 125–145.

Eagly, Alice H., Mona G. Makhijani, and Bruce G. Klonsky. 1992. "Gender and the Evaluation of Leaders: A Meta-Analysis." *Psychological Bulletin* 111, no. 1: 3–22.

Hyde, Janet Shibley, and Laurie A. Frost. 1993. "Meta-Analysis in the Psychology of Women." Pp. 67–103 in *Psychology of Women: A Handbook of Issues and Theories,* ed. Florence L. Denmark and Michele A. Paludi. Westport, CT: Greenwood Press.

Hyde, Janet Shibley, and Marcia C. Linn, eds. 1986. *The Psychology of Gender: Advances through Meta-Analysis.* Baltimore: Johns Hopkins University Press.

Lytton, Hugh, and David M. Romney. 1991. "Parents' Differential Socialization of Boys and Girls: A Meta-Analysis." *Psychological Bulletin* 109, no. 2: 267–296.

Maccoby, Eleanor E., and Carolyn N. Jacklin. 1974. *The Psychology of Sex Differences.* Palo Alto, CA: Stanford University Press.

Mednick, Martha T., and Veronica G. Thomas. 1993. "Women and the Psychology of Achievement: A View from the Eighties." Pp. 585–626 in *Psychology of Women: A Handbook of Issues and Theories,* ed. Florence L. Denmark and Michele A. Paludi. Westport, CT: Greenwood Press.

Meece, Judith L., Jacquelynne (Eccles) Parsons, Carolyn M. Kaczala, Susan B. Goff, and Robert Futterman. 1982. "Sex Differences in Math Achievement: Toward a Model of Academic Choice." *Psychological Bulletin* 91, no. 2: 324–348.

Whitley, Bernard E., Jr., M. C. McHugh, and I. H. Frieze. 1986. "Assessing the Theoretical Models for Sex Differences in Causal Attributions for Success and Failure." Pp. 102–105 in *The Psychology of Gender: Advances through Meta-Analysis,* eds. Janet Shibley Hyde and Marcia C. Linn. Baltimore: Johns Hopkins University Press.

Sexual Harassment

Sexual harassment refers to any unwelcome sexual advances by one person or group to another. The overwhelming majority of victims of sexual harassment are female, and the perpetrators are mostly male. Sexual harassment falls into two broad categories, "hostile environment" and "quid pro quo" harassment. Hostile environment harassment generally refers to sexual behavior that is unsolicited and creates an intimidating, offensive environment that interferes with an individual's work or educational performance. Specific hostile environment behaviors represent a continuum of harassment ranging from put-down jokes, leering, and offensive words and displays of pornographic materials to molestation, sexual assault, and battery (Reilly, Lott, and Gallogy 1986).

"Quid pro quo" literally means "this for that" in Latin. In this type of harassment, the abuser requires sexual compliance as a condition for an educational benefit, economic reward, job promotion, or some other type of exchange. Quid pro quo harassment involves an abuse of power, in which the harasser is in a position of authority or privilege over the victim. For example, a male professor may require a female student to perform a sexual act for him in exchange for a particular grade in the class.

Frank J. Till (1980) created a typology of sexual harassment to classify behaviors by their severity. Gender harassment includes generalized sexual statements, insults, or degradations against an individual woman or women as a collective group. Examples include offensive graffiti, obscene jokes, or insulting remarks. Seductive behavior refers to unwanted, inappropriate sexual advances, including repeated, unwanted sexual invitations, persistent phone calls, requests for dates, and so on. Sexual bribery (quid pro quo) involves sexual activity in exchange for a reward. Sexual bribery may be either overt or subtle. It is important to note that even if an individual gives her consent for this exchange, it is still considered sexual harassment by law because it involves an abuse of power. Sexual coercion involves sexual activity under duress or threat (also quid pro quo). Examples include holding back a promotion or the threat of a failing grade until the victim agrees to sexual intercourse. The last classification is sexual imposition, which involves molestation, assault, or any unwanted physical contact such as pinching, groping, or intentionally brushing against another's body. This typology of harassment does not imply that one form of harassment or another is perceived as any less significant by the victim. All forms of sexual harassment have serious implications for the victim. They include detrimental changes in mental and physical health, loss of achieved and potential professional status, and the diminishment of learning opportunities.

Sexual harassment has permeated women's academic experiences since their inclusion within institutions of higher learning, and it is a common occurrence. Research has suggested that the sexual harassment of students ranges from 20 percent to 50 percent of all students (Sandler and Shoop 1997; Fitzgerald et al. 1998). However, when one examines the breakdown of harassment by collegiate level, as many as 70 to 90 percent of undergraduate women have experienced harassment by male students. Graduate women tend to experience sexual harassment more from male instructors than their peers. It is theorized that this shift is

Sexual Harassment
Sexual Harassment is not wrong because it is illegal. It is illegal because it is wrong.
-Berniece Sandler
Experience has demonstrated that many complaints of sexual harassment can be effectively resolved through informal intervention. For information about informal and formal resolution options available contact:
The Women's Center
893-3778
Human Resources
893-4119
Sexual Harassment Complaint Office
893-2546
The names of other contact people can be accessed though our web page: http://www.sa.ucsb.edu/women'scenter/harass
MUTUAL RESPECT
What friendships and relationships are built upon.
What is Sexual Harassment?
Sexual harassment occurs when unwanted or uninvited attention of a sexual nature interferes with a person's ability to obtain an education, work, or participate in recreational or social activities at UCSB. Sexual harassment is an abuse of informal or formal power or authority.
Sexual Harassment may include:
Derogatory remarks about one's clothing, body or sexual activities based on gender
Disparaging comments, jokes and teasing based on gender
Verbal harassment or abuse
Subtle pressure for sexual activity
Unnecessary and unwanted touching, patting, or pinching
Demanding sexual favors accompanied by overt threats concerning such things as one's job, grades, letters of recommendation or promotion
Physical assault
For Sexual Harassment Prevention Education Training call (805) 893-3778
Printed for your assistance by the Sexual Harassment Prevention Education Program and the Office of the Executive Vice Chancellor. (4/00)

Women's centers at universities offer many programs and services regarding sexual harassment (Courtesy of the University of California at Santa Barbara)

due to the close working relationship between graduate students and their instructors. The American Psychological Association (1996) reports that approximately 13 percent of female graduate students have been sexually harassed and 21 percent avoided classes for fear of sexual harassment.

Positive changes in sexual harassment law now conceptualize harassment as a form of gender discrimination under both civil rights law and Title IX of the Education Amendments Act of 1972. Donna J. Benson and Gregg E. Thomson affirm that since women "can no longer be openly denied access to educational and professional training legally, sexual harassment may remain an especially critical factor of more covert discrimination" (1982, 240). Colleges and universities provide established power differentials and are dictated by different sets of sexual mores regarding appropriate sexual behavior (Murrell and Dietz-Uhler 1993). The power differential between students and instructors is strong, as instructors are the knowledge givers and the grade givers and are often the key to successful academic networking. However, female professors report high rates of sexual harassment by their male students. Catharine MacKinnon writes that "the sexual harassment of women occurs not only when women are on the bottom of the formal hierarchal ladder, but also when they are in lateral positions or even on top of the hierarchy" (1997, 101). Therefore, female professors may have institutional power yet experience harassment because they are a woman living in a society that continues to privilege men over women. Highly autonomous faculty, diffusion of authority, and a shortage of female faculty are all characteristics linked to institutions where sexual harassment is frequent between instructors and students.

Student-to-student harassment is also rampant on campuses. Peer harassment may not be held as seriously accountable as faculty-student harassment, however. Peer harassment is often misconceived, even by the victim at times, as flirting, sexual attraction, or just "boys being boys." Hostile environment harassment is frequently the chosen form of harassment between students. It may not even be aimed at any woman in particular. For example, Bernice R. Sandler and Robert J. Shoop report of a tunnel at a large southern university where there is a life-size painting of a Raggedy Ann doll, legs spread apart with blood flowing out. The words "I raped Raggedy Ann" are painted below (1997, 52). This display creates an offensive environment for the students that have to pass it everyday, and serves as a remembrance to female students of their vulnerability and lack of power at the university.

Gender differences are evident in nearly every aspect of research on sexual harassment. Women experience sexual harassment more, conceptualize it differently, and even attribute responsibility for it in another way than do men. Probably because of greater personal experience, women perceive sexual harassment more broadly than men. Higher acceptance of stereotypical gender roles is also related to higher tolerance of sexual harassment by women. Since women are socialized to be passive and accepting of male dominance, they may be predisposed to accept sexual harassment as the inevitability of being a woman. Men are more likely to place blame with the victim, returning to the evolutionary argument that they cannot control their sexuality. The sexual harassment of women is strongly correlated to men's perception of dominance over women. Too often, institutions simply reproduce this dominant paradigm.

Victims of harassment cope with their abuse in a variety of ways. Women's notions of stereotypical gender roles also influence their coping abilities. Women who have moved beyond traditional gender-role ideology tend to respond to harassment with a more active, direct approach. They are more likely to use institutional or organizational reporting procedures or confront their harasser or both. Women who employ more traditional gender-role ideas rely on strategies such as denial, avoidance, or ignorance of the problem. Regardless of how the victim responds to it, sexual harassment has adverse effects on women's academic achievement. In addition to its effects on the victim's psychology (e.g., anxiety, insomnia, depression) and physiology (e.g., gastrointestinal disturbances, nausea), sexual harassment affects women's learning opportunities. By avoiding the threatening situation, women may remove themselves from classrooms, lose confidence in themselves and their intelligence, become emotionally unstable, and become reluctant to form mentoring relationships with male faculty. Their experience with sexual harassment in academia can ultimately lead some women to conclude that their success in college comes not from being a diligent student but rather from their sexual attractiveness.

An overwhelming number of colleges and universities have a formal policy for reporting harassment, but it is often there only on paper. Students who are being sexually harassed are often effectively silenced when they even suggest the possibility of harassment by an instructor. Like other victims of violence against women, students often find themselves on the defensive and are held responsible for the actions that occurred. One study has suggested that on average, only five complaints are officially reported at any particular academic institution each year (Riger 1991), which may be due to gender biases within reporting policy. Victims may be reluctant to pursue official grievance procedures for fear that no one will believe them and that no significant repercussions will occur for the harasser, and they are strongly afraid of retaliation.

Changes in institutional sexual harassment policy, such as anonymous reporting and serious investigation of charges, although important, are not the only changes that academic institutions need to make. Gender equity for students, faculty, and employees is necessary to subvert the dominant belief system that perpetuates sexual harassment. Students have led the battle for increasing awareness and responsiveness to sexual harassment in higher education. Women against Sexual Harassment (WASH) and similar organizations across campuses nationwide have actively demanded the eradication of sexual harassment and all forms of violence against women on college campuses. It is the responsibility of administrators and educators to be active listeners and form appropriate, gender-conscious responses to this violence.

Jeanette Reichmuth

See also Part 5: Gender Inequality; Students' Rights; Title IX; Part 6: Classroom Climate; Sexual Assault

References

American Psychological Association. 1996. *Sexual Harassment: Myths and*

Realities. Washington, DC: American Psychological Association Press.

Argos, V. P., and Tatiana Shohov. 1999. *Sexual Harassment: Analyses and Bibliography.* Commack, NY: Nova Science Publishers.

Benson, Donna J., and Gregg E. Thomson. 1982. "Sexual Harassment on a University Campus: The Confluence of Authority Relation, Sexual Interest, and Gender Stratification." *Social Problems* 29: 236–251.

Fitzgerald, Louise F., Lauren M. Weitzman, Yael Gold, and Mimi Ormerod. 1998. "Academic Harassment: Sex and Denial in Scholarly Garb." *Psychology of Women* 12: 329–340.

MacKinnon, Catharine. 1993. *Only Words.* Cambridge, MA: Harvard University Press.

Murrell, Audrey J., and Beth L. Dietz-Uhler. 1993. "Gender Identity and Adversarial Beliefs as Predictors of Attitudes toward Sexual Harassment." *Psychology of Women Quarterly* 17: 169–175.

Reilly, Mary Ellen, Bernice Lott, and Sheila M. Gallogy. 1986. "Sexual Harassment of University Students." *Sex Roles* 15: 333–358.

Riger, Stephanie. 1991. "Gender Dilemmas in Sexual Harassment: Policies and Procedures." *American Psychologist* 46: 497–505.

Sandler, Bernice R., and Robert J. Shoop. 1997. *Sexual Harassment on Campus: A Guide for Administrators, Faculty and Students.* Boston: Allyn and Bacon.

Till, Frank J. 1980. *Sexual Harassment: A Report on the Sexual Harassment of Students.* Report on the National Advisory Council on Women's Educational Programs. Washington, DC: U.S. Department of Education.

Part 3

FEMINISM IN THE ACADEMY

Overview

Feminist efforts have greatly shaped academic environments for more than a century. When, in the mid–nineteenth century, Elizabeth Cady Stanton asserted that women must be given opportunities equal to those of men if they were to achieve their greatest potential, she was attempting to pry open the doors of education for women. Since that time, women both inside and outside the academy have stressed the importance of education for women.

"Feminism" is a term that has many definitions. The following three-part definition characterizes feminism's many forms. First, feminism suggests that women have something valuable to contribute to every aspect of the world. Second, since women as a group experience oppression, they have been unable to achieve their potential or gain the rewards of full participation in society. This oppression permeates all aspects of society. Third, feminists assert that this situation should change.

With this orientation as a backdrop for their work, feminists have affected academic environments in many ways. First, they have attempted to ensure that women have full access to all positions in higher education: as students, faculty and staff members, and administrators. They have further drawn attention to the disproportionate number of men (and white men in particular) in high-paying, high-prestige positions and to the disproportionate number of women (and women of color in particular) in low-paying, low-prestige positions. They have also pointed out the ways in which academic structures affect women and men differently, paying attention to such issues as "women's ways of knowing" (Belenky et

Elizabeth Cady Stanton fought for women's education for more than fifty years of her life (Library of Congress)

al. 1986), the need to balance work and family issues (Hensel 1991), sexual harassment (Sandler and Shoop 1997), and the gender gap in higher education leadership (Chliwniak 1997). Finally, feminists have attempted to transform teaching and learning environments. In this sense, they have questioned didactic approaches that do not support many women's preference for learning that is holistic and relational. They have also attempted to reform curricular materials such that they represent the efforts, accomplishments, and lives of women as well as men. In both of these efforts, it has been important to ensure that women are not seen as a monolithic category devoid of difference. Instead, feminists have increasingly become attuned to the necessity of including all women in their efforts and analyses by embracing a variety of identities related to class, race, gender expression, sexual orientation, and ability.

Women in Higher Education: Positioning Equality

Feminism has drawn attention to the positions and roles that women and men perform in academic settings. It has asserted that since gender matters in teaching, learning, researching, and leading, it is important to ensure women's access to all those positions in higher education. Historically, women were only first admitted to higher education (at Oberlin College) in 1837—approximately 200 years after Harvard University opened its doors to men. And even though a great deal has changed since that time, ongoing struggles to ensure equal opportunities to participate fully in higher education continue. For example, Title IX was initiated in 1972 to ensure equal opportunities for women and men in publicly supported institutions, yet challenges continue to be levied against its enforcement, particularly in collegiate athletic programs. In this section, I review the positions that women hold in higher education institutions, drawing attention to conditions of both parity and inequality.

Students. Women students now constitute over 50 percent of all students in United States higher education institutions. In some respects and at many levels, then, women have achieved parity with men (see Table 3.1).

It is important to recognize that in some regard, trends of gendered participation differ among racial groups. For example, white women earned 46.5 percent of all doctorates awarded to white persons during the 1997–1998 academic year, but American Indian women earned 55.6 percent of all doctorates among American Indian people, and African American women earned 60.1 percent of all doctoral

Table 3.1 Percentage of Degrees Conferred to Women

	Associate's Degree	*Bachelor's Degree*	*Master's Degree*	*Doctorate*
1970–1971	42.9	43.4	40.1	14.3
1997–1998	61.1	56.1	57.1	42.0

Source: National Center for Education Statistics, U.S. Department of Education.

Table 3.2 Degrees Conferred by Racial and Ethnic Group, 1997–1998

	American Indian	*Asian*	*Black*	*Hispanic*	*White*
Associate's					
Male	2,243	10,885	18,584	19,006	160,346
Female	3,977	14,162	36,424	26,621	250,990
Bachelor's					
Male	3,148	33,405	34,469	27,648	399,105
Female	4,746	38,187	63,663	38,289	501,212
Master's					
Male	780	10,239	9,631	6,499	125,343
Female	1,269	10,849	20,466	9,716	182,244
Doctorate					
Male	83	1,390	824	649	15,368
Female	104	944	1,242	621	13,379
Professional					
Male	291	3,993	2,303	1,971	35,069
Female	270	3,719	3,180	1,576	24,204

Source: National Center for Education Statistics (2001).

degrees among African American people. One trend is consistent among racial groups, however. In the associate's, bachelor's, and master's degree categories, women outnumber men in the degrees received in all racial categories (see Table 3.2).

It is also important to recognize that women's participation has increased steadily in a variety of fields. In psychology, for example, women earned 24.0 percent of the bachelor's degrees in 1970–1971. By 1997–1998, this percentage had risen to 67.5 percent. In 1970–1971, women earned only 0.6 percent of all engineering bachelor's degrees, but by 1997–1998, women earned 12.2 percent of those degrees. In sum, although women have achieved majority status in most degree categories in higher education today, their racial background and their disciplinary affiliation makes a difference in their representation.

Faculty. Similar to the expansion of women's participation in higher education as students, women's participation as faculty is growing as well. However, it is important to look at the numbers associated with faculty carefully, as many factors affect women's participation as faculty members in higher education. In 1997, women represented 36.3 percent of the full-time faculty in all higher education institutions but 46.9 percent of the part-time faculty (U.S. Department of Education). As such, women are disproportionately represented in ranks that are generally not tenured and do not enjoy the institutional decisionmaking power and stability that full-time faculty possess. In evaluating women's participation as faculty in higher education, it is also important to consider the institutions at which women and men work. As seen in Table 3.3, women represent nearly 50 percent of faculty at public two-year

Table 3.3 Characteristics of Faculty Members with Teaching Duties by Type of Institution, Fall 1997 (percentage)

Institution	*Male*	*Female*
Public Research	70.5	29.5
Private Research	73.9	26.1
Public Doctoral	66.7	33.3
Private Doctoral	63.6	36.4
Public Comprehensive	61.7	38.3
Private Comprehensive	63.3	36.7
Private Liberal Arts	62.2	37.8
Public Two-year	51.3	48.7
Other	67.9	32.1
Total	63.7	36.3

Source: National Center for Education Statistics (2001).

institutions but only 26.1 percent at private research institutions.

This disparity has implications for the ways that women can engage as scholars. Faculty members at two-year institutions typically spend a greater percentage of their time engaged in teaching students, whereas those at research universities both teach and have support to conduct research and disseminate their findings to a broader audience. In large part, they are responsible for creating disciplinary knowledge that is then used within their own and other institutions. In many of the disciplines, then, what is considered to be foundational knowledge is created in institutions from which women were once excluded and in which they are now underrepresented.

In order to ascertain the true status of women in the faculty ranks, this analysis can be taken one step further. Since faculty members at the assistant professor ranking are generally not tenured, they have less decisionmaking power and scholarly autonomy than do tenured associate and full professors. In Table 3.4 below, it is clear that as rank (and corresponding benefits of that rank) increases, the percentage of women decreases. In fact, it is only in

Table 3.4 Distribution of Faculty by Sex and Rank (1997)

	Male	*Female*	*Total*	*Percentage Female*
Professor	129,974	32,133	162,107	19.8
Associate Professor	83,390	43,126	126,516	34.1
Assistant Professor	67,239	55,824	123,063	45.3
Instructor/Lecturer	38,899	41,432	80,331	51.6

Source: National Center for Education Statistics (2001).

Table 3.5 Number of Full-Time Faculty Members by Sex, Rank, and Racial and Ethnic Group, Fall 1997

Rank	*American Indian*	*Asian*	*Black*	*Hispanic*	*White*
Professor					
Male	321	7,265	3,316	2,154	116,918
Female	92	1,243	1,924	767	28,107
Associate Professor					
Male	231	5,434	3,373	1,891	72,461
Female	145	1,633	2,674	1,088	37,586
Assistant Professor					
Male	261	5,787	3,758	2,198	55,235
Female	285	3,113	4,288	1,753	46,385
Instructor					
Male	263	1,348	1,985	1,385	27,598
Female	200	1,264	2,590	1,269	28,797
Lecturer					
Male	34	301	367	251	5,367
Female	29	354	438	302	6,189

Source: National Center for Education Statistics (2001).

the least permanent and stable position of instructor/lecturer that women hold the majority of the faculty positions.

Again, as with women's participation as students, current statistics reveal both similarities and differences by racial category. As seen in Table 3.5, men outnumber women in all racial categories when considering the associate and full professor rankings. However, at the assistant professor ranking, men outnumber women only in the Hispanic, Asian, and white racial categories. It is clear from the following numbers that women's participation in upper-level, more prestigious, and higher-paying positions still lags behind that of men.

Administration. Women are also underrepresented in the upper levels of administration in higher education. According to a recent report issued by the American Council on Education (2000), the percentage of women presidents has nearly doubled in the past fifteen years. In 1986, women held 9.5 percent of the presidencies, but by 1998, 19.3 percent of college presidencies were held by women. However, there are differences in the types of institutions that women serve. In 1998, only 2 percent of all women presidents served at major research universities, and 39 percent were presidents of two-year community colleges (Glazer-Raymo 1999). Overall, despite their majority as students, women are underrepresented in all types of academic leadership (Chliwniak 1997).

In sum, the general trend is that the higher the position in higher education, the fewer women one can expect to find. Feminist analyses have drawn attention to the gendered implications of this phenomenon. What does it mean when the majority of students are women, but the majority of decisionmakers and tenured faculty members are men? Are decisions about teaching and learning being made without an acknowledgement that there are social differences that tend to exist between most women and most men? What does it mean for women of color that they do not often see role models who share their identities in key leadership positions on higher education campuses? What does it mean for knowledge production when nearly three-fourths of all faculty at research institutions are men? The presence of women and men in certain positions has implications in itself. However, feminist analyses have gone beyond numbers to suggest how the ways of knowing and interacting in higher education environments are themselves gendered. Thus feminists move beyond the "Who?" to the "How?"

Teaching and Learning: Changing the Academic Climate

Teaching and learning come in many forms, all of which are gendered. People engage in classroom dialogue, residence hall programming, and one-on-one meetings with advisers. In each case, their identities as gendered persons are present in their interactions. Faculty members and students engage in a variety of types of research, all of which have been developed by people who have various perspectives related to their identities. Feminists have suggested that this situation calls for a concerted effort to pay attention to interactions related to teaching and learning in higher education through feminist lenses. Both through women's studies and many other disciplines, scholars have taken this charge seriously.

In teaching and learning, students and scholars construct and (re)present knowledge in certain ways. Their epistemology, or "theory of knowledge" (Harding 1987), guides their research questions, teaching practices, methodologies, analyses, and writings. As Sandra Harding suggested more than a decade ago, although feminist methodologies and epistemologies may certainly influence the direction and outcome of research, the methods of feminist researchers are often used by researchers with varying epistemologies. Simply put, the adoption of specific tools or ideas does not in itself constitute a feminist analysis. Instead, it is the use of tools and strategies paired with the epistemologies that leads to a feminist analysis.

Recognizing the Value of Women's Interpretations

As they approach their work, feminist scholars have stressed the importance of asking questions related to the assumptions they are making about *how* they know, as well as about *what* they know. These questions lead scholars to better understand the ways their stances affected their creation of knowledge. Scholarship on feminist research and pedagogy has provided useful responses to the questions: What constitutes knowledge? And who are accepted as knowers? What practices facilitate knowledge development? Feminist epistemology prompts approaches to knowledge that both acknowledge the limitations of what we know and seek to ensure that women's perspectives are valued as both creators and subjects of knowledge. In this way, feminism values knowledge that is interpreted by women and that has the potential to improve society for women. It also recognizes that women's and men's understandings and interactions with/in the world will be affected by their gender.

Jane Flax suggests that feminist theory is based on the assumptions that men and women have different experiences, that women's oppression is not a subset of some other social relationship, that the oppression of women is part of the way the structure of the world is organized, and that one task of feminist theory is to explain how and why this structure evolved (1996, 18–19). This cognizance of gender's effects on men and women's private and public lives suggests different understandings of social phenomena. Women's interpretations of their social situations can offer different views of social interactions and potentially provide possibilities for change. Yet, feminist epistemology also asserts that all knowledge is shaped by its constructors' and interpreters' multiple and intersecting identities. As such, feminists have increasingly recognized that oppression does not take the same form or have the same effects for all women. The diversity represented by women is a key element of feminist teaching and learning.

The Reclamation of Women's Voices

Feminists are aware that women have traditionally not been allowed the same access to knowledge and knowing that men have. In some cases, their experiences in classrooms have been met with both overt and subtle hostility. Although this situation has arguably changed dramatically, the foundational knowledge upon which most disciplines and fields of study are based is gendered. More specifically, when teachers point students to the parents of the discipline they are studying, they are generally pointing to fathers. Cheris Kramarae and Dale Spender point out that in women's studies, which serves as an academic arm of feminism:

> Knowledge was constructed thus: that there was no knowledge without knowledge makers, and that those who were responsible for making the knowledge were almost exclusively male: that far from being objective, and impartial, disciplinary knowledge was the product of a particular group of men whose subjectivity, partiality, priorities, and power base were deeply embedded in the knowledge-making process. (1992, 1–2)

This understanding led feminist scholars to assert that a critical analysis of current knowledge and knowledge processes was needed.

Another concern articulated in feminist epistemology and pedagogy is that women have not often been asked to write down their own experiences. As such, they may doubt their own abilities to engage in the construction of knowledge (Bloom 1998; Lewis 1993), even when it is about their own lived experiences. This problem is particularly difficult since both feminist methodology and feminist pedagogy rely upon the soliciting and honoring of women's experiences—as articulated by women (Collins 1991; Harding 1987). These dilemmas affect the ways that women are able to express their own experiences and interpret their own lives in publicly accessible ways. Research participants', students', and faculty members' positions—in relation to the larger society, their own personal context, and the researcher herself or himself—need to be taken into account when soliciting and hearing their stories and perspectives.

The feminist belief that the oppression of women should be alleviated also affects the relationships that feminist seek to establish with participants in their research, as well as the relationships feminist teachers seek with their students. Since, in our society, women's participation in knowledge construction and interpretations of their own lives has been limited, feminist researchers are careful not to reproduce the exclusion of women participants in knowledge construction. Although not always enacted in every piece of research, feminist researchers have suggested some general principles to guide feminist research relationships. These themes or guidelines fall into the following areas: (1) research participants should have the opportunity to be equal partners in the research endeavor, even if "equality" may mean different things, depending on the research context; (2) research relationships should be reflexive; and (3) research relationships should be empowering ones, encouraging or enabling participants to take action to improve their situations. Feminist pedagogy often struggles to embrace similar tenets, although it is sometimes difficult to do so within an academic context. Feminists attempt to empower students to be conscious shapers of their own educational experiences, as well as critics of practices and curricula that exclude them. From the types of relationships developed in feminist research and feminist pedagogy, knowledge is formed that both honors the perspectives of women and seeks understanding for positive change.

The Importance of Teaching and Learning for Change

Feminist research and teaching seeks to provide information for women that will be useful for them in transforming their lives. This orientation leads feminist scholars into places where women are enacting change or seeking information from which to enact change. It also leads feminist teachers to include content and teaching practices that engage students. In the questions they ask, the interactions they promote, the critiques they offer, and the texts they choose to discuss, feminists seek to engage others in purposeful teaching and learning.

Knowledge derived with a feminist viewpoint attempts both to create new knowledge based on women's authoring of their own experiences and to deconstruct or critique current knowledge that did not take women's voices into account in its construction. Achieving these goals is difficult for several reasons. First, much "foundational" knowledge omits or misinterprets women's experiences. Second, many women struggle to construct their own experiences in a society that has deemed certain styles of communication and ways of thinking as inappropriate. Third, traditional methods in social science research and teaching were generally not developed to represent the ways that women tend to learn and understand their worlds. The teaching and learning practices that are overly attentive to some experiences and accomplishments while remaining silent about others are taken up by feminist teaching and learning, deconstructed, and reconstructed in purposefully more gender-attentive ways.

Although feminists use a variety of methods to engage in their academic work, their belief that women's contributions have been restricted or unacknowledged has led them to tend toward certain ways of teaching and learning. Much feminist scholarly work concerns itself with finding, making sense of, and telling women's stories and experiences to reclaim the importance of women's lives. Feminism in the academy suggests the importance of processes that allow women's perspectives to be heard, while simultaneously offering a feminist criticism of the contexts in which those perspectives are shaped, spoken, and heard. Feminist teaching and learning involves an acknowledgement of the diversity of women's experiences, the diversity of research processes that are available for better understanding gendered lives, and, in addition, the variety of audiences that can be—and perhaps should be—reached through feminist education.

It is important to remember that although feminists have produced a great deal of scholarly work related to epistemological questions about knowledge, knowers, and the processes of constructing knowledge, there is no ideal type of feminist teaching and learning. Instead, feminism is sensitive to context and participants, attempting to adapt and adopt methods to ensure that the issues discussed above are addressed fairly and ethically. When making efforts to develop scholarly practices that honor the contributions and experiences of women, feminist researchers and teachers both draw and wipe away lines in the sand. That is the process of knowing.

The entries in this section describe several ways in which feminism has taken shape in academic environments. Feminist scholars and activists have increasingly become attuned to the differences among and between women. The entry on black feminism and womanism summarizes the scholarly thought that has grown out of black women's articulation of their own epistemological and experiential position. The entries on feminist epistemology and feminist research methods emphasize how feminist thought has drawn attention to and shaped ways of knowing that expand traditional and scientific methods that often ignored the experiences of women. The discussion of feminist ethics encourages scholars and practitioners to remember that what is deemed "good" or moral may depend on one's (gendered) vantage point. Finally, the entry on feminist pedagogy and the transformation of the curriculum demonstrates that feminism has effects both on what is taught in classrooms and on the manner in which teachers and students interact around academic content.

In sum, this section conveys the different ways that feminism has taken shape in and been shaped by academic dialogues. In many cases, feminists have strongly resisted traditional ways of teaching and learning that exclude women. Simultaneously, feminists have encountered the resistance of others as they have tried to transform academic environments. The struggle to improve colleges and universities—both in terms of women's access to all positions and opportunities and in terms of the content and form of academic teaching and learning—continues.

Rebecca Ropers-Huilman

References and further reading

American Council on Education. 2000. *The American College President: 2000.* Washington, DC: American Council on Education.

Belenky, Mary Field, Blythe McVicker Clinchy, Nancy Rule Goldberger, and Jill Mattuck Tarule. 1986. *Women's*

Ways of Knowing: The Development of Self, Voice, and Mind. New York: Basic Books.
Bloom, Leslie. 1998. *Under the Sign of Hope: Feminist Methodology and Narrative Interpretation.* New York: State University of New York Press.
Chamberlain, Mariam K. 1991. *Women in Academe: Progress and Prospects.* New York: Russell Sage Foundation.
Chliwniak, Luba. 1997. *Higher Education Leadership: Analyzing the Gender Gap.* ASHE-ERIC Higher Education Report 25, no. 4. Washington, DC: George Washington University.
Collins, Patricia Hill. 1991. *Black Feminist Thought: Knowledge, Consciousness, and the Politics of Empowerment.* New York: Routledge.
Flax, Jane. 1996. "Women Do Theory." Pp. 17–20 in *Multicultural Experiences, Multicultural Theories,* ed. M. F. Rogers. 1979. Reprint, New York: McGraw-Hill.
Glazer-Raymo, Judith. 1999. *Shattering the Myths: Women in Academe.* Baltimore: Johns Hopkins University Press.
Harding, Sandra. 1987. "Introduction: Is There a Feminist Method?" Pp. 1–14 in *Feminism and Methodology,* ed. S. Harding. Bloomington: Indiana University Press.
Hensel, Nancy. 1991. *Realizing Gender Equality in Higher Education: The Need to Integrate Work/Family Issues.* ASHE-ERIC Higher Education Report no. 2. Washington, DC: George Washington University.
Kramarae, Cheris, and Dale Spender. 1992. "Exploding Knowledge." Pp. 1–24 in *The Knowledge Explosion: Generations of Feminist Scholarship,* ed. C. Kramarae and D. Spender. New York: Teachers College Press.
Lewis, Magda Gere. 1993. *Without a Word: Teaching beyond Women's Silence.* New York: Teachers College Press.
National Center for Education Statistics. 2001. Digest of Education Statistics. Washington, DC: U.S. Department of Education.
Sandler, Bernice R., and Robert J. Shoop. 1997. *Sexual Harassment on Campus: A Guide for Administrators, Faculty and Students.* Boston: Allyn and Bacon.

Black Feminism and Womanism

A black feminist is a person, historically an African American woman academic, who believes that female descendents of American slavery share a unique set of life experiences distinct from those of black men and white women. Black feminists believe that the lives of African American women are oppressed by combinations of racism, sexism, classism, and heterosexism. In order to help alleviate the suffering and poor living conditions of black women and to help them gain political power, black feminists advocate a separate area of study that focuses exclusively on the lives of black women. Black feminists believe that when the lives of African American women are improved, there will be progressive development also for African American men, families, and community.

The contemporary black feminist movement took most of its shape during the late 1960s and early 1970s. Black feminist groups such as the Combahee River Collective, an organizing group that became famous for its statements confronting racism in the gay movement and homophobia in the black community, and the National Black Feminist Organization expressed their dissatisfaction with the sexism of black civil rights organizations and the racism of white feminist organizations.

Sage: A Scholarly Journal of Black Women, the first explicitly black feminist periodical devoted exclusively to the experiences of women of African descent, was founded in 1984 at Spelman College, a traditionally black women's college in Atlanta, Georgia. Barbara Smith and Audre Lorde were cofounders of Kitchen Table: Women of Color Press, the first independent press to focus on the work

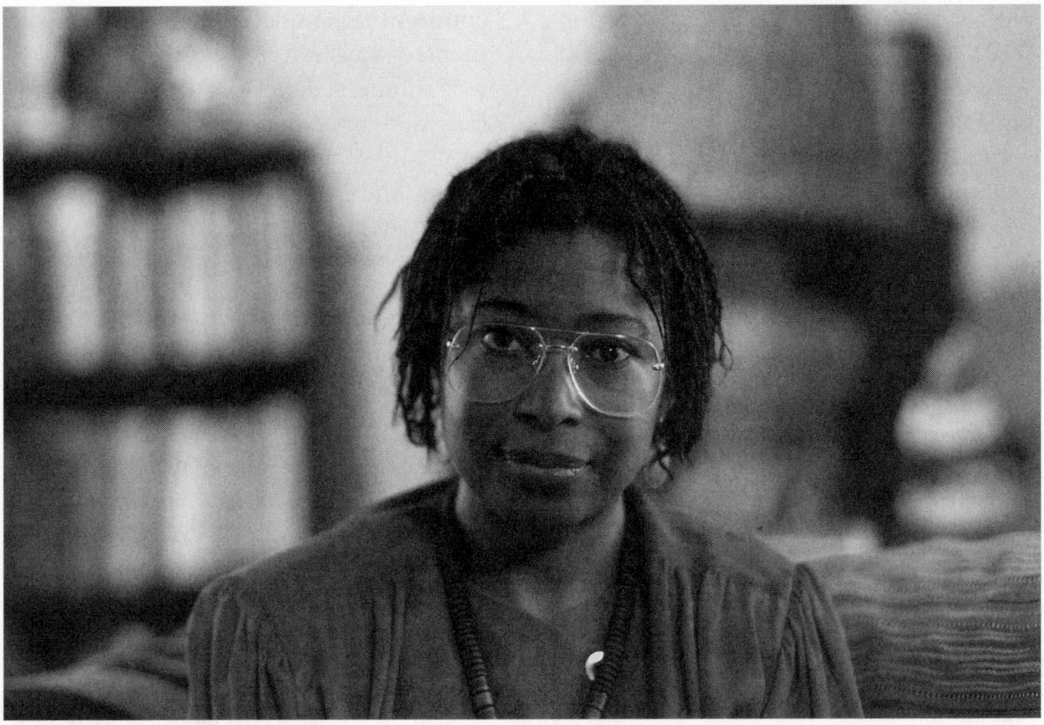

Writer Alice Walker coined the term "womanism" to make the point that feminism did not always include women of color (Corbis)

of feminists of color. Among its publications were the now-classic *Home Girls: A Black Feminist Anthology* and *This Bridge Called My Back: Writings by Radical Women of Color.* In 1983, Alice Walker introduced the term "womanist" as a more culturally acceptable label for people uncomfortable with the label of black feminist.

In her landmark book, *Black Feminist Thought,* Patricia Hill Collins describes major themes in the construction of black feminist thought, all generated from a black woman's point of view. She states that black feminist thought consists of specialized knowledge created by African American women. First, black women empower themselves by creating self-definitions and self-valuations that enable them to establish positive self-images and to repel negative, controlling representations of black womanhood created by other people. Some of these negative, controlling images are "mammies," "matriarchs," "welfare queens," and "jezebels." Black feminists stress the importance of positive self-definition as part of the journey toward empowerment.

Second, black women confront and dismantle the interlocking structure of political oppression in terms of race, class, and gender. Black feminism can be described as the nexus between the black liberation struggle and the women's liberation movement, but it has its own distinct ideologies and notions of collective action. Black feminists are highly critical of dichotomous, hierarchical, and oversimplified additive models of oppression that suggest that black women must identify as either black or women, women first and black second, or black first and women second, or that their reality is simply "the black experience" in addition to "the woman experience." Black feminist perspectives stress how various forms of gender, race, and class oppression interlock, forming a matrix of social domination. Gender, race, and class represent interrelated systems of oppression that profoundly affect black women.

Third, black feminists combine academic intellectual thought and political activism. Scholars first describe their activist traditions dating from abolitionist times and then they investigate instances of contemporary activism in formal organizations and in everyday life and work. Black women intellectuals often use examples of lived experiences like working in factories, working as domestics, obtaining good health care, organizing communities, and mothering in their theorizing and written scholarship. They have the job of reinterpreting experiences so that African American women are aware of their collective knowledge, enabling them to feel empowered instead of oppressed. Black feminism may be seen in part as a reaction to the racist history of the white women's feminist movement, but it must also be identified with the glorious tradition of black female activists' trenchant commitment to empowering themselves to create a humanistic community for all.

The black feminist movement does not mobilize through an institutionalized formal organization. Black feminist collectives have operated through local communities in decentralized, often segmented ways referred to in the literature as "submerged networks." Some informal networks include self-help groups, book clubs, "girlfriend" parties and gatherings, and explicit political education (or consciousness-raising) groups.

Evangeline Wheeler

See also Part 1: Black Women's Colleges; Part 2: Demographics of Gender and Race; Intersection of Gender and Race; Part 6: Black Sororities; Part 7: Women of Color at Predominantly White Institutions

References and further reading

Collins, Patricia Hill. 1991. *Black Feminist Thought: Knowledge, Consciousness, and the Politics of Empowerment.* New York: Routledge.

Guy-Sheftall, Beverly, ed. 1995. *Words of Fire: An Anthology of African-American Feminist Thought.* New York: New Press.

Feminist Epistemology

Academic feminism addresses the relationship between knowledge and its social uses and how patriarchal values have shaped the content and structure of knowledge. Driven by both a moral and intellectual commitment to social justice, feminist scholarship aims to be a transformative force in higher education. By introducing a new paradigm for knowledge production that blends inquiry and advocacy, feminists have challenged core academic values and enlarged the range of perspectives, theories, and methodologies that comprise the scholarly enterprise. As one of several "emancipatory knowledges" that have emerged in contemporary academic organizations over the past several decades (e.g., critical, postcolonial, queer theories), feminist epistomology represents a radically different way of knowing.

At the turn of the twenty-first century, the value-neutral claim of positivist science was being challenged. It is within this larger context, which Jurgen Habermas calls a "legitimation crisis," that feminist perspectives have contributed to the critique of science, producing an "awareness of the complexity, historical contingency, and fragility of the practices we invent to discover truth about ourselves" (Lather 1990, 80). Over the past few decades, the critical voices of those who have been formerly marginalized have jointly challenged many of the prevailing assumptions about what constitutes knowledge and how it is produced.

To understand academic feminism and its constitutive values, it is important to note that values are infused into all academic cultures and knowledge production and that feminism is only one value system among many in the academy. Researchers' values affect their choice of topic and the questions they ask about a topic. Valuing women's experiences, consciousness raising, and social transformation has raised social issues that had not and could not have been addressed by an androcentric paradigm (e.g., rape, sexual harassment, battered women, and sexism in psychotherapy). Sample selection or interpretation and analyses that do not take into account the different social worlds inhabited by men and women, for example, are value-based research decisions that result in "bad science."

Neither academic feminism nor the larger academic culture are monolithic. There is, however, a set of traditions deeply engrained in the structure of the academy and in the conventional norms for conducting research. Similarly, definitions of feminist scholarship typically concede that as a broad intellectual framework, it includes diverse priorities, perspectives, activities, and methodologies. Still, a cohesive culture can be identified through analyses of how feminist scholars have consistently identified basic values that define their ethos and through which they construct this emanicipatory knowledge.

Michele A. Paludi and Gertrude A. Steuernagel (1990) identified the following traditional academic norms: (1) implicit conservatism, (2) objectivity, (3) the value of cumulative scholarship, (4) the association of power with expertise, (5) the superiority of pure knowledge over applied knowledge, (6) the value of specialist knowledge, and (7) the value of individuality and competition. These norms contrast with the values, beliefs, and assumptions of feminist culture in varying degrees and in specific ways.

Various definitions of academic feminism have been supplied, suggesting that feminists who work in the academy share three overarching concerns: "a normative commitment to women's emancipation, a scientific commitment to the explanation of women's oppression, and a practical commitment to social transformation." Academic feminism's primary curricular manifestations, women's studies, "takes gender as its primary category of analysis; emphasizes the relations of power between women and men; foregrounds women's experience in a way that does not objectify, victimize, romanticize, or overgeneralize; and seeks to effect social change. It also recognizes the importance of race, class, and sexual identity" (Boxer 1998, 14).

Epistemology is the system of thought through which questions of truth, authority, what counts for knowledge, and how one comes to know are addressed. Understanding feminist epistemology is critical to understanding academic feminism. Several key assumptions and values drive academic feminism. These conceptions of knowledge and truth reflect the values and material conditions of the socially constructed female world, or feminist standpoints.

The social construction of gender and the centrality of gender as a category of analysis are the basic assumptions of academic feminism. Historically, women have had their choices constrained and rights curtailed through social, legal, and economic forces. That has raised women's consciousness about the social construction of gender and provided the impetus for the larger feminist movement in which the academic form is rooted. In feminist scholarship, gender is the central theoretical dimension.

Feminist inquiry blurs the boundaries between pure and applied knowledge. As problem-focused scholarship, academic feminism challenges the intellectual superiority and status of theoretical or pure courses and programs as opposed to applied or practical research. Feminists and others whose research is conducted for the purpose of effecting social change are challenging the traditional notion that advocacy and scholarship are incompatible.

This boundary crossing relates to the disciplinary structure of academic knowledge as well as to dichotomous concepts that predominate in academic culture. In addition to integrating theory and experience, academic feminists challenge other deeply engrained dichotomous concepts (e.g., body-mind, practice-theory, personal-professional, women-men) and their implicit hierarchical relationships. For example, feminist scholarship disrupts the norm of discrediting emotional or personal modes of knowledge in favor of cognitive or impersonal processes.

Through consciousness raising, women become empowered to reconceptualize social reality, based on their awareness of how their own experiences do not fit within the dominant discourse. Academic feminists engage in a self-conscious struggle to reject patriarchal perceptions of women and to reinterpret social reality based on women's experiences and values. Consciousness raising for academic feminists involves a struggle to embrace a consciousness that questions all oppressive social structures and to use that consciousness to create knowledge.

Feminist scholarship is problem-focused, action-oriented, and value-based in its commitment to the emancipation of women. Despite the great variability among feminist scholars in their beliefs about the most effective way to promote social change, effecting such change is a unifying principle. Academic feminists' commitment to transforming institutions of higher education into pluralistic and caring communities is reflected in the mission of the National Women's Studies Association (NWSA), which is to realize "a vision of a world free not only from sexism but also from racism, class-bias, ageism, heterosexual bias—from all the ideologies and institutions that have consciously or unconsciously oppressed and exploited some for the advantage of others" (Boxer 1998, 18).

Feminist epistemology is reflected in methodology, the processes and practices feminist scholars use to produce knowledge. As researchers, feminists use a multiplicity of methods, ranging from traditional to innovative, and often combine these methods in new ways. One interpretation of feminist methodology at the level of practice includes the perspective that women's intuitive rationality and feminist political commitment results in a distinctive method (Stanley and Wise 1983). Another view avoids the search for a distinctive feminist method and instead inquires into the ways feminist research uses the three primary techniques of listening to informants, observing behavior, and examining historical records (Harding 1987).

Syntheses of feminist research methodology suggest nine characteristic elements, including (1) reflexivity, (2) consciousness raising, (3) reconceptualization of the relationship between subject and object, (4) concern for ethical issues, (5) emphasis on empowerment and transformation of institutions through research, (6) attention to the affective components of the research, (7) use of the situation at hand, (8) openness to transdisciplinarity, and (9) recognition of diversity (Reinharz 1992; Cook and Fonow 1990). Feminist researchers do not necessarily employ all of these elements in any one research project; instead, they represent features that distinguish feminist research from other research paradigms.

Feminist scholarship uses a revisionist approach to reexamine traditional interpretations, conventional wisdom, and existing frameworks. The tendency of feminist researchers to reflect upon, examine critically, and explore analytically the nature of the research process is referred to as reflexivity. Feminist scholarship questions the "dominance of methodologies of research, categories of analysis, and ways of interpreting evidence that distort or block understanding of women and gender" (Boxer 1998, 18). Shulamit Reinharz (1992) refers to this as "feminist distrust." This critical stance applies to feminist scholarship itself; feminists are reflexive about the extent to which their work is inclusive, nonessentializing, and action-oriented. By identifying their race, class, and gender in the research process, feminists recognize and make explicit the influence of their social location in conducting research.

As revisionist scholarship, academic feminism challenges the tendency of institutions of higher education toward conservatism. The conservative norm in higher education places a value on models and theories based on an accumulative body of knowledge; thus paradigms of inquiry that undercut existing frameworks are resisted. Expertise, or specialist knowledge, is highly valued in the academy. This value permeates the teacher-student relationships. The teacher-as-expert model is challenged by feminists, who bring a philosophy of shared power and responsibility to the classroom.

Consciousness raising is integrated into feminist research in various ways. Feminist consciousness is first used as a kind of "double vision" through which the researcher sees the world both as a scholar and a woman; she is able to use her experiences with and responses to oppression to provide insight into the research. Second, feminist researchers may use research for its consciousness-raising effects, that is, to motivate participants to take action against oppressive structures and processes (Fonow and Cook 1991).

In rejecting the rigid dichotomy of subject and object, feminist scholars challenge the norm that strict separation of the researcher from the researched produces more valid knowledge. In locating the researcher as a gendered being (or as having a certain class, race, or sexual orientation), feminist research recognizes how the web of social relations influences the analytical and interpretive processes of research and shapes the life of the researcher. The recognition that the beliefs, interests, desires, and behaviors of the researcher affect the results of the analysis underlies feminist researchers' attempts to make these subjective elements explicit in their work, rather than to ascribe to an illusory objectivity. Many feminist researchers recognize the importance of the personal experience of the researcher and are reflexive about the relationship between experience and research in the presentation of data (Reinharz 1992).

Feminists' contributions to the philosophy of science have intensified the dialogue with a critique of objectivity that investigates how participatory values enhance objectivity and upholds the legitimacy of perspectival knowledge. In this conception of objectivity, openly political and value-laden research produces more complete and less distorted versions of social realities because it does not presume to seek universal truth or essentialize human experience.

Ethical questions in feminist scholarship are typically concerned with the level of empathy and respect established in the researcher and participant relationship. This feminist ethic of egalitarianism contrasts with the scientific ethic of detachment and role differentiation between the researcher and the subject. Issues of reciprocity between researcher and researched and other ethical concerns are frequently addressed in all aspects of the research process.

For many feminist scholars, the goals of social change and institutional transformation are obligatory and can be accomplished either through implementing the results of research or through its consciousness-raising effects. The statement of purpose, topic selection, theoretical orientation, choice of method, view of human nature, and definitions of the feminist researcher's role are based in the value of women's empowerment. Even when conducting basic research, feminists typically derive policy implications that address how their research can contribute to the welfare of women. Feminists employ a wide range of ways to engage the reader in the research, such as allowing participants to speak for themselves in the interview process, producing these direct quotes in the written report, and revealing themselves in the interpretation and analysis.

Feminists recognize the affective dimension of research as an important source of insight. In interpreting the female world, feminist researchers attend to and validate the "private, emotional, interiorized, intimate world" (Cook and Fonow 1990, 73). Carol Gilligan's pathbreaking research on female moral development discovered the centrality of caring in women's worldview and approach to resolving moral dilemmas (1982). Patricia Hill Collins developed an alternative epistemology in her work on black feminist thought, based on the ethic of caring. When the ethic of caring is used to validate knowledge claims, it includes an emphasis on individual uniqueness, the acceptance of the appropriateness of emotions in dialogue, and the cultivation of the capacity for empathy (1990).

The use of the situation at hand, or an emphasis on creativity, spontaneity, and improvisation in the selection of topic and method, is a characteristic of feminist approaches that comes from the traditions of ethnomethodology and phenomenology. Feminists' use of ordinary situations to reveal otherwise hidden processes may be viewed as a survival mechanism, given the underrepresentation of women in traditional research institutions and inadequate funding for feminist research (Fonow and Cook 1991).

Feminist research draws upon empirical data, analyses, and methodologies from multiple disciplines. Feminists work within the traditions of their disciplinary homes and across the borders of other disciplines in an effort to be "connected knowers" (Belenky et al. 1986). Reinharz (1992) suggests that the ability to *cross disciplinary boundaries* is related to women's sense of connectedness in moral reasoning as found by Carol Gilligan.

Recognition of women's diversity has become "the new criterion for feminist research excellence" (Reinharz 1992, 253). Since the early 1970s, feminist scholars have challenged themselves to increasingly confront all diversity issues in their work, including racism, classism, and ethnocentricity. As a field, women's studies strives to maintain a balance in the curriculum with respect to gender, race, ethnicity, sexual orientation, and social class. Feminists believe that diversified participant samples and case studies lead to more precise conceptualizations. A predominant feature of feminist research is to criticize one's lack of attention to diversity issues, thus creating a new methodological norm. The feminist ideal of recognizing human diversity in research has contributed to a more socially conscious science. The development of multicultural, global, and postcolonial feminisms has transformed central ideas about the philosophy of science (Narayan and Harding 2000).

Although these features of feminist research methodology have been identified through an examination of feminist research studies, they comprise a collection of methods used, not a prescription for how to conduct feminist research. Scholars who have undertaken syntheses of feminist methodology have noted the ambiguity and controversy that are associated with many of these stated tendencies in feminist inquiry.

Lynn Safarik

See also Part 3: Feminist Pedagogy; Feminist Research Methodology

References and further reading

Belenky, Marie Field, Blythe McVicker Clinchy, Nancy Rule Goldberger, and Jill Mattuck Tarule. 1986. *Women's Ways of Knowing: The Development of Self, Voice, and Mind.* New York: Basic Books.

Boxer, Marilyn Jacoby. 1998. *When Women Ask the Questions: Creating Women's Studies in America.* Baltimore: Johns Hopkins University Press.

Collins, Patricia Hill. 1990. *Black Feminist Thought: Knowledge, Consciousness, and the Politics of Empowerment.* New York: Routledge.

Cook, Judith A., and Mary M. Fonow. 1990. "Knowledge and Women's Interests: Issues of Epistemology and Methodology in Feminist Sociological Research." Pp. 69–93 in *Feminist Research Methods: Exemplary Readings in the Social Sciences,* ed. Joyce M. Nielsen. Boulder, CO: Westview Press.

Fonow, Mary M., and Judith A. Cook. 1991. "Back to the Future: A Look at the Second Wave of Feminist Epistemology and Methodology." Pp. 1–15 in *Beyond Methodology: Feminist Scholarship as Lived Research,* ed. M. M. Fonow and A. J. Cook. Bloomington: Indiana University Press.

Gilligan, Carol. 1982. *In a Different Voice: Psychological Theory and Women's Development.* Cambridge, MA: Harvard University Press.

Harding, Sandra, ed. 1987. *Feminism and Methodology.* Bloomington: Indiana University Press.

———. 1991. *Whose Science? Whose Knowledge? Thinking from Women's Lives.* Ithaca, NY: Cornell University Press.

Lather, Patti A. 1990. "Reinscribing Otherwise: The Play of Values in the Practices of the Human Sciences." In *The Paradigm Dialogue,* ed. E. G. Guba. Newbury Park, CA: Sage.

Narayan, Uma, and Sandra Harding, eds. 2000. *Decentering the Center: Philosophy for a Multicultural, Postcolonial, and Feminist World.* Bloomington: Indiana University Press.

Paludi, Michele A., and Gertrude A. Steuernagel, eds. 1990. *Foundations for a Feminist Restructuring of the Academic Disciplines.* New York: Hawthorne.

Reinharz, Shulamit. 1992. *Feminist Methods in Social Research.* New York: Oxford University Press.

Stanely, Liz, and Susan Wise, eds. 1983. *Breaking Out: Feminist Consciousness and Feminist Research.* Boston: Routledge and Kegan Paul.

Feminist Ethics

Feminist ethical theories provide unique lenses for helping to determine what one ought to do and deciding on a course of action in the face of competing ethical principles. Such lenses can guide the higher education practitioner to make more adequate ethical decisions.

Feminist ethicists claim that ethical action is required of the feminist enterprise and is central to all feminist dialogue. They describe the moral obligations of feminist thought and action, which contribute to an understanding of ethical psychological practice. Although feminist ethics involves much of what traditional ethics does—that is, examination of the nature, consequences, and motives of action—feminist ethics goes beyond this by asserting a mandate to empower individuals to create just social structures that ensure that people are attentively and justly cared for and to nurture each person's potential within her or his particular context.

Feminist thought is not unitary; there exist multiple feminisms, including liberal Marxist, radical, relational, and postmodern. Each feminist theory has its own perspective that informs ethical thought. Although feminist ethicists and theorists dispute some issues, there is general agreement on the broad, central themes that define feminist ethics. They assert that women and their experiences have moral significance; attentiveness and subjective knowledge can illuminate moral issues; ethical practitioners should engage in an analysis of context and the power dynamics inherent in that context; an ethical feminist critique of male distortions of reality must be accompanied by a critique of racist, classist, and homophobic distortions; and ethical psychological practice requires action directed at achieving social justice. Each of these themes is discussed more fully in what follows.

Feminist ethicists insist that women and their experiences have moral significance. This theme draws on the feminist observation that moral philosophy has been largely a male enterprise. Thus, the "understanding" of women has developed under a patriarchy that privileges male insights, beliefs, and experiences. Under patriarchy, rigid, narrow roles that women are assigned often are transformed into pervasive caricatures that fail to capture the complexity of women's experiences. Feminists call for the need to eradicate the misrepresentation, distortion, and oppression of women resulting from a historically male interpretation of women's experiences. They voice the need to expose individual and institutional practices that have denied women access to education and jobs and have devalued and suppressed women. Feminist ethicists attend to women's experiences to achieve a more adequate understanding of the complexities and diversities of women. They claim that the experiences of women, such as mothering, women's friendships, peace making, and collective and collaborative decisionmaking, are important areas for identifying ethical concerns and issues. From the experiences of women, feminists have described feminine values, such as attentive love, connectedness, responsibility for others, and the ethic of care.

The last value was described by Carol Gilligan in 1982. She claimed that care is a moral orientation that could be identified by examining the voices of women and girls as they face moral dilemmas. Gilligan and other relational feminists argued that experiences of subordination and inequality that circumscribe the lives of women and girls give rise to a moral self grounded in human connections and concern for others. Relational feminists emphasize the differences between men and women and distinguish between the "feminine self" and associated values characterized by the "feminine voice." In contrast, they claim the "masculine voice" is socialized to be concerned with abstract rules of justice.

Relational feminists have generally advanced three notions. First, they offer a critique of the Kantian moral theory that posits abstract reasoning as the pinnacle of human thought. Relational feminists claim that women's subjective knowledge is just as valid. Although Immanuel Kant argued in the latter 1700s that women were less able to reason than men and therefore should be excluded from moral decisionmaking, relational feminists argue that women's more subjective epistemology gives them greater ethical sensibility than men. They do not claim women as incapable of abstract, principled reasoning but rather suggest that the attention they give to others provides women access to subjective knowledge informed by both rationality and affect. Second, relational feminists emphasize the values of empathy, nurturance, and caring over or in addition to justice, rights, and moral rules. They see women's qualities as equal to men's; for example, what might be called "women's passivity" is thought of as peacefulness, and dependence can be redefined as helpfulness. Finally, relational feminists challenge the ideas of individualistic moral choice derived from Kant's moral imperatives. Instead, they emphasize relationships and connections with others. As opposed to a rights-based morality that values autonomy and independence, relational feminists suggest relationship-based morality, grounded in interdependence, connections to one another, and responsibilities for each other. They offer the mother-child relationship as an alternative paradigm to the autonomous man.

Empirical research shows that although the ethic of care can be identified in individuals' moral responses, gender differences are not found to the degree originally asserted by relational feminists. In fact, feminists have argued that the "woman equals care, and man equals justice" dichotomy is dangerous because it essentializes gender, maintains women as subordinate, and fails to attend sufficiently to the diversity among women. Liberal feminists advocate that rather than celebrate women's caring attributes, the oppressive structures that relegate women to the private sphere and men to the public must be changed. Liberal feminists argue that the ethic of justice and the ethic of care are important for both men and women and should be integrated into one moral theory.

The second theme of feminist ethics asserts that attentiveness and subjective knowledge can illuminate moral issues. In placing greater knowledge on women's experiences than on preordained categories (e.g., right and wrong, good and evil), feminist ethics places great importance on grounded knowledge. Ethical feminists examine the cognitive, affective, and subjective realities of women's experiences. In part out of reaction to the hegemony of rational objective science, feminist ethics demands that one constantly analyze the process and outcomes of knowledge construction from a gendered sociocultural perspective. Being subjective means that the ethical feminist (administrator, researcher, therapist) is obliged to consider the other's (student, research participant, client) point of view and to integrate that reality into the knowledge process, so as to reflect both scientific and personal integrity.

Although most feminists urge the celebration of women's values, relationships, and unique moral perspectives, they do not claim that men cannot attain them, nor do they devalue male virtues and attributes. However, radical feminists (e.g., Daly 1984; Raymond 1986) view women's attributes, moral sensibilities, and affective relational skills as innately different or arising from biologically based experiences, such as women's ability to give birth and to nurse. Thus, they claim that women's values and virtues are unique to women and unavailable to men. Radical feminists raise the question of how to separate the true nature, ethics, and epistemology of women when their subjectivities have developed within patriarchy. They envision the moral course of women collectively living separate from men and outside patriarchy. Women may not be able to dismantle patriarchy, but, radical feminists argue, they can save themselves through feminist-womanist ways of knowing, doing, and being that are separate from males and the masculine. Radical feminists denounce patriarchal attempts to name and thereby assert power over and determine the limits and boundaries of women's experiences and subjectivities. In place of irredeemably male assertions such as "truth" and "the good," radical feminists propose normative and separate women's ways of knowing and being.

Although recognizing the value of the critique of patriarchy, many feminists view separatism as counterproductive. These feminists claim that engagement in oppressive structures is necessary to achieve the feminist social agenda of working for the collective good. They caution that embracing women's subjectivity as "women's ways of knowing" may reinforce stereotypes. Moreover, radical theories based on the essential nature of women create a false universalism that assumes *all* women share a "common nature," regardless of race, ethnicity, class, or attributes that influence how their identities are constructed. Such claims to universality are not supported by empirical research.

Feminist ethicists make a third assertion that a feminist critique must be accompanied by a critique of all discriminatory distortions. Feminists caution against focusing only on gender oppression, thereby privileging experiences of Caucasian heterosexual middle-class women over those of women of color, lesbians, poor women, or any woman who lives outside North American and North European dominant contexts. Treating women as a unitary group may unwittingly endorse restrictive rather than emancipatory views of women. Although gender has been located at the intersection of other important loci of oppression (e.g., ethnicity, culture, class, age, sexual orientation, ability, linguistic status), for most women, gender is not the most salient variable on which they experience interpersonal and sociopolitical oppression. Out of ethical concern for liberating oppressed people, feminists embrace human diversity as a requirement and a foundation for practice and have a mandate to work for the empowerment of all oppressed groups. The goal of feminist ethics is not only to liberate women from oppression but to rid the world of all oppressions.

Feminist standpoint theory raises the question of how various standpoints arise out of the conditions surrounding them and how they are constructed within subjective consciousness. By grounding claims to women's virtues in the unique particularities of each woman's experiences, standpoint theory can thereby account for the differences among women as well as between men and women. Moral adequacy depends on paying loving attention to the particularities of individuals' and communities' narratives while examining these particularities in light of their unique sociocultural contexts and entering into their perspectives. Thus, the ethical feminist (administrator, researcher, therapist) is obliged to take the other's (student, research participant, client) point of view.

Fourth, feminist ethics obliges people to engage in an analysis of the context and the power dynamics inherent in any context. Because both just and caring attention reveals the power hierarchies inherent in each particular situation, feminist ethics requires that practitioners critique the ways in which their own positions in the hierarchy of power within any context affects their perceptions and moral sensitivities. This self-critique and analysis of power relationships must occur in all ethical responses.

Postmodernism has offered important tools for analyzing power and a method for deconstructing how "woman" has been constructed in patriarchy. Like feminists, postmodernists challenge the assertion of absolute objectivity and interrogate ways of knowing and inherent power hierarchies that affect what is accepted as "knowledge." However, postmodernism is problematic for most feminists, for if realities are merely constructions rising out of specific contexts, then no universal experience may be claimed. In the absence of a moral absolute or universal truth, how can one speak of moral arguments against oppression or ethical action required of an ethical feminist practitioner? Postmodernism rejects all grand narratives or overarching explanatory theories, including the one that provides a theoretical explanation for forces such as patriarchy and sexism. Thus, although postmodernism does not legitimize oppression, neither does it challenge it, thereby maintaining the status quo. Feminists, on the contrary, assert that analysis of gender oppression can illuminate oppression and dominance over other groups and that, once revealed, practitioners then have a responsibility to act.

The final theme of feminist ethics requires action directed at achieving social justice. Feminist ethics is concerned not only with what ought to be but with how to bring about what is more in line with what ought to be. Ethical feminists have a mandate to use their knowledge to bring about individual, familial, communal, educational, institutional, legal, and social change. Where structures are not amenable to equity for all, they must be altered to be made more just.

As a prerequisite for ethical action, virtue ethicists have argued that moral character or virtue is necessary. Virtue ethics intersects with both principle ethics and feminist consciousness to name the characteristics of a virtuous agent of change: autonomy, nonmaleficence, beneficence, justice, and fidelity. However, some feminists have worried that virtue ethics can become too individualistic and can shift focus away from the structures that maintain a meritocracy that rewards individual men and Caucasian women. They argue that feminists should place more importance on the shared process of discovery, expression, interpretation, and adjustment between people and seek solutions that affect entire communities rather than only individuals and occur in collaboration rather than competition.

Because all persons are embedded in their own social context, as they critique and strive to change the status quo, they must confront the same system that gives them privilege. It is at this point that people tend to walk away from the challenge. However, feminist ethics demands moving beyond individual moral action to the place where ethics intersects with political action. Ethical feminist practice works to create the structural and cultural conditions for self-determination. The ultimate goal of feminist ethics is to enhance the human condition and to create a more just and caring world for all. Feminist ethics is emerging and being refined and will continue to offer more adequate lenses for higher education and all who seek better ways to make ethical decisions and to achieve social justice.

Kalina M. Brabeck and
Mary M. Brabeck

See also Part 8: Ethics and Practice

References and further reading

Daly, Mary. 1984. *Pure Lust: Elemental Feminist Philosophy.* Boston: Beacon Press.

Gilligan, Carol. 1982. *In a Different Voice: Psychological Theory and Women's Development.* Cambridge, MA: Harvard University Press.

Raymond, Janice. 1986. *A Passion for Friends: Toward a Philosophy of Female Affection.* Boston: Beacon Press.

Feminist Pedagogy

The term "pedagogy" commonly refers to teaching practices, the approaches teachers use to convey their subject matter to students. "Feminist pedagogies" are explicitly designed to foster equal access, participation, and engagement for all students in the learning process. Their practitioners seek to oppose sexism, racism, social class prejudice, and homophobia as barriers to equality. Moreover they wish to enable students, particularly female students, to create an education that fosters personal awakening and growth as well as social equality and justice.

Although originally focused primarily on methodologies, as distinct from subject matter, the term "feminist pedagogy" increasingly embraces the whole process of classroom knowledge construction. Although originally conceived primarily in terms of women's perspectives, feminist pedagogies increasingly reflect students' and teachers' multiple identities and positions in settings of educational diversity—identities given by class, race, culture, age, and other dimensions, as well as gender. The exploration of participants' social positions, both consciously understood and unconsciously felt, both vis-à-vis each other and as they reflect wider societal networks, becomes central to the educational process. Knowledge for both personal liberation and egalitarian social change comes from exploring these relationships.

The principles behind the development of feminist pedagogies in the last twenty years reflect many strands of progressive historical educational thought. They include the work of John Dewey and his followers in the 1920s and later, who believed in the classroom as a student-centered learning community whose values could help lead to a more egalitarian social order; and more recently the work of Paulo Freire, whose "liberation" model of pedagogy stems from his literacy work with Brazilian peasants and is rooted in Marxism and Latin American liberation theologies. Freire sought the empowerment of oppressed peoples in opposition to the repressive ideology and practices of dominant groups who robbed them of their language, identity, and power. However, his work has been criticized for ignoring the multiple and contradictory locations that make people simultaneously members of both oppressed and oppressor groups; in particular, exploited men's subjugation of women but also white women's racism toward women of color.

Feminist teachers, while sharing Dewey's and Freire's commitments to student empowerment, also diverge from these schools in that they claim a commitment to women students, a concern with gender as a category of analysis for their teaching practices, and a notion that women and men (and by extension other diverse groups) might have different, even oppositional educational needs and interests. The particular concern for women students as different from men in the classroom is representative of the challenges posed by women's studies scholarship and feminist theorists in the 1980s and 1990s to the universalism and false objectivity of male-dominated Western thought. Both feminist and postmodern scholars assert that knowledge is always constructed in a social context; the fact that the "norm" is always male, white, and privileged and that other perspectives are ignored represents societal power arrangements and the dominance of a repressive minority over educational and cultural institutions. As women's studies scholarship has transformed the academic disciplines to include the experiences of women, people of color, and other marginalized groups, so the classroom has increasingly become an arena for the intersection of these new and previously silenced perspectives.

The 1960s women's liberation movement was the second inspiration for feminist pedagogies. Along with creating women's studies programs in colleges and universities worldwide, the women's liberation movement engendered the consciousness-raising groups by which women began to explore and articulate their own experiences and feelings publicly for the first time. In resistance to the more abstract, intellectualized, and global focus of the New Left in general (as well as its sexism) but sharing its commitment to fundamental political change, these groups delved into their subjective experiences, feelings and emotions, and personal histories to articulate theories that could lead to common social action on behalf of improving women's lives. These groups were leaderless, localized, collective, and unstructured, assuming and relying on a commonality of concerns among all women to realize their goals. They bequeathed to formal educational settings and to feminist pedagogy an attentiveness to student personal experience, a respect for the emotions as a valid source of learning, and a view of the teacher as a facilitator and equal participant rather than a distant authority.

A third inspiration for feminist pedagogies has been the ongoing research on female students at all levels from kindergarten through college, which shows that girls and women are consistently disadvantaged by the practices and atmosphere of traditional, male-dominated, and hierarchically organized classrooms. At every educational level and in every country that has been studied, it has been shown that female students speak less than males and receive less teacher attention and mentoring. Although females on the whole do well in school, it is males who have traditionally excelled, particularly in the higher grades and in math and science.

Although many aspects of institutional sexism have been identified, feminist theorists in the fields of education and psychology specifically suggested that traditional teaching approaches favor males; girls and women benefit from classroom atmospheres that are collaborative rather than competitive and concerned with "connected" and relational approaches to learning rather than separate, analytical, and rational ones. Whatever strides have been made, however, it is clear that women still lag behind in important areas linked to success in later life, most notably in the new realms of computers, engineering, and educational technology.

In weaving together these complex legacies and lessons, feminist teachers had evolved a variety of specific teaching methods by the mid-1980s. They included collaborative learning groups and projects, the evocation of students' personal reactions and experiences in journals, shared classroom decisionmaking, student-led discussions, and many more. Moreover, just as in the evolution of feminist theory itself, major upheavals in the feminist classroom have transformed the early models of feminist teaching since 1980. Women of color and lesbians, particularly the former, have pointed out that white middle-class academic feminists have created women's studies scholarship in their own image, ignoring more marginalized and oppressed women just as male theory had ignored all women. In educational settings, the emphasis on sharing individual "personal experiences" tends to silence the women, often women of color, who are in the minority in any particular classroom.

Simultaneously, the classroom search for commonalities in the experiences of all women thwarted the evolution of theory from contradictory and different perspectives, leaving its construction to the dominant group—white heterosexual women—and leaving women of color and others at the margins. White students often resist seeing themselves as socially positioned and privileged by their whiteness. They like to speak simply as individuals (or globalized "human beings, just people") while preferring to treat women of color as anomalies. As bell hooks (1990) puts it, "Black students sometimes sense that feminism is really a private cult whose members are white"

(29). Black students' relentless efforts to link all discussions of gender with race may be contested by white students, who see this as deflecting attention away from feminist concerns. And so suddenly the feminist classroom is no longer the safe haven many women students imagined. Instead it presents conflict, tension, and hostility. Faced with such challenges, which split apart the presumed unities of both women of color and white women and lesbian and heterosexual women, as well as the assumed dichotomies between males and females, feminist teachers have begun to write about and explicate these "conflicts, tensions, and hostilities" in the feminist classroom.

The recent work in feminist pedagogy has embraced what Carmen Luke in Australia calls a "foundation of difference," what Kathleen Weiler calls a "feminist pedagogy of difference," and what Frances A. Maher and Mary Kay Thompson Tetreault call "pedagogies of positionality" (Luke 1992; Weiler 1991; Maher and Tetreault 2000). Differences of power, learning styles, cultural and class backgrounds, and other variables that students and teachers bring to the classroom are the persistent stumbling blocks, once avoided by feminist teachers, where feminist pedagogies now begin. The goal is not to replicate these power relationships but to challenge and change them. For example, much work has recently been done on the concept of "whiteness" and other positions of privilege; pedagogies of positionality encourage the excavations of privilege in the classroom (McIntosh 1992; Maher and Tetreault 1997). If white students come to see that whiteness is a position, just like gender, then race and gender can be seen as relational and interactive: each side constructs the other in a constantly shifting dynamic that feminist teachers can work both to reveal and transform. The resulting knowledge is not hierarchically ordered but rather always contextualized—and evolving.

The challenges mounted by lesbians and students and faculty of color to false commonalities of experience and theory have been joined by another false assumption underlying early ideas of feminist pedagogy—namely, that feminist teachers could relinquish their authority in the name, again, of a common sisterhood. As academics, they have had to come to terms with the hierarchical nature of the academy, the need for feminists to establish themselves within their academic fields, the expectations of both female and male students for their teachers to be experts, and the responsibilities of evaluating students. Unable to relinquish it altogether, practitioners of feminist pedagogy are challenged to come up with new grounds for their authority, in the context of creating democratic and feminist classrooms within undemocratic and androcentric educational institutions.

Feminist professors tend to see classroom authority as not fixed but rather as a set of relations that can be acknowledged as grounded in teachers and students evolving various connections to each other and the material. Such teachers emphasize their scholarly expertise as an important part of their own experience that they bring to bear on their courses. Their stance challenges the traditional dichotomy in academia between "experience" and "expertise."

The acknowledgement of these dynamics of difference, whether of gender, race, culture, or pedagogical authority, illustrates the ongoing challenges faced by feminist teachers and the difficulties they encounter. Experimentation continues with collaborative classroom dynamics, in which teachers position students as authorities and push them to articulate their varying positions in relation to a vibrant and growing literature. Feminist teachers are always "in process" (Maher and Tetreault 2000). Furthermore, positional pedagogies reflect the current tensions in feminist theory between the postmodern construction of "woman" as a shifting product of relational discourses and an emphasis on the real oppression of many women. In the classroom, to see everyone as positioned is not to see every position as equally valid, but rather to uncover the complex and shifting relations of privilege that are masked by any one ideological position, even that of "all women." Moreover, to shift "feminist pedagogy" toward "pedagogies of positionality" does not mean giving up commitments to social justice and equality for actual women and others beyond the classroom and beyond our local and national borders. The future of pedagogy, feminist pedagogy, and pedagogies of difference and positionality lies, like other educational issues, in societal changes beyond the classroom and beyond educational institutions. Yet although classrooms reflect the power dynamics of the larger society, they also offer arenas in which to observe and challenge them.

An earlier version of this essay appears as pp. 1526–1529 in *The Routledge International Encyclopedia of Women,* eds. Cheris Kramarae and Dale Spender, London, UK: Routledge, 2000.

Frances A. Maher,
with Mary Kay Tetreault

See also Part 3: Feminist Epistemology; Feminist Research Methodology; Part 4: Women's Studies

References and further reading

American Association of University Women. 1992. *How Schools Shortchange Girls.* Washington, DC: American Association of University Women.

Belenky, Mary Field, Blythe McVicker Clinchy, Nancy Rule Goldberger, and Jill Mattuck Tarule. 1986. *Women's Ways of Knowing: The Development of Self, Body, and Mind.* New York: Basic Books.

Boxer, Marilyn. 1998. *When Women Ask the Questions: Creating Women's Studies in America.* Baltimore: Johns Hopkins University Press.

Bunch, Charlotte, and Sandra Pollack, eds. 1983. *Learning Our Way: Essays in Feminist Education.* Trumansburg, NY: Crossing Press.

Cohee, Gail, Elizabeth Daumer, Theresa D. Kemp, Paula M. Krebs, Sue A. Lafky, and Sandra Runzo, eds. 1998. *The Feminist Teacher Anthology: Pedagogies and Classroom Strategies.* New York: Teachers College Press.

Culley, Margo, and Catherine Portuges, eds. 1985. *Gendered Subjects: The Dynamics of Feminist Teaching.* London: Routledge and Kegan Paul.

Dewey, John. 1956. *The Child and the Curriculum* and *The School and the Society.* 1900 and 1915. Reprint (2 vols. in 1), Chicago: University of Chicago Press.

Downey, Gary Lee, and Juan C. Lucena. 1997. "Engineering Selves: Hiring In to a Contested Field of Education." Pp. 117–141 in *Cyborgs and Citadels: Anthropological Interventions in Emerging Sciences and Technologies,* ed. G. L. Downey and J. Dunit. Santa Fe, NM: School of American Research Press.

Ellsworth, Elizabeth. 1989. "Why Doesn't This Feel Empowering? Working through the Repressive Myths of Critical Pedagogy." *Harvard Educational Review* 59, no. 4: 297–324.

Epstein, Debbie, ed. 1994. *Challenging Lesbian and Gay Inequalities in Education.* Philadelphia, PA: Open University Press.

Epstein, Debbie, Janette Elwood, Valerie Hey, and Janet Maw, eds. 1998. *Failing*

Boys? Issues in Gender and Achievement. Philadelphia, PA: Open University Press.
Freire, Paulo. 1993 [1970]. *The Pedagogy of the Oppressed.* Reprint, New York: Continuum.
Gilligan, Carol. 1982. *In a Different Voice: Psychological Theory and Women's Development.* Cambridge, MA: Harvard University Press.
Hall, Roberta, and Bernice Sandler. 1982. *The Classroom Climate: A Chilly One for Women.* Project on the Status and Education of Women. Washington, DC: Association of American Colleges.
Hoffman, Frances, and Jayne Stake. 1998. "Feminist Pedagogy in Theory and Practice: An Empirical Investigation." *National Women's Studies Journal* 10, no. 1: 79–97.
hooks, bell. 1990. "From Skepticism to Feminism." *Women's Review of Books* 7 (February): 29.
———. 1994. *Teaching to Transgress.* New York: Routledge.
"Lesbian, Gay, Bisexual and Transgender People in Education." 1996. *Harvard Educational Review* 66, no. 2 (special issue).
Luke, Carmen. 1992. "Feminist Politics in Radical Pedagogy." Pp. 25–53 in *Feminisms and Critical Pedagogy,* eds. Carmen Luke and Jennifer Gore. New York: Routledge.
Luke, Carmen, and Jennifer Gore, eds. 1992. *Feminisms and Critical Pedagogy.* New York: Routledge.
Maher, Frances. 1987. "Toward a Richer Theory of Feminist Pedagogy." *Journal of Education* 169, no. 3: 91–99.
Maher, Frances A., and Mary Kay Thompson Tetreault. 1994. *The Feminist Classroom: An Inside Look at How Professors and Students Are Transforming Higher Education for a Diverse Society.* New York: Rowman and Littlefield.
———. 1997. "Learning in the Dark: How Assumptions of Whiteness Shape Classroom Knowledge." *Harvard Educational Review* 67 (Summer): 321–349.
Martin, Jane Roland. 2000. *Coming of Age in Academe: Rekindling Women's Hopes and Reforming the Academy.* New York: Routledge.
Mayberry, Maralee, and Ellen Rose, eds. 1999. *Innovative Feminist Pedagogies in Action: Meeting the Challenge.* New York: Routledge.
McIntosh, Peggy. 1992. "White Privilege and Male Privilege: A Personal Account of Coming to See Correspondences through Work in Women's Studies." Pp. 70–81 in *Race, Class and Gender: An Anthology,* ed. M. Andersen and P. H. Collins. Belmont, CA: Wadsworth Publishing.
Nussbaum, Martha. 1997. *Cultivating Humanity: A Classical Defense of Reform in Liberal Education.* Cambridge, MA: Harvard University Press.
Patai, Daphne, and Noretta Koertge. 1994. *Professing Feminism.* New York: Basic Books.
Ropers-Huilman, Becky. 1998. *Feminist Teaching in Theory and Practice: Situating Power and Knowledge in Poststructural Classrooms.* New York: Teachers College Press.
Sadker, David, and Myra Sadker. 1994. *Failing at Fairness: How America's Schools Cheat Girls.* New York: Scribner's.
Schniedewind, Nancy. 1985. "Cooperatively Structured Learning: Implications for Feminist Pedagogy." *Journal of Thought* 20 (Fall): 74–87.
Schniedewind, Nancy, and Frances Maher, eds., 1987, 1993. *Women's Studies Quarterly* 15, nos. 3–4, special issue on "Feminist Pedagogy." Reissued, with additions, in 1993, vol. 21, nos. 3–4.
Sommers, Christina Hoff. 1994. *Who Stole Feminism?* New York: Simon and Schuster.
———. 2000. *The War against Boys: How Misguided Feminism Is Harming Our Young Men.* New York: Simon and Schuster.
Spender, Dale. 1983. *Invisible Women: The Schooling Scandal.* London: Writers and Readers.
Weiler, Kathleen. 1991. "Freire and a Feminist Pedagogy of Difference." *Harvard Educational Review* 61 (November): 449–474.

Feminist Research Methodology

Feminist methodology is a way of conducting research with sensitivity toward feminist goals. It is the composite of a feminist political perspective and research techniques, theoretical approaches, and epistemologies used to guide research. Feminist research generally has advanced the position of women in higher education by promoting the development of women's studies as an academic discipline and by bringing a critical gender perspective to the study of the core realms of other disciplines, especially those in the social sciences. The development of a feminist methodology arises from feminist critiques of conventional ideas about how to do research. A number of feminisms exist. Employing them as guides to the conduct of research and the selection of techniques and epistemologies constitutes feminist methodology.

Three specific goals are common to feminist inquiry: to make gender visible as an oppressive structure, to critically examine theories that are nonfeminist or androcentric, and to work toward social change. Qualitative techniques are often employed by feminist researchers because they are compatible with feminist political goals. They share concern for multiple viewpoints, the potential exploitative relationship between researcher and respondent, reflexivity, and the use of personal experience in research. However, we can distinguish between qualitative methods and feminist methodology as different analytically: one is constructed around a set of research techniques, whereas the other emphasizes a political perspective.

Although feminist scholars have contributed new methodologies to the academy, there is much debate over exactly what it is that they have provided and how it has changed methodology. The debates stem from two fundamental issues. The first involves determining what constitutes a method. The word "method" refers to the techniques used for gathering data, whereas methodology is "a theory and analysis of how research does and should proceed" (Harding 1987). The second is linked to discussions of feminist theory and the existence of multiple feminisms. Shulamit Reinharz (1992) claims that a feminist perspective is guided by feminist theory. The existence of three feminist epistemologies—feminist empiricism, feminist standpoint theories, and postmodern feminism—complicates using feminist theory as a guide for defining a feminist methodology or for even identifying a common link in a class of feminist methodologies. The question of what distinguishes a feminist methodology from qualitative methods involves these issues.

As an element of research design, methods are one part of a variety of decisions that must be made about how research will be conducted. These decisions include the selection of (1) techniques for collecting and analyzing data, (2) political perspectives that set the objectives of the research, (3) theoretical approaches that identify the theories employed to interpret the data, and (4) epistemological (and ontological) positions that describe the theories of knowledge acquisition (and knowledge itself), which are used to determine who has knowledge and what kinds of evidence are needed to validate knowledge (as well as what things can be known). Although methodology is a synthesis of these four decisions, each one can be considered analytically distinct such that a variety of combinations exist in the practice of research. However, some combinations are more likely than others. Certain techniques are better suited to fulfilling the political objectives of a research project or are more consistent with specific

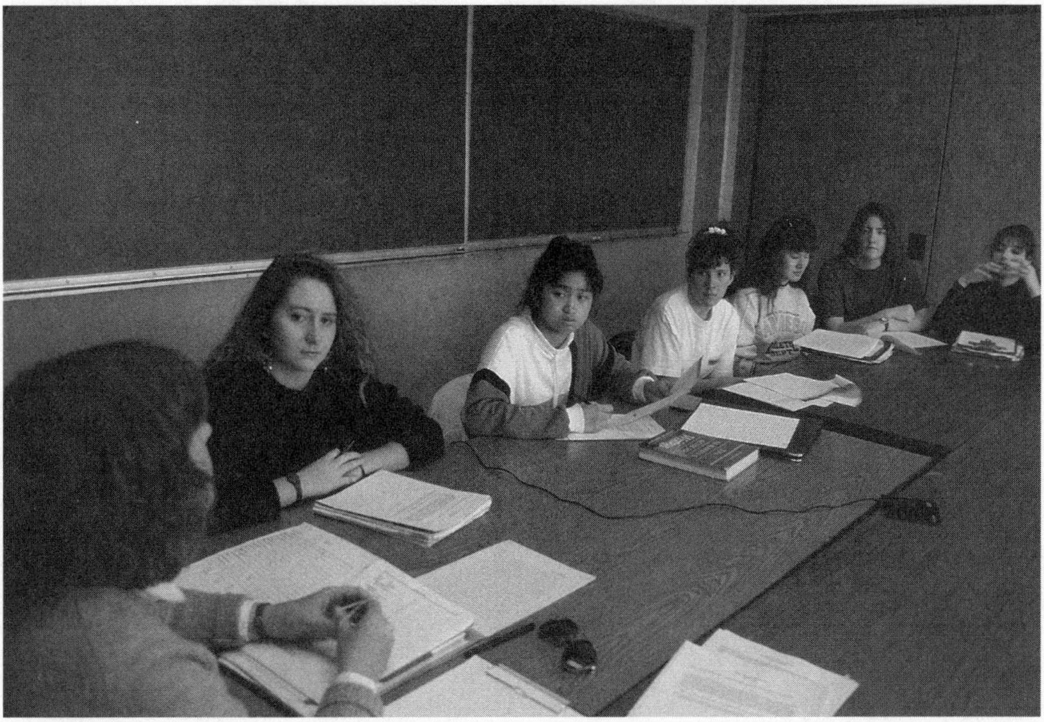

Feminist research methodology takes into account the diverse personal and cultural experiences of researchers in how they interact with their subjects (Painetworks)

theoretical approaches and epistemological positions.

This issue of compatibility has made it difficult to distinguish qualitative methods from feminist methodologies, but several distinctions separate the two. First, they emphasize different elements of the four decisions described above. Qualitative methods are a category of research techniques employed to collect data that reveal information about quality and process rather than about quantity or magnitude. Particular data collection techniques are interviews, participant observation, and textual and semiotic analyses. Types of interviews include oral histories, semistructured in-depth interviews (conversational-style interviews), and focus groups in which participants are interviewed collectively and discuss issues with each other and the researcher. Participant observation involves the interaction of the researcher in the setting of his or her informants. Data are collected from observation using the five senses, through interaction with participants as they go about their daily lives and participate in events, and through conversation. Textual and semiotic analyses are used to interpret documents (archival or other) and forms of material culture such as pictorial signs or building.

Although qualitative methods emphasize research technique, feminist methodologies embrace a feminist political perspective that defines the subject of the inquiry. Feminism is a broad perspective that is applied to the research methods of individual disciplines. The feminist researcher exists at the intersection. All of the techniques used in the researcher's discipline—both quantitative and qualitative—are available to her or him. However, the methods are employed from the perspective of a feminist. The goals of a feminist political perspective are making the invisible visible, bringing the margin to the center, rendering the trivial important, focusing on women as competent actors, studying women as subjects rather than objects for men, and paying attention to how the lack of knowledge about gender is constructed.

Similarly, Sandra Harding rejects the idea that specific techniques produce high-quality feminist research and focuses instead on the incorporation of three features into the research: (1) drawing on women's experiences in political struggles as a resource for social analysis; (2) designing research for women that addresses problems of interest to women from a perspective that helps them to understand how they might change their experience of oppression; and (3) rejecting the objective stance that hides a researcher's positionality in relation to her subjects and instead directly acknowledges the conditions of the relationship. These factors "can be thought of as methodological features because they show us how to apply the general structure of scientific theory to research on women and gender. They can also be thought of as epistemological ones because they imply theories of knowledge different from the traditional ones" (Harding 1987, 9–10).

A coherent feminist methodology is complicated by the existence of multiple feminisms. Multiple feminisms arise, in part, from the variety of epistemological positions adopted by different groups of feminists. There are three feminist epistemologies commonly used today. The first, feminist empiricism, is a way of knowing that incorporates a sensitivity to feminist concerns into the practice of empiricism. It improves the practice of science by showing how sexist and androcentric prejudices in the practice and institutions of science have informed how we think. Some argue this perspective creates a more objective knowledge claim because women are more likely to recognize the importance of gender in an analysis than nonfeminist researchers (Harding 1987). However, there is no reason to focus on objectivity if one of the projects of feminism is to show how objectivity is an impossible goal and rigorous adherence to the tenets of the scientific method cannot eliminate gender bias by itself. That is the position of the second epistemology, feminist standpoint theory, which argues against scientific objectivity, claiming it promotes a "view from nowhere" (Haraway 1991).

Standpoint theory presents a view centered on the feminine because a marginal perspective is thought to be better suited for showing a less distorted picture than one coming from a masculine, hegemonic perspective. This theory, rather than breaking down the masculine-feminine dualism, privileges feminine concepts instead. "In this sense, feminist scholarship remains a modernist project with political and progressive aims" (McDowell 1999, 228). That is the criticism of standpoint theory from the postmodern feminist position, the third epistemology. Postmodernist feminism rejects the masculine-feminine dualism, challenges the idea that a women's perspective is different from a man's perspective, and argues that women cannot have a unified identity. Instead of a women-centered inquiry, postmodern feminists focus on gender and power relations as a subject constituted through discourse.

The debates among the three epistemological positions present two major problems for defining a coherent feminist theory: "One is the dilemma of how to generalize about women while recognizing the inexhaustible differences among them; the other is the dilemma of how to assert the truth of one's claims while recognizing that intelligent women may disagree" (Jaggar and Rothenberg 1993, 79).

Women, and feminist men, for that matter, may subscribe to different epistemologies. Judith Grant attributes these problems to feminists' attempts to ground theory in the concepts of "woman" and women's experiences in the early conceptions of feminist empiricism and feminist standpoint theories. These two concepts serve to essentialize the characteristics of women and fix a feminist perspective that neglects differences among women and women's experiences. Providing an explanation as to why early feminism tended to define "woman" as white and middle-class, Grant argues that it is a consequence of the focus on experience in feminism. The preferred methodological tool of early feminists for defining oppression was one that emphasized their personal experiences. Personal experience was tied to a universal womanhood. Because most early feminist writers were white women, the focus on their personal experience served to neglect differences between women in early feminism (Grant 1993). The rejection by postmodernists of the concepts of "woman" and women's experiences and the debates mentioned previously serve to fragment feminism and complicate the creation of a feminist methodology.

Despite very contentious debates among proponents of each epistemology, there is ample evidence to suggest that a set of common goals have emerged, particularly from modifications made to each of the three in response to criticism. First, feminist empiricism does not adhere strictly to the tenets of empiricism. It diverges in three important ways that have the consequence of transforming the traditional idea of objectivity: (1) the feminist views of a researcher will matter to her or his ability to engage in good science; (2) research and political values cannot be separated; and (3) the existence of the gender system in institutions will affect the practice of good research. This interpretation of feminist empiricism offers some overlap with standpoint theory regarding questions about who has knowledge. Second, Grant (1993) shows how feminist standpoint and postmodern feminist theories have been appearing more similar, in that both are concerned with the recognition of difference in women's experiences. Rather than grounding feminist theory in a woman's standpoint, a variety of standpoints exist to account for differences among women. In addition, a feminist standpoint provides an interpretation of women's experiences such that alliances can be established despite differences. Feminists have adopted the postmodern focus on gender and power relationships, emphasizing the social construction of femininity and masculinity and the existence of multiple gendered identities (McDowell 1999). These changes open up the possibility that all three epistemologies share a feminist political perspective in which feminist methodologies have some common objectives.

Christine L. Jocoy

See also Part 3: Feminist Epistemology; Feminist Pedagogy

References and further reading

Grant, Judith. 1993. *Fundamental Feminism: Contesting the Core Concepts of Feminist Theory.* New York: Routledge.

Haraway, Donna J. 1991. *Simians, Cyborgs, and Women: The Reinvention of Nature.* New York: Routledge.

Harding, Sandra, ed. 1987. *Feminism and Methodology.* Bloomington: Indiana University Press.

Jaggar, Allison M., and Paula S. Rothenberg, eds. 1993. *Feminist Frameworks: Alternative Theoretical Accounts of the Relations between Women and Men.* 3rd ed. New York: McGraw-Hill.

McDowell, L. 1999. *Gender, Identity and Place: Understanding Feminist Geographies.* Minneapolis: University of Minnesota Press.

Reinharz, Shulamit. 1992. *Feminist Methods in Social Research.* New York: Oxford University Press.

Part 4

WOMEN IN THE CURRICULUM

Overview

The integration of material by and about women into the higher education curriculum in the United States grew out of the women's liberation movement of the late 1960s and early 1970s. In fact, women's studies is often referred to as "the academic arm of the women's movement." Women students and faculty members who in the 1960s had been involved in the civil rights movement, the antiwar movement, and organizations with a focus on social class like Students for a Democratic Society challenged the power relations involved in defining what was truth and what counted as knowledge. In some colleges and universities, separate women's studies courses were established, whereas in others the strategy was to work toward gender balance in existing courses. Since the 1970s, work to include women has developed along a continuum, starting with a few famous women or a special lecture added to an existing course and progressing to gender-balanced courses in various disciplines, departmental courses on women's issues, and finally interdisciplinary women's studies courses housed in their own department or program. The efforts along this continuum have also broadened by extension into more disciplines (including professional programs and the sciences) and by the inclusion of the contributions and concerns of a much more highly diverse group of women, both nationally and internationally. This work has been supported by the growth of centers for research on women. As new content has made its way into the curriculum, questions about teaching and learning have led to the development of a broader range of strategies, often referred to as "feminist pedagogy." Additionally, many institutions try to expand the community of teachers and learners involved in the study of women by offering lunch seminars, discussion groups, public lectures, and annual conferences. As the twenty-first century begins, there is also an emphasis on the expansion of the teaching and learning community by using new technologies, especially the Internet.

Moving in Many Directions: The 1970s

The transformation of the curriculum began in different disciplines depending on the institution, sometimes as new departmental or interdisciplinary courses, sometimes as special units in existing courses. In the earliest years, books and other course materials were very few. Pamphlets and position papers picked up at political meetings and women's health centers were the subject of study in academic courses. One of the best examples of these materials is *Our Bodies, Ourselves,* first a

Simone de Beauvoir's The Second Sex *was one of the earliest books used in women's studies courses to recover women's history and perspective (Corbis)*

booklet printed on newsprint and priced at 35 cents. It was the first product of the Boston Women's Health (Book) Collective, an offshoot of a socialist-feminist organization called Bread and Roses, which was active in the Boston area in the late 1960s and early 1970s. Some books written earlier were retrieved, such as *The Second Sex* (1949) by Simone de Beauvoir, *Women as a Force in History* (1946) by Mary Ritter Beard, and *The Feminine Mystique* (1963) by Betty Friedan. Other instructors turned their feminist consciousness and that of their students onto the work of Karl Marx,

Sigmund Freud, or Charles Darwin. Records of the content of these earliest courses are found in collections of syllabi published yearly, starting with *Female Studies I* assembled by Sheila Tobias in 1970 (Boxer 1998, 11).

By the middle of the 1970s, not only were there books and articles in established disciplinary journals, but new interdisciplinary, feminist journals had appeared, such as *Feminist Studies* (1972), *Women's Studies Quarterly* (1972), *Frontiers: A Journal of Women's Studies* (1975), *Signs: Journal of Women in Culture and Society* (1975), and *Women's Studies International Forum* (1978). In addition, discipline-specific journals on women's issues sprang up, such as *Psychology of Women Quarterly* (1976). These materials were used across the continuum from the isolated lecture in an existing disciplinary course to an interdisciplinary course in women's studies.

Although the sites of academic work on women varied across institutions, some of the most frequently found were in English literature, history, psychology or sociology, and education. In English literature, women writers of novels and poetry were rediscovered and became the subject of study—English authors such as Jane Austen, the Brontë sisters, and Virginia Woolf and U.S. authors such as Emily Dickinson and Harriet Beecher Stowe. The newly formed Feminist Press aided in the recovery of such nineteenth-century works as *Life in the Iron Mills* by Rebecca Harding Davis. Louise Bernikow anthologized four centuries of women's poetry in *The World Split Open* (1974), and Elaine Showalter published *A Literature of Their Own* (1977) on British women novelists.

The challenges to the political status quo that many of these academic feminists had mounted in the 1960s were carried over into challenges to the disciplinary status quo. Students and faculty in English literature, for example, asked why there were not more women writers in the canon of great works. This question led them back to Virginia Woolf's 1929 essay, *A Room of One's Own,* but also to a critique of that essay from a social class perspective. Scholars also questioned the criteria for inclusion of work in the canon, especially the privileging of the public sphere over the private one. These questions led to the inclusion of a wider variety of written work in the curriculum—journals, letters, travelogues, and so on—and to the search for contemporary women authors, including women of color such as Alice Walker, Toni Morrison, Maxine Hong Kingston, Leslie Marmon Silko, and more.

In the field of history, the most immediate (U.S. history) received the first attention. Besides Beard's work, the book most widely read early on was Eleanor Flexner's *Century of Struggle* (1975) on the women's suffrage movement. By the mid-1970s, Gerda Lerner had published *Black Women in White America* (1972), Linda Gordon *Woman's Body, Woman's Right: A Social History of Birth Control in America* (1976), and William Chafe *The American Woman: Her Changing Social, Economic, and Political Roles, 1920–1970* (1972). There were many edited volumes on U.S. women's history and both edited and singly authored works on European women's history.

Although some of this work could be (and was) criticized for its focus only on white, middle- or upper-class women, again the political consciousness of the 1960s led historians of women to focus on the diversity of women's experience. Doing so required new methods and sources besides the study of public documents. Private documents such as letters and diaries were used as sources, but in addition, new methodologies developed by class-conscious social historians in the 1960s proved useful. Oral history interviews and quantitative analysis of census data provided information on women who left no written records. Not only did historians of women use a wider variety of source material, but they also began to challenge the structure of their discipline. The concept of periodization based on male experience came under attack, most notably by Joan Kelly in her 1977 essay, "Did Women Have a Renaissance?"

In psychology, early work focused on mental illness (Phyllis Chesler's 1973 book, *Women and Madness*) or on stages of women's development (Jean Baker Miller's 1976 work, *Toward a New Psychology of Women*). There was also a major focus on sex differences in a wide range of abilities and characteristics and on their possible causes, ranging from gender socialization to genetic and hormonal differences between males and females. *The Psychology of Sex Differences* (1974) by Eleanor Maccoby and Carol Jacklin was an exhaustive review of this work and very influential. Again, however, critiques of earlier work characterized the field, as women psychologists found that many psychological constructs had been generalized from all-male samples and that gender socialization could explain many of the differences presumed immutable. An example is Julia Sherman's 1978 book, *Sex-Related Cognitive Differences.*

Education was a field that overlapped considerably with psychology, especially in the areas of cognitive abilities and stages of human development. However, there were other topics that were introduced into the education curriculum. An early element was the examination of gender bias in textbooks and children's literature, which was accompanied by efforts to change publishers' offerings and by publication of new works for children by both mainstream presses and alternatives like the Feminist Press. Later in the 1970s, educational research and the college curriculum in education also focused on gender differences in K–12 classroom interactions (work led by Myra and David Sadker) and on examining and redressing performance differences in certain subjects, especially mathematics (Jacobs 1978).

Although the feminist scholarship and curriculum transformation described in the preceding paragraphs were occurring in history, psychology, English literature, and education, the study of women in interdisciplinary women's studies courses was also moving forward. Greater numbers of institutions developed a course, a minor, a major, and even graduate work in women's studies. Many of the materials developed in the disciplines were useful in these interdisciplinary courses as well. However, by the end of the 1970s, textbooks based on interdisciplinary scholarship became available. Although many disciplinary professional organizations had established women's caucuses or committees, some of which held conferences or published journals, the National Women's Studies Association (NWSA), founded in 1977, offered an annual meeting where scholars could present interdisciplinary research and discuss teaching interdisciplinary women's studies courses. These meetings attracted not only those actually teaching women's studies courses but also those working at the boundaries of the traditional disciplines. Indeed, that is still true for NWSA today.

Focus and Specialization: 1980–2000

As interest in women's studies spread, other disciplines became sites for women's studies scholarship as feminist scholars moved into departments other than those mentioned above. Not only did this mean extension to other disciplines in the arts, humanities, and social sciences, but also courses on women were developed in professional programs such as nursing, social work, law, and medicine. By 1980, questions were being asked in various institutions: Why isn't material by and about women a part of every course? Doesn't an accurate curriculum demand the inclusion of the experience of half the human race?

Curriculum Transformation. Efforts to answer those questions in some institutions led to faculty development projects labeled "curriculum transformation," "curriculum integration," "gender balancing the curriculum," or "women in the curriculum." One of the earliest of these efforts took place in 1979 at Wheaton College, formerly a women's college but now coeducational. Other institutions that quickly developed projects were Smith College (a women's college with an active women's studies program), the University of Maine (a state university with very little women's studies presence at that time), Montana State University, and the University of Arizona (a state university with an established women's studies program).

In surveying a range of such early programs, Marilyn Schuster and Susan Van Dyne (1985) identified three models. The *top-down model* involves an administrative mandate, works within the existing departmental structure, and targets introductory courses for maximum effect. The *piggy-back model* uses existing interdisciplinary programs or structures as demonstration sites. The *bottom-up model* presumes the existence of a network (even if loosely organized) of feminist scholars and existing women's studies courses. The University of Maine's program was an example of the first; Smith College's program was an example of the last. All had the same eventual goals, but the route to those ends depended on the conditions and climate on the individual campus.

Programs such as these were initially funded in the early 1980s by government agencies and private foundations. The federal support ended when the Reagan and Bush administrations did not reauthorize funding for such projects after their multiyear grants had ended. Those that have continued are funded internally or by statewide or regional sources. In 1997 the National Center for Curriculum Transformation Resources on Women, housed at Towson University in Baltimore, published a directory of past and present projects numbering over 400. The center also publishes materials specific to various disciplines and offered a national summer institute in 2002.

But what did it mean to integrate material by and about women into the curriculum? The development of women's studies as a field in the 1970s led to an analysis of curriculum transformation as progressing in stages. The stages originally identified by Peggy McIntosh (1983) were modified and used in books on curriculum transformation by JoAnn Fritsche (1984) and by Schuster and Van Dyne (1985). Although there are some differences among them, the premises are the same. In stage 1, women are absent, and the definition of standards for inclusion are traditional and male-centered. In stage 2, women's absence is noticed, and the few women whose lives and contributions fit male-defined standards are included. (This stage has been referred to as "add women and stir.") At stage 3, questions are raised about women's exclusion and the standards for inclusion. Women as a group are studied as a group and their exclusion and oppression are paramount. (Students and faculty sometimes get stuck here in the rage and despair of victims.) At stage 4, women are studied on their own terms, as a group but with attention to their diversity. At this stage, new methodologies broaden the information available, and consciousness of the interaction of gender, race, class, and other forms of diversity is central. Stage 5 challenges the structure of the disciplines and the criteria for inclusion. Stage 6 is the ultimate goal of complete gender balance, an inclusive vision of human experience.

The methods used to accomplish such curriculum transformation have been high-profile seminars and workshops on campus, summer grants to individual faculty members or departmental teams, an ongoing series of presentations by colleagues and visiting scholars, and mentoring relationships with peers who are engaged in women's studies research and teaching. At some institutions, the programs publish newsletters for faculty to highlight successful curriculum revisions and to publicize the availability of resources (especially videos that can be shown in classes).

Although at some institutions curriculum transformation programs grew out of women's studies, at others women's studies developed out of well-funded curriculum transformation programs. At the University of Maine, for example, which in 1981 had neither the faculty resources nor the institutional support for a women's studies program, an externally funded curriculum transformation program was institutionalized in 1985 and became its own women's studies program by 1989. More commonly (at the University of Maryland, for example), a strong women's studies program spawned the curriculum transformation program. In either case, however, the relationship between the two has proved mutually supportive. In many institutions, women's studies faculty are departmentally based and want to carry what they do in women's studies into the rest of their teaching. Students in women's studies classes also bring that gender analysis with them into their other courses and challenge their professors when it is absent. Students in gender-balanced courses further their interests by choosing women's studies courses, either departmental or interdisciplinary. At campuses with active curriculum transformation projects, women's studies is usually more widely understood and politically supported. Resources such as discussion sessions, lecture series, and library and media centers are more broadly used and supported.

Diversity. Although material by and about women was being integrated into the curriculum along a continuum ranging from adding a few famous women to departmental courses to creating interdisciplinary women's studies courses, a similar progression was observable in recognizing differences among women and embracing diversity. It happened first with respect to the study of U.S. women. Then with the demise of the Soviet Union, the rise of the United States as the major world power, and the globalization of capitalism, the study of women increasingly focused on women around the world, especially those in Asia, Africa, and Latin America.

Although it is not true, as sometimes alleged, that the beginnings of women's studies and curriculum transformation were only white, straight, and middle class, it is true that most of the faculty had those characteristics. However, their involvement in the social movements of the 1960s led many of them to include diverse perspectives in their courses. This development can be seen in the syllabi from the 1970s and in the books most widely used. *Sisterhood Is Powerful,* by Robin Morgan (1970), *Black Women in White America* by Gerda Lerner (1972), and novels and poetry by women of color are some examples. There was certainly room for improvement, both in the range of texts available and in their use in the classroom. By the 1980s, it was also probably the case that many of the faculty teaching material by and about women had come from the women's movement without any prior involvement in the other social justice movements of the 1960s. It is also arguable that feminist academics of the 1970s may have used the analogy of racism to identify sexism without truly analyzing and developing strategies for overcoming the double jeopardy of being a woman of color (Boxer 1998, 104).

The challenge to diversify content by and about women in the curriculum was mounted in the beginning of the 1980s, first in terms of women of color and lesbians, including those who claimed both identities. Cherrie Moraga and Gloria Anzaldúa confronted the whiteness of women's studies in their edited volume, *This Bridge Called My Back: Writings by Radical Women of Color* (1981). They challenged women's studies to use the book as a text, a challenge many faculty accepted. A similar challenge was made in the 1982 volume, *Lesbian Studies,* edited by Margaret Cruikshank. As the decade progressed, diversity concerns broadened to include age, religion (especially not Christian), ethnicity not defined by race, and disability/ability status. Class analysis was usually present as a factor interacting with all the other definitions of diversity.

In a sense, one can trace a similar progression of integrating diversity through stages as that observed in efforts to balance the curriculum with regard to gender. From near absence in the curriculum, "add diversity and stir" efforts led to chapters on diversity in women's studies texts or the inclusion of one book written by an African American or lesbian author. Similarly, feminist academics began to question the selection criteria for inclusion in the women's studies curriculum and to seek new methodologies for scholarship on underrepresented groups. As consciousness of diversity issues increased, feminist academics questioned the unity of women's experience and recognized multiple perspectives on a given issue. For example, reproductive freedom for white, middle-class, straight women might mean primarily access to contraception and abortion, for straight women of color an end to coerced sterilization, and for lesbians or bisexual women the right to artificial insemination and custody of children.

The final stage of a diversified women's studies and gender-balanced curriculum is still being envisioned, and there are differing views. Whether the multiple positions will become even more numerous and isolated or whether they will yield to a greater recognition of human interdependence is still uncertain. Although the battle over differences has sharply divided advocates for women's studies and has several times threatened the very existence of NWSA, the struggle to overcome difference continues. A good discussion of the future possibilities is found in the chapter on diversity in Marilyn Boxer's 1998 book, *When Women Ask the Questions: Creating Women's Studies in America.*

In some institutions and regions, the work on diversity and gender balance is integrated. For example, since 1989 the University of Maryland has run a summer institute for faculty entitled "Thinking about Women, Gender, and Race." The New Jersey Project, which involves public postsecondary institutions in that state, not only runs institutes and symposia but has published a teaching sourcebook entitled *Creating an Inclusive College Curriculum* (Friedman et al. 1996) and, since 1990, a semiannual journal, *Transformations: The Journal of Inclusive Scholarship and Pedagogy.* There are other important publications on the intersection and interaction of various forms of diversity. A new journal focused on women and diversity is *Meridians: Feminism, Race, Transnationalism.* Some other relevant books include *Transforming the Curriculum: Ethnic Studies and Women's Studies* (1991), edited by Johnella Butler and John Walter, and *Teaching What You're Not: Identity Politics in Higher Education* (1996), edited by Katherine Mayberry.

Mathematics, Science, and Technology. Other fields influenced by women's studies and curriculum transformation, although somewhat later, are those of mathematics, science, and technology. Influenced by feminist work in psychology—on the border between the social and natural sciences—women scientists as well as philosophers and historians of science challenged the masculine domination of their fields. They identified three perspectives regarding women's participation in science: women cannot do science or at least cannot do it as well as men; women can do science as well as men if they are given equal opportunity; and it is not enough for women merely to get into science—they should bring their culturally defined differences with them to use as a platform for critique and change. (These stages could apply equally well to other "outsiders"—people of color in the United States, people from non-Western cultures.)

The stage theory useful in describing both the processes of gender balancing the traditionally male curriculum and of diversifying the women's studies curriculum have also been applied to the integration of women's contributions and issues into the study of science. Sue Rosser's *Female Friendly Science* (1990) and *Re-Engineering Female Friendly Science* (1997) discussed these stages. First the absence of women is not noticed, either in the science studied or in the ranks of the scientific workforce. Second, the absence of women is noticed, and a few women who have achieved in the male world of science are noted. There is now a rich body of material on women scientists who contributed, despite the odds against them: Londa Schiebinger's *The Mind Has No Sex: Women in the Origins of Modern Science* (1989), Margaret Rossiter's *Women Scientists in America* (1982), Louise Grinstein and Paul Campbell's *Women of Mathematics* (1987), Evelyn Fox Keller's *A Feeling for the Organism: The Life and Work of Barbara McClintock* (1983), Anne Sayre's *Rosalind Franklin and DNA* (1975), and Marcia Bonta's *Women in the Field* (1991).

Close reading of the biographies above led to the third stage, that of looking for reasons why there are not more women in science. The National Science Foundation now publishes status studies every two years on the participation of "outsiders" in science and engineering. At first these studies were just focused on women, then on women and minorities, and by 2000 on women, minorities, and people with disabilities. Notable in the search for the reasons for the exclusiveness of the science and engineering workforce is the work of Carolyn Merchant. (Her work also serves as an example of the expanding diversity of the subjects discussed above.) *The Death of Nature: Women, Ecology, and the Scientific Revolution* (1980) dealt with the rise of capitalism in Europe and the masculinization of science and medicine. *Ecological Revolutions: Nature, Gender, and Science in New England* (1989) considered the roles of the American Indians compared to those of the European settlers, as science developed later on that side of the Atlantic. *Earthcare* (1995) summarized points from the first two books but expanded its scope to global perspectives.

In the fourth stage, the search for more women scientists uncovers the contributions of women who did not get credit for their work. Methods useful in other fields of history have been employed here as well (searching for letters and diaries, using oral interviews, redefining what counts as science, etc.). As more women become involved in science and science focuses more on women, topics may broaden (stage 5), analysis may become more sophisticated, and the language in which data and theories are described may change, all leading to the construction of new knowledge. The ultimate goal is an inclusive science redefined and reconstructed (stage 6).

Another example of the movement toward a science that includes us all is found in the work of Sandra Harding. From her earlier work (*The Science Question in Feminism* [1986] and *Whose Science? Whose Knowledge? Thinking from Women's Lives* [1991]), which focused primarily on gender, Harding moved to editing a book including perspectives diverse along other dimensions as well—racial and global, for example. *The "Racial" Economy of Science* (1993), which she edited, includes worldwide consideration of premodern sciences and visions of the egalitarian science of the future.

Feminist Pedagogy and the Issue of Language. The substantial changes in the gender content of the college curriculum were also accompanied by changes in teaching methods and the learning environment in general. That is not surprising, given the demands of students in the 1960s for a democratic society, not only nationally and internationally but also on campus. Their demands were reinforced by feminist social and political organizations, which criticized both mainstream and social change organizations for their silencing of women's voices. *Women's Ways of Knowing* (Belenky et al. 1986) was widely discussed, as was a volume of essays edited ten years later by the same group of authors, *Knowledge, Difference, and Power* (Goldberger et al. 1996).

In other disciplines, but certainly in women's studies and gender-inclusive courses, teacher-centered classrooms gave way to student-centered ones. Students sat in a circle, called on each other, and worked in collaborative small groups. Students took responsibility for presenting topics that they knew more about than their instructors did. The slogan of the women's movement of the 1970s, "the personal is political," was translated in the classroom to "the personal is academic," as both students and instructors sought connections between lived experience and academic theories and constructs. Implementing and managing these drastic changes in classroom practices became the subject of seminars and discussion groups of faculty, eager to empower their students without abdicating their responsibility as teachers. How safe a place was the classroom for personal disclosure? What to do with students who talked all the time—or never? How to respond to student opinions that were sexist, racist, homophobic, or factually incorrect? Again, these issues became the subject for discussions at national meetings and for books and articles (see especially Fisher, *No Angel in the Classroom: Teaching through Feminist Discourse* [2001], and Maher and Tetreault, *The Feminist Classroom* [1994]).

Language used in the classroom and in student writing was also an issue. A move to nonsexist or gender-inclusive language in printed material was a result of feminist analyses starting in the 1970s. On the one hand, many publishers and professional organizations moved early on to establish guidelines on language, but most colleges and universities did not have language policies until the 1980s. Some applied only to the institutions' publications, but others applied to classroom communication and student's written work. Some campuses included sexist language in their "hate speech" policies, some of which have recently been struck down in court. Without the use of any sanction or "stick" to implement language policies, most institutions that have the policies use "carrot" approaches such as appeals to fairness or descriptions of the requirements of post-college job markets. Backing them up is a body of scholarship demonstrating that use of male nouns and pronouns does, in fact, limit the perception of the reader and listener to a male subject. Dale Spender (1980), Deborah Tannen (1990), and others have demonstrated that language—at least spoken and written English—is still certainly gendered, in ways that may work to women's disadvantage.

Conservative Backlash and Feminist Cautions

Although the growth of both women's studies and gender balance in disciplinary courses since 1970 has been enormous, there is still much to be accomplished. New faculty, especially in the liberal arts and professional programs that train significant numbers of women, have often been exposed to women's studies and gender analysis in graduate school, but some have not. There are still plenty of faculty members with no graduate training in gender issues who resist any tampering with their professional preparation. Even those with some feminist consciousness often get stuck at the earlier stages of curriculum transformation. Arguments that there is no time or space in a crowded curriculum to add material on women are frequently heard. An unintended outcome of the development of women's studies programs and the hiring of disciplinary departmental specialists in gender issues sometimes seems to be that the rest of the faculty members in a department feel they have received permission to ignore women's experiences and contributions in their own courses. Finally, students can be very resistant to perspectives different from their own and the ones they were expecting from a course, based on their past experience with its discipline.

The years of the Reagan and Bush administrations (1981–1992) also saw a conservative backlash supported politically. Curriculum transformation efforts that had been supported by federal government agencies lost their funding when multiyear grants ran out. Alan Bloom's book, *The Closing of the American Mind* (1987) was widely read and quoted. The book called not only for a return to the classical texts written by privileged white men, common in the college curriculum before the 1960s, but also for an end to open admissions. It specifically attacked women's studies and black studies. Lynne Cheney, who served as director of the National Endowment for the Humanities at that time, was also influential and widely quoted. Her own book, *Telling the Truth: Why Our Culture and Our Country Stopped Making Sense and What We Can Do About It,* did not appear in print until 1995, but her ideas were very much in the public eye in the late 1980s. Some faculty members joined a conservative organization called the National Association of Scholars, while conservative students formed Students for Accuracy in Academia.

The integration of scholarship for, by, and about women into postsecondary curriculum is by no means complete. Efforts continue, strengthened by new developments in research.

Ann K. Schonberger

References and further reading

Beard, Mary Ritter. 1946. *Women as a Force in History: A Study in Traditions and Realities.* New York: Macmillan.

Beauvoir, Simone de. 1949. *The Second Sex.* New York: Alfred A. Knopf.

Belenky, Mary, Blythe Clinchy, Nancy Goldberger, and Jill Tarule. 1986. *Women's Ways of Knowing: The Development of Self, Voice, and Mind.* New York: Basic Books.

Bernikow, Louise. 1974. *The World Split Open: Four Centuries of Women Poets in England and America.* New York: Vintage Books.

Bloom, Alan. 1987. *The Closing of the American Mind: How Higher Education Has Failed Democracy and Impoverished the Souls of Today's Students.* New York: Simon and Schuster.

Bonta, Marcia. 1991. *Women in the Field: America's Pioneering Women Naturalists.* College Station: Texas A & M University Press.

Boxer, Marilyn. 1998. *When Women Ask the Questions: Creating Women's Studies in America.* Baltimore: Johns Hopkins University Press.

Butler, Johnella E., and John C. Walter, eds. 1991. *Transforming the Curriculum: Ethnic Studies and Women's Studies.* Albany: State University of New York Press.

Chafe, William. 1972. *The American Woman: Her Changing Social, Economic, and Political Roles, 1920–1970.* London: Oxford University Press.

Cheney, Lynne. 1995. *Telling the Truth: Why Our Culture and Our Country Stopped Making Sense and What We Can Do about It.* New York: Simon and Schuster.

Chesler, Phyllis. 1973. *Women and Madness.* New York: Avon Books.

Cruikshank, Margaret, ed. 1982. *Lesbian Studies: Present and Future.* Old Westbury, NY: The Feminist Press.

Davis, Rebecca Harding. 1972. *Life in the Iron Mills.* Old Westbury, NY: The Feminist Press.

Fisher, Berenice. 2001. *No Angel in the Classroom: Teaching through Feminist Discourse.* New York: Rowman and Littlefield.

Flexner, Eleanor. 1975. *Century of Struggle: The Woman's Rights Movement in the United States.* Cambridge, MA: Belknap Press of Harvard University Press.

Friedan, Betty. 1963. *The Feminine Mystique.* New York: W. W. Norton.

Friedman, Ellen, Wendy Kolmar, Charley Flint, and Paula Rothenberg. 1996. *Creating an Inclusive College Curriculum: A Teaching Sourcebook*

from the New Jersey Project. New York: Teachers College Press.
Fritsche, JoAnn. 1984. *Toward Excellence and Equity: The Scholarship on Women as a Catalyst for Change in the University.* Orono: University of Maine Press.
Goldberger, Nancy, Jill Tarule, Blythe Clinchy, and Mary Belenky, eds. 1996. *Knowledge, Difference, and Power: Essays Inspired by Women's Ways of Knowing.* New York: Basic Books.
Gordon, Linda. 1976. *Woman's Body, Woman's Right: A Social History of Birth Control in America.* New York: Grossman.
Grinstein, Louise, and Paul Campbell. 1987. *Women of Mathematics: A Biobibliographic Sourcebook.* New York: Greenwood Press.
Harding, Sandra. 1986. *The Science Question in Feminism.* Ithaca, NY: Cornell University Press.
———. 1991. *Whose Science? Whose Knowledge? Thinking from Women's Lives.* Ithaca, NY: Cornell University Press.
Harding, Sandra, ed. 1993. *The "Racial" Economy of Science: Toward a Democratic Future.* Bloomington: Indiana University Press.
Jacobs, Judith, ed. 1978. *Perspectives on Women in Mathematics.* Columbus, OH: ERIC.
Keller, Evelyn Fox. 1983. *A Feeling for the Organism: The Life and Work of Barbara McClintock.* New York: W. H. Freeman.
Kelly, Joan. 1977. "Did Women Have a Renaissance?" In *Becoming Visible: Women in European History,* ed. Renate Bridenthal and Claudia Koonz. Boston: Houghton Mifflin.
Kolodny, Annette. 1998. *Failing the Future: A Dean Looks at Higher Education in the Twenty-First Century.* Durham, NC: Duke University Press.
Lerner, Gerda. 1972. *Black Women in White America: A Documentary History.* New York: Pantheon Books.
Maccoby, Eleanor E., and Carol N. Jacklin. 1974. *The Psychology of Sex Differences.* Stanford, CA: Stanford University Press.
Maher, Frances, and Mary Kay Tetreault. 1994. *The Feminist Classroom: An Inside Look at How Professors and Students Are Transforming Higher Education for a Diverse Society.* New York: Basic Books.
Martin, Jane. 2000. *Coming of Age in Academe: Rekindling Women's Hopes and Reforming the Academy.* New York: Routledge.
Mayberry, Katherine, ed. 1996. *Teaching What You're Not: Identity Politics in Higher Education.* New York: New York University Press.
McIntosh, Peggy. 1983. *Interactive Phases of Curriculum Re-Vision: A Feminist Perspective.* Working Paper no. 124. Wellesley College Center for Research on Women.
Merchant, Carolyn. 1980. *The Death of Nature: Women, Ecology, and the Scientific Revolution.* San Francisco: Harper and Row.
———. 1989. *Ecological Revolutions: Nature, Gender, and Science in New England.* Chapel Hill: University of North Carolina Press.
———. 1995. *Earthcare: Women and the Environment.* New York: Routledge.
Miller, Jean Baker. 1976. *Toward a New Psychology of Women.* Boston: Beacon Press.
Moraga, Cherrie, and Gloria Anzaldúa, eds. 1981. *This Bridge Called My Back: Writings by Radical Women of Color.* Watertown, MA: Persephone Press.
Morgan, Robin. 1970. *Sisterhood Is Powerful: An Anthology of Writings from the Women's Liberation Movement.* New York: Vintage Books.
Rosser, Sue. 1990. *Female-Friendly Science: Applying Women's Studies Methods and Theories to Attract Students.* New York: Pergamon Press.
———. 1997. *Re-Engineering Female-Friendly Science.* New York: Teachers College Press.
Rossiter, Margaret W. 1982. *Women Scientists in America: Struggles and Strategies to 1940.* Baltimore: Johns Hopkins University Press.
Sayre, Anne. 1975. *Rosalind Franklin and DNA.* New York: W. W. Norton.
Schiebinger, Londa. 1989. *The Mind Has No Sex: Women in the Origins of Modern Science.* Cambridge, MA: Harvard University Press.
Schuster, Marilyn, and Susan Van Dyne. 1985. *Women's Place in the Academy; Transforming the Liberal Arts Curriculum.* Totowa, NJ: Rowman and Allanheld.

Sherman, Julia. 1978. *Sex-Related Cognitive Differences: An Essay on Theory and Evidence.* Springfield, IL: Thomas.

Showalter, Elaine. 1977. *A Literature of Their Own: British Women Novelists from Bronte to Lessing.* Princeton, NJ: Princeton University Press.

Spender, Dale. 1980. *Man Made Language.* London: Routledge and Kegan Paul.

Tannen, Deborah. 1990. *You Just Don't Understand: Women and Men in Conversation.* New York: William Morrow.

Woolf, Virginia. 1929. *A Room of One's Own.* New York: Fountain Press.

Academic Caucuses and Committees

The first women's caucuses and committees were formed on campuses roughly in 1969–1971 to address gender equity issues and discrimination in academic disciplines. The second wave of feminism in the 1960s encouraged the formation of professional organizations. These groups sought to provide a voice for women and counter institutional sexism or discrimination by empowering women in academe. Once founded, they were places of skill building, mentorship, job announcements, and publication opportunities. The committees also conducted examinations of gender-equity statistics to determine the current status of women in the field.

Women's organizations on campus or within professional networks merged the activist and academic cultures of the post–civil rights era. The caucuses wanted to make academia or, at the very least, their home discipline more accountable to the needs of women. Anecdotal evidence of disparities in hiring, merit, tenure promotions, and support were found to exist across campuses in the United States. However, thanks to caucuses or committees, by 1972 more than thirty studies had been conducted that illustrated women's status across fourteen disciplines (Morlock 1973).

The first known organized women's caucus was formed by women political scientists in 1969. Within weeks afterward, other women academics in other fields formed their own women's professional organizations at their annual meetings. In the field of history, the Coordinating Committee on Women in the Historical Profession was established in 1969. (It is now called the Coordinating Council for Women in History.) The American Sociological Association established its Committee on the Status of Women in 1970, as did the American Philosophical Association and the Africana Studies Association. The American Economics Association established the Committee on the Status of Women in the Economic Profession in 1971.

By 1972, there were reportedly more than 200 committees on the status of women in local chapters of the American Association of University Professors (Freeman 1973). Most professional organizations saw the need to support one for their women members. For instance, the Committee on the Status of Women in Physics was established in 1972 as a means of redressing issues important to women in physics and as an outreach committee of the American Physics Society. The Committee on the Status of Women in the American Musicological Society was founded in 1974. Since its formation in 1988, the Association for Feminist Anthropologists has advocated on issues germane to women by establishing various working commissions.

The Modern Language Association's (MLA) Commission on the Status of

Women of the MLA published its findings in *Female Studies 6: Closer to the Ground: Women's Classes, Criticism, Programs—1972.* The volume spoke to some of the pedagogical concerns women had about teaching books by women writers, about the best ways to teach women in English programs across the United States, and about the treatment of women professors and students (Hoffman, Secor, and Tinsley 1972).

A women's caucus supports not only women but also the promotion of research on women. At some campuses, the caucus might actually work under the rubric of a women's faculty association, a women's faculty committee, or a committee on the status of women; however, nomenclature aside, these organizations share a common interest in advancing the needs of women on campus. Some even went so far as to publish reports or books based on their studies. The Council of Ontario (Canada) Universities Committee on the Status of Women supported the publication of Paula J. Caplan's book *Lifting a Ton of Feathers: A Woman's Guide to Surviving in the Academic World* (1994). The book provides a lucid examination of the gendered ways in which women experience higher education.

The American Psychological Association (APA) has multiple affiliates that focus on the concerns of women in the organization. The Association for Women Psychologists was instrumental in creating feminist activism in the APA. The Women's Program Office of the APA founded the Committee on Women in Psychology and has been instrumental in the field by ensuring that its members have reports to guide their attempts to survive in academe, such as the 1992 *Survival Guide to Academia for Women and Ethnic Minorities.* In 2000 the APA published a report of the Task Force on Women in Academe titled *Women in Academe: Two Steps Forward, One Step Back.* Its major findings include the predominance of subtle sexism rather than the overt sexism of the past and the overrepresentation of women at the lower ranks, where they endure increased service loads, lack leadership positions, and encounter difficulty conducting research about gender, race, ethnicity, or sexual orientation.

The Association for Women in Mathematics (AWM) was founded in 1971 at the joint mathematics meeting of the American Mathematics Society and the Mathematical Association of America, held in Atlantic City, New Jersey. In "A Brief History of the Association for Women in Mathematics: The Residents' Perspectives," Lenore Blum (1991) notes the parallel between activism off campus and activism within the departments. Specifically, she notes how she reviewed the programs for the meetings, looking for the names of other women, and developed a sense of renewed activism as a result. She explained that the paucity of women presenters caused her to become more involved in the field and seek out other women. Many of the other women involved in AWM share similar sentiments.

In the physical and biological sciences, women's caucuses and similar organizations were slower to establish themselves, compared to the humanities and social science disciplines. *Analytical Chemistry,* which is published by the American Chemical Society, ran an article in April 2000 by Elizabeth Zubritsky, "Women in Analytical Chemistry Speak," that delved into women's concerns in the field. The stories of twenty-eight women interviewed emphasize that women predominate on the lower rungs of the academic ladder.

The concern regarding equity on campus or in academic disciplines has extended into other communities. Commissions on the status of Chicano/as, Latino/as, African Americans, Asians and Asian Americans, and others sprouted up in professional organizations, campuses, and university systems. It is not uncommon to find a status committee or caucus for multiple ethnic groups. Academics of color or those from other underrepresented groups note the disparate numbers along the academic ladder and have been repoliticized to ensure that equal opportunities continue (Lim, Herrera-Sobek, and Padilla 2000). Furthermore, they have conveyed that racialized sexism and an overall sense of isolation are unique to their experience in academia and attempt to shed light on their situation.

Committees on lesbian, gay, bisexual, and transgendered groups have also been established to deal with issues of discrimination, climate, and scholarly research on campuses, in professional organizations, and in the disciplines. The Committee on Lesbian and Gay History, an affiliate of the American Historical Association, was founded in 1978. The Lesbian and Gay Caucus for Political Science was founded in 1987, and the American Philosophical Association's Committee on the Status of Lesbian, Gay, Bisexual, and Transgender People in the Profession was established in 1997. These groups continue the struggle against academic hegemony on their campuses. They demonstrate that advocacy networks are imperative for countering the invisibility and isolation of women; faculty of color; and lesbians, gays, bisexuals, or transgendered faculty (Pinar 1998; Tierney 1997). Thus, much like women's caucuses, these other caucuses have taken a multilayered approach that addresses the needs of faculty and their specific areas of research.

Various states have also formed committees to review the status of women in higher education. In Arizona, the Commission on the Status of Women was formally founded in July 1989; the long-term vision is one of continued work toward gender parity in the state higher educational system. The Arizona Board of Regents released its findings in the *Millennium Project* in 2001. The project was a quantitative and qualitative examination of the "institutional culture" in Arizona's higher educational system. Part 2 of the project will focus on women faculty and faculty of color.

The Wisconsin Commission on the Status of Women was established in 1998. Its 1999 report, which followed up an earlier report undertaken at the behest of the 1980 Regents' Task Force on the Status of Women, notes problems with the lack of representation along gender and racial lines for faculty in the state higher educational system and suggests ways to reach parity. Both studies find that women predominate at the bottom of the academic ladder as adjuncts and assistant professors, whereas men are more likely to hold full professorships. Like most reports about women in the academia, the Wisconsin reports conclude by noting that networking, mentoring, and an overall supportive environment are essential.

In California, We Advocate Gender Equity is a strong advocate for women in the University of California system. Its biannual meetings not only keep members up-to-date with court cases but also offer a safe space for advocacy and information.

Janni L. Aragon

See also Part 2: Feminist Assessment; Part 5: Affirmative Action and Employment; Part 6: Campus Climate

References and further reading

American Association of University Professors. www.auup.org. Cited June 11, 2002.
American Psychological Association. 1992. *Survival Guide to Academia for Women and Ethnic Minorities.* Washington, DC: American Psychological Association.
———. 2000. *Women in Academe: Two Steps Forward, One Step Back.* Washington, DC: American Psychological Association.
Blum, Lenore. 1991. "A Brief History of the Association for Women in Mathematics: The Residents' Perspectives." *Notices* 38 (September): 7.
Boris, Eileen, and Nupur Chaudhuri, eds. 1999. *Voices of Women Historians: The Personal, the Political, the Professional.* Bloomington: Indiana University Press.
Caplan, Paula J. 1994. *Lifting a Ton of Feathers: A Woman's Guide to Surviving in the Academic World.* Toronto: University of Toronto Press.
Freeman, Jo. 1973. "Women on the Move: Roots of Revolt." Pp. 1–32 in *Academic Women on the Move,* ed. A. S. Rossi and A. Claderwood. New York: Russell Sage Foundation.
Hoffman, Nancy, Cynthia Secor, and Adrian Tinsley, eds. 1972. *Female Studies VI: Closer to the Ground: Women's Classes, Criticism, Programs—1972.* New York: The Feminist Press.
Lim, Shirley Geo-Lin, Maria Herrera-Sobek, and Genaro Padilla, eds. 2000. *Power, Race, and Gender in Academe.* New York: Modern Language Association.
Morlock, Laura. 1973. "Discipline Variation in the Status of Academic Women." Pp. 255–312 in *Academic Women on the Move,* ed. A. S. Rossi and A. Claderwood. New York: Russell Sage Foundation.
Pinar, William F., ed. 1998. *Queer Theory in Education.* Mahway, NJ: Lawrence Erlbaum.
Tierney, William G. 1997. *Academic Outlaws: Queer Theory and Cultural Studies in the Academy.* Thousand Oaks, Ca: Sage.
University of Arizona. 2001. *Millennium Project Enhancing Campus Climate for Academic Excellence: Phase 1, Faculty.* Tucson: University of Arizona.
We Advocate Gender Equity. http://www.wage.org. Cited June 10, 2002.
Wisconsin Commission on the Status of Women. 1999. "Equality for Women in the UW System: A Focus for Action in the Year 2000." Madison: University of Wisconsin.
Zubritsky, Elizabeth. 2000. "Women in Analytical Chemistry Speak." *Analytical Chemistry* 72 (April): 272A–281A.

Distance Education

Distance learning refers to those modes of teaching and learning that do not rely on face-to-face interaction between student and instructor or among students themselves. Technology has dramatically transformed distance learning from old-fashioned "correspondence courses" to online courses, certificate programs, and degrees. The rush for educators to keep up with technological advances creates the potential for a digital divide and greater gender gap between males and females.

History

Gene T. Sherron and Judith V. Boettcher explained four generations of distance-education technologies in their 1997 book. The first generation (from the1850s to the 1960s), began predominantly with the use of one-way distance-learning communication technology. That technology may have been print (from the 1890s), radio (from the 1930s), or television (1950s–1960s). These first-generation technologies were primarily one-way communications that provided interaction between faculty and student, with additional communication through telephone and mail,

Students in a distance-learning class (Charles Gupton/Corbis)

both augmenting the learning process much as they still do today in distance learning. The first generation was occasionally supplemented with on-site facilitators and student mentors.

The second generation incorporated multiple technologies without computers. Between the 1960s and 1985, distance learning included the use of audiocassettes, televisions, videocassettes, fax, and print. Faculty and student still interacted by telephone, fax, and mail, though communication was still primarily one-way. The second generation was occasionally supplemented by face-to-face meetings at the resident campus.

Third-generation distance learning incorporated multiple technologies, including computers and computer networks. From 1985 to 1995, distance learning was revolutionized with electronic mail, chat sessions, and bulletin boards. For the first time, computer programs and resources packaged on disks, compact discs, and the Internet were employed. Two-way audioconferencing, as well as seminar and large-room videoconferencing via terrestrial, satellite, cable, and new telephone technologies, became a reality. Fax and print continued to be used, along with new broadband communications between faculty and students. Computer programs and videoconferencing provided two-way audio and video, enabling asynchronous and synchronous communications. The Internet provided text, graphics, short videos, and easy access to research information.

Multiple technologies are the norm in the fourth generation of distance learning, including the beginning of high-bandwidth computer technologies. The years 1995 to approximately 2005 will continue to emphasize the use of electronic mail, chat rooms, and bulletin boards in distance learning. Computer networks and high-bandwidth transmission of individualized, customized, and real-time video will provide new interactive learning experiences. Desktop videoconferencing through the Internet is becoming affordable and practical. Video streaming and multicasting with full 30-frame-per-second digital video transmission provide lengthy, high-quality programming on demand. Hand-held, wireless, and teleportation technologies will continue to revolutionize distance learning in the fourth generation and lead us to a fifth generation that can only be imagined.

Distance Learning Today: E-learning

Distance learning has come to be called online learning, web-based learning, distributed learning, and e-learning. E-learning, which includes Internet-based and videoconferencing technologies, is the focus of this discussion. Whatever term is used, new distance-learning initiatives provide flexibility, accessibility, and new options and opportunities for both men and women that we have never seen before.

According to a recent congressional study, the average e-learning student is a part-time employee, thirty-four years of age, who has earned some previous college credits and, most important, is a woman (U.S. Senate 2001). The Department of Education estimated there were 6,000 accredited web-based courses in 2000. More than 700,000 distance-learning students enrolled in 1998, and department officials predicted that more than 2 million students will enroll in 2002 (U.S. Department of Education 2000).

Many people have argued that education changes at glacial speed and that higher education has remained basically the same for many centuries. They have ignored, however, "what, for women, has been a revolutionary change during the last century and a half: The admission of women into colleges and universities has evolved from a statistical rarity to women slightly outnumbering men overall in undergraduate programs" (Kramarae 2000, 4). According to Kramarae's study called *The Third Shift,* sponsored by the American Association of University Women, two major trends are converging in education today: the growth of technology and e-learning in colleges and universities and a demographic shift toward a predominantly female population of nontraditional-age college students (60 percent of students over the age of twenty-five are women).

Women and the E-learning Experience

Learning online requires both motivation and self-direction. There has been tremendous polarization in retention of online students: They either do extremely well or fail miserably. Without the motivation and ability to manage time and projects, the e-learner becomes frustrated and lost and eventually drops out. Many women experience problems similar to the ones they face in traditional education. Studies have documented that women have greater anxiety using computers than do men. These experiences can lead to stress and subsequent withdrawal from an online class. Some studies have reported up to a 50 percent dropout rate in online learning programs.

E-learning is not for everyone, whether male or female. Today's new technologies provide virtual face-to-face communication through videoconferencing and teleportation conferencing. These experiences can create socialization and humanization much like the traditional classroom and, when incorporated into the online learning initiative, can actually transform the distance-learning experience into a more real and social experience for the learner. Desktop videoconferencing, an Internet-based technology, is quickly becoming a feasible, practical, and economical communication tool for business, industry, and education. It is already having a tremendous impact in all areas of education, training, and development.

Studies of Videoconferencing as a Form of Distance Learning

Women in nursing have excelled in the use of videoconferencing. This technology has been used effectively to deliver continuing education units to geographically bound nursing students as well as provide critical health care information to rural patients. In nursing education, videoconferencing is an effective medium for conducting problem-based learning, case studies, and group discussions. On an international level, nurses are using videoconferencing to discuss health care issues with their colleagues around the world. In a recent study involving the United States and Great Britain, nursing students were exposed to diverse nursing perspectives focusing on communication issues, women's health, advocacy, empowerment, and family-centered care. A conclusion of the study was that there should not be a high expectation of knowledge acquisition in such interactions. Instead, the project objectives should be focused on "broadening of perspective, changing attitudes, increasing cultural awareness and experiencing information technology and distance learning" (Waddell et al. 1999).

These findings have significant implications. For example, since the 11 September 2001 terrorist attacks in the United States, videoconferencing equipment sales have increased worldwide. In the aftermath, the plight of women in patriarchal cultures was broadcast to the world through telecommunication satellite technologies. Social discrimination and violence, along with isolation and censorship, have been a way of life that they have had to tolerate. Awareness of such situations and global studies, such as those being implemented by the nursing profession using state-of-the-art videoconferencing technologies, will play an important role in bringing about change for women and children around the world and empowering new learners for the twenty-first century.

Distance Learning and the Workplace

Although it is still true that men on the average make higher salaries than women, technology has helped to level the playing field. Early in the twentieth century, many jobs were more easily performed by men. Technology has helped to change the nature of work, and today almost all jobs can be done as easily by women as by men. "This gender shift may be the most significant change in the history of the American workplace" (Judy and D'Amico 1998, 52). Previously, women mostly worked in gender-specific jobs such as nursing, the clerical profession, and teaching, and others held bottom-end jobs in mills and sweatshops or as domestics. With these few exceptions, the workplace was chiefly a masculine domain. Men were needed for physical labor and worked in jobs that did not require much schooling; most skills were learned on the job. Since the mid–twentieth century, machines and technology have replaced human power, and U.S. society has shifted from producing goods to providing services.

Gender is considered a particularly irrelevant characteristic in the service sector, which will be the largest employment sector in the early twenty-first century. According to the authors of *Workforce 2020,* "if occupationally relevant gender differences exist [in the service sector] today, they are as likely to favor women as men. Thus women seem to be preparing themselves more assiduously than men for professional careers in the information age: Women now garner 55 percent of bachelor's degrees, 53 percent of master's degrees, and nearly 40 percent of doctorates" (Judy and D'Amico 1998, 52–53). An important trend is emerging: in the decades ahead, men will lose whatever workplace advantage they may still retain.

As employers work to recruit and retain a highly skilled workforce, researchers predict additional emphasis on the corporate university. Employers will provide training and education for their employees through the use of advanced learning technologies such as the Internet and videoconferencing. Some companies, such as Ford Motor Company, already provide laptops for their employees so they may access online learning programs during flexible hours. Some employees, however, view this phenomenon less as a benefit than as a requirement to work outside regular work hours.

The Phenomenon of the "Third Shift"

The "second shift" was a metaphor describing work and family conflicts for women in Arlie Russell Hochschild's landmark 1989 study. Women reported that they worked one shift in the workplace and a second shift in the home. Cheris Kramarae adds education to this equation as a third shift. "As lifelong learning and knowledge become ever more important to economic well-being, women and men find they juggle not only work and family, but also demands of further schooling and education throughout their lives" (Kramarae 2000, 3). Although more women are going online to take courses, for many of them it requires juggling a full-time job, family responsibilities, homemaking, and a heavy course load. As women try to schedule learning time around their family and work responsibilities, a "third shift" is created.

Online learning can eliminate problems with accessibility, which is a common drawback of traditional postsecondary and adult education programs. Many "third shift" learners appreciate the flexibility that online learning provides. Many educators note that women need to have more involvement in the planning and evaluation of online programs. According to Kramarae, women are underrepresented in all countries as software designers, network engineers, college administrators, and teachers, so their needs may not be met when distance-learning programs are designed primarily by men.

LuAnn Hiniker

See also Part 4: Gender and Technology; Internet-based Distance Education

References and further reading

Duin, Ann Hill, Linda L. Baer, and Doreen Starke-Meyerring. 2001. *Partnering in the Learning Marketspace.* EDUCAUSE New Directions for Institutional Research, Vol. 4. San Francisco: Jossey-Bass, PricewaterhouseCoopers.

Hochschild, Arlie Russell. 1989. *The Second Shift: Working Parents and the Revolution at Home.* New York: Viking.

Judy, Richard W., and Carol D'Amico. 1998. *Workforce 2020: Work and Workers in the Twenty-First Century.* Indianapolis: Hudson Institute.

Katz, Richard N., and Julia A. Rudy. 1999. *Information Technology in Higher Education: Assessing Its Impact and Planning for the Future.* EDUCAUSE Leadership Strategies no. 102. San Francisco: Jossey-Bass.

Kramarae, Cheris. 2000. *The Third Shift: Women Learning Online.* Washington, DC: American Association of University Women Education Foundation.

Ponce, Theta C. 1988. "Some Basic Considerations on the Role of Women in the Development of Science and Technology." Pp. 158–160 in *The Role of Women in the Development of Science and Technology in the Third World,* ed. Akhtar M. Faruqui, Mohamed H. A. Hassan, and Gabriella Sandri. Teaneck, NJ: World Scientific Publishing.

Sherron, Gene T., and Judith V. Boettcher. 1997. *Distance Learning.* Boulder, CO: College and University Systems Exchange Publishing.

U.S. Department of Education, Web-Based Education Commission. 2000. *The Power of the Internet for Learning: Moving from Promise to Practice.* http://www.hpcnet.org/webcommission. Cited June 10, 2002.

Waddell, Donna L., Barbara A. Tronsgard, Ann Smith, and Gill Smith. 1999. "An Evaluation of International Nursing Education Using Interactive Desktop Videoconferencing." *Computers in Nursing* 17 (July): 186–192.

Ecofeminism

Ecofeminism is the position that the oppression of women and the domination of the natural environment are linked. Examining ecofeminism is important in higher education because it is representative of the diversity of feminism and women's studies and provides students, faculty, and educators with basic information on emerging research, theories, and teaching strategies.

The term "ecofeminism" is usually credited to Françoise d'Eaubonne. In 1974, her article "Le Feminisme ou la Mort" (Feminism or death) linked environmental issues to the patriarchal ideologies of power, domination, and hierarchy. Today, ecofeminism is connected to a wide range of ideologies from the cultural, such as Native American myths and goddess spirituality, to the socialist, which focuses on the connections between capitalism and the environment, to women's issues. Ecofeminist issues include animal rights, environmental racism, food safety, health and reproductive rights, and Third World development. Ecofeminism applies to most academic disciplines, including the humanities, social sciences, natural sciences, and business.

After d'Eaubonne's article was published in 1974, the ecofeminist movement emerged spontaneously in Asia, Europe, and the United States. The Chipko Movement of the Garhwal Himalayas, in the mid-1970s, is often used to symbolize the emerging ecofeminist movement. The women of the area hugged trees in order to stop them from being logged. The term "tree-huggers" stems from this social action. Ecofeminism became part of European politics in 1983 when Petra Kelly founded Die Grünen, the West German Green Party. Kelly blended environmental issues with feminist issues to create a political party. In 1998, the Greens became part of Germany's governing coalition. About the same time as the start of Die Grünen, as a response to the Three Mile Island nuclear accident, Ynestra King launched ecofeminism in the United States when she helped organize "Women's Life on Earth: A Conference on Ecofeminism in the Eighties" in Amherst, Massachusetts. At this conference, King and other feminist environmentalists explored and expanded d'Eaubonne's relationship between ecology and feminist ideology. Grassroots ecofeminist efforts in the early 1980s were also successful in changing United States environmental policy. Lois Gibbs, a housewife turned activist, is often cited for her success in connecting the health problems of the families in Love Canal, New York, and the toxic waste dump on which the town was built. Although early ecofeminists organized into political parties, held high-profile conferences, and created grassroots movements, no formal, umbrella, ecofeminist organization was ever formed. Today, it is represented primarily in publications that provide contrasting ideologies in many fields of study, each of which employ pedagogical strategies to help understand its basic concepts.

The four ideologies that address ecofeminism today are liberal, cultural, social, and socialist. Each ideology shares ecofeminism's basic tenets that humans are part of nature, not separate from it, that treatment of humans and the natural environment cannot be separated, and that all life on earth functions as an interconnected community. By examining these differing ideologies, we can understand the richness of ecofeminism.

Liberal ecofeminism is grounded in the liberal feminist ideals of public voice and political change. Mainstream political methods are used to make better laws and policies to solve problems and to protect human rights. Like liberal ecofeminism, cultural ecofeminism involves public voice through grassroots political action using rituals. This group often employs Native American myth and traditions as part of their actions. Starhawk and the Reclaiming Collective, for example, led a series of Wiccan rituals in the late 1990s to help save the old-growth forests of the Pacific Northwest in the United States. Cultural ecofeminists believe that women have an innate ability to be closer to nature than men. Each sex is equal, but each also has different powers, skills, and talents. For example, women's intuition is considered to be a powerful alternative to mechanism and technology.

Social ecofeminists acknowledge the biological differences between women and men but reject the social and economic hierarchies that patriarchy attaches to these differences. They challenge capitalism and embrace the idea of decentralized communities. Chiah Heller is a social ecofeminist. Heller believes interdependence, complementarity, and spontaneity apply to personal and community relationships. She writes of abandoning the dualisms of man and culture versus woman and nature and of how nature provides a potential realm where these dualisms can be challenged.

Although the terms "social ecofeminism" and "socialist ecofeminism" sound similar, they represent two different ideologies. Socialist ecofeminists repudiate capitalism and add the idea that capitalism views both women and the natural environment as commodities. Ynestra King and Carolyn Merchant are both socialist ecofeminists. King is a radical political activist, and Merchant writes about the ways in which women and men interact with nature and how capitalist ideologies circumscribe women's roles in the economy. For example, originally midwives took care of women in childbirth, but men displaced them as medical knowledge and technology expanded, eventually controlling natural reproduction. Related to socialist ecofeminism is the idea that women and nature are both victims of colonization. According to Val Plumwood, colonization involves the belief that women and nature are inferior to men and culture. This patriarchal idea focuses on the differences between women and men while ignoring their similarities. Colonization also ignores the complexity of the relationship between humans and their environment and asserts that nature is replaceable. In a colonized world, technology, not nature, is considered essential for expanding human life.

In addition to the four ideologies that represent ecofeminism, one must also understand the fields of study that use ecofeminism. The humanities, social sciences, hard sciences, and business all have ecofeminism applications. In the humanities, philosopher Karen Warren writes and teaches about environmental ethics and ecofeminism. She argues that in patriarchy, "a logic of domination" attempts to justify men's control and oppression of both women and the natural environment. Ecofeminism, Warren asserts, challenges this logic. Social scientists use ecofeminism to understand the relationships between people and their environment. In linguistics, some researchers study the links between naturist and sexist language and the subjugation and domination of women and the environment. For example, women are often referred to in animal terms, such as "fox," "bitch," or "mother hens." Since animals are seen as inferior to humans in patriarchal societies, applying animal names to women reinforces women's inferior status. Patriarchal domination of women and nature is also reinforced by terms that feminize nature: "virgin" timber is cut down, mines "penetrate" Mother Earth, and fallow fields are "barren."

The hard sciences also use ecofeminist concepts. Ecofeminism complements the basic principles of care in the medical sciences. In biology, it is connected to the deep ecology movement and the notion of biodiversity. An ecofeminist geologist could study environmental racism and the impact of mining on minority communities. Green businesses and organizations such as Businesses for Social Responsibility advocate ecofeminist concepts of community and teach corporations to value both environmental resources and humans equally. Ecofeminism can be valuable in most disciplines in some manner, but it also has critics.

First, critics claim that sex roles found in society today express personal preferences, not coercion. Those who make this argument assume that men run things because they want to and women prefer their supportive roles. A second criticism is that ecofeminism essentializes gender when biological traits, like male aggression and women's inherent connection to Mother Earth, are used to amplify gender differences while ignoring similarities. Critics who say this often believe that men and women are basically biologically different but that culture is the dominant influence creating gender differences. Third, some people find the terms "oppression" and "domination" to be too vague and complain that those who use those terms assume that all women are oppressed and dominated in the same manner as the environment. The final criticism centers on the ecofeminist claim that, in patriarchal cultures, a higher position in the hierarchy implies a higher value. In fact, according to the critics, the focus of ecofeminism is on the person, not nature, and therefore it is anthropocentric and women-centered, thus perpetuating the value-laden hierarchy and devaluing men instead of women.

Ecofeminism links environmental issues to women's issues. It is applicable to many fields of study and is grounded in different ideologies. Those who use ecofeminism in their classrooms realize that it is a controversial perspective that links theory to action. Therefore, the pedagogical strategies are important to note as well. In addition to traditional classroom lectures and activities, ecofeminism lends itself to nontraditional strategies. Examples of these strategies include field trips, lab exercises, community service projects, and the construction of social action networks on the Internet. In fact, since ecofeminism challenges traditional views on the environment and women's roles, it is common to find pedagogical techniques that do so as well.

Tess Pierce

References and further reading

Levin, Margarita Garcia. 1994. "A Critique of Ecofeminism." Pp. 134–140 in *Environmental Ethics: Readings in Theory and Application,* ed. L. P. Pojman. Boston: Jones and Bartlett.

Mellor, Mary. 1997. *Feminism and Ecology.* New York: New York University Press.

Merchant, Carolyn. 1992. *Radical Ecology: The Search for a Livable World.* New York: Routledge.

Plumwood, Val. 1997. "Androcentrism and Anthropocentrism: Parallels and Politics." Pp. 327–355 in *Ecofeminism: Women, Culture, and Nature,* ed. Karen J. Warren. Bloomington: Indiana University Press.

Warren, Karen. 1994. "The Power and Promise of Ecological Feminism." Pp. 124–134 in *Environmental Ethics: Readings in Theory and Application,* ed. L. P. Pojman. Boston: Jones and Bartlett.

Family and Consumer Sciences

Family and Consumer Sciences (FCS) is the name for the new and broader vision of the field previously called home economics. This new conceptualization evolved because of changes in U.S. families, culture and resources, ethnic and racial demographics, knowledge in the basic disciplines, and higher education. FCS professionals use an integrative, interdisciplinary approach to address concerns related to the reciprocal relationships among individuals, families, and communities, and the environments in which they function. The field's purpose is to improve individual, family, and community well-being; affect the development, delivery, and evaluation of consumer goods and services; influence policy creation; and shape social change, thereby enhancing the quality of life (American Association of Family and Consumer Sciences 2001). Although FCS originally emerged to provide opportunities for educated women to make a difference when there were few careers open to women, the field now provides many career options for both men and women.

Education for careers is provided through FCS programs in higher education, but academics in the field also conduct research and provide service and outreach to the public and to other professionals. FCS higher education programs offer associate's, bachelor's, master's, and doctoral degrees in FCS and its specializations. Graduating thousands annually, the field prepares professionals to work in a wide range of careers in all levels of public and higher education, as well as human services organizations, government, business, and industry. Examples include product design and development in the food, textiles and apparel, and financial industries; retail buying and management; journalism; community education; all levels of education; family and community services; admin-

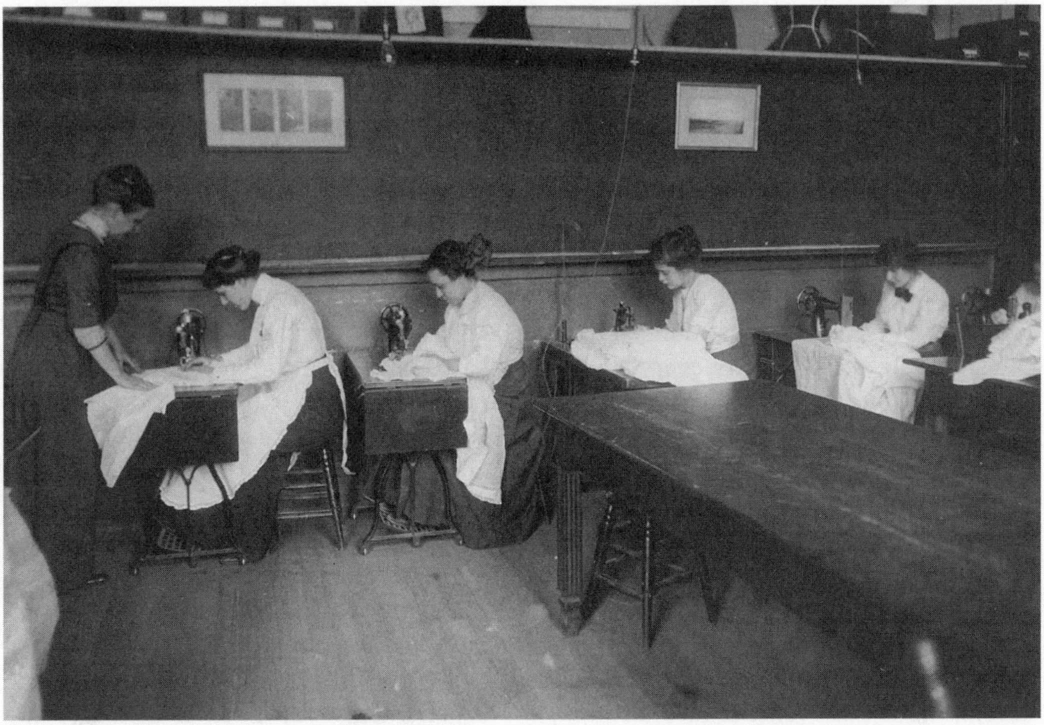

Girls are taught to sew at Washington Irving High School in New York City, 1911 (Library of Congress)

istration; wellness; research in public institutions and industry; certified financial planning and debt counseling; consumer protection; consumer affairs; housing and multifamily property management; and indoor environmental health, safety, and energy efficiency.

Although the concept of FCS originated in Aristotle's philosophy, Catharine Beecher created the modern conceptualization in the mid-1800s. In her seminaries for young girls, Beecher offered a more intellectually challenging education than was generally available then. Her publications were also popular among adult women. Others interested in providing higher education for women developed programs in public land grant colleges (now universities). Iowa State University established the first home economics program in 1871, followed by Kansas State University in 1873 and Illinois Industrial University (now the University of Illinois, Urbana-Champaign) in 1874. By 1895, there were ten FCS departments in land grant colleges, and by 1900 there were thirty (East 1982, 4).

During the Progressive era (approximately 1890–1920) in the United States, a group of educated women and men facilitated formalization of this movement into a discipline and profession. They were particularly concerned about the growing poverty during the Industrial Revolution in their increasingly prosperous nation. Living conditions were overcrowded; housing and sanitation were poor; food was often adulterated; few health, safety, and pollution regulations existed; and communicable diseases were the leading cause of death. However, in spite of their education and commitment, the female pioneers found it difficult to find professional employment; it was almost impossible if they were married. Not to be stifled, these scientifically trained women (and men) created their own discipline and profession to study and address the problems of everyday life (Stage and Vincenti 1997).

Melvil Dewey, inventor of the Dewey Decimal System, and Ellen Richards, chemist and first woman graduate of Massachusetts Institute of Technology (MIT) and later MIT instructor of chemistry, initiated the Lake Placid Conferences on Home Economics (1899–1908) to convene women and men interested in developing the movement into an organized discipline and profession. Richards was concerned with consumer education; nutrition; child protection; industrial safety; public health; career education; women's rights; the purity of air, food, and water; and the application of science and management principles to the family. She led the 1902 conferees in defining the field as the study of the laws, conditions, principles, and ideals concerned with the relationship between humans' immediate physical environment and their nature as social beings. They considered it a philosophical field dependent on scientific subjects such as economics, sociology, chemistry, and hygiene (Lake Placid Conferences).

The conferees developed a college-level curriculum. At first, they emphasized the application of science to improve sanitation and diets, to ensure the safe handling of food, and to reduce the drudgery of housework so that all women could have time and energy for life's loftier pursuits. As the social sciences emerged in the early 1900s, the profession and the curriculum broadened to include child development, the social and emotional quality of daily life, and the acquisition and management of resources needed as families changed from producing to consuming units. These newer programs prepared graduates for teaching, as well as for new careers in dietetics, social services, community-based education through the Department of Agriculture's Cooperative Extension Service, business, and industry, when few opportunities existed for women. Today, there are hundreds of FCS higher education programs nationally and many in other countries.

During and after World War II, the economy bustled, public education increased eligibility for higher education, research exponentially expanded knowledge, and public support for higher education grew. All prompted the creation of specializations in many fields. Family and consumer sciences developed specializations in human nutrition and food management (dietetics); human development (child development); family relations and family therapy; apparel and textiles; housing and home furnishings (interior design); and consumer economics and family resource management.

The discipline and profession experienced further changes during the second half of the twentieth century. Americans, including FCS professionals, had come to believe that science was capable of solving almost all problems, but by the 1970s, this unrealistic confidence had begun eroding. In 1978 Marjorie Brown, professor of home economics education at the University of Minnesota, and Beatrice Paolucci, professor of family economics and management at Michigan State University, urged the field to embrace a different vision of itself. They based their new conceptualization on the work of contemporary German philosopher Jurgen Habermas, who acknowledged the usefulness but also the insufficiency of the sciences in addressing problems requiring ethical action, the most challenging problems in everyday life. Brown and Paolucci (1979) argued that critical reflection, ethical reasoning, and collaborative participation are needed to increase the profession's effectiveness in defining the most important and fundamental problems and empowering individuals and families with the knowledge and higher order thinking skills needed to address such problems.

They redefined the mission of the profession as enabling families—both as individual units and generally as a social institution—to create and maintain ways of thinking and acting that lead to the physical, social, emotional, and intellectual formation of all family members into mature individuals. They argued that the field's mission should also include empowerment of families to participate in enlightened, cooperative critique and formulation of social goals (within and beyond the family) and the means for accomplishing them. Not all in the field accepted Brown and Paolucci's view. Some favored the long-standing view of the field that emphasized technical knowledge and skills.

Since the mid–twentieth century, programmatic and philosophical changes within the field and external societal changes have increased the need for a new name for the field. Various names developed for higher education programs, including human ecology, human environmental science, human sciences, and FCS. Because of the confusion these names created, five home economics professional organizations sponsored a conference in 1993 in Scottsdale, Arizona, to position the profession for the twenty-first century. Attendees redesigned the field and chose "Family and Consumer Sciences" as the profession's new name. Since then, many college and university programs across the United States have changed their names to be consistent with this new name, but for many local reasons, others have retained the names they had.

The linkages among home economics, feminism, and FCS during the twentieth century have evolved in distinct stages. In the 1960s, feminists in the women's movement outside the field sharply criticized home economists for preparing women for a life limited to domestic responsibilities. By the 1990s, some feminist historians began reinterpreting the field, recognizing that this new profession actually provided professional opportunities for educated women, using strategies and compromises deemed necessary at the time (Stage and Vincenti 1997).

Virginia B. Vincenti

References and further reading

American Association of Family and Consumer Sciences. www.aafcs.org. Cited December 9, 2001. The American Association of Family and Consumer Sciences has an archive and collection of historical artifacts related to the profession at 1555 King St., Alexandria, VA 22314.

Brown, Marjorie M. 1985. *Philosophical Studies of Home Economics in the United States: Our Practical Intellectual Heritage.* Vol. 1. East Lansing: College of Human Ecology, Michigan State University.

Brown, Marjorie M., and Beatrice Paolucci. 1979. *Home Economics: A Definition.* Washington, DC: American Home Economics Association.

East, Marjorie. 1982. *Caroline Hunt: Philosopher for Home Economics.*

University Park: Division of Occupational and Vocational Studies, Pennsylvania State University.
Hunt, Caroline. 1980. *The Life of Ellen H. Richards.* 1912. Reprinted with new preface and forward. Washington, DC: American Home Economics Association.
Lake Placid Conferences on Home Economics (Proceedings of First through Tenth Conferences). Lake Placid, NY. 1899–1908.
Rossiter, Margaret W. 1982. *Women Scientists in America: Struggles and Strategies to 1940.* Baltimore: Johns Hopkins University Press.
———. 1997. "The Men Move In: Home Economics in Higher Education, 1950–1970." Pp. 96–117 in *Rethinking Home Economics: Women and the History of a Profession,* eds. Sarah Stage and Virginia B. Vincenti. Ithaca, NY: Cornell University Press.
Stage, Sarah, and Virginia B. Vincenti, eds. 1997. *Rethinking Home Economics: Women and the History of a Profession.* Ithaca, NY: Cornell University Press.

Gender and Technology

Information and communications technologies (ICTs), such as computer-mediated conferences, interactive CD-ROMs, and web-based courses, are playing an increasingly important role in tertiary education, but there is consistent evidence that differences exist in how many females and males perceive and use these technologies. To date, research has focused on the barriers that female learners face. More recently, attention is turning to the experiences of female instructors who use technology to teach on campus and at a distance. Studies of female experience with learning technologies reveal a consistent pattern, established in the early years in school, in which girls are discouraged from computing both as a process and as a career choice. Elements of exclusion include attitude, anxiety level, motivation, access, socialization and culture, learning context, learning design, nature of content, and learning and cognitive style differences.

Research on females and technology has been paralleled by the evolution of feminist thought and of the entire field of instructional and communications technology since the 1980s. For example, there is general acceptance of the view that learning is a social process that embeds the use of ICTs in a sociocultural practice. There is no *inherently* negative relationship between women and technology, but there appears to be one that is socially *constructed.* However, the view that technology is a social and political phenomenon that excludes women has been challenged from within feminist circles as well as from more traditional paradigms.

Although this debate continues, there is agreement that the design of much of the commercially available software and learning environments actively discourage female teachers and learners from participating. These learning products and environments have tended to be self-contained, applications-based, and designed for the individual learner. Computer-based simulations and learning activities based on game designs are examples of highly structured, autonomous learning contexts. Web-based environments encourage more collaborative activities, yet access remains a concern. Barriers to teaching and learning in technological environments are related to personal, political, and sociological factors, including institutional practices.

Personal Factors

Personal barriers include attitudes and motivation, self-efficacy, stress and anxiety, and achievement. Females, especially older females, have tended to assess computers as less effective instructional tools, but as access to technology increases, motivation and attitude improve. It is well documented that females have felt less competent than males using computers, feelings that have often led to the personalization of a stressful and unsuccessful experience. It is not unusual to hear women remark that if something does not work, it must be their fault for not performing the right task. Sherry Turkle (1995) describes this attitude as the "don't touch it, you'll get a shock" phenomenon. Computer anxiety is learned through experience at home and in school. It is reinforced by the relative absence of females in informal technological contexts such as video arcades and computer clubs and formal ones such as technical professions. Adult women may enter technology-based learning activities with low self-esteem, which is compounded by the inevitable problems every computer user has with networks and equipment.

Women remain underrepresented in scientific and techological fields (Courtesy of the Association of Women in Science)

Political, Sociological, and Institutional Factors

Social and political factors in technological environments are interrelated. Unequal access to computers and, by extension, information is of concern across the world because computer ownership and computer use remains predominantly male and North American. That is also true of the pattern of online use and access. Unequal access begins in the home and at school, ranging from a 2 to 1 ratio to a 5 to 1 ratio in favor of male ownership of computers. The nature of access has changed over the past several years in regions with greater technological development, and estimates of access by sex vary substantially. However, women are still more likely to remain at a relative disadvantage to men in both the personal and professional spheres. Although approximately 38 percent of North American Internet users are reportedly female, the quality of their access may be unequal (Brown and Jolly 1999). The quality of access is affected by factors such as limited time to be online or access through older computers and slower connection speeds, which affect the type and amount of information available. Males tend to participate in more informal computing experiences than females and feel more comfortable with technology. Access relates directly to experience through attitude and achievement.

There have been relatively few technological role models for women. Male teachers are more likely to be involved in computing; and a discriminatory environment exists in many classrooms in which technology is a focus (see Campbell 1999). Although the numbers of women receiving graduate degrees in many science and technology-related fields, such as engineering, have increased since 1990, the proportion of women receiving graduate degrees in computer science has actually declined. The design of software and the language of computing are often uncomfortable for women. Themes typically concern sports, various forms of destruction, and physical adventures. Even course development tools for faculty can exclude women. For example, the "tool" and "workshop" metaphors used by many productivity tools reflect a male-oriented vocation (e.g., carpentry). Learning tasks in computer-based learning environments are often set up to support individual, procedural problem solving or competitive and abstract activities, rather than being cooperative, collaborative, and narrative-based.

In recent years, more attention has been paid to the technology-related needs of the adult learner in nontraditional learning environments. A high proportion of these learners are women. Financial support for learning is one problem for this group. The lack of support for the family issues that concern women translates into inflexible schedules and deadlines for assignments and exams, requirements for technological tools that may be out of their financial and technological reach, isolation from other learners and their teacher, and activities that may require extra fees, such as videoconferencing. Families and other social structures in the community have been found to marginalize some women by destroying materials, increasing demands for attention and help, or refusing to set aside time or space for women to study. Ironically, women may place higher demands and standards on themselves to compensate for what they perceive as selfishness in pursuing their own goals and interests. Faculty and administrators in distance education departments and institutions need to consider these issues when planning new courses and programs.

The Internet

The Internet can bring women together in communities across national and cultural boundaries and enhance women's creative potential. Previously inaccessible information sources are now available and may be embedded in online support structures. Hypertext writing and computer-mediated conferencing (CMC) may encourage social activism through the building of online, activist communities. Online environments may be empowering in their potential support of women whose cognitive styles are connected, interrelational, collaborative, and nonlinear. The Internet may offer the most equitable context yet for women learning with technology.

With improved bandwidth over the Internet and multimedia technologies such as streaming audio and video, multiple representations of information are possible. Multimodal designs that include graphical and dynamic representations (such as video, audio, and animation) will support more diverse cognitive and learning styles. Educational websites are emerging that offer information in a diversity of forms and represent content from multiple perspectives by using problem-based learning designs. Examples of these environments for higher learning include Blue Web'n (http://www.kn.pacbell.com/wired/bluewebn) and Merlot (http://www.merlot.org).

Female learners may come to communication activities affected by social practices associated with gender, such as the tendency to attenuate to others. In face-to-face classroom interactions, inequalities can emerge through nonverbal cues related to sex, appearance, size, and demeanor, as well as through verbal cues such as conversational dominance. Until recently, researchers and teachers assumed that some gender inequalities would be lessened by online communications. A lack of social cues, plus the advantage of asynchronicity, can make the online conversation more equitable and safer for women. But despite the potential for gender equity in CMC, many women have been silenced, criticized, and even pursued and frightened in the online environment.

Support for Female Teachers and Learners

There are ways to create learning environments that feel supportive to women and to all learners of varying learning styles, experiences, ages, cultures, and values. To create these environments, Sherry Turkle argues that "a new social construction of the computer" is needed (as cited by Kirkup 1992, 280). In these environments, the cultural context in which knowledge is produced will be examined with the questions *whose authority?* and *whose knowledge?* as critical lenses.

Since the late 1990s, attention has turned to learning designs based on *cognitive flexibility theory.* This approach encourages learners to "crisscross the landscape" of multiple perspectives and constructions of reality. Learning is based on social interaction. Approaches include problem-based and case-based models in which learners work together to gather evidence to support critical solutions. Social discourse is central to this process and is often supported through online conversations or threaded discussions.

Gender-neutral, technology-based learning designs with the following elements have been found to be appropriate for all adult learners: cooperative learning environments that stimulate attention by changing organization and presentation of content; content that is designed to relate to prior experience and knowledge; appropriate levels of challenge; content that is "chunked" for short learning periods; and frequent interaction accompanied by mediated feedback. Providing opportunities to try new knowledge in authentic, collaborative contexts is important. In these designs, content is immediately accessible, well-organized, has good visual and interface design principles, and includes multiple forms available through several choice points and self-selected paths. Language is active rather than passive, personal rather than abstract, devoid of bias and cultural connotations, and of moderate difficulty. Sentence structures are simple rather than complex, with important ideas made immediately apparent and abstract ideas related to the real world of action.

Additional suggestions for successful learning and teaching experiences for women include cooperative environments; scheduled orientation sessions in which students learn to use the technology; use of online conversation, supported with CMC or email lists; use of social protocols such as language use, acceptable methods of disagreement, and equal distribution of conversation; more flexible deadlines for assignments submitted at a distance; creative solutions to computer ownership and access, such as rent-to-buy arrangements and free modem pools; development of community access points; and better security arrangements in computer labs that are open for extended hours.

Katy Campbell

See also Part 4: Distance Education; Internet-based Distance Education; Part 6: Learning and Knowing

References and further reading
Brown, Mark Malloch, and Richard Jolly. 1999. "New Technologies and the Global Race for Knowledge." Pp. 57–76 in *Human Development Report.* New York: United Nations.
Campbell, Katy. 1999. "Designs for Computer-Based Learning: Designing for Inclusivity." *Technology and Society: Gender and Computer Technologies* 18, no. 4: 28–34.
Ganguly, Keya. 1992. "Accounting for Others: Feminism and Representation." Pp. 60–79 in *Women Making Meaning: New Feminist Directions in Communication,* ed. Lana F. Rakow. New York: Routledge.
Herring, Susan C. 1996. "Gender and Democracy in Computer-Mediated Communication." Pp. 476–489 in *Computerization and Controversy: Value Conflicts and Social Choices,* ed. R. Kling. 2nd ed. San Diego: Academic Press.
Kirkup, Gill. 1992. "The Social Construction of Computers: Hammers or Harpsichords?" Pp. 267–283 in *Inventing Women; Science, Technology and Gender,* eds. Gill Kirkup and Laurie S. Keller. Cambridge, MA: Basil Blackwell.
———. 1995. *The Importance of Gender as a Category in Open and Distance Learning.* Paper presented at the conference "Putting the Learner First: Learner-Centred Approaches in Open and Distance Learning." Cambridge, UK, July.
Spender, Dale. 1995. *Nattering on the Net: Women, Power, and Cyberspace.* North Melbourne, Victoria, Australia: Spinifex Press.
Spiro, Rand J., Richard L. Coulson, Paul J. Feltovich, and Daniel K. Anderson. 1988. Pp. 375–383 in *Cognitive Flexibility Theory: Advanced Knowledge Acquisition in Ill-Structured Domains.* Proceedings of the Annual Conference of the Cognitive Science Society. Hillsdale, NJ: Lawrence Erlbaum.
Taylor, Jenifer. 1997. "Warming a Chilly Classroom." *ASEE Prism:* 29–33.
Turkle, Sherry. 1995. *Life on the Screen: Identity in the Age of the Internet.* New York: Simon and Schuster.

Internet-based Distance Education

Online instruction delivered via the Internet is a global educational innovation that is fundamentally altering the way people engage in formal systems of higher education. Current debate regarding this educational innovation tends to fall into two camps. There are those who see Internet delivery of formal instruction as personally empowering to users because of its greater flexibility, the more numerous choices available to learners, and the user's control of the content and process of learning. Alternatively, critics are concerned that expanding adoption will exacerbate existing power differentials between the information rich and information poor, which will then increase already strained and distant relations across class, race, and gender group identities (Miller 2001, 188). At the most basic level, delivering courses via the Internet removes the disciplinary elements of the traditional classroom in terms of time and space. Students are responsible for attendance in the virtual classroom through an Internet connection. Although this trait affords great flexibility, it also poses some problems. Likewise, instructors trade spaces limited by bricks, mortar, and semester schedules for territory as yet uncharted in terms of educational efficacy, effects on student outcomes, institutional policy and support, and the inevitable uncertainty of continuous connectivity.

Complete undergraduate and graduate degree programs are now available online and can be completed without ever going to campus. Registration, advising, and instruction comprise the virtual university. Unheard of in the early 1990s, online instruction is now a major strategic initiative at nine out of ten public universities and six out of ten private colleges or universities in the United States. Statistical data on this fast-growing phenomenon are outdated as soon as they are reported. However, the National Center on Education Statistics surveys electronically mediated instruction, and results are reported regularly at www.nces.ed.gov.

Learning Online

Reliable connectivity, the learning environment, barriers to participation in learning, and interaction preferences that lead to "sense making" or learning are just a few of the variables that may affect women differently from men who enroll in online courses. These issues deserve careful consideration and analysis on their own merits, along with the reasons for the absence of these issues at the planning and policy levels.

Connectivity. Reliable connectivity, much like the need for reliable transportation to campus, is a multifaceted issue. Given the economic disparity between the earnings of men and women and the number of women who are single parents and belong to the working poor, access to state-of-the-art computing capability and high-speed Internet connections at work or at home is not a given. In many ways, the explosion of online course offerings transfers institutional expansion costs to students and other community resources such as public libraries. The allure of flexibility of time and place for learning diminishes when the reality is frequently interrupted online service, inadequate software to support transfer of attachments and messages, and competing demands at home or work. Even when computers are provided at little or no charge, home-based Internet connections may require setup or maintenance from a service provider. For some women whose religious faith prohibits any interaction with males who are not family members, a search for female technicians requires time, energy that could be devoted to learning, and an invasion of privacy.

Learning Environment. A consideration of the learning environment includes both the physical location of the student computer and the quality of the virtual classroom. In a recent study, women reported that success in online courses requires greater self-discipline and direction when it comes to setting aside time for learning at home or work. However, some women in the late stages of pregnancy or recently postpartum noted that online courses provided an opportunity for continuing uninterrupted in their degree program. These women found late-night participation provided speedy transmission, a quiet home learning environment, and a sense of empowerment culminating in a high level of satisfaction with online learning (Jeris 2001). Whether the task is to participate in a synchronous discussion (chat room) or contribute asynchronously (e.g., threaded discussion), students must negotiate with family members or colleagues to share resources such as phone lines and computers. Although it is true for men and women, the life circumstances for many women may not favor consistently successful negotiations.

For other women, online learning has proven to be as difficult and personally threatening as taking night classes in buildings with dimly lit parking lots. Cheris Kramarae (1997), a legal scholar who tracks educational policy developments related to online instruction, noted that online aggression against women takes many forms, from male domination of online interaction to anonymous verbal harassment and transmission of pornographic material. She posited that a more pressing priority than making online credit card transmissions secure is making the Internet safe for women. What is more troubling is that large university library systems are now using electronic certification to secure and authenticate users of their costly online research databases, but these same institutions have not addressed hostile online learning environments in any manner or setting other than faculty development workshops.

Electronic Surveillance. Software designers of online courseware add new features to each upgrade. Tracking mechanisms for student participation have gone from simple counting of "hits" on various locations within the virtual classroom to elaborately detailed surveillance systems. In a recent address to the Franke Institute for the Humanities, Andrew M. Rosenfield noted, "We know where you've been. We have the technological ability to figure out not only who's learned but who's learned quickly. We don't externalize that feature because we think that's private" (2001, 17). Not only are system administrators and faculty able to access these data for the purpose of improving instruction, but they may also use them to track utilization patterns by students throughout the day and night. This information was recently used at one institution as justification for not providing more comprehensive technical support because the "students are mostly stay-at-home moms; they can get online anytime" (Jeris 2001). In this case, both the content of the students' comments and the contribution patterns were appraised, a gender-based stereotype was assigned, and a resource allocation decision was made from information accessed without the students' knowledge or permission. An even more disturbing possibility is that this detailed information regarding an individual's participation pattern in an online course could wind up in the hands of someone who intends to use it for personally threatening or violent purposes. Although the information is password protected, the fact remains that the students are not informed of the depth and breadth of the surveillance.

Participation. Although factors that support or hinder women from participating in adult education are well documented (Merriam and Caffarella 1998), current enrollment data–gathering practices virtually preclude the possibility of this information reaching policy development conversations. Since 1995, adult part-time students have comprised over 50 percent of the for-credit enrollment in higher education (National Center for Education Statistics 2001). However, the major interest in tracking these statistics is to provide accurate counts of full-time equivalents (FTEs) for funding purposes. Hence, one FTE may be a composite statistic of three or four part-time adult students (the majority of whom are women). Rich information on race, class, and gender, along with reasons for participating in higher education, are of no interest to funding bodies at the state and federal levels.

An FTE is a unitary, deracinated, supposedly value-neutral signifier of enrollment. Given the recursive relationship between policy development and funding priorities, adult part-time students' diverse needs remain marginal to strategic needs analysis and planning within higher education. This bias is coupled with the reality that online instruction is an overwhelmingly adult education phenomenon in higher education because many institutions do not permit traditional-age undergraduates to enroll in online courses. The net effect is to provide borderless recruiting and enrollment regions, greatly expanding the number of potential adult students who can pay full tuition or are eligible for unsubsidized loans. Further, many corporations are reluctant to provide tuition reimbursement for online courses (Palloff and Pratt 1999, 34). For many women, this means that an attractive educational option that has the potential for removing some of the traditional barriers to participation (child care, family responsibilities, etc.) is beyond their reach financially.

Interaction Preferences. Online courses, particularly those that use asynchronous or threaded discussions as the primary interaction method, show promise for providing a more student-centered virtual space for learning. Teacher-researchers report that their course evaluations reveal numerous expressions of appreciation from students regarding the absence of competition for "air time," more confidence in their responses, and less worry about quick comebacks or disparaging remarks from male students (Alsgaard 2000; Daley 2000; Jeris 2001). In other words, the hierarchical structure of the teacher-centered traditional classroom that often places teachers at the helm, male students as second in command, and female students as the quiet audience for interactions between teachers and male students is modified online. Often, a key determinant of frequent and substantial contributions to discussions is keyboarding skills, and it is not unusual for women returning to higher education to be highly proficient in this area.

Freed from "twenty-five pairs of eyes" (Alsgaard 2000, 22), women in online courses actively construct meaning in the quiet of their homes or after hours at work. These familiar spaces, along with the students' appropriation of time for learning, set the stage for a qualitatively different experience. Women participate more often, at greater length, comment more frequently on other student's contributions, quote other students more in their papers, and communicate more frequently with instructors online than in traditional classrooms. They are also more likely to ask clarifying questions about assignments and negotiate assignment guidelines that allow them to adapt papers and projects to their life experiences and work-based needs (Alsgaard 2000; Jeris 2001). In short, virtual classrooms have the potential for empowering women as they seek information regarding course content and logistics.

Teaching Online

Not unlike their female students, women who teach online face many of the same challenges of renegotiating time and space for teaching, as well as the potential hazards of virtual classrooms, such as electronic surveillance and online harassment. Flexible schedules, home-based electronic access (often at personal expense), and reduced commuting time may relieve stress and provide time management options. However, the professional consequence of drastically reduced time spent on campus interacting with colleagues is a factor that should not be dismissed. Women who decide to develop and deliver online courses in higher education are often faced with a professional development predicament. Already beleaguered in successfully navigating the tenure process, the decision to teach online has the potential for placing untenured women professors at even greater risk.

Progress toward Tenure. According to the *Fall 1997 Staff Survey* of the Integrated Postsecondary Data System, of tenured full-time faculty nationwide, 72 percent are men and 28 percent are women. Given that 72 percent of all full-time faculty range from thirty to fifty-four years of age, women professors are building careers, working toward tenure, and raising children concurrently. Anne Keating (1999) documents the significant increase in development and delivery time for online courses, which is often unrecognized and unrewarded through the traditional tenure process. Not wanting to appear averse to educational innovations, untenured women professors may be at risk for taking on the time-intensive labor of online courses without realizing the long-term impact on their careers.

Although relationship building with colleagues may diminish, women who teach online are finding virtual classrooms a rich context for relationship building with students. Contrary to their initial expectations, screen-to-screen interaction is surprisingly intense, intellectually stimulating, and rewarding. However, factors that may interfere with positive interaction are abundant. These include the amount and type of technical support for students and teachers; the reliability of the network system; the learning curve, complexity, and reliability of course software packages and features; and the quality of faculty development for novice instructors of virtual classrooms.

Technical Support. The most disturbing words an online instructor ever hears are, "The system is down." Granted, circumstances arise that interfere with traditional classroom meetings, but many of those factors (except weather) are under faculty control, and they have time to plan alternatives. Not so with online courses. A complicating factor is that many institutions elect to do major upgrades and overhauls of systems during periods when many traditional undergraduates are not on campus, such as summer terms or holiday breaks. Typically, online courses do not adhere rigidly to the traditional academic calendar, so work-arounds, standby servers, and backup systems may be temporarily put in place to enable the online courses to continue during network maintenance. In addition, staff that normally provide technical support to online students and faculty may be diverted to work on network maintenance. Consequently, for significant periods, online courses may be poorly supported through human and technical resources. Moreover, many institutions are reluctant to provide 24-7 technical support to online faculty and students, although problem resolution is often available within twenty-four hours. Without question, these interruptions pose challenges for both men and women who are teaching and learning online, and research has yet to document a differential impact on men and women related to technical reliability and support. But if, in the course of a degree program, women take more online courses than men, or more women choose to teach online than men, then these resource allocation decisions may impede women students' progress in earning degrees or even women faculty's ability to gain tenure.

Instructional Support. Learning to teach online and learning to learn online are collaborative efforts among faculty, students, information system staff, and instructional support staff. Heretofore rigid boundaries around faculty and student rights and responsibilities must be renegotiated in ways that maintain the integrity of teaching and learning processes. Like many technological innovations, deployment is far ahead of policy development. Expediency, cost containment, and rapid change place technical experts in an authoritative role as key decisionmakers. They are the experts senior administrators turn to for input on institutional resource allocation decisions for both instructional and technical support. As a result, differential needs of adult learners based on gender, or any other group identity, for that matter, have yet to become central issues in the expansion of higher education through Internet-based courses.

Laurel Jeris

See also Part 4: Distance Education; Gender and Technology

References

Alsgaard, Melissa. 2000. "Digital Feminism: Reaching Women through Web-Based Courses." *Feminist Collections* 22, no. 1: 22–27.

Daley, Barbara J. 2000. "Learning Human Resource Development through Electronic Discussion." Pp. 25–31 in *Academy of Human Resource Development Conference Proceedings,* ed. K. Peter Kuchinke. Raleigh-Durham, NC: Academy of Human Resource Development.

Jeris, Laurel. 2001. "Comparison of Power Relations within Electronic and Face-to-Face Classroom Discussions: A Case Study." Paper presented at the annual meeting of the Adult Education Research Conference, Lansing, MI, June 1–3.

Keating, Anne B. 1999. *The Wired Professor: A Guide to Incorporating the World Wide Web in College Instruction.* New York: New York University Press.

Kramarae, Cheris. 1997. "Technology Policy, Gender, and Cyberspace." *Duke Journal of Gender Law and Policy* 4, no. 1: 149–158.

Merriam, Sharan B., and Rosemary S. Caffarella. 1998. *Learning in Adulthood.* 2nd ed. San Francisco: Jossey-Bass.

Miller, Ned. 2001. "The Politics of Access and Communication: Using Distance Learning Technologies." Pp. 187–205 in *Power in Practice: Adult Education and the Struggle for Knowledge and Power in Society,* ed. Ronald M. Cervero and Arthur L. Wilson. San Francisco: Jossey-Bass.

National Center for Education Statistics. 2001. *Digest of Education Statistics.* Washington, DC: U.S. Department of Education.

Palloff, Rena M., and Keith Pratt. 1999. *Building Learning Communities in Cyberspace: Effective Strategies for the Online Classroom.* San Francisco: Jossey-Bass.

Rosenfield, Andrew M. 2001. "The Online University." A lecture presented at the Franke Institute for the Humanities, February 12, 2001. Quoted in "Voices on the Quads," *University of Chicago Magazine* (April): 17. http://www.alumni.uchicago.edu/magazine. Cited October 24, 2001.

Medical Education

Since the 1960s, women medical student enrollees have increased from 6 to 8 percent of enrollees nationwide in U.S. medical academies to more than 40 percent of enrollees (Bickel, Galbraith, and Quinnie 1995). Since 1980, a medical curriculum based on didactic teaching and immersion in a hard science core has given way to student-centered instruction emphasizing problem-based learning and an integrated science curriculum. The profession and its training institutions have moved from an empiricist, paternalistic, and sovereign "world of power" to a consumer-oriented and pluralistic organization with ever-increasing diversification in its health care and heath maintenance options. Medical school curricula have moved from a strictly "science" model to include greater emphasis on applied behavioral sciences, the humanities, and patient-centered care (Stewart et al. 1995). As a result of the changes in the way doctors are trained, the hierarchical notion of the professional as expert and the patient as passive recipient has been challenged. Today, many health practitioners seek to empower the patient and to share decisionmaking with other health care practitioners, thus renouncing physicians' traditional control.

A major force behind maintaining medicine's traditional paradigm was the profession's exclusionary practices regarding race, social class, and gender. The high price of medical education maintained medicine's social uniformity by eliminating applicants from the lower and working classes. Deliberate policies against Jews, women, and people of color guaranteed social homogeneity and, therefore, strict control over medical training and medical practice. Women were not admitted to the nation's medical schools in appreciable numbers until the mid–twentieth century. Prior to the passage of Civil Rights Act in 1964, medical schools limited women enrollees to 5 percent of total student enrollment (Starr 1982).

With the inclusion of women into the medical profession, new ideas regarding how physicians are trained and the way in which medical care is provided have emerged. Traditional medical sovereignty has given way to patients' right to informed consent and their right to refuse treatment. Doctors and hospitals, once free to override patient preferences, now must share medical information as well as decisionmaking authority with patients. Female physicians have demanded that male physicians change both their attitudes and traditional institutional practices, and these demands have resulted in new rules of professional behavior and practice as well as new ways to train future physicians. Under the new rules, medical students now can choose from a variety of instructional and curricular formats. Problem-based learning is replacing traditional didactic teaching, tutoring in the ambulatory care unit has replaced bedside teaching on hospital wards, and continuity clinics are replacing standard clinical rotations (Peterson et al. 1980).

Women in Medicine: The First Wave

The history of women in American medicine is a tale of both inclusion and exclusion. In colonial America, most medical care was provided by women in the home. Women were prominent lay practitioners in childbearing activities; in some areas of the country, medical practice belonged almost entirely to women as late as 1818. By the Jacksonian period, however, women no longer held as dominant a position in lay medical practice. Furthermore, women confronted opposition if they attempted to join the emerging professional medical practice (Kett 1968).

In the 1840s, the work of the suffragists and a growing feminist movement created opportunities for women to receive formal medical training separate from but equal to male physicians. Boston's New England Medical College, founded in 1848, was the world's first medical school exclusively for women (Walsh 1977). Nonetheless, the establishment of gender-segregated medical schools did little to change the established exclusionary practices of the professional medical associations. Almost all practicing physicians were opposed to the admission of women into the profession, and the policy of existing medical societies was strict ostracism (Shyrock 1966).

By the mid-1800s, the nation had seventeen female medical colleges. Competition among small private medical schools as well as academically weak medical departments in some universities opened opportunities for women medical students. Some less successful university-affiliated medical schools actively recruited women medical students in an effort to increase school revenue. Nonetheless, women in the nineteenth century were not satisfied to be accepted only in second-rate proprietary schools or gender-segregated schools. In 1893, women's struggle for admission to the country's elite medical schools was accomplished when Johns Hopkins University agreed to accept women medical students in exchange for a $500,000 endowment contributed by wealthy women (DeAngelis 1999).

Johns Hopkins University's women's endowment committee, known as the Women's Fund Committee, attached certain conditions to the gift, including the agreement to accept women on the same basis that men were accepted, as opposed to admitting equal numbers of men and women. M. Carey Thomas, dean and later president of Bryn Mawr College, was the individual behind the stipulations attached to the endowment. Her requirements maintained that entering students have a full college degree, coursework in biology, chemistry, and physics, and the ability to read French and German (DeAngelis 1999).

Elizabeth Blackwell was the first woman in the United States to graduate with a medical degree (U.S. National Library of Medicine)

Enrollment statistics from 1893 indicate that women represented 10 percent or more of the students at nineteen coeducational medical schools. Between 1880 and 1900, the percentage of women doctors increased nationally. In the nation's large cities, women physicians were even more prevalent. In late-nineteenth-century Boston, women comprised more than 18 percent of practicing physicians, in Minneapolis more than 19 percent, and in San Francisco almost 14 percent (Starr 1982).

The private and weak university-affiliated medical schools had been training grounds for many women physicians, but these schools suffered greatly from medical education reform efforts in the United States. By the turn of the twentieth century, only three out of the original seventeen female medical colleges existed. Because of economic problems and the closing of so many medical schools, the number of women medical students declined by 65 percent. By 1920, medicine had grown more uniform in its social composition. Increased medical education costs, more stringent requirements limiting student applications from the working classes, and deliberate policies banning Jews, women, and blacks enabled medicine to become the sole domain of white, male, upper-class Americans (Starr 1982).

Women in Medicine: The Second Wave

By the mid–twentieth century, the exclusion of women and minorities by the medical profession had become part of American culture. In the United States, however, the role of the judiciary in interpreting the Constitution encourages the dissatisfied to organize in social movements and to present their demands as a claim under the Bill of Rights. Over time, the appropriate legislative body articulates such claims into constitutional amendments. Unlike civil laws or rules and regulations that limit specific behaviors, constitutional amendments dismantle and rebuild the structures that form the basis of existing culture.

The particular form of social activism found in the United States has been successful in breaking through barriers of the most sovereign institutions, including medicine. The U.S. civil rights movement advocated the rights of women, children, students, tenants, gays, Chicanos, Native Americans, black Americans, and welfare clients. Medicine, medical care, and medical education figured prominently in the nation's generalization of rights, particularly as a concern by the women's movement. As a result of these movements, female enrollees in the nation's medical schools rose from 6 to 8 percent of students in 1960 to more than 40 percent of students by the mid-1990s (Dickstein 1996).

The second wave of women in medicine began in the mid-1960s, following the passage of the Civil Rights Act. The nation's growing social consciousness led to a renewed interest in health care as a matter of right, not privilege. Hospitals that accepted federal funds were now obligated to provide charity care. Newly articulated health rights issues ushered in policies addressing an individual's right to make informed consent, refuse treatment, access personal medical records, participate in therapeutic decisions, and receive due process for involuntary commitment to mental institutions.

Patients' rights policies now obligated doctors and hospitals to share medical information and decisionmaking authority with their patients, thus challenging the solidification of power and expertise within the profession. Since the Progressive era (about 1890 to 1920), reformers had assumed that professionals would always act in the interest of those they were trying to help. By the 1970s, however, reformers had become skeptical of professionals and the institutions they supervised, and nowhere was the distrust of professional domination more apparent than in the women's movement. Feminists claimed that as patients, nurses, and other health care providers, they were denied the right to participate in medical decisions. Paternalistic doctors, they claimed, refused to share information or take women's intelligence seriously. Feminists further claimed that much of what passed for scientific knowledge was sexist prejudice and that male physicians had deliberately excluded women from medical competence by keeping them out of medical schools and suppressing alternative medical practitioners such as midwives (Starr 1982).

An equally striking change took place in the consciousness of contemporary women physicians. The older generation of women physicians felt they had to prove they could be successful in medicine on the dominant males' terms. In contrast, the new feminist physician demanded that male physicians change their attitudes and modify institutional practices to accommodate their needs as women.

Women Leaders' Influence in Academic Medicine

The inclusion of women in medical practice and in the medical academy is connected to feminist influences in political movements, social activism, and medical practice. The core of the feminist movement is the search for women's voice. In regard to medicine, the feminist "voice" advocates an ethic of care, nurturance, and compassion.

Feminists and women academic physicians ushered in a revival of therapeutic counterculture similar to the medical counterculture of the nineteenth century. Folk, non-Western, and novel therapies gained clientele and respectability. The medical counterculture went under the rubric of "holistic medicine" and presented itself as a humane alternative to an overly technical, disease-oriented, and impersonal medical system. Just as nineteenth-century medicine advocated therapeutic dissent, twentieth-century technological medicine gave way to pressure for a democratization of medical knowledge and self-care advocacy. Left-wing advocates from feminists to neo-Marxists linked national health insurance and community-lay participation on health service boards with individual patient rights. The issue was professional dominance, and the aim of the new social consciousness was to increase the power of the consumer (Starr 1982).

A new medical consciousness shaped intellectual developments in medical ethics, medical education, and medical sociology. Traditionally, medical policy was the exclusive domain of physicians, but the civil rights movement and the accompanying women's movement gave voice to philosophers, attorneys, sociologists-historians, and feminists. These new voices portrayed the medical profession as a dominating, monopolizing, self-interested force. Furthermore, these voices for change have been instrumental in shaping new roles for physicians and new methods of health care delivery (Starr 1982).

Academic medicine has a long and powerful history and is supported by a profession that maintains profound opposition to change. Until the mid-1990s, the medical curriculum maintained its traditional teaching methods, course content, and specialized treatment of disease that seemed incompatible with the feminist notion of individual autonomy, patient-centered care, and interdisciplinary patient care teams (Enarson and Burg 1992).

For the first time in American history, women have advanced to positions of power in academic medicine. As a critical mass of women physician faculty take their place in U.S. medical academies, they provide a foundation of support that allows women deans, department chairs, and program directors to lead from a woman's perspective.

Twenty-first-century women physicians are composites of egalitarian principles and the product of a role-liberating society. As a group, women physicians are more aware of home and community as sources to be tapped. They are more amenable to the fusion of preventive and clinical services in patient care, less inclined to substitute technical procedures for human services, and more discerning of the essence of the complicated hurt that brings patients to health care personnel (Bluestone 1978). As leaders, women physician faculty support a liberating educational environment. Student-centered curricula, a sense of connectedness among faculty and students, mutual respect at all levels of the academic organization, and an educational purpose that supports personal discovery and connected knowing characterize the feminist-led, twenty-first-century medical academy.

Kay Beaver

See also Part 6: Graduate and Professional Education; Graduate Students

References and further reading

Bickel, Janet. 1995. *Women in U.S. Academic Medicine: Statistics.* Washington, DC: Association of American Medical Colleges.

Bluestone, Naomi. 1978. "The Future Impact of Women on American Medicine." *American Journal of Public Health* 68: 760–763.

DeAngelis, Catherine D., ed. 1999. *The Johns Hopkins University School of Medicine Curriculum for the Twenty-First Century.* Baltimore: Johns Hopkins University Press.

Dickstein, Leah J. 1996. "Overview of Women Physicians in the United States." Pp. 3–10 in *Women in Medical Education: An Anthology of Experience,* ed. Delese Ware. Albany: State University of New York Press.

Enarson, Cam, and Frederic Burg. 1992. "An Overview of Reform Initiatives in Medical Education: 1906 through 1992." *Journal of the American Medical Association* 268: 1141–1143.

Kett, Joseph F. 1968. *The Formation of the American Medical Profession: The Role of Institutions, 1780–1860.* New Haven, CT: Yale University Press.

Peterson, E. S., A. E. Crowley, J. Rosenthal, and R. Boerner. 1980. "Undergraduate Medical Education." *Journal of the American Medical Association* 244: 2810–2868.

Shryock, Richard H. 1966. "Sylvester Graham and the Popular Health Movement, 1830–1870." Pp. 111–125 in *Medicine in America: Historical Essays,* ed. Richard H. Shryock. Baltimore: Johns Hopkins University Press.

Starr, Paul. 1982. *The Social Transformation of American Medicine.* New York: Basic Books.

Stewart, Moira, Judith B. Brown, Wayne W. Weston, Ian R. McWhinney, Carol L. McWilliam, and Thomas R. Freeman. 1995. *Patient-Centered Medicine: Transforming the Clinical Method.* Thousand Oaks, CA: Sage.

Tong, Rosemarie. 1997. *Feminist Approaches to Bioethics: Theoretical Reflections and Practical Applications.* Boulder, CO: Westview Press.

Walsh, Mary Roth. 1977. *Doctors Wanted: No Women Need Apply.* New Haven, CT: Yale University Press.

Physical Education

Physical education for women in higher education has been a combination of ideas and practices derived from medical and social understandings of the female body, from the ever-developing notions about the purposes of higher education for women, and from the administrative and political acumen of women leaders within higher education.

Throughout the nineteenth century, arguments were made for and against involving women in any form of physical exertion. For example, Emma Hart Willard (1787–1870), founder of the Troy Female Seminary, Catharine Beecher (1800–1878), founder of the Hartford Female Seminary, and Mary Lyon (1797–1849), founder of Mount Holyoke Seminary, each established important institutions of higher learning to prepare women to be teachers. A major component of the curriculum at these institutions included physical education. These nineteenth-century leaders wrote convincingly about the necessity of regular exercise for bodily health and sharpness of thought. For example, Catharine Beecher's *Physiology and Calisthenics for Schools and Families* (1856) directly connected physical education to public health issues and to strengthening the republic. Beecher believed that women were the moral guardians of the country and that they were obligated to stay healthy to fulfill their domestic responsibilities. German and Swedish gymnastics grounded the curriculum of the female seminaries. The students took daily walks, participated in calisthenics, and performed strenuous domestic work.

These curricular developments were happening in the midst of vigorous debates about the harmful effects of physical education for women, not to mention the challenges to conventional notions of femininity. In 1873 these debates were renewed when Dr. Edward Clarke instilled fear in the general public with his pronouncement that women who studied college subjects reduced their capability to reproduce. It would take the collective effort of women scientists such as physiologist Clelia Mosher (1863–1940), physical educators such as Amy Morris Homans (1848–1933) and Mabel Lee (1886–1985), and others studying the experiences of educated women to counter these claims.

In the mid–nineteenth century, growing numbers of women were completing higher education programs that prepared them to be physical education teachers in the public schools, as well as university professors focusing on women's physiology, women's health, and physical education for women. Physical education, as a field, was bringing women into professional positions within colleges and universities. Historians Geraldine Clifford (in *Lone Voyagers*) and Joan S. Hult (in "The Governance of Athletics") each have identified some of the earliest female faculty within coeducational institutions of higher education as physical educators, broadly defined. For example, in the 1870s and 1880s, women faculty were hired to direct a college gymnasium and teach gymnastics and calisthenics and often were named the dean of women. As early as 1885, a physical education curriculum was present in all women's colleges in the East, and "sports for women" were organized in many colleges and universities in the Midwest. These conditions led to expanded roles for women hired to direct women's physical education on college campuses. For example, at Syracuse University in the early twentieth century, Katherine Sibley had a dual appointment of professor of physical education and hygiene and president of the Women's Athletic Association. In 1918 the physical education department at Syracuse University was created under the direction of Sibley, who remained in the director's position until her retirement in 1950. In 1919 the first class of women "phys-ed majors" graduated from Syracuse University. By 1922, the bachelor of science degree was awarded to those completing a four-year course in physical education, and certificates were given to students completing a two-year sequence in physical education. In 1922, nineteen bachelor's degrees in physical education were earned by women.

Although women faculty and administrators were entering coeducational institutions in greater numbers during the first half of the twentieth century, vigorous debates continued about the role of physical education for women. Originally, the attainment of muscular strength was the goal for women in physical education courses. By the late 1890s and 1900s, games were introduced into programs, although they were viewed by some as a deviation from the programs' rigor and seriousness. According to Dorothy S. Ainsworth, the director of physical education at Smith College in the 1940s, "With the changes brought in by the modern education method between 1910 and 1920 physical educators now are concerned with not merely the physical (muscular and organic well being) but all sides of the human being. No longer have we done our duty if we produce a muscular and organic marvel. In fact, the fear that we may produce muscles is rather against us" (*Report of Symposium* 1940).

On the national level, professional organizations were gaining strength and started building an agenda for how college and university physical education programs ought to be focused. For example, the slogans "A sport for every girl" and "Every girl in a sport" represented the ideals that guided the Committee on Women's Athletics and the National Section of Women's Athletics (NSWA). In the 1920s and 1930s, the argument made by members of both organizations was that athletic opportunities needed to be available for all girls and women, not just a select few who would be competing against another select few. Competition between women was not completely disdained, as in earlier times. Rather, criticism was directed at the type of organizational structures that eliminated the vast majority of females from participation in the name of improved competition. This debate echoed other debates within higher education that addressed the tension between those who believed that the purpose of higher education was to identify and support the elite (in this case the most athletically talented) and those who advocated reducing competition in favor of wider participation.

Understanding the power of organization, women physical educators knew that they would need to be a stronger entity in the American Physical Education Association if they were to effectively fight the "elitism and exploitation" that had come to characterize men's athletics and was beginning to creep into women's athletics (Hult 1985). The *Sport Guides,* published by the NSWA in the 1930s, were meant to help create quality standards that would be embraced by the larger profession. The *Guides* included skill development, coaching strategies, techniques of officiating, and direct and implied statements of belief regarding what values should occur from sports, as well as problems to be avoided. Joan Hult understood the *Guides* to be powerful tools to educate and persuade readers to accept a new authoritative organization whose purpose was to guide and direct all activities related to each sport in which women participated. The *Guides* were widely used by women physical educators.

Professional alliances between women faculty and women administrators at institutions of higher education were also strengthening the 1930s and 1940s. For example, Eunice Hilton, the dean of women at Syracuse University, specifically advocated for a professional alliance between deans of women and physical educators that would position them as a united front working for the best in curriculum, services, and policies for women students, as well as for the best working conditions for women faculty and administrators. This alliance would prepare deans of women to speak on behalf of the physical educators of women when matters of policy were being discussed. This suggestion implies that policies influencing physical educators of women and their programs could be shaped by deans of women, who were often consulted regarding what other women employees at the institution should be doing. Hilton called the director of physical education the "chief ally of the dean of women," indicating that she perceived the relationship as mutual, but recognized the political reality that on most campuses, deans of women carried more clout with the administration than physical educators did. Hilton points out: "General education has not paid much attention to physical education, which has suffered a long time from the departmentalization in modern colleges and universities. Set off by itself, often without devices for integrating the various courses properly with the total academic program, frequent difficulties have arisen" (*Report of Symposium* 1940). Physical educators did not perceive Hilton as an outsider giving advice but rather an insider sharing strategy and wisdom about carrying out an effective plan for change. This example of collaboration was representative of many efforts underway on college and university campuses.

Women were organizing to promote inclusion of physical education for women at all levels of education. The power of women's organizations to affect the curriculum at institutions of higher education has been evident throughout the history of higher education. For example, as early as 1885 the American Association for the Advancement of Physical Education gathered professionals in the fields of education, public health, and medicine. In the early part of the twentieth century, the National Association for Physical Education of College Women (NAPECW) was organized. In her 1986 biography of Amy Morris Homans, the widely recognized leader of physical education for women, Betty Spears notes that NAPECW was the first organization that brought together women physical educators working at the collegiate level. Although focusing on preparing college physical educators, NAPECW often relied on the publications produced by NSWA, a precursor to today's National Association of Girls and Women in Sport (NAGWS). These organizations and others regularly shaped the norms of the profession.

World War II altered the physical education curriculum at institutions of higher education. Linking educational reforms for women to the larger national, democratic agenda was considered an effective strategy in the 1940s. Physical educators on college campuses were called on by the leaders of their professional organizations to assist the country's defense program. For example, with the guidance of the NSWA's "War Time Credo," special training, sports, and recreation programs were designed for the U.S. Army Air Forces female personnel; public service announcements were created emphasizing the need for the women of the country to participate in exercise and recreational programs in the midst of serving the war effort; and women physical educators turned to other female campus leaders, such as deans of women, for advice regarding safeguarding women's programs.

Another emerging dimension of the physical education curriculum for women increasingly included recreational sports and, later, intercollegiate competitive athletics. Certainly with the passage of Title IX of the Education Amendments of 1972, leaders in higher education faced questions of equity within the curriculum and within athletic programs. A significant part of the history of physical education can be located in the tensions that emerged between the Association of Intercollegiate Athletics for Women (AIAW) and the National Collegiate Athletic Association (NCAA). When the NCAA subsumed the AIAW, many women leaders within higher education were directly affected. Mergers almost always resulted in women losing authority as they were demoted from director positions to assistant director positions reporting to the male athletic director.

Thalia M. Mulvihill

See also Part 6: Growth of Women's Athletics; Women Athletes

References and further reading

Ainsworth, Dorothy. 1975. *The History of Physical Education in Colleges for Women (USA).* New York: Barnes.

Bouchier, Nancy B. 1998. "Let Us Take Care of Our Field: The National Association for Physical Education of College Women and World War II." *Journal of Sport History* 25(1): 64–85.

Clifford, Geraldine J. 1989. *Lone Voyagers.* New York: The Feminist Press.

Hult, Joan. 1985. "The Governance of Athletics for Girls and Women: Leadership by Women Physical Educators." *Research Quarterly for Exercise and Sport,* Centennial Issue (April).

Lee, Mabel. 1983. *A History of Physical Education and Sports in the USA.* New York: John Wiley and Sons.

Mulvihill, Thalia M. 2000. "The Extended Influence of Dean M. Eunice Hilton and Katherine Sibley: A Case Study of the Collegial Integration of Programs for Women University Students, 1930s–1950s." *Initiatives* 59 (Fall).

Report of Symposium for Deans of Women and Directors of Physical Education. Topic: Integration of the Student Program from the Points of View of the Dean, the Personnel Officer, and the Director of Physical Education. 1940. Under the Auspices of Eastern Association of the Directors of Physical Education for College Women. October 11–12. American Woman's Club, New York City. George Arents Research Library, M. Eunice Hilton Collection, Box 17, p. 8.

Spears, Betty. 1986. *Leading the Way: Amy Morris Homans and the Beginnings of Professional Education for Women.* New York: Greenwood Press.

Teacher Education

The historical development of women as teacher-educators in the United States illustrates the transition of a woman's place from the domestic sphere to the public sphere. Certain historical circumstances supported this transition. The present status of women as teacher-educators is largely an effect of its historical development.

Before European settlement, women were long accepted as educators in many Native American tribes. In fact, one of the problems that the Founding Fathers had with Native Americans was the degree of authority exercised by Native American women within the tribal structure.

In 1637 Governor John Winthrop banished Anne Hutchinson from her New England community of Newton for teaching her ideas to the adult members of the community. Her crime was not teaching but that she was teaching adults. At that time, dame schooling was a generally accepted practice in New England. Women conducted dame schools in their homes, where they taught letters and sums to young children. This arrangement allowed women to stay safely in their own homes and fit society's perception of them as nurturers of young children. Therefore, it was not Hutchinson's act of teaching that was criminal, nor the place in which she taught, but rather whom she taught. Anne Hutchinson was guilty of sharing her learning and thoughts with other adults. The authorities deemed her a criminal and unfit for human society for doing so. Before women could safely teach adults in higher education, societal conceptions of women's appropriate place had to be transformed.

Three events ushered in by the common school movement brought about the conditions whereby women assumed the role of teacher-educators. The first was acceptance of the idea that women be employed to teach children in public places rather than their homes. The second event was the requirement of formal preparation or training for women who wished to become teachers, which also required the development of teacher colleges (initially, normal schools). The third was the acceptance of women as teacher-educators within these public institutions of higher education. Horace Mann, Cyril Peirce, Catharine Beecher, Henry Barnard, and other New Englanders promoted the common school movement during the early nineteenth century. The 1840s and 1850s heralded the movement's first attempts to create a state-supported school system.

Founders of the state-supported school systems desired to ameliorate or prevent problems in society by reforming public education. The common school movement supported the idea that male and female children of all socioeconomic statuses in the United States—race was not addressed—should attend free public schools taught by well-trained teachers. Such an educational reform sought to address several societal concerns at that time: (1) form a common American of good character, (2) be the great equalizer of opportunity, (3) increase the wealth of all, and (4) prevent social conflict. Among the strategies to achieve this goal was the proposal that the teaching force become largely female. This decision is often referred to the feminization of the teaching profession.

Arguments for a female teaching faculty included the following: Because of their natural inclination to nurture, women were better with children than men. In addition, having women teach provided a role for the excess numbers of single women caused by the largely male migration to the West and later by the Civil War. Finally, because women would accept lower wages than men, the public could afford many more teachers. The foregoing arguments were useful for developing societal acceptance of women as public school teachers, but they had unfortunate consequences. The first argument settled women ever more firmly into the role of emotional nurturers and excluded women from the role of scholar. The second argument resulted in the stereotype of the spinster schoolmarm. Finally, the third argument set the precedent for the present second-class status of teaching, in terms of both pay and valuation.

These arguments gained credibility, and thus the feminization of teaching occurred, first in the northeastern United States and then in the South and West. Catharine Beecher makes note that in 1848, five out of seven teachers in Massachusetts were women, but only one out of six teachers in Kentucky were female (Hoffman 1981, 45). In 1850, 60 percent of

Maria Montessori was one of the first female innovators of teacher training methods (Library of Congress)

the nation's teachers were women. By 1900, the proportion had risen to 70 percent and by 1910 to 80 percent (Ransom 1988, 22).

Initially, the women hired as teachers were mostly white. There was about a fifty-year lag before women of other ethnic groups were included. Patricia Carter, an educational historian, notes that in 1890, fewer than 4 percent of the nations teachers were black women, whereas between 1890 and 1900 the number of black women teachers increased by 72 percent. Furthermore, the feminization of teaching occurred at an even greater rate among blacks than it did among whites. Carter indicates that in 1890, there were approximately equal numbers of black men and women paid to teach—7,864 women and 7,236 men. However, by 1910, women had filled over two-thirds (or 29,772) of all the teaching positions held by blacks (Carter 1992, 134). The same pattern held among other minorities as well. In 1890 there were only ten women teachers who were of American Indian or Asian American descent, but by 1900 this number climbed to 255 (Carter 1992, 134).

The large influx of women during the middle of the nineteenth century stamped teaching as a woman's profession. Because women were considered to be inferior and subordinate to men at that time, the profession of teaching was stamped as inferior and subordinate to professions such as law, theology, or medicine. Such a reputation lingers today.

The proliferation of women as professors of normal schools followed a later but similar progression. The first normal school (school for the training of teachers) opened in 1839 in Massachusetts. Twenty-five young women composed the first cohort of students. Cyril Peirce and visiting professors (all male) taught the classes. The 1840s and 1850s saw the establishment of normal schools in Ohio, Illinois, Iowa, and Wisconsin.

Women faculty entered public higher education largely through traditionally "female" professions of nursing, home economics, and teacher education. For example, Agnes Fay Morgan, one of the few women to earn a Ph.D. in organic chemistry prior to 1915, could only gain employment as a faculty member in the area of home economics at Berkeley. If a woman wanted to be a "professor," her best chance lay in those disciplines, such as teacher education, that had been deemed feminine. By 1900, 63.4 percent of the faculty members of teachers' colleges were women. This statistic contrasts vividly with the meager 7.9 percent of faculty members that were women in other public institutions of higher education (Graham 1978).

As in teaching itself, the feminization of teacher education faculty had the effect of creating a second-class status for the profession—a status that continues today in terms of both valuation and pay. In addition, when research began to assume the same status as teaching within public institutions of teacher education, a corresponding drop in the percentage of women faculty occurred, so that by 1950 only 44.9 percent (Graham 1978) of the faculty of teachers' colleges was female, a drop of 18.5 percent from the high of 1900. As the emphasis on nurturing others through teaching became de-emphasized, faculty positions were seen as inappropriate for women, according to historians such as Patricia Graham.

The largest percentage of female full-time higher education faculty is still found in teacher education. The National Center for Education Statistics (NCES) reports that in 1998, women comprised 54.1 percent of the full-time teacher education faculty. This statistic compares favorably to the average percentage of women employed by other disciplines, which is 28.2 percent, as indicated by NCES (2001, 27). Unfortunately, this feminization still results in a subordinate status for those in this discipline. For example, the average salary of full-time faculty in education is $58,527, third from the lowest among the disciplines. The two disciplines ranking lower are humanities and fine arts, also considered to be somewhat feminized disciplines. Additionally, the average teacher education faculty salary compares quite unfavorably to the average salary of other disciplines, which is $72,570 (NCES 2001, 46).

Yet even in the feminized discipline of teacher education, women still operate at a disadvantage. In part, this disadvantage results from lingering stereotypes of women as nurturers rather than as scholars that limit their progression through the professorial ranks in colleges of education. In part, the discrepancy results from the conflict that women experience between fulfilling their role as nurturers (as exemplified by the time put into service and teaching) and publishing their research. Finally, women face difficulty in being accepted as serious professionals in academia because of conflicts in expected interactional styles. When women act in the hesitant passive manner of "traditional women," they are seen as nonserious, but when they act as men do, they are seen as cold and heartless. At this time, there is apparently no "correct" interactional style for a woman in academia. These barriers result in fewer hires and slower promotion of women faculty.

The obstacles faced by women who are teacher-educators are revealed by the proportion of women found in the different ranks of academia. Several studies have shown that women are more likely than men to be at the lowest ranks in colleges of education and that men are more likely than women to be at the highest rank in colleges of education. Furthermore, men are far more likely to be deans of colleges of education than are women. However, these discrepancies are less glaring in colleges of education than in disciplines such as math and science.

Where once women were considered criminals for teaching adults, they now are accepted as professors in public institutions of higher education. Teaching and later teacher education provided an avenue for women to enter into higher education. Unfortunately, the very feminization of these professions in a society that saw women as inferior to men in all but nurturing qualities ensured that teaching and teacher education would assume a second-class status among other professions and disciplines in higher education. Furthermore, even though it is a highly feminized profession, women still do not advance within it to the same degree that men do. This latter phenomenon is caused by lingering stereotypes about women that present barriers for both tenure and promotion. Yet these stereotypes little by little are losing their hold upon society, and in some institutions, an equal playing ground for men and women exists in the field of teacher education.

Felecia M. Briscoe and
Linda C. Pacifici

See also Part 7: Disciplinary Socialization; Socialization

References and further reading

Aisenberg, Nadya, and Mona Harrington. 1988. *Women of Academe: Outsiders in the Sacred Grove.* Amherst: University of Massachusetts Press.

Carter, Patricia. 1992. "Social Status of Women Teachers." Pp. 127–138 in *The Teacher's Voice: A Social History of Teaching in Twentieth-Century America,* ed. Richard J. Althenbaugh. London: Falmer Press.

Graham, Patricia A. 1978. "Expansion and Exclusion: A History of Women in American Higher Education." *Signs* 3: 759–773.

Hoffman, Nancy. 1981. *Woman's "True" Profession: Voices from the History of Teaching.* New York: The Feminist Press.

National Center for Education Statistics. 2001. "Background Characteristics, Work, Activities, and Compensation of Faculty, Staff in Postsecondary Institutions: Fall 1998." Washington, DC: U.S. Department of Education.

Ransom, Nancy A. 1988. "A Comparative History of Faculty Women at George Peabody College for Teachers and Vanderbilt University, 1875–1970." Ph.D. diss., George Peabody College for Teachers of Vanderbilt University, Nashville, TN.

Transformation of the Curriculum

The collegiate curriculum in the United States is a dynamic and adaptive course of study spanning a panoply of academic disciplines and areas of intellectual inquiry. From the nascence of American higher education, the curriculum has represented the zeitgeist of educational philosophy and has evolved in tandem with the combined influences of historical events, popular sentiment, and governmental intervention. In its original manifestation, the curricular aim of higher education was rigidly focused upon the preparation of young men of character for the ministry or the learned professions, such as law or medicine. The contemporary American college curriculum has weathered numerous shifts in educational philosophy, often controversially, and currently embodies a broad spectrum of study tailored to the missions of the various institution types and myriad program requirements subsumed within postsecondary education in the United States. At present, the curriculum includes a number of areas of study that were previously given little consideration or outright ignored by academia, including women's studies. The female collegiate experience has evolved steadily during the course of the history of American higher education, from the very early programs of study focused specifically for women through coeducation and into the twenty-first century. Programs of women's studies are now an established part of the collegiate curriculum, marking a distinct shift in curricular theory from the days when colleges offered courses for women rather than about them.

The history of the curriculum in higher education began with the founding of Harvard College in 1636, which was established to educate a pious and learned future clergy as well as young men of status who were destined to assume positions of public leadership (Lucas 1994, 104). This dual mission of educating clergymen and future civic leaders was shared by other colonial colleges, for which the curriculum, a hybrid of arts and religious studies, was also a faithful rendering of the studies pursued at Oxford and Cambridge Universities by promoters of higher education in the new world (Foster 1911). The rudimentary subjects required in the education of an erudite young man were Greek and Latin, and all academicians embraced the notion that a foundation in the classics was essential to professional or ecclesiastical success. In the 1700s, new subjects were added to the curriculum, including modern languages, mathematics, literature, and natural sciences, but the emphasis remained upon classical training in colonial colleges. Indeed, the curriculum endured for 200 years as a uniform program of liberal arts and was emulated by nearly all liberal arts colleges that emerged over the course of the 1800s (Lucas 1994, 109–110).

By the late 1700s, a curricular question arose as to whether higher education was focused too stringently on classical education and was not providing proper coverage of subjects considered more practical to daily life (Brubacher and Rudy 1976, 101). During this period, many institutions experimented with the curriculum by including a number of scientifically oriented subjects as a supplement to the required liberal arts subject matter. In 1824, for example, Thomas Jefferson experimented with allowing students to choose among different courses offered through eight specialized units or schools, an idea that garnered close scrutiny from proponents of enlarging the curriculum. Controversy over the proper course of study to be pursued dominated higher education during the 1800s (Lucas 1994, 131–132).

In 1827, President Jeremiah Day of Yale University, in response to the movement for curricular reform, selected a committee of college fellows to draft a position paper that ultimately addressed a broad range of educational issues. The document, which became known as the Yale Report upon its publication in 1828, was a defense of classical learning and quickly became the most widely read and influential pronouncement on education of the time. The Yale Report acknowledged that the traditional education system was imperfect and should remain open to improvement but suggested that a college education should be directed to the larger task of establishing a foundation of learning common to all endeavors and that professional studies should commence upon one's entrance into a profession (Hofstadter and Smith 1961). Conservatives were greatly heartened by so forthright a defense of traditional learning, and classicists felt vindicated in opposing demands for more popular and practical learning. Many hailed the Yale Report as the definitive statement on the nature and purpose of a liberal arts education. The report, however, brought no conclusion to the heated argument over the collegiate curriculum—that debate was to continue unchecked throughout the nineteenth century and into the next (Rudolph 1962, 131–135).

Antebellum institutions of higher learning for women were scant in number at best and represented little more than "finishing schools" focused on the development of refined young women suitable for the domestic life. Elmira Female College, which began conferring degrees in 1859, provided a signpost for other women's institutions to follow and predated the foundation of numerous women's colleges in the 1870s, such as Smith, Vassar, and Wellesley (Lucas 1994, 154–158). Women's colleges had a significant impact in the South and East, where the influence of the prestigious all-male institutions and local predisposition for single-sex education precluded women from enjoying coeducational higher education until the 1900s. Women's colleges offered unique institutional structures and traditions distinct from their male counterparts, and founders argued that their schools met the demand for women's higher education without detriment to the feminine persona. Young women, according to this philosophy, were afforded the opportunity to strengthen their minds at women's colleges without becoming similar to men (Gordon 1997).

Also crucial to the advancement of women in American higher education was the movement toward coeducation at formerly exclusively male institutions. Popular sentiment had long dictated that women were unfit for serious academic pursuits—indeed, it was thought that too much strain on the female mind would render a woman unfit for her role as wife and mother. The movement was irrepressible, however, and the earliest advances took place in the midwestern land grant institutions, beginning in the 1850s. By 1880, almost one-third of colleges had adopted a modest form of coeducation, and three-fourths of institutions were coeducational by 1900 (Lucas 1994, 156). Proponents of coeducation argued that the two sexes coexist throughout life in familial and social contexts, and therefore the notion of coeducation was not as unnatural as the creation of academic monasteries and nunneries for an arbitrary four-year segment of human life (Sill 1972). Though the experience of women on the campus was often disparate from the one afforded men, they were at least given the opportunity to engage in higher education in a forum previously unavailable.

In the postbellum period, the outcome of decades of turmoil supplanted the quaint "old-time" college with the model of the modern university. Accelerating industrialization and urbanization, development of new scientific and technological knowledge upon which business and industry relied, and growth in capital from the accumulated fortunes of industrial entrepreneurs and business magnates were contributing factors to the movement to restructure higher education. A major theme in discussions of the university during this period turned on the pragmatism of knowledge and the importance of creating a nexus between academic theory and professional practice. The clear tendency in higher education throughout the last quarter of the nineteenth century was to embrace the demand for more utilitarian learning (Lucas 1994, 142–146).

The dissatisfaction with the traditional liberal arts education and the resulting movement toward more utilitarian learning was manifest in the development of the land grant college (Brubacher and Rudy 1976, 62–64). The establishment of nonsectarian state institutions originated prior to the Civil War, but virtually all such institutions lacked the characteristics later associated with universities. Federal land grants provided significant opportunity for founding state land grant colleges, but the federal land grants were insufficient to maintain college operations. The Morrill Acts of 1862 and 1890 established the funding to "promote the liberal and practical education of the industrial classes in the several pursuits and professions of life," and the resulting public institutions became a source of civic pride and progress in the community (Lucas 1994, 147–153). The land grant colleges were the first institutions to embrace an applied and practical curriculum, undergirding the shift away from classical liberal learning, and to embody the nonelitist notion that every American could receive some form of postsecondary education (DeVane 1965).

In 1869, Charles Eliot's inaugural address as president of Harvard made again salient the controversy in academia regarding the nature and substance of the academic curriculum, when he embraced the elective curriculum as a means of reform (Rudolph 1977, 135–138). Under his leadership, students would have more freedom to select from among different classes and courses of study, and he suggested that the elective system would foster scholarship by giving freedom to natural preferences and predilections toward areas of study (Carnochan 1993). Conservatives found this idea unpalatable, and the controversy endured unabated through the end of the twentieth century, even as the elective principle took hold in higher learning. The idea of a disciplinary hegemony began to be replaced by the philosophy that no academic discipline should outweigh any other in importance.

Throughout the last third of the 1800s, the issue of which factors constituted distinguishing characteristics between a college and a university remained in dispute, though there was a gradual genesis of popular sentiment. The university attracted larger enrollments, offered a broader array of subjects of study, was more professional and utilitarian in orientation, and its mission focused on research and graduate study (Lucas 1994, 166–171). Until this period, graduate study had been somewhat of a rarity in American higher education, but it was soon to be embraced through the context of the German model of the university, which emphasized scholarship and research through scientific inquiry (Rudolph 1962, 272–274). The metamorphosis of the college into the university was marked by several changes: the introduction of electives, reluctance to serve in loco parentis, addition of career training, emphasis on graduate and professional study, and increasingly specialized scholarship within discipline-based academic departments. At the beginning of the twentieth century, it became abundantly clear that the prevailing philosophy of higher education had shifted substantially from half a century before. Most private liberal arts colleges lacked the resources to transform themselves into true universities, so many redefined themselves exclusively as teaching institutions serving as purveyors of liberal culture.

A marked movement toward curricular reform and experimentation in American higher education took place during the first four decades of the twentieth century. The replacement of the nineteenth-century uniform liberal curriculum with an elective system and the introduction of a multitude of practical areas of study by the end of the nineteenth century indicated an incremental shift in curricular philosophy. Between 1900 and 1940, however, this philosophy began yet another shift in the opposite direction, away from pedagogical pragmatism and back toward liberal learning. As reaction to the elective curricula set in, many former advocates of the idea reversed themselves, seeking a better parity between the broad elective curriculum and the uniform liberal one because of what seemed at the time as a lack of coherence and intellectual integration in the academy. The question again became one of balance between professional training through the practical curriculum and the classic principles of liberal learning, which led to the gradual establishment of the first two years of the collegiate experience as a period of general education (Lucas 1994, 185–187, 210–214).

In 1930 at the University of Chicago, President Robert Maynard Hutchins announced a controversial curricular experiment that became known as the Chicago Plan. It was intended to resurrect the liberal program of study through the creation of an autonomous undergraduate college and a curriculum focused on the study of the 100 "great books" of Western civilization (Fuhrmann 1997). This broad cast of study, which became one of the most discussed reorganizations during the second quarter of the twentieth century, was to include subject matter considered indispensable to any learned person and to be preparatory to any professional or personal calling (Brubacher and Rudy 1976, 274). Though he conceded the need for professional training, Hutchins felt that there was excessive emphasis on specialization and utility in higher learning and that the university should focus on preparation of the broad understanding that predicates the development of professional acumen (Rudolph 1977, 278–280). Perceived as incompatible with modern needs, the program met with criticism, but at least some of its elements were replicated in colleges and universities across the country.

Illustrative of the renewed emphasis on liberal education was the production of a 1945 Harvard faculty committee report entitled *General Education in a Free Society* but popularly referred to as the Harvard Redbook, a moniker it earned from its red binding. This report focused on the need for the general education of the populace and was rendered just as the last vestiges of World War II had again focused the lens of the curriculum toward specialization. The Redbook sought to explore the critical issue of how general education could be adapted to meet the needs of many, yet emphasize core subject areas. To this question, the report offered no definitive answer, and though Harvard's own faculty rejected it, support for the Redbook elsewhere was substantial, and variations of its recommendations were adopted in numerous American institutions of higher learning.

The 1950s also bore witness to changes in the collegiate experience for women. After World War II, as issues of efficient use of manpower and prudent use of educational resources surfaced, a debate on the necessary extent of women's education ensued. By 1950, the proportion of women enrolled in postsecondary education dropped to 30 percent, lower than any point in the twentieth century, and the first significant challenge arose to equal education for women in the 1900s. Some scholars found the remedy in providing women with education more focused on their domestic duties, whereas others sought to emphasize women's professional preparation, such as teacher training in the normal schools. This debate helped to provide a framework for a later widespread renewal of academic and professional aspiration for women in the United States (Fass 1997).

From the 1950s to the 1970s, another movement toward specialization was engendered by the technological exigencies experienced during World War II, the practical and vocational mindset of returning veterans preparing to take advantage of the Servicemen's Readjustment Act of 1944 (the G. I. Bill), and the tension created by the Russian launch of Sputnik, which sparked the "space race." In the wake of these events, the curriculum began to shift its focus back toward the mathematics and sciences, and even some private liberal arts colleges introduced new career-oriented majors to remain technologically current and maintain their market share. The community college, which emerged in the early 1900s, began developing rapidly during this period by offering a number of career study options and practical vocational training (Stark and Lattuca 1997). The idea of technical proficiency and expertise was reinforced during the Kennedy years of the 1960s, a decade that soon became an age of turmoil on American college campuses. Once the era of collegiate unrest in the 1960s came to a close, academia again focused on the curriculum. In the aftermath of Vietnam, some critics called for a more global curriculum to impart an enlarged consciousness, but others urged moral and ethical education on the heels of the Watergate scandal. Critics of the professionalized curriculum looked again to liberal studies as a remedy for the vocational philosophy that had beset higher education.

The 1980s and 1990s could be characterized by a controversy turning on "political correctness," which arose out of campus debates over an array of social and political issues in which were subsumed the ideas of freedom of speech, multiculturalism, feminism, and the overall role of higher education in American society (Lucas 1994, 267–277). Critics of the curriculum held that it was permeated with the study of Eurocentric and elitist literary, historical, and cultural topics and argued that it was often sexist, racist, and homophobic (Mayhew and Ford 1971). These critics asserted that the curriculum should be refreshed and replenished with courses devoted to the study of other cultures and political and cultural genres. Multiculturalism, feminist studies, and gay and lesbian studies as reform initiatives began to flourish, while detractors of the political correctness movement assailed that fear of being labeled sexist, racist, or homophobic unfairly compelled compliance with these curricular philosophies (Lucas 1994, 272–273).

Regardless of intent, as a result of the multicultural education movement, the doors of higher education opened to the study of numerous subjects that had been repressed or outright ignored in the history of the American collegiate curriculum, including women's studies (Haworth and Conrad 1990). The current proliferation of programs in women's, African American, and gay and lesbian studies are in large part a product of this reform. Higher education now seeks proper methodologies for integrating these new curricular components into the amorphous contemporary college curriculum in an effort to address the disparity between the need for both broad liberal and focused professional education in American society.

Kerry Brian Melear

See also Part 1: Women's Colleges; Part 3: Feminist Pedagogy; Part 6: Curricular and Professional Choices

References and further reading

Brubacher, John S., and Willis Rudy. 1976. *Higher Education in Transition: A History of American Colleges and Universities, 1636–1976.* 3rd ed. New York: Harper and Row.

Carnochan, William B. 1993. *The Battleground of the Curriculum.* Stanford, CA: Stanford University Press.

DeVane, William C. 1965. *Higher Education in Twentieth-Century America.* Cambridge, MA: Harvard University Press.

Fass, Paula S. 1997. "The Female Paradox: Higher Education for Women, 1945–1963." Pp. 699–723 in *The History of Higher Education,* eds. Lester F. Goodchild and Harold S. Wechsler. Needham Heights, MA: Simon and Schuster.

Foster, William T. 1911. *Administration of the College Curriculum.* New York: Houghton Mifflin.

Fuhrmann, Barbara S. 1997. "Philosophies and Aims." Pp. 86–99 in *Handbook of the Undergraduate Curriculum,* eds. Jerry G. Gaff and James L. Ratcliff. San Francisco: Jossey-Bass.

Gordon, Lynn D. 1997. "From Seminary to University: An Overview of Women's Higher Education, 1870–1920." Pp. 481–482 in *The History of Higher Education,* eds. Lester F. Goodchild and Harold S. Wechsler. Needham Heights, MA: Simon and Schuster.

Haworth, Jennifer G., and Clifton F. Conrad. 1990. "Curricular Transformations: Traditional and Emerging Voices in the Academy." Pp. 191–204 in *Curriculum in Transition: Perspectives on the Undergraduate Experience,* eds. C. F. Conrad and J. G. Haworth. Needham Heights, MA: Ginn Press.

Hofstadter, Richard, and Wilson Smith, eds. 1961. *American Higher Education: A Documentary History.* Chicago: University of Chicago Press.

Lucas, Christopher J. 1994. *American Higher Education: A History.* New York: St. Martin's.

Mayhew, Lewis B., and P. J. Ford. 1971. *Changing the Curriculum.* San Francisco: Jossey-Bass.

Rudolph, Frederick. 1962. *The American College and University: A History.* Athens: University of Georgia Press.

———. 1977. *Curriculum: A History of the American Undergraduate Course of Study since 1636.* San Francisco: Jossey-Bass.

Sill, Elizabeth R. 1972. "Shall Women Go to College?" P. 169 in *Early Reform in Higher Education,* ed. David Portman. Chicago: Nelson-Hall.

Stark, Joan S., and Lisa R. Lattuca. 1997. *Shaping the College Curriculum: Academic Plans in Action.* Boston: Allyn and Bacon.

Women's Studies

Women's studies is a relatively new academic discipline in higher education that focuses on the experiences, accomplishments, and struggles of women and contributes feminist perspectives to the construction of knowledge. Women's studies uses gender as the primary tool of analysis and recognizes the power imbalances between women and men: "The term *women's studies* is used to cover a wide range of activities, from scholarship and teaching that are traditional in all but their focus on women to innovative attempts to revise methods of inquiry, develop new categories of analysis, reconceptualize pedagogies, and restructure institutional relationships" (Boxer 1998, 3). Women's studies in the United States grew out of the women's movement in the 1960s and consequently has its roots in social and political activism. Programs are offered at higher education institutions across the country at the associate's, bachelor's, master's, and doctoral levels as majors, minors, concentrations, and certificates.

Women's studies has experienced tremendous growth since the founding of the first undergraduate program at San Diego State University in 1969–1970. There are currently over 600 women's studies departments, programs, and research centers in the United States.

Women's studies classes boost the self-esteem of female students by reclaiming important role models in women's history (Courtesy of Mount Holyoke College)

There are 7 Ph.D. programs as well as over 100 graduate programs. In 1996–1997, 602 bachelor's degrees, 71 master's degrees, and 5 doctoral women's studies degrees were conferred by institutions of higher education (National Center for Education Statistics 2000).

Women's studies programs typically combine women's studies courses and those from other disciplines, including history, English, philosophy, psychology, sociology, political science, anthropology, religion, and the sciences. At the undergraduate level, core requirements for women's studies majors usually include an introductory course on women's studies and courses on feminist theory, methodology, and cultural diversity. Examples of titles of required courses include "Critical Perspectives in Women's Studies," "Sex and Gender in American Society," "Modes of Feminist Inquiry," and "Women of Color in the U.S." Examples of elective courses include "Psychology of Women," "Asian Women: Myths of Deference, Arts of Resistance," "Lesbian Literature," "Women, Work, and Protest in the Twentieth Century," and "The Political Economy of Women." A typical program is interdisciplinary in nature; about half the work falls under the rubric of social sciences and half under that of the humanities (Morgan and Broyles 1995).

Since women's studies has its roots in the women's movement of the 1960s and was conceived as the academic arm of the women's movement, there is a general understanding that its pedagogy, research, epistemology, and service will be feminist and activist in nature. Women's studies and women's liberation were intermeshed, and "the majority of teachers came to this work as seasoned political activists and were ready to transfer techniques of organizing from the community to the campus" (Buhle, 2000, xx). Many professors teaching the first women's studies courses were also involved in local community efforts like creating battered women's shelters and organizing community women's centers. Their activism informed not only their areas of research but also their pedagogy. In the classroom, traditional norms were replaced with a new focus on active student engagement, reflection on personal experience, and the de-centering of professorial authority. Women's studies faculty tried to bridge academic and activist pursuits.

During the late 1960s and 1970s, much of the research in women's studies focused on women's history. Scholars realized that much of women's history had been left out or erased from history books and that those women who were written about were often devalued. Women's history needed to be rediscovered and introduced into contemporary society. A similar process took place in the humanities, where women writers were unearthed and women characters were reinterpreted from feminist perspectives. Gradually, an academic feminist awareness of women's contribution across all disciplines started to emerge.

As the number of women's studies programs, scholars, and publications proliferated and diversified, so did feminist theories. In the 1980s, women of color, lesbians, and poor women gained increased visibility, and classes and publications focusing on race, sexuality, and class multiplied. These groups forced the reexamination of the original assumptions about feminism and called for an account of the experiences and lives of all women, not just middle- and upper-class white heterosexual women. Gender as the exclusive tool of analysis gave way to a more complex system including race, class, sexuality, and ethnicity. Essentialism, standpoint theory, postmodernism, French feminism, and womanism brought various understandings and perspectives on the cause and nature of women's position in society. At present, postcolonial and transnational feminist perspectives offer new conceptual avenues that blur the boundaries often produced by theory based upon sex, race, and class categories. Women's studies faces the current challenge of recognizing and valuing numerous feminisms, both domestic and global, while also trying to find commonalities among women.

Women's studies has always been and continues to be challenged and invigorated by internal debates and external criticisms. Criticisms of women's studies are often based upon the assertion that women's studies practitioners politicize and attribute gender to topics that are presumably objective and gender-neutral. Scholarly work is supposedly undermined by political and ideological agendas. Allegations of man hating and male bashing are also frequently made. In the 1990s, much media attention was given to critics who accused women's studies of sloppy scholarship, ideological policing, and deference to political activism. Despite such faultfinding, women's studies scholars have refuted these allegations or have reflected upon them to improve the goals of the discipline.

There are a variety of ways that women's studies programs are housed in universities. Some programs have become fully established departments offering majors and retaining tenured full professors whose "home" is in the department. Other programs are amalgamations of professors from various departments whose homes are in other disciplines and are granted tenure through their respective home departments. Some argue that the departmentalization of women's studies has strengthened and legitimized the role of women's studies in the academy, whereas others believe that the further incorporation of women's studies into mainstream academia weakens and dilutes its historic activist nature.

The National Women's Studies Association (NWSA), founded in 1977, is "a forum fostering dialogue and collective action among women who are dedicated to feminist education and change" (National Women's Studies Association 2002). It sponsors a yearly conference and publishes books, newsletters, and other projects to foster the growth and development of women's studies. According to the NWSA, the following journals have the closest affiliation to women's studies: *Feminist Studies; Feminist Teacher; Frontiers: A Journal of Women's Studies; Meridians: Feminism, Race, Transnationalism; NWSA Journal; Sage; Signs: A Journal of Women in Culture and Society; Transformations; Women's Studies Quarterly; Women's Studies: An Interdisciplinary Journal;* and *Women's Studies International Forum.*

Francesca B. Purcell

See also Part 3: Feminist Epistemology; Feminist Pedagogy; Feminist Research Methodology; Part 4: Transformation of the Curriculum

References and further reading

Boxer, Marilyn Jacoby. 1998. *When Women Ask the Questions: Creating Women's Studies in America.* Baltimore: Johns Hopkins University Press.

Buhle, Mary Jo. 2000. "Introduction." Pp. xv–xxvi in *The Politics of Women's Studies: Testimony from 30 Founding Mothers,* ed. F. Howe. New York: The Feminist Press.

Morgan, Frank B., and Susan G. Broyles. 1995. "Degrees and Other Awards Conferred by Institutions of Higher Education, 1992–93." Washington, DC: Office of Educational Research and Improvement, U.S. Department of Education.

National Center for Education Statistics. 2000. *Digest of Education Statistics.* Washington, DC: U.S. Department of Education.

National Women's Studies Association. http://www.nwsa.org. Cited June 13, 2002.

Part 5

WOMEN AND HIGHER EDUCATION POLICY

Overview

Public and educational policy have played a crucial role in determining the fate of women of all races, classes, sexual orientations, and abilities in the postsecondary academy. From the opening of the first institutions of higher education in the United States in the seventeenth century until the present, policy has shaped women students' admissions, support, and graduation and female faculty recruitment, compensation, and promotion. Legislative, academic, financial aid, employment, public, legal, and social policies—and challenges to those policies—have shaped and altered academe in profound and enduring ways.

The original impetus for establishing colleges in America was the desire for an educated clergy (Chamberlain 1988, 12). Harvard was founded in 1636, and William and Mary was established before the close of the seventeenth century for that purpose. The first educational and public policies were unspoken but absolute: they mandated that only white, propertied men "of good character" had the right to an education in the United States (Kates 2001, 3). It was more than 200 years after Harvard opened its doors that policy changes allowed the first cohort of women to be admitted to a college in the United States.

In 1837 four young women enrolled at Oberlin College; three of them received college degrees four years later (Chamberlain 1988, 6). Antioch College opened its doors to women in 1853. Both colleges exercised a policy that facilitated young women's entry into academia on a very limited basis. It mandated that Oberlin women study the "ladies course," be prohibited from delivering graduation oratories or any other public speeches, and perform domestic work (Gordon 1990, 18). Policy engendered similar conditions at Antioch, where men and women remained separate except in the classroom (Chamberlain 1988, 5).

Oberlin and Antioch became pioneers in coeducation after years of formal and informal policy debate. Advocates of women's education in the nineteenth century had linked their cause to the formation of domesticity and "cultured motherhood." Evangelical Christian leaders had sanctioned limited education for women as a means of enhancing their spiritual authority within the home (Chamberlain 1988, 6). In other cases, the women who attended seminaries or normal institutes did so in preparation for teaching children, an occupation that befit "respectable" young women. By the middle of the nineteenth century, most Americans accepted coeducation in secondary schools, but policy meant to facilitate and support women in "higher education . . . was another matter" (Gordon 1990, 17).

Belva Ann Lockwood, the first woman to practice law in the United States, was turned down by Columbia, Georgetown, and Harvard because they thought her application was a joke (Library of Congress)

Women's education continued to be controversial despite the success of Oberlin and Antioch. In 1862 Congress passed the Morrill Land Grant Act, providing for the funding of public institutions with no prohibition on female students. Yet female students continued to exist only on the social margins of college life. Throughout the nineteenth century, little official educational policy existed to ensure the rights of women or those similarly denied access to higher education. Rather, a system of informal regulations ensured that for the most part, higher education remained the domain of privileged white males (Kates 2001, 5, 22).

Despite discriminatory policy and practices, by 1880 there were about 56,000 women in attendance at colleges and universities in the United States. The number increased to 85,000 by 1900. Many of these students attended women's colleges that opened in rapid succession in the late nineteenth century. The last of these schools opened a full twenty-one years before women won the right to vote in 1920. These private colleges continued to implement policy that produced and supported a socioeconomically and ethnically homogenous student population, admitting a few minority students while resisting diversification (Kates 2001, 4, 7).

Women were able to gain access to state universities in larger numbers when parents and women's organizations petitioned legislators and boards of regents to change policy to provide for vocational preparation for the daughters of taxpayers. Yet higher education for women remained controversial; many believed that women's health and the well-being of the nation would suffer as result of women's "unnatural pursuit"(Newcomer 1959, 21, 25). Women of color and poor women were multiply disenfranchised by educational policy in this era. Legislative, social, and legal policy worked with academic policy to prohibit those who were considered "unfit" for college and university work and life from entering educational institutions. Even the Morrill Land Grant Act of 1862 made no provision for "Negro colleges," and only three states in the South designated black colleges to receive funds. In 1890 Congress passed a second Morrill Land Grant Act, requiring that black colleges receive land grant monies. This act had the negative effect of fashioning "academically oriented black colleges as institutes that fostered vocational training as especially suited for Negroes" (Kates 2001, 10). Policy restricted educational opportunities for students of color, the poor, and the disabled throughout the United States, and studies by scientists gave academic gatekeepers empirical proof to keep racist, sexist, classist, and able-ist admission policies in place (2001, 3–8).

From 1900 to 1930, the proportion of women receiving bachelor's or professional degrees increased from 19 percent to 40 percent (Newcomer 1959, 12). The proportion remained steady during the 1930s; despite the impact of the Depression, both men and women increased their enrollment in colleges around the country. After World War II, with the advent of the G. I. Bill—which many consider to be the major policy created to increase access to postsecondary education in the United States—the nation witnessed a dramatic rise in the number of male students of all classes and races and a concomitant reduction in the ratio of women attending college. By 1950, women represented only 24 percent of those receiving bachelors degrees, compared with 41 percent a decade earlier (1959, 7). Policy enacted an even greater toll on women who did enroll in the wake of the G. I. Bill. Because priority was given to veterans, undergraduate and graduate women found it more difficult to be admitted and were denied financial aid and opportunities for further advancement. During this period, "women students were being treated openly as second class citizens" (Chamberlain 1988, 16). Nevertheless, by the fall of 1957, the number of women enrolled in American colleges exceeded 1 million for the first time (1988, 7).

In the 1960s and 1970s, a spate of legal and legislative actions fostered administrative, curricular, and financial aid policy changes designed to address the unequal access to education for women, nonwhites, and the poor. Patterns of admissions and financial support that in the past had heavily favored white men began to change during the 1960s and 1970s, when the federal government established massive programs of grants and loans for higher education without distinction for race or gender (Chamberlain 1988, 11). Similarly, legislation influenced policy determining student recruitment and admission practices and shaped the college environment, faculty, student services, athletics and physical education, and curriculum.

In the early 1970s, numerous federal laws and regulations were passed in an effort to create and reinforce policy meant to equalize opportunities for women in higher education. In 1972 the U.S. Congress approved an Omnibus Higher Education Bill. This legislation included Title IX of the Education Amendments enacted to prohibit sex discrimination in all federally assisted educational programs. Title VII of the 1964 Civil Rights Act, prohibiting sex discrimination in employment, was also extended to include all educational institutions, and the Equal Pay Act of 1963 was expanded to cover executive, administrative, and professional employment. Subsequent policy changes were based on legislation including the Pregnancy Discrimination Act, Age Discrimination and Employment Act, Equity in Athletics Disclosure Act, and the Civil Rights Act of 1991. Additionally, in 1972 guidelines were issued to implement executive orders requiring federal contractors to institute affirmative action goals to ensure equal treatment of all employees. Affirmative action has been a premier force in theory and practice for women in higher education to secure fair and equal treatment.

Impact of Contemporary Policy on Women Students

Significant legal decisions followed passage of federal laws and regulations that addressed discrimination in admissions, employment, and contracting and strengthened protection for women, "as did Supreme Court decisions on pension equity, sexual harassment," student life and faculty tenure reviews (see "Gender Inequality," this volume). As a result of Title VII and Title IX legislation, women students and faculty have been able to use the courts—albeit with limited success—to change the campus climate and to address gender bias in sports, testing, admissions, and financial aid. Yet, despite a "history of institutional violations of civil, constitutional and contract laws," women's claims have for the most part been unsuccessful against colleges and universities (see "Legal Issues," this volume).

By 1979, in large part as a result of legislation and legal challenges leading to policy changes, women became a majority on campuses, and in 1982 they were awarded more bachelor's degrees than men. From 1999 to 2000, women students received 58 percent of master's degrees and about 44 percent of professional degrees and Ph.D.'s (National Center for Education Statistics 2002, table 274). Although many around the country celebrated these figures as proof of gender equity in higher education, they represent only a very small and misleading part of the picture. For the most part, it is still white, middle-class, able-bodied women who earn these degrees. Women of color, poor women, and women with disabilities remain vastly underrepresented in this celebratory figure. Additionally, women are not equally distributed in institutions of equal rank, the degrees women earn are disproportionately in fields with lower status and lower pay, women receive less financial aid than do men and as a result end up owing more money, and when they enter the job market, their degrees are worth less than their male counterparts' credentials.

Despite the fact that the law essentially requires nondiscrimination in college admissions, athletic programs, student life, and testing, women students continue to suffer as a result of gender bias. Admissions policy reflects both gender equity and gender bias (Jacobs 1999). In athletics, only 37 percent of college athletes are women, although they constitute 53 percent of undergraduates (Mickleson and Smith 1998, 335). Seventy percent of women reported having experienced sexual harassment in sports and in the classroom in 1996 (Larocca and Kromrey 1999). Researchers have also identified standardized test bias that acts against women students. These studies suggest that there is a systematic bias in the tests and that utilizing Scholastic Aptitude Test (SAT) scores as the sole indicator of qualification leads to admissions policy that is not gender-neutral (Childs 1980, 4).

Gender bias is also evident in policy determining the offer of financial aid in colleges and universities across the nation. Educational and financial aid policy determines the total resources available to pay for college costs, the amounts and percentages derived from different sources, and the way financial aid is distributed among students. Even though since 1970, college enrollment for women has increased by 77 percent (as compared to a 23 percent increase for men), and regardless of the fact that women far surpass men as adult, part-time, independent, low-income, and thus "financially needy" students, women receive only 68 percent of what male students receive in financial aid earnings, 73 percent of what men are awarded in grants, and 84 percent of what they receive in loans for low-income undergraduates. An even "more significant difference between genders appear in discretionary programs like college work study, research and teaching assistantships and corporate benefit programs that pay tuition" (Moran 1987, 2, 3).

Financial aid policy also results in women being underrepresented in academic merit scholarships, even though as a whole, they have higher grade point averages than males in both high school and the first year of college (Moran 1987, 1). In 1995, 42 percent of students eligible for the National Merit Scholarship were female, despite comprising 56 percent of the scholarship competitors (Fairtest 1995). Perhaps as a result of these inequities, women students' parents pay more for their daughters' education than they do for their sons' schooling (Jacobs 1999). As a result of these policy mandates, women—although entering into and completing degrees in impressive numbers—choose to enroll in less expensive and less prestigious schools, enter into fields with less financially rewarding credentials, and receive less pay when they are employed after graduation (216). Women with a college degree earn on average the equivalent of men with a high school degree (Jacobs 1999, 162; U.S. Bureau of the Census 1997).

Increasingly, women are coming to college later in life and are twice as likely as men to be classified as independent students and as part-time students (Wolff 2001b, B20). Students from low-income families made up only 6 percent of the student population in 1996, as opposed to 18.7 percent from middle-income families and 41.1 percent from high-income families (National Education Association 1998, 18). Profoundly poor women, especially those on public aid, are dissuaded from entering into educational programs because of recent welfare legislation that emphasizes and supports "work first" rather than educational advancement. As a result of 1996 welfare policy legislation, "the number of families reported as participating in activities that would lead to postsecondary degrees was cut in half," from 648,763 in 1995 to 340,000 in 1998–1999 (Adair 2001, 226). Similarly, despite the passage of the Americans with Disabilities Act in 1990, women with disabilities have yet to become full participants in the American educational system (Jordan 1999).

Although they must continue to deal with the impact of racism, sexism, and homophobia on college campuses, women students of color and women students who identify as sexual minorities have fared somewhat better than have poor and disabled female students. As the result of legislation, policy was developed in the 1970s that increased enrollments for males and females of each major racial group (Kates 2001, 22). In 1997 students of color accounted for 27 percent of the undergraduate student population and 18.4 percent of graduate students (National Education Association 1998, 16). Also, as a result of policy changes involving recognition of same-sex partners and legal protections, increasing numbers of students enrolled in undergraduate programs identify themselves as "sexual minorities" (Mills 2001, 1).

Impact of Contemporary Policy on Female Faculty

When women enter the academy as faculty, they are less likely than males to work in prestigious institutions and more likely to teach more and for less pay, be hired on a part-time or adjunct basis, suffer the effects of sexual harassment, and feel unsupported in their efforts to raise families and be productive scholars. Women faculty also receive fewer promotions and as a result are dramatically underrepresented in the ranks of higher paid chairs and academic and business officers (Nicklin 2001, A30).

Women faculty are underrepresented on many college and university campuses. Several studies found that women comprised about one-fourth of the faculty but only about one-tenth of the tenured faculty in the United States; 50 percent of women were tenured in 1998, compared to 70 percent of their male colleagues (Hensel 1991, 1). Women faculty make up 58 percent of part-time faculty, compared to 35 percent of full-time faculty (National Education Association 1998, 21). As full-time faculty, the higher the rank, the more women are underrepresented. For example, in 1995 almost 55 percent of lecturers were women, whereas only 22 percent of full professors were women faculty (National Education Association 1998, 23). Furthermore, the attrition rate among women in academe is higher, and women who stay in colleges and universities are promoted at a slower pace than are their male counterparts (Hensel 1991, 1). When gender discrimination exists, it is often subtle and systemic. Male perspectives dominate policy development, performance assessment, and interpersonal interactions (Hensel 1991, 2; Miller and Wilson 1999, A18).

Promotion policy adversely affects women faculty's ability to secure positions of authority and increased pay in the academy as well. Women comprise only 19 percent of total college and university presidents, about 28 percent of department chairs, and 26 percent of trustees or boards of regents (Chiliwniak 1997, 2). In addition to being hired at lesser institutions and levels and receiving fewer career advancement opportunities, women faculty are paid less and valued less for the work they do as a result of administrative policy. In 1972–1973 women at the assistant professor level made 91 percent of what men made, and in 1996–1997, twenty-four years later, they made 93 percent (Chamberlain 1988, 14). This continuing pay gap increases as women climb the career ladder. In 1996 women who were assistant or associate professors made 93.5 percent of their male counterparts' salaries, whereas women who were full professors earned 87.7 percent (*Chronicle of Higher Education* 1998, 29). Finally, and not surprisingly, many studies reveal low satisfaction with policy among women faculty—particularly among women faculty of color and women faculty from working-class and impoverished backgrounds—in the postsecondary academy (Tack and Patitu 1992, 2).

In the entries that follow, it is clear that women students and faculty in the United States have benefited greatly from policy changes. These changes have had particularly positive impacts on women's admission into school and faculty ranks, increased sports participation, and sexual harassment litigation. Yet policy continues to both enact and remedy the unequal treatment of women of all races, classes, sexual orientations, and abilities in academe.

Vivyan C. Adair

References and further reading

Adair, Vivyan. 2001. "Poverty and the (Broken) Promise of Higher Education." *Harvard Educational Review* 71, no. 2: 217–239.

Chamberlain, Mariam K. 1988. *Women in Academe: Progress and Prospects.* New York: Russell Sage Foundation.
Childs, Ruth Axman. 1980. "Gender Bias and Fairness." *ERIC Digest.* http://www.ed.gov/databases/ERIC_Digests/ed.328610.html. Cited April 30, 2001.
Chiliwniak, Luba. 1997. *Higher Education Leadership: Analyzing the Gender Gap.* ASHE-ERIC Higher Education Report 25, no. 4. Washington, DC: George Washington University.
Chronicle of Higher Education. 1998. "Average Faculty Salaries of Full-Time Faculty Members." *Chronicle of Higher Education* Vol. XVL, no 1: 29.
Fairtest. "Gender Bias in College Admissions Test. www.fairtest.org/examarts/spring1995/nmerit.htm. Cited June 10, 2002.
Gordon, Lynn. 1990. *Gender and Higher Education in the Progressive Era.* New Haven, CT: Yale University Press.
Hensel, Nancy. 1991. *Realizing Gender Equality in Higher Education: The Need to Integrate Work/Family Issues.* ASHE-ERIC Higher Education Report 2. Washington, DC: George Washington University.
Jacobs, Jerry. 2001. "Gender and Stratification of Colleges: Gender and Stratification." *Journal of Higher Education* 70, no. 2: 161–187.
Jordan, I. King. 2001. "Colleges Can Do Even More for People with Disabilities." *Chronicle of Higher Education* (June 15): B14.
Kates, Susan. 2001. *Activist Rhetorics and American Higher Education, 1885–1937.*Carbondale: Southern Illinois University Press.
Larocca, Michela A, and Jeffrey D. Kromrey. 1999. "The Perception of Sexual Harassment in Higher Education: Impact of Gender and Attractiveness." *Sex Roles: A Journal of Research* 40, nos. 11–12: 921–940.
Mickleson, Roslyn, and Stephen Smith. 1998. "Can Education Eliminate Race, Class and Gender Inequality?" Pp. 328–340 in *Race, Class and Gender: An Anthology,* eds. Margaret Anderson and Patricia Hill Collins. New York: Wadsworth Publishing.
Miller, D. W., and Robin Wilson. 1999. "MIT Acknowledges Bias against Female Faculty Members." *Chronicle of Higher Education* (April 2): A18.
Mills, Richard. 2001. "Lawsuit Challenges University Housing Policy for Gay Graduate Students." *The Daily Californian.* http://www.dailycal.org/article.asp?id=5375&ref. Cited June 10, 2002.
Moran, Mary. 1987. "Student Financial Aid and Women." *ERIC Digest.* www.ed.gov/databases/ERIC-Digests/ed284525.html. Cited June 12, 2002.
National Center for Education Statistics. 2002. *Digest of Education Statistics.* Washington, DC: U.S. Department of Education.
National Education Association. 1998. *NEA 1998 Almanac of Higher Education.* Washington, DC: NEA Communication Services.
Newcomer, Mabel. 1959. *A Century of Higher Education for American Women.* New York: Harper and Brothers.
Nicklin, Julie. 2001. "Few Women Are among Presidents with the Largest Compensation Packages." *Chronicle of Higher Education* (November 9): A30.
Tack, Martha, and Carol Patitu. 1992. *Faculty Job Satisfaction: Women and Minorities in Peril.* ASHE-ERIC Higher Education Report 5. Washington, DC: American Association for Higher Education.
Wolff, Paula. 2001a. "Part-Time Students in Academe." *Chronicle of Higher Education* (March 16): B20.
———. 2001b. "Very Part Time Students Are Hobbled by Very Little Financial Aid." *Chronicle of Higher Education* (March 16): B20.

Affirmative Action and Employment

Affirmative action—the use of special efforts to promote the education and employment of women and minorities—has been the topic of intense debate over the last decade, in society as a whole as well as in the academy. Conflicting legal decisions, differing definitions, misperceptions, and an emotional backlash on the part of some has heated this debate.

The term "affirmative action" refers to a wide range of voluntary and mandatory activities in the areas of employment, education, and government contracts. This discussion of affirmative action is limited to the activities required of all federal nonconstruction contractors (i.e., businesses, colleges, or universities that receive federal grants or contracts totaling $50,000 or more and that have fifty or more employees) by President Lyndon Johnson's 1965 Executive Order 11246 (as amended in 1967 to include gender by Executive Order 11375). The guidelines for implementing affirmative action are included in Revised Order 4, which for colleges and universities is administered by the U.S. Department of Education.

The guidelines require a written affirmative action plan that is publicly available to all applicants and employees, a labor force analysis, and goals and timetables for correcting any imbalances by gender and ethnicity. Institutions are required to analyze the labor availability for various job categories, indicate the current levels of employment in these categories by race and gender, and propose how they will correct any imbalances. For example, for clerical or janitorial positions, the recruiting would be local, and one would expect the institution to have a goal of hiring women and minorities for these two positions roughly equivalent to their presence in the local workforce. For a midlevel staff or administrative position, the market might be regional, and for faculty and administrative positions, the market would be national. In both instances, the plan should determine the availability of women and minorities in these labor markets and set hiring goals and timetables accordingly.

The hostility toward affirmative action comes in the interpretation of these goals and timetables as being inflexible quotas that ignore merit. The perception is that much more qualified white males are passed over in favor of much less qualified women and minorities for hiring and promotion. This contradicts the idea of or belief in meritocracy in American universities and society. However, prior to affirmative action, faculty, staff, and administrative applicants were hired informally. Ads were rarely placed in newspapers or journals. Formal search committees were unusual. Rather, the word went out from one colleague to another that a position was available. These colleagues were usually white and male. Clearly affirmative action, with its job posting, advertising, and other search requirements, has changed the antiquated hiring process. In doing so, however, there are more candidates, more accountability, and more possible misunderstandings.

Underlying the debate over affirmative action are philosophical differences about how to remedy discrimination (Freeman 1990). The first is the "victim perspective," which focuses on whether conditions associated with racist or sexist practices exist and, if so, whether those conditions trigger broad actions as remedies. Under this definition, affirmative action has been only partially effective. The second approach is the "perpetrator perspective," which concentrates on isolating and punishing employers who have discriminated and providing remedies for actual victims. Using this definition, discrimination continues, but the violators will be rooted out, and only the actual victims will be provided a remedy. This second approach ensures that no "innocent bystanders" are damaged by systemic remedies. Many opponents of affirmative action consider themselves innocent bystanders who are victims of remedies provided for long ago acts of discrimination perpetrated against long-lost victims. In periods of economic slowdown, the paranoia about being passed over in favor of women and minorities for jobs, promotions, or layoffs fuels the fires of opposition.

A key issue in affirmative action for colleges and universities is its proscribed nature. In legal terms, affirmative action is required of colleges and universities "under color of" government action. Where there is government action, it must follow constitutional guidelines. In particular, the Fourteenth Amendment to the U.S. Constitution requires that the action must not deny "equal protection of the laws" to any person.

In the early days of affirmative action, there were a few lawsuits claiming that affirmative action promoted "reverse discrimination," which violated the Fourteenth Amendment. An important early case, *Regents of the University of California v. Bakke* (1978) found that race could be used as a "plus" factor (but not "the" factor) in medical school admissions decisions. The Supreme Court said that a properly constructed affirmative action plan could be a "benign" use of race and serve a "legitimate government interest." The Court also mentioned the university's legitimate concern for diversity, an issue that would be revisited later.

The Reagan era ushered in an assault on affirmative action. One important case involved "minority set-asides," a type of affirmative action that reserves a portion of government construction contracts for minority and women contractors. In *City of Richmond v. J. A. Crosson Co.* (1989), very modest set-asides in city projects were struck down. The Court ruled that any racial classifications were suspect and subject to the legal concept of "strict scrutiny." Gone were the "compelling public interest" and "benign discrimination" of the *Bakke* decision, which used a much more liberal legal concept of "intermediate scrutiny" to view affirmative action programs.

The 1990s brought more contradictory decisions, a more deeply divided Supreme Court, and very narrow decisions on affirmative action. The first such case was *Adarand Constructors v. Peña* (1995), which also used strict scrutiny to challenge federal government minority set-asides. The Court tightened the parameters for such programs: past and present discrimination against minorities in the market must be documented, and the government must show that the set-aside benefits only the victims of such discrimination. Additional issues are being litigated in *Adarand II,* which is pending action in the Supreme Court.

The second case was *Hopwood v. University of Texas* (1996). Although this is an important case, it is discussed in detail in the affirmative action in admissions section.

The third case was *Taxman v. Board of Education of Township of Piscataway* (1996). Sharon Taxman was a business education teacher at a high school in New Jersey. The school district had financial problems, and one position in the business education department was abolished. Two teachers, one African American and one white, with equal experience and training, were considered for the layoff. Taxman, the white teacher who had slightly more seniority, was laid off. She sued and won (although by then, she had been rehired). The defense of affirmative action in this case was weak because of the overreliance on the diversity argument and the unexplored possible biases in how the recruiting area for teachers in the affirmative action plan was chosen (e.g., the southern, "white" suburbs over the more diverse urban areas north of the town). When Taxman won her case in the Court of Appeals, a coalition of groups supporting affirmative action reached a settlement with her, strategizing that the case was not a strong one to present to the Supreme Court.

The debate over affirmative action will continue. In addition to *Adarand II*, admissions cases from Georgia, Washington, and Michigan are headed to the Supreme Court. Since all consider the touchstone issue of whether affirmative action required by government action violates the Fourteenth Amendment's equal protection provisions, they will all influence the future of affirmative action in employment. Ballot initiatives to limit affirmative action at the state and local level, like California's Proposition 209, will likely continue. Much of this legal and political action is a concerted effort to challenge affirmative action by conservative groups. Whether affirmative action will be revised or discarded altogether is open to debate.

Patricia Somers

See also Part 5: Legal Issues; Title IX

References and further reading

Adarand Constructors v. Peña, 515 U.S. 200 (1995) (*Adarand I*).

Adarand Constructors v. Mineta (*Adarand II*), 534 U.S. 103 (2001).

Americans United for Affirmative Action. http://www.affirmativeaction.org. Cited June 10, 2002.

Cahn, Steven. 1993. *Affirmative Action and the University: A Philosophical Inquiry.* Philadelphia: Temple University Press.

Chin, Gabriel. 1998. *Judicial Reaction to Affirmative Action, 1989–1997: Things Fall Apart.* Affirmative Action and the Constitution. Vol. 3. New York: Garland Publishers.

City of Richmond v. J. A. Crosson Co., 488 U.S. 469 (1989).

Curry, George, ed. 1996. *The Affirmative Action Debate.* Reading, MA: Addison-Wesley.

Freeman, Alan. 1990. "Antidiscrimination Law: The View from 1989." *Tulane University Law Review* 64: 1407.

Garcia, Mildred, ed. 1997. *Affirmative Action, Testament for Hope: Strategies for a New Era in Higher Education.* Albany: State University of New York Press.

Hopwood v. University of Texas, 518 U.S. 1033 (1996) (*cert. denied*), 78 F 3d 932 (1996, Fifth Circuit).

Lindsay, B., and M. Justiz, eds. 2001. *The Quest for Equity in Education: Towards a New Paradigm in an Evolving Affirmative Action Era.* Albany: State University of New York Press.

Regents of Univ. of California v. Bakke, 98 S. Ct. 2733 (1978).

Revised Order 4, 41 *Code of Federal Regulations* 60.

Rosenfeld, Michael. 1991. *Affirmative Action and Justice: A Philosophical and Constitutional Inquiry.* New Haven, CT: Yale University Press.

Taxman v. Board of Education of Township of Piscataway, 91 F 3d 1547 (1996, Third Circuit).

Class

Higher education plays a fundamental role in promoting and enhancing the progress and well-being of citizens and society. For women, education is essential to increase earnings, escape poverty, enhance self-esteem, and provide adequately for their families; it is key to development, a major source of women's empowerment and number one on women's diverse range of concerns. Decades of research and scores of studies document the undeniably positive impact of education on earnings, success, achievement, and individual and national well-being: each year of postsecondary education generates a 6–12 percent increase in earnings (Sweeney et al. 2000). By 2006, 32 percent of all new jobs (6 million) will require applicants to have a bachelor's degree; 38 percent will require some postsecondary education (Carnevale and Desrochers 1999, 8). Eighty-seven percent of adults recently surveyed by Public Agenda agreed that getting a college education has become as important as a high school diploma used to be (Hebel 2000b, 1). Women's progress—increased labor force participation, earnings, and general well-being—over the last twenty-five years has been almost solely attributable to their rising rate of participation in higher education (Blau 1998, 136).

In 1996, however, the enactment of the Personal Responsibility and Work Opportunity Reconciliation Act (PRWORA)—welfare "reform"—rescinded access to higher education for low-income parents on welfare. These predominantly female-headed families, among the poorest and most vulnerable in the country, were confronted with a daunting challenge: "end dependency" and "become self-sufficient" without access to advanced education. PRWORA restrictions had a devastating impact on the 750,000 welfare recipients enrolled in college: decreases in college enrollments ranged from 29 percent to 82 percent (Finney 1998, 2). Federal restrictions and corresponding sanctions forced many college-bound women to leave school for work, despite the long-term consequences. Recently available data on the impact of PRWORA show that although many welfare recipients are finding work, most of these jobs are unstable and do not pay enough to bring families out of poverty (Berstein et al. 2000; Hartmann 1999, 31–33; "New Studies" 1998, 4, 12–13; Primus 2000, 5–6).

The principal intent of current policy under PRWORA, to move mostly poor women off "welfare" and into jobs, was promulgated to promote job training and thus financial independence for parents receiving public assistance. States were discouraged from allowing recipients to meet federal work participation requirements by attending college: only two states, Maine and Wyoming, retained access to higher education in their state welfare plans. At present, less than half the states provide recipients some relief from work requirements to attend college, and nearly all impose limits of two years or less of postsecondary education. Only thirteen states allow participation in postsecondary education *alone* to meet work requirements within established time limits (Greenberg, Strawn, and Plimpton 2000).

Welfare in Historical Context

In 1935, the passage of the Social Security Act (SSA) stipulated that four categories of aid be designated to assist the "worthy poor"; one of these was for children. Title IV created Aid to Dependent Children (ADC) "for the purpose of encouraging the care of dependent children in their own homes or in the homes of relatives . . . to help maintain and strengthen family life and to help such parents or relatives to attain or retain capability for the maximum self-support and personal independence" (42 U.S.C. 601). Through ADC, aid was extended to the child, a caretaker relative, or any other essential member of the household. Eligibility for aid required that the child be "needy and deprived" because of the death or continued absence of a parent and "deprived of support" by reason of the death, absence, or incapacity of a parent, usually the father (LaFrance 1987). When the program began, the focus was on the provision of financial assistance to needy children living with their mothers or relatives.

Since its inception, three major policy changes—in 1962, 1967, and 1988—altered both the focus and intent of ADC. Amendments in 1962 brought the first substantive changes in welfare policy, including a name change to Aid to Families with Dependent Children (AFDC). These amendments emphasized the provision of rehabilitative services to AFDC recipients; they established community work and training programs for adult recipients and day care facilities for children, increased incentives to work, provided rehabilitative social services, expanded efforts to locate absent fathers, and afforded states the opportunity to extend coverage to poor two-parent families with an unemployed father (AFDCUP).

In 1967 the Social Security Act was again amended; the focus was now on work. New strategies constituted a move from "soft" rehabilitative services to "hard" work-related services. The amendments were, in large part, a reaction to the perceived failure of the 1962 "social services" approach, representing disillusionment with a strategy that had fallen short on its promise to "rehabilitate" welfare recipients. All recipients with children over six were now required to register for work and training through the Work Incentive Program (WIP). The new work emphasis included financial incentives—an "earnings disregard"—which allowed recipients to retain the first $30 of their earnings and one-third of every dollar thereafter.

By the late 1970s, the welfare system was widely considered to be inadequate, inequitable, fiscally burdensome, and nearly uncontrollable. A proclaimed "welfare crisis" directed attention toward changing the relationship between government and citizen, reducing public dependency on government, and reestablishing the work ethic, especially among the able-bodied poor.

The passage of the Family Support Act (FSA) in 1988 marked Congress's third try since the 1960s to revamp AFDC. The focus of this act was twofold: to transform welfare from an income maintenance program to a transitional support system by requiring recipients to participate in programs designed to facilitate their preparation for employment and to enforce parental obligations to support children. Strategies for accomplishing these goals included enforcing collection of child support payments from absent parents, requiring participation of recipients in education or work training or both, securing government provision of time-limited transitional services such as child care and medical care to recipients moving into the labor market, and emphasizing the adoption of a *new* "social contract." The last item reflected a shift from "entitlement" to income to a social obligation to work and support children on the part of recipients and a corresponding societal obligation to provide supportive resources to facilitate work.

The enactment of PRWORA in 1996 brought sweeping changes to AFDC. It made two significant changes to the welfare system: it established a five-year lifetime limit on benefits, eliminating the sixty-one-year-old entitlement to cash assistance program for low-income mothers and children, and it required welfare recipients to work in exchange for their benefits. It also changed the name of the program to Temporary Assistance to Needy Families (TANF). The work requirements radically reduced opportunities for women to pursue postsecondary education. Although states were free to allow recipients to go to college to satisfy their individual work requirements, college does not count toward a state's mandated aggregate work participation rate. PRWORA was intended to give states greater latitude in designing programs for recipients, which extended to allowing states to decide what activities would satisfy the work requirements. For the most part, it was acceptable for a state to include postsecondary education in its definition of work. However, the federal government also put forth aggregate work participation requirements, for which the states are not the primary decisionmakers. Under PRWORA, recipients who attend college do not count toward the state's aggregate work participate rate: PRWORA does not consider postsecondary education to be a "work activity." States are thus discouraged from allowing recipients to meet the work requirement by attending college (Butler and Deprez 2002).

The fear of federal financial reprisal, coupled with the political hazards inherent in the failure to follow the path of tough, work-based reform, led most states to abandon programs offering postsecondary education to welfare recipients. Although higher education was an option adopted by states as part of the Job Opportunities and Basic Skills (JOBS) program established under the Family Support Act of 1988, by 1996 this "window of opportunity" for poor women had shut with the passage of PRWORA. "Work first" became the mantra in welfare offices throughout the nation, as thousands of poor women were diverted from classrooms to workfare sites. Many more have been forced into the paid labor market, concentrated in low-paying jobs averaging $6.61 per hour with few, if any, benefits (Weinstein 1999, C6). Although "a popular perception holds that present and former welfare recipients who start in low-wage jobs can gain skills in the workplace and move on to better jobs, analyses conducted by the U.S. Department of Labor . . . show that most of those workers increase their earnings by only $500 or $600 annually by advancing in their current employment or changing jobs"(Carnevale and Sylvester 2000, B7).

Unlike past federal welfare-to-work law that considered most education and training activities "work," PRWORA did not. A person participating in a job-related education or training program lasting more than one year could not be "counted" in a state's work participation rate. As a condition of receiving federal welfare block grants, states were required to meet participation rates demonstrating that they were moving significant numbers of parents into "work" activities. In 1997 states were expected to have 25 percent of their single-parent families working at least twenty hours per week; by 2002, 50 percent of these families had to be working at least thirty hours a week. Success is being judged by the number of families leaving the welfare rolls, not those leaving poverty.

Higher Education and Welfare Policy

When the precursor to TANF (and AFDC), Aid to Dependent Children, was first established within the Social Security Act of 1935, women raising children alone were provided financial benefits to enable them to remain home and care for their children. The provision of care for children in these single-parent, mostly widowed, families was an issue of concern to the act's architects. Traditional notions of women as caretakers and nurturers, not as providers or workers, dictated this thinking. No programs were established for workplace training or advanced education. None were needed. Women were thought to belong in the home to care for their children. As the population of what became known as "welfare recipients" grew and the ethnic and racial composition and marital status of recipients changed, welfare policy grew more stringent, restrictive, and prescriptive. The initial aim of keeping women in their homes to care for their children gave way to requirements forcing them to work outside the home, handing over to others the care of their children. Although welfare policy became more restrictive, higher education began to slowly open its doors to and encourage applications from women. Only since the mid-1960s has education been clearly linked to "women's economic status and their employment opportunities" (Stetson 1997, 137–138). Now, according to a Department of Education report, *Trends in Education Equity of Girls and Women,* "achieving a bachelor's degree . . . increased women's annual median income by as much as 71 percent" (Hebel 2000a, 1).

Higher Education Matters

In an exhaustive contemporary study tracing trends in the well-being of American women from 1970 to 1995, economist Francine Blau (1998, 112–165) affirmed the well-known strong positive associations between educational attainment and labor force participation, increased earnings, and general well-being. She found that although women had made substantial progress since the mid-1970s, it was the rising rate of participation in higher education that made the most difference. Findings of note revealed real wage gains of 20.3 percent for female college graduates, compared to 8 to 9 percent for women with high school degrees or some college: high school dropouts experienced a 2.2 percent decline. Rising educational attainment was also a factor in women's increasing labor force participation: rates increased 19 percent among college-educated women and 29 percent for highly educated women, but among the least educated women, rates rose by only 4 percent. By 1995, only 47 percent of women with less than a high school education were in the labor force, compared to 83 percent of college graduates (Blau 1998, 131, 124–125).

A recent Federal Reserve study concluded that "education levels played a key role in determining economic success . . . across education groups: mean income grew between 1995 and 1998 *only* for families headed by individuals with at least some college education . . . median income between 1989 and 1998 rose appreciably *only* for families headed by college graduates" (italics ours; Stevenson 2000, A1). *Women's Voices 2000,* a comprehensive polling and research project on women's values and policy priorities, found education level to have a significant, "direct correlation with income level" (2000, 23). Other national data also favor higher education attainment: between 1979 and 1995, women with a high school diploma experienced a 3.6 percent drop in wages, whereas college-educated women experienced a 19.5 percent increase (Fitzgerald 1997, 37). A recent study found that a college education enabled the majority of women surveyed (81 percent) to become financially independent: an average of 70 percent attributed their success in securing employment to a college degree (*Welfare Reform* 1998). A 1992 Upjohn study of college attendees, technical school attendees, and nonattendees (those not attending any postsecondary institution) disclosed that "postsecondary technical education attendees had a 16 percent hourly wage advantage over nonattendees and a 21 percent annual earnings advantage. Higher education attendees, in turn, had a 22 percent wage advantage and 32 percent annual earnings advantage over individuals who pursued postsecondary technical education" (Hollenbeck 1992, 3–4).

In *Maine Families: Poverty Despite Work,* a survey of welfare recipients revealed that those with college degrees earned 20 percent more per hour than those with less than a high school education: "This suggests that access to postsecondary education can enhance the ability of welfare recipients to escape poverty through work" (Lazere 1996, 43). And, in a 1996 study of welfare recipients, Kathleen Harris confirmed that "women who finish high school or who obtain any post secondary education significantly reduce their chances of repeat dependency" (1996, 407–426). Predictably, recipients with post–high school education have a 41 percent lower chance of returning to welfare than do those who did not graduate from high school. Education, she concludes, "is more important in maintaining welfare exits than is contact with the labor force prior to entering welfare" (Harris 1996, 416).

In an interim report to Congress, *Indicators of Welfare Dependence and Well-Being,* the Department of Health and Human Services cited educational attainment as indicative of the "ability to work and earn wages: individuals, with no more than a high school education, have the lowest amount of human capital and are the most at risk of being poor despite their work effort" (1996, V-2). In a recent national comparative study on wage flexibility, employment, and education, Andrew Glyn and Wiemer Salverda confirm that "the assertion that lower relative wages enable less-educated American workers to find jobs more easily is simply not supported by the data." They further conclude that "the entry of women into the labor force has generally had a greater effect on better-educated women and an extremely uneven effect on low-educated women" (Glyn and Salverda 1999, 1). In fact, by the mid-1990s, 59 percent of individuals in families headed by a single woman with a high school education or less were in the bottom earnings quintile (Heintz and Folbre 2000, 48–59).

Higher education is crucial for families who are poor. Without it, low-wage work, with its correspondingly high rates of unemployment and underemployment (11.5 percent and 20.2 percent for females with less than a high school education and 5.7 percent and 12.1 percent for those with a high school diploma), is often a family's only work opportunity, exacerbating their already desperate situations (Economic Policy Institute 2002). For poor women whose access to postsecondary education is now restricted, the prospects of securing meaningful, stable, and adequately paid work is dismal. Recent information from a 1998 joint study by the Children's Defense Fund and the National Coalition for the Homeless found that over 70 percent of welfare recipients who moved from welfare to work earned below the three-person poverty line amount of $250 a week (Children's Defense Fund 1998). A 1994 survey of welfare recipients in Maine, for example, revealed that for the women in the sample (96 percent of the total sample), 22 percent had less than a high school education, and only 5 percent had a college degree; the wages of those who had worked over the last twelve months averaged $5.37 per hour (Women's Development Institute 1995, 4). Further events deteriorating the lives of low-wage workers were the national 2.4 percent hourly wage decreases between 1989 and 1996, with declines as high as 10.6 percent in New England, 9.3 percent in the Pacific, and 6.7 percent in the mid-Atlantic regions (Economic Policy Institute 2002).

A recent survey published by Educational Testing Services (ETS) warned that immediate job placement, the current federal imperative, "can represent a lost opportunity to pursue further education . . . that could result in better job prospects" (Carnevale and Desrochers 1999, 9). Although states have developed elaborate work placement and training programs to move recipients into jobs averaging $6.61 per hour, the ETS study also found that 69 percent of all welfare recipients *do* have skills that qualify them for some postsecondary education, enabling them to increase their advantage in the labor market, position them for job advancements, and secure their family's stability and security (1999, 7).

Luisa S. Deprez and
Sandra S. Butler

References

Berstein, J., E. C. McNichol, L. Mishel, and R. Zahradnik. 2000. *Pulling Apart: A State-by-State Analysis of Income Trends.* Washington, DC: Center on Budget and Policy Priorities.

Blau, Francine D. 1998. "Trends in the Well-Being of American Women, 1970–1995." *Journal of American Economic Literature* 36 (March): 112–165.

Butler, Sandra S., and Luisa S. Deprez. 2002. "Something Worth Fighting For: Higher Education for Women on Welfare." *Affilia* 17, no. 1 (February): 30–54.

Carnevale, Anthony, and Donna Desrochers. 1999. *Getting Down to Business: Matching Welfare Recipient's Skills to Jobs that Train.* Princeton, NJ: Educational Testing Service.

Carnevale, Anthony P., and Kathleen Sylvester. 2000. "As Welfare Rolls Shrink, Colleges Offer the Best Route to Good Jobs." *Chronicle of Higher Education,* February 18, B7.

Children's Defense Fund. 1998. "Welfare to What? Early Findings on Family Hardship and Well-Being." http://publicagenda.org/issues/news.cfm?issue_type=welfare. Cited December 17, 2001.

Economic Policy Institute. "Hourly Wages of Low-Wage Workers by State, 1979–1996," and "Low-Wage Labor Market Indicators by Region, 1979–1996." http:www.epinet.org/datazone. Cited January 27, 2002.

Finney, Johanna. 1998. "Welfare Reform and Post-Secondary Education: Research and Policy Update." *IWPR Welfare Reform Network News* 2, no. 1 (April): 2.

Fitzgerald, John. 1997. *Working Hard, Falling Behind: A Report on the Maine Working Parents Survey.* Augusta, ME: Maine Center for Economic Policy.

Glyn, Andrew, and Wiemer Salverda. 1999. "Employment Inequalities." Working Paper no. 293 (December): 1. Annandale-on-the-Hudson, NY: Levy Institute.

Greenberg, Mark, Julie Strawn, and Lisa Plimpton. 2000. "State Opportunities to Provide Access to Postsecondary Education Under TANF." Washington, DC: Center for Law and Social Policy.

Harris, Kathleen Mullan. 1996. "Life After Welfare: Women, Work, and Repeat Dependency." *American Sociological Review* 61 (June): 407–426.

Hartmann, Heidi. 1999. "Women Are Paid Less—They and Their Families Deserve Pay Equity." *Civil Rights Journal* (Fall): 31–33.
Hebel, Sara. 2000a. "Education Department Report Notes a Quarter-Century of Strides by Women in Academe." *Chronicle of Higher Education Daily News,* April 26, 1.
———. 2000b. "In a Shift, Most Americans Say They Value College Education." *Chronicle of Higher Education Daily News,* May 3, 1.
Heintz, James, and Nancy Folbre. 2000. *Field Guide to the U.S. Economy.* New York: New Press.
Hollenbeck, Kevin. 1992. "Postsecondary Education as Triage: Returns to Academic and Technical Programs." Upjohn Institute Staff Working Paper 92–10. Kalamazoo, MI: W.E. Upjohn Institute for Employment Research, April.
Kennickell, Arthur B., Martha Starr-McCluer, and Brian J. Surette. "Recent Changes in U.S. Family Finances: Results from the 1998 Survey of Consumer Finances. www.federalreserve.gov/pubs/bulletin/2000/0100lead.pdf. Cited March 3, 2001.
LaFrance, Arthur B. 1987. *Welfare Law: Structure and Entitlement in a Nutshell.* St. Paul, MN: West Publishing.
Lazere, Edward B. 1996. *Maine Families: Poverty Despite Work.* Washington, DC: Center on Budget and Policy Priorities.
"New Studies Look at Status of Former Welfare Recipients." 1998. *CDF Reports: Newsletter of the Children's Defense Fund* 19, nos. 4–5 (April–May): 4, 12–13.
Primus, Wendall. 2000. "Success of Welfare Reform Unclear." *News and Issues: Newsletter of the National Center for Children in Poverty* 10, no. 1 (Winter): 5–6.
Stetson, Dorothy McBride. 1997. *Women's Rights in the U.S.A.: Policy Debates and Gender Roles.* 2nd ed. New York: Garland Publishing.
Stevenson, Richard W. 2000. "Fed Says Economy Increased New Worth of Most Families." *New York Times,* January 19, A1,C6.
Sweeney, Eileen, Liz Schott, Ed Lazere, Shawn Fremsted, Heidi Goldberg, Joselyn Guyer, David Super, and Clifford Johnsons. 2000. *Windows of Opportunity: Strategies to Support Families Receiving Welfare and Other Low-Income Families in the Next Stage of Welfare Reform.* Washington, DC: Center on Budget and Policy Priorities.
U.S. Department of Health and Human Services. 1996. *Indicators of Welfare Dependence and Well-Being.* Interim Report to Congress. Washington, DC: Government Printing Office, October, V-2.
Weinstein, Michael M. 1999. "When Work Is Not Enough." *New York Times,* August 26, C6.
Welfare Reform and Higher Education. 1998. Fact Sheet. Washington, DC: One Dupont Circle Coalition, 2.
Women's Development Institute. 1995. *Who Gets Welfare in Maine? A Survey of AFDC Families.* Hallowell, ME: Women's Development Institute.
Women's Voices 2000: The Most Comprehensive Polling and Research Project on Women's Values and Policy Priorities for the Economy. 2000. Washington, DC: Center for Policy Alternatives.

Gender Inequality

The status and role of women in higher education gained momentum throughout the last three decades of the twentieth century, as women mobilized in defense of their basic rights to equality with men as students, faculty, and academic leaders. They made significant strides following passage of federal laws and regulations that made it illegal for academic institutions to discriminate in admissions, employment, and contracting. Women academics have traversed difficult terrain in arriving at a central role in higher education, and judging from the observations and the data on women's participation, much remains to be done on the precipitous road ahead.

Background

In June and July 1970, congressional hearings held by Representative Edith Green (D-OR) documented persistent patterns of institutional discrimination against academic women. Acrimonious debates on the issues generated demands for protective legislation, and in November 1972 the U.S. Congress approved an omnibus higher education bill with far-reaching consequences. Among its provisions, Title IX banned sex discrimination in all programs and activities of educational institutions, including postsecondary education, which received federal grants and contracts. It mandated that goals and timetables be adopted for admissions, hiring, promotion, and tenure and granted compliance responsibility to the Office of Civil Rights and the Department of Health, Education, and Welfare (which then housed the U.S. Office of Education). It also extended Title VII of the Civil Rights Act of 1964 to employees in public and private higher education and the Equal Pay Act of 1963 to executive, professional, and administrative employees, essentially prohibiting discrimination in higher education based on race, sex, religion, color, and national origin. In the ensuing years, the Pregnancy Discrimination Act, Age Discrimination and Employment Act, Equity in Athletics Disclosure Act, and Civil Rights Act of 1991 strengthened protection for women, as did Supreme Court decisions on pension equity, sexual harassment, hostile environment, and tenure reviews. Commissions on the status of women, professional women's caucuses, class action challenges, and other forms of advocacy proved to be effective strategies in increasing public and institutional awareness of and support for women's equity in higher education.

Charting the Progress of Women Students

Data on enrollment and degrees are derived from U.S. Department of Education databases, especially *Digest of Education Statistics, Projections of Educational Statistics,* and *Integrated Postsecondary Education Data Systems (IPEDS) Surveys;* as well as *Doctorate Recipients from United States Universities.* The latter is an analysis of data contained in the annual Survey of Earned Doctorates sponsored by six federal agencies (NSF, NIH, NEH, USDE, USDA, and NASA) and conducted since 1958, originally by the National Research Council and, since 1999, by the National Opinion Research Center (NORC) at the University of Chicago.

Enrollment. Of the 14.5 million students enrolled in higher education in 1998, women comprised 8.1 million, or 55.9 percent. They are in the majority at all levels: undergraduate (56 percent), graduate (56.7 percent), full-time (54.2 percent), and part-time (58.7 percent). The National Center for Education Statistics (NCES) forecasts growth in the number of women students to 10.2 million by the year 2010, an increase of 22 percent, or an average annual growth rate of 1.7 percent; men's enrollment are projected to increase at a slower rate, from 6.3 million to 7.3 million, or 1.2 percent, by 2010 (Gerald and Hussar 2000). NCES projections are based on low, intermediate, and high estimates of national data for the decade from 2001 to 2010. Consistent with earlier projections, it forecasts a continued increase in degrees awarded to women, also predicting that men's share of degrees will increase at the undergraduate and first professional levels but not at the master's or doctoral levels.

Women have also made substantial inroads in professional schools: since 1970, the percentage of women students in medicine has increased from 9 to 42 percent; in dentistry, from 1.5 to 38 percent; and in law, from 5 to 44 percent. Minority enrollments also escalated from 16 percent in 1975 to 26.2 percent by 1997 (27.2 percent of all undergraduates and 18.4 percent of all graduate students). Women of color, who are almost 15 percent of all women students, account for a larger proportion of minority enrollments than minority men.

Degrees. By 1998, women earned 55.7 percent of all academic degrees awarded in a highly diversified system of 4,070 accredited colleges and universities (1,727 two-year and 2,343 four-year and graduate institutions). They now earn 59.5 percent of all associate degrees, 54.6 percent of bachelor's degrees, 57.8 percent of master's degrees, 44 percent of first professional degrees, and 42 percent of doctorates. The National Opinion Research Center's analysis of data from the *Survey of Earned Doctorates* showed that by 1999, 392 universities awarded a total of 41,140 research doctorates, a decline of 3.6 percent from the previous year (4.8 percent for men and 2 percent for women), and the first annual decline in fourteen years (Sanderson, et al. 2000). The number of doctorates awarded by broad field was greatest in the life sciences, followed by social sciences, physical sciences and mathematics, education, humanities, engineering, and business and other professional fields. However, women's share of research doctorates rose to 42.7 percent in 1999, the fourth year in which it has exceeded 40 percent: in the social sciences, women earned 54.5 percent of all degrees awarded; in the humanities, 48.9 percent; in education, 64.2 percent; in business and other professional fields, 40 percent; in the life sciences, 44.7 percent; in the physical sciences, 23.4 percent; and in engineering, 14.9 percent. When subfields are compared by gender, women earn the majority of research doctorates in anthropology and sociology, art history, the health sciences, language and literature, linguistics, psychology, and most areas of education. At the first professional level, they also earn more degrees in veterinary medicine (66.6 percent), pharmacy (64.5 percent), and optometry (53.2 percent), and are reaching parity in medicine (41.4 percent) and law (43.7 percent).

By 1999, women of color who are U.S. citizens earned 52 percent of all doctorates awarded to minorities. African American women received 62.2 percent; Native Americans, 55.3 percent; Latinas, 56.2 percent; and Asian American women, 41.7 percent (Sanderson, et al. 2000, 15). These gains can be attributed to several factors: affirmative action recruiting; the availability of fellowships, scholarships, and grants; a larger critical mass of women baccalaureates; and a relative stasis in U.S. male doctoral enrollments in an expanding graduate sector. Survey data also show that 44.3 percent of women obtaining doctorates in 1999 had definite employment commitments, 16.8 percent held postdoctoral appointments, and 20.6 percent were still seeking employment. Of those who indicated their employment goals, women were much more likely than men to give teaching as their goal (41 percent versus 30 percent) and less likely to cite business and industry (11.8 percent versus 22 percent) (Sanderson et al. 2000, 84). Almost 51 percent of women as well as 59.2 percent of men intended to work in a state other than the one in which they earned their degree, confirming the general understanding that doctorate recipients are highly mobile and move across state boundaries to attend college, select their doctoral program, and accept employment, with marital status and other variables influencing their decisions to relocate for professional reasons (Sanderson et al. 2000, 35).

Women in the Professoriate

The remarkable expansion in the past three decades of higher education from a meritocratic system into a diversified agglomeration of institutions has provided greater opportunities for women, not only in admission to selective institutions and male-dominated professional schools but also as faculty and in positions of academic leadership. Women comprise 34.6 percent of 550,822 full-time instructional faculty, compared to 24 percent in 1975. Between 1975 and 1995, the percentage of women faculty grew proportionately at every rank: from 9.6 to 17.8 percent of full professors, from 17 to 31.7 percent of associate professors, from 29 to 43.5 percent of assistant professors, from 41 to 54.2 percent of lecturers, from 41 to 50.4 percent of instructors, and from 33 to 44.3 percent of faculty with no academic rank. Faculty of color accounted for 13.5 percent of full-time and 12.5 percent of part-time faculty. (Data on women faculty are derived from two main sources: the U.S. Department of Education's *Digest of Educational Statistics* and *National Survey of Postsecondary Faculty—93;* and *Professional Women and Minorities: A Total Human Resource Data Compendium,* compiled biannually by the Commission on Professionals in Science and Technology.)

Tenure. From these data, it would be natural to assume that hiring, tenure, and promotion policies now facilitate women's advancement in the professoriate, but that is far from the case. The National Center for Education Statistics reports a persistent gender gap of 20 percent in tenure rates since the 1980s: by 1998, 50.1 percent of women faculty were tenured, compared to 70.2 percent of their male colleagues. White male faculty outnumber white females (53 percent versus 35 percent) and people of color, who account for about 13 percent (5 percent African American, 4 percent Asian Pacific islander, 3 percent Latino, and 0.4 percent Native American). Gains made since 1990 indicate that the number of women holding doctorates in science and engineering is increasing, and they now comprise a total of 35 percent of tenure-track faculty and 16 percent of tenured faculty in these fields.

Consistent with data on women doctorates generally, findings from the *National Survey of Postsecondary Faculty* (NSOPF—93) also reveal that throughout the 1990s, women faculty have entered the professoriat in greater numbers than before. Indeed, by 1992, they constituted almost 41 percent of "the new academic generation," junior faculty with seven years' or less experience. However, one troubling sign is the greater likelihood of junior women faculty now being employed in non–tenure track positions. As Martin Finkelstein, Robert Seal, and Jack Schuster (1998) point out, "while the proportion of women full/tenured professors increased from one in eight to one in four between 1969 and 1988, the proportion of men professors increased from one in three to one in two; proportionately women remained at about 10 percent of full professors" (1998, 58). Furthermore, among new faculty, men are still nearly twice as likely as their female colleagues to have achieved tenure (29.1 percent versus 16.5 percent): "Yet one more indicator of a gender gap is seen in the breakout by rank: among new-cohort full professors, many more men (80.6 percent) than women (66.8 percent) have attained tenure" (Finkelstein, Seal, and Schuster 1998, 58). Also operating to women's disadvantage, fully one-third of new entrants are not in tenure-eligible positions. Women, we may conclude, are in a double bind: They constitute 4 percent of full-time instructional faculty but 48 percent are in non–tenure track positions. Without the possibility of earning tenure as well as job-related pensions and health benefits, non–tenure track faculty are relegated to the ranks of instructor and lecturer or to itinerant roles as they travel between campuses to teach mainly undergraduate students. Considered "teachers" and not "scholars," despite their doctorates and other credentials, they obtain few rewards and little recognition for conducting research, mentoring colleagues, or serving their institutions or professions. As a result, higher education drifts toward dichotomous patterns of professional employment, in which a minority of full-time tenure-track faculty conduct research, direct programs, advise students, and sustain academic standards with the aid of a large part-time workforce.

Salaries. The dissatisfaction among women faculty regarding persistent salary inequities in their fields mirror American women's general disappointment with public inattention to their professional concerns. Not only do women still earn less than men, but they tend to be employed in less prestigious subfields of their disciplines, at less prominent institutions, and in lower-paying jobs. Data from a College and University Personnel Association survey show that the best-paid professors are in male-dominated fields: law, financial management, public health, chemical engineering, and enterprise management. Not surprisingly, the lowest salaries are in such feminized fields as English composition, health and physical education, nursing, speech, and teacher education.

NSOPF-93 data also show the extent to which full-time women faculty average lower salaries than men: in 1992, 66 percent of women earned base salaries of less than $40,000, compared to 37 percent of men; in contrast, only 5 percent of women faculty reported salaries of $60,000 or more, compared to 19 percent of men. In determining the relative value of traditional faculty roles of research, teaching, and service, studies support accepted beliefs that monetary rewards and professional recognition accrue more readily to those who do research and publish scholarly works than to those whose primary activity is classroom teaching. Michael Nettles, Laura Perna, Ellen Bradburn, and Linda Zimbler's analysis of NSOPF data shows clearly that women faculty were more likely to teach and to engage in applied research than their male colleagues, who produced more basic, funded research (2000, 8). Moreover, salary differentials tend to be greater for women than men in both percentages and actual dollars in every academic rank, regardless of age or years of experience. More important, these differentials exist at every type of public and private institution and have become more pronounced in the past decade.

NCES *IPEDS* data underscore these disparities in annual comparisons of faculty salaries. In 1972–1973, following extension of the Equal Pay Act to higher education, women earned on average 82.6 percent of what men earned, but twenty-six years later, in 1998–1999, they earned only 81.6 percent of their male cohort's salaries. What is most troubling is that the gap increases as women climb the career ladder: for women who are assistant or associate professors, the average pay difference by sex is 93.5 percent, but for women full professors, it is 87.7 percent. Even for women instructors and lecturers, who are not likely to enjoy the prospect of tenure-track positions, the gender pay gap persists: 90 percent for lecturers and 95 percent for instructors. In comparing institutions by type of control, the gender pay gap is 79 percent in private institutions and 82.8 percent in public colleges and universities. By institutional level, salary disparities by gender are most pronounced in four-year comprehensive and two-year community colleges, where more women faculty are employed and where teaching workloads are higher.

Women in Academic Leadership

Since colleges and universities are labor-intensive institutions and human resource costs may range from 65 to 85 percent of operating expenditures, universities seek to control costs by monitoring hiring and compensation packages. Higher education is a big business, employing 2.8 million people: 1.8 million professional and 0.9 million nonprofessional staff. Women account for almost 52 percent of all employees: 45 percent of the professional staff and 64 percent of the nonprofessional staff.

Presidents. According to an American Council on Education survey of 3,124 university and college presidents, women now comprise 19.3 percent of the total. Their biggest gains have been in two-year colleges, where they account for 22.4 percent, and at doctoral universities, where they rose to 13.2 percent. Despite these gains, they are least likely to head research universities: Women constitute 9.5 percent of presidents at private institutions and 15.2 percent of those at public institutions and are most likely to be at the helm of women's colleges, community colleges, and public four-year colleges. Women presidents of research universities now include Nannerl Keohane at Duke University; Judith Rodin at the University of Pennsylvania; Donna Shalala at the University of Miami; Ruth Simmons at Brown University; and Mollie Corbett Broad, who heads the University of North Carolina system.

Deans and Department Chairs. A growing number of women are now moving through the administrative ranks. Professional association data report an increase each year in the number of women deans; however, upward mobility is a slow process, and they remain a distinct minority in the status professions: business, law, medicine, dentistry, pharmacy, engineering, and the sciences. Their participation as department chairs, generally acknowledged to be a stepping-stone to academic leadership, is estimated to be 28 percent, based on data compiled by the Women's Research and Education Institute. As of 1998, women in nonacademic administrative positions in higher education were most highly represented in external affairs (51 percent), student services (49 percent), and academic affairs

(43 percent). Nevertheless, the 1998–1999 survey of the College and University Personnel Association reveals that women administrators still earn less than men in most categories, even when they are in the majority, and in doctoral institutions where salaries are higher, the median salary for men in senior-level positions continues to outpace women's salaries.

Trustees. Of the 38,000 trustees now serving as voluntary, unpaid members of college and university governing boards, women's participation ranges from 26.4 percent on private or independent boards to 30 percent in public institutions. The political dimension of public sector trustee selection is demonstrable: for multicampus systems, they are either elected by popular vote or appointed by the governor or state legislature based largely on their compatibility with the dominant political party; for institutional boards, two-thirds are selected in this way. In state community college systems that have either coordinating or governing boards, the state and local governments that provide the bulk of their funding make appointments jointly. In contrast to the public sector, private higher education boards tend to be self-perpetuating, encouraging the appointment of like-minded, influential, and wealthy members of the business community. Minorities fare less favorably than women in board appointments. On boards of private or independent universities, whites account for 89.6 percent of the trustees, African Americans 6.5 percent, Latinos 2.1 percent, Asian Americans 2 percent, and Native Americans 0.5 percent (Madsen 1998). On boards of public institutions, whites comprise 82.7 percent of members, African Americans 11.7 percent, Latinos 3.1 percent, Asian Americans 1 percent, and Native Americans 0.8 percent (Madsen 1997). The interrelationship among boards of trustees, the political power structure, and economic wealth is inextricably tied to gender hierarchies. Until women are perceived as power brokers who can influence public policy at the local and state levels as well as control the distribution of economic resources, boards of trustees will remain male-dominated.

Outlook

Women's status in higher education has improved greatly in the past three decades, and this success can be attributed to a number of factors. Bolstered by the civil rights and women's movements of the 1960s and 1970s, legislators, judges, and the educational establishment now recognize the social, political, and economic advantages inherent in bringing women into the mainstream as educated and informed citizens. For almost two decades, women have been the majority of students at almost every level. Furthermore, their growing presence in the academic pipeline enhances their credibility as a formidable intellectual resource. Women's studies and gender studies programs have transformed curriculum, pedagogy, and scholarship in many academic and professional fields, particularly in the humanities and social sciences. Unfortunately, gender bias against women in positions of leadership and at the senior levels of their chosen fields has not been eradicated. Compounding these factors are shifts in public perception about the importance of intellectual pursuits in a world driven by the uncertainties of the globalized marketplace, the promise of high technology and distance learning, and the high cost of operating universities. Mentoring by senior administrators and senior faculty, subsidized child care policies, modifications in tenure and promotion criteria, and other strategies will do much to improve women's status in the coming decade.

Judith Glazer-Raymo

References and further reading

Finkelstein, Martin J., Robert K. Seal, and Jack H. Schuster. 1998. *The New Academic Generation: A Profession in Transformation.* Baltimore: Johns Hopkins University Press.

Gerald, Debra E., and William J. Hussar. 2000. *Projections for Educational Statistics.* Washington, DC: National Center for Education Statistics. http://nces.ed.gov/pubs2000/2000071.pdf. Cited June 14, 2002.

Glazer-Raymo, Judith. 1999. *Shattering the Myths: Women in Academe.* Baltimore: Johns Hopkins University Press.

Madsen, Holly. 1997. *Composition of Boards of Public Colleges and Universities.* Occasional Paper no. 36. Washington, DC: Association of Governing Boards of Universities and Colleges.

———. 1998. *Composition of Governing Boards of Independent Colleges and Universities.* Occasional Paper no. 37. Washington, DC: Association of Governing Boards of Universities and Colleges.

Nettles, Michael, Laura Perna, Ellen Bradburn, and Linda Zimbler. 2000. *Salary, Promotion, and Tenure Status of Minority and Women Faculty in U.S. Colleges and Universities.* Washington, DC: National Center for Education Statistics, Office of Educational Research and Improvement. http://nces.ed.gov/pubs2000/2000173.pdf. Cited February 14, 2002.

Sanderson, Allen R., Bernard L. Dugoni, Tom B. Hoffer, and Sharon L. Myers. 2000. *Doctorate Recipients from United States Universities: Summary Report 1999.* Chicago, IL: National Opinion Research Center.

Legal Issues

Women in higher education have benefited greatly from judicial and legislative willingness over the last thirty years to expand the scope of antidiscrimination law. Women have also benefited greatly from affirmative action in all areas of higher education, and courts have significantly expanded the theories and remedies available for sexual harassment. When the expansion of antidiscrimination law is combined with the traditional legal theories available under constitutional law, contract law, and tort law, the evidence is clear that women have more legal options at their disposal than men.

Nevertheless, women are still marginalized in many areas in higher education, and their legal claims against colleges and universities have generally been unsuccessful. Indeed, colleges and universities, perhaps more than other institutional litigants, have been remarkably successful at fending off lawsuits and winning them. To the dismay of many individual litigants, courts generally support the concept of academic autonomy. They rely on a definition of the academy as an essential but unique and complex social institution that functions on the basis of special expertise (not available to judges) and requires special exemption from most legal requirements so that educational decisions are determined by educators. The litigants, however, point to a history of institutional violations of civil, constitutional, and contract laws. They argue that a judicial doctrine of academic autonomy would insulate academia from laws and policies necessary to maintain a fair and just society.

One area in which the courts are less likely to accept the academic autonomy concept is in the area of discrimination, and it appears that the scope of sex discrimination law, in particular, has expanded greatly over the last thirty years. What has been remarkable about the judicial and legislative willingness to expand the scope of sex discrimination law is that during the same period, courts and legislatures have become more conservative and less willing to entertain claims by racial and ethnic minorities. The successes of women in higher education may be attributable to politically organized groups, such as the National Organization for Women and the American Association of University Women, or to the fact that judges and legislatures, in limiting the rights of minorities, have expanded the rights of white litigants. Indeed, despite efforts to diversify higher education, the reasons that whites still predominate can be attributed largely to successes of white women.

Women as a whole, however, have benefited greatly from recent changes in law. Their successes are particularly evident in faculty employment, affirmative action, sexual harassment, college athletics, and college admissions. Given their successes in these areas, special attention should be paid to them.

Faculty Employment

Women faculty face barriers to employment and promotion. These barriers include the glass ceiling on promotion, overt sexism, extremely subjective promotion and tenure criteria, and inadequate socialization processes. Given these barriers, women faculty, and white women faculty in particular, have resorted to the judicial system to seek a remedy for discrimination. Indeed, the most common litigation involves single white females suing historically white institutions. Despite the number of women who sue institutions of higher education, few have prevailed, as courts usually grant extensive deference to institutional decisionmaking.

Women of color have been the least successful litigants against colleges and universities. The lack of success by women of color is attributable partly to their extremely low numbers in most positions. More likely, however, women of color have been unable to successfully assert a legal theory that accounts for the intersection of race and gender. Legal conventions require that women assert either a gender discrimination or race discrimination claim, rarely allowing women of color to prove how their marginalization results from the complex intersection of both. Furthermore, courts have become conservative in race matters over the last thirty years, and so women of color may find their gender discrimination claims more successful than their race discrimination ones. This judicial conservatism in race matters seriously limits the options available to women of color.

Women who file class action gender discrimination lawsuits, however, have been relatively successful. Yet, the rules of antidiscrimination law, in combination with academic notions of merit and individualism, force women to couch complaints against their institutions in terms of individual acts of discrimination rather than systemic patterns of discrimination. The law privileges an understanding of discrimination as resulting from the intentional actions of individuals acting outside society's rules. The privilege given to individual and intentional discrimination in law does not permit judges to situate faculty women's work aspirations within the context of historical labor market discrimination.

Nevertheless, despite the flaws of antidiscrimination law, women have been able to resort to such law with some success. Most commonly, women faculty resort to Title VII of the Civil Rights Act of 1964, which prohibits race and gender discrimination in employment. The Equal Pay Act of 1963 also prohibits sex discrimination in salaries and wages. More recently, women have taken advantage of the protection afforded by Title IX of the Education Amendments of 1972. The Fourteenth Amendment of the U.S. Constitution, though prohibiting illegal discrimination, plays a very small role in employment discrimination cases for a number of reasons. First, the Fourteenth Amendment lacks the implementation and enforcement mechanisms of the various federal civil rights laws. Second, it protects only faculty members at public institutions. Finally, it requires a showing of clear individual and intentional discrimination.

Title VII of the Civil Rights Act of 1964. Title VII, which applies to all employers with fifteen or more employees, is the most important legislation in employment discrimination. Indeed, Congress was concerned with sex discrimination in higher education when it amended Title VII in 1972 to cover private and public institutions (the law excluded colleges and universities before then). Despite this effort, colleges and universities usually prevail in the cases against them, most likely because Title VII requires a showing of intent to discriminate by institutional actors. Title VII, however, allows faculty to show an "inference" of intent to discriminate, which then must be counteracted by the institution. Even though the institution can often assert a legally justifiable reason for its decision, the availability of the inference standard requires it to show some justification for its decisions, something that is not required under the Fourteenth Amendment. And once an institution indicates a reason, the faculty members have the opportunity to rebut it (even if they often fail to do so). Title VII also permits faculty to show that the institution's policies and practices, though apparently neutral, actually have a negative and disproportionate impact on women or minorities. Such claims do not require proof of discriminatory intent, and they often are filed as class action claims. Institutions usually prevail in such cases as well.

Compared to other social groups, women have been somewhat successful under Title VII, although they are most successful when they combine their claims in class action suits. Courts will rarely award reinstatement and tenure in these cases, choosing instead to award back pay and compensation for lost wages. But in two very important tenure cases, single women plaintiffs were not only victorious but were awarded tenure by the courts. In *Kunda v. Muhlenberg College* in 1980, a federal appeals court affirmed an award to a female plaintiff of back pay, promotion to associate professor, and tenure upon her completion of a master's degree. And in *Brown v. Boston University* in 1989, another federal appeals court affirmed an award to a female faculty member of $200,000 and reinstatement to the position of associate professor with tenure.

The Equal Pay Act of 1963. Congress amended the Equal Pay Act in 1972 to protect women employees in higher education (the act excluded colleges and universities before then). The purpose of the act was to ensure that women were paid the same as men for "equal work." Because women are underrepresented in most high-status positions, the requirement of "equal work" is very difficult to meet. As a result, the act is not as important in eliminating sex discrimination as Title VII, which allows women to sue for salary disparities in "comparable work." Nevertheless, once women have established that they have performed equal work, they usually can prove easily that they do not receive equal pay.

Title IX of the Education Amendments of 1972. Although the case law is still undeveloped, women faculty (and other female employees) likely may gain successes under Title IX, which prohibits gender-based discrimination in educational institutions receiving federal financial aid. For a number of reasons, Title IX is an important statute for female faculty and administrators who may be victimized by gender discrimination. First, Title IX allows faculty members direct access to a court, whereas Title VII requires them to pursue administrative remedies through the Equal Employment Opportunity Commission before initiating a lawsuit. Second, Title IX permits faculty members to receive uncapped compensatory and punitive damages, but Title VII limits the amount of damages one may recover to two years' back pay and $300,000 in punitive damages. Finally, Title IX borrows the statute of limitations from an analogous state law, whereas Title VII claims must be filed within 180 days of the discrimination (or 300 days in states with an approved civil rights agency). Title IX suits for gender discrimination, therefore, are likely to increase.

Affirmative Action

Affirmative action is extremely controversial and contentious, but the crux of the arguments for and against it focus on race-conscious policies. All the evidence supports the conclusion that women, and white women in particular, have benefited most from affirmative action. All racial and ethnic minorities have made gains in higher education, and white male predominance has diminished in many areas since the start of affirmative action in the 1960s. Yet whites still predominate in the higher-status positions, a phenomenon that is attributable to the successes of white women, which keeps whites overrepresented in faculty and administrative positions and in most student bodies. Despite the emphasis on race, it is clear that white women, not minorities, are replacing white males in higher education.

The courts have been largely unsupportive of affirmative action, although in one of the most important Supreme Court cases, the Court upheld a promotion policy that benefited women. In *Johnson v. Transportation Agency* in 1987, the Court upheld a voluntary affirmative action policy under Title VII, which promoted women (and minorities) to jobs in which they were "traditionally underrepresented" to correct a "manifest imbalance" in the workforce. This case is still good law; the recent Supreme Court decisions invalidating affirmative action have focused entirely on race-conscious policies.

Sexual Harassment

If there is any area in which the courts have been most receptive, it is sexual harassment. Feminist theory has been instrumental in establishing the recognition of sexual harassment as a legal wrong, which is based on a feminist understanding of sex discrimination. Such a theory was originally proposed by feminists such as Catharine MacKinnon. Indeed, before MacKinnon's work, the law did not recognize sexual harassment as such because it was deemed to be sexually based behavior (so anyone can be victimized by it) rather than gender-based misconduct, which involves the systemic and structural subordination of women through the aggressive expression of male sexuality.

MacKinnon's influence has been instrumental in defining sexual harassment under Title VII. The Equal Employment Opportunity Commission, which enforces Title VII, has defined sexual harassment as either (1) "quid pro quo," which is harassment that occurs when submission to or rejection of such conduct by an individual is used as the basis for employment decisions; or (2) "hostile environment," which is harassment that occurs when discriminatory conduct creates a "hostile or abusive work environment." The Supreme Court accepted the commission's definition of sexual harassment in *Meritor Savings Bank v. Vinson* in 1986. Since then, the law has recognized sexual harassment as a form of sex discrimination in the workplace.

The question remained whether students could sue for sexual harassment. Students cannot sue under Title VII since they are not employees, so their only option is Title IX. Following *Meritor Savings Bank*'s line of reasoning, the sexual harassment cases under Title IX have similarly held that sexual harassment constitutes sex discrimination. In *Franklin v. Gwinnett County Public Schools* in 1991, the Supreme Court held that the sexual harassment of students is a form of sex discrimination under Title IX and that individuals can recover damages from school districts for teacher-on-student harassment. In *Gebser v. Lago Vista Independent School District* in 1998, the Supreme Court held that school districts are liable for damages for teacher-on-student harassment only when they have actual notice of the harassment. And in *Davis v. Monroe County Board of Education* in 1999, the Supreme Court held that school districts may be liable for damages under Title IX for student-on-student sexual harassment under two conditions: (1) when schools act with "deliberate indifference" toward the harassment and (2) when the harassment is "severe, pervasive, and objectively offensive." Thus, in just over fifteen years, the law of sexual harassment has evolved from a point at which there was no legal recognition of sexual harassment to a point at which institutions can be held liable for the actions of their students.

College Athletics

This area has grown in importance because women still face gender discrimination in athletic programs. The passage of Title IX has been instrumental in opening up opportunities for women athletes, not only through its expansion of sex discrimination law but through its specific provisions on athletics. The law essentially requires nondiscrimination in athletic programs, but it permits separate teams for men and women where the participation is based on competitive skill or the activity involved is a contact sport.

Until recently, however, the mandates of Title IX were not enforced, as men's and women's participation in sports was deemed a cultural matter, not a legal one. But in recent cases, women athletes were successfully able to sue their colleges or universities under Title IX for failing to adequately provide them with an equal opportunity to participate in sports. In these cases, the institutions usually sought to reduce the number of athletic teams for budgetary reasons. The courts applied one of three tests to determine institutional liability: (1) whether the level of participation for men and women was substantially proportionate to their respective enrollments; (2) when one sex has been underrepresented in athletics, whether the institution showed a history and continuing practice of program expansion; or (3) when one sex has been underrepresented and the institutions could not show a history of program expansion, whether it demonstrated that the interests and abilities of the underrepresented sex were fully and effectively accommodated. Few institutions will be able to meet any of these tests, and thus women should make great gains in college athletics.

College Admissions

Women now make up the majority of college students, a phenomenon that is attributable to changing cultural norms, better precollegiate education, affirmative action policies, and antidiscrimination laws. Title IX has been instrumental in prohibiting overt sex discrimination in educational programs, and the successes of women have in turn influenced changes in the practices that implicitly discriminated against them.

Recent litigation has focused on single-sex admissions programs. Although single-sex institutions have a long and important history, recent case law has shed doubt on the legality of public single-sex institutions. Title IX prohibits gender discrimination, but it excludes private undergraduate single-sex institutions. The Fourteenth Amendment, however, has been used to challenge public single-sex institutions. This type of case has shed some doubt on the viability of women's colleges, but these colleges are private, and recent Fourteenth Amendment cases do not apply to them.

Two of these Fourteenth Amendment cases are worthy of note. In *Mississippi University for Women v. Hogan* in 1982, the Supreme Court invalidated an admissions policy that excluded males from a professional nursing school. In doing so, however, the Court made clear that policies that discriminate on the basis of gender have to be carefully justified. The tendency of courts before this case was to determine whether gender-based policies were rational, but then the courts deferred to states to determine rationality. This case, with its mandate for careful justification, was important for gender discrimination as a whole. In *United States v. Commonwealth of Virginia* in 1996, the Supreme Court invalidated Virginia Military Institute's single-sex admissions policies, holding that the institution's exclusion of women discriminated against them. Women as a whole have benefited from these admissions decisions (even from *Hogan*) because the courts have been concerned with gender stereotypes and they have made the justification for gender-based policies much more stringent than before.

In conclusion, women have benefited greatly from antidiscrimination law. The expansion of the concept of sex discrimination has occurred despite Ronald Reagan's and George H. W. Bush's appointments of conservative judges to the federal courts. It appears that as cultural norms change, so do the laws and case decisions. Women can expect greater gains in higher education as the case law evolves and as norms consequently change.

Benjamin Baez

See also Part 2: Sexual Harassment; Part 5: Affirmative Action and Employment; Students' Rights; Title IX; Part 6: Sexual Assault; Part 7: Disciplinary Socialization; Socialization; Tenure and Promotion

References and further reading

Abel, Emily. 1987. "Collective Protest and Meritocracy: Faculty Women and Sex Discrimination Lawsuits." Pp. 347–377 in *Women and Symbolic Interaction,* eds. Mary Jo Deegan and Michael R. Hill. Boston: Allyn and Unwin.

Brown v. Boston and Maine Railroad, 124 N. E. 322 (1933).

Crosby, Faye J., and Cheryl Van DeVeer. 2000. *Sex, Race and Merit: Debating Affirmative Action in Education and Employment.* Ann Arbor: University of Michigan Press.

Davis v. Monroe County Board of Education, 119 Sup. Ct. 1661 (1999).

Dziech, Billie Wright, and Linda Weiner. 1990. *The Lecherous Professor: Sexual Harassment on Campus.* 2nd ed. Urbana: University of Illinois Press.

Franklin v. Gwinnett Public Schools, 112 Sup. Ct. 1028 (1991).

Gebser v. Lago Vista Independent School District, 118 Sup. Ct. 1989 (1998).

Johnson v. Transportation Agency of Santa Clara, 480 U.S. 616 (1987).

Kaplin, William A., and Barbara A. Lee. 1995. *The Law of Higher Education: A Comprehensive Guide to Legal Implications of Administrative Decision Making.* 3rd ed. San Francisco: Jossey-Bass.

Kunda v. Muhlenberg College, 621 F. 2d 532 (1980).

LaNoue, George R., and Barbara A. Lee. 1987. *Academics in Court: The Consequences of Faculty Discrimination Litigation.* Ann Arbor: University of Michigan Press.

MacKinnon, Catharine. 1979. *Sexual Harassment of Working Women: A Case of Sex Discrimination.* New Haven, CT: Yale University Press.

Meritor Savings Bank v. Vinson, 477 U.S. 57 (1986).

Mississippi University for Women v. Hogan, 458 U.S. 718 (1982).

Rai, Kul B., and John W. Critzer. 2000. *Affirmative Action and the University: Race, Ethnicity, and Gender in Higher Education Employment.* Lincoln: University of Nebraska Press.

Tierney, William G., and Estella Mara Bensimón. 1996. *Promotion and Tenure: Community and Socialization in Academe.* Albany: State University of New York Press.

United States v. Commonwealth of Virginia, 116 Sup. Ct. 2264 (1996).

Students' Rights

For most of the history of higher education in America, college students were considered to have few, if any, rights at all. Only in the past forty years, have the courts acknowledged and defended the rights of college students under the Constitution, federal legislation, and contract theory. Prior to this time, institutions were viewed as standing in loco parentis (in the place of parents) and were given broad authority over students with little, if any, court intervention or oversight. The legal theory of in loco parentis was most clearly established by the Kentucky Supreme Court in *Gott v. Berea College* (1913). Although the court first expressly articulated this legal theory in 1913, the philosophy of in loco parentis had been the defining force in the relationship between the college and the student since the founding of Harvard College and had been evidenced but not specifically expressed in early cases such as *Pratt v. Wheaton College* (1866). This legal theory would hold sway until the ruling of the Court of Appeals for the Fifth Circuit in *Dixon v. Alabama State Board of Education* (1961). In the years that followed *Dixon,* the courts expanded upon these rights and defined the relationship between the college and the student in constitutional or contractual terms. In the mid-1960s, Congress began to further expand the rights of college students through legislative action.

The case before the court in *Gott v. Berea College* (1913) concerned a policy established by the college that prohibited students from frequenting certain eating establishments, including a tavern recently purchased by Gott. The court rejected Gott's claims and strongly supported Berea's right to establish almost any rule it wished governing student behavior. The court opined,

> College authorities stand in loco parentis concerning the physical and moral welfare and training of the pupils, and we are unable to see why, to that end, they may not make any rule or regulation for the betterment of their pupils that a parent could for the same purpose. Whether rules or regulations are wise or their aims worthy is a matter left solely to the discretion of the authorities or parents as the case may be, and, in the exercise of that discretion, the courts are not disposed to interfere, unless the rules and aims are unlawful or against public policy. (156 Ky. 376, 379; 161 S.W. 204, 206)

However, the court did not create the legal theory of in loco parentis from whole cloth. In 1765, William Blackstone's commentaries on English law included a discussion of the delegation of a father's right to discipline to the schoolmaster who stood in loco parentis (as cited in Bickel and Lake 1999).

Two cases involving women college students help to illustrate the lack of basic rights afforded to college students prior to the *Dixon* ruling. In *Woods v. Simpson* (1924), Vivian Simpson was expelled from the University of Maryland for refusing to disclose whether she wrote a letter to a Washington newspaper that accused members of the faculty of making untoward propositions to female students. She brought suit, but the Maryland appeals court upheld her expulsion, noting that discipline was a matter left to the faculty and requiring great delicacy, "especially in dealing with girl students" (146 Md. 547, 551; 126 A. 882, 883). The unwillingness of the courts to intervene on behalf of students can also be seen in *Anthony v. Syracuse* (1928). Beatrice Anthony was expelled from Syracuse University without any hearing because it was believed that she was not "a typical Syracuse girl" (224 A.D. 487, 489; 231 N.Y.S. 435). The court ruled on behalf of Syracuse University, holding that the registration card that Anthony signed, which afforded Syracuse the right to expel her without notice or reason, was a binding contract. However, the contracts during this period were interpreted exclusively to the benefit of the institutions, not as other contracts between parties of unequal standing would have been.

With *Dixon v. Alabama State Board of Education*, the courts began to dismantle in loco parentis as a legal theory. In late February 1960, twenty-nine students from Alabama State College, a historically black college, engaged in a lunch counter sit-in at the small lunch grill in the basement of the Montgomery County courthouse, following the model established by college students in Greenville, North Carolina, earlier that month. The protests by Alabama State College students would continue for several days, growing in size each day. The six plaintiffs in *Dixon* were expelled from Alabama State College without a hearing for their roles as the "ringleaders" of the protests. The students, with support from the National Association for the Advancement of Colored People, brought suit in federal court challenging their expulsions. The district court upheld the actions of the college, but this decision was reversed by the Court of Appeals for the Fifth Circuit. The Court of Appeals ruled that institutions must provide some basic constitutional rights for college students at public institutions, noting: "We are confident that precedent as well as a most fundamental constitutional principle support our holding that due process requires notice and some opportunity for hearing before a student at a tax-supported college is expelled for misconduct" (294 F.2d 150, 158). The ruling the following year in *Carr v. St John's* (1962) sent a signal to private institutions that the courts would look differently upon the contract between the college and students and interpret those documents in a manner more favorable to students.

In the years that followed *Dixon,* the Supreme Court ruled in several cases that would help to bring the rights provided by the First Amendment to students. In *Tinker v. Des Moines Independent Community School District* (1969), the Supreme Court addressed the free speech rights of students in a case that involved the suspension of three high school students, including Mary Beth Tinker, for wearing black armbands to school to protest U.S. involvement in the Vietnam War. In overturning the school's disciplinary action, Justice Abe Fortas wrote, "First Amendment rights, applied in light of the special characteristics of the school environment, are available to teachers and students. It can hardly be argued that either students or teachers shed their constitutional rights to freedom of speech or expression at the schoolhouse gate" (393 U.S. 503, 506; 89 S. Ct. 733, 736). Although this case originated in the high school setting, it remains to this day the Supreme Court's most significant ruling on the free speech rights of students and has shaped the many cases that followed involving college students. In *Healy v. James* (1972), the Supreme Court addressed the associational rights of college students. The case arose from Central Connecticut State College's refusal to grant recognition to a local chapter of Students for a Democratic Society for fear of campus disruption. In rejecting the institution's arguments for this refusal, Justice Lewis Powell stated for the Court, "Although the freedom of association is not explicitly set out in the [First] Amendment, it has long been held to be implicit in the freedom of speech, assembly, and petition. There can be no doubt that denial of official recognition, without justification, to college organizations burdens or abridges that associational right" (408 U.S. 169,181; 92 S. Ct. 2338, 2346). The Court's ruling in *Healy v. James* served as the basis for number of later court rulings ordering the recognition of gay, lesbian, and bisexual college student groups.

Students' rights have been secured not only by the courts but by Congress. The Family Educational Rights and Privacy Act of 1974, commonly referred to as the Buckley Amendment, was designed to grant students the right to review their education records and limit the disclosure of information from their education records without their consent. More recently, Congress has passed several pieces of legislation that require institutions to share information with students about issues related to alcohol (Drug-Free Schools and Communities Act, 1989) and crime on campus (Jeanne Clery Disclosure of Campus Security Policy and Campus Crime Statistics Act, 1990). The Clery Act was amended in 1992 to mandate the creation of campus policies on sexual assault and establish certain aspects of those policies.

John Wesley Lowery

See also Part 5: Affirmative Action and Employment; Legal Issues; Title IX

References and further reading

Americans with Disabilities Act of 1990, 42 U.S.C. § 12101 et seq.

Anthony v. Syracuse, 224 A.D. 487; 231 N.Y.S. 435 (1928).

Bickel, Robert D., and Peter F. Lake. 1999. *The Rights and Responsibilities of the Modern University: Who Assumes the Risks of College Life?* Durham, NC: Carolina Academic Press.

Carr v. St. John's, 12 N.Y.2d 802; 187 N.E.2d 18 (1962).

Civil Rights Restoration Act of 1987, 20 U.S.C. § 1687.

Dixon v. Alabama State Board of Education, 294 F.2d 150 (Fifth Circuit, 1961).

Drug-Free Schools and Communities Act, 20 U.S.C. § 1102i.

Family Educational Rights and Privacy Act of 1974, 20 U.S.C. § 1232g.

Gott v. Berea College, 156 Ky. 376, 161 S.W. 204 (1913).

Healy v. James, 408 U.S. 169; 92 S. Ct. 2338 (1972).

Jeanne Clery Disclosure of Campus Security Policy and Campus Crime Statistics Act, 20 U.S.C. § 1092f).

Kaplin William A., and Barbara A. Lee. 1995. *The Law of Higher Education: A Comprehensive Guide to Legal Implications of Administrative Decision Making.* 3rd ed. San Francisco: Jossey-Bass.

Pratt v. Wheaton College, 40 Ill. 186 (1866).

Section 504 of the *Rehabilitation Act of 1973,* 29 U.S.C. § 794.

Tinker v. Des Moines Independent Community School District, 393 U.S. 503; 89 S. Ct. 733 (1969).

Title VII of the Civil Rights Act of 1964, 42 U.S.C. § 2000d.

Title IX of the Educational Amendments of 1972, 20 U.S.C. § 1681 et seq.

Woods v. Simpson, 146 Md. 547; 126 A. 882 (1924).

Title IX

Title IX of the Education Amendments of 1972 provides that "No person in the United States shall, on the basis of sex, be excluded from participation in, be denied the benefits of, or be subjected to discrimination under any education program or activity receiving Federal financial assistance" (Section 1681 (a)). From the beginning, Title IX has been fraught with controversy and foot dragging. Yet this piece of legislation has had almost as much impact on education as Title VII of the Civil Rights Act of 1964, which prohibited discrimination by ethnicity in education programs and forced the wholesale desegregation of higher education. Key issues with Title IX include employment, sexual harassment, athletics, admissions and scholarships, and pregnancy.

Title IX was birthed by the Women's Equity Action League (WEAL), the National Organization for Women (NOW), congressional representatives, and academic women across the country. In 1969, Bernice Sandler, a recent Ph.D., discovered that Executive Order 11246 (as revised) forbade discrimination against women as well as minorities on the part of federal contractors (i.e., all postsecondary institutions receiving federal funds). Under the aegis of WEAL, Sandler filed a class action complaint against all universities and colleges in the country, charging gender discrimination. The ensuing outpouring of information from academic women, support of key members of Congress, and complaints of sex discrimination filed by WEAL and NOW against over 250 colleges and universities led to hearings on the issue by Representative Edith Green. The seven days of hearings in June and July of 1970 were a wake-up call to academic women and congressional representatives

Not until Title IX of the Education Act of 1972 was passed did women's teams like this basketball team from Temple University receive funding for their uniforms and travel. (Joseph V. Lavolito/ Courtesy of Temple University)

(specifically, Representatives Green, Martha Griffiths, and Shirley Chisholm, and Senator Birch Bayh). As a result of the nearly 1,300 pages of transcripts, Title IX was born and attached to the Education Amendments of 1972. There was little opposition to Title IX, but college representatives did demand exemptions for private undergraduate admissions and football. Title IX was passed on 23 June 1972 and signed into law on 1 July. There was little recognition of the broad coverage that Title IX would command, especially in athletics, but also in all areas of academic life.

However, it soon became evident that the enforcement of Title IX would be an uphill battle. The Department of Health, Education, and Welfare (HEW) delayed issuing guidelines to implement the legislation. After three years and heavy pressure from Congress, HEW issued regulations (34 C.F.R., sec. 106 et seq.; available online at http://www.ed.gov/offices/OCR/regs/34cfr106.html). Another year passed before the regulations took effect.

Two important court cases challenged the scope and coverage of Title IX. *North Haven Board of Education v. Bell* (1982) challenged whether Title IX applied to the employment practices of education institutions and if so, whether this function was consistent with the statute. The court answered "yes" to both issues. Two years later, in *Grove City College v. Bell* (1984), the Supreme Court ruled that Title IX applied only to the program or entity receiving federal funds (such as the college's student aid program) and not the entire college. Civil rights groups and congressional representatives criticized this narrow interpretation, which also applied to Title VII of the Civil Rights Act of 1964, Section 504 of the Rehabilitation Act of 1973, and the Age Discrimination and Employment Act of 1975 because the other three pieces of legislation contained the same definition of "program." As a result, the Civil Rights Restoration Act of 1987, passed over the veto of President Ronald Reagan, amended the four laws to define program or activity as "all the operations of . . . a college, university, or other postsecondary institution . . . any part of which is extended federal financial assistance" (U.S. Department of Justice 1998).

Title IX has had an important influence on the admission of women to postsecondary institutions. Although the original legislation had special admissions exemptions, Title IX and the Fourteenth Amendment have combined to provide strong protection to women in this area. Title IX prohibits preference by gender and "actual or potential parental, family, or marital status" in admissions. The most famous admissions cases involve two public all-male military academies: the Virginia Military Institute (VMI) and the Citadel. In arguments that echoed those used to prevent racial desegregation of higher education, the State of Virginia argued that it had created separate, "parallel" programs for women at other institutions and that these programs were "sufficiently comparable." In *United States v. Commonwealth of Virginia* (1996), the Supreme Court disagreed and found that VMI's exclusion of women violated the Fourteenth Amendment. So, although Title IX allows narrow exceptions in admissions, primarily in religious institutions, the Fourteenth Amendment provides a stronger tool for the admission of women into all types of postsecondary programs.

A related issue is that of financial aid and gender. Title IX orders that financial aid funds administered by the institution not discriminate based on sex, marital, or parental status (34 C.F.R. Sec. 106.37(a)(1)). Again, the original legislation permitted exceptions to nondiscrimination in financial aid, including funds from foreign governments or foreign trusts (the Rhodes Scholar exception), athletic scholarships, and winners of pageants based on "personal appearance, poise, and talent" (the Miss America exception).

Another important and unresolved issue is the use of standardized test scores in the scholarship selection process. In *Sharif by Salahuddin v. New York State Department of Education,* a group of female high school students filed suit using the Fourteenth Amendment to prevent the state of New York's practice of awarding Regents and Empire State Scholarships based exclusively on Scholastic Aptitude Test (SAT) scores. The women argued that although women as a group tended to score about sixty points lower on the SAT, they had higher high school and college grades than men. The New York district court agreed and ordered the state not to use the SAT as the sole criterion for selection. This decision raises the intriguing question of whether women are discriminated against in the National Merit Scholarship selection process. The selection of semifinalists for this prestigious scholarship is based on test score (PSAT) alone, but the finalists are judged on several factors, including test scores and high school record. Although more girls than boys take the PSAT, boys garner nearly 60 percent of the semifinalist spots (Poe 1998).

The admissions regulations, which prohibit discrimination based on actual or potential parental, family, or marital status, mirrors the language throughout Title IX that prohibits discrimination against pregnant students and employees. This protection for pregnant employees predated the Title VII prohibition of discrimination based on pregnancy. The provision has had a much stronger impact on K–12 students, however, for in the past, a pregnant student or a student-mother was routinely discriminated against in terms of extracurricular activities, courses, and academic placement. There were no such sanctions, however, for the student-father. Title IX eliminated this disparity.

Another issue that has received wide attention is sexual harassment. Title IX prohibits sexual harassment of both employees and students, and Title VII of the Civil Rights Act prohibits the sexual harassment of employees, including student employees. The victim of the harassment may be male or female, and the harassment may be either heterosexual or homosexual. Two types of sexual harassment are recognized in employment cases. Quid pro quo sexual harassment involves the exchange of sexual favors in return for certain benefits: a better grade, promotion, or recommendation for tenure. Likewise, it is also sexual harassment if negative action is threatened if such favors are not granted. The second type is hostile environment harassment, which is offensive conduct directed at an employee by colleagues, potential students, visitors, or vendors, for example. Although a victim of sexual harassment has various legal options, an institution of higher education should have a written policy on sexual harassment and a grievance procedure that protects the rights of both the victim and harasser. Further, the Supreme Court declared that, at least in employment-related cases (*Harris v. Forklift Systems* 1993), the harassing conduct is unlawful whether or not it produces a psychological, financial, or other impact on the victim.

Harassment cases involving faculty-student or student-student harassment have taken a different path. Many of the court cases and incidents reported in the media come from the K–12 sector and are either shocking cases of sexual abuse or blatant overreaction. In the higher education cases, however, both the harasser and victim are adults. Although university sexual harassment policies forbid unwanted sexual advances between faculty and students, consensual affairs are viewed in different ways. Some would argue that any affair between a faculty member and student in his or her class could not truly be consensual because of the power relationship. Others argue that consensual affairs should not be subject to scrutiny. The key word in most such cases is *unwanted* sexual attention of any type. Under Title IX, harassment cases may be pursued only against the institution (not the individual harasser), although tort and various criminal laws may allow victims of physical abuse to take legal action directly against the harasser in state or local courts.

Moreover, there are different standards for adjudicating Title IX sexual harassment cases, depending on whether the individual seeks redress through the courts or through the U.S. Department of Education. Federal courts must follow the Supreme Court's guidance in *Gebser v. Lago Vista Independent School District* (1998) for faculty-student harassment and *Davis v. Monroe County Board of Education* (1999) for peer harassment. Generally, these two cases require that to be held liable for harassment, an official of the institution must have "actual knowledge of, discrimination [the sexual harassment] . . . and fails to adequately respond" (*Gebser v. Lago* 1998, section C). Thus, the victim must go to an appropriate college official and make a complaint of sexual harassment, preferably in writing. If the victim files sexual harassment charges with a campus hearing officer or directly with the U.S. Department of Education, then the Office of Civil Rights "Sexual Harassment Guidance: Harassment of Students by School Employees, Other Students, or Third Parties" guidelines apply.

A vexing recent development in sexual harassment case law in higher education is the pitting of Title IX against the First Amendment. In a technical writing class at the University of New Hampshire, a faculty member made perceived sexual comments. One such comment was that "Belly dancing is like jello on a plate with a vibrator under the plate." Because of this and other incidents, several women filed charges against the faculty member, and the university found him guilty of sexual harassment. However, the federal district court sided with the faculty member, citing, among other reasons, that the sexual harassment policy "fails to take into account the nation's interest in academic freedom and therefore is not *reasonably* related to the legitimate pedagogical purpose of providing a congenial academic environment" (*Silva v. University of New Hampshire* 1994, 314). In another case involving classroom speech, the Court of Appeals for the Ninth Circuit said that neither appellate courts nor the Supreme Court had determined the scope of protection to be given to a professor's classroom speech when charges of sexual harassment were involved. Rather, the court attacked the vagueness of the university's sexual harassment policy, saying that "Cohen was simply without any notice that the Policy would be applied in such way as to punish his longstanding teaching style—a style that, until the College imposed punishment upon Cohen under the Policy, had apparently been considered pedagogically sound and within the bounds of teaching methodology permitted at the college" (*Cohen v. San Bernadino Valley College* 1996, 972). Finally, by extension, liability for peer-to-peer verbal sexual harassment is limited due to the Supreme Courts rejection of "hate speech" codes for public college campuses. Thus, there is controversy over whether verbal sexual harassment conflicts with First Amendment free speech rights at public colleges and universities, and it will not be resolved until the issue is addressed by the U.S. Supreme Court.

Title IX has had far-reaching effects on athletics. Even though the regulations on Title IX in athletics were developed in 1975, they were not enforced until the late 1980s, after the 1984 *Grove City College* case made clear that all programs in the institutions, whether or not they received federal funds, were covered. Beginning at Section 106.31, the regulations spell out equal opportunity requirements for interscholastic, intercollegiate, club, or intramural athletics; athletic scholarships; physical education classes; and extracurricular activities (cheerleading, booster clubs, etc.). The regulations include all sports and do not exclude any revenue-generating sports from the calculation of funds available to the athletic programs.

According to William A. Kaplin and Barbara A. Lee (1995), by far the greatest controversy generated by Title IX is over segregated versus unitary (gender-integrated) teams. The regulations (Section 106.41(b)) require that where a sports team is composed of members of a single sex and opportunities for separate competition are not available and have been historically limited, members of the excluded sex must be allowed to try out for the team in question, unless it is a contact sport (boxing, wrestling, rugby, ice hockey, football, or basketball). The overall athletic program should "effectively accommodate the interests and abilities of members of both sexes" (Section 106.41 (c)(1)).

Although the requirements do not mandate equality of aggregate expenditures for members of each sex, they do stipulate that the "failure to provide necessary funds for teams for one sex" is a relevant measure of compliance. Section 106.41 (c)(1) does list ten factors to help measure overall equity: whether the selection of sports and levels of competition effectively accommodate the interests and abilities of members of both sexes; the provision of equipment and supplies;

scheduling of games and practice times; travel and per diem allowances; opportunity to receive coaching and academic tutoring; assignment and compensation of coaches and tutors; provision of locker rooms, practice, and competitive facilities; provision of medical and training facilities and services; provision of housing and dining facilities and services; and publicity. Additional, detailed information on athletic compliance is contained in the "Policy Interpretation" and the "Investigator's Manual" for the Office of Civil Rights.

Both male and female athletes have filed many cases under Title IX. The first case (*Haffer v. Temple University* 1987) ended with a settlement rather than a court order. However, the case inspired women athletes at other colleges to challenge the amount of money allocated to women's athletics. The leading case (actually a series of four cases) on athletics involves Brown University. In the most recent decision (*Cohen v. Brown University* 1996) and the one most likely to influence other cases because it was issued by an appellate court, the decision discussed the fallacy of basing funding for women's athletics based on "relative interest."

> Thus, there exists the danger that, rather than providing a true measure of women's interest in sports, statistical evidence purporting to reflect women's interest instead provides only a measure of the very discrimination that is and has been the basis for women's lack of opportunity to participate in sports . . . [E]ven if it can be empirically demonstrated that, at a particular time, women have less interest in sports than do men, such evidence, standing alone cannot justify providing fewer athletics opportunities for women than for men. Furthermore, such evidence is completely irrelevant where, as here, viable and successful women's varsity teams have been demoted or eliminated. (179–180)

However, the court left to the university to decide exactly how to obtain substantial proportionality (44 Fed. Reg. 71413), including cutting men's teams to do so.

Several male athletes have sued under Title IX when their teams (usually swimming or wrestling) were cut. The courts have consistently ruled that whether the issue is budgetary or compliance with Title IX, the institutions have the freedom to decide how to allocate funds, including cutting teams, as long as they maintain proportionality. As a result, participants in "mat sports" are trying to rally support against Title IX, including modification of the regulations to classify extracurricular activities such as cheerleading and dance teams as intercollegiate sports.

In a very recent case, courts have challenged the "contact sports" exception to Title IX. In *Mercer v. Duke University* (1998; *reversed* 1999) the Court of Appeals for the Fourth Circuit ruled that Title IX does not provide a blanket exception to contact sports; rather the exception is for the "tryout requirement" (34 C.F.R. sec. 106.41(b)). Heather Sue Mercer, a kicker, was allowed to try out for the Duke University football team and practiced with the team for two seasons. Indeed, she kicked the winning field goal in the Blue-White scrimmage in 1995. Ultimately, however, she was excluded from the team. The court ruled that once the university allowed her to try out for the team, it was "subject to Title IX and therefore prohibited from discriminating against [the person trying out] on the basis of his or her sex." As this is being written, Heather Mercer was awarded $1 in actual damages and $2 million in punitive damages. The award is currently on appeal.

The impact of Title IX on sports has been dramatic. The U.S. Department of Education indicates that since 1972 women's participation in collegiate athletics has increased from 15 percent of all athletes to 37 percent, college scholarship money for women athletes increased from $100,000 to $180 million, and operating expenses per female athlete increased from $1 per year to $4,100 ("Title IX: 25 Years of Progress").

Yet as successful as Title IX has been in promoting equity for women and girls, there is further to go. Title IX has made many changes since 1972 that have affected women and girls in all types of educational settings. The two most controversial issues, athletics and sexual harassment, will continue to draw popular and media attention and be the subject of lawsuits and lobbying for years to come. In all other areas of academic life, Title IX will continue to promote small, incremental changes for women for decades to come.

Patricia Somers

See also Part 2: Sexual Harassment; Part 5: Affirmative Action and Employment; Gender Inequality; Legal Issues; Part 6: Growth of Women's Athletics; Sexual Assault; Women Athletes; Part 7: Hiring; Tenure and Promotion

References and further reading

Burns, Beverly H. 2000. *A Practical Guide to Title IX in Athletics: Law, Principles, and Practices.* Washington, DC: National Association of College and University Attorneys.

Civil Rights Restoration Act, 20 U.S.C. sec. 1687 (1987).

Cohen v. Brown University, 101 F.3d 155, First Circuit (1996).

Cohen v. San Bernadino Valley College, 92 F.3d 968, Ninth Circuit (1996).

Cole, Elsa Kircher, ed. 1997. *Sexual Harassment on Campus: A Legal Compendium.* Washington, DC: National Association of College and University Attorneys.

Cole, Elsa Kircher, and Thomas P. Hustoles. 1997. *How to Conduct a Sexual Harassment Investigation.* Washington, DC: National Association of College and University Attorneys.

Davis v. Monroe County Board of Education, 119 Sup. Ct. 1661 (1999).

Fair Test: The National Center for Fair and Open Testing. *Gender Bias in College Admissions Test.* http://www.fairtest.org/facts/genderbias.htm. Cited June 12, 2002.

Gebser v. Lago Vista Independent School District, 118 Sup. Ct. 1989 (1998).

Grove City College v. Bell, 465 U.S. 555 (1984).

Haffer v. Temple University, 678 F. Supp. 517, E.D. Pa. (1987).

Harris v. Forklift Systems, 115 Sup. Ct. 367 (1993).

Kaplin, William A., and Barbara A. Lee. 1995. *The Law of Higher Education: A Comprehensive Guide to Administrative Decision Making.* 3rd ed. San Francisco: Jossey-Bass.

———. 2000. *Year 2000 Cumulative Supplement to the Law of Higher Education.* 3rd ed. Washington, DC: National Association of College and University Attorneys.

Mercer v. Duke University, 32 F. Supp. 2d 836, M.D. N.C., 1998; *reversed* 190 F.3d 643, Fourth Circuit (1999).

National Center for Education Statistics. 2000. *Trends in Educational Equity of Girls and Women.* NCES 2000–030. Washington, DC: U.S. Department of Education.

North Haven Board of Education v. Bell, 456 U.S. 512 (1982).

Poe, Kristen. 1998. "Blinded by the Results: Is Looking to GPA in Addition to Standardized Test Scores Truly a Less Discriminatory Solution to Merit Scholarship Selection?" *Women's Rights Law Reporter* 19 (Winter): 181–196.

Sandler, Bernice. 2000. "'Too Strong for a Woman'—The Five Words That Created

Title IX." *Equality and Excellence in Education* (April): 9–13.
Sharif by Salahuddin v. New York State Department of Education, 709 F. Supp. 345, S.D.N.Y. (1989).
Silva v. University of New Hampshire, 888 F. Supp. 292, D.N.H. (1994).
Title IX of the Education Amendments, 20 U.S.C. sec. 1681 et seq. (1972).
"Title IX: 25 Years of Progress." http://www.ed.gov/pubs/Title IX. Cited June 12, 2002.
United States v. Commonwealth of Virginia, 116 Sup. Ct. 2264 (1996).
U.S. Department of Education, Office of Civil Rights. *Case Resolution Manual.* http://www.ed.gov/offices/OCR/docs/ocrcrm.html. Cited June 12, 2002.
———. *How to File a Discrimination Complaint with the Office of Civil Rights.* http://www.ed.gov/offices/OCR/docs/howto.html. Cited June 12, 2002.
———. "Investigator's Manual." http://www.ed.gov/offices/OCR. Cited June 12, 2002.
———. *Nondiscrimination in Employment Practices in Education.* http://www.ed.gov/offices/OCR/docs/hq53e8.html. Cited June 12, 2002.
———. 1977. "Sexual Harassment Guidance: Harassment of Students by School Employees, Other Students, or Third Parties." 62 Fed. Reg, 12034. http://www.ed.gov/offices/OCR/docs/sexhar00.html as revised January 21, 2001. Cited June 12, 2002.
———. 1979. "Policy Interpretation," 44 Fed. Reg. 71413. http://www.ed.gov/offices/OCR/docs/t9interp.html. Cited June 12, 2002.
———. 1997. *Title IX: Twenty-five Years of Progress.* http://www.ed.gov/pubs/TitleIX/title.html.
———. 1999. *Impact of the Civil Rights Laws.* http://www.ed.gov/offices/OCR/docs/impact.html. Cited June 12, 2002.

Women with Disabilities

An organized effort to provide access to higher education for people with disabilities began in the United States during the mid-1940s in response to the return of disabled World War II veterans. Even though several U.S. postsecondary institutions made efforts to make their campuses more accessible to people with mobility disabilities throughout the 1940s, 1950s, and 1960s, the first legislation to address access issues did not occur until 1973. The passage of the Rehabilitation Act of 1973, specifically Section 504, prohibits institutions receiving federal funding from discriminating against people with disabilities by stating, "no otherwise qualified handicapped individual in the U.S. shall, solely by reason of his/her handicap, be excluded from the participation in, be denied the benefits of, or be subjected to discrimination." In essence, Section 504 obligates postsecondary institutions to make "reasonable accommodations" for students who say they have a disability.

Modeled after the Civil Rights Act of 1964, the 1990 Americans with Disabilities Act (ADA) reaffirms Section 504 and extended civil rights protection for people with disabilities to include public and private entities. The ADA enhances Section 504 by providing a definition of disability and guidelines for accessibility. The definition of disability has long been debated by disability rights activists and disability studies theorists. Most political activists consider disability not as a medical category but rather as a social one, perpetuating the belief that disability is socially constructed. "Just as feminists pointed out that 'sex,' as a physiological marker, differed from the vast social meanings assigned to women in the name of 'gender,' disability activists have stressed that social, and not biological, definitions of disability determine the makeup of the minority group and account for its oppression" (Longmore and Umansky 2001). However, to provide civil rights protection to people with disabilities, the ADA defines disability as a: "physical or mental impairment that (1) substantially limits one or more major life activities of such individual; (2) a record of such an impairment; or (3) being regarded as having such an impairment" (U.S. Department of Justice 1990).

The Status of Women with Disabilities as Postsecondary Students

The National Center for Education Statistics has collected data illustrating the significant increase of students with disabilities attending institutions of higher education. Since the 1970s, the number of students with disabilities attending colleges has tripled. According to a 1998 national survey, students with disabilities comprise approximately 9 percent of enrolled undergraduates at both two-year and four-year institutions (Henderson 1999, 16). However, according to a national survey in 2000 of four-year institutions only, the proportion of first-year students reporting disabilities averaged 6–8 percent between 1988 and 2000 (Henderson 2001, 23). The results of this survey also highlighted specific differences related to gender.

In general, on several questions in the freshmen survey, gender appeared to be a more significant characteristic of students than disability status. For example, women with disabilities considered themselves more similar to women without disabilities than to men with disabilities. Students with disabilities were more likely to be male than were students without disabilities (52 percent versus 45 percent). In addition, compared to students without disabilities, white/Caucasian men were overrepresented among freshmen with disabilities (72 percent of students with disabilities were white; 38 percent were white men). In contrast, at 35 percent of the total first-year students with disabilities, white/Caucasian women were underrepresented within this group (Henderson 2001, 26).

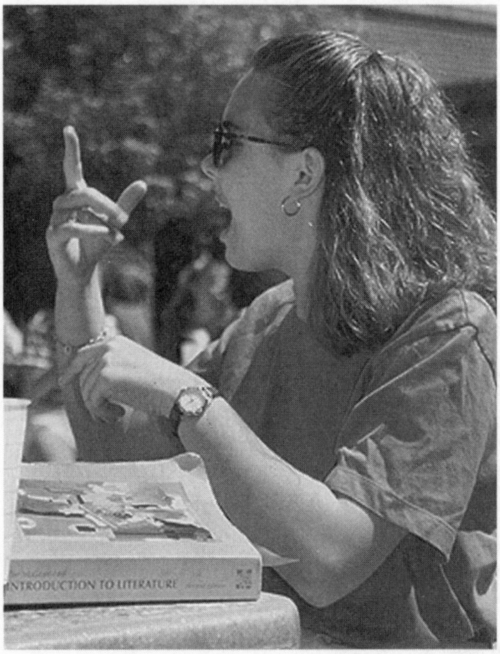

Women with disabilities have had to fight especially hard for access to higher education (Courtesy of Gallaudet University)

Given the historical marginalization of people with disabilities and women in higher education, examining the gender differences within this population provides insight into the increased invisibility experienced by women with disabilities on college campuses. One significant statistic highlighted by the 2000 survey suggests women were more likely to report health-related disabilities, whereas men reported higher incidences of learning disabilities. Of students at four-year institutions, 15 percent described their disability as "health-related," 60 percent were women, and about 34 percent were students of color (Henderson 2001). The virtual invisibility of many health-related disabilities illustrates a current concern about access and accommodation for people with invisible disabilities on college campuses.

Although physical barriers to access still exist on college campuses, attitudes and behaviors toward students with disabilities form the most prominent barrier to educational access. A deficit paradigm exists in which the student with a disability is considered deviant and therefore is provided separate services to individually address the deficit. The "problem" remains with the individual rather than with the academic system that labels and defines the "problem." When a disability is not readily visible, legitimacy issues are raised, and the needs of these students with invisible disabilities are often dismissed.

The Academic Field of Disability Studies

Much like the development of women's studies as an academic discipline, disability studies has emerged as an interdisciplinary field of study that focuses on disability as a social phenomenon and provides a social, political, and cultural analysis as a departure from the popular, individually focused, impairment-oriented medical model. However, "the extraordinarily low representation of people with disabilities in academic settings as students, faculty, and administrators, as well as the general failure to recognize them as an underrepresented minority, has excluded their perspectives from both current discussions of curricular reform and ongoing intellectual discourse" (Longmore and Umansky 2001, 26).

Susan M. Pliner

References and further reading

Henderson, Cathy. 1999. *1999 College Freshmen with Disabilities: A Biennial Statistical Profile.* HEATH Resource Center and American Council on Education.

———. 2001. *2001 College Freshmen with Disabilities: A Biennial Statistical Profile.* HEATH Resource Center and American Council on Education.

Linton, Simi. 1998. *Claiming Disability: Knowledge and Identity.* New York: New York University Press.

Longmore, Paul K., and Lauri Umansky, eds. 2001. *The New Disability History: American Perspectives.* New York: New York University Press.

U.S. Department of Justice. 1990. Americans with Disabilities Act. http://www.usdoj.gov/crt/ada/statute/html. Cited June 12, 2002.

U.S. Department of Labor. Rehabilitation Act of 1973, Section 504. http://www.dol.gov/oasam/regs/statutes/sec504.htm. Cited June 12, 2002.

Part 6

WOMEN STUDENTS

Overview

The percentage of women college students enrolled in higher education has steadily increased since the 1970s. At 56 percent of the undergraduate student population in 1999, women are more academically successful than their male counterparts. In fact, in 1999 women received 61 percent of associate's degrees, 56 percent of bachelor's degrees, 57 percent of master's degrees, and 42 percent of the doctoral degrees awarded. Unless a dramatic shift occurs, women in the United States will soon receive more doctorates than U.S. men, making women the number one recipients of all degrees in U.S. colleges and universities at all educational levels. Not only are women receiving more degrees than men, but in 2001 the National Center for Education Statistics reports that the number of undergraduate women in two- and four-year institutions has exceeded men since 1978. Women students from underrepresented populations, including African American, Hispanic, Native American, and Asian American, are also matriculating in increasing numbers. The changing demographics of college and university students favor women: students are more likely to be older, attend part-time, live off-campus, work, and have a family. When relationships or jobs dead end or children enter school, older women return to the academy to fulfill their dreams and concentrate their efforts on their personal and professional development. Some individuals are concerned about the feminization of higher education, whereas others rejoice in the changes brought to the academy. Ultimately, women on campus are as diverse among themselves as they are compared to men.

Women bring more to campus than just their presence. The years since the 1960s, during what Rob Rhoads calls the "freedom struggles" of the multicultural student movements, including the women's movement, civil rights movement, and gay liberation movement, brought unheralded changes to U.S. colleges and universities. Changes in admissions and financial aid, parietal rules in residence halls, gendered leadership and governance roles, the treatment of women students by faculty and men students, and the campus culture for women are all gaining attention on many campuses. Changes in the social realm consist of limited social and sexual restrictions, more legislation dealing with women's safety on campus, more curricula to frame women's experience through women's studies and interdisciplinary classes, and more career options than even a generation ago. Universities responded to these changes in different ways, but many created women's centers, set up commissions to study the status of women, and created programs to combat sexual harassment on campus.

Women students are graduating in record numbers (Courtesy of Spelman College)

Academic changes that favor women in this time of change include feminist pedagogy, which focuses on discussion, inclusiveness, and experience as legitimate ways of knowing in the classroom. A learning style preference of many women, these new patterns open the way for more dialogue, interaction, and connected learning in and out of the classroom. In spite of some change, in *Women in Higher Education: A Feminist Perspective* (1993), Judith Glazer-Raymo, Estela Bensimón, and Barbara Townsend lament the paucity of research on women students in community colleges; returning women students; Asian American, Native American, and Latina women students; and recent immigrants from eastern Europe. They recommend a better understanding of the intersections of race, class, and gender by looking through the lens of feminist paradigms and methods. These changes and others are a harbinger of the continuing evolution of women's influence in the academy.

Historical Influences

The first women students to enter a collegiate institution in the United States did so in 1837 at Oberlin College in Ohio. Although women (and other underrepresented populations) were a part of the entering class, they were not encouraged or allowed the same academic and social privileges as their male peers. In 1865 Vassar was the first self-declared college to open its doors exclusively for women, who were expected to study a curriculum as rigorous as the one studied by men at the elite private institutions. Private coordinate women's colleges, attached and connected to institutions for men only, offered a compromise. However, in the second half of the nineteenth century, options for women's higher education multiplied. Land grant institutions were created by the 1862 Morrill Act, and since the attendance of women was not addressed specifically in the bill, women could not be excluded from these institutions. In addition to the women-centered private colleges and single-sex vocational institutions, women could also choose to attend religiously oriented coeducational colleges and private and public secular coeducational institutions. By the 1870s, coeducation was seen as the norm and gave women more options than the single-sex institutions offered. However, women were by no means treated equally to men, often being required to enroll only in curricula deemed acceptable for women (teacher training, domestic science, etc.) and sometimes not being permitted to attend classes with their male peers.

By the late 1800s, the noticeable numbers of women in higher education led to administrative need for student control. Faculty concern about students' extracurricular and anti-intellectual activities increased. A growing student body, no longer homogeneous, and with less interest in scholarship, a more complex and involved social life, less faculty-student contact, and more problems framed as discipline, set the stage for deans of women in U.S. higher education. At the twilight of the nineteenth century in 1892, the first deans of women were hired at the Universities of Chicago, Michigan, and Wisconsin. In *Pioneering Deans of Women* (2000), Jana Nidiffer maintained that college presidents resented what they described as the "woman problem," too many female students and not enough control over them. Freeing the president and faculty from undesirable duties, deans of women assumed responsibility for the health, virtue, and on-campus housing of women students and attempted to ensure their proper supervision.

The twentieth century saw unimagined change in the numbers of women on college and university campuses, and although progress did occur in many arenas, some feminist scholars frame these 100 years as one of marginality for college women. In the 1920s, female college students, predominantly white, were the first modern college women; as Barbara Solomon noted in her book, *In the Company of Educated Women* (1985), they were ladylike yet demanded expression of their individuality. In the 1930s, women students learned about commitments to serve society while holding on to frivolity and breaking many sexual taboos, mainly those forbidding premarital and lesbian sex. College women in the 1940s, still primarily white, entered the workforce to assist in the war effort. Yet when large numbers of young men returned from World War II, many women abandoned work for domesticity. As the purpose for educating college women came into question in the late 1940s, the Serviceman's Readjustment Act of 1944 (commonly known as the "G. I. Bill") reduced access to higher education for women. Veterans represented 49 percent of those enrolled in higher education and 69 percent of all college men. Conversely, women usually married within three years of graduation, and many worked until they began a family.

In the 1950s, a more diverse, egalitarian student body than ever before began showing up in larger numbers on U.S.

college campuses, including more women, more veterans, and more people of color. These ever-increasing numbers of women college graduates elected to chose work after marriage and even after children. In *Campus Life: Undergraduate Cultures from the End of the Eighteenth Century to the Present* (1987), Helen Lefkowitz Horowitz described a study of Vassar College alumnae in the 1950s. Women students serious about their studies but from families of modest means sought careers, whereas more social women from privileged backgrounds aspired upon graduation to the roles of wives and mothers. Most who held jobs joined fields traditionally considered appropriate female employment, such as teaching, social work, and low-level management. Competing with men for highly prized graduate and professional school programs, women college graduates were bright and determined to succeed, studied and worked persistently, moved forward in spite of setbacks, and defied conformist expectations.

The 1960s and 1970s brought social upheaval and change to the country and U.S. higher education. The Vietnam War, the civil rights and women's movements, and the assassinations of John F. Kennedy and Martin Luther King, Jr., created dramatic social and legislative action affecting higher education. Title VII of the Civil Rights Act of 1964 and the Higher Education Act of 1965 were created, and in loco parentis (campus policies designed to place the institution, literally, "in place of parents" in overseeing the safety and morality of students) dropped out of favor. The civil rights movement was partially spawned by four black students protesting segregation at a sit-in at Woolworth's lunch counter in Greensboro, North Carolina. Seeking direct action and following the moral legitimacy of the movement, thousands of northern students, many of whom were women, picketed lunch counters, participated in freedom rides in the South, and registered voters in Mississippi.

Protests on college campuses lasted into the 1970s. The most well-known protest occurred in May 1970 at Kent State University, where four students protesting the Vietnam War were shot and killed by National Guardsmen. As the women's movement took hold on campus and in loco parentis became passé, women students gained access to the birth control pill and demanded unlimited sexual freedom. As social mores changed, women could choose to initiate sex that was in public view, casual, and unconnected to commitment. Paradoxically, although college students opposed most parental limits on activities such as excessive drinking, taking drugs, and indulging in permissive sex, obtaining academic achievement for the purpose of occupational success was a common mantra among college students. As the women's movement gained impetus and Betty Friedan's book *The Feminine Mystique* was published in 1963, women students met in consciousness-raising groups on campus to talk about what it meant to be female in U.S. society. These groups were the forerunners of women's studies programs created in the years that followed.

As a kind of backlash to the liberalism of the preceding decades, the late 1980s and early 1990s were a conservative time in the United States as the economic, political, and social climates changed. Higher education was no exception and felt the effects of this wave. A qualitative study by Dorothy Holland and Margaret Eisenhart (1990), described in *Educated in Romance* and conducted during the 1980s at two southern universities, highlighted a culture in which female students were valued by how they looked and dated, rather than by their intellectual and career aspirations. College women's battles with anorexia, bulimia, and other eating disorders have been partially explained by this phenomenon. *The Morning After* (1993), a backlash memoir of Katie Roiphe's undergraduate and graduate days at Harvard and Princeton Universities, framed a conservative feminist debate by waxing right-wing philosophical on women students in higher education, ignoring gender power differences in the academy, and waging war against campus feminist activists who wanted to eliminate date rape and sexual harassment.

Although not based on scientific evidence, Roiphe's argument framed a politically conservative response to feminism on campus; the publication of this book and the debates it sparked on campuses illustrated the complexity of the women's movement as a new millennium commenced. During this time, primarily white female students and faculty kept alive the conversation about women in the academy through their participation in the growing number of women's studies programs across the United States. In this increasingly contentious society, new rules were created to protect women and the campus community from criminal acts.

In the new millennium, a renewed sense of social justice around women's issues in the academy is taking hold. A national teleconference in 2000 used a constructivist method to create a social action agenda for the twenty-first century, *Women's Lives, Women's Voices, Women's Solutions: Shaping a National Agenda for Women in Higher Education,* sponsored by the National Initiative for Women in Higher Education: Improving Campus Climates and the Status of Women in Higher Education and the University of Minnesota, had more than 5,000 participants at four regional and 200 satellite sites. First Lady Hillary Rodham Clinton served as honorary chair. Sensing a need to move beyond issues of access, the agenda focused on issues of inclusion and leadership by women workers, teachers, and students in higher education. In facilitated caucus sessions, participants developed action plans to improve the campus climate and status of women on campus in teaching, learning, research; work and life; partnerships and outreach; and leadership in a new century. (A complete report of these action plans can be found at www.umn.edu/women/wihe.html.) Participants at the conference were invited to submit "Commitment to Action" plans for their campuses to the above website address and to keep the discussion of women's issues alive on their campuses with a discerning eye toward the future.

Social Influences

The social influences on women in higher education in recent years are prominent and diverse. Fewer social rules, more crime against college women, and ever-increasing numbers of women with different racial, ethnic, sexual, class, ability, and religious backgrounds are the norm. Roberta Hall and Bernice Sandler described the assumptions and conditions apparent in our society and on college campuses in their 1984 report, *Out of the Classroom: A Chilly Campus Climate for Women?* They explained how women are perceived as different and deficient since men's behavior is accepted as the norm, men receive more pay for the same kind of work as women, and men's work is assigned more importance than women's work. On campus, the result is differential treatment of women and men. Students, faculty, and campus administrators engage in behaviors that single out women (e.g., focusing on women's appearance and not their accomplishments), behaviors that overlook women (e.g., giving less time and attention to women than men), and mixed patterns of communication between women and men (e.g., impersonal styles for men and personal styles for women). Hall and Sandler further asserted that the effects of a chilly climate translate into fewer opportunities for women and enhance their feelings of inadequacy, isolation, frustration, and helplessness. Their report, which was widely distributed throughout the United States, offered specific suggestions for how admissions, financial aid, academic advising, career counseling, lab and field work, work study and campus employment, health care, campus safety, athletics, student government and leadership could make the campus a more hospitable place for women students. Hall and Sandler also reevaluated the residential, social, and cultural climate for women on campus.

Sexual Harassment, Sexual Assault, and Campus Safety. Sexual harassment by employees and employers is prohibited under Title VII of the Civil Rights Act of 1964 and is recognized by the courts as a cause of action under Title IX of the Education Amendments of 1972; in some localities, state and local laws also prohibit it. Institutions frame definitions in various ways but usually include language prohibiting the three forms of harassment that have been defined in the legislation and subsequent case law: quid pro quo harassment (literally, "this for that"), unwelcome sexual attention, and hostile working or learning environment. Quid quo pro behavior is defined as an attempt to coerce an individual into sexual favors by promising rewards or making threats of punishment (such as in grades or workplace evaluation). Unwelcome sexual attention is just that; it can occur between individuals of the same or different genders. Hostile learning or working environments may include offensive, degrading, or intimidating behavior, but specific benefits are not promised for sexual cooperation. Examples of creating a hostile environment include using sexually degrading words or sounds to describe a person, repeatedly making sexually explicit comments that are not legitimately related to the learning or working setting, or asking recurrent questions about an individual's sexual activities.

Many people, female students included, do not know what sexual harassment means. Many cannot tell the difference between flirting and persistent inappropriate behavior. Yet sexual harassment, date rape, obscene graffiti, and threatening phone calls are common on college and university campuses. Men's residential social fraternities have been specifically singled out as creating exclusionary and divisive environments regarding class, race, and especially sex. It is estimated that as many as 50–70 percent of undergraduate women have personally experienced some type of sexual harassment. At one university in a multi-university study, 30 percent of female graduate student respondents were prey to unwelcome sexual attention from professors, and 15 percent received direct propositions. Women students from underrepresented populations are particularly in danger of verbal and physical abuse.

Because of an increase in the number of reported cases, sexual assault on college and university campuses gained national awareness as a violent crime in the late 1980s and early 1990s. In spite of increased reporting during this time period, forcible rape was the most common unreported violent crime on campus. Research has shown that most date and acquaintance rapes on colleges and university campuses involve excessive consumption of alcohol and other drugs, often encouraged by peer pressure. Large numbers of violent crimes on campus forced the nation's lawmakers to create legislation to protect college and university community members, particularly women.

For years universities underplayed campus dangers, but finally in 1990 Congress took action and passed the Student's Right-to-Know and Campus Security Act. This legislation holds institutions responsible for informing the university community of a crime and for protecting the university community from crime. This legislation also required that the outcomes of disciplinary hearings involving a violent crime be made known to the victim. An amendment of the initial bill, the 1991 Sexual Assault Victim's Bill of Rights, holds institutions of higher education accountable for informing the campus community of sex offenses and for educating the community in sex offense prevention. President Bill Clinton signed the 1994 Violence against Women Act, which states specifically that college campuses must allocate restitution monies for continuous training of campus security; psychological, medical, and legal assistance for victims; and peer education programs.

Women Students' Leadership. Leadership opportunities for graduate and undergraduate women on campus are plentiful, although breaking through the male stronghold of campus leadership has not been easy. Authors such as Sally Helgesen in *The Female Advantage: Women's Ways of Leadership* (1990) and Margaret Hennig and Anne Jardim in *The Managerial Women* (1976) made popular theories about the ways in which women lead differently than men. They asserted that women are more likely to lead in a cooperative instead of competitive way, stay connected to instead of separate from those they lead, and try to find ways to resolve conflict with a win-win instead of win-lose outcome.

Often the "chilly climate" for women on college and university campuses, combined with a lack of female mentors, particularly for women students of color, leaves women lower in the campus leadership hierarchy than their male peers. However, Renee Romano studied fifteen women presidents or copresidents of campus-wide coeducational student governing or social-cultural organizations representing African American, Asian American, Jewish, and Caucasian women and women with disabilities at three large institutions. She found new points of reference for women student leaders. For example, these leaders discovered role models in strong and powerful mothers and grandmothers who had never held formal leadership positions, rather than women administrators and faculty in the higher education context. Emphasizing their relationships with organizational members, women in the study used words like "nonhierarchical, interactive, accessible, one-to-one, and equality" to describe their leadership practices. Women student leaders in this study were developing ways to lead that reflected practices and development different from those experienced by their male counterparts.

Developmental Influences

The development of collegiate women has received important consideration in the last twenty years, as higher education tries to meet their needs. Much of what is known about student development is carved out of research conducted on students. However, the overwhelming majority of research conducted prior to the 1970s on the development of college students used men as its subjects and generalized the findings to women. Additionally, most research conducted on men used rational-modernist methodology and quantitative methods, whereas the newer scholarship on women typically employs more constructivist methodologies and qualitative methods. Testing hypotheses is no longer the norm, as feminist scholarship creates knowledge by entering into conversation with study participants and often seeks social change as an outcome. To date, moral and intellectual development of women and the formation of their identity are the domains examined most closely by scholars.

Gender-Related Moral Development. Carol Gilligan published her highly acclaimed book, *In a Different Voice* (1982), using data she collected in the late 1970s. Gilligan's research was influenced by the research of, among others, Jean Baker Miller and Nancy Chodorow. Miller argued for a gender-based psychological perspective in *Toward a New Psychology of Women* (1976), whereas Chodorow, in *The Reproduction of Mothering* (1978), observed a psychological separation of male children from their mothers, whereas female children connected to theirs. In her own research, Gilligan concluded that women were more likely to use an "ethic of care" to make moral decisions, which she contrasted with Lawrence Kohlberg's "ethic of justice." According to Gilligan, a care ethic frames women in relationship with others, whereas a justice ethic sees men as separate, autonomous, and rule-bound.

Gilligan's work sparked an examination of gender differences in scholarship and in the media. Research in student affairs, including counseling, residence life, leadership development, and career planning, and in academic disciplines such as teaching, social work, and developmental psychology, stressed the need for less emphasis on traditional models that focus on rules and objectivity and more on the application of new models that focus on connection. Gilligan published more than fifteen works in about the same number of years, some with her colleagues at Harvard University, on the moral development of young women, including *Mapping the Moral Domain* (1988) and a chapter in Arthur Chickering's *The Modern American College* (1981). Many scholars agree that both the ethics of care and justice are necessary for a satisfying moral life.

Not without its critics, many of whom are feminists, Gilligan's work is perceived by some as a way to encourage gender stereotyping of social expectations or to glorify women. In *Caring: A Feminine Approach to Ethics and Moral Education* (1984), Nel Noddings claimed that care and justice are discordant moral positions and that choosing care over justice is the appropriate moral choice. Regardless of the position taken by scholars or the press, Gilligan's work added richness to the discussion of moral development and explicated a view different from the idea that there was a single, objective reality. Despite all that has been written about Gilligan's work, no new theories have been created on the moral and ethical development of women, but new theories related to women's identity have been explored.

Gender-Related Identity Development. Over a fifteen-year period from the early 1970s to the late 1980s, Ruthellen Josselson studied what was essential in women's experience to create a uniquely female identity. She discovered that female college students thought it was more important *who* they become rather than *what* they become, the opposite of what male college students sought. Josselson's longitudinal study, published in 1987 as *Finding Herself: Pathways to Identity Development in Women,* concluded that many college women find their identity in relationship, whereas college men find their identity in competence. Her theory identifies four identity patterns in women—foreclosure, achievement, moratorium, and diffusion—all tied to commitment and crisis. Scant research has been conducted in this area, and more is needed to distinguish the identity development nuances of women of color in particular.

In student affairs, womanist theology, and educational anthropology, a paucity of literature addresses the identity of women and women of color, but scholars are beginning to look at this subject in more complex ways. Scholars who study women's identity argue that it is more complicated than explained in the past. Extending the work of their student affairs colleagues Amy Reynolds and Raechele Pope, who defied the androcentric, single-focus models of identity development and explored multiple oppressions, Susan Jones and Marylu McEwen sought a clearer understanding of the many identities a woman possesses. Derived from Jones's grounded theory study of ten college women with diverse racial backgrounds ranging from twenty to twenty-four years of age, McEwen and Jones presented a fluid model that addresses the intersecting identities of race, class, gender, sexual orientation, and culture. They underscored the importance of understanding how students see and define themselves as an alternative to putting them in boxes based on visible or unseen characteristics. Derived from a small sample of women at one institution, this model needs more qualitative and quantitative empirical testing. However, it is of particular importance to understanding how higher education influences the intersecting identities of an increasingly diverse population of college women.

Gender-Related Intellectual Development. In 1986, Mary Field Belenky, Blythe McVicker Clinchy, Nancy Rule Goldberger, and Jill Mattuck Tarule published their landmark work on the different ways women come to know their world in *Women's Ways of Knowing* (updated in 1997). This foundational work changed the way scholars and practitioners examine how women learn and interpret what they come to know. Taking a constructivist approach by encouraging women to tell their stories, these scholars also worked in a constructivist way by "creating conversations" with each other in many aspects of the project, especially when identifying their findings. Challenging their assumptions derived from earlier work by William Perry (1970), who viewed intellectual development from a linear, universal, singular, and authoritarian perspective, these women created a theory based solely on women's experience. In 1996, this same group of scholars edited a book entitled *Knowledge, Difference, and*

Power, highlighting prominent feminist thinkers such as Sara Ruddick, Aída Hurtado, and Sandra Harding. This book sheds new light on how to look at differences in women's knowing and to acknowledge and respect women's perspectives in this increasingly complicated, diverse world. Grounded in the scholarship of Belenky and her colleagues, as well as Perry, Marcia B. Baxter Magolda's book *Knowing and Reasoning in College* (1992) was the first to demonstrate to postsecondary educators *how* both women and men students think, not *what* they think, so that academics could teach them more effectively. In doing so, Baxter Magolda distinguished between the thought patterns of women and men college students and showed how these patterns could be used for enhancing students' development inside and outside the classroom.

In a monograph entitled *Understanding and Applying Cognitive Development Theory* (1999), Patrick Love and Victoria Guthrie compared and contrasted several theories of intellectual development, including William Perry's *Forms of Intellectual and Ethical Development in College: A Scheme* (1970); Belenky, Clinchy, Goldberger, and Tarule's *Women's Ways of Knowing;* and Baxter Magolda's *Epistemological Reflection Model.* Love and Guthrie created new condensed groupings for understanding similar notions presented in these theories and showed how students may move from unequivocal knowing to radical subjectivity to generative knowing. In their model, unequivocal knowers look at the world as knowable, singular, and made legitimate by authorities. Radical subjectivist knowers move away from absolute knowing to a position at which all knowledge, regardless of source, is equally worth knowing and true. At some point in this stage or position, students move to a "great accommodation" where they recognize the complexity and ambiguity underlying all perspectives. Thus, generative knowers diverge in their outcomes. At this level, Belenky and her colleagues and Baxter Magolda recognize complex and multiple ways of knowing. Baxter Magolda breaks them down by gender and states that as absolute knowers, women are more likely to receive knowledge, whereas men are likely to master it. As transitional knowers, women are more likely to maintain an interpersonal approach, but men are more likely to take an impersonal approach to knowing. Finally, as independent knowers, women are more likely to take an interindividual approach that involves listening to others and then determining their own approach, whereas men are more likely to take an individual approach to knowing. Ultimately, more research is needed to understand the patterns of women's knowing, from all races, classes, sexual orientations, disabilities, and the like, and how these themes manifest themselves in and out of the classroom to enhance women's learning.

Curricular and Occupational Influences

Women's presence on campus has brought substantive changes within academe and beyond. As one of a multitude of critical and cultural perspectives, feminism brings changes to the curriculum and scholarship in many academic fields. Feminist perspectives are woven into the curriculum in women's studies courses and across disciplines, transforming higher education in the process. Using teaching strategies geared toward women's attitudes, values, and beliefs and employing women faculty who are attuned to the gender and cultural differences in graduate and undergraduate epistemological development bring women's experience to the heart of academe. Often described as feminist pedagogy, these models offer more emancipatory approaches encompassing women's ways of knowing than the traditional models that delight in transmitting one correct truth. Encouraging participants to become more active learners, feminist pedagogies express multiple points of view. In *The Feminist Classroom* (1994), Frances A. Maher and Mary Kay Thompson Tetreault describe how teachers, students, and subject content intertwine to produce learning based on relationships and interaction, instead of transmitting knowledge in one direction. They encourage the excluded voices in the classroom to be heard to educate for a multicultural world.

Guiding feminist assessment principles, such as those articulated in Caryn Musil's book *Students at the Center* (1992), embrace interactive pedagogies and encourage classroom assessment that is student-centered; participatory; affected by institutional culture; compatible with feminist activists' beliefs; and shaped by feminist pedagogy, scholarship, and methodology. Although the contributors to Musil's book acknowledge that some of the principles are found in other kinds of assessment, it is the underlying feminist paradigm from which the process unfolds that makes this form of assessment unique and important to women students and faculty. Musil asserts that opening the conversation to students and faculty who differ by race, class, gender, ethnicity, sexuality, age, and disabilities makes space for new insights into and approaches to student learning.

In addition to a feminist change in the way knowledge is presented in higher education, women students are now entering academic fields traditionally considered male domains. Both women and men are moving away from education, the humanities, and the social sciences—all long-established fields of study for women. However, women are not studying in large numbers in the physical sciences, mathematics, or engineering and thus are being locked out of these professional arenas. In *Educating Women for Success in Science and Mathematics* (1994), Sue Rosser and Bonnie Kelly offered suggestions for how the hard sciences might be taught in ways to make them attractive fields of study for women and other underrepresented populations. They described a model for transforming the curriculum to reflect social factors that affect students both inside and outside the classroom, to include women and women's ways of knowing in the content of the curriculum, and to promote social action methods in teaching and scholarship related to science, although other disciplines could also benefit from these changes. Since women typically have higher grade point averages than men, their exclusion from science cannot be explained by lack of ability. In their chapter in *Women Succeeding in the Sciences* (2000), Michelle Smoot Hyde and Julie Gess Newsome discuss university factors, such as positive interaction with professors, access to role models, well-delineated curriculum plans, supportive lab research, and positive associations with other majors on campus, and external factors, such as a supportive network of female friends, family support, work-related experience, and multidimensional experience, as examples of conditions that produce success for women science students. Hyde and Gess Newsome suggested that all of these strategies could enrich women's experience across all academic disciplines.

Most women enter the workforce after completing their higher education, though in lower-paying occupations than men and thus they do not receive the same benefits from their education. In a study presented in *Education Statistics Quarterly*, graduates of colleges and universities in 1992–1993 who did not pursue graduate education within four years represented 70 percent of all college graduates. Four years after this cohort received bachelor's degrees, nearly all who had not enrolled in graduate studies were employed. In 1997, men earned more than women in all fields except engineering, health care (but not nursing), and humanities and arts. Women who were thirty years old or older when they earned their degrees received higher salaries than women twenty-two years old or younger. Asian American and Pacific Islander women earned more than white women upon graduation. In congruence with other findings of women's identity, women indicated that they chose their work based on what was interesting to them, in contrast with men, who looked for job advancement or income possibilities.

Summary

The entries that follow discuss in more detail some of the topics covered in this overview, as well as issues unexplored here. Information on particular populations of female students (e.g., African Americans, American Indians, Asian Americans, biracial and biethnic students, Jewish students, Latinas), campus environment (e.g., classroom climate, community colleges, graduate students and science), and activities of students (e.g., athletics, sororities, extracurricular activities) complements information about critical issues in the lives of women students (e.g., curricular and professional choices, identity development, socioeconomic status, sexuality, persistence).

Florence Guido-DiBrito

References and further reading

American Association of University Women and the AAUW Educational Foundation. 1999. *Higher Education in Transition: The Politics and Practices of Equity, Symposium Proceedings.* Washington, DC: American Association of University Women and the AAUW Educational Foundation.

Baxter Magolda, Marcia B. 1992. *Knowing and Reasoning in College: Gender-Related Patterns in Students' Intellectual Development.* San Francisco: Jossey-Bass.

Belenky, Mary Field, Blythe McVicker Clinchy, Nancy Rule Goldberger, and Jill Mattuck Tarule. 1986. *Women's Ways of Knowing: The Development of Self, Voice, and Mind.* New York: Basic Books.

Chickering, Arthur W., and Associates, eds. 1981. *The Modern American College: Responding to the New Realities of Diverse Students and Changing Society.* San Francisco: Jossey-Bass.

Chodorow, Nancy. 1978. *The Reproduction of Mothering.* Berkeley: University of California Press.

Edwards, Rosalind. 1993. *Mature Women Students: Separating or Connecting Family and Education.* London: Taylor and Francis.

Evans, Nancy J., Deanna S. Forney, and Florence Guido-DiBrito. 1998. *Student Development in College: Theory, Research, and Practice.* San Francisco: Jossey-Bass.

Friedan, Betty. 1963. *The Feminine Mystique.* New York: W. W. Norton.

Gilligan, Carol. 1982. *In a Different Voice: Psychological Theory and Women's Development.* Cambridge, MA: Harvard University Press.

Gilligan, Carol, Jane Victoria Ward, and Jill Mclean Taylor, eds. 1988. *Mapping the Moral Domain.* Cambridge, MA: Harvard University Press.

Glazer, Judith S., Estela M. Bensimón, and Barbara K. Townsend, eds. 1993. *Women in Higher Education: A Feminist Perspective.* ASHE Reader Series. Needham Heights, MA: Ginn Press.

Gmelch, Sharon Bohn. 1998. *Gender on Campus: Issues for College Women.* New Brunswick, NJ: Rutgers University Press.

Goldberger, Nancy, Jill Tarule, Blythe Clinchy, and Mary Belenky, eds. 1996. *Knowledge, Difference, and Power: Essays Inspired By Women's Ways of Knowing.* New York: Basic Books.

Guido-DiBrito, Florence, and Alicia F. Chávez. 2002. "Student Development Theory." Pp. 596–603 in *Higher Education in the United States: An Encyclopedia,* ed. James F. Forest and Kevin Kinser. Santa Barbara, CA: ABC-CLIO.

Hall, Roberta M., and Bernice Resnick Sandler. 1984. *Out of the Classroom: A Chilly Campus Climate for Women?* Report on the Status and Education of Women. Washington, DC: Association of American Colleges.

Helgesen, Sally. 1990. *The Female Advantage: Women's Ways of Leadership.* New York: Doubleday.

Hennig, Margaret, and Anne Jardim. 1976. *The Managerial Woman.* New York: Pocket Books.

Holland, Dorothy C., and Margaret A. Eisenhardt. 1990. *Educated in Romance: Women, Achievement and College Culture.* Chicago: University of Chicago Press.

Horn, Laura J., and Lisa Zahn. 2001. "From Bachelor's Degree to Work: Major Field of Study and Employment Outcomes of 1992–1993 Bachelor's Degree Recipients Who Did Not Enroll in Graduate Education by 1997." *Educational Statistics Quarterly: Postsecondary Education.* http://nces.ed.gov/pubs2001/quarterly/sping/q5_2.html. Cited June 12, 2002.

Horowitz, Helen L. 1987. *Campus Life: Undergraduate Cultures from the End of the Eighteenth-Century to the Present.* New York: Alfred A. Knopf.

Hyde, Michelle Smoot, and Julie Gess Newsome. 2000. "Factors That Increase Persistence of Female Undergraduate Science Students." Pp. 115–137 in *Women Succeeding in the Sciences: Theories and Practices across Disciplines,* ed. Jody Bart. West Lafayette, IN: Purdue University Press.

Jones, Susan Robb, and Marylu K. McEwen. 2000. "A Conceptual Model of Multiple Dimensions of Identity." *Journal of College Student Development* 41, no. 4: 405–414.

Josselson, Ruthellen. 1987. *Finding Herself: Pathways to Identity Development in Women.* San Francisco: Jossey-Bass.

Lott, Bernice, and Mary Ellen Riley, eds. 1996. *Combating Sexual Harassment in Higher Education.* Washington, DC: National Education Association.

Love, Patrick, and Victoria Guthrie. 1999. *Understanding and Applying Cognitive Development Theory.* New Directions for Student Services no. 88. San Francisco: Jossey-Bass.

Maher, Frances A., and Mary Kay Thompson Tetreault. 1994. *The Feminist Classroom: An Inside Look at How Professors and Students Are Transforming Higher Education for a Diverse Society.* New York: Basic Books.

Miller, Jean Baker. 1976. *Toward a New Psychology of Women.* Boston: Beacon Press.

Musil, Caryn McTighe, ed. 1992. *Students at the Center: Feminist Assessment.* Washington, DC: Association of American Colleges and National Women's Studies Association.

Nidiffer, Jana. 2000. *Pioneering Deans of Women: More Than Wiser and Pious Matrons.* Athene Series. New York: Teachers College Press.

Noddings, Nel. 1984. *Caring: A Feminine Approach to Ethics and Moral Education.* Berkeley: University of California Press.

Perry, William G. 1970. *Forms of Intellectual and Ethical Development in the College Years: A Scheme.* Troy, MO: Holt, Rinehart & Winston.

Reynolds, Amy L., and Raechele L. Pope. 1990. "The Complexities of Diversity: Exploring Multiple Oppressions." *Journal of Counseling and Development* 70: 174–180.

Roiphe, Katie. 1993. *The Morning After: Sex, Fear and Feminism on Campus.* Boston: Little, Brown.

Romano, C. Renee. 1996. "A Qualitative Study of Women Student Leaders." *Journal of College Student Development* 37, no. 6: 676–683.

Rosser, Sue V., and Bonnie Kelly. 1994. *Educating Women for Success in Science and Mathematics.* Columbia, SC: Division of Women's Studies, University of South Carolina.

Solomon, Barbara M. 1985. *In the Company of Educated Women: A History of Women and Higher Education in America.* New Haven, CT: Yale University Press.
Stalker, Jacqueline, and Susan Prentice, eds. 1998. *The Illusion of Inclusion: Women in Post-Secondary Education.* Halifax, NS: Fernwood Publishing.

Activism

Student activism has historically been a tool of resistance and transformation for women in higher education who voice discontent with a particular aspect of society, governmental regulations, or their educational institutions. Students have protested issues such as war, sexism, patriarchy, heterosexism, homophobia, racism, capitalism, exclusion, xenophobia, and other aspects of subordination. Women have especially focused their activist goals on the liberation, education, and self-empowerment of women. Reproductive rights and sexual liberation have also been key aspects of women's struggle. Even the right to gain entry and inclusion into institutions of higher education has come as a result of activism and protest.

In the middle to late nineteenth century, the nation saw an increase in college-educated women in certain parts of the country, and as these women gained access, they learned to organize and fight for equal rights for women on a national level. The face of student activism in higher education has included women with different identities, including many different kinds of feminists, environmentalists, peace makers, Marxists, socialists, Chicanas, Latinas, African Americans, Asian and Pacific Islander Americans, Native Americans, international women, Third World women, lesbians, and queer women, among others. Student activism has also been largely responsible for increasing the numbers of feminist, gender, ethnic, and sexuality studies professors, centers, conferences, programs, and departments at universities across the world.

Research shows that students who enter postsecondary education from marginalized or disadvantaged backgrounds often engage in a process of resistance to oppressive practices and environments within those institutions while continuing their education. Although a higher education has proven to be a form of liberation for many of these students, it has simultaneously been oppressive to some. As these students learn how to negotiate both privilege and oppression in the college setting, they develop tools for understanding their conditions. These tools are political and social consciousness, which are often internalized and acted upon in the form of student activism. Research further indicates that student activism has a direct effect on these students' retention at their universities. It is through involvement in on- and off-campus student organizations that many marginalized students create meaning from their education. In their efforts to accomplish their goals or visions of social justice, these students develop intimate connections between their education and their lived experience. It is important to note that not all student activism is progressive or justice-oriented; nevertheless, historically, student movements are remembered and documented for their positive effects and achievements.

Activism can be defined in many different ways. One definition incorporates critical consciousness and action, or praxis. Brazilian educator and philosopher Paulo Freire popularized the concept of

Take Back the Night marches have become a popular form of protesting violence against women on campuses (Painetworks)

conscientización, meaning "critical consciousness." He argued that oppressed people have the power to transform their conditions of oppression through a process of *conscientización* and praxis. He defined praxis as reflection and action rooted in a theoretical self-understanding of the lived conditions of the oppressed. Critical consciousness and praxis are central elements of student activism. Student activists have made calls for grassroots movements that connect theory with action and further connect academia with their communities. Theory, reflection, and action are motivated by the lived experiences of the students and their communities.

Chicana critical education scholar Dolores Delgado Bernal examined the oppositional behavior of students from a critical racial and feminist perspective. She documented the experience of Chicana high school student activists who participated in the 1968 East Los Angeles Blowouts, a massive act of student resistance that was motivated by both critical consciousness and a desire for justice. Delgado Bernal found this event to be transformational resistance, that is, resistance working toward liberation and social change. Her work further indicated that traditional forms of leadership in activist movements need to be reevaluated from a feminist perspective to include multiple forms of student leadership. Delgado Bernal challenged traditional interpretations of women in student movements and recognized that women have been at the forefront of student movements all along, even when they were not recognized as leaders.

Delgado Bernal urged further consideration of both internal and external resistance as different types of activism. The experiences of women in male and female student activist organizations throughout the civil rights movement and into the present can attest to this form of exclusion. For example, Elaine Brown wrote about her personal experiences in the Black Panther Party. She described the treatment she received from her male counterparts once she gained leadership in the party. Essentially, men who had previously supported her began to view her as a threat; consequently, she was forced to leave her leadership position in the movement. Likewise, in 1970 Gloria Arellanes, the minister of correspondence and finance of the East Los Angeles chapter of the Brown Berets, resigned her position along with all the other women members of the chapter, who felt that the male membership of the Brown Berets had not treated them as equals and "revolutionary sisters" in their movement (Espinoza 2001).

Feminist, lesbian, and women's organizations during the 1960s and 1970s were created in direct opposition to gender and sexual subordination. Widespread activism throughout the movement had great success, especially for white women from upper-level income backgrounds. Unfortunately, women of color and poor and working-class women did not enjoy the success of the women's student movement at the same level. Chicana, Latina, African American, Asian and Pacific Islander, Native American, and other Third World activists often found that they were being asked to choose between their race, sexuality, and gender, and they encountered obstacles at every turn. Hence, even within women's organizations, sexuality, class, race, and politics remain subjects of contention because of issues of identity and inclusion. Even so, movements of women students have continued to have success, and they remain an important element of student life and the struggle for social justice. As students gain critical consciousness on multiple levels (including, but not limited to race, class, gender, sexuality, and spirituality), they gain a more inclusive sense of activism and build necessary coalitions for their efforts. They become agents of social change on their campus and in their communities.

Anita Tijerina Revilla

See also Part 2: Demographics of Gender and Race; Part 3: Black Feminism and Womanism; Part 4: Women's Studies; Part 5: Students' Rights; Part 6: Development of Multiple Social and Cultural Identities

References and further reading

Aguilar-San Juan, Karin, ed. 1994. *The State of Asian American Activism and Resistance in the 1990s.* Boston: South End Press.

Brown, Elaine. 1993. *A Taste of Power: A Black Women's Story.* New York: Anchor Books.

Crow Dog, Mary, with Richard Erdoes. 1991. *Lakota Woman.* New York: Harper Perennial.

Delgado Bernal, Dolores. 1998. "Using a Chicana Feminist Epistemology in Educational Research." *Harvard Educational Review* 68, no. 4: 555–581.

Espinoza, Dionne. 2001. "'Revolutionary Sisters': Women's Solidarity and Collective Identification among Chicana Brown Berets in East Los Angeles, 1967–1970." *Aztlán: A Journal of Chicano Studies* 26, no. 1: 17–58.

Freire, Paulo. 1970, 1993. *Pedagogy of the Oppressed.* New York: Continuum.

Rhoads, Robert. 1998. *Freedom's Web: Student Activism in an Age of Cultural*

Diversity. Baltimore: Johns Hopkins University Press.
Solórzano, Daniel, and Octovio Villalpando. 1998. "Critical Race Theory: Marginality and the Experience of Students of Color in Higher Education." Pp. 211–224 in *Sociology of Education: Emerging Perspectives*, eds. Carlos Torres and Theodore Mitchell. Albany, NY: State University of New York Press.

African American Students

Rarely have the history, status, or unique experiences of African American women in higher education been the subject of academic inquiry. Until recently, the experiences of African American women were assumed to be identical to or less important than those of African American males, ignoring the "double burden" of race and gender prejudices that African American women must confront in their daily lives. In addition, African American women are forced to contend with the myth that African American females in the United States have had significant advantages over African American males. This myth leads to the further marginalization of black women by elevating the importance of men's issues above their own and by portraying black men as "victims" of black women's success. Further, it obscures the fact the black women, past and present, confront substantial discrimination attributed to the interlocking mechanisms of racism and sexism and that African American men have sometimes participated in that oppression. African American women on college campuses often view themselves as outsiders in both the white-dominated and male-dominated world.

It is true that black women in general fare batter than men on some educational indicators. According to William B. Harvey (2001), of those aged twenty-five and over, 15.4 percent of African American women but only 13.9 percent of African American men had completed four or more years of college compared with 23 percent of white women and 27 percent of white men (Harvey 2001, 63). African American women in National Collegiate Athletic Association (NCAA) Division I institutions have a six-year graduation rate of 41 percent, whereas African American men have a rate of only 31 percent (Harvey 2001, 61). Yet these statistics are hardly evidence of an African American female advantage. In fact, white, Latino, and Asian American women's graduation rates also outpaced those of men in the same racial category. It is more likely evidence of a societal trend than specific evidence of African American female advantage. In fact, other indicators, such as black women's lower rates of tenure and promotion and their lower income returns than men with comparable education levels, reveal that African American men fare better than women in some respects. In addition, African American women tend to be heavily concentrated in lower-paying, female dominated fields such as education.

The Historical Context of African Americans in Higher Education

Historically, African Americans in the United States have faced considerable adversity in most political, social, and economic realms; education has been no exception. After slavery was abolished in 1865, policies and practices of racial exclusion, including Jim Crow laws in the South, perpetuated racial inequality and denied African Americans equal access to education. Legal barriers ensured that African Americans remained in segregated schools, which were mired in

Students at the entrance to Spelman College (Courtesy of Spelman College)

poverty and lacked basic resources. In general, the educational attainment of African Americans was poor, and few African Americans were able to attend college. "From 1826, when the first black American graduated from Bowdoin College, to 1890, only thirty black Americans graduated from predominantly white colleges and universities in the United States. By 1910 the number was still fewer than 700" (Feagin, Vera, and Imani 1996, 10).

It was not until the 1954 *Brown v. Board of Education of Topeka, Kansas* decision, when the Supreme Court declared that racial segregation in public education was unconstitutional and ordered that schools be desegregated "with all deliberate speed," that the foundation was laid for any significant changes. Yet these changes were often slow, sporadic, and highly contested. Whites, including many elected officials, fought bitterly to maintain racial exclusion. African American students enrolling at several predominantly white universities in the South during this period had to be escorted by the National Guard and faced crowds of unruly protesters, severe harassment, and death threats. Discriminatory practices, however, were not limited to the southern states. Many northern colleges and universities also employed discriminatory tactics to exclude African Americans entirely or limit them to very small numbers. Most of the people who were granted admission to predominantly white colleges and universities often faced severe restrictions and were not allowed to reside on campus. The eventual effects of the *Brown v. Board of Education* decision and the civil rights movement in the 1960s brought about some important changes; for the first time, significant numbers of African Americans were granted admission to predominantly white universities from which they had previously been excluded. Between 1950 and 1970, the number of African Americans enrolled in all colleges and universities more than tripled, and African Americans enrolled in predominantly white colleges and universities accounted for the majority of these gains.

Historically black colleges and universities (HBCUs) are an important exception in the history of African American education. HBCUs continue to serve an important role in the education of African Americans and provide opportunities to African Americans from disadvantaged backgrounds. In 1950, 90 percent of African American college students (approximately 100,000) attended HBCUs (Fleming 1984, 7). Although by 1998 HBCUs enrolled only 14 percent of all African American college students, they awarded 26 percent of all bachelors degrees earned by African Americans that year (National Center for Education Statistics 2001, table 222). HBCUs also conferred nearly 15 percent of all master's degrees awarded to blacks and nearly 13 percent of all doctorates earned by blacks (National Center for Education Statistics 2001, tables 222, 265, 268, and 271). There is also some evidence that HBCUs provide more supportive learning environments, which are often lacking at predominantly white colleges and universities. In addition, black women at HBCUs have higher grade point averages and receive their bachelors degrees at significantly younger ages than their counterparts at predominantly white institutions.

African American Educational Attainment

African Americans experienced slow but steady gains in college enrollment and degree attainment throughout the 1990s. Among African Americans, women showed a larger growth than men in both these categories. African American women receive 65 percent of bachelor's degrees, 68 percent of master's degrees, and 60 percent of doctoral degrees awarded to African Americans. These figures obscure the fact that African American women still represent only a small portion of degree recipients when all races are included (National Center for Education Statistics 2001, table 222).

Although conditions have slowly improved in the decades that followed the civil rights movement, African Americans still face considerable educational disadvantages. Research on African American students in the United States has shown that they continue to enroll in colleges and universities at lower levels than whites, graduate at lower levels, and have lower grade point averages than their white counterparts. According to the 2000 U.S. Census, among eighteen to twenty-four year olds in 1998, 77 percent of African American women and 65 percent of African American men completed high school, compared with 83 percent of white women and 78 percent of white men (Varson n.d., slide 22). There were more than 1.5 million African Americans enrolled in institutions of higher education, but of this group, only 58 percent were enrolled in four-year colleges or universities; the remainder were enrolled in community colleges or other two-year institutions. African Americans represent approximately 11 percent of all undergraduate students but receive only 7.5 percent of all bachelor's degrees conferred (*Chronicle of Higher Education Almanac Issue* 2000, 24–25). Overall, African Americans had a 38 percent graduation rate from NCAA Division I institutions; that number reflects some decreases in recent years and lags behind Latinos (46 percent), whites (59 percent), and Asian Americans (66 percent) ("Freshman-Cohort Graduation Rates" 2001).

African Americans on Predominantly White College Campuses

Since 86 percent of all African American undergraduates attend predominantly white universities, the experiences of this population provide important insights into the status of African Americans in higher education (National Center for Education Statistics 2001, table 222). Despite the fact that predominantly white colleges and universities in the United States began large-scale racial integration nearly forty years ago, there are continuing problems with racism and race relations on these campuses. African Americans on predominantly white college campuses often find a chilly racial climate. They must continually justify their presence to white students, faculty, and administrators who openly question their qualifications and intellectual abilities and treat them as tokens of undeserved affirmative action.

During the 1990s and the early part of the twenty-first century, there has been a widespread resurgence of open racial hostility and aggression toward African American students and other students of color. African Americans on many predominantly white college campuses have reported threats, harassment, and other incidents of racial intimidation involving black student organizations and black cultural centers. Black students are often treated by their white peers as undesirable group members for class projects and are excluded from social activities and networking. This treatment has lead to feelings of alienation and isolation among many black students on predominantly white campuses and is compounded by the severe lack of African American faculty members. Previous studies have revealed that African American students often had negative interactions with white faculty inside and outside the classroom. African American students often stated that white faculty members had low expectations of them, did not seem to care about their learning, made assumptions about "all students" that did not apply to African Americans, stereotyped African Americans and failed to see them as individuals, treated them like "experts" or "spokespersons" of their race, excluded them from the curriculum and interaction in class, seemed awkward in personal interactions, and took overt stances against multicultural and diversity programs.

African Americans have made many advances in educational attainment since the civil rights era. However, they still face considerable obstacles to advancement in higher education. To improve their educational experiences and outcomes, further research must be conducted to understand the unique challenges of African American women and men and to explore how educational environments can be improved to facilitate their future success and advancement.

Rochelle L. Woods

See also Part 1: Black Women's Colleges; Hispanic-Serving Institutions; Historically Black Colleges and Universities; Part 6: Black Sororities; Part 7: African American Faculty

References and further reading

Allen, Walter R., Edgar G. Epps, and Nesha Z. Haniff. 1991. *College in Black and White: African American Students in Predominantly White and in Historically Black Public Universities.* Albany: State University of New York Press.

Brown v. Board of Education of Topeka, Kansas, 347 U.S. 483 (1954).

Chronicle of Higher Education Almanac Issue 45, no. 1. 2000.
Feagin, Joe R., Hernan Vera, and Mikitah Imani. 1996. *The Agony of Education: Black Students at White Colleges and Universities.* New York: Routledge.
Fleming, Jacqueline. 1984. *Blacks in College: A Comparative Study of Students' Success in Black and in White Institutions.* San Francisco: Jossey-Bass.
"Freihman-Cohort Graduation Rates." 2001. http://www.ncaa.org/grad_rates/2001/d1/aggregate/d1.html. Cited June 23, 2002.
Harvey, William B. 2001. "Minorities in Higher Education 2000–2001: Eighteenth Annual Status Report." Washington, DC: American Council on Education.
Higginbotham, Elizabeth. 2001. *Too Much to Ask: Black Women in the Era of Integration.* Chapel Hill: University of North Carolina Press.
Ihle, Elizabeth L. 1992. *Black Women in Higher Education: An Anthology of Essays, Studies, and Documents, Educated Women.* New York: Garland.
Jackson, Lisa R. 1998. "The Influence of Both Race and Gender on the Experiences of African American College Women." *Review of Higher Education* 21, no. 4: 359–375.
National Center for Education Statistics. 2001. *Digest of Education Statistics.* Washington, DC: U.S. Department of Education.
St. Jean, Yanick, and Joe R. Feagin. 1998. *Double Burden: Black Women and Everyday Racism.* Armonk, NY: M. E. Sharpe.
Varson, Alex. "The 18–23 Year Old Population." Washington, DC: U.S. Census Bureau. http://www.census.gov/mso/www/pres_lib/dod99/sld022.htm. Cited June 24, 2002.

American Indian Students

American Indian (also known as Native American) students include American Indians from more than 161 distinct tribes and 210 distinct tribal languages (Pavel et al. 1998). American Indians include indigenous populations from the continental United States, including Alaska natives and native Hawaiians. As of 2000, American Indians comprised 2.5 million, or 0.9 percent, of the U.S. population; New Mexico has the largest percentage of American Indians (9.5 percent), followed by South Dakota (8.3 percent), Oklahoma (7.9 percent), Montana (6.2 percent), and Arizona (5 percent) (U.S. Census Bureau 2001). As of 2000, 9 percent of American Indians lived in the Northeast, 3.1 percent in the South, 17 percent in the Midwest, and 43 percent in the West. Some of the larger tribes are the Cherokee, Navajo, Chippewa, Sioux, Choctaw, Seminole, and Pueblo. Smaller tribes include the Miccosukee, Cupeno, Mohegan, Oregon Athabascan, and Tonkawa (Pavel et al. 1998). About 1 percent of the total American Indian population, or 142,000 students, attended college in 1997 (Wilds 2000).

Despite overall low levels of educational attainment and achievement, American Indian women receive the majority of the associate's (64 percent), bachelor's (60 percent), master's (62 percent), and doctoral (56 percent) degrees awarded to Indians (National Center for Education Statistics 2001). Nevertheless, researchers have pointed out that studies on American Indian women have been ignored, especially when the results indicated that high school and college women have distinctly different experiences regarding the educational paths that prevented them from graduating from college. This disparity is attributed to the patriarchal system of educational removal and assimilation of American Indians that arose during the colonial period and continues today in the United States (Almeida 1997; Bowker 1993).

In her pivotal study of 991 female American Indians from several tribes, Ardy Bowker (1993) examined why these students dropped out of high school. Bowker found that American Indian students' notions of dropping out formed as early as kindergarten and the first grade.

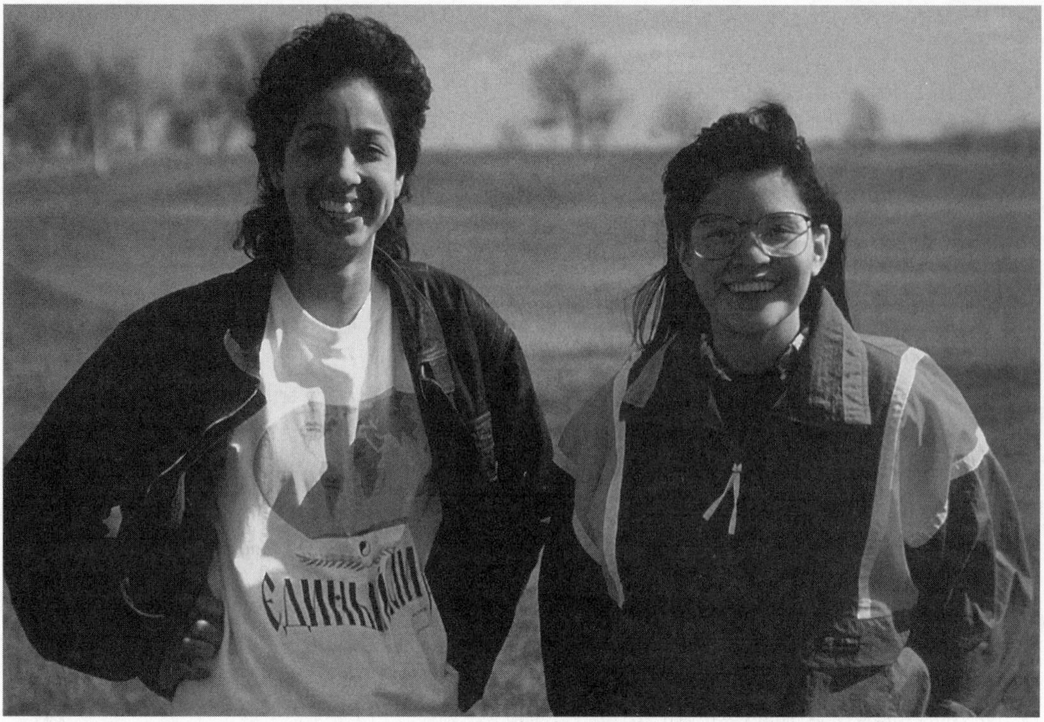

Students of Haskell Indian Nations University in Lawrence, Kansas (Painetworks)

The specific reasons for dropout among female American Indian students included (1) teachers' low expectations and racist and uncaring attitudes; (2) a negative school environment in which rules were used as a tool to isolate and remove American Indian students; (3) teen pregnancy; and (4) poverty. One of the surprising findings was that most of the dropouts had aspirations to go to college and that some eventually did. She also found that successful female graduates (1) had caring teachers and role models, (2) experienced a strong sense of spirituality defined as having a moral purpose, and (3) had families who cared for and nurtured them.

The poor condition and failure today of female American Indians' education is attributed directly to the majority educational system in the United States. Most female American Indians today live in urban areas, and they have the highest rates of poverty of any other minority group in the United States (Pavel et al. 1998). They also have the lowest level of high school completion rates and the lowest level of associate's, bachelor's, and professional degree attainment of any minority group in the United States. Research on American Indian high school and college students is also relatively sparse compared to that for other ethnic minority groups in the United States, and the study of American Indian women in high school and college is even more rare.

The History of American Indian Education

Formal education for American Indians began with the systematic removal of

American Indian children from their families and their placement in off-reservation boarding schools. The purpose of these boarding schools was to eliminate American Indian sovereignty, language, and culture and to forcibly assimilate them into mainstream society. One of the very first American Indian cultural traits to disappear was the unique and central roles women played in these societies (Almeida 1997). The role of most women in American Indian societies before the colonial period was to educate their children in the traditional ways, participate equally in political and cultural decisions, and maintain their central living environments, in which the women were in charge. American Indian women at this time were heads of the families, and it is through the matrilineal lines that they passed down their heritage. With the imposition of the inchoate, patriarchal educational system, women's roles in American Indian societies were diminished.

During the Native American historical period of "Contact with Europeans" (1492–1800), a main goal of the colonists was to convert American Indians to Christianity. Harvard, William and Mary, and Dartmouth Colleges were founded to provide education for English colonists and American Indians (Pavel et al. 1998). These institutions were unsuccessful because of the vast cultural and religious differences between the English colonials and the varying American Indian tribes, as well as American Indian resistance to "colonial" education and assimilation. Only a very small number of American Indians graduated from these institutions.

In the "Removal Era" (1800–1830), thousands of American Indian children were removed from their families and placed in boarding schools. They were established because American Indians were resisting earlier assimilation efforts. The philosophy behind the schools was to remove American Indian children as early as possible and educate them in European American values so that they would forget their own language and culture and readily assimilate into the majority society. These schools prevented Native American children from speaking their language, practicing their native customs, dressing according to their tribal ways, and interacting with their families. Many of these children did not see their families until many years later. Education for women at these schools focused exclusively on training them for domestic work in European American homes.

During the "Reservation Era" (1830–1930), American Indians began to be removed from their native lands and placed in reservations. Some tribes, like the Miccosukee of Miami, Florida, resisted removal and hid until 1928 in the Everglades without European American contact. During this period, American Indian women started losing their value and place within the purview of European American research and education. The traditional training and education of American Indian women by their female elders disappeared because of the new and inchoate reliance on federal education caused by the reservation system.

During the "Reform Era" (1930–1969), boarding schools were closed after many complaints by native tribes, but only when the government decided they were detrimental to American Indians. Currently, there are four types of institutions American Indian students attend for primary and secondary education: schools run by the Bureau of Indian Affairs (BIA), which is part of the Department of Interior; schools run by tribes; schools with high American Indian enrollments; and schools with low American Indian enrollments (Pavel et al. 1998). Most American Indian students attend BIA and tribal schools.

American Indian Higher Education Today

The tribal college movement, started during the Reform Era, was established to respond to the detrimental effect European American education was having on American Indians and also so that tribes would have control over their own advanced education (American Indian Higher Education Consortium 1999). In 1968, the Navajo Nation created Diné College, the first tribally controlled college. Today, there are thirty-two tribally chartered colleges and three federally charted colleges for American Indians in twelve states. Most tribal colleges offer two-year degrees. The main focus of tribal colleges is to ensure that American Indian students receive training in their own culture as well as the European American model and to provide a pathway to four-year institutions.

Even though American Indian women overall receive a large portion of the degrees conferred to all American Indians, there are no separate studies on their specific experiences from primary through higher education; instead, the only information available comes in the form of both quantitative and qualitative aggregate data that includes both men and women. Bowker (1993), Almeida (1997), and others have shown that American Indian women's education, culture, worth, and value needs to be reappropriated from the European American patriarchal purview and resituated to express their specific experiences and points of view regarding their own education.

Roger Geertz González

See also Part 1: Tribal Colleges; Part 6: Development of Multiple Social and Cultural Identities; Part 7: American Indian Faculty; Part 8: American Indian Administrators

References and further reading

Almeida, Deirdre A. 1997. "The Hidden Half: A History of Native American Women's Education." *Harvard Educational Review* 67, no. 4: 757–771.

American Indian Higher Education Consortium. 1999. "Tribal Colleges: An Introduction." http://www.aihec.org/intro.pdf. Cited September 26, 2001.

Bowker, Ardy. 1993. *Sisters in the Blood: The Education of Women in Native America,* Washington, DC: Office of Educational Research and Improvement.

Collins, LaVerne Vines. 1997. Census Facts for Native American Month. http://www.census.gov/Press-Release/fs97-11.html. Cited October 11, 2001.

National Center for Education Statistics. 1999. *Digest of Education Statistics.* Washington, DC: U.S. Department of Education.

Pavel, D. Michael, Rebecca Rak Skinner, Margaret Cahalan, John Tippeconic, and Wayne Stein. 1998. *American Indians and Alaska Natives in Postsecondary Education.* Washington, DC: National Center for Education Statistics.

Peacock, T. D., and D. R. Day. 1999. "Teaching American Indian and Alaska Native Languages in the Schools: What Has Been Learned." *ERIC Digest.* http://www.ael.org/eric/digests.htm. Cited November 18, 2001.

U.S. Census Bureau. 2001. http://www.census.gov/population/cen2000. Cited June 11, 2002.

Wilds, Deborah J. 2000. *Minorities in Higher Education, 1999–2000.* Washington, DC: American Council on Education.

Asian American Students

The subject of Asian American women as college students is a research area clearly in its infancy; in fact, little

An Asian American student works on her homework (Courtesy of the Association of Women in Science)

research has been conducted specifically on Asian American female students. Instead, Asian American issues remain largely subsumed within studies of race or gender. To develop some understanding of Asian American women as college students, it is vital to extrapolate from the existing research on Asian Americans, Asian American students, Asian American women, and women of color.

The recognition of the racial and ethnic group known as Asian Americans, or, more comprehensively, Asian Pacific Americans (APA), is a relatively recent phenomenon that began in the 1960s as an offshoot of the American civil rights movement. Since that time, APAs have regularly been grouped together as a singular ethnic identity group, though their nations of familial origin are diverse and include any countries on the Asian continent, South Asia subcontinent, and any of the islands of the Pacific Rim. These different ancestries do not, in most cases, share similar languages, ethnic heritage, religions, or political structures and histories. The grouping, therefore, rests more in regional proximity of their nations of origin and, to some extent, physical appearance. This assignment of a single racial and ethnic classification also serves to distinguish between Americans of Asian descent and Asians who are not American but are living or studying in the United States. Ultimately, this creation of a singular minority group for people of Asian descent in the United States has produce both positive and negative outcomes, which is certainly true within the realm of higher education.

Asian Americans account for 5.6 percent of all college enrollments in the

United States, though they make up only about 3.5 percent of the overall U.S. population (Hune and Chan 1997). Among APAs in general, women earn over 51 percent of all bachelor degrees, 46 percent of all master's degrees, 45 percent of all professional degrees, and 41 percent of all doctorates (Hune 1998). Along the course of the academic pipeline, APA women decrease as a percentage of overall APA graduates, certainly affecting the opportunities for female APA students to become APA faculty. In addition, APA women doctoral graduates overwhelmingly earn their degrees in sciences and engineering, further limiting the preparation of APA women for faculty roles in other areas, such as the liberal arts. Creating faculty role models for APA women students is especially challenged by the preparation of APA women for doctoral studies in all areas of college and university academic work.

In examining and understanding the range of academic experiences of APA women, existing stereotypes deserve consideration. APA students are expected to excel in the classroom and are often blamed for the difficulties white American students may face in the admission processes of elite higher education and in the grading of coursework, with APA students earning a disproportionate share of spaces in an entering class or skewing the curve in their coursework.

Asian American student stereotypes are academic: they study hard, they are talented at math and science, and they are quiet and respectful of their instructors. There are also social stereotypes of Asian American students, as well: they have domineering parents, are reserved and passive, are not involved in extracurricular activities, and are not interested in having active social lives. Asian American students are often perceived as a "model minority": a minority group of students who do not require extra assistance in their acclimation and adaptation to the requirements of higher education.

This "model minority" stereotype has had negative ramifications for APA women, from feeling extreme pressure to be exceptional academically to being directed toward majors in math and science, without consideration for their individual interests and talents. In addition, this sense that APA students are disproportionately successful in college leads to their being overlooked in student services and outreach. Although many APA students do come from multigenerational American families, many APA students are also first-generation college attendees and have the same socioeconomic class, preparation, and acclimation issues as any other first-generation college student. The assumption, then, that being Asian makes for an easy college experience in the classroom has proven to be a significant disadvantage for many APA women.

APA women have reported feeling isolated on college campuses, as if they are invisible. They face racial and gender biases, as well as class and cultural stigmas or stereotypes (Hune 1998). These biases and stereotypes appear both within and outside of the APA communities on campus. Internal biases can involve national origin, with some APA groups having more visibility and experience as a campus community than others. Students of Chinese, Japanese, and Korean heritages often make up the majority of campus APA populations and are the majority involved in APA groups. South Asians—Indians, Pakistanis, and Bangladeshis—often create their own student groups and find their own communities on campus. Smaller Asian populations, including Thais, Hmong, and Cambodians, have little to no visibility on campus or power within Asian student organizations and may even feel ostracized from the general Asian community. With the added factors of class and preparation for college, these inter-Asian distinctions can become even more pronounced.

APA students often find themselves disregarded as a minority group by other students. White students often perceive APA students as a threat and a group that receives privileges from admission officers and faculty. Other students of color often view APA students not as students of color or a campus minority group but as being connected with the white majority. In being misunderstood and devalued by both the majority and other students of color, APA students face a distinct kind of isolation on their campuses.

APA women students may feel this isolation even more acutely than APA male students because they experience both racial and gender biases. APA women face stereotypes of being demure and passive, which affect their relationships inside and outside the classroom. In the classroom, this cultural shyness may, in fact, merely be cultural politeness. APA women are not necessarily more shy than any other group of women. They may, however, be more culturally sensitive than their non-Asian peers to being respectful of individual speakers or to authority figures like professors, and this sensitivity can work against them in the classroom, by limiting their opportunities to engage in dialogues and ask questions. APA women report feeling especially challenged by white women in discussions on women's experiences because white women speak as authorities on all women. Literature on women of color also minimizes the experiences of APA women, often focusing on the experiences of African American women as the defining experiences of all women of color. Again, issues for Asian American students are often subsumed in a general analysis of people of color, and APA women's issues are often subsumed in a general analysis of women. In both areas, APA women are doubly marginalized.

APA women could benefit from many important innovations and developments in American higher education. Increased number of mentors—in faculty and staff roles—would be an important start. Improving awareness of APA issues among faculty, staff, and students on campus would lead to greater understanding and acceptance of APA students within the general student population. Developing Asian studies programs and incorporating APA interests and issues into existing programs will also lead to greater and more comprehensive exploration of APA experiences—for APA and non-Asian students alike. Bridging the existing gaps between APA students and other members of their higher education communities should be the primary goal for anyone interested in moving APA students, and especially APA women students, forward in college and university settings. The academic and social issues facing APA women are significant and deserving of further research and action in American higher education.

Roberta Malee Bassett

See also Part 6: Curricular and Professional Choices; Development of Multiple Social and Cultural Identities; Undergraduates and Science; Part 7: Asian American Faculty; Part 8: Asian American Administrators

References and further reading
Chan, Sucheng C., and Ling-chi Wang. 1991. "Racism and the Model Minority: Asian-Americans in Higher Education." Pp. 43–67 in *The Racial Crisis in American Higher Education,* eds. Philip G. Altbach and Kofi Lomotey. Albany: State University of New York Press.
Cheng, Lucie, and Philip Q. Yang. 2000. "The 'Model Minority' Deconstructed." Pp. 459–482 in *Contemporary Asian America: A Multidisciplinary Reader,* eds. Min Zhou and James V. Gatewood. New York: New York University Press.
Hune, Shirley. 1998. *Asian Pacific American Women in Higher Education: Claiming Visibility and Voice.* Washington, DC: Association of American Colleges and Universities.
———. 2000. "Doing Gender with a Feminist Gaze: Toward a Historical Reconstruction of Asian America." Pp. 413–430 in *Contemporary Asian America: A Multidisciplinary Reader,* eds. Min Zhou and James V. Gatewood. New York: New York University Press.
Hune Shirley, and Kenyon S. Chan 1997. "Special Focus: Asian Pacific American Demographic and Educational Trends." Pp. 39–67 in *Minorities in Higher Education,* eds. Deborah J. Carter and Reginald Wilson. Vol. 15. Washington, DC: American Council on Education.
Osajima, Keith. 2000. "Asian American as the Model Minority: An Analysis of the Popular Press Image in the 1960s and 1980s." Pp. 449–458 in *Contemporary Asian America: A Multidisciplinary Reader,* eds. Min Zhou and James V. Gatewood. New York: New York University Press.

Biracial and Biethnic Students

College students who are biethnic (sometimes called biracial, multiracial, mixed race, or mixed heritage) are those whose parents are from different ethnicities or races as designated by the U.S. Office of Management and Budget (OMB). The number of biethnic college students is not known but can be estimated from results of the most recent U.S. Census. The 2000 Census indicated that 6.8 million of the 281.4 million respondents, or 2.4 percent, identified with more than one race. Of those 6.8 million people, 42 percent, or about 2.9 million, were under eighteen. If the number of biethnic students who go to postsecondary education is proportionate to their presence in the population, in the coming years approximately 3–5 percent of college students will fall into this category.

Multiracial college women have identified a number of gender-specific concerns (Renn 1998). Social life and dating are seen by some women to be complicated by their mixed racial and ethnic heritage; they cite other students' concerns about dating someone who is not of the same race or ethnicity. Another gender-specific issue for multiracial women is the exotification by media and advertisers of racially ambiguous female models and celebrities; some multiracial college women find that this effect permeates campus life as well, leading to a social environment in which they feel fetishized and exotified. Finally, some mixed-race students find that although they experience racism and sexism on campus, the social, political, and academic support available generally to women of color is sometimes not fully available to them; women reported not feeling comfortable, for example, in the overwhelmingly white residential sororities or the black and Latina sororities on one campus (Renn 1998).

Biethnic and Biracial Individuals in the United States

Even with the new census data, the number of individuals who are actually of mixed heritage is not known. Experts estimate there are between 1 and 10 million biethnic adults in this country. The ambiguity in the actual number of biethnic individuals is caused by skewed statistics and governmental policies. The OMB subscribes to a policy requiring biethnic children born in the United States to be assigned to the racial status of the minority parent indicated on the birth certificate. Also, this policy states that if both parents are minorities, the child will be assigned the race of the father.

U.S. history is replete with examples of people being defined, categorized, and generalized in terms of race. Paul R. Spickard (1997) suggests that labeling is a social construct, making it easier for whites to generalize about the qualities of minorities. Some suggest that labeling is important for self-identification and pride, whereas others claim labeling polarizes our society. The U.S. Census has promulgated the labeling debate.

In the 1990s, the census statistics drew congressional boundaries for ethnic groups based on counts of minorities who had to identify themselves as one of four minority groups (Black or African American, Asian American, Native American or American Indian, or Hispanic). Many biethnic people felt that the directive to be defined by only one racial category was evidence confirming the exclusion of biethnic people from society. Others believed the census forced biethnic people to reject part of their heritage, an activity that is believed to promote a negative self-concept. Following significant political and social action, the 2000 Census was changed to allow individuals to "check all that apply" for racial and ethnic categories: 2.4 percent of respondents checked more than one category.

The self-identification option in the 2000 Census has come under considerable social, political, and economic scrutiny. It is believed that self-identification in a single minority group shows unity and power but identifying biethnically or biracially will diminish minority power in race-based organizations, representation in government, and program funding. Advocates of maintaining the policy that biethnic and biracial individuals should identify only with their minority heritage claim that creating a separate multiracial category would diminish the strength of established minority groups, requiring federal and state governments, school boards, and civil rights agencies to redraw districts, funding appropriations, and programmatic efforts. It is not yet clear how the results of the 2000 Census will affect policy and programs.

Biethnic and Biracial Students in Higher Education

The changing demographics of the United States will usher in comparable changes in the student population at institutions of higher education. By 2010, students of color, mostly African Americans, Latinos, and American Indians, are projected to comprise 24 percent of total postsecondary enrollment. Many students in these categories are biethnic, and their experience of inclusion, visibility, and acceptance differs from those with a single ethnicity or race.

Within postsecondary education, a main issue faced by minority and biethnic students is identity formation. Identity has been found to affect the development of self-esteem and positive self-concepts. Erik Erikson (1968) suggests identity development is a critical developmental task faced by adolescents. Identity development involves establishing autonomy, finding independence, and negotiating a sense of self in relationship to society.

According to both lifespan and student development theories, identity formation is a process, and its emergence coincides with adolescence. Identity development is a focal point in many student development theories, centering on the notion that colleges help students strengthen their sense of identity. Furthermore, literature reveals that attending college increases a student's acquisition of values and ethics, an integral part of identity development. According to student development theory, if students do not find an individual identity, then identity confusion will prevail, hindering a student's growth and persistence in college.

For biethnic and biracial students, identity formation is not a simple matter. Societal response to biethnic individuals has not been particularly positive. In 1937, Everett V. Stonequist wrote *The Marginal Man,* in which he concluded biethnicity was a psychological disorder, which he called *marginality.* Stonequist viewed marginality as a problem residing within an individual, resulting from a mixture of personality characteristics and societal expectations. He characterized the marginal personality as having mental contrasts, tension, and inner conflict. Furthermore, cultural or racial hybrids were socially maladjusted and were unable to develop normal and healthy identities. Stonequist's claim that individuals of mixed heritage were mentally unstable prevailed throughout most of the twentieth century.

By 1970, sociologists and psychologists redefined the construct of ethnicity as a socially based paradigm, rather than the individually based paradigm they had previously believed it to be. Considering race and ethnicity as socially based paradigms, researchers began to see the social influences affecting ethnic identity development. Christine Hall (1980) concluded that group antagonism created identity development difficulties for mixed-race individuals. The terms "biethnic" and "biracial" were introduced into the literature in an attempt to move toward a paradigm that views mixed-race people as capable of a normal, healthy identity.

Since the 1980s, several theorists, including William Poston, Maria P. P. Root, and George K. Kich, have brought forth models of identity development. Poston's model (1990) has a lifespan focus, indicating that biracial individuals tend to struggle with identity confusion and social adjustment. It encompasses five developmental stages an individual passes through in a lifetime to develop a healthy biracial identity. In the first stage, personal identity, children's sense of self is dependent on their familial beliefs about ethnicity. As individuals mature, they are forced to choose an ethnic label to use as a self-descriptor. Poston contends that a variety of factors can influence this decision, with the primary factor being choosing between the dominant and minority cultures. He argues that people at this stage are typically adolescents who do not have the cognitive ability to choose both identities.

According to Poston, after choosing a label, the biracial person may be filled with guilt, confusion, and questions regarding having chosen one culture over the other, which manifests in depression, anger, and withdrawal. The individual must resolve this conflict and learn to appreciate both cultures or remain at this level of uncertainty. However, through education and experiences, the individual's understanding of the hidden or repressed ethnicity broadens until an appreciation of both cultures emerges. Poston postulates that only then can individuals develop a secure, integrated identity.

Kich (1992) presents a heuristic developmental model, with three major stages of development leading to resolution of biethnicity. Development is viewed similarly to other minority identity development models, in which the stages mark a series of transitions leading to a secure identity. However, in Kich's model, the biracial individual struggles with choosing one ethnicity over the other. Teresa LaFromboise, Hardind L. K. Coleman, and Jennifer Getron (1993) suggest that to navigate through this struggle, biethnic individuals need to acquire competencies regarding cultural beliefs and values. Specifically, the individual needs to have a positive attitude and the ability to effectively communicate with both ethnic groups involved.

Root (1990) provides a model that is not based on stages in which identity is determined in part by socialization. Root describes how a multiracial person seeks identity in relation to social, familial, and political systems. She contends that there are four ways a person can resolve identity: (1) accept the identity society assigns, (2) identify with both racial groups, (3) identify with single race group, or (4) identify as biracial. In Root's model, a person can identify with any of these groups simultaneously or move among them throughout a lifetime. Kendra R. Wallace (2001) studied mixed-race college students and found Root's model to be an accurate description of students' experiences. Renn (1998) also found Root's four identity resolutions to be present in college students, and she added a category in which students "opted out" of or deconstructed racial categories altogether.

Samantha J. Ortiz

See also Part 2: Intersection of Gender and Race; Part 6: Development of Multiple Social and Cultural Identities; Developmental Issues

References and further reading

Erikson, Erik. 1968. *Identity, Youth, and Crisis.* New York: W. W. Norton.

Hall, Christine I. I. 1980. "The Ethnic Identity of Racially Mixed People: A Study of Black-Japanese." Ph.D. diss., University of California, Los Angeles.

Kich, George K. 1992. "The Developmental Process of Asserting a Biracial, Bicultural Identity." Pp. 304–317 in *Racially Mixed People in America,* ed. Maria P. P. Root. Newbury Park, CA: Sage.

LaFromboise, Teresa, Hardin L. K. Coleman, and Jennifer Getron. 1993. "Psychological Impact of Biculturalism: Evidence and Theory." *Psychological Bulletin* 114: 395–412.

Poston, William S. C. 1990. "The Biracial Identity Development Model: A Needed Addition." *Journal of Counseling and Development* 69: 152–155.

Renn, Kristen A. 1998. "Patterns of Situational Identity among Biracial and Multiracial College Students." *Review of Higher Education* 23: 399–420.

Root, Maria P. P. 1990. "Resolving 'Other' Status: Identity Development of Biracial Individuals." *Women and Therapy* 9: 185–205.

Spickard, Paul R. 1997. "What Must I Be? Asian Americans and the Question of Multiethnic Identity." *Amerasia Journal* 23: 43–60.

Stonequist, Everett V. 1937. *The Marginal Man: A Study in Personality and Culture Conflict.* New York: Russell and Russell.

Wallace, Kendra R. 2001. *Relative/ Outsider: The Art and Politics of Identity among Mixed Heritage Students.* Westport, CT: Ablex Publishing.

Black Sororities

There are four black sororities: Alpha Kappa Alpha, Delta Sigma Theta, Zeta Phi Beta, and Sigma Gamma Rho. The forces that helped shaped black sororities were sexism, racism, and a sense of racial obligation. The majority of black sororities were shaped by the pressures on pre-

Members of a black sorority in Washington, D.C., early 1900s (Library of Congress)

dominantly black colleges during segregation. Over the decades, they have expanded to other historically black colleges and universities (HBCUs) and predominately white universities.

All the sororities have active undergraduate and graduate/alumnae chapters. Community outreach programs sponsored by the sororities include economic empowerment; drug prevention; teen pregnancy; health care ranging from breast cancer to acquired immunodeficiency syndrome (AIDS); the elderly; programs with black empowerment and making connections to the continent of Africa; and preparing young women to be academically, physically, psychologically, and technologically prepared in society.

Among college organizations, the black sororities have become leaders in community service. Today more than 250,000 black women belong to these four sororities. Unlike the predominantly white sororities, association does not end with an undergraduate education but continues past college to include activities related to careers, families, and civic and community involvement.

The four organizations are brought together under the National Pan-Hellenic Council (NPHC), an official umbrella organization that coordinates the activities and philosophies of all nine of the black sororities and fraternities. Established at Howard University in 1930, the NPHC incorporated under the laws of the State of Illinois in 1937. The purpose of the NPHC is to strive to maintain a cooperative environment for its member organizations, encourage interaction among them, and act as a mutual forum for addressing social issues.

Alpha Kappa Alpha

Alpha Kappa Alpha became the first Greek letter organization established by and for black women on 15 January 1908. Ethel Hedgeman Lyle, a faculty member at Howard University whose purpose was to provide intellectual and social stimulation for black college women, founded the sorority. It expanded its membership and its vision under Nellie Quander, a Howard graduate, four years later. Alpha Kappa Alpha has grown into an international and national sorority with more than 170,000 women members in over 900 chapters around the world.

Alpha Kappa Alpha has a five-point international program that targets education, the black family, health, the arts, and economics. A signature program of the sorority is organizing, nurturing, team building, respecting, achieving, character building, and knowledge (ON-TRACK). The program is designed to assist 20,000 at-risk third through sixth graders in making the right choices in their lives academically, socially, and personally.

Delta Sigma Theta

Delta Sigma Theta was the first black sorority committed to public service. Twenty-two undergraduate black women founded the sorority at Howard University in Washington, D.C., on 13 January 1913. That same year, the members participated in the women's suffrage march, also in Washington, D.C. Delta Sigma Theta is the largest black women's organization in the world, with a membership of over 190,000 predominantly African American college women. The sorority currently has more than 900 chapters located in the United States, Japan, Germany, Bermuda, Haiti, Liberia, the Bahamas, the Republic of Korea, and the Virgin Islands.

The major programs of the sorority are based upon the organization's Five-Point Program Thrust, which fosters economic development, educational development, international awareness and involvement, physical and mental health, and political awareness and involvement. The sorority is involved with Habitat for Humanity, voter registration, and the Dr. Betty Shabazz Delta Academy.

Zeta Phi Beta

Five female students—Pearl A. Heal, Viola Tyler Goings, Arizona Cleaver Stemmons, Myrle Tyle Faithful, and Fannie Pettie Walls—founded Zeta Phi Beta Sorority on 16 January 1920 on the campus of Howard University. These women sought to establish a new organization predicated on the precepts of scholarship, service, sisterhood, and finer womanhood. The sorority was the first Greek-letter organization to charter a chapter in Africa (1948) and to be constitutionally bound to a brother group, Phi Beta Sigma fraternity.

The sorority has a Seven-Point Plan of Action, which includes economic development, drug and substance prevention, education, and health. The sorority is known for such programs as "Girl Power," and other self-esteem programs, conflict resolution and anger management programs, and the promotion of creative arts. There are more than 600 chapters of Zeta Phi Beta worldwide, with a membership of over 100,000.

Sigma Gamma Rho

Sigma Gamma Rho Sorority was founded by seven young teachers (Mary Lou Allison Little, Dorothy Hanley Whiteside,

Vivian White Marbury, Nannie Mae Gahn Johnson, Hattie Mae Dulin Redford, Bessie M. Downey Martin, and Cubena McClure) on 12 November 1922 on the campus of Butler University in Indianapolis, Indiana. Sigma Gamma Rho is the only African American sorority founded on a predominantly white campus.

The sorority is a leading service organization, promoting sisterhood, scholarship, and service. It sponsors the Mwanamugimu Essay Contest, which aims to increase knowledge about the history and culture of African nations and improve the writing and research skills of students. The sorority has become an international service organization comprising women from every profession. There are over 100,000 members in over 460 chapters in the United States, Africa, and the Caribbean.

Tiffany Gayle Chenault

See also Part 1: Historically Black Colleges and Universities; Part 6: African American Students; Sororities

References and further reading

Alpha Kappa Alpha. www.aka1908.com. Cited June 12, 2002.

Delta Sigma Theta. www.deltasigmatheta.org. Cited June 12, 2002.

Giddings, Paula. 1988. *In Search of Sisterhood: Delta Sigma Theta and the Challenge of the Black Sorority Movement.* New York: William Morrow.

Gregory, Sheila T. 1995. *Black Women in the Academy: The Secrets to Success and Achievements.* Lanham, MD: University Press of America.

Parker, Marjorie H. 1990. *Alpha Kappa Alpha: Through the Years 1908–1988.* Chicago: Mobium Press.

Sigma Gamma Rho. http://www.sgrho1922.org. Cited June 12, 2002.

Zeta Phi Beta. http://www.2phib1920.org. Cited June 12, 2002.

Classroom Climate

"Classroom climate" refers to the sum total environment of a classroom, including the physical structure, power dynamics, teaching styles, curriculum, and relationships among students. Classrooms have become an important focus of educational research on teaching and learning since they serve as the primary setting in which formal schooling occurs from grade school through graduate school. One outgrowth of the research on classrooms has been a growing body of scholarship documenting differential treatment that may disadvantage girls and women in coeducational settings. Among the most influential and widely cited of these studies is Roberta Hall and Bernice Sandler's 1982 report, *The Classroom Climate: A Chilly One for Women?* The problems described in this report spawned numerous follow-up investigations in postsecondary institutions as well as primary and secondary schools. As a consequence of these studies, classroom climate has come to be more widely understood as an important indicator of educational equity for women.

From a historical perspective, the systematic scholarly investigation of women's experiences in classrooms has been a relatively recent development. Women have long understood that participating in formal education and gaining entry into classrooms that were considered "male territory" marked an important step toward equal standing in a democratic society. As women increasingly gained access to classrooms, it was assumed they would benefit from an education equal to male students in those same classrooms. It was not until the U.S. women's movement in the 1960s that academic women began to systematically examine the classroom

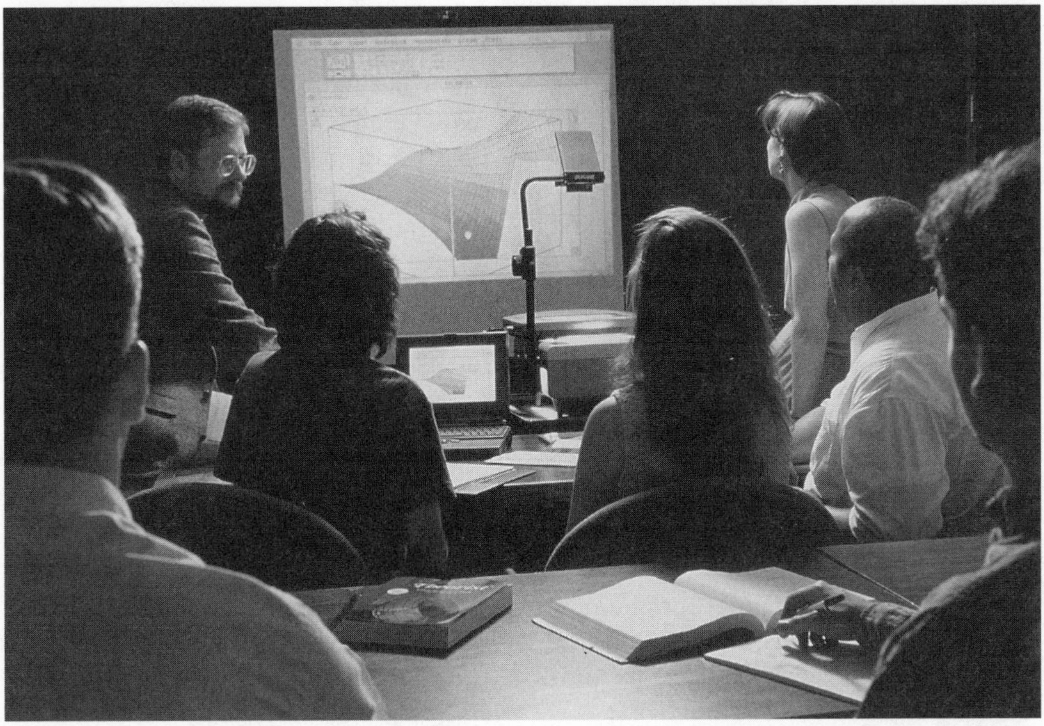

Classroom climate is partly determined by the attitude of the professor (George Disario/Corbis)

experiences of women in coeducational environments. By introducing the labels "classroom climate" and "chilly climate," Hall and Sandler gave a name to a problem that had long existed but remained largely invisible. Along with "chilly climate," the terms "gender bias" and "gender discrimination" are also used in the literature to describe classroom environments that harm girls and women. In general, this body of research considers the impact of classroom structure, content (curriculum), and process, with a particular focus on gender. More recently, "classroom climate" has been used to describe ways in which classroom practices may disadvantage students, not only because of gender but because of other factors (i.e., sexual orientation, race, social class, disability) as well.

Both overt and subtle faculty behaviors, including gendered communication patterns and sexual harassment, are pervasive themes in the literature. In addition, the climate for women in science classrooms, differences among women in classrooms, and strategies for warming classroom climates have received significant attention, though often in specialized journals with a women's studies or feminist focus. In general, the body of scholarship is primarily descriptive and can be divided into three major types: (a) observational studies—sometimes termed "behavioral research"—that rely on data from researchers who observe classrooms and record incidences of gender bias; (b) self-report studies that rely on student appraisals of the nature and frequency of inequities in their classrooms; and (c) meta-analyses that synthesize and analyze findings from a number of smaller studies (e.g., Brady and Eisler 1995; Sandler, Silverberg, and Hall 1996). Some of these studies rely on quantitative analyses only, whereas others incorporate interview and anecdotal data. In many cases, findings are accompanied by recommendations for improvement.

Chilly Classroom Characteristics

Claims made in the 1982 chilly classroom climate report emerged from an understanding that classrooms reflect the strengths, weaknesses, and biases of the larger society in which they are situated. It is from this vantage point that numerous faculty behaviors, largely unconscious, came to be understood as contributing to classroom environments that disadvantage women. Some specific examples of these behaviors include calling on men more often than on women; asking follow-up questions of men and not women, thus coaching them to arrive at a more complete answer; waiting longer for men students to answer questions; using classroom examples that reflect stereotypes about men and women (i.e., always referring to a doctor or police officer as "he" whereas the teacher and victim are "she"); addressing women in ways that emphasizes their social roles rather than intellectual ones ("honey," "dear," "cutie"); focusing more on a woman's appearance rather than her accomplishments; downgrading women who are not attractive or attentive to their appearance; nodding, gesturing, and paying more attention when men speak; viewing marriage and parental status differently for males and females; and attributing women's achievements to something other than their abilities.

Identifying Chilly Climates

Discerning the subtle types of behaviors that contribute to creating a "chilly climate" requires a familiarity with gender theory—an understanding that different social and behavioral expectations for women and men can result in sex and gender discrimination. Sometimes gender-biased behaviors in classrooms are easily identified—overtly sexist comments and sexually harassing behavior, for example. At other times, gender bias can be more subtle and difficult to detect, especially when the behavior reflects gender role expectations that have become so ubiquitous that they go unnoticed by most people (including faculty and students themselves). According to gender theory, when people conform to these expectations, those around them are likely to be comfortable and at ease with a situation, and when people transgress these expectations, others are more likely to notice. Thus, when a woman acts in ways that conform to predominant cultural expectations about femininity (being polite, waiting her turn in conversation, for example), others rarely take note. Likewise, when men act in ways that conform to gender expectations (interrupting in a conversation, for instance), others are unlikely to think it out of the ordinary. But it is not the gender differences that matter; rather what matters is the ways in which these differences can result in classroom practices that advantage men and disadvantage women.

Aside from faculty behaviors, the chilly climate literature describes a number of other aspects of the classroom that likely contribute to inequitable environments. Some of these include differential use of speech and language by gender (i.e., men are more likely to view verbal aggression in classroom discussions as positive, except when women engage in it); the behaviors of some male students (i.e., interrupting, dominating, or controlling the discussion) that may discourage women's participation; physical arrangement of classroom that may discourage face-to-face discussions and encourage a more competitive atmosphere; absence of women faculty role models (especially in engineering, math, and physics); peer sexual harassment both inside and outside classrooms; lack of women's contributions and perspectives in classroom textbooks; and discounting or ridiculing women when they raise "women's issues" in class (Hall and Sandler 1982; Sandler, Silverberg, and Hall 1996).

Mary Rowe of the Massachusetts Institute of Technology coined the term "microinequities" to describe the kinds of subtle behaviors that might appear to be inconsequential when taken alone but that constitute a significant pattern of gender inequity when taken together. Researchers contend that the cumulative effects of such practices can have deleterious consequences for girls and women, including diminished self-esteem, lower scores on standardized tests, and lowered career aspirations. Since both men and women learn cultural expectations of gender roles, it is not surprising that *both* male and female faculty behave in ways that create "chilly" classrooms for women. Hidden assumptions about gender also help to explain why many female students may not even recognize these behaviors as gender-biased (see Sadker and Sadker 1994; Sandler, Silverberg, and Hall 1996).

Many of the behaviors identified in classroom climate studies are not necessarily unique to the differential treatment of women. Indeed, there is much agreement that the chilly climate concept can extend beyond gender and apply to other groups of students who are marginalized in mainstream higher education because of their race, cultural heritage, sexual orientation, age, social class, disability, or some other attribute that has been historically disadvantaged in American society.

Since the early 1980s, a number of researchers have attempted to identify possible confounding variables and tease out the relative influence of various factors that might contribute to the chilly classroom climate. Studies have examined in depth the impact of particular variables, such as sex of the faculty member, pedagogical style, course content, class size, institutional differences, identity differences among women and how the classroom climate may affect self-esteem, cognitive development, choice of major, and career path. Limitations of the initial chilly climate report have been addressed by the authors in a 1996 follow-up, *The Chilly Classroom Climate: A Guide to Improve the Education of Women* (Sandler, Silverberg, and Hall 1996). Most notable among its points were the need to focus further attention on the behaviors students bring to the classroom and how these might compound teacher behaviors and the ways in which power dynamics and other forms of identity differences contribute to shaping a student's classroom experience.

Classroom Climates in the Sciences

In general, the scholarship on science classrooms finds that gender bias is exacerbated for most women. It is believed to result from the facts that women are still in the minority in math, engineering, and physics and that these areas, more than others, have long been considered "male or masculine" domains (Sandler, Silverberg, and Hall 1996). The research in this area also examines the environments of laboratory and fieldwork settings as well as pedagogical styles. Drawing on cognitive development theories, a number of scholars have considered how changing pedagogical styles, classroom structure, and group dynamics might help to attract and retain more women in these fields. In some cases, postsecondary institutions have experimented with offering courses specifically designed to create less competitive environments in male-dominated disciplines, and Smith College created the first undergraduate engineering program at a women's college in an effort to provide high quality, single-sex engineering education.

Differential Impact of the Chilly Climate

Understanding the dynamics of classroom climates is a complex undertaking because any analysis must reflect the larger sociopolitical forces that shape identity and status in U.S. society. Unfortunately, most research in this area was conducted in predominantly white middle-class environments. Not surprisingly, it is largely white, middle-class, traditional-aged women students who have been the primary beneficiaries of the research recommendations for improving classroom climates for women. Increasingly, more researchers have made clear that theories of gender cannot be evenly applied to understand the experiences of *all* women—thus, identity differences among women such as race, ethnicity, sexual orientation, religion, social class, disability, and age must be considered in both research focus and classroom intervention strategies.

Warming Classroom Climates

If many women experience a chilly climate to some extent in postsecondary education, how can faculty "warm up" classrooms? This question is the basis for research related to classroom climates and pedagogy in which faculty training and development, curriculum transformation, and feminist pedagogy are the major emphases. Some of the themes include promoting faculty awareness of how to eliminate the subtle behaviors that may unwittingly perpetuate gender bias in the classroom; training faculty to recognize power dynamics among students that create a climate that may disadvantage women in the classroom; creating nonhierarchical classroom spaces with a focus on shared knowledge among participants rather than simply communicating knowledge from professor to student; promoting collaborative rather than competitive learning environments in classrooms; using textbooks and teaching materials that portray women's contributions to the field; and identifying faculty behaviors that can enhance student responsibility for participation.

Directions for Further Research

A few studies have concluded that evidence of the chilly climate for women in higher education classrooms is thin (see Drew and Work 1998). Such findings are typically associated with studies that rely solely on data derived from self-report surveys that may not be best suited to assessing the subtle types of behavior that contribute to creating a chilly climate. More research is needed to enhance understandings of classroom climates. Bernice Sandler, Lisa Silverberg, and Roberta Hall (1996) suggest the following questions as a guide for further research in this area:

1. Which faculty and student behaviors have an impact on student classroom behavior and why?
2. Do teachers reinforce already existing student classroom behaviors? If so, how?
3. How can faculty members change students' classroom behavior?

Elizabeth J. Allan

See also Part 3: Feminist Pedagogy; Part 7: Campus Climate

References and further reading

AAUW. 1998. *Gender Gaps: Where Schools Still Fail Our Children.* Washington, D.C.: American Association of University Women Educational Foundation.

Astin, Alexander W., and Helen S. Astin. 1993. *Undergraduate Science Education: The Impact of Different College Environments on the Educational Pipeline in the Sciences.* Los Angeles: Higher Education Research Institute, University of California at Los Angeles.

Brady, Kristine L., and Richard M. Eisler. 1995. "Gender Bias in the College Classroom: A Critical Review of the Literature and Implications for Future Research." *Journal of Research and Development in Education* 29, no. 1: 9–19.

Drew, Todd L., and Gerald G. Work. 1998. "Gender-Based Differences in Perception of Experiences in Higher Education: Gaining a Broader Perspective." *Journal of Higher Education* 69 (September–October): 542–555.

Hall, Roberta, and Bernice Sandler. 1982. *The Classroom Climate: A Chilly One for Women?* Washington, DC: Project on the Status and Education of Women, Association of American Colleges.

Sadker, Myra, and David Sadker. 1994. *Failing at Fairness: How Our Schools Cheat Girls.* New York: Touchstone.

Sandler, Bernice R. 2001. *Eighteen Ways to Warm Up the Chilly Climate.* http://www.Bernicesandler.Com/Id41.htm. Cited June 12, 2002.

Sandler, Bernice Resnick, Lisa Silverberg, and Robert M. Hall. 1996. *The Chilly Classroom Climate: A Guide to Improve the Education of Women.* Washington, DC: National Association of Women in Education.

Whitt, Elizabeth J., M. I. Edison, Ernest T. Pascarella, Amaury Nora, and Patrick T. Terenzini. 1999. "Women's Perceptions of a 'Chilly Climate' and Cognitive Outcomes in College: Additional Evidence." *Journal of College Student Development* 40, no. 2: 163–177.

Community College Students

Over 3 million women elect to study in the 1,155 American community colleges annually, pursuing degrees, certificates, and special interest areas. Consistently comprising 58 percent of the total two-year college enrollment, women elect to study at community colleges to take advantage of the convenient locations, affordable tuition rates, academic programs, and special services provided by this sector of higher education. Community colleges, sometimes referred to as junior or technical colleges, are designed to serve students living in a specific geographic region by offering programs that meet the unique educational needs of the area. Typically, community colleges offer associate's degrees that facilitate the transfer to four-year baccalaureate programs, vocational and career preparation providing a professional degree or certification, remedial education opportunities (including high school equivalency programs), and adult and continuing education programs.

Female college students—like two-year colleges in the United States—have a long history of struggling to find legitimacy in the higher education world. Women students were nonexistent in the colonial colleges, and it was not until the mid-nineteenth century that women found their places in higher education—primarily in separate institutions aligned with colleges for men and designed to extend the traditional high school studies. However, social and cultural influences combined with increased federal legislation and economic realities led to the uncoupling of the first two years of college from the university curriculum and the influx of women students into postsecondary institutions. The 1944 Servicemen's Readjustment Act, also known as the G. I. Bill, had the biggest influence upon women students entering community colleges. Not only did it underwrite costs for over 60,000 women, but also it provided nontraditional students entry into the higher education classroom. With these veterans came a maturity and experience that would significantly influence the typical college student. Following closely on the heels of this legislation was President Truman's Commission on Higher Education in 1946, which urged the establishment of scholarship programs, aid for public institutions, and legislation banning discrimination in admissions practices. These influences opened the doors of community colleges more widely to female students.

The statistical profile of community college students in the United States today indicates that the most typical student on the two-year campus is female, aged twenty-five or older, probably with dependents, and probably employed while commuting to classes part-time (American Association of Community Colleges 2000). Despite this profile, there has been little study of the community college woman student, and that which exists is primarily focused on the adult reentry woman described above. There are many reasons why traditional-aged students may attend the community college. Proximity to home and work may provide financial, social, and personal support as they complete college courses. They may have a level of comfort with the community college in their neighborhood or wish to take advantage of a quality education that is supported in good measure by local or state funds, resulting in tuition costs that are significantly lower than university or proprietary school programs. They may be undecided about future careers and want to explore various program options before making the adjustment to a residential college or institution with programs specifically tailored to their interests and career goals. Some students want to continue involvement in athletics begun in their high schools and recognize that their chance to compete intercollegiately is increased when teams are selected from regional pools of athletes rather than nationally recruited pools. Others began their education at a four-year institution and found the adjustment too difficult, so they returned to their homes to take advantage of family structure and support while they mature and, often, work to recapture a respectable grade point average.

Many traditional-aged women students attend community colleges because they are interested in pursuing vocational or career programs, which are not a part of the typical liberal arts or university curriculum. Programs to develop credentials in fields historically occupied by women, such as health care, office systems, or education, are readily available at most community colleges; additionally, women may easily explore nontraditional fields such as engineering, construction trades, or criminal justice in the community college classroom. Whatever draws her to a community college, the traditional student is often using the program as a bridge to further education or the workplace. As a young woman moving toward adulthood, she may be working to establish her independence, determine her personal and professional life goals, and establish relationships with fellow students that will provide social outlets and opportunities.

Reentry women also use community colleges as a means of facilitating life changes. However, they often have responsibilities and concerns different from their younger colleagues. Reentry women students delayed entering college for various reasons, often related to poor past performance, marriage or children, or subtle messages that they were not worthy or capable of pursuing a college education. Given that all women over the age of twenty-two are considered reentry students, it is clear that their college entrance may have been greatly influenced by the economics, values, politics, and gender expectations that governed social, cultural, family, and career norms during the twentieth century. At a younger age, they may have seen their brothers receive assistance for college but not find the same resources available to them. They may have been handicapped by undiagnosed learning disabilities or encouraged to marry or assume an entry-level job rather than pursue a career or profession. Others may have become pregnant as teens or college students and been required to refocus their goals on short-term needs of child rearing and survival rather than the personal and professional long-term benefits that an education offers. They may not have entered college because they did not complete high school. Whatever their reasons, these women identify a need or desire to attend college at a nontraditional age, often turning to the local community college to begin this endeavor. Now, they enter their college years as mature women often unfamiliar with educational protocol and clearly aware that they are outside the norm.

Community colleges are well situated to serve the needs of women students at any age. Child care, on-campus employment, athletics, financial assistance, tutoring, remedial education, counseling, computer laboratories for student use, and a varied curricula offered both during the day and in the evening provide the flexibility and support needed for success. Since the majority of students in community colleges are women, the environment offers many opportunities for establishing relationships and networks that will assist them in meeting their goals. At the two-year college, students are able to explore lifelong learning options. They may complete a general education development certificate, transition into remedial studies, and ultimately pursue a degree or professional certificate without needing to adjust to new settings or systems. Frequently, federal or state subsidized programs will assist the female student as she pursues additional sources of support for housing, transportation, or basic needs.

The welfare-to-work legislation of the 1990s has also facilitated the presence of women in the community college classroom. The two-year colleges are able to deliver short-term, career-oriented programs adapted to the student who must quickly train for a career or lose state or federal assistance. Almost half the community colleges in the United States offer welfare-to-work programs.

A community college education makes a difference. The average expected lifetime earnings for an individual who has earned an associate's degree are more than $1 million. This sum represents an increase of $250,000 over that of an individual who has earned only a high school diploma.

Jean V. Kartje

See also Part 1: Community Colleges; Part 6: Nontraditional Students

References and further reading

American Association of Community Colleges. 2000. *National Community College Snapshot.* http://www.aacc.nche.edu/Template.cfm?Section=AboutCommunityColleges.htm. Cited June 12, 2002.

Cohen, Arthur M., and Florence B. Brawer. 1996. *The American Community College.* San Francisco: Jossey-Bass.

LaPaglia, Nancy. 1993. *Storytellers: The Image of the Two-Year College in American Fiction and in Women's Journals.* DeKalb, IL: LEPS Press, Northern Illinois University.

Witt, Allen A., James L. Wattenbarger, James F. Gollattscheck, and Joseph E. Suppiger. 1994. *America's Community Colleges: The First Century.* Washington, DC: Community College Press.

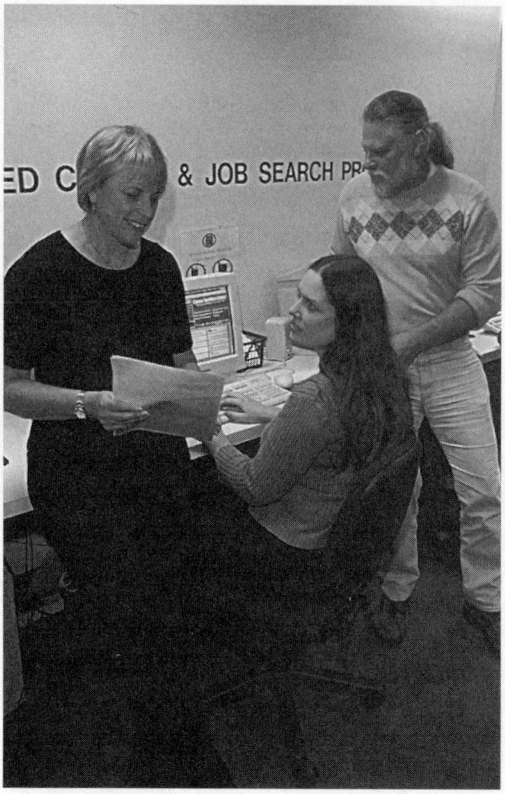

Employment counselors help a student find resources (Painetworks)

Counseling Issues and Services

As the growing majority of college students, women present a unique set of counseling issues for campus counseling professionals. Research indicates that women face personal development and maturity from a different perspective than do men. Developmental theory indicates that men define themselves and mature by developing autonomy, whereas women define themselves and mature through connection and relationships built with others. These developmental differences may call for different counseling approaches and have prompted counseling services on campus to focus on the experience of female as well as male students in their service and program delivery.

There are many counseling areas that specifically attend to the needs of women students. Relationships, reproductive concerns, career issues, and the role of violence and fear in women's lives are salient counseling issues for women students. Issues of physical and sexual abuse, body image and eating disorders, and self-esteem are also typical concerns found among women in college.

As the population of women has continued to rise on college campuses, the need for professionals trained in such counseling areas has also risen. From 1960 to 1972, the number of women attending college rose by 367 percent, although women remained the minority on campus. That is no longer the case, as percentages of women have surpassed those of men on campus. In the 1980s, reports of a "chilly" campus climate reinforced the need for attention to women students' experiences and support mechanisms on campus. In these reports, the effects of the chilly climate on women students included feelings of isolation, being ignored, and a differentiation from men on campus.

Many women were also struggling with other barriers. Nontraditional-age women (generally defined as those students older than age twenty-two) found the campuses as uninviting as other groups of women. These students faced identity issues as they exchanged parental dependence for marital dependence. Many counseling centers developed programs specifically targeting women students in transition as they struggled to develop their identities and independence. For those with children, child care concerns represented another barrier. Both the practical side of care for children while students attended classes, as well as the emotional side of the tendency of women to neglect their needs for the needs of their children or others around them, represented great strains for many students. Counseling centers stepped up to provide self-esteem development sessions and one-on-one counseling for women suffering from the weight of these psychological strains.

Counseling services on campus are estimated to be used twice as often by women as by men. At one time, this difference in those seeking counseling would have been attributed to an inferior developmental process in women. In contrast, Carol Gilligan's work demonstrated that the standard to measure moral development was based on the male experience and was not appropriate for women. The quality of women's development and thinking were inadequately assessed using a male model. Although now generally accepted, Gilligan's work expressing women's experiences "in a different voice" broke ground for women to acknowledge and appreciate their differences from men. Ruthellen Josselson's model for women's development added to the theoretical base for improving counseling services for women.

Counseling services on campuses acknowledged women's experiences and built services to provide a bridge for college women in transition. Services were added to aid women in coping with gender-based barriers on campus and helping students find their identity in what was a new world to many women students. Women found these services to be a strong resource when coping with their multiple roles as they juggle the demands of being a college student and a woman.

Debra J. Blanke

See also Part 6: Curricular and Professional Choices; Developmental Issues; Learning and Knowing; Nontraditional Students

References and further reading

Carter, J. O., ed. 1978. *Second Wind: A Program for Returning Women Students.* U.S. Department of Education, Women's Educational Equity Act Program. Newton, MA: Education Development Center.

Gilligan, Carol. 1982. *In a Different Voice: Psychological Theory and Women's Development.* Cambridge, MA: Harvard University Press.

Grayson, Paul A., and Kate Cauley, eds. 1989. *College Psychotherapy.* New York: Guilford Press.
Josselson, Ruthellen. 1987. *Finding Herself: Pathways to Identity Development in Women.* San Francisco: Jossey-Bass.
———. 1996. *Revising Herself: The Story of Women's Identity from College to Midlife.* New York: Oxford University Press.

Curricular and Professional Choices

Although similar in many respects, the processes of curricular choice and professional choice are defined somewhat differently. Curricular choice is a decision about the major course of study individuals choose to follow as students at the postsecondary level. Professional choice is the decision individuals make to determine a full-time profession or occupation that will be suitable to them.

For decades, women were underrepresented in higher education in the United States. Although they now constitute the majority of postsecondary students, women remain underrepresented in many of the sciences and business-related academic disciplines and in many professional fields. It is important to recognize that there are several obstacles females must overcome in the classroom and in the workplace. Research suggests that some factors contributing to why females are underrepresented in certain majors and professions include societal views and stereotypes, parental influence, and absence of female role models in the field.

Despite these hindrances, women have made great strides both educationally and professionally since the 1970s. Studies indicate that women have been making progress in fields that have traditionally been dominated by men, such as medicine, business, and law. Since the early 1980s, women have been more likely than men to enroll in college after high school graduation and currently earn nearly 55 percent of the degrees awarded from four-year institutions. Other studies suggest that despite women's progress, they still make up less than 20 percent of those graduating with degrees in computer science, mathematics, and engineering. Although these numbers have remained constant in math and science, they have dropped slightly in the area of computer science in recent years. Studies also indicate that upon graduation, roughly the same number of male and female high school students will have completed enough math courses required to pursue a degree in one of these fields, but a significantly smaller percentage of women will actually select a science or technical discipline when choosing a major. However, research also indicates that women who do opt for a science or technical major are more likely than men to graduate with the technical degree, as well as continue on to graduate school in the same field (Olsen 2000).

Majors traditionally studied by men include biological and natural sciences, business, engineering, math, and computer science. Although more female college students have been choosing these fields of study, their perceptions of math and science remain largely negative, and they are consequently overrepresented in the fields of arts and letters (Dowd 1999). Some researchers claim that the attitude that science is overly intellectual and unfeminine discourages women from pursuing the field, both academically and professionally (Packard and Wong 1999). They argue that women have been conditioned by society from an early age to believe that these fields signify masculinity and that because science is objective, it is inappropriate for women to pursue these areas of study. Another societal viewpoint is that science is outcome-oriented and women do not prefer this style of learning. This line of thinking concludes that women should be represented in areas such as home economics, the humanities, or teaching, where a more interactive approach to learning is applied (Packard and Wong 1999). Attitudes about women and the sciences vary, however, by type of institution: women at single-sex colleges are one and a half times more likely to major in science or math than women at coeducational institutions (Rayman and Brett 1995).

Women have received contradictory messages about the meaning of success for years, and they affect women's curricular choices in college. For example, some women have been told that success means tending to their home and family, whereas others learned from an early age that success for a woman involves aspiring to a professional career. Many people believe that a successful woman can be happy in a career and continue with the daily responsibilities of a family, whereas others believe women should avoid some careers altogether. Girls and women have been taught to be polite, quiet, and agreeable; they have learned to seek others' approval instead of acknowledging their individual abilities and knowledge (Advancing Women 2002). These messages and values influence women in college as they begin to make decisions about their curricular and professional development. Women may internalize gender stereotypes, accept them as fact, and therefore choose majors and professions that do not challenge these societal views (Canes 1995). This phenomenon may explain why females are more likely than males to declare majors in the health-related professions, English, psychology, communications, and the arts and foreign languages at both the undergraduate and graduate education levels.

In addition, studies have demonstrated that parental actions and attitudes, including a parent's occupation, can be especially influential in a woman's curricular and professional decisionmaking (Kennedy and Parks 2000). For example, one way that parents can influence a decision to enter the traditionally male fields is to be positive about their daughter's education in math and science and to encourage the use of critical thinking and problem solving in these courses. Parents who continue to support these abilities and interests in their daughters as they move into higher education can also have a significant influence on a woman's curricular choice. In one in-depth study, results indicated that those women who persisted in the field after graduating with a science degree were more likely to have had more family and faculty encouragement throughout their undergraduate years (Rayman and Brett 1995).

Female role models also significantly influence women's curricular choices. From a young age, girls may dismiss science or math because they think the preparation for these careers is too difficult. Extensive research conducted via case studies and surveys has concluded that females, especially mothers and female professors, are important to the curricular and professional decisions women make during and after college, when they recognize that members of their sex can be successful in male-dominated majors and professions. In contrast, other studies yielded no positive correlation between same-sex role models and impact on women college student curricular or professional decisions, claiming instead that women base their professional and curricular decisions primarily on their interests and capabilities. In this line of argument, the absence of sufficient numbers of female role models does not explain why women do not choose science-related majors in college (see Canes 1995).

Curricular choice has an influence on the lives of graduates beyond the college years. Depending on the chosen field of study, average salaries of young females with a four-year degree in the early to mid-1990s were lower than those of males in their graduating class. For example, salaries of entry-level professionals who studied the humanities, computer science, and other technical degrees in college were similar, with males receiving average salaries only slightly greater than those of females. In contrast, males majoring in business and management had higher average starting salaries of approximately $4,000 than females in the same graduating class (Bae et al. 2000). Although males continue to have earnings relatively greater than those of females, the gap has been slowly declining from 1970, when the average salary for females was equivalent to only 57 percent of average salaries for males. Today, female salaries are equivalent to nearly 78 percent of males in the same fields of study (Bae et al. 2000).

Courtney A. Little

See also Part 1: Medical Education; Part 4: Transformation of the Curriculum; Part 6: Graduate and Professional Education; Undergraduates and Science; Part 7: Disciplinary Socialization; Socialization

References and further reading

Advancing Women. "Does Society Encourage Girls to Develop Career Goals?" http://www.advancing women/grrls4.html. Cited June 12, 2002.

Bae, Yupin, Susan Choy, Claire Geddes, Jennifer Stable, and Thomas Snyder. 2000. *Educational Equity of Girls and Women.* NCES 2000–030. Washington, DC: U.S. Government Printing Office.

Canes, Brandice J. 1995. "Following In Her Footsteps? Faculty Gender Composition and Women's Choices of College Majors." *Industrial and Labor Relations Review* 48: 486–504.

Dowd, Alicia C. 1999. "Understanding Women's Career Choices Using Taylor's Concept of Authenticity." Paper presented at the annual convention of the American Education Research Association, Montreal, Quebec, Canada, April 19–23. Dialog ERIC, ED434291.

Kennedy, Helen L., and Joe Parks. 2000. "Society Cannot Continue to Exclude Women from the Fields of Science and Mathematics." *Education* 120: 529.

Olsen, Florence. 2000. "Institute for Women and Technology Works to Bridge Computing's Gender Gap." *Chronicle of Higher Education* 25 (February): A47.

Packard, Becky Wai-Ling, and E. David Wong. 1999. "Future Images and Women's Career Decisions in Science." Paper presented at the Annual Meeting of the American Education Research Association, Montreal, Canada, April 19–23. Dialog ERIC, ED430805.

Rayman, Paula, and Belle Brett. 1995. "Women Science Majors: What Makes a Difference in Persistence after Graduation. *Journal of Higher Education* 66, no. 4: 388–414.

Development of Multiple Social and Cultural Identities

Multiple social and cultural identity development refers to the ways in which race, gender, and other socially meaningful markers intersect and are integrated in the articulation and experience of one's identity. Understanding and exploring this theoretical concept is necessary to better address the needs and conditions of women in higher education institutions, which are predominantly both white and male. This subject is also particularly important for those women in the academy whose particular experiences with multiple paradigms of domination (i.e., racism and patriarchy) uniquely locate them in the often hegemonic social and political relationships carried out in American higher education institutions. As Diane Goodman (1990) assessed in her study of African American women's identity development, the ways in which race, gender, and class interact and intersect need further study. Although an important topic, social and cultural identity development has received little theoretical or empirical attention. More empirical research and theoretical development are needed in this area to assess the nature of social and cultural identity development in women and to document the process in women over time. Also, the role of higher education and other educational institutions in the development of social and cultural identity should be explored and assessed.

Social and Cultural Identity in Student Development

Research on African American women has more often contributed to the understanding of social and cultural identity development than other bodies of scholarship. Alice R. Brown-Collins and Deborah R. Sussewell's 1986 study on African American women's emerging selves highlighted the complexities of integrating race and gender, a topic that until then rarely had been given scholarly consideration. Their research also showed that an African American woman perceives her notion of her self in relationship to others. The study's conclusions identify multiple self-referents for African American women: the psychophysiological, an African American referent, and what Brown-Collins and Sussewell termed "myself." The first referent represents the black woman's knowledge of herself as a woman. The second involves knowledge of social and political realities, in which knowledge obtained and understood about the self is a collective-affective experience. The "myself" referent is self-knowledge that is unique to a woman's personal history, is a by-product of both her blackness and her femaleness, and needs to be studied simultaneously.

This emphasis on self-knowledge is carried on in Diane Goodman's work to include the voices of African American women in theories of women's development. Goodman sought to address deficiencies in feminist research by explicitly focusing on the experiences of African American women and considering the interaction of sex and race. She argued that identity development in African American women results from the interaction of two factors, an Afrocentric cultural ethos and a socialization in their families to be independent and self-reliant. Resulting from this interaction are three areas of self in which Goodman's respondents spoke about themselves and their identities: sense of self, sense of self in relationship, and sense of being in the world, or ontology. Goodman noted that the capacity for self-reflection was most developed in those subjects with the most integrated self-concept and who were most seriously preoccupied with moral and spiritual issues.

Models of Integration of Social and Cultural Identities in Students

Susan Jones, Marylu McEwen, Amy Reynolds, and Raechelle Pope were among the first scholars to address the integration of social and cultural identity issues directly within the field of student development. Jones (1997) looked specifically at the multiple dimensions of identity development in women college students. She found that the multicultural group of women she interviewed dealt with many issues previously unaddressed in the literature on women's development. Among those issues were the multiple ways in which race mattered, the multiple layers of identity, and the braiding of gender identity with other dimensions of self. In addition, the more dimensions of identity that the women perceived, the more complex became their negotiations between inside (personal) and outside (societal) worlds. The ability to define their identity was then critical as these women sought ways to live peacefully with multiple dimensions of identity.

Jones and McEwen (2000) updated the findings presented by Jones in 1997 and developed a conceptual model of multiple social and cultural dimensions of identity. It portrayed the intersections and interactions among dimensions of identity development not seen in other models. The model attends theoretically to the myriad ways in which personal self-definitions and differing contexts dynamically interact with the development of socially constructed identities. Significantly, the model demonstrates that it is possible to live successfully with multiple identities. The authors also found that the respondents spoke of having a core identity, defined as personality characteristics that were more authentic and complex than their socially constructed, or external identities.

Reynolds and Pope (1991) explored identity development for individuals possessing what they term as multiple oppressed identities, such as a female person of color who is also lesbian. Basing their analysis in an Afrocentric worldview as articulated by Linda Myers (1993), they asserted that to be oppressed was to be socialized into a worldview that was suboptimal and led to a fragmented sense of self, making it difficult for people to embrace all their identities. Reynolds and Pope proposed their multidimensional identity model, based on a model of biracial identity development, to describe the process of facing an internal conflict over one's essential sense of self. This nonhierarchical, nonevaluative model has four patterns of identity resolution: (1) identification with only one aspect of self that is assigned by society, (2) identification with only one aspect of self that is consciously chosen by the individual, (3) identification with multiple aspects of the self in a segmented fashion, and (4) identification with combined aspects of self (Reynolds and Pope 1991, 179).

Linda J. Myers, Suzette L. Speight, Pamela S. Highlen, Chikako I. Cox, Amy L. Reynolds, Eve M. Adams, and C. Patricia Hanley (1991) framed identity development as a process of continuous integration and expansion of one's sense of self. They used Myers's notion of optimal theory as the foundation for what they suggested was a more inclusive, "pancultural" model of identity development. According to an optimal model of identity development, it is a process of expanding self-knowledge regarding one's relationship to a spiritual universe. The authors argued that such knowledge then makes possible the integration of all the material manifestations of being (such as race, gender, class, age, color, and ethnicity) into a whole sense of self. The resultant identity development model proposed by the authors, grounded in research interviews and counseling sessions, is identified as optimal theory applied to identity development (OTAID). The OTAID is a six-phase process that is sequential but neither linear nor categorical. Therefore, individuals may or may not move through all the phases of the model in one lifetime, nor is there a predictable amount of time that an individual may spend in a phase. The OTAID is described instead as an "expanding spiral" in which the end of the process looks similar to the beginning. At the beginning in phase 0, absence of conscious awareness, individuals experience themselves as connected to all life but are lacking in self-knowledge. At the end of the process in phase 6, transformation, through self-knowledge individuals again become aware of their connection to the universe and all life. Through each phase, the individual comes to know himself or herself in a fuller, more complete way and begins to understand that individual identities as raced, gendered, classed, or aged are actually interrelated and interdependent.

Dafina Lazarus Stewart

See also Part 2: Intersection of Gender and Race; Part 3: Black Feminism and Womanism; Part 6: African American Students; American Indian Students; Asian American Students; Biracial and Biethnic Students; Developmental Issues; Latina Students; Sexuality

References and further reading

Brown-Collins, Alice R., and Deborah R. Sussewell. 1986. "The Afro-American Woman's Emerging Selves." *Journal of Black Psychology* 13: 1–11.

Goodman, Diane J. 1990. "African-American Women's Voices: Expanding Theories of Women's Development." *Sage* 7: 3–14.

Jones, Susan Robb. 1997. "Voices of Identity and Difference: A Qualitative Exploration of the Multiple Dimensions of Identity Development in Women College Students." *Journal of College Student Development* 38: 376–385.

Jones, Susan Robb, and Marylu McEwen. 2000. "A Conceptual Model of Multiple Dimensions of Identity." *Journal of College Student Development* (July–August): 405–413.

McEwen, Marylu K., Larry D. Roper, Deborah R. Bryant, and Miriam J. Langa. 1990. "Incorporating the Development of African-American Students into Psychosocial Theories of Student Development." *Journal of College Student Development* 31: 429–436.

Myers, Linda J. 1993. *Understanding an Afrocentric World View: An Introduction to Optimal Psychology.* Dubuque, IA: Kendall/Hunt.

Myers, Linda J., Suzette L. Speight, Pamela S. Highlen, Chikako I. Cox, Amy L. Reynolds, Eve M. Adams, and C. Patricia Hanley. 1991. "Identity Development and Worldview: Toward an Optimal Conceptualization." *Journal of Counseling and Development* 70: 54–63.

Reynolds, Amy L., and Raechelle L. Pope. 1991. "The Complexities of Diversity: Exploring Multiple Oppressions." *Journal of Counseling and Development* 70: 174–180.

Developmental Issues

Although human development has not been adopted as the overarching goal of higher education, there is little doubt that higher education aims to foster enduring intellectual and personal growth in students. College outcomes research confirms that undergraduate students change in patterned ways as a result of the college experience—not just through age-related maturation—and that these changes persist after graduation. Postsecondary educators have drawn from developmental psychology theories of growth and change within individuals over time. Theories of psychosocial identity development, cognitive development, moral development, and career development are rich in descriptions of the early and midlife adults that compose the college population. Understanding normative development can enable faculty, administrators, and counselors to provide effective educational conditions and assist individual students.

Developmental psychology of women has been an active and contentious field since the mid-1970s, when psychologists began writing about the androcentrism of traditional developmental theory. In Sigmund Freud's psychosexual theory of human development, women's inability to traverse the Oedipus complex meant a failure to develop fully as moral beings. Instead, Freud contended, women were dependent, incompetent, hysterical, and masochistic. Similarly, Erik Erikson and Lawrence Kohlberg cast women as less autonomous and principled than men and therefore less highly developed than males.

Women developmentalists began identifying the masculinist bias in these theories and questioning the claim that such models were universal in their applicability. Critics began by highlighting the all-male samples that formed the research base for major theories of development and noting that women were seen as deficient because they were defined in relation to male development patterns. Feminists identified androcentric assumptions shared by traditional theories. Early theories assumed development had to do with striving for a separate, autonomous identity, agency, mastery, and reasoning through logic. Traditional notions of development follow Freud in presuming that a healthy transition to adulthood requires disconnecting from family and other primary relationships in order to become a fully autonomous adult. These theories assume that successful adulthood means a firmly bounded self with distinct separation between self and others. Finally, the experience of conflict is seen as integral to the appropriate process of separation and individuation.

Jean Baker Miller's landmark 1976 book, *Toward a New Psychology of Women,* identified the antifemale bias in Freudian and Eriksonian psychoanalytic theory, situated women's development within gendered social roles, and proposed an alternative to the autonomous, bounded self. Originally termed "self-in-relation" theory, the relational approach of Miller and her colleagues at the Stone Center holds that women develop their sense of self within and through connections to significant others. Actual relationships and inner constructions of the relational process involve perspective taking, feeling empathy, sharing, and paying attention to the well-being of others and of the relationship itself. Development occurs as women simultaneously strive for full selfhood—"being-within-relation"—and the achievement of deep, complex, responsive relationships "being-in-relation." Studying women college students from the relational approach, Stone Center researchers demonstrated that young female undergraduates deal with conflict and values exploration within relationships, rather than by disconnection. Traditional models of college learning and interaction that feature individual, isolated, competitive, impersonal, and success-oriented ideologies and practices provide poor matches with relational development.

The mother-daughter relationship is both prototype and facilitator of a relational sense of self. From an object-relations perspective, Nancy Chodorow theorized that women's affiliative development begins with the primary connection between girls and their mothers. Unlike boys, girls have no need to disconnect from their early identification with female caregivers in order to develop gender identity. From the beginning of life, women develop a sense of self within connection. For the majority of college women, mothers continue to serve as models of affiliation and to enable young women to practice individuation within the mother-daughter relationship.

Ruthellen Josselson (1987) found that mothers were central to the identity passage of college women in early adulthood. Josselson conducted a longitudinal study of thirty-four women, whom she interviewed as college seniors and twenty-four years later. The study used James Marcia's ego identity status framework (1966) to assess the relevance of Erikson's male-derived developmental theory. Josselson discovered that Erikson's assumptions of disconnection and autonomy were not descriptive of women's psychological growth. Instead, women anchored themselves in different relational structures as they accomplished various degrees of individuation within interpersonal connections. Female college students who remained embedded in their family of origin, whom she labeled "foreclosures," remained inflexible and closed to self-exploration but actually functioned well and were satisfied with their stereotypically female lifestyles. "Identity achieved" women were more introspective and open to change. The most disconnected college seniors, the "identity diffuse," were those who could not form a healthy self-structure. Twenty-four years after college graduation, women who had been exploring the "moratorium" status had moved into foreclosure or achieved identity. The other women continued in the identity status of their college years, indicating that the identity passage in late adolescence and early adulthood is pivotal and lasting. In company with other theorists of women's development, Josselson concluded that women construct identity around issues of communion, connection, relational embeddedness, spirituality, and affiliation.

With the publication of *In a Different Voice: Psychological Theory and Women's Development* in 1982, Carol Gilligan challenged the universality of Kohlberg's influential theory of moral development. Kohlberg's stage theory characterized development as a progression from self-centered moral positions through conventional judgments to the highest level, in which moral reasoning relies on principles of justice. Gilligan questioned why females consistently scored below males at conventional positions in Kohlberg's framework. Based on an interview study of women facing the real moral dilemma of whether to have an abortion, Gilligan suggested that women might follow a different moral trajectory than that of principled justice and individual rights. Instead, she identified in women a central concern with caring and relationships in resolving moral dilemmas. The developmental trajectory for women, according to Gilligan, involves balancing one's own needs with concern and care for others in the context of particular circumstances and specific relationships. Although associated with males and females, respectively, the ethic of justice and the ethic of care are present and available to both men and women.

Another major book followed Miller's and Gilligan's groundbreaking work in addressing the missing perspective of women in developmental theory: *Women's Ways of Knowing: The Development of Self, Voice, and Mind* (1986). Authors Mary Belenky, Blythe Clinchy, Nancy Goldberger, and Jill Tarule considered the cognitive and epistemological development of women and found that college women's meaning making showed a limited fit with the perspective of William Perry's male-derived cognitive development theory. Belenky and her colleagues interviewed a sample of 135 women who were geographically, economically, and educationally heterogeneous. Their analysis of women's life stories revealed five perspectives on knowledge incorporating different ways of thinking about self, authority, truth, and decisions. The five perspectives were (1) silence, a position in which the woman sees herself as powerless, lacking voice, and not making independent meaning; (2) received knowing, in which women accept authoritative truths from powerful others and understand knowledge as outside the self; (3) subjective knowing, in which women rely on intuitive, private, feeling-based knowledge rather than on articulated formal reasoning; (4) procedural knowing, in which women acknowledge and use systems of developing and evaluating knowledge claims, either through "separate knowing" (a distanced, impartial, analytic stance) or "connected knowing" (a believing stance connected to ideas and fellow learners); and (5) constructed knowing, in which women recognize the contextual nature of knowledge, see themselves as constructors of knowledge, value multiple approaches to knowing, and integrate knowledge with self and individual commitments. Belenky and her colleagues deny that the perspectives form a hierarchical stage theory; however, Goldberger argue in a later coauthored book that "constructed knowing can be considered 'superior' in its flexibility and in the sense that it represents a metaperspective on knowing" (Goldberger et al. 1996, 13). Subjective and connected knowers, according to this conception, would struggle within postsecondary classrooms that stress debate, dispassion, and impersonality.

Characterized as "different voice" or "relational" theories, the works of Miller, Gilligan, and Belenky and her colleagues have been both influential and controversial. Feminist and other critics accuse these works of being essentialist—that is, defining gender differences as inherent or natural rather than socially constructed. Accompanying this criticism is the charge of "alpha bias," in which male and female characteristics are seen as distinct rather than overlapping distributions. Essentializing and separating qualities of "womanness," critics say, ignores the social construction of gender, masks variability among women, reinforces gender stereotypes, and implies that men and women are more different than alike. Some feminists point to limitations in research methods and instrumentation, imprecise theoretical constructs, and inconsistent empirical results to conclude that evidence of gender differences in epistemology have not been empirically demonstrated.

Goldberger and her colleagues and Gilligan have refuted claims of essentialism on two main grounds. Having studied only women as a corrective to all-male studies, they do not claim that the resulting new "voice" or knowledge perspectives are necessarily distinctly female. More important, theorists who use this perspective accept the social construction of gender. Jean Baker Miller describes women's subordinate position in hierarchies of social power, for instance, and locates the relational self in female roles that emphasize nurturance and empowerment of others. Goldberger and her colleagues argue that structural power relations privilege certain epistemologies, leaving marginalized individuals feeling devalued but also developing "strategies for knowing that are unique to their social positionality and history of oppression" (1996, 9). Women thus develop gender-related (though not unique) identity and cognitive pathways precisely because of their socially constructed positionality.

The theories reviewed here are the major contemporary models specifically dedicated to women's psychological development. Many other theories treat gender as a key variable, including the cognitive development theories of Marcia B. Baxter Magolda, Karen Kitchener, and Patricia King. Some feminist developmentalists argue that treating gender as a variable perpetuates androcentric assumptions and places male development as the normative center. Instead, they call for female-centered developmental models that view gender as a social status. Multiple recent theoretical strands within developmental psychology support this position, including the work of Lev Vygotsky on socially mediated learning and cultural psychologists' accounts of the ways in which self and culture construct each other. Theories that focus on the effects of historically embedded, broad social structure and events on individual development include Urie Bronfenbrenner's human ecology theory and the life course analysis approaches of Glen Elder, Björgulf Claussen, and others. Social constructionists such as Campbell Leaper characterize gender in terms of social interactions within inequitable power structures, whereas narrative theorists like Bruner, Scholnick, and others locate meaning making within discursive practices. Finally, postmodernists deny the existence of a stable, coherent, self-constructed identity, dissolving the possibility of representing the universalized experience of women.

Drawing from these interdisciplinary theoretical approaches, Miller and Scholnick have described the varied work of feminist developmental psychologists as centering around three large concepts. First, humans are connected, relational beings who are "embedded in social relationships more than they are separated, autonomous, and distanced from others" (2000, 4). This view challenges traditional dichotomies, such as mind/body or reason/emotion, and emphasizes relational mutuality and coconstruction rather than conflict and competition. Second, human development is situated and particular. As standpoint theorists insist (e.g., Susan Bordo, Patricia Hill Collins, Lorraine Code, Sandra Harding), there is no "view from nowhere." Instead, gender is situated in a social, political context and intertwined with race, ethnicity, social class, and sexuality. These feminists insist on the variability of women's experience. Third, feminist developmental psychology draws specific attention to the gendered construction of society, noting that androcentric cultural values permeate and shape the lives of girls and women. Politics and power are thus inseparable from development and from the research process. Woman's "voice" might differ from dominant epistemologies and discourses, in fact, because of her "dual consciousness" as a member of a marginalized group who can see both dominated and dominating perspectives.

Karen D. Arnold

See also Part 3: Feminist Epistemology; Feminist Ethics; Part 6: Learning and Knowing.

References and further reading

Belenky, Mary F., Blythe M. Clinchy, Nancy Goldberger, and Jill Tarule. 1986. *Women's Ways of Knowing: The Development of Self, Voice, and Mind.* New York: Basic Books.

Chodorow, Nancy. 1978. *The Reproduction of Mothering.* Berkeley: University of California Press.

Erikson, Erik. 1980. *Identity and the Life Cycle.* New York: W. W. Norton.

Gilligan, Carol. 1982. *In a Different Voice: Psychological Theory and Women's Development.* Cambridge, MA: Harvard University Press.

Goldberger, Nancy R., Jill M. Tarule, Blythe Clinchy, and Mary B. Belenky, eds. 1996. *Knowledge, Difference, and Power: Essays Inspired by* Women's Ways of Knowing. New York: Basic Books.

Jordan, Judith V., Alexandra G. Kaplan, Jean B. Miller, Irene P. Stiver, and Janet L. Surrey. 1991. *Women's Growth in Connection: Writings from the Stone Center.* New York: Guilford Press.

Josselson, Ruthellen. 1987. *Finding Herself: Pathways to Identity Development in Women.* San Francisco: Jossey-Bass.

Marcia, James E. 1966. "Development and Validation of Ego Identity Status." *Journal of Personality and Social Psychology* 3, no. 5: 551–558.

Miller, Jean. B. 1976. *Toward a New Psychology of Women.* Boston: Beacon Press.

Miller, Patricia H., and Ellin K. Scholnick. 2000. *Toward a Feminist Developmental Psychology.* New York: Routledge.

Extracurricular Issues

The cocurriculum is the group of experiences that contribute to a college student's learning but are not part of the structured academic curriculum, which is traditionally credit bearing. Cocurricular (also called extracurricular) activities are not simply the sum of all the time a student spends in places other than the classroom or laboratory. A student's out-of-class activities need to contribute in some way to her learning to be considered part of the cocurriculum. What students do outside the classroom is rarely neutral—it usually either complements the academic experience or detracts from it.

The terms are fairly interchangeable, but using "cocurriculum" in place of "extracurriculum" is a way, perhaps idealistically, to demonstrate that what happens in residence halls, study lounges, corridors of academic buildings, student organization meeting rooms, and the gym is indeed partnering with academic coursework. The term "extracurricular" suggests that these experiences are peripheral and thus marginalizes the realm outside the classroom.

The cocurriculum warrants attention when one considers that the majority of college students' time is spent outside formal instruction. Recent research indicates that approximately 30 percent of a full-time student's waking hours is spent in the classroom, demonstrating the relative importance of the cocurriculum (National Survey of Student Engagement 2001). If the majority of students' time is relegated to nonclass activities, the quality and nature of those activities are critical to students' overall collegiate experience. There should be a rich and constructive experience that contributes to educational endeavors, facilitates personal development, and strengthens connection with the institution. Here the peer group has the strongest influence and skills are practiced that are not always used inside the classroom. Additionally, cocurricular activities provide significant opportunities for students to build a sense of community, which links them to the institution and has implications for student persistence as well as satisfaction.

The American educational system dates back to the colonial period, when institutional control over students was stringent and extracurricular activities were almost nonexistent. Higher education transformed as the United States grew more industrialized. During this period, beginning around 1870, a full complement of structured, out-of-class activities emerged: sporting teams, debating clubs, literary societies, fraternities and sororities, campus publications, and religious organizations. College administrators at this time often discouraged such social organizations and activities, fearing that they undermined the formal academic curriculum. These early extracurricular activities were initiated by students and actively squelched by the administration. As students persisted, college officials eventually sanctioned the organizations and activities. As higher education researchers revealed the potential of the cocurriculum to contribute positively to student retention and satisfaction, institutions have provided more support to these out-of-class experiences.

Effects of Cocurricular Involvement

Ernest Pascarella and Patrick Terenzini summarized the literature on the effects of extracurricular involvement. The majority of the research suggested that involvement in cocurricular activities had a positive effect on educational persistence and attainment, as well as strong positive effects on social self-concept (1991, 625). The authors implied that even more positive effects are probably attributable to the cocurriculum, but the research lacked consistency, so findings might have been obfuscated. For example, many studies explored "peer involvement or influence," which could arguably be a proxy for cocurricular involvement.

Alexander Astin's landmark 1977 publication, *Four Critical Years,* accessed longitudinal data on thousands of college students and reported on myriad outcomes associated with postsecondary education. Based on this extensive quantitative research, Astin posited his involvement theory in 1984, which lent considerable credibility to the activities included in the cocurriculum. Involvement theory suggests that the amount and nature of a student's involvement outside the classroom is directly related to a student's learning. The five postulates are simple and perhaps now intuitively obvious, but Astin's articulation of them represented the first data-driven support of the positive impact of the cocurriculum.

1. Involvement refers to the investment of physical and psychological energy in various objects. The objects may be highly generalized (the student experience) or highly specific (preparing for a chemistry examination).
2. Regardless of its object, involvement occurs along a continuum; that is, different students manifest different degrees of involvement in a given object, and the same student manifests different degrees of involvement in different objects at different times.
3. Involvement has both quantitative and qualitative features. The extent of a student's involvement in academic work, for instance,

can be measured quantitatively (how many hours the student spends studying) and qualitatively (whether the student reviews and comprehends reading assignments or simply stares at the textbook and daydreams).
4. The amount of student learning and personal development associated with any educational program is directly proportional to the quality and quantity of student involvement in that program.
5. The effectiveness of any educational policy or practice is directly related to the capacity of that policy or practice to increase student involvement. (Astin 1984, 298)

This initial theory was supported by quantitative research showing that students who lived on campus were more likely to persist to graduation, that students who had interaction with faculty outside the classroom were more satisfied with all aspects of their institutional experience (academic as well as social), and that the student peer group was the most influential factor in a student's collegiate experience.

Astin's follow-up publication, *What Matters in College: Four Critical Years Revisited* (1993), confirmed the important role that cocurricular involvement plays in student learning. Astin found that self-reported increases in a student's leadership ability were positively correlated with cocurricular involvement activities such as participation in student organizations, being elected to office, tutoring other students, participating in a cultural awareness workshop, being a member of a social fraternity or sorority, and socializing with students from different racial backgrounds. These kinds of cocurricular involvement variables suggested that student-to-student interactions were also positively correlated with an overall satisfaction measure. Quantitative research findings supported the anecdotal evidence collected by campus administrators and faculty members. The findings bolstered what many intuitively believed to be true about how involvement not only improved an individual student's collegiate experience but enhanced the overall sense of community on campus.

Challenging student affairs professionals around the country, Ernest Boyer raised this issue: "Colleges like to speak of the campus as community, and yet what is being learned in most residence halls today has little connection to the classrooms, indeed it may undermine the educational purposes of the college.... A question that must be asked is, 'How can life outside the classroom support the educational mission of the college?'" (1987, 5). This question motivated researchers and practitioners to attempt to link the cocurriculum to the core academic mission—with varying degrees of success. In 1996 the American College Personnel Association (ACPA) issued its *Student Learning Imperative,* calling on institutions to provide a "seamless learning environment" that included the curriculum and the cocurriculum. For a variety of reasons, campuses have experienced different levels of success with these collaborative efforts between faculty and student affairs staff, even though the research suggests that community on campus plays a role in recruitment and retention of students.

Cocurricular Effects and Gender

Research clearly documents the relationship of the cocurriculum to student learning, but little of it directly addresses the different experiences women in particular may have in their out-of-class activities. The landmark studies of how the cocurriculum contributes to learning are large-scale, overarching studies, which do not often address gender differences. The notable exception is the body of research that explores how women experience leadership development in the college years.

Pascarella and Terenzini reported a critical cocurricular finding pertaining specifically to women students: women who took a leadership role in cocurricular activities were more likely to select careers in male-dominated fields. Given this information, increasing women students' participation in cocurricular leadership activities could have a long-term impact, not only on women students but indeed on American society, by encouraging women leaders to enter nontraditional sex-role professions.

Certainly research on sororities addresses women's experiences in single-sex organizations. In fact, Astin's 1993 study found that women who were involved in sororities were more likely to report increased leadership abilities at the end of their collegiate experience than women who did not join sororities. Adriana Kezar and Deb Moriarty's follow-up study of gender and leadership indicated that joining a fraternity did not similarly predict an increase in leadership abilities for men students. Thus, sorority membership can positively affect women's leadership development. However, it has been argued that sororities reinforce more traditional leadership structures and style and do not introduce women to more collaborative leadership models.

Other studies of women's leadership development focus on women who attend women's colleges. Elizabeth Whitt's (1994) qualitative study of three women's colleges identified the similarities of the students' experiences and outcomes. Participation in leadership activities in the cocurriculum was linked to many positive intellectual and affective outcomes for women students. Astin (1977, 1993) showed that attending a women's college had a positive effect on many leadership outcomes, both behavioral and perceptual. Women's college graduates were more likely to be elected to office in college, and they were more likely to report increases in their leadership abilities.

The research on gender differences in collegiate leadership experiences is not without controversy. For example, one issue of the *NASPA Journal,* published by the National Association of Student Personnel Administration, featured back to back entries using the same leadership assessment tool, one finding gender differences and one finding no gender differences (see Komives 1994; Posner and Brodsky 1994).

When the research is not contradictory, it is often confusing. Kezar and Moriarty (2000) compared the leadership outcomes of four groups of college students, African American women and men and white women and men. They found that being elected to office is a predictor for increased leadership ability among white men and African American women and that being involved in a student organization is a predictor for increased leadership ability among white women. They were puzzled at the finding for African American women but posited that among the whites in the study, the men were more responsive to the traditional leadership hierarchy. They suggested that the white women were more responsive to collaborative or group approaches to leadership since membership in an organization enhanced their leadership self-concept.

Thus, the cocurriculum—the series of activities outside the classroom (and thus outside the formal academic curriculum) that enhance one's educational experience—has been found critical to the persistence and development of college students. Yet, women students' experiences in the cocurriculum have been underexplored, except for the generally positive role that leadership opportunities play in women's confidence, development, and success.

Emily Langdon

See also Part 1: Women's Colleges; Part 6: Persistence; Sororities

References and further reading

American College Personnel Association. 1996. *The Student Learning Imperative.* http://www.acpa.nche.edu/sli/sli.htm. Cited June 12, 2002.

Astin, Alexander W. 1977. *Four Critical Years: Effects of College on Beliefs, Attitudes, and Knowledge.* San Francisco: Jossey-Bass.

———. 1984. "Student Involvement: A Developmental Theory for Higher Education." *Journal of College Student Personnel* 25, no. 4: 297–308.

———. 1993. *What Matters in College: Four Critical Years Revisited.* San Francisco: Jossey-Bass.

Boyer, Ernest. 1987. *College: The Undergraduate Experience in America.* New York: Harper and Row.

Kezar, Adriana, and Deb Moriarty. 2000. "Expanding Our Understanding of Student Leadership Development: A Study Exploring Gender and Ethnic Identity." *Journal of College Student Development* 41, no. 1: 55–69.

Komives, Susan R. 1994. "Women Student Leaders: Self-Perceptions of Empowering Leadership and Achieving Style." *NASPA Journal* 31, no. 2:102–112.

Kuh, George D., John Schuh, Elizabeth Whitt, and Associates. 1991. *Involving Colleges: Successful Approaches to Fostering Student Learning and Development Outside the Classroom.* San Francisco: Jossey-Bass.

"National Survey of Student Engagement." 2001. http://www.indiana.edu/%7Ensse/acrobat/overview-2001.pdf. Cited June 12, 2002.

Pasceralla, Ernest T., and Patrick T. Terenzini. 1991. *How College Affects Students: Findings and Insights from Twenty Years of Research.* San Francisco: Jossey-Bass.

Posner, Barry Z., and Barbara Brodsky. 1994. "Leadership Practices of Effective Student Leaders: Gender Makes No Difference." *NASPA Journal* 31, no. 2: 113–120.

Whitt, Elizabeth J. 1994. "'I Can Be Anything!': Student Leadership in Three Women's Colleges. *Journal of College Student Development* 35, no. 3: 198–207.

Graduate and Professional Education

Graduate and professional education involve the continuation of academic study beyond the baccalaureate degree. Graduate education is distinguished from professional education in that the student is preparing for a career in academe, the government, or business-related professions. Those continuing in professional education are in degree programs that will prepare them for work in law, medicine, or other professional fields. Both graduate programs and professional education have been well established in the United States for over 100 years, although it was only in the latter part of the twentieth century that the face of the graduate student began to change and the higher education system became more diversified.

In the early nineteenth century, the leaders in graduate education were in German universities, although leadership in this area passed to the United States in the twentieth century as American universities advanced their programs. Harvard, Yale, and Johns Hopkins Universities, are credited with the development of postbaccalaureate education (Miller 1971). Although Harvard took the lead, in 1847 Yale developed a model that made the distinction between undergraduate and graduate education. Johns Hopkins University was the first institution to be founded primarily as a graduate education institution.

Graduate education is divided into two main areas: the master's degree and doctoral study. Obtaining a master's degree typically requires a minimum of thirty credit hours past the baccalaureate degree, or about two years of coursework, although some programs may require more or less depending on the university and discipline requirements. At the completion of class work, either a comprehensive exam is administered or a written thesis is submitted, and either of these may be followed by an oral defense in which the student is posed questions by the department faculty. However, there are hundreds of different types of master's degrees offered in the United States, and each program has unique characteristics and requirements.

The traditional master's degrees grounded in the arts and sciences curriculum are the master of arts (M.A.) and the master of science (M.S.). Examples of other master's degrees that have a more practical or professional approach are the master of business administration (M.B.A.), the master of education (M.Ed.), and the master of engineering (M.Eng.). Although there are still a significant number of students who attend graduate school immediately following their undergraduate experience, more students choose to return for a master's degree several years later. For these more mature students, the general reason for pursuing a master's degree is that it provides a stepping-stone for career advancement, and more businesses now make it possible for their employees to attend graduate school by offering tuition reimbursement or time off from work. At the same time, universities are offering more options for students who choose to remain employed while pursuing their master's degree. Examples include offering evening or weekend classes and conducting classes in the work environment rather than on the college campus. With the increased availability and visibility of master's education, the number of master's degrees awarded in the United States has grown

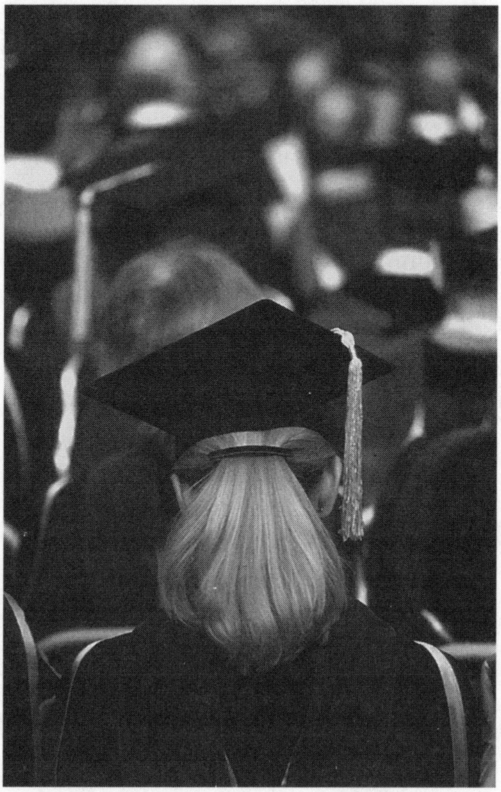

About one-third of women graduates go on to postgraduate education (Painetworks)

from 203,509 in 1970–1971 to 430,164 in 2000 (National Center for Education Statistics 2001, table 268).

A doctoral program is considered the basis for socialization into the professoriat. It has always been considered a first step for developing the skills, knowledge, and competencies associated with teaching and research (Fox 1996). For this reason, requirements for doctoral degrees are similar throughout the United States. Although there are differences in course requirements and completion rates, the basic doctoral degree begins with one to two years of coursework and ends with the oral defense of the dissertation. The dissertation, which is reviewed by a panel of faculty members, must show a thorough knowledge of the subject being studied and present original research and findings that add to the body of knowledge for their discipline. Many doctoral students hold research or teaching assistantships in addition to taking classes and conducting original research.

The Ph.D. (doctor of philosophy) is the typical doctoral degree received at universities, although areas of study range from the basic humanities to the sciences and education. Those receiving Ph.D.'s have traditionally gone on to faculty positions at colleges or universities. However, it is not uncommon today for Ph.D. recipients to go immediately into careers outside academe. Not only do many choose to forgo teaching or research opportunities, but many are forced to look elsewhere for work because of the lack of available faculty positions. With the proliferation of doctoral recipients, it is natural to assume that not all Ph.D.'s will find the ideal job at a college or university.

Other doctorates are available for those selecting a less traditional, more practical course of study. Some examples are the educational doctorate (Ed.D. or D.Ed.) and the doctor of engineering (D.Eng.) degree. It is normal for these graduate students to focus their studies and dissertations on more applied areas.

Professional education, as previously mentioned, is postbaccalaureate study in the professions. Two of the most established professional education fields are medicine and law. The requirements for obtaining an M.D. or J.D. are rigid and do not vary greatly at different universities. Students enter as a cohort and graduate within the recommended time period unless serious circumstances delay their progress. The process may not be as rigid in other professional areas like engineering or divinity programs, but the curriculum focuses on more applied areas of study. Unlike a Ph.D., in which the dissertation is the culmination of study, graduates in medicine, law, and nursing are required to take state-regulated exams in order to practice their profession.

Women have been included in graduate and professional education almost as long as these courses of study have been offered, but it was not until fairly recently that women began to enroll in greater numbers in postbaccalaureate study. In fact, not until the 1990s did the number of master's degrees awarded to women surpass the number awarded to men (Johnsrud 1995). However, disparities remain in that more men than women are awarded doctorates each year, even though women have made steady gains in admission to doctoral programs and completion of those degrees. There is one exception to this trend: women outnumber men in doctorates earned in educational fields. There are also demographic differences between men and women doctoral students, the greatest being that women tend to be older than men and are more likely to be single. Trends have also shown that women take longer to complete their doctoral studies than men.

It is interesting to note that in her 1969 book, *The Woman Doctorate in America,* Helen Astin wrote that despite the increase in numbers of educated women, they were still underrepresented in the professional and scientific fields. Years later, research shows that women are still the minority in doctoral programs, although the picture is much brighter for master's students.

Patricia Helland

See also Part 6: Curricular and Professional Choices; Graduate Students; Graduate Students and Science

References and further reading

Astin, Helen S. 1969. *The Woman Doctorate in America: Origins, Career, and Family.* New York: Russell Sage Foundation.

Fox, Mary F. 1996. "Publication, Performance and Reward in Science and Scholarship." Pp. 408–428 in *Faculty and Faculty Issues in Colleges and Universities,* eds. Dorothy E. Finnegan, David Webster, and Zelda F. Gamson. Needham Heights, MA: Simon and Schuster.

Johnsrud, Linda K. 1995. "Women in Graduate Education: Reviewing the Past, Looking to the Future." Pp. 69–80 in *Student Services for the Changing Graduate Student Population,* eds. Anne S. Pruitt-Logan and Paul D. Isaac. San Francisco: Jossey-Bass.

Miller, John P. 1971. "Graduate Education." In *The Encyclopedia of Education,* ed. Lee C. Deighton. 10 vols. New York: Macmillan.

National Center for Education Statistics. 2001. Washington, DC: U.S. Department of Education. http://www.nces.ed.gov/pubs2001/digest. Cited June 12, 2002.

Graduate Students

Graduate study is academic work beyond the baccalaureate degree. Within higher education, graduate study usually refers to programs leading to a master's or doctoral degree. However, graduate study can also involve credential programs (including teaching credentials and other certification programs) and professional programs (including medical school, law schools, business administration programs, etc.). Students enrolled in these various programs are referred to as graduate students. Historically, the representation of women enrolled in graduate programs has been significantly lower than that of men. Since 1990, enrollments of women have been increasing in graduate programs, but in some disciplines, the representation of women is still extremely low, particularly in business, the physical sciences, and engineering.

Women's Participation in Graduate Study

At the start of the new millennium, women comprised the majority of students enrolled in graduate programs. In 1974 female representation was 44 percent of graduate enrollments and totaled 526,000, but by 1998 the 679,155 women students represented 55 percent of graduate enrollments. This emergence into the majority also paralleled the presence of a significant number of women in traditionally masculine disciplines, including the biological and physical sciences, where enrollments by women continue to increase.

In "The New Majority: CGS/GRE Survey Results Trace Growth of Women in Graduate Education," Peter D. Syverson reported that in 1998, Asian and Hispanic/Latina women were the two most rapidly

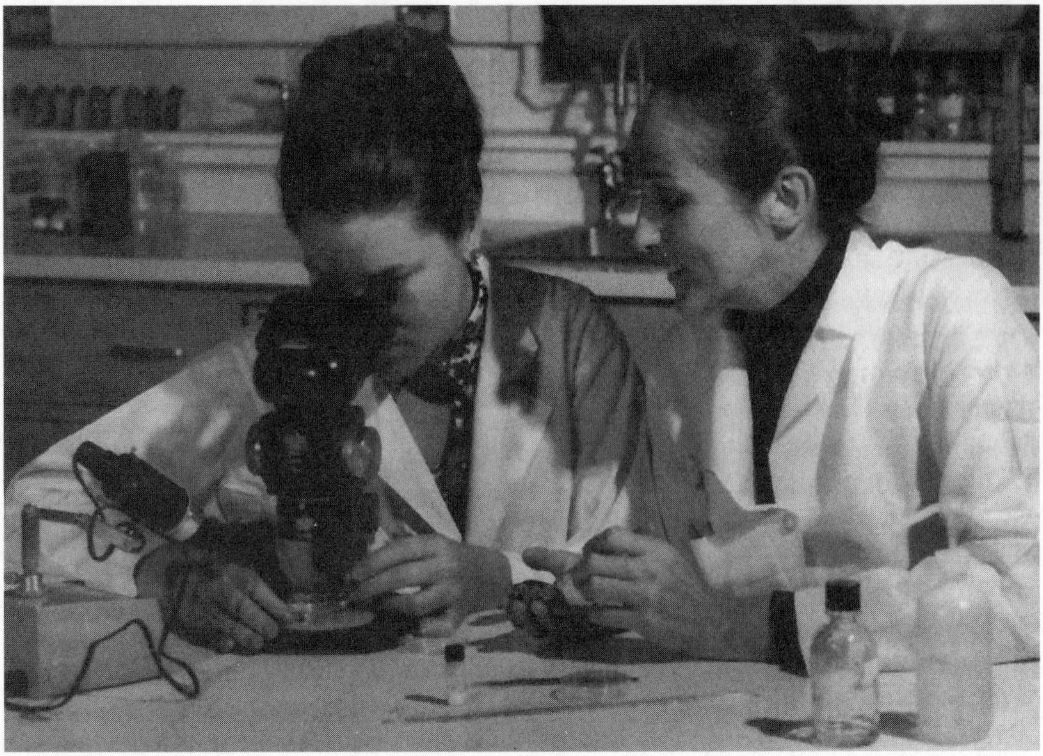

A graduate student scientist and her faculty advisor (Courtesy of the Association of Women in Science)

growing subgroups of female graduate students. He found that African American women comprised the largest single minority group among graduate students, representing 46 percent of the enrollment of minority women but only 10 percent of all female students enrolled in graduate school. White women constituted the largest group of female graduate students enrolled during this period. Their numbers totaled 407,918, comprising 78 percent of the female graduate student population and nearly double the combined total population for all minority groups. Hispanic/Latina women represented 6 percent of the graduate student population, Asian Americans 5 percent, and American Indians 1 percent. Enrollments were larger for women than for men in each ethnic group.

When their enrollment is examined according to academic discipline and degree type, women dominated master's degree programs in the health sciences, totaling 78 percent of students enrolled in those fields. They reached 75 percent of students in education and 72 percent of those in public administration and services. Percentages for these disciplines diminish in doctoral programs, where women represented 42 percent of the enrollment, as opposed to the 57 percent of the matriculated students in master's programs (Council of Graduate Schools 2001).

According to an analysis of graduate enrollment trends completed by the Council of Graduate Schools, women students were the recipients of 55 percent of the graduate degrees awarded in 1998. However, only 42 percent of the doctoral degrees conferred were awarded to women. An examination by discipline reveals that only 32 percent of the doctoral degrees in business were awarded to women, 25 percent of those in the physical sciences, and 15 percent of those in engineering. Although female attainment of master's degrees in these areas was more proportionate to their percentage of the population, women were still highly underrepresented in these traditionally male-dominated fields. Women were overrepresented in institutions categorized as master's-granting institutions according to the Carnegie Classifications of Institutions of Higher Education and underrepresented at those categorized as Research I institutions.

The analysis of graduate enrollment trends also revealed that more women (55 percent) than men (46 percent) pursue graduate degrees on a part-time basis. Syverson (2001) explained that although the higher percentage of women enrolled part-time is consistent across all disciplines, the large number of women in education programs, where part-time study is the norm, profoundly impacts the overall part-time percentage.

Women's Experiences as Graduate Students

Increases in the numbers of women in graduate education address some of the concerns articulated by scholars in the late 1960s and 1970s, but many of the dilemmas prevalent in the academic literature of that era remain unresolved. As summarized by Nancy Fischer and Sharon D. Peters (1979), women graduate students were less likely to obtain a doctorate than male students, did not enjoy the same support networks within their disciplines as their male counterparts, were less likely to experience mentoring by a professor than were men, were excluded from many traditionally masculine fields of study, and felt that courses were arranged to suit the needs of full-time students.

In 1998, almost two decades later, scholars continue to discuss many of the same issues. Many women in graduate school struggle to establish mentoring relationships with faculty members. Discussions of discrimination on the basis of gender, ethnicity, or both are recurrent themes within the literature on women students in graduate education since the 1960s.

Equity, discrimination, and issues of exploitation of women graduate students were pervasive in the academic literature from the 1960s through the 1980s. In the early 1990s, scholars began to address the increase in enrollments of female graduate students and to examine the need for the full participation of women in all areas of the academy, especially within faculty ranks and in administration.

Pamela Merchant Christian

See also Part 1: Medical Education; Part 6: Graduate and Professional Education; Graduate Students and Science; Part 7: Disciplinary Socialization; Socialization

References and further reading

Council of Graduate Schools. 2001. *Graduate Enrollment and Degrees, 1986 to 1998.* http://www.cgsnet.org/VirtualCenterResearch/graduateenrollment.htm. Cited June 12, 2002.

Fischer, Nancy A., and Sharon D. Peters. 1979. "The Cost for Women in Graduate and Professional Schools: More Than a Question of Money." Paper presented at the Annual Meeting

of the Mid-South Sociological Association. Memphis, TN.
Goldberg, Julie L., and William E. Sedlacek. 1995. *Graduate Women in Engineering.* College Park: University of Maryland, College Park Counseling Center.
Hansen, Ellen, Susan Kennedy, Doreen Mattingly, Beth Mitchneck, Kris Monzel, and Cheryl Narve. 1995. "Facing the Future, Surviving the Present: Strategies for Women Graduate Students in Geography." *Journal of Geography in Higher Education* 19, no. 3 (November): 307–315.
Hollenshead, Carol, Patricia Soellner Younce, and Stacy A. Wenzel. 1994. "Women Graduate Students in Mathematics and Physics: Reflections on Success." *Journal of Women and Minorities in Science and Engineering* 1, no. 1 (January–March): 63–88.
Syverson, Peter D. 2001. "The New Majority CGS/GRE Survey Results Trace Growth of Women in Graduate Education." http://www.cgsnet.org/pdf/cctr706.pdf. Cited June 12, 2002.
Wenniger, Mary Dee. 1998. *Women in Higher Education, 1998.* Madison, WI: Wenniger Co.
Woods, Rochelle L. 2001. "Invisible Women: The Experiences of Black Female Doctoral Students at the University of Michigan." Pp. 105–115 in *Sisters of the Academy: Emergent Black Women Scholars in Higher Education,* ed. Reitumetse O. Mabokela and Anna L. Green. Sterling, VA: Stylus.

Graduate Students and Science

In recent decades, women have made significant gains in scientific and technical areas, based on the number of advanced degrees earned. Studies at both the national and institutional levels have raised awareness of deficiencies in the campus climate for female students and faculty. This awareness resulted in an agenda of reform to ensure full participation for women in academia. Today most academic institutions provide advocacy for women in the sciences, either through formal structures or through funding and vigorous promotion of women's work.

Despite recent gains, women remain poorly represented in some fields of graduate study and academia, such as engineering and computer science. *Trends in Educational Equity of Girls and Women,* a report published in 2000 by the National Center for Education Statistics (NCES) of the U.S. Department of Education, which tracks the progress of women in higher education, presents data on graduate degrees awarded to women since 1970. Since then, there have been significant gains in masters and doctoral degrees awarded to women in the physical sciences, mathematics, and computer sciences. The most dramatic increases were realized from 1970 to 1985. Since then, the curve has become flat in most disciplines. In 1970, women earned 1.1 percent of engineering master's degrees, compared to 17.2 percent in 1996. Only 0.7 percent of engineering Ph.D.'s were conferred on women in 1970, but the percentage had risen to 12.5 percent by 1996. Although these are admirable gains, they are also a reminder that there is great potential for improvement. On a more optimistic note, the Ph.D.'s awarded to women in the biological sciences, a field that tends to attract women, went from 14.3 percent in 1970 to 42 percent in 1996—almost half of the biological science doctorates.

In September 2000, the Congressional Committee on the Advancement of Women and Minorities in Science (CAWMSET) released the report *Land of Plenty: Diversity as America's Competitive Edge in Science, Engineering, and Technology.* This report confirms data reported by NCES on the trends in graduate degrees earned by women in recent years. It also reviewed and documented the barriers that lead to underrepresentation of women in science and technology fields. An important factor for female graduate students is the academic climate. The variables comprising academic climate are faculty interactions; integration into departmental functions; attitudes toward marriage, childbearing, and family responsibilities; the composition of the faculty (lack of mentors, role models, and female faculty); and other discipline-specific factors. A set of strategies and recommendations for recruitment and retention of women in higher education also came from CAWMSET. They included broadening access to higher education for underrepresented groups through systematic changes in the educational system.

As students, women often report feeling isolated, being marginalized, and having difficulty communicating with male faculty, feelings that persist throughout their careers. A 1999 research report from the Office of Educational Research and Improvement of the U.S. Department of Education, *A Closer Look at Women's Colleges,* points out that women are more likely to succeed when they perceive that their institution cares about diversity and gender equity (1999, 3). The structure of postgraduate programs now often includes research fellowships and cooperative arrangements specifically for women. These opportunities integrate women into their discipline's mainstream. Today's institutions also better understand the safety concerns of women graduate students and have worked to improve conditions for those who must work in labs until late at night.

The campus climate for female graduate students reflects the climate for female faculty. In all fields of science, technology, and mathematics, more women than ever before have enrolled in graduate school and have completed degrees since 1980; during this same time span, the number of women faculty in these fields has not seen a significant increase. Many feel that the "supply" problem does not really exist today, based on the number of degrees earned by women in science and mathematics, but women seem to be less successful at becoming tenured, and they are naturally attracted to climates where they believe they can be successful.

In January 2001, representatives of nine research universities (the California and Massachusetts Institutes of Technology; Harvard, Princeton, Stanford, and Yale Universities; the University of California, Berkeley; the University of Michigan, Ann Arbor; and the University of Pennsylvania) met to discuss specific steps they could take to improve conditions for women at their respective institutions. Also present were representatives of the American Association for the Advancement of Science and the Ford Foundation (which sponsored the meeting). Although this major initiative is being implemented at only a few institutions, women in graduate school should realize that success in the sciences is attainable with persistence, particularly in graduate programs such as these that are aware of the need to support female students and faculty.

In addition to institutional efforts to support women, there are a number of organizations whose purpose is to help improve the climate for women students in higher education, with the long-term goal of repairing the leaky academic pipeline. The oldest and largest of these organizations are described here. Institutions affiliated with the Committee on Institutional Cooperation (CIC) have Women in Science and Engineering (WISE) programs. WISE institutes on campuses have as their goal the improvement of gender equity and the campus climate for female students and faculty at all levels. Through various types of programming, WISE institute staff encourage women to pursue academic majors in science and mathematics and encourage these women to pursue careers in academia.

The oldest organization for women in the sciences, Sigma Delta Epsilon–Graduate Women in Science (GWIS), was formed at a meeting of the American Association for the Advancement of Science (AAAS) in December 1921. Since women were banned from men's organizations, women scientists and graduate students from Cornell University and the University of Wisconsin formed this national organization affiliated with AAAS to help them face the unique challenges of women in science. Even then, the organization's goals were clear: to further scientific thought and education and to improve women's standing in the scientific community by establishing awards, grants, and fellowships. Recognizing that financial assistance was an important need, GWIS created trust funds for women's research. GWIS chapters exist throughout the United States. Membership is open to women who hold a baccalaureate degree or higher in a scientific discipline and have some research experience. Graduate students and postdoctoral fellows, in particular, benefit from the advice and networking that GWIS offers since most members hold advanced degrees. Although women are no longer excluded from the mainstream scientific organizations, GWIS provides a venue in which they can meet other women scientists with diverse backgrounds and interests, develop the leadership skills essential in today's workplace, and gain insight into balancing personal and professional life.

The Association for Women in Science (AWIS) was established in 1971 with the goal of achieving equality and full participation for women in science, mathematics, engineering, and technology. AWIS also provides mentoring and scholarships and conducts research on the status of women in higher education. The organization is affiliated with AAAS, is headquartered in Washington, D.C., and has chapters in most states. AWIS membership is open to anyone interested in supporting women in science.

The Society of Women Engineers (SWE), founded in 1950, supports engineering graduate students. SWE's goals are to help women realize their potential as engineers and leaders and to expand the image of engineering. The Institute of Electrical and Electronics Engineers and American Institute of Physics both have women's divisions to support women as students and professionals. Both organizations base their involvement on the underrepresentation of women in physics and engineering at all levels.

A newer organization is the Women in Engineering Programs and Advocates Network (WEPAN), a national educational organization founded in 1990. WEPAN aims to foster positive change in the engineering infrastructure to promote the academic and career growth of women. It has centers at Purdue University, the University of Michigan, Stevens Institute of Technology, and the University of Washington and sponsors fellowships and research awards for female graduate students and faculty.

Carol L. Hodes

See also Part 6: Graduate Students; Undergraduates and Science

References and further reading

American Institute of Physics. http://www.aip.org. Cited June 10, 2002.

Association for Women in Science: http://www.awis.org. Cited June 10, 2002.

Congressional Committee on the Advancement of Women and Minorities in Science, Engineering, and Technology Development. 2000. *Land of Plenty: Diversity as America's Competitive Edge in Science, Engineering and Technology.* Washington, DC: U.S. Government Printing Office.

Graduate Women In Science. http://www.gwis.org. Cited June 14, 2002.

Institute of Electrical and Electronics Engineers. http://www.ieee.org. Cited June 14, 2002.

National Center for Education Statistics. 2000. *Trends in Educational Equity of Girls and Women.* Washington, DC: U.S. Department of Education.

Society of Women Engineers. http://www.swe.org. Cited June 14, 2002.

U.S. Department of Education, Office of Educational Research and Improvement. 1999. *A Closer Look at Women's Colleges.* Washington, DC: U.S. Department of Education.

Women in Engineering Programs and Advocates Networks. http://www.wepan.org. Cited June 14, 2002.

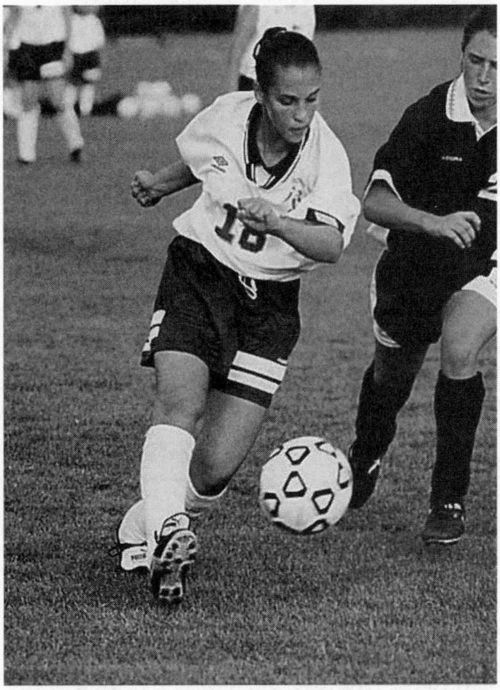

A women's soccer game at Mount Holyoke (Courtesy of Mount Holyoke College)

Growth of Women's Athletics

The history and growth of women's athletics in higher education paralleled the struggle women experienced to attain access to higher education. Women did not gain entry into higher education until the 1800s, with the founding of all-women institutions of higher learning. Many of the reasons given for excluding women from higher education were similar to those provided for restricting their athletic opportunities. For example, it was thought a woman would compromise her childbearing capacities if she strained herself with higher education; the same was expected to happen if a woman participated in vigorous exercise involving competition.

To help combat these concerns, the first all-female higher education institutions made physical education programs part of the required curriculum. These programs helped make women stronger and healthier and disproved the idea that higher education would have ill effects on women. The first women's athletic associations were founded at Bryn Mawr College in 1891 and at Wellesley College in 1896. These athletic associations were dissimilar to the associations of today. Competition was discouraged, and they were more akin to physical education clubs. The emphasis in physical education was on the improvement and maintenance of health, a quality upon which all but the most severe critics could agree. Physical education programs were the norm for women in higher education until the 1960s, when a form of intramurals began to gain popularity, leading to the first significant numbers of women competing in intercollegiate athletics in the 1970s.

Concern for the health of women inspired colleges to develop physical education programs beyond mere exercise opportunities. For example, among the goals of Mary Lyon, founder in 1837 of the women's seminary that became Mount Holyoke College, was the preparation of future mothers and teachers. To this end, she realized that regular "calisthenics" were necessary to make women healthier to endure everyday life. Calisthenics consisted of exercises using Indian clubs and hoops. For Lyon, known as a dedicated educator who raised standards at the collegiate level to force secondary schools to improve, the addition of physical education to the curriculum was yet another way to prove that women were fit for higher education and that they were ultimately entitled to this education.

Through the incorporation of required exercise into the curriculum, students became physically fit, enabling them to perform better academically. The early women's colleges had demonstrated that an educated woman was a healthy woman by emphasizing physical education as part of the total educational experience; women graduated better educated and more healthy.

The Age of Health

Physical education programs were founded in colleges and universities for a number of reasons, of which addressing and hopefully disproving the accusations and myths surrounding ill effects for women who participated in higher education was one. Thus the physical education programs established in the early 1900s focused almost exclusively on health benefits and did not evolve into intercollegiate athletics until the 1970s. The reason for the slow development was the long-held belief by many—including parents, donors, college officials, and even students—that competitive athletics were harmful to women's health and well-being.

Although women participated in calisthenics and active games from their entry into higher education, these activities were not recognized as "sport" because if they consisted of competition at all, the competition was among women from the same school. These "competitions" were called play days and involved two or more schools competing in a sport. Instead of one school playing another school, all the teams were mixed with players from among the participating schools, thus downplaying competition while emphasizing team play, cooperation, and physical fitness. A so-called telegraphic form of competition and sports days were also utilized. The telegraphic form took place in sports such as swimming and bowling. Each school would perform at its respective school and then compare results with other schools by telegraph. "Sports days" consisted of many schools competing together in mixed teams at one college. It was more accepted for women to compete among each other if the emphasis was on participation as opposed to results.

Female physical educators in the early 1900s agreed that they did not want women's athletics to follow the same route that men's athletics had taken. Female physical educators felt that intercollegiate men's sports were too violent and intense because of the contact that took place and the injuries incurred. Men's sports were also thought to exploit athletes because of the money involved. Money—as direct payments to athletes and as bribes and slush funds—was a common feature in the early days of men's intercollegiate sports. To establish more control in intercollegiate athletics for men, faculties and administrations stepped in to oversee athletics programs. To that end, the National Collegiate Athletic Association (NCAA) was established in 1910 as a means of providing oversight and control.

In contrast, women were not permitted to engage in such competition and participated in sports in environments tightly controlled by female physical educators. Observant of the flaws in men's athletics programs and instilled with an obligation to uphold morality in society, female physical educators strongly held to the belief that competition could bring out the same negative consequences in women as it had in men; competition was therefore to be avoided at all costs. In 1923, this attitude of discouragement toward competition for the female athlete was reinforced by the National Amateur Athletic Federation (NAAF). At the first NAAF conference, a statement was issued that reemphasized that athletics should be for all participants rather than focusing solely on the better performers.

Intercollegiate athletic competition was the rare exception rather than the rule. During the period from 1920 to 1930, female physical educators reinforced the concept of sports for all rather than any emphasis on the elite athlete. Mabel Lee notes "that in the early 1920s about 22 percent of the colleges sponsored some form of intercollegiate sports for women, but by 1930 only 12 percent were engaging in intercollegiate competition, whereas intramurals sponsored jointly by women's athletic associations and the departments of physical education gained popularity" (1983, 160).

In spite of the emphasis on cooperation among participants, individual sports were more popular than team sports among women. Individual sports such as archery, tennis, golf, and swimming were thought to be more feminine sports and thus more socially acceptable. These sports were incorporated into physical education programs more than team sports, with the exception of basketball. Female physical educators made such games as basketball "safe" for women by changing the rules from those used for men's games. Thus, they avoided what they felt was the heavy competition of male's sports and instead pursued "a sport for every girl and a girl in every sport," a motto that characterized this era of women's sports.

If the NAAF had lobbied for competition, women's intercollegiate athletics probably would have evolved more quickly. But the NAAF chose not to do so, endorsing the status quo of cooperative sporting ventures for women. Although teams of women from different institutions played against one another throughout the first half of the twentieth century, women's competitive intercollegiate athletics programs did not really begin to grow significantly until the 1960s.

There were a few important exceptions to women's lack of involvement in intercollegiate athletics and athletics internationally. One such exception was the Olympic Games, although women were allowed to participate only in certain events. Attitudes concerning women's involvement in track and field and swimming were generally more supportive outside the United States. Even so, Mildred "Babe" Didrikson was an Olympic medallist in track and field and later dominated women's golf. In addition, Gertrude Ederle won a bronze medal in the 1924 Paris Olympic Games. In 1926, she became the first woman to swim the English Channel. Such events were rare, but the athletic successes of Didrikson and Ederle contributed to the slow but growing acceptance of women's involvement in sports.

Another catalyst for change occurred during World War II, when women were needed in the workforce to replace men who had been drafted into the armed forces. Through their work experience, women became more independent. It has been argued that wartime work opportunities brought women into the economic mainstream and influenced their participation in a variety of public social activities, including sports. With men off to war, there was also a void in leisure activity. In partial response, the professional All-American Girl's Baseball League was founded in 1943 and lasted twelve years. Although it was initially well received, the novelty soon wore off, and despite the league's many successes and visibility, it did not make team sports more acceptable for women.

From the 1940s through the 1960s, college women athletes continued to participate mainly in noncompetitive play days. An exception was created by Gladys Palmer who, in 1941, organized the first Women's National College Golf Tournament. However, the Executive Committee of the National Section of Women's Athletics of the American Association for Health, Physical Education, and Recreation adamantly went on record in opposition to such a competition. The golf tournament and other one-time competitions like it were the exception during the postwar era.

In some ways, women may have impeded their own progress. Women's sports were organized and overseen by women's physical education departments from the 1880s until the 1960s. Roberta Park and Joan Hult explain that "women's physical education departments replicated the 'separate spheres' ideology of the larger society" (1993, 36). Women physical educators pushed for facilities and opportunities but considered men's version of competitive athletics flawed. Thus, female physical educators "reinforced a separate but equal zone of female athletics that reconciled play and womanhood" (Verbrugge 1988, 372). The result was separate but not equal opportunities for college women.

The "age of health" broke significant barriers regarding the participation of women in sports. The initial argument that sports damaged women evolved into a belief that physical activity facilitated learning and well-being. From this foundation, further change could occur.

The Age of Change

The 1960s brought a significant change to the attitude that women must be protected from competitive athletics. With the women's movement helping to broaden the definition of female roles and female physical educators more open to competition, formal women's intercollegiate athletics programs began to take shape. Legal decisions and federal statutes also promulgated sport opportunities for female students. A significant increase in opportunities for girls and women was realized because of the passage of Title IX of the Education Amendments of 1972: "No person in the United States shall, on the basis of sex, be excluded from participation in, be denied the benefits of, or be subjected to discrimination under any education program or activity receiving Federal financial assistance" (U.S. Department of Health, Education, and Welfare, Office of Civil Rights 1975, 901A). The impact of Title IX rippled through higher education into women's professional sports and then back to intercollegiate sports. Title IX had an immediate impact on intercollegiate sports by prompting colleges and universities to establish women's intercollegiate athletic programs.

The National Association of Girls and Women in Sport initially oversaw women's intercollegiate athletics; a significant increase in participation led to the organization of the Association of Intercollegiate Athletics for Women (AIAW), which monitored women's athletic competitions nationally. In 1983, the NCAA co-opted the AIAW and began to oversee women's intercollegiate athletics. The NCAA remains the dominant governing body for women's and men's collegiate athletics, creating and enforcing policies related to student athletes and organizing national tournaments.

In 1984, the *Grove City College v. Bell* legal decision caused a major setback in the growth of girls' and women's athletics. In this challenge to Title IX, the Supreme Court decided that since athletic programs did not receive direct federal funds, these programs did not have to comply with the statute. It was not until the Civil Rights Restoration Act was passed in 1987 that the interpretation of Title IX was broadened to include athletic programs. In addition, in 1991 the Court ruled in *Franklin v. Gwinnett County* that a person can sue for damages if that person can prove that opportunities were denied related to Title IX. With such rulings, colleges and universities, as well as the NCAA, took more seriously their obligation to address gender inequities in collegiate athletics.

The Age of Gender Equity

A number of agencies and organizations, including the NCAA and the American Association of University Women (AAUW), have conducted research that has promoted a better understanding of women, sports, and higher education. Their reports acknowledge the struggles girls and women have faced in sports and education and assert that the time has come to address the inherent discrimination that women have faced in sports. For example, based on a survey of its 7,000 members, the Women's Sports Foundation, sponsored by the Miller Brewing Company, produced the *Miller Lite Report on Women in Sports* (1985). One of the major findings of this report was that girls who participated with boys in early play tended later to have a better body image, showed a greater tendency to seek leadership positions in sports, and participated more in sport or fitness activities as adults.

Through a longitudinal study, R. Vivian Acosta and Linda J. Carpenter (2000) have documented that in spite of the benefits to women who participate in sports, there persists a lack of opportunities for women in sports and a decreased number of women in leadership positions in athletics. Two of the perceived causes include success of the "old boys' club" network and the lack of support systems for females. Acosta and Carpenter claim that fewer females in leadership positions in sports means that fewer people have an awareness of equity in sports. Consequently, the inherent inequities persist.

To help attempt to address inequities, the Knight Foundation Commission on Intercollegiate Athletics (1993), established by the NCAA, was charged to investigate abuses in college athletics and to offer suggestions for the reform of athletics, including in the area of gender equity. Because of the gross inequities identified by the Knight Foundation Commission, the NCAA formed a Gender Equity Task Force. It identified a number of major problems that must be overcome for gender equity to occur in sports and higher education. These problems included a pervasive attitude that women lack the interest and ability to compete, a "turf problem," and the availability of supporting monies. The "turf problem" is caused by existing men's teams' reluctance to give up field space, equipment, and so on in order to give women equitable opportunities. Based on the work of this task force, in January 1994 the NCAA membership committed to establishing gender equity in sports.

In 1997, the NCAA Committee on Women's Athletics was formed. One of its responsibilities is to promote institutional progress in implementing gender equity plans. After the Committee on Women's Athletics examined the 1999 Gender-Equity Audit Report, a number of concerns were raised. The committee was disappointed at the lack of female and ethnic minority employment in athletic administration positions. The committee also met with Donna Lopiano, executive director of the Women's Sports Foundation. Lopiano highlighted the following ongoing needs:

> Women of color are underrepresented in most sports, creating the need for additional opportunities to reach the minority female population.
>
> Female participation in nontraditional and extreme sports (such as pole vault, football, wrestling, and rowing) should be pursued.
>
> Outspoken leadership by the committee and the NCAA is necessary to counter anti–Title IX rhetoric.
>
> Employment issues for women coaches are on the rise.
>
> Lack of media coverage of women's sports needs to be addressed.
>
> More complaints regarding equitable benefits are occurring at all levels of competition.
>
> Strong leadership is needed to address sexual harassment and homophobia.
>
> Sponsorship opportunities and television coverage should be pursued for more women's sports. (National Collegiate Athletic Association 1999, p. 2)

Through the heightened awareness of the twentieth anniversary of Title IX and the NCAA's increased commitment to gender equity, colleges and universities have generally become more committed to addressing historical inequities between men's and women's intercollegiate athletics. Such mandates as the Equity in Athletics Disclosure Act, requiring coeducational postsecondary institutions receiving federal funds to compile and make available gender-specific data on their athletic programs, makes institutions more accountable. Today in intercollegiate athletics, even with more than 8,000 NCAA-sanctioned women's intercollegiate teams, female sports participation rates and allocated financial resources remain well below levels for male participants.

Shawn Ladda

See also Part 1: Women's Colleges; Part 5: Title IX; Part 6: Women Athletes

References and further reading

Acosta, R. Vivian, and Linda J. Carpenter. 2000. "Women in Intercollegiate Sport: A Longitudinal Study—Twenty-Three Year Update, 1977–2000." Unpublished manuscript, Brooklyn College, Brooklyn, NY.

Franklin v. Gwinnett County, 112 Sup. Ct. 1028 (1991).

Gerber, Ellen. 1975. "The Controlled Development of Collegiate Sport for Women, 1923–1936." *Journal of Sport History* 2, no. 1: 1–28.

Grove City College v. Bell, 465 U.S. 555 (1984).

Knight Foundation. 1993. *Reports of the Knight Foundation Commission on Intercollegiate Athletics, March 1991–March 1993.* Charlotte, NC: Knight Foundation.

Lee, Mabel. 1983. *A History of Physical Education and Sports in the U.S.A.* New York: John Wiley and Sons.

Miller Lite Report on Women in Sports. 1985. Iselin, NJ: New World Decisions.

National Collegiate Athletic Association. 1999. "Committee on Women's Athletics Seeks Quicker Solutions for Gender-Equity Issues." *NCAA News,* August 16.

Park, Roberta J., and Joan Hult. 1993. "Women as Leaders in Physical Education and School-Based Sports, 1865 to the 1930s." *Journal of Physical Education, Recreation, and Dance* 64, no. 3: 35–40.

U.S. Department of Health, Education, and Welfare, Office of Civil Rights. 1975. "Final Title IX Regulation Implementing Educational Amendment of 1972. *Federal Register* 40, no. 108 (June 4): 901A.

Verbrugge, Martha. H. 1988. *Able-Bodied Womanhood: Personal Health and Social Change in Nineteenth-Century Boston.* New York: Oxford University Press.

Jewish Students

Jewish women in the United States have faced the dual challenges of sexism and anti-Semitism in their quest for higher education. Since the birth of the women's colleges and the advent of coeducation in the mid-1800s, Jewish women have had to overcome not only religious and cultural ideals that assigned women to the home but also stringent opposition to members of their religion from college administrators, faculty, fellow students, and parents. Although in the final decades of the twentieth century, Jewish women not only achieved parity with their male counterparts but also surpassed their non-Jewish counterparts in terms of percentage enrolled on American collegiate campuses, they won these feats only after many decades of struggle.

The mass immigration of Jews to the United States between 1881 and 1924 occurred at precisely the same time as the development of public education for the masses, yet Jewish women did not reap the benefits of this educational movement to the same extent as their brothers. Most newly arrived families were not willing to forgo the financial and physical assistance Jewish daughters provided in terms of household care and wages. Indeed, although many saw a college degree as key to advancement for their sons, few considered the education of their daughters in similar light.

This parental preference for sending sons to school while keeping daughters home was common to many religious groups, not just to Jews. In fact, although more Jewish males than females attended school at the turn of the twentieth century, Jewish women were more likely to receive an education than any other group of women in the United States. At times, Jewish daughters pursued their education

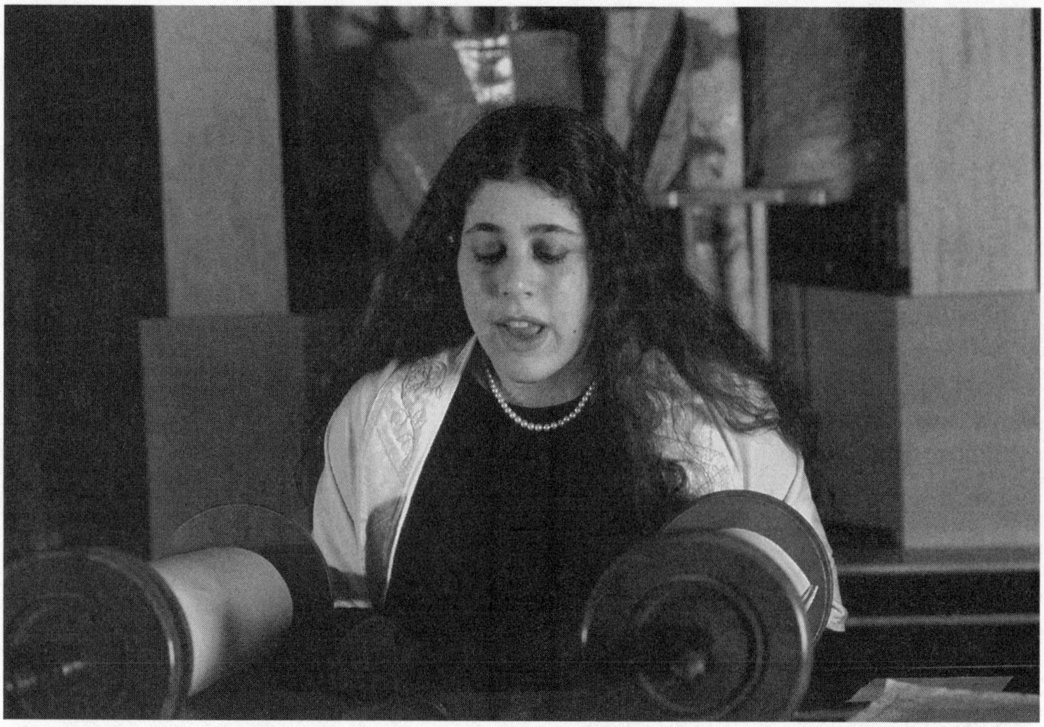

A Jewish student reads the Torah at her Bat Mitzvah (Richard T. Nowitz/Corbis)

in addition to holding down jobs and helping out with family chores, but the number of women willing to pursue an education even after a long day's work did not translate into a significant Jewish female presence on college campuses.

In the 1870s and 1880s, less than 2 percent of women aged eighteen to twenty-one attended college in the United States. Of the small group of "pioneers" who did enroll, nearly all came from Protestant backgrounds. The few women who might have been Jewish either hid their religious identities or else blended in with their fellow collegians and thus escaped comment and notice on the basis of their religion. Amelia D. Alpiner, a student in the class of 1896 at the University of Illinois, Urbana-Champaign, was the first Jewish female collegian to be identified according to her religion. A prominent student on campus, she played a visible role in many campus activities and served as a charter member of Pi Beta Phi sorority. Two years after Alpiner graduated, another identified Jewish woman, Gertrude Stein, graduated from the Harvard Annex, or Radcliffe College, the women's division of Harvard College. Other than these two prominent women, the Jewish females who attended college during the latter decades of the nineteenth century and the first decade of the twentieth century did so in relative anonymity.

In the 1910s, the number of Jewish women enrolled in college increased, though in aggregate, they still constituted a tiny percentage of their religious and age cohorts. According to a survey of American colleges in 1916, Jewish women comprised only a tiny fraction of the college population. Where responses indicated that Jewish men attended college in higher proportions than did their non-Jewish counterparts—3.6 for every 1,000 Jewish men, as opposed to 2.2 for every 1,000 non-Jewish men—female Jews in college comprised only one-ninth the number of male Jews and attended college in numbers less than half of their non-Jewish female counterparts. Although the study located only a tiny number of Jewish women collegians enrolled at colleges nationwide, it found that at the all-women's colleges of the Northeast, such as Barnard, Radcliffe, Smith, Wellesley, Vassar, and Bryn Mawr, 335 Jewish women held 5 percent of the enrolled places (Sapinsky 1981, 702–703).

The wave of Jewish immigration at the turn of the twentieth century increased the Jewish population in the United States from less than 1 million to more than 3.3 million. The new arrivals, mainly from eastern Europe, proved poorer, less educated, less cultivated, and more ostentatious in their habits and behaviors than their better-assimilated German predecessors. When the children of these recent immigrants began to arrive in numbers on college campuses in the late 1910s and 1920s, their presence attracted greater societal and institutional notice than had the earlier Jewish students.

The increased presence of Jewish women on campus and the poorer, less "Americanized" brand of Jewish student who was attending combined to raise notice from fellow students and the public. Concurrent societal paranoia and fear of foreigners mixed with institutional concerns regarding the expanding number of Jewish students enrolled on campus to produce a wave of anti-Semitism that reached high proportions during the 1920s and 1930s. During these two decades and extending into the 1950s, students, alumni, and administrators of many institutions, eager to preserve the so-called Anglo-Saxon superiority of their colleges, instituted explicit and tacit policies both to limit Jewish enrollment and to restrict Jewish participation in campus activities.

At many institutions, deans of women and other powerful administrators adopted the practice of interviewing every student who applied and evaluating each on the basis of mental ability, character, personality, health, and background. This practice enabled them to single out for rejection the students whom they considered "undesirable," "crude," and "lacking in refinement," a high proportion of whom were Jewish. When Jewish groups publicly pressured institutions to ease their restrictions, the schools simply altered their processes of selection and placed limits on the number of commuter students they would admit. This policy proved effective in curbing Jewish admissions because in the 1920s and 1930s, many Jewish families chose to keep their daughters close to home in the hopes of both saving money and keeping an eye on their female offspring.

Both the commuter students and their counterparts at distant colleges felt the dual sting of sexism and anti-Semitism from institutions unused to the visible presence of Jewish female collegians. Attending schools resistant to their presence proved difficult and at times lonely for women trying to earn a higher education. The Jewish Greek system, founded in the 1910s and 1920s, sought to aid the new collegians in their quest to belong. For many Jewish females, the religious-based sororities provided opportunities for campus involvement that might otherwise have been closed to them.

The 1930s brought a turbulent mood to college campuses across the United States, as the Depression took its toll on student and institutional bank accounts. Jewish students played active and important roles in the student peace and protest movement of the 1930s, and this association served to increase displays of public anti-Semitism in college towns. Outraged citizens, responding to what they perceived as the socialist and communist leanings of the peace and protest movement, labeled those who belonged as anti-American. Jewish women in particular bore the brunt of these accusations, suffering the effects of inflamed anti-Semitism to a greater extent than their male counterparts. The rise of Nazism in Europe added to the pressures placed on Jewish collegians, as they struggled with the question of whether to abandon the peace movement and turn their energies instead to opposing Nazism and supporting Adolf Hitler's foes. When the United States finally entered World War II, Jewish female collegians played active roles on the home front, volunteering for war-related causes and hosting teas and other festivities for those in uniform.

The American victory overseas in 1945 brought the servicemen home, and the Servicemen's Readjustment Act of 1944 (known as the G. I. Bill), providing for their free college education, brought them to campus. The female students who had populated the colleges and universities during the war now found space for them limited and their presence discouraged. Jewish women of the 1950s, like their non-Jewish counterparts, chose to forgo higher education in greater percentages than they had prior to the war. Instead, they married younger and bore children at an earlier age than did their mothers. What higher education they did receive often centered around traditionally "womanly" concerns such as health and education, and for them as well as for non-Jews, domesticity, beauty, and other "traditional" values held great sway.

By 1960, 63 percent of Jewish men and women aged eighteen though twenty-four attended college. Despite the postwar decline in the percentage of females enrolled in institutions of higher education, the real number of Jewish women collegians continued to rise. Their numbers crept close to the figures for Jewish male attendance, and by the early 1970s, Jewish women began to surpass their non-Jewish counterparts in terms of the percentage of females compared to males of the same religious faith.

The 1972 passage of Title IX of the Education Amendments added the weight of law to the equality of opportunity that collegiate women had struggled so hard to achieve. For Jewish women, the heightened social, sexual, and ethnic consciousness on campuses of the late 1960s and 1970s combined to create campus environments more favorable to their presence. Accepted in ways that heretofore eluded them, Jewish women flocked to college in increased numbers and with greater prominence.

According to the Current Population Survey performed by the Department of Labor in 1990, Jewish women had achieved a higher level of education than their non-Jewish white female counterparts by the late 1980s. The study found that over half of the Jewish women in the United States held at least a bachelor's degree and that over 25 percent of Jewish women held a graduate or professional degree as of 1990, whereas only 17 percent of white female non-Jews had received a bachelor's degree and fewer than 5 percent of them had earned a graduate or professional degree. This high level of educational achievement signaled a shift within the Jewish community away from drawing a sharp distinction between the opportunities for advanced study offered female and male children. At the same time, although both Jewish males and females possessed higher levels of education than their non-Jewish white counterparts, Jewish men still outranked Jewish women in number of years of education.

In the final years of the twentieth century, the number of Jewish women receiving a collegiate education reached parity with Jewish men. In 1997, an estimated 85 percent of the Jewish female population between the ages of eighteen and twenty-four attended college, a percentage that mirrored that of Jewish men earning a collegiate degree. Although Jewish collegians still encountered pressures and discrimination as a result of their religion, Jewish women at the turn of the twenty-first century succeeded in establishing a place for themselves in college on par with their Jewish brothers and ahead of their non-Jewish female counterparts.

Diana B. Turk

See also Part 7: Campus Climate

References and further reading

Greenberg, Michael, and Seymour Zenchelsky. 1993. "Private Bias and Public Responsibility: Anti-Semitism at Rutgers in the 1920s and 1930s." *History of Education Quarterly* 33 (Fall): 295–319.

Gurock, Jeffrey S. 1988. *The Men and Women of Yeshiva: Higher Education, Orthodoxy, and American Judaism.* New York: Columbia University Press.

Hartman, Moshe, and Harriet Hartman. 1996. *Gender Equality and American Jews.* Albany: State University of New York Press.

Horowitz, Helen Lefkowitz. 1987. *Campus Life: Undergraduate Cultures from the End of the Eighteenth Century to the Present.* New York: Alfred A. Knopf.

Marcus, Jacob R. 1981. *The American Jewish Woman: A Documentary History.* New York: KTAV Publishing.

Ritterband, Paul, and Harold S. Wechsler. 1994. *Jewish Learning in American Universities: The First Century.* Bloomington: University of Indiana Press.

Rosovsky, Nitza. 1986. "The Jewish Experience at Harvard and Radcliffe: An Introduction to an Exhibition Presented by the Harvard Semitic Museum on the Occasion of Harvard's 350th Anniversary, September 1986." Cambridge: Harvard Semitic Museum, distributed by Harvard University Press.

Sapinsky, Ruth. 1981. "The Jewish College Girl." Pp. 701–708 in *The American Jewish Woman: A Documentary History,* ed. Jacob R. Marcus. New York: KTAV Publishing.

Schneider, Susan Weidman. 1985. *Jewish and Female: Choices and Changes in Our Lives Today.* New York: Simon and Schuster.

Solberg, Winton. 1992. "Early Years of the Jewish Presence at the University of Illinois." *Religion and American Culture: A Journal of Interpretation* (Summer): 215–245.

Solomon, Barbara Miller. 1985. *In the Company of Educated Women: A History of Women and Higher Education in America.* New Haven, CT: Yale University Press.

Wechsler, Harold S. 1977. *The Qualified Student: A History of Selective College Admissions in America.* New York: John Wiley and Sons.

Latina Students

"Latina" is an umbrella term referring to women originating from Latin America, regardless of immigration status. At least 66 percent of Latinas/Latinos are of Mexican descent or origin (Chicanas/Chicanos). Although the 2000 Census estimated that at least 12.5 percent of the

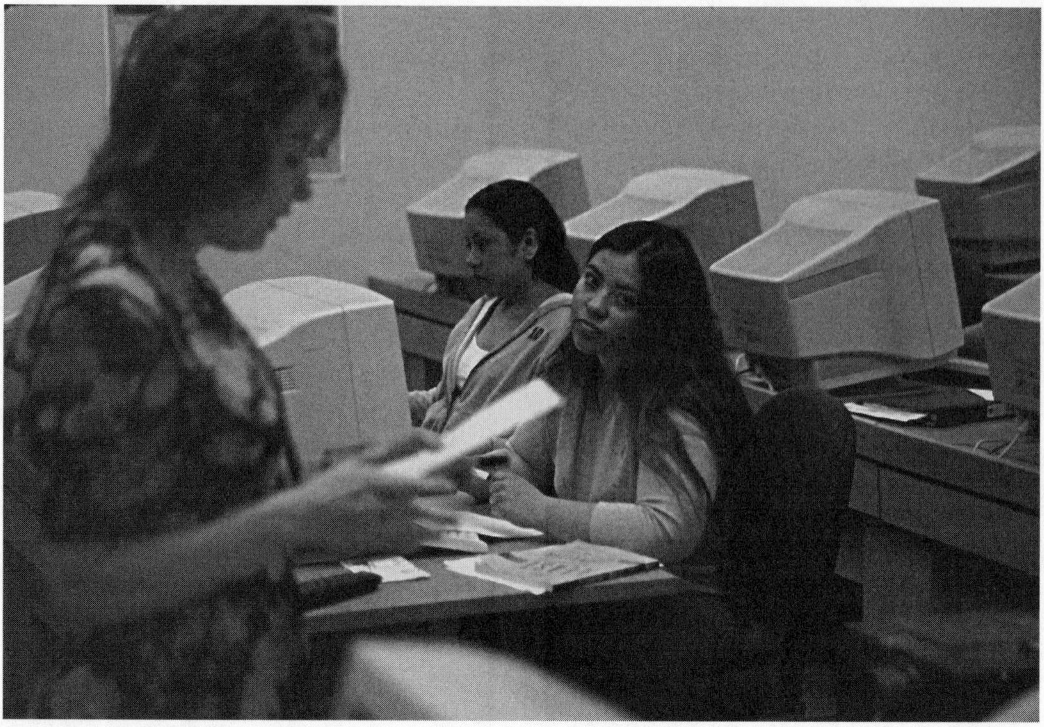

These Latina students participate in an internet-guided lecture at the University of Pennsylvania (Painetworks)

U.S. population is classified as "Hispanic or Latino," just over 5 percent of postsecondary students are Latina/Chicana women (National Center for Education Statistics 1999).

Chicanas/Latinas in Postsecondary Education

Of every ethnic group of women in the United States, Chicanas/Latinas are the least likely to complete a bachelor's degree. Sylvia Hurtado and Deborah Faye Carter (1997) find that beyond the inequality of elementary and secondary educational conditions described below, other structural barriers may contribute to these dismal statistics, including the effects of a negative campus racial climate. In such an environment, women and people of color experience racial discrimination in academic and social campus settings from faculty, staff, and students. Often, these experiences are characterized by being the target of racialized verbal or nonverbal insults, being rendered invisible in class discussions, being deemed "the representative" of all Latinas/os, and being belittled in terms of academic merit. The effects of a negative campus racial climate include changing majors (often away from math, science, or engineering), extending time to degree, leaving school, earning a lower grade point average, and having a lowered self-concept. In comparison to white men, women, and even Chicanos, Chicana undergraduate students experience the highest levels of stress. Chicanas admit to being worried about financing their education, adjusting to their academic environment, and continuing to support their families financially, yet they are often unaware that these concerns are causing them stress, which in turn depresses their academic performance.

Research also demonstrates that "stereotype threat" diminishes higher education opportunities for women and African Americans. In standardized testing situations (e.g., Scholastic Aptitude Test, Graduate Record Exam), students were found to be more susceptible to societal stereotypes about race, gender, and intelligence, and they underperformed when reminded of their race, gender, or both. The prevalence of racial and gender stereotypes also functions to depress the academic performance of Chicanas/Latinas. As part of a negative campus racial climate, stereotype threat causes "self-doubt" and can eventually undermine the success of Chicana/Latina doctoral students and faculty. Undergraduate experiences with a negative campus racial climate are often followed by experiences of racialized and gendered marginalization in graduate school and isolation in faculty positions.

Indeed, Chicana/Latina college students seeking role models in the form of Chicana/Latina faculty are most often disappointed. Although discriminatory hiring practices exacerbate the already low numbers of Chicana/Latina faculty, the conditions leading up to the doctorate and the doctoral process itself also contribute to the very small number of Chicana/Latina academics. Daniel Solórzano found that in comparison to every other group (white, black, Asian American, Native American, men, and women), Chicanas are the most underrepresented population in terms of doctoral production. In Patricia Gandara's seminal 1982 work addressing the difficulties in surmounting the barriers to earning a doctorate, she likens this process to "passing through the eye of a needle."

The underrepresentation of Chicanas/Latinas in higher education translates into an overrepresentation in the service sector and in low-wage employment and few opportunities to move up the socioeconomic ladder. Furthermore, structural restrictions on higher education means an underrepresentation of Chicana/Latina medical doctors, lawyers, and educators, which further limits the quality of services made available to their communities. In addition, the lack of a strong Chicana/Latina presence in positions of power makes it less likely that legislators and policymakers will address Chicana/Latina education as a priority for change.

The Educational Pipeline

Chicana/Latina women continue to be seriously underrepresented in higher education, although they constitute a significant and growing portion of the K–12 student population. In a 2001 report from the American Association of University Women (AAUW), Angela Ginorio and Michelle Huston found that Latinas are the largest "minority" group of girls in the U.S. K–12 system. For example, Chicanas/Latinas comprise 50 percent of California's public school kindergarten class for the 2001–2002 school year. The educational opportunities made available to these young Californians have larger societal repercussions, as the population growth pattern in California begins to evidence itself in major cities across the nation. Unfortunately, although Chicanas/Latinas are numerous within primary and secondary schools, researchers note many structural barriers that continue to hinder Chicana/Latina access to postsecondary education. It is important to contextualize the disparities between the educational attainment of Chicanas/Latinas and other women in higher education within a critical examination of the Chicana/Latina educational pipeline.

At the elementary school level, "dropout" or "push-out" factors often begin with a pattern of underfinanced, overcrowded schools that lack basic human and material resources for students. In these early years of schooling, Chicanas/Latinas are often faced with dilapidated school buildings, overcrowded classrooms, and inexperienced teachers. Low per-pupil expenditures are exacerbated by lack of access to a quality curriculum. Few Chicanas/Latinas have access to a well-trained teacher who appropriately implements bilingual/multicultural education by drawing on the cultural and linguistic knowledge Chicana/Latina students bring from their homes and communities to the classroom. In contrast, the most inexperienced teachers are often placed in the most low-income, overcrowded schools. Frequently, educators view Chicana/Latina students' culture and language as deficits to overcome instead of strengths on which to draw. Race, class, and gender stereotypes prevail in many explanations for the failure of Chicana/Latina students. Unfortunately, these stereotypes make their way into schools and inform lowered teacher expectations and biased intelligence tests. Because schools do a poor job of reaching out to Chicana/Latina parents as educational partners, they rely on standardized tests and teacher recommendations to provide or limit students' access to knowledge. Well before high school, most schools do not nurture a college-going culture for Chicanas/Latinas, instead restricting access to enrichment programs, magnet schools, and gifted and talented education programs.

High schools tend to continue the patterns of inequality evidenced earlier. The high schools most Chicanas/Latinas attend are racially segregated, underresourced, and overcrowded. Standardized tests from elementary and junior high or middle school may be used in conjunction with teacher and counselor recommendations to restrict Chicana/Latina access to college preparatory curricula. High school textbooks often ignore the multiple contributions Chicana/Latina communities have made to the United States and the world. In addition to being outdated and inappropriate, textbooks are often in short supply, along with other classroom resources such as computers and, sometimes, even desks. Low-income schools may not offer the basic courses required for college entrance. Even if their school offers the basic college requirements, Chicanas/Latinas may be placed on a curriculum track that restricts access to those courses. Moreover, predominately white, affluent schools offer multiple opportunities for students to earn college credit and extra grade points (above the 4.0 scale) through Advanced Placement (AP) courses, whereas many of the schools Chicanas/Latinas attend do not. Even within schools that offer AP courses, Chicanas/Latinas are usually tracked away from these college-preparatory opportunities. The result is that Chicanas/Latinas are sorely underrepresented in AP courses.

Unequal elementary and secondary conditions restrict the flow of Chicanas/Latinas through the educational pipeline. Chicanas/Latinas are more likely to begin their college career in a community college, rather than a four-year college or university. The structural nature of the community college tends to push Chicanas/

Latinas into vocationally oriented two-year terminal degree programs (e.g., child care providers, medical assistants). Poor counseling, overcrowding, and limited financial resources are some of the factors implicated in the low transfer rates of Chicanas/Latinas from community colleges to four-year colleges and universities.

Theoretical and Practical Approaches

In the midst of dismal statistical realities, hope remains. Scholars such as Daniel Solórzano and Tara Yosso (2001) are using critical race theory as a framework to examine racial and gender disparities in education and are challenging the structures, processes, and discourses that maintain racialized and gendered inequalities. Chicanas/Latinas are resisting racism and sexism as they survive the journey to and through higher education. Chicana/Latina college graduates are also giving back to their communities by sharing their struggles and successes with young Chicana/Latina students. Finally, researchers are validating these struggles by documenting the resources, barriers, and critical life events of successful Chicana/Latina scholars.

A number of initiatives have evolved to improve the situation of Chicanas/Latinas in higher education. For example, to help each other prosper in graduate school and academia, a small group of Chicana/Latina women from several northern California universities founded Mujeres Activas en Letras y Cambios Sociales (MALCS) in 1982. Today, MALCS serves as a national network for faculty, administrators, community workers, and graduate and undergraduate students who are working toward four common goals: (1) to recruit and support Chicana/Latina women in higher education and advanced studies; (2) to encourage and promote the distribution of research on Chicana/Latina women; (3) to promote the development and institutionalization of Chicana/Latina studies; and (4) to address issues of concern to Chicana/Latina communities. Each year, MALCS organizes a summer institute, which serves as a forum for presenting research as well as a place/space for Chicana/Latina community activists and scholars to encourage and mentor each another.

Tara J. Yosso

See also Part 1: Hispanic-Serving Institutions; Historically Black Colleges and Universities; Part 6: Development of Multiple Social and Cultural Identities; Developmental Issues; Part 7: Latina Faculty; Part 8: Latina Administrators

References and further reading

Cuadraz, G. 1997. "Chicana Academic Persistence: Creating a University-Based Community." *Education and Urban Society* 30: 107–121.

Gandara, Patricia. 1982. "Passing through the Eye of the Needle: High-Achieving Chicanas." *Hispanic Journal of Behavioral Sciences* 4: 167–179.

———. 1995. *Over the Ivy Walls: The Educational Mobility of Low-Income Chicanos.* Albany: State University of New York Press.

Ginorio, Angela, and Michelle Huston. 2001. *Sí Se Puede! Yes We Can: Latinas in Education Report.* Washington, DC: American Association of University Women Educational Foundation.

Hurtado, Sylvia, and Deborah Faye Carter. 1997. "Effects of College Transition and Perceptions of the Campus Racial Climate on Latino College Students' Sense of Belonging." *Sociology of Education* 70: 324–346.

National Center for Education Statistics. 1999. *Digest of Education Statistics.* Washington, DC: U.S. Department of Education.

Rendon, Laura. 1992. "From the Barrio to the Academy: Revelations of a Mexican American 'Scholarship Girl.'" *New Directions for Community Colleges* 80 (Winter).

Solórzano, Daniel. 1995. "The Baccalaureate Origins of Chicana and Chicano Doctorates in the Social

Sciences." *Hispanic Journal of Behavioral Sciences* 17: 3–32.
Solórzano, Daniel, and Tara Yosso. 2001 "Critical Race and Latcrit Theory and Method: Counterstorytelling Chicana and Chicano Graduate School Experiences." *International Journal of Qualitative Studies in Education* 14: 371–395.

Learning and Knowing

Women's Socialization toward Connection

Women's development and learning have been mediated by women's socialization in American society. Historically, American women have been socialized to care for others, regard their interests and needs as secondary to those of others, and generally subordinate themselves to patriarchal domination. Social roles and gender-related identities are promoted in multiple contexts, including the home, family, community, workplace, and educational institutions. Lyn Mikel Brown and Carol Gilligan (1992) used adolescent girls' narratives to portray the power of gender socialization in the lives of adolescent girls. The pressure to be good women—that is, nice, polite, and never mean—caught girls in a tension between the authentic relationships of their childhood and inauthentic relationships in which open conflict was discouraged. The self-assertive expression of thoughts characteristic of younger girls changed to self-doubt and confusion when they became adolescents. Brown and Gilligan captured this movement toward the desired female image as approaching the wall of feminine socialization. Some girls gave in to inauthentic relationships to become the perfect girl; others resisted. Dorothy Holland and Margaret Eisenhart (1990) witnessed a version of this socialization on two college campuses where African American and white college women became caught up in a culture of romance through which they anticipated, interpreted, and evaluated their experience. The majority of the women studied devoted more energy to gaining prestige through making themselves attractive to men than they did to academics, downsizing their academic and career aspirations.

In addition to gender-related marginalization, many women are further marginalized by socialization related to race, ethnicity, class, and sexual identity. Lyn Mikel Brown's work with white adolescent working-class girls revealed that class mediated feminine socialization. For the working-class girls in her study, femininity included "toughness, a self-protective invulnerability to sadness and fear, an often direct and unapologetic expression of anger, as well as a deep capacity for love and nurturance toward those who need them" (1998, 69). These characteristics did not yield self-confidence, however, because the girls often saw their futures as bleak and viewed themselves harshly. Wendy Luttrell's research portrays how working-class women, both African American and white, distinguish "common sense from schoolwise intelligence, pitting experience against schooling" (1997, 35). This distinction reflects a gendered view of knowledge that assigns emotion, affect, intuition, and relatedness to women's knowing, whereas thought, cognition, reason, and autonomy are viewed as characteristic to men's knowing. Although the African American women recognized the intelligence women exhibited to survive in a racist environment, they viewed men as more powerful intellectually. Work with adult women who live in poverty and rural isolation revealed that they did not view themselves as knowledgeable or consider their perspectives to be important (Belenky, Bond, and Weinstock 1997). Lesbian women face complications in the socialization to connection because romantic connection is framed as connection to the opposite sex. Natalie Eldridge, Julie Mencher, and Suzanne Slater indicate that when lesbian women act on their romantic feelings for other women, they must do so in opposition to societal pressure (Jordan 1997).

In exploring women's ways of knowing in the writings of feminists of color, Aída Hurtado examined five mechanisms women of color use to negotiate their multiple group memberships in generating and comprehending knowledge (Goldberger, Tarule, Clinchy, and Belenky 1996). Anger resulting from injustice can block or facilitate access to knowledge, as can silence and outspokenness. When these mechanisms can be used to counteract marginalization, they promote women of color's knowledge; yet knowing when to negotiate these mechanisms in various settings is important to avoid further oppression. Another mechanism, the ability to withdraw from men because of structural conditions such as incarceration or economic hardship, contributes to women of color establishing their own authority. Membership in multiple social realities also helps women of color develop the ability to shift consciousness or to shift to the current group's perception of reality. This ability enhances the capacity to suspend knowledge temporarily to resist oppression and make acting against oppression possible. Finally, this ability to shift among realities yields multiple voices or the ability to talk to different groups without losing the self. These latter capacities reflect complex forms of knowing.

Women's socialization, despite its complexity and variation because of race, ethnicity, class, and sexual identity, supports their emphasis on communion with others more so than it supports their emphasis on agency. The terms "communion" and "agency" were coined by David Bakan, who defined agency as focused on "the existence of an organism as an individual" (1966, 15). He offered self-protection, self-assertion, and self-expansion as dynamics of agency. Bakan used the term "communion" to refer to "the participation of the individual in some larger organism of which the individual is a part" (1996, 15). Bakan described communion as "being at one with other organisms, . . . manifest in contact, openness, and union" (1996, 15). The different values assigned to these two concepts in American society resulted in a view of them as dichotomous, with agency perceived as the more desirable of the two.

Developmental theory perpetuated this dichotomy and the devaluing of communion. Initially, development (based primarily on studies of men) was conceptualized as a story of increasing independence and individuation from others. This conceptualization called for the development of agency, or the ability to separate from others and function as an autonomous individual. Increasing individuation and separation from others to achieve control, autonomy, and independence in relationship to others marked developmental progress. A focus on agency often led to sacrificing others' needs in relationships to maintain autonomy. The individual freedom and achievement valued in Western, democratic societies created a preference for agency as the guiding characteristic of maturity. From this vantage point, persons who exhibited communion (primarily, although not exclusively, women) were viewed as dependent and deficient. Thus developmental theory, created by men through the study of men, formed yet another layer of women's socialization as secondary and deficient.

A More Complex View of Communion

Studying the complexities of women's development revealed that it was developmental theory, not women, that was deficient. Moral development based on studying men was portrayed as a move from an egocentric perspective, through a conventional concern regarding others, to a principled perspective that extended beyond tangible relations with others, with a focus on rights or justice throughout. Carol Gilligan's concern that women's care for others was interpreted as morally deficient to principled reasoning led her to sketch a parallel version of women's moral development (Gilligan 1982; Gilligan, Ward, and Taylor 1988). Her study of women revealed that an ethic of care stood at the core of women's moral development, which led them to focus on responsibility rather than rights in moral contexts. Like the justice version of the story, the care version moved from egocentric to principled, but did so with communion or connection in the foreground.

Theorists in other developmental dimensions were working simultaneously to generate the story of women's learning and development. After substantial work with adult women in both college and public agency settings, Mary Belenky, Blythe Clinchy, Nancy Goldberger, and Jill Tarule (1986) offered a comprehensive theory of ways of knowing that conveyed women's connections to others in the knowledge production process. Perhaps their most important contribution was the concept of "connected knowing," a version of knowing in which the knower enters into the subject to be known rather than standing at arms length from it, as had been the traditional expectation of complex intellectual development. These authors also emphasized the crucial link between who we are and how we know that had been overlooked in the male versions of intellectual development theory. Both Gilligan's and Belenky and her colleagues' work clarified that the communal dimension of women's experience developed into complex forms of viewing knowledge and morality.

Women's identity development theory was also reconstructed with the recognition that communion is a component of mature identity development. Jean Baker Miller (1976) was an early proponent of the centrality of relationship and connection to women's identity development. While studying college women, Ruthellen Josselson (1996) concluded that identity development described as agency was less important to women than identity development characterized by communion. The integration of autonomy and relationship development emerged in both white and African American college women; connection to others in learning was typical in African American students (Evans, Forney, and Guido-DiBrito 1998). Findings like these contributed to Arthur Chickering and Linda Reisser's 1993 revision of Chickering's earlier model to reflect the communion dimension. Women's proclivity toward connection was integrated into new relational versions of development, with extensive work coming from researchers affiliated with the Stone Center at Wellesley College. Using this relational view, Julie Mencher reframed the concept of fusion in lesbian women's development from a pathological overreliance on attachment to a view of mutual engagement, empathy, and empowerment in lesbian women's development (Jordan 1997). Collectively, research on women's development yielded a new understanding of communion, or the ability to connect with others and to function in a collaborative way, as a component of maturity.

Further research including women and men simultaneously helped address the question of equality of the agentic and communal versions of development. Marcia B. Baxter Magolda's 1992 research on college student's intellectual development extended Belenky and her colleagues' concept of connected knowing. Baxter Magolda found two gender-related patterns within ways of knowing, one focused on the individual separate from others and one focused on connection and collaboration with others. These patterns emerged in early ways of knowing in which students looked to external authorities for knowledge and continued through students' transition to constructing knowledge for themselves. The existence of these patterns through the three ways of knowing evident in college demonstrated that the connected and separate styles of knowing are equally complex because they exist within the same overall assumptions about knowledge. Robert Kegan's 1994 study of adult self-evolution supports the equality of the communal and agentic dimensions. Kegan's portrayal of self-evolution proceeds from an adolescent focus on self-interest to a focus on external others to define the self and eventually to an internal self-definition that interprets external influence. Kegan emphasized that the phase of focusing on others can be approached from either a relational or separate stance, as can the internal self-definition. Thus tendencies toward agency or communion are preferences within phases of self-evolution.

Contemporary research moves beyond the debate about the equality of developmental theories to reveal that the most complex forms of development require both communion and agency. Baxter Magolda's fifteen-year longitudinal study of intellectual development demonstrated that the most complex form of knowledge construction, "contextual knowing," required both the relational and separate patterns the participants had previously used. To acquire relevant evidence, analyze and interpret that evidence, and come to their own judgments, Baxter Magolda's participants reported that both the capacity to go into the subject and to stand apart from it were crucial (2001). Clinchy's most recent work advances the benefits of both capacities in constructed knowing; thus she advocates the marriage of the two (Goldberger, Tarule, Clinchy, and Belenky 1996).

The marriage of agency and communion appears in contemporary theories of identity and self-evolution. Kegan's most complex phase of self-evolution is characterized by interdependence between self and other in which self-authorship is maintained in the context of genuine interdependence with others. This interdependence is central to Judith Jordan's concept of "mutuality." Jordan defined it as "involv[ing] commitment to engage in the development and support of both people; it involves respectfully building a relationship together that both sustains and transcends the individuals engaged in it" (1997, 32). As such, mutuality requires that each person be able to "represent her or his own experience in a relationship, to act in a way that is congruent with an 'inner truth' and with the context, and to respond to and encourage authenticity in the other person" (1997, 31). Mutuality sacrifices neither self nor other too much.

In Jordan's definition of mutuality, autonomy takes the form of being clear in our thoughts and actions, acting with intention, but at the same time recognizing the impact of our actions on others. The concept of mutuality constitutes the marriage of agency and communion. Baxter Magolda's (2001) longitudinal participants experienced this blend of the two as they constructed their adult identities. Theories of racial identity development emphasize the necessity of connection with one's own racial group in the process of establishing a self-authored and interdependent racial identity in a white-dominated world; the same emphasis is found in theories of sexual identity development (Evans, Forney, and Guido-Dibrito 1998).

Contemporary developmental theory, by virtue of women's inclusion in its construction, portrays a developmental trajectory from self-interest and reliance on external influence to self-authorship in the context of mature relationships with others. To promote women's (and men's) development along this trajectory, higher education must abandon the traditional male-oriented model of separate education in favor of a transformed model that merges agency and communion.

Practices to Promote Women's Development and Learning

Merging agency and communion in higher education requires acknowledging communion, or connection, as a legitimate form of learning and development to welcome women of all colors, classes, and sexual orientations into learning. Further, it requires acknowledging that maturity in connection is necessary for complex forms of learning and development and is thus essential to the education of all learners. Contemporary conceptualizations of pedagogy advance these notions. Feminist pedagogy centers on communion yet does so in the context of agency. It emphasizes helping learners find and express their voices in order to participate in knowledge construction. Critical and liberatory pedagogy (e.g., Shor 1996) focuses on analysis of oppressive social structures to empower learners to authorize their own voices. Constructivist pedagogy (e.g., Twomey Fosnot 1996) looks at joint construction of knowledge among educators and learners. Culturally relevant pedagogy (e.g., Ladson-Billings 1994) emphasizes connection to learners' cultures and mutual construction to facilitate authorization of voice and knowledge.

Constructive-developmental pedagogy (e.g., Baxter Magolda 1999; Belenky et al. 1986; Kegan 1994) focuses on learners' development of the capacity to construct knowledge and identity, an extension of the notion of authorization of voice and knowledge. Belenky and her colleagues' articulation of connected teaching to bring forward women's knowing advanced the metaphor of teacher as midwife, describing an educator as assisting "students in giving birth to their own ideas, in making their own tacit knowledge explicit and elaborating it" (1986, 217). This metaphor captured learners moving toward agency in the context of connection. Pedagogy to create culturally responsive learning environments for students of color and gay, lesbian, and bisexual students (e.g., Baxter Magolda 2000; Ladson-Billings 1994) emphasizes connection to students' worldviews and identities to promote self-authorship.

Baxter Magolda's (2001) fifteen-year longitudinal study of young adults' learning in educational, employment, and personal contexts yielded a model for promoting self-authorship that reflects the merger of communion and agency. Three core educational assumptions form the foundation of the model: knowledge is complex and socially constructed, the self is central to knowledge construction, and expertise and authority are shared in the mutual construction of knowledge. These three assumptions demand complexity in how educators and learners construct knowledge, themselves, and their relations with others. The three assumptions are linked to learners' current capacity in these three dimensions of development via three educational principles: validating learners as knowers, situating learning in learners' experience, and defining learning as mutually constructing meaning. When these three principles are pedagogical mainstays, learners are invited into knowledge construction, supported in viewing themselves as constructors of knowledge and authors of their own lives, and accompanied in the process of learning self-authorship. Thus the achievement of agency takes place in the context of communion, and self-authorship is portrayed much like Jordan's (1997) mutuality.

New insights from the development of women, particularly the study of women's development as mediated by gender, race, class, and sexual orientation structures in the twentieth-century United States, strengthen our understanding of human development and learning. Translation of these insights to transform American higher education is crucial to providing quality education for all learners.

Marcia B. Baxter Magolda

See also Part 3: Feminist Pedagogy; Part 6: Developmental Issues

References and further reading

Bakan, David. 1966. *The Duality of Human Existence: An Essay on Psychology and Religion.* Chicago: Rand McNally.

Baxter Magolda, Marcia B. 1992. *Knowing and Reasoning in College: Gender-Related Patterns in Students' Intellectual Development.* San Francisco: Jossey-Bass.

———. 1999. *Creating Contexts for Learning and Self-Authorship: Constructive-Developmental Pedagogy.* Nashville, TN: Vanderbilt University Press.

———. 2001. *Making Their Own Way: Narratives for Transforming Higher Education to Promote Self-Development.* Sterling, VA: Stylus Publishing.

———, ed. 2000. *Teaching to Promote Intellectual and Personal Maturity: Incorporating Students' Worldviews and Identities into the Learning Process. New Directions for Teaching and Learning.* Vol. 82. San Francisco: Jossey-Bass.

Belenky, Mary, Lynne A. Bond, and Jacqueline S. Weinstock. 1997. *A Tradition That Has No Name: Nurturing the Development of People, Families, and Communities.* New York: Basic Books.

Belenky, Mary, Blythe McVicker Clinchy, Nancy Goldberger, and Jill Tarule. 1986. *Women's Ways of Knowing: The Development of Self, Voice, and Mind.* New York: Basic Books.

Brown, Lyn Mikel. 1998. *Raising Their Voices: The Politics of Girls' Anger.* Cambridge, MA: Harvard University Press.

Brown, Lyn Mikel, and Carol Gilligan. 1992. *Meeting at the Crossroads: Women's Psychology and Girls' Development.* Cambridge, MA: Harvard University Press.

Chickering, Arthur W., and Linda Reisser. 1993. *Education and Identity.* 2nd ed. San Francisco: Jossey-Bass.

Evans, Nancy J., Deanna S. Forney, and Florence Guido-Dibrito. 1998. *Student Development in College: Theory, Research, and Practice.* San Francisco: Jossey-Bass.

Gilligan, Carol. 1982. *In a Different Voice: Psychological Theory and Women's Development.* Cambridge, MA: Harvard University Press.

Gilligan, Carol, Jane Victoria Ward, and Jill Mclean Taylor, eds. 1988. *Mapping*

the Moral Domain. Cambridge, MA: Harvard University Press.
Goldberger, Nancy, Jill Tarule, Blythe Clinchy, and Mary Belenky, eds. 1996. *Knowledge, Difference, and Power: Essays Inspired by Women's Ways of Knowing.* New York: Basic Books.
Holland, Dorothy C., and Margaret A. Eisenhart. 1990. *Educated in Romance: Women, Achievement and College Culture.* Chicago: University of Chicago Press.
Jordan, Judith V., ed. 1997. *Women's Growth in Diversity: More Writings from the Stone Center.* New York: Guilford Press.
Josselson, Ruthellen. 1996. *Revising Herself: The Story of Women's Identity from College to Midlife.* New York: Oxford University Press.
Kegan, Robert. 1994. *In over Our Heads: The Mental Demands of Modern Life.* Cambridge, MA: Harvard University Press.
Ladson-Billings, Gloria. 1994. *The Dreamkeepers: Successful Teachers of African American Children.* San Francisco: Jossey-Bass.
Luttrell, Wendy. 1997. *Schoolsmart and Motherwise: Working-Class Women's Identity and Schooling.* New York: Basic Books.
Miller, Jean Baker. 1976. *Toward a New Psychology of Women.* Boston: Beacon Press.
Shor, Ira. 1996. *When Students Have Power: Negotiating Authority in a Critical Pedagogy.* Chicago: University of Chicago Press.
Twomey Fosnot, Catherine, ed. 1996. *Constructivism: Theory, Perspectives, and Practice.* New York: Teachers College Press.

Nontraditional Students

Reentry, or nontraditional-age, students are those who are over age twenty-five and enter postsecondary education for the first time or return to continue postsecondary study begun at an earlier time. Reentry women have been entering institutions of higher education in increasing numbers since the 1960s, and since 1980, women over age twenty-five have been the fastest-growing sector in higher education. The number of nontraditional-age women in college has increased rapidly since 1970. In 1950, the number of women in college over the age of twenty-five was 10,000, and those over age thirty-five were not even counted. By 1986, more than 2.5 million women over the age of twenty-five were attending college, and over 1 million of these women were over the age of thirty-five.

Not only have the numbers of reentry students increased, but the characteristics of these students have changed as well. Initially, reentry women were mostly married, white, middle-class women with husbands and grown children who had decided to continue their education in order to feel more fulfilled. Between 1960 and 1974, as divorce rates rose and more women entered the labor force, this trend started to change. Women began to attend college for many reasons but predominantly to prepare themselves for more varied and flexible work possibilities. Other reasons for entering or returning to higher education included personal growth and intellectual stimulation, the need to become financially independent, and the desire to look forward to a profession. In the 1980s the reentry population diversified, with a greater number of single parents, older single women, low-income women, and women of color attending institutions of higher education than ever before. Reentry women were an important part of the higher education landscape and a population not to be dismissed. Researchers attempted to characterize this population; the major questions they asked were who are these women, why are they returning to school, what changes are

Student, age fifty-two, at her graduation from Saint Thomas University (Painetworks)

they experiencing, and are they encountering any specific problems?

In the 1970s the average age of reentry women was thirty-eight, and the majority had previously attained some formal education beyond high school. However, this profile changed as more racial and ethnic minority and lower-income women enrolled in college programs. Typically, though not always, students from this newer population had dropped out of formal education at an early age and were single parents and heads of their own households.

Because of the large age span encompassed by the label "reentry students," members of this group have different needs and concerns. Nontraditional women students are likely to fall within two categories: (a) those who are in their twenties and early thirties, have younger children, and are juggling a variety of roles (student, parent, wage earner, etc.); and (b) those in their thirties and forties whose children are older and who experience less pressure to be involved in multiple roles. The first group may feel guilty about time spent away from family while they are at school or doing homework. They fear that their family structure will loosen and tend to blame themselves for time devoted to school-related issues. The other group of women experience a sense of "identity disorientation" because of the shift in roles. Part of this effect may be due to the "empty nest syndrome," a phrase that has been used to describe the feelings women have when their children have grown and are no longer dependent on them for their survival. These phenomena suggest that as reentry women make the transition into higher education, they have to cope with many challenging psychological issues about roles, priorities, and identity.

For many reentry women, beginning or returning to higher education initiates particularly stressful situations, those caused by societal changes in areas such as finance and technology and those instigated by personal concerns such as marriage, family, and relationship issues. It is often difficult to separate the two, and women may experience stress from a combination of societal and personal concerns. In recent decades, societal and economic changes have accelerated in the United States and abroad. The world has experienced economic recession and inflation, increased longevity, and economic demands that have led families to depend on two incomes for survival. These economic factors are among the reasons nontraditional-age women have entered higher education; many women cite issues related to employment, either to help in the search for a better job or to find surcease from employment that is presently unfulfilling, among their reasons for entering postsecondary education.

Personal and psychological development issues of reentry women may be many, with an emphasis on their desire to develop an identity and the need to feel fulfilled. There are other personal variables, but many returning female students cite an increase in personal fulfillment as being of paramount importance. The decision to return to school is usually an issue that has assumed major importance in the lives of nontraditional-age women. Some of these women express a profound desire for personal growth and believe that going to school is a vehicle for accomplishing this goal.

Psychological issues can also be a determining factor for the overall success of reentry women. Like other students, the female nontraditional student enters the world of higher education with all her life experiences and expectations; and like other students, she may experience this setting as frightening or threatening. There is much within the higher education system that may cause these feelings to emerge. Reentry students may encounter alien cultures—both the youth culture of traditional-age undergraduates and the academic culture of faculty—with unfamiliar languages and norms. Many women feel that they have been denied opportunities that others have experienced in terms of education, culture, or finances. Often, these students are concerned with whether they are entitled to be in school. They may feel that they will be found out and identified as imposters, as if they were merely posing as college students.

The fear of not "making it" as a college student is the primary self-expressed fear of many reentry women. It is often expected that women will fail, and little notice is paid to female reentry students when they withdraw from a class, receive a failing grade, or decide not to register for another semester. Typically, this fear is expressed in a variety of ways but is most easily divided into the fear of academic work and the fear of academic failure. The former is the expressed particularized fear of being unable to master the necessary skills to pass the curriculum. The latter is the generalized fear that the student will not survive or succeed in the academic world. Often, reentry women have used their fears as motivators to help them succeed. Many times, they are women who persist and defy the odds against academic success. Their concerns influence them to work harder, ask more questions, use more support services, and move through the system of higher education.

Reentry issues may be magnified for women of color. The dynamics of the larger society, which often negatively impact the lives of racial and ethnic minority women, are played out in higher education. The social context in which students learn is culture-bound, and issues of gender, class, and race are often taken for granted or unexplored by traditional-age undergraduates and many faculty. For many reentry students of color, what they are learning in the classroom is not what they are experiencing in real life; the experiences and knowledge they bring to higher education are in conflict with curricula based on modernist epistemologies and the unstated meritocratic ethos of the academy. Institutions of higher education too often adhere to a hierarchy that precludes women and most people of color from assuming positions of power, thereby placing reentry women of color at the bottom of the ladder. Many of these women returned to school in hopes of becoming successful in gaining access to better jobs and a better life; at the same time, they realize that being successful in school is not necessarily going to ensure their career advancement. In addition to the challenges faced by white reentry women, reentry women of color may have to overcome institutional racism and societal expectations that they will not succeed in higher education.

Estelle Miller

See also Part 1: Community Colleges; Part 6: Persistence; Socioeconomic Status

References and further reading

Cohen, Rosetta Marantz. 1998. "Class Consciousness and Its Consequences: The Impact of an Elite Education on Mature, Working-Class Women." *American Educational Research Journal* 35, no. 3: 353–375.

Kates, Erika. 1993. *Access to Higher Education Project.* Project on Women and Social Change; Final Report. Northampton, MA: Smith College.

LaPaglia, Nancy. 1994. *Storytellers: The Image of the Two-Year College in American Fiction and in Women's Journals.* Dekalb, IL: LEPS Press, Northern Illinois University.

Mezirow, Jack. 1978. *Education for Perspective Transformation: Women's Reentry Programs in Community Colleges.* New York: Columbia University Center for Adult Education.

Rifenbary, Deborah C. 1995. "Reentering the Academy: Voices of Returning Women Students." *Initiatives* 56, no. 4: 1–10.

Tisdell, Elizabeth J. 1993. "Interlocking Systems of Power, Privilege, and Oppression in Adult Higher Education Classes." *Adult Education Quarterly* 43: 203–226.

Persistence

Persistence in higher education can be defined as the collective actions and behaviors taken by students that result in the acquisition of a degree. Although persistence is frequently assumed to be synonymous with retention, in reality, the two terms are not identical. Persistence is a human activity or behavior, whereas retention is the subsequent outcome or result.

The difference between the two may be best illustrated by the following example: When a woman transfers from College A to College B with the intention of continuing her degree, she is performing an act of persistence in higher education. However, from the viewpoint of College A, this woman was not retained. Consequently, the phrase "institutional persistence" has been coined to refer to those actions resulting in degree completion at a single institution.

Persistence to degree completion is an important activity at multiple levels (e.g., individual, economic, and social). Women who successfully complete their degrees reap significant individual benefits such as higher salaries and professional advancements commensurate with their abilities. However, when a woman drops out of college, those institutional resources that were expended for her benefit were wasted and could have been put to better use on another student. Since access to college is a limited commodity, the admittance of one student generally means that a college seat was made unavailable for another student. Hence, nonpersistence is costly to many different parties.

Further, there are multiple reasons for nonpersistence—most have very little to do with postsecondary policies. The American College Testing Program (1995)

defined three basic types of nonpersistence: (1) natural nonpersistence, such as illness or job transfer; (2) stop outs, a temporary leave, such as for pregnancy; and (3) unnecessary nonpersistence caused by situations such as adjustment difficulties or academic problems.

A Historic Struggle

The historical omnipresence of gender discrimination has forced women to take very active roles in their persistence to degree completion. From the earliest accounts of women in college, the road to a degree was an uphill one. Although many historical records from early coeducational colleges have praised these institutions for being open-minded, in fact, women students frequently faced harsh discrimination (Miller-Bernal 2001; Solomon 1985). Federal laws in the nineteenth century required individual states to provide equal educational opportunities to both sexes, but many instructors subtly but firmly suggested to girls that their place was at home. Thus, young women had first to overcome obstacles to enroll in college and then to stand firm against multiple challenges to persist.

With the advent of the women's rights movement in the 1960s, the struggle for gender equity in higher education reached a climax. By 1972, Title IX of the Education Amendments had been passed, prohibiting sex discrimination in any institution that received federal assistance. Despite legislated efforts of this sort, gender discrimination has not yet been eradicated. Still, these policies have contributed to a steady rise in women's access to and persistence in higher education.

Enrollment and Persistence Trends

Since the 1970s, women's attendance in institutions of higher education has soared, outpacing that of men (National Center for Education Statistics 2001, table 173). Many female students enroll on a part-time basis, juggling classes with family and job demands. Even full-time enrollment does not indicate that women students can devote themselves fully to their studies. Many full-time female students are heads of families, have child care responsibilities, are in charge of domestic chores, and are concurrently employed. Persistence by most women, therefore, requires superior time management skills.

Despite these obstacles, typically more women than men persist to graduation from college within the traditional four-year sequence. However, when women drop out, they are less likely to reenroll. The abundant research in the area of college persistence lists the most common reasons for dropping out as boredom with classes, financial problems, time crunches, issues related to institutional requirements and regulations, and changes in career goals.

Since there is firm evidence that persistence and a high degree of integration in the campus environment are closely correlated, many female students are at a disadvantage. Female students who have familial and work obligations cannot spend large blocks of time at the student union or interacting with other students and faculty members after classes. Many are also commuters who arrive at the last minute to class and then leave quickly afterward. This circumstance may lead to a sense of isolation. Another obstacle to female persistence is the lack of student-sensitive institutional policies.

In spite of the many barriers, female students are well represented among the approximately 15 million students now enrolled in higher education. Women's gains became especially noticeable in the

1970s and 1980s. Although enrollment rates for men increased 6 percent from 1988 to 1998, female enrollment increased by 16 percent. By 1980, women earned more associate degrees than men (217,173 to 183,787). The number of women who persisted to obtain either a bachelor's or master's degree was roughly equal to that of men (National Center for Education Statistics 2001, table 248).

By 1990, women had surpassed men in earned bachelor's degrees (53 percent of the total) and master's degrees (also 53 percent). By 1997, women were earning 41 percent of doctoral degrees, predominantly in the fields of education and psychology. They also accounted for 42 percent of all professional degrees (National Center for Education Statistics 2001, table 248).

Recent Evidence

The National Center for Education Statistics (2000) published a report on students who began attending college for the first time in 1995–1996. Persistence was defined as continued enrollment or the acquisition of a degree or certificate and was measured after three years. For students in four-year institutions, the persistence rate was 80 percent, but at two-year colleges, the rate was much lower, at 60 percent. In terms of the students' persistence at the same institution, the four-year institutional retention rate was 67 percent. Results from two-year institutions found that the retention rate was 45 percent. At institutions with programs lasting less than two years, the retention rate was 61 percent.

Women by Field

Overall, women persist to completion of their programs at about the same rates as men—even in the once male-dominated physical sciences. Although the evidence indicates that the gender gap in persistence has closed in many fields, there is still some variation by student ethnicity and major field of study.

In business programs, women now account for 49 percent of all degrees. In the social sciences in general, the number of women has continued to grow and is on a par with or even exceeds that of men. In math, computer science, the earth sciences, and the physical sciences, women earn approximately one-third of all undergraduate degrees.

In engineering, the numbers remain low. Women in undergraduate engineering programs total 17 percent of all students; in master's programs, 17 percent; and in doctoral programs, just 12 percent (National Center for Education Statistics 2001, table 254). There are several reasons for women's historical underrepresentation. One is that they simply have not received the same encouragement to enter and persist in these programs as have men. Issues surrounding persistence have often included feeling singled out, being less often acknowledged, and being less academically prepared in this field. More often, parents have not presented significant resistance when daughters express a desire to switch out of engineering studies, as compared to their reactions to a son's similar decision. As for the lower numbers entering graduate school, this statistic has often been due to less mentoring in undergraduate years and the conflicting demands of family and career (Seymour 1995).

The American Association of University Women and the National Science Foundation, as well as other support organizations for women in science and engineering, have addressed the lower participation and persistence rates for women in engineering programs. These groups have made inroads in championing opportunities for young women via scholarship programs. Organization such as the Society of Women Engineers have also helped women by creating campus groups that offer them support and social integration within their majors.

The persistence of women in the sciences has been given much attention. As a result of concerted efforts, undergraduate women in the sciences and engineering are finally beginning to achieve higher undergraduate completion rates than men. The reasons vary but have been attributed to stronger family support and encouragement, better advising and preparation, higher levels of self-esteem, and more support from campus organizations and from student affairs offices.

Graduate Education

Since 1984, the number of women in graduate school has exceeded that of men. During the years 1987–1997, the number of male graduate students grew by 22 percent, compared to a 68 percent growth rate for women (National Center for Education Statistics 2001, table 189). It should be noted that in the humanities and in psychology, women have attained more graduate degrees than men and that the two groups are approximately equal in number of life sciences degrees granted. To date, though, women have not yet caught up to men in mathematics and the physical sciences.

Racial and Ethnic Minority Women

In spite of this tangible and undeniable evidence of progress among women in general, minority women continue to underperform in relation to white women. Certainly, income and race far outweigh gender as determining factors in who enters and persists until college graduation. Still, enrollments of minorities in higher education have been increasing since 1976, when they accounted for only 16 percent of all students. Today, minority enrollments total 27 percent. However, to further underscore the differences based upon race, 37.3 percent of white females aged twenty-five to twenty-nine have attained at least a bachelor's degree; the comparable figures for black and Hispanic women are 18.6 percent and 15.8 percent (National Center for Education Statistics 2001, table 207).

Moreover, in the sciences, minority students are still dramatically underrepresented in number and overrepresented among those who do not persist. Minorities comprise approximately 12 percent of the science and engineering student bodies (National Center for Education Statistics 2001, table 202). The major barriers to gifted minorities persisting in their science studies appear to be linked to inadequate preparation, financial difficulties, and discriminatory practices of institutions.

The lower persistence rates of minority students are likely the result of the overrepresentation of minorities with the following risk factors: lack of a regular high school diploma; delayed postsecondary enrollment; enrollment in college on a part-time basis; full-time employment while enrolled; or enrollment as a self-supporting student, as a student with children, or as a single parent. As with all students, the likelihood of persistence diminishes with each of the aforementioned risk factors.

Among the first-time students in the 1995–1996 study, only 16 percent of students with no risk factors left postsecondary education without a degree after three years, whereas 32 percent of students with one risk factor left and 49 percent of students with two or more risk factors left (National Center for Education Statistics 2001, ii). Four-year institutional students tended to be younger, nonworking, higher income students—a profile that excludes a large part of the minority student population. However, even with numerous barriers, minority women have gained access to higher education at significantly higher rates than minority men.

Older Female Students

Women students over the traditional college age face many obstacles to persistence. White married females make up the bulk of students in the nontraditional age groups. As a rule, most attend college on a part-time basis. Adult females are appearing on campuses in increasing numbers and will continue to do so, with students over forty becoming the fastest-growing group in higher education (Rowley, Lujan, and Dolence 1998). Regardless of the obstacles in their paths, students over forty have high persistence rates and attain better grades than younger, more traditional students (Noel et al. 1985).

Linda Serra Hagedorn, Faith I. Womack, Christina Vogt, Shelly Westebbe, and Jeffrey Kealing

See also Part 1: Community Colleges; Part 6: Classroom Climate; Graduate and Professional Education; Graduate Students and Science; Undergraduates and Science

References and further reading

American College Testing Program. 1995. "Data Compiled from the ACT Institutional Data File for 1994." Iowa City, IA: American College Testing Program.

Miller-Bernal, Leslie. 2001. *Separate by Degree: Women Students' Experiences in Single-Sex and Coeducational Colleges.* New York: Peter Lang.

National Center for Education Statistics. 2000. *Descriptive Summary of 1995–96 Beginning Postsecondary Students: Three Years Later.* Washington, DC: U.S. Department of Education.

———. 2001. *Digest of Education Statistics, 2000.* Washington, DC: U.S. Department of Education.

Noel, Lee, Randi Levitz, and Diana Saluri. 1995. *Increasing Student Retention: Effective Programs and Practices for Reducing the Dropout Rate.* San Francisco: Jossey-Bass.

Rowley, Daniel James, Herman D. Lujan, and Michael G. Dolence. 1998. *Strategic Choices for the Academy: How Demand for Lifelong Learning Will Re-Create Higher Education.* San Francisco: Jossey-Bass.

Seymour, Elaine. 1995. "The Loss of Women from Science, Mathematics, and Engineering Undergraduate Majors: An Explanatory Account." *Science Education* 79, no. 4: 437–473.

Solomon, Barbara Miller. 1985. *In the Company of Educated Women: A History of Women and Higher Education in America.* New Haven, CT: Yale University Press.

Romantic Relationships

Of those factors that affect student development during college, peer relationships are among the most influential. Romantic relationships constitute a critical subset of peer relationships, particularly since the features of romance during young adulthood often mimic characteristics of highly adaptive infant-caregiver attachment bonds. Romantic relationships, in other words, might enhance levels of adjustment and achievement among college women if they encourage feelings of security and self-worth. Two interconnected topics are relevant to a discussion of college women's romantic relationships: (1) cultural forces that shape women's experiences with their romantic partners and (2) concepts and characteristics of romance during adolescence.

The Cultural Context

According to prevailing cultural scripts in the United States and elsewhere, love should come "naturally" to women. In part because of the implicit bias of instruments that measure love (Cancian 1986) and in part the effects of early childhood socialization, women appear to be more comfortable with "matters of the heart" than are men. Women are allegedly fluent in the language of intimacy and nurture or look after romantic partners with intuitive skill. Women seem to be more sensitive to the dynamics of romantic relationships and more involved in negotiations with a romantic partner. Women also self-disclose with less reservation than men do, which suggests that women are more adept at forging closeness with others.

However, although cultural scripts expect women to be interpersonal experts, they are to remain sexual ingénues. The sexual desire of men is largely condoned, whereas the sexual desire of women is often condemned. Women should be sexually attractive to men, but only to a point. Past this vague point, women are either "promiscuous" or "self-degrading." In short, women are to specialize in platonic forms of intimacy. Sexually expressive women are antithetical to the feminine ideal. Passion is allowed in a conjugal context, but mostly for the purposes of pleasing the male partner. This implies that women are to enjoy the cerebral rather than physical aspects of romance, despite the fact that romantic love flourishes in the presence of both.

Still, women increasingly report sexual attitudes and experiences similar to those reported by men. Gender disparity in self-reported feelings of closeness to one's romantic partner also seems to be declining. Perhaps the cultural scripts are changing in response to different socioeconomic roles that women are playing today. Greater financial leverage and vocational opportunities allow women to hone skills in areas outside the interpersonal. Women may be able to enjoy more freely multiple dimensions of romantic relationships as a result of these contextual shifts.

Romance during Adolescence

Relative to other individuals at different stages in the life cycle, adolescents seem to be particularly preoccupied with romance. Some debate exists as to where and how adolescent girls acquire and process information about romantic love. One line of argument suggests that girls actively shape the culture of romance during adolescence. From this vantage point, adolescents' romantic behavior and interactions are largely self- (or intragroup-) regulated. However, another line of argument stresses that girls are passive receptors of cultural messages about romance. Here, girls do not decide for themselves what constitutes appropriate forms of romantic behavior or appropriate romantic feelings. Rather, girls learn how to think and act in romantic ways from adults, who themselves are bound by cultural codes that delimit "right" or "wrong" romantic behavior and feelings. To some, this latter argument explains why heterosexuality is so common. Dominant cultural codes, in other words, rarely "condone" same-sex romantic love.

A middle-ground perspective suggests that adolescent girls construct "romance" within a larger cultural framework. Their awareness of and attitudes toward romance do not develop in a vacuum, but they do not internalize dominant cultural codes without critical reflection either. In this light, adolescent concepts of romance emerge from local interpretation of more global symbolic systems.

What might romance during adolescence look like? Early adolescents often value the companionship of romantic relationships, using close friendships as an interpersonal template against which to describe and measure their experiences with romantic partners. As adolescents enter young adulthood, however, their romantic relationships derive less from infatuation and companionability than intimacy and commitment. Shared values, emotional closeness, care giving and care receiving, and mutual support characterize the romantic relationships of older adolescents, thereby signifying the onset of attachment transfer from parents to romantic partners. Romance during early and middle adolescence is more affiliative in nature, whereas romance during late adolescence and young adulthood is more akin to mature affectional bonds that typify marital relationships. Notably, interactions with friends and family members remain decisive factors in the quality and course of romantic relationships at all points in the adolescent life cycle.

College Women's Romantic Relationships

The brief discussion above sets the stage for a closer examination of women's romantic relationships during college. In many cases, traditional-age female college students are moving toward more serious types of romantic relationships but also are more conscious of cultural expectations that limit the extent to which they can enjoy the many dimensions of adult romance. The bind they face is complex. From a developmental perspective, women's romantic relationships can be more intimate and supportive in college than those experienced in high school, but with intimacy and closeness comes a newfound awareness of cultural codes that are perhaps more personally relevant than ever before. Stated differently, teenage girls are privy to female stereotypes but still somewhat shielded from them, since romance in early and middle adolescence is more camaraderie-based. Therefore, the "interpersonal expert–sexual ingénue" dichotomy is less proximate and less pronounced. In college, by contrast, romantic relationships assume several dimensions of adult romance (commitment, trust, respect), which may heighten the salience of the feminine ideal. For example, college women, now familiar with intimacy and care giving, can better apprehend their culturally sanctioned role with respect to such. The appropriate parameters of sexual desire may seem particularly problematic, given the increased freedom that characterizes college life, although the struggle to reconcile "being good" with sexual desire begins as early as age twelve for girls.

Depression is not uncommon among college women who are involved in romantic relationships. The physical proximity of the romantic partner, the balance of power between partners, and the communication strategies employed by each partner together increase or decrease the likelihood of depressive symptoms reported by women. Such symptoms also may surface in the aftermath of a breakup with a romantic partner. In line with maturational models, romance can be quite serious in college, and breakups can precipitate a sense of tremendous loss or sadness. Connections to peers are critical to a host of key student outcomes (e.g., retention, academic achievement) for a number of reasons, not the least of which is the security that close peer relationships can provide. When romantic attachments to peers are forged and then broken, adjustment can be disrupted considerably. Some women, however, may feel less depressed following a breakup if the relationship itself was conflict-laden or unsatisfying.

The quality of women's romantic relationships in college owes to factors both intrinsic and extrinsic to the student. A young woman's feminist orientation might influence her relationships with opposite-sex partners, as might the strategies that she employs to assert power within the dyad (Falbo and Peplau 1980). Men's beliefs and assumptions about women generally and their female partners specifically also play into relationship dynamics.

For many female college students, the importance of friends may wane as a romantic relationship becomes more serious. To maintain the romantic relationship, young women may chose to spend most of their time with their romantic partner, much to the detriment of close camaraderie with friends. Given the many developmental advantages conferred by close friendships, this conflict can be problematic.

In a groundbreaking study of women's romantic relationships during college, Dorothy Holland and Margaret Eisenhart (1990) concluded that both academic pursuits and same-sex friendships fell by the wayside in the presence of romantic relationships among women in their sample. Being sexually attractive to men and "having a boyfriend" promised much greater clout on campus than did scholarly achievement. Moreover, the cultural premium placed on romance virtually barred these women from establishing and sustaining close friendships with other female students, who were viewed as competitors in a zero-sum romantic climate. For the women in Holland and Eisenhart's study, internalized cultural dictums prompted women to prioritize romantic relationships at the expense of academic achievement and female solidarity, which attests further to the pervasive cultural forces that circumscribe female students' interactions with others. Here, the culture of romance on the college campus inhibits rather than encourages women's sense of intrinsic self-worth (their "value" is determined not by their intellectual accomplishments but by their sexual appeal to men). Although the implications of this study are considerable, a large body of educational research that follows up on these findings has yet to emerge.

Research on the experiences of lesbian and bisexual female college students also is scarce. The discussion above has been limited largely to heterosexual romantic relationships because same-sex romance in both adolescence and college receives relatively little scholarly attention. A recent movement to acknowledge the fluidity of women's sexual identity over the life cycle also merits further attention (see Peplau 2001). Precisely because college is, for many, a period of much freedom and experimentation, women's sexual identities may be particularly elastic during the college years.

Shannon K. Gilmartin and Linda J. Sax

See also Part 6: Developmental Issues; Sexuality

References and further reading
Cancian, Francesca. 1986. "The Feminization of Love." *Signs: Journal of Women in Culture and Society* 11: 692–709.
Falbo, Toni, and Leticia Anne Peplau. 1980. "Power Strategies in Intimate Relationships." *Journal of Personality and Social Psychology* 38: 618–628.
Hazan, Cindy, and Phillip Shaver. 1987. "Romantic Love Conceptualized as an Attachment Process." *Journal of Personality and Social Psychology* 52: 511–524.
Holland, Dorothy C., and Margaret A. Eisenhart. 1990. *Educated in Romance: Women, Achievement, and College Culture.* Chicago: University of Chicago Press.
McCormick, Naomi B. 1979. "Come-Ons and Put-Offs: Unmarried Students' Strategies for Having and Avoiding Sexual Intercourse." *Psychology of Women Quarterly* 4: 194–211.
Peplau, Leticia Anne. 2001. "Rethinking Women's Sexual Orientation: An Interdisciplinary, Relationship-Focused Approach." *Personal Relationships* 8: 1–19.
Rose, Suzanna. 2000. "Heterosexism and the Study of Women's Romantic and Friend Relationships." *Journal of Social Issues* 56: 315–328.
Shulman, Shmuel, and Offer Kipnis. 2001. "Adolescent Romantic Relationships: A Look from the Future." *Journal of Adolescence* 24: 337–351.
Simon, Robin W., Donna Eder, and Cathy Evans. 1992. "The Development of Feeling Norms Underlying Romantic Love among Adolescent Females." *Social Psychology Quarterly* 55: 29–46.

Service Learning and Community Service

Community service and service learning encompass involvement in a service activity for another person, community, or agency for which the participant receives no tangible benefits. Service learning is distinguished by its focus on the learning aspect of this involvement, which is usually structured through intentional reflection by the participant on the activity and on what she has learned from her involvement. Most research has found that college women participate in service learning, community service, and volunteer experiences more than men do. Women appear to have a greater interest in participating in community service and service learning than do men and to be interested in different types of activities than are men. Involvement in these activities has been found to lead to many changes in participants; through their involvement women seem to accrue even more gains than men in academic skills, social responsibility, and self-concept.

Service learning and community service, although often used interchangeably, actually have distinct definitions. "Community service" generally refers to activities in which participants engage in some uncompensated activity for the benefit of those served. It does not necessarily connect in any formal or structured way with a student's academic experience, nor does the participant necessarily reflect upon or learn from her experiences. "Service learning," in contrast, involves both community service and intentional, explicit connection to students' academic experiences and necessarily involves structured reflection on the project, those served, and the student herself. Service learning has been described as having two aspects that are critical to efforts to renew the contemporary university. First, it is an extension of both traditional and transformational pedagogies in such a way that "it transforms and renews the educational enterprise as a whole. By linking the classroom to the world of praxis, it allows induction to complement deduction, personal discovery to challenge received truths, immediate experience to balance generalizations and abstract theory" (Zlotkowski 1998, 3). Second, service learning teaches students that knowledge is necessary for the public good as well as for individual gain.

Service learning has gained national visibility in the last twenty years, but it actually has roots that go as far back as the development of land grant universities and John Dewey's philosophies of active learning. Dewey believed that both communities and the students' academic experience would be enriched by the involvement of students.

Little research or writing exists that specifically focuses on the role or experience of women in community service and service learning. Indeed what literature on the matter exists primarily compares women's participation to men's, rather than exploring women's experiences in their own right. The literature is mixed on the question of gender and participation. The majority of studies addressing the relative participation of women and men in service learning and community service cite greater participation by women; however, other studies find no gender difference in participation. Explanations for the greater involvement of women include women's greater "affinity" for service work, their preparation for careers in service areas, and their greater openness to nontraditional forms of education. Several authors have argued that participation in community service and service learning is congruent with Carol Gilligan's "ethic of care." This moral orientation, which Gilligan found more often in women than in men, is "an activity of relationship, of seeing and responding to need, taking care of the world by sustaining the web of connection so that no one is left alone" (Gilligan 1982, 62). Although holding this ethic might predispose women to involvement in service activities, students also may participate in community service and service learning for personal gain as well, for example, to feel good about themselves, to develop career-related skills, or to meet others.

Only a few studies have documented dynamics specific to women, or gender differences beyond participation rates, in the context of service learning and community service. The small number of studies reflects the relative youth of research in this area and the lack of research focused on outcomes of participation rather than descriptors of participants or predictors of participation.

Ann H. Shiarella, Anne M. McCarthy, and Mary L. Tucker (2000) found significant gender differences in students' attitudes toward community service. They found that women as a group scored higher than men in all aspects measured in their study, including measures of attitudes that people should help the community, beliefs that one is part of one's community and should help, the costs of helping, awareness of needs in the community, desire to participate in community service, perceptions of the seriousness of the needs of the community, and career benefits. Kimberlee J. Trudeau and Ann S. Devlin (1996) found that female undergraduates were more likely to express interest in volunteering than were male undergraduate students and were more likely than men to be motivated to participate by altruistic feelings.

Trudeau and Devlin also found some significant gender differences in the types of service that interested female and male college students. Women were more likely than men to be interested in working with those socially discriminated against, with groups focusing on medical issues and disaster relief, and with teaching and mentoring programs. Women were more likely than men to be interested in long-term rather than short-term projects and more willing to participate in service projects requiring training.

Research has pointed to differential effects of service learning and community service for women and men. In 1999, Janet Eyler and Dwight E. Giles reported their findings from a national study of more than 1,500 college students. They found that women demonstrated more positive outcomes from their participation in service-learning projects than did men. Eyler and Giles found women had greater growth in the following areas: personal efficacy, communication skills, career skills, systemic problem locus, sense of the importance of social justice and the importance of volunteering time, and the beliefs that everyone should volunteer and that service should be required in schools. However, men showed greater growth in tolerance and community efficacy. Women, more so than men, reported learning more in service-learning classes than other classes and being intellectually challenged in service-learning settings. They were more likely to report that participation helped them to know themselves better and that it was rewarding to help others and to learn to work with others. They also perceived more academic learning benefits from their participation, in that they better understood the complexity of the issues and saw the issues in a new way. Participation also led to greater gains for women in feeling connected to the community.

Although female students seem to be more likely than their male counterparts to participate in service learning, volunteer efforts, and community service, their participation has not been reflected in the leadership in the field. There is much still to learn about the role of women in service learning and community service, be it as student participants, community members, or instructors. However, the findings to date indicate that women play a significant role in service-learning and community service experiences and are strongly affected by them.

Ellen M. Broido

References and further reading

Eyler, Janet, and Dwight E. Giles, Jr. 1999. *Where's the Learning in Service Learning?* San Francisco: Jossey-Bass.

Gilligan, Carol. 1982. *In a Different Voice: Psychological Theory and Women's Development.* Cambridge, MA: Harvard University Press.

Rhoads, Robert A., and Jeffery P. F. Howard, eds. 1998. *Academic Service Learning: A Pedagogy of Action and Reflection.* New Directions for Teaching and Learning no. 73. San Francisco: Jossey-Bass.

Shiarella, Ann H., Anne M. McCarthy, and Mary L. Tucker. 2000. "Development and Construct Validity of Scores on the Community Service Attitudes Scale." *Educational and Psychological Measurement* 60: 286–300.

Trudeau, Kimberlee J., and Ann S. Devlin. 1996. "College Students and Community Service: Who, With Whom, and Why?" *Journal of Applied Social Psychology* 26: 1867–1888.

Waterman, Alan S. 1997. "Student Characteristics in Service Learning." Pp. 95–106 in *Service Learning: Applications from the Research,* ed. Alan S. Waterman. Mahwah, NJ: Lawrence Erlbaum.

Zlotkowski, Edward. 1998. *Successful Service-Learning Programs: New Models of Excellence in Higher Education.* Bolton, MA: Anker.

Sexual Assault

Sexual assault involves all forms of forced, unwanted, or nonconsensual sexual activity (rape, oral or anal intercourse, or sexual experiences not involving intercourse). Men as well as women can be victims of sexual assault, but the majority of cases involve males violating females. Therefore, this entry refers to male perpetrators and female victims. Historically, sexual assault has been treated as a shameful secret that no one talked about; yet as long as coeducational institutions have existed, sexual assault on college campuses has occurred. In 1957, for instance, Eugene J. Kanin found that more than 20 percent of college women in the United States had been sexually victimized. It was not until the women's movement of the late 1960s and early 1970s that the issue became more public. Feminists demanded that issues considered personal and private, including rape, domestic violence, and sexual assault, deserved public scrutiny as evidence of pervasive gender inequality in and outside the home. Women's activists sparked media attention, put rape on the political agenda, increased empirical research on the subject, and inspired the creation of rape crisis centers, domestic violence shelters, and antirape advocacy organizations. They also encouraged campus change. In the early 1980s, *Ms.* magazine teamed with the Center for the Prevention and Control of Rape and psychology professor Dr. Mary Koss to conduct a three-year research project on sexual assault on college campuses. The study revealed that one in four undergraduate women had experienced rape or attempted rape. These stunning statistics forced college campuses across the country to begin to seriously address the issue. By 2000, sexual assault and acquaintance rape were household terms.

The incidence rates of women who are sexually assaulted on college campuses range from 15 to 25 percent, depending on the methodologies, questions, sampling, and definitions used in the research. Disturbingly, however, only about 5 percent of sexual assaults are reported. Low reporting rates are attributed to several factors, including embarrassment, fear of reprisal, memory error, lack of desire to recall the traumatic experience, the feeling that the victim is to blame, or reluctance to recognize the experience as sexual assault. In addition, the way an institution responds affects whether or not a student will report an incident.

Although there are situational factors and personality characteristics that put some women at greater risk for sexual assault, the most important risk factors are alcohol, myths, and stereotypes. Studies show that when a man initiates a date, pays the expenses, takes a date "parking," or drives his automobile, the risk for sexual aggression is greater. Also, a man's acceptance of traditional sex roles, involvement in interpersonal violence, or adversarial attitudes about relationships also contribute to sexual aggression in dating situations. Women who are victims of childhood abuse, hold liberal sexual attitudes, use alcohol, or have a number of sex partners are twice as likely to be victimized by rape as those without such risk profiles, according to some studies. Researchers disagree on whether or not there are specific personality characteristics putting women at greater risk for sexual assault. Some say there are no personality characteristics that put women at risk, whereas others suggest that low self-regard or negative self-image increases the risk. The disagreement stems from the difficulty in determining cause and effect when studying this very sensitive issue.

Alcohol use is associated with many campus sexual assaults and is frequently cited as a reason by women who blame themselves. Research has shown that up to 75 percent of men and 50 percent of women involved in campus sexual assaults were consuming alcohol at the time of the assault. Cultural biases are thought to permit the man who is drinking to be considered "not responsible for his actions," but the woman who is drinking "should have known better." Alcohol does not have a direct physiological effect that causes men to become sexually stimulated, but it is thought to influence or intensify sexual aggression and to decrease impulse control. A woman who drinks may be perceived as "loose" or interested in sex, and some men think nonconsensual sex is justified and acceptable if the woman is drunk. Although some argue that men pressure women to drink alcohol as a ploy to get them intoxicated and to then gain sexual favors, others feel that women need to be responsible for their choices, including the choice to drink. Either way, alcohol is clearly related to the incident rates of sexual assault on college campuses.

Gender stereotypes and rape myths are also associated with sexual assault. Some common rape myths and stereotypes include the following: women want it, they enjoy it; women ask for it, women deserve it; it only happens to certain types of women or to women from certain kinds of families; women tell lies and exaggerate; men are justified in their behavior and are not responsible for unintentional effects; and it's not really harmful. "It" in all of these myths or stereotypes refers to rape and sexual assault. Such myths perpetuate violence by placing the blame on the victim rather than on the perpetrator, which ultimately leads to the denial of assistance to victims. These misleading ideas also explain why so much research and so many intervention efforts focus on the victim and also sometimes blame the victim. For example, numerous programs exist for training women how to defend themselves or ways to avoid being an easy target. Less victim-focused approaches involve educating men about how to end rape.

Sexual assault is a problem that is not diminishing on college campuses. Whether by failing to take appropriate steps to prevent sexual assault or by mishandling cases once they occur, some colleges and universities contribute to the problem and may even perpetuate the violence rather than helping to end it. A key to addressing sexual assault is the open acknowledgement that sexual assaults do happen on campus, that is, promulgating public dialogue rather than disclaimers or lack of disclosure. If an institution's administration does not believe there is a problem, its policies defining sexual assault, handling sexual assault cases, and condemning the behavior are of little value. Policies and policy enforcement differ from campus to campus, depending on how each administration views the problem and potential solutions. Helpful policies regarding sexual assault must, at minimum, identify the behaviors that are prohibited, ensure enforcement of the procedures that will take place at and after the time of an incident, and provide protection for both male and female students, whether they are alleging an assault or are alleged to have assaulted another student. College campuses can and usually do offer a variety of services that can help victims, such as counseling, medical services, and victim advocacy.

Publicizing campus crime rates, sponsoring programs on ways to avoid sexual assault (for men and women), and offering ways to assist victims of rape are educational programming efforts that may help reduce incidence rates of sexual assault on college campuses. Many campuses have been offering self-defense programs for women for some time, and more recently programs for and by men have been added. Colleges and universities are realizing that rape is not just a woman's issue and that women alone cannot prevent the crimes from occurring.

Lee Scherer Hawthorne

See also Part 5: Legal Issues; Students' Rights

References and further reading

Bohmer, Carol, and Andrea Parrot. 1993. *Sexual Assault on Campus.* New York: Lexington Books.

Kanin, Eugene J. 1957. "Male Aggression in Dating-Courtship Relations." *American Journal of Sociology* 63: 197–204.

Parrot, Andrea. 1991. "Recommendations for College Policies and Procedures to Deal with Acquaintance Rape." Pp. 368–380 in *Acquaintance Rape: The Hidden Crime,* eds. Andrea Parrot and Laurie Bechhofer. New York: Wiley.

Rosen, Ruth. 2000. *The World Split Open: How the Modern Women's Movement Changed America.* New York: Viking.

Schwartz, Martin D., and Walter S. DeKeseredy. 1997. *Sexual Assault on the College Campus: The Role of Male Peer Support.* Thousand Oaks, CA: Sage.

Warshaw, Robin. 1988. *I Never Called it Rape: The* Ms. *Report on Recognizing, Fighting, and Surviving Date Rape and Acquaintance Rape.* New York: Harper and Row.

Sexuality

Students' sexuality includes expressions of emotional and physical affection between a women and a man and between two women. The development of college students' sexuality in the United States is entwined with social, cultural, and historical factors related to gender and higher education. Women have been pursuing degrees in higher education at institutionalized facilities in the United States since the early 1800s, with the opening of Mount Holyoke Female Seminary in 1837. With the growth throughout the 1800s of women's colleges and the increasing number of women on coeducational campuses, the issue of sexuality became extremely important for female students themselves and for the way in which they would come to be perceived. Initially, women who attended colleges or universities represented a challenge to the traditional ideologies of gender (and in some cases, race and class) and they were often threatened with the social stigma of lesbianism, frigidity, or promiscuity. These threats served as a form of baiting to keep women from pursuing advanced degrees or to control and constrain their sexuality within the public realm of the university campus. Because the college experience is often marked by an increased awareness of sexuality, this entry examines sexuality as it pertains to female students through two lenses, "Women's Movements and Sexual Liberation" and "Lesbianism and Bisexuality," to encompass a breadth of information regarding this topic.

Women's Movements and Sexual Liberation

With the success of Mount Holyoke Female Seminary, a number of other women's institutions, including Vassar (1865), Smith (1872), Wellesley (1875), and Bryn Mawr (1886) Colleges, were established for the benefit of women's higher education. These openings and the growing number of women entering colleges in general had multiple and interconnected effects. Not only did they increase the number of women receiving public education and degrees, but they simultaneously challenged the traditional expectation of white middle-class women to move from the domestic sphere of their father's home to that of their husband's home. In general, they changed what women perceived as their life goals, offering new opportunities and an escape from heterosexual domesticity. Those women for whom a college education was possible discovered that economic survival did not require marriage or a man.

By the 1920s, faculty and administrators at the women's colleges became concerned about the attitudes and behaviors of the new "college girl," who seemed more interested in socializing than in studying. Policies designed to maintain chasteness and to limit opportunities for heterosexual activity were only marginally successful, as students found ways to thwart regulations regarding smoking, drinking alcohol, dancing, and socializing with men. The influx of military veterans after World War II further exacerbated the situation, as campus social climates were marked by an emphasis on heterosexual activity and marriageability.

In 1960, the Food and Drug Administration (FDA) approved distribution of the birth control pill, which began to alter the public perception of premarital sex, in addition to placing additional responsibility within heterosexual relationships on women. This period, often called the "sexual revolution," happened in tandem with the growing strength of the women's liberation movement during the mid- to late 1960s. Liberation was equated with the sexual freedom that the birth control pill provided. As women left their families to enter college, they were forced to deal with many contradictory messages—the notions of being a "good girl" and the freedom of sex without consequences. Female college students faced new choices regarding careers and marriage, as well as contraception, and quickly began to earn a reputation as sexually "free" and "liberated."

Lesbianism and Bisexuality

Not only did the emergence of women's colleges introduce an alternative form of education, but also they created a space where newly recognized forms of intimate and sexual relationships between women became tacitly accepted. Before terms such as "lesbian," "bisexual," or even "homosexual" entered the mainstream lexicon in the early 1900s, emotional and sometimes physical relationships between women were referred to as romantic friendships or Boston marriages. As Lillian Faderman describes in *Odd Girls and Twilight Lovers* (1991), these friendships were encouraged within academia, where women found the time and the occasion to meet with one another and form such relationships. Certainly, romantic friendships existed before and outside the confines of the university, but it was the formation of public spaces for women, such as at women's colleges, that made romantic friendships and (later on) lesbian life possible in the twentieth century.

Although people were already organizing in places such as Los Angeles, San Francisco, and New York City, the beginning of the gay liberation movement is historically marked by riots at the Stonewall Inn in New York City in June 1969. Along with the women's liberation movement and other social movements of the time, gay liberation largely manifested itself among college students on various campuses. It was not until after the Stonewall riots, though, that so-called homophile—now called lesbian, gay, bisexual, and transgender (LGBT)—student groups began to flourish on a variety of college campuses. As such, the issue of sexuality for college students and lesbian and bisexual female students in particular became one about oppression, personal identity, and freedom of expression.

As LGBT student groups continued to organize socially, politically, and institutionally, many universities were forced to deal with sexual diversity in terms of administrative structures and curriculum. In "Historicizing Outsiders on Campus," Kathleen O'Mara explains that as "cultural diversity" became a university mission in the 1980s and 1990s, "sexual difference achieved official recognition" (1997). With such recognition, some campuses succeeded in establishing and maintaining LGBT program offices and resource centers specifically to provide student support services, networking, counseling, and information and to serve as a meeting place and as a means of connection among faculty, administrators, and students. The first of these program offices was established as the Lesbian–Gay Male Program Office at the University of Michigan in 1971.

In addition to the formation of such offices and centers, gay, lesbian, and bisexual students began to speak out about the homophobic and heterosexist climate of the university. Students spoke of feeling alienated in the classroom, in their residence halls, and on campus in general. As new LGBT program offices and resources centers are established, the climate for gay, lesbian, bisexual, and transgender students seems to be getting warmer. To aid in this process, reference guides such as Jan-Mitchell Sherrill and Craig A. Hardesty's *The Gay, Lesbian, and Bisexual Students' Guide to Colleges, Universities, and Graduate Schools* (1994) have been published to assess the climate of university campuses, faculty, and curriculum, thus allowing LGBT students to make more informed choices regarding their education.

There is a difference, however, in the way lesbian and bisexual women experience the university and their relationship to LGBT program offices, women's resource centers, the women's liberation movement, and the gay liberation movement. Lesbians and bisexual women often feel that issues specifically dealing with gender or female sexuality are ignored for the sake of solidarity, public recognition, and acceptance. Even with the recent promotion of "queer" as a label for student groups and campus newspapers, lesbian and bisexual women have argued that the pervasiveness of patriarchy has led to the reformulation of "gay" as "queer," thus perpetuating the marginality they feel as women. To address concerns about marginality, women's colleges have persevered, and women's studies programs and departments have been developed and persist. Furthermore, the creation of sexuality studies, specifically lesbian studies, has offered lesbian and bisexual female students an academic avenue within the university.

The issue of sexuality for female college students is a historically complicated and multifaceted situation. It combines the admission of women to colleges in general, the birth of women's colleges, changing perceptions of gender roles at the turn of and throughout the twentieth century, the women's liberation movement, the birth control pill, the gay liberation movement, the creation of women's studies as well as LGBT campus offices and resource centers, and queer activism. Developments are always in flux, combining in different ways and at different moments in time to create multiple individual experiences. As the strict division of gender roles is blurred in accepting women's presence in higher education, so too is it blurred in accepting the various ways in which women represent and express their sexuality.

Sarah M. Tillery

See also Part 1: Lesbian, Gay, Bisexual, and Transgender Issues on Campus; Part 6: Activism; Romantic Relationships; Sexual Assault

References and further reading

Bailey, Beth. 1999. *Sex in the Heartland.* Cambridge, MA: Harvard University Press.

Faderman, Lillian. 1991. *Odd Girls and Twilight Lovers: A History of Lesbian Life in Twentieth-Century America.* New York: Penguin Books.

Horowitz, Helen Lefkowitz. 1987. *Campus Life: Undergraduate Cultures from the End of the Eighteenth Century to the Present.* New York: Alfred A. Knopf.

Mallory, Sherry L. 1998. "Lesbian, Gay, Bisexual, and Transgender Student Organizations: An Overview." Pp. 321–328 in *Working with Lesbian, Gay, Bisexual, and Transgender College Students: A Handbook for Faculty and Administrators,* ed. Ronni L. Sanlo. Westport, CT: Greenwood Press.

O'Mara, Kathleen. 1997. "Historicizing Outsiders on Campus: The Re/production of Lesbian and Gay Insiders." *Journal of Gender Studies* 6, no. 1 (March): 17–32.

Pharr, Suzanne. 1998. "Homophobia as a Weapon of Sexism." Pp. 565–574 in *Race, Class, and Gender in the United States,* ed. Paula S. Rothenberg. 4th ed. New York: St. Martin's Press.

Sherrill, Jan-Mitchell, and Craig A. Hardesty. 1994. *The Gay, Lesbian, and Bisexual Students' Guide to Colleges, Universities, and Graduate Schools.* New York: New York University Press.

Zemsky, Beth. 1996. "GLBT Program Offices: A Room of Our Own." Pp. 208–214 in *The New Lesbian Studies: Into the Twenty-First Century,* eds. Bonnie Zimmerman and Toni A. H. McNaron. New York: The Feminist Press.

Socioeconomic Status

Women's access to college education differs by the social class background of the student. From their initial entry into higher education in the mid-1800s, women from middle and upper classes usually attended elite women's colleges, whereas women from farm and other working-class families often enrolled in normal schools, which were teacher-training institutions. As state colleges grew and normal schools declined in the period following World War I, women from low socioeconomic status (SES) backgrounds began to shift their enrollment to four-year public teaching colleges. However, rising tuition costs and the Depression forced many low-SES women out of public four-year colleges, whereas the numbers of women from higher status backgrounds in these institutions began to grow. High-SES students also continued to be the vast majority at the elite private women's colleges. Some of the low-SES women who no longer had access to state colleges turned to the new junior colleges to continue their education. These institutions saw an increasing proportion of low-SES students after World War II, more than a third of whom were women. Two-year colleges disproportionately attracted low-SES women in the period from the 1950s onward; currently, the majority of community college students are women from low-SES backgrounds. Women from high-status families continue to matriculate at prestigious private and public four-year institutions, whereas low-SES women enroll in less prestigious four-year colleges and community colleges. Although the majority of women in college are segregated by social class, throughout the history of women's higher education in the United States, low-SES women have gained access to prestigious institutions in small numbers. This access has come at a price, however, as these women often feel isolated and uncomfortable.

Women's access to postsecondary education began in 1837 with the founding of Mount Holyoke by Mary Lyon. Herself the product of a poor farm background, Lyon strove to keep tuition costs low in order to keep access to education affordable. Although Lyon wished to attract mature women from poor farm families, the other women's colleges that were to become the "seven sisters" targeted the daughters of higher status families. The proportion of women from all social class backgrounds participating in higher education increased rapidly. Prior to 1900, although only 4 percent of the population went to college, women were 40 percent of all students.

The growing demand for teachers also affected women's education because the majority of teachers were women from a range of social class backgrounds. Believing that an educated citizenry was essential to the new republic, many states began sponsoring the study of teaching. As a result, the normal school, a new type of postsecondary institution, was founded to increase the quality of teaching.

Women from lower status farm and working-class families flocked to the new normal schools and quickly became the majority. By 1900, more than half of all women pursuing postsecondary education did so at normal schools and teachers' colleges. One reason for the popularity of normal schools was free tuition in many states, sometimes offered in exchange for teaching in common schools after graduation. Women from farm and other working-class backgrounds were encouraged to teach as a means of self-support and to make themselves useful after finishing common school and before marrying. Normal school attendance and teaching were vehicles of upward mobility for immigrants and African Americans as well. Irish Americans took advantage of normal schools in the late 1800s and by 1910 had become the largest group of teachers in New York City.

In contrast to the free tuition at many normal schools, tuition costs at many private women's institutions increased during the late 1800s and early 1900s. As women's participation in higher education increased, so did the need for financial aid, especially for low-SES students. This need was particularly acute at the elite women's colleges, and although only 6 percent of women received any type of aid in 1900, more than 20 percent did so by 1920. The majority of students at elite institutions did not work, but working while pursuing an education was increasingly common between 1900 and 1919 at these institutions. Administrators at these colleges worried that only the wealthy would be able to attend and so publicized student budgets and the fact that students could work their way through in an effort to attract poorer students.

Some schools also assisted students in finding employment and tried to raise scholarship money. Securing scholarship funding was difficult, and the scholarships were minimal, requiring students also to work. Additionally, scholarships were not given to first-year students and so could not be utilized to attract poor students who could not afford to enroll initially. Furthermore, some schools placed working students in separate living quarters or assigned them the smallest and least expensive rooms. These actions highlighted social class differences among students.

Following World War I, as the number of college students grew, normal schools declined and were replaced by the public four-year city and state college systems. Women from low-SES backgrounds shifted their enrollment to these four-year public colleges as well as to the new Catholic women's colleges. Women from high-SES backgrounds continued to have advantages in accessing higher education and to comprise the majority at private elite women's colleges.

During the period between the two world wars, low-SES Jewish women, like their male counterparts, began to gain access to higher education in larger numbers than before. For example, many Jewish women in New York City attended public colleges such as Brooklyn College and Hunter College, and some also attended elite private institutions such as Barnard. These women were largely commuter students, an important factor for those who could not afford the costs of paying for room and board at other, more rurally situated private schools. Barnard was also the least expensive of the elite women's colleges prior to 1920 and had the highest number of Jewish students of the sister institutions. Additionally, low-SES African American women began to gain access to the northern system of city and state colleges during this period. Regardless of race or ethnicity, many low-SES women continued to be self-supporting and worked their way through college.

However, rising tuition costs during the 1920s and later the Depression forced many low-SES women out of public four-year colleges. At the same time, particularly following the Depression, the numbers of women from higher status backgrounds in these institutions began to grow. Some of the low-SES women who no longer had access to state colleges turned to the new junior colleges to continue their education.

Two-year institutions saw an increasing proportion of low-SES students after World War II, more than a third of whom were women. Throughout the 1950s and 1960s, low-SES students, including a high proportion of women, became increasingly concentrated at the two-year colleges. At prestigious institutions, including private women's colleges, however, high-SES students remained heavily overrepresented. Daughters of manual laborers comprised less than 10 percent of students at private women's colleges in the late 1950s, compared to just over 30 percent at state teachers' colleges. One study found that low-SES women had more barriers to overcome to enroll in college than did their male counterparts from the late 1950s to the late 1960s.

In the mid-1960s, however, national legislation tied economic progress directly to college attendance for poor youth and provided the financial aid to do so. As a result, the proportion of students entering higher education from the lowest segments of the economy nearly doubled, from 12 to 22 percent. Many of those entering higher education, however, did so at the least prestigious institutions. By the mid-1970s, women became the majority at two-year colleges, almost ten years before they became the majority at four-year colleges and universities. The vast majority (75 percent) of two-year students during the 1970s were from low-SES backgrounds, and women attending two-year institutions were from lower social class backgrounds than men.

The gains following the 1965 legislation were lost by the late 1980s, however. Currently, like the attendees of normal schools before them, the majority of community college students are women from low-SES backgrounds. Women from high-status families continue to matriculate at prestigious private and public four-year institutions, whereas low-SES women enroll in less prestigious four-year colleges and community colleges.

Although the majority of low-SES women have always enrolled in a different segment of the U.S. higher education system, a few have historically and are currently enrolled in prestigious colleges and universities. Whether or not the prestigious institutions highlight differences in amenities or activities for students from different classes, the students know the background from which other students come. The possibility of feeling isolated or uncomfortable may dissuade a young woman from attempting to gain admission and in that sense may help perpetuate the segregated nature of women's college experiences.

MaryBeth Walpole

See also Part 1: Community Colleges; Part 2: Class; Part 4: Teacher Education; Part 6: Persistence

References and further reading

Faragher, John M., and Florence Howe, eds. 1988. *Women and Higher Education in American History.* New York: W. W. Norton.

Goodlad, John I., Roger Soder, and Kenneth A. Sirotnik, eds. 1990. *Places Where Teachers Are Taught.* San Francisco: Jossey-Bass.

Levine, Arthur, and Jana Nidiffer. 1996. *Beating the Odds: How the Poor Get to College.* San Francisco: Jossey-Bass.

McDonough, Patricia M. 1997. *Choosing Colleges: How Social Class and Schools Structure Opportunity.* Albany: State University of New York Press.

Touchton, Judith G., and Lynne Davis. 1991. *Fact Book on Women in Higher Education.* New York: Macmillan.

Sororities

Sororities, or Greek-letter societies for college women and alumnae, have a distinct purpose within American higher education and are more than mirror images of men's fraternities. On a surface level, sororities share the characteristic mottoes, crests, colors, badges, grips, passwords, songs, rivalries, and initiation rites of men's fraternities and other literary and secret societies, which first flourished in the 1800s. Like fraternities, sororities improved the quality of student life by fulfilling member needs for friendship, housing, and dining. However, on coeducational college campuses where male students dominated campus life, sororities also served as an important vehicle for enhancing women's position within the campus political structure. Yet because sororities served as exclusive voluntary associations for collegiate women just as higher educational opportunities were expanding for some American women, their existence confirms the stronghold of American values related to competition, exclusion, personal success, and sponsored mobility. Thus, sororities' mixed legacy of privilege and exclusion of some women in the face of campus discrimination against all women reveals much about women's autonomy and the prevailing collegiate notions of womanhood and gender expectations over time.

The oldest sororities trace their heritage to the Adelphean (Alpha Delta Pi) and Philomathean (Phi Mu) literary and "secret" societies at Wesleyan Female College in Macon, Georgia, founded in 1851 and 1852, respectively. These groups did not identity as "fraternities" or seek to expand their membership to other campuses until after the turn of the century. I. C. Sorosis was founded as the first national women's fraternity in 1867 at Monmouth College in Monmouth, Illinois. Although the society quickly established associate chapters in other locations, these chapters soon closed, and the organization became Pi Beta Phi Fraternity in 1888, when advantage was gained by the adoption of Greek letters. The organization of Kappa Alpha Theta and Kappa Kappa Gamma occurred in 1870, the first at what is now DePauw University and the second at Monmouth College. Interestingly, these two women's groups were intentionally created to adopt the principles and methods of men's organizations. The years 1872 and 1873 brought the creation of Alpha Phi at Syracuse and later, Delta Gamma in Oxford, Mississippi. Most important, Gamma Phi Beta (1874, Syracuse University) was the first group to identify as a "sorority" after a Latin professor on the faculty coined the term. The West Coast experienced its first sorority founding in 1909, when Beta Phi Alpha was established at the University of California, Berkeley. Yet even this brief period of the sorority movement evidences that new Greek-letter groups most often began either where the first group(s) gave a model to emulate or where exclusivity and discrimination created the demand for new opportunities.

As different kinds of educational opportunities expanded to new female populations, new Greek-letter societies were created. The membership, purpose, and mission of these new organizations were originally designed to meet the needs and interests of women in growing academic fields and institutions. For example, women created their own professional recognition societies in many academic fields, such as Pi Kappa Sigma (1894, education), Nu Sigma Phi (1898, medicine), Delta Omega (1904, osteopathy), Kappa Beta Pi (1908, law), Delta Omicron (1909, music), Phi Upsilon Omicron (1909, home economics), Phi Beta (1912, music and drama), Delta Psi Kappa (1916, physical education), Gamma Epsilon Pi (1918, commerce), Pi Delta Nu (1919, chemistry), Kappa Epsilon (1921, pharmaceuticals), and Alpha Alpha Gamma (1922, architecture). These trends were also present in the creation of social sororities as well. For example, Alpha Chi Omega (1885, DePauw) was assisted in its founding by the dean of the school of music and maintained an interest in the fine arts throughout the school's early years. Several national sororities were founded at Longwood College (then the Virginia State Normal School in Farmville, Virginia), including Zeta Tau Alpha (1898), Kappa Delta (1897), Sigma Sigma Sigma (1898), and Alpha Sigma Alpha (1901). Where African American women had educational opportunities, they also founded Greek-letter societies. Three of these groups originated at Howard University in Washington, D.C.—Alpha Kappa Alpha (1908), Delta Sigma Theta (1913), and Zeta Phi Beta (1920). Another, Sigma Gamma Rho, was founded in Indianapolis, Indiana, in 1922 and gained incorporation as a national collegiate sorority when chartered at Butler University in 1929.

Even junior colleges were not immune from the influence of Greek-letter societies, for Stephens College in Columbia, Missouri, witnessed the birth of three national junior college sororities in 1921—Kappa Delta Phi, Zeta Mu Epsilon, and Theta Tau Epsilon.

Other social sororities responded to religious diversity at colleges by incorporating new practices into their rituals and membership drives to attract females other than Anglo-Saxon Protestant women. Theta Phi Alpha (1912) was founded at the University of Michigan as a sorority for Catholic women at nonsectarian, coeducational institutions. Iota Alpha Pi (1903, Hunter College), Alpha Epsilon Phi (1909, Barnard College), and Delta Phi Epsilon (1917, Washington Square College of New York University) began as sororities for Jewish women. Still, another group, Phi Sigma Sigma (1913, Hunter College) was organized as explicitly nonsectarian by its Jewish and non-Jewish founders. Interestingly, a map of the chapter rolls for many of these groups, combined with the advance of the professional Greek-letter societies for women, gives insight into the spread of educational opportunities for women in general and the access of female minority groups to higher education as well. For example, the creation of Nu Sigma Phi in 1898 as a sorority for women in medicine and Delta Omega in 1904 as a sorority for women in osteopathy confirms that some educational opportunities existed for women that would only later be decreased as the field of medicine became "professionalized" in the twentieth century. Another example challenges notions about regional diversity and patterns of chapter colonization and support. Although four of the first five chapters of Alpha Epsilon Phi, an organization for Jewish women (1909, Barnard College), were founded in New York, the fifth chapter colonized at Sophie Newcomb College in New Orleans, the twenty-second at Vanderbilt University (1925), the twenty-fourth at the University of Texas (1925), and the twenty-ninth at Duke University (1933). Also, in 1935 Alpha Epsilon Phi located its national office "centrally" in New Orleans. Although the South had not witnessed as many sorority births as the Northeast and was considered a major prospect for sorority expansion in the first quarter of the century, the southern advance of a "Jewish" sorority remains worthy of note.

Even this brief history of the sorority movement confirms that Greek-letter societies for women truly flourished, as did the Progressive spirit and the university movement around the turn of the century. By 1935, sororities' philanthropic work included but was not limited to support for social science research, missionary societies, settlement houses and schools, child welfare reform, nurseries and home for orphans, care for "crippled and underprivileged children," frontier nursing services, hygiene and health clinics, mountain schools, and war relief overseas. In black sororities, the philanthropic mission was amplified and took on the additional dimension of racial uplift, social activism, and support for civil rights. For example, the first public act of Delta Sigma Theta (1913, Howard University) was to march in a women's suffrage parade down Pennsylvania Avenue in Washington, D.C. (13 March 1913). The activities of black sororities in partnership with black fraternities have included providing leadership for the American Council on Human Rights and support for the National Council of Negro Women, the National Urban

League, and the National Association for the Advancement of Colored People, to name a few.

The Progressive eye of reform also focused inward, and a new emphasis on democratic student government resulted in the creation of many new organizations, alliances, and federations. In this matter, sorority women pioneered. At the urging of Kappa Kappa Gamma (1870, Monmouth), the first national pan-Hellenic convention occurred in 1891. By 1902, the National Panhellenic Congress (later "Conference") had formed for the purpose of maintaining on a "high plane fraternity life and interfraternity relationship, to cooperate with college authorities in their effort to maintain high social and scholastic standards throughout the whole college, and to be a forum for the discussion of questions of interest to the college and fraternity world" (National Panhellenic Conference website). By contrast, the National Interfraternity Conference, the cooperative association for fraternities, did not form until 1909. In 1929, the National Pan-Hellenic Council took shape as an association for the eight fraternities and sororities that were "interracial in character" but whose membership was "dominantly Negro." But even these early efforts at reform and promotion through national association could not always head off anti-Greek sentiment on the part of faculty, and sorority chapters were chartered and closed during the same era at Barnard, Swarthmore, Hollins, Wesleyan, Winston-Salem, and Mary Baldwin.

Combined with the strong legacy of sorority philanthropic work, the rituals and early songs of almost every social sorority are artifacts of the clubwoman era and offer some variation on the theme of "ideal or true womanhood." Yet the much more permissive behaviors of sorority women today suggests that over time, sororities achieved for college women what women's clubs achieved for women in the larger community. Just as clubwomen faced constraints upon public participation in the larger community, college women not only faced academic restrictions but also encountered many barriers when attempting to participate in campus life. For example, historian Helen Horowitz reveals that by the later nineteenth century, fraternities and their secular, affluent, competitive, and ambitious members gained an inordinate influence on American campus life. In Horowitz's typology of students as insiders, outsiders, and rebels, fraternity men were privileged as the classic campus insider with control of the lively extracurriculum. As women gained access to higher education, the more affluent and conventional college women embraced sororities as a tool for aligning themselves with campus leaders to avoid being "outsiders." Besides making inroads into the campus political structure, the Greek system and its "gender-differentiated prestige system" gave college women increased control over their identity and sexuality. Joining a sorority in general and a "better" sorority in particular offered college women instant validation of self-worth and entrée to acceptable romantic partners and future marriage prospects. Over time, sorority women have parlayed their increasing autonomy into new ideals, behaviors, and expectations for themselves and their organizations.

Today the campus branches of the twenty-six sororities in the National Panhellenic Conference and the four sororities in the National Pan-Hellenic Council together claim more than 3.8 million initiated members and 9,950 collegiate and alumnae chapters. An unknown host of "local" sororities adds to these impressive numbers. Together, these sororities raise millions of dollars annually for various philanthropic and nonprofit organizations and provide countless hours of volunteer and community service work. Elaborate education programs enhance members' quality of life. In the case of collegians, for example, sororities raise awareness of problems such as eating disorders, date and acquaintance rape, sexual harassment, depression, and alcohol abuse. Furthermore, these organizations furnish an arena in which members can strengthen skills related to leadership, parliamentary procedure, business operation, collaboration, communication, and coalition building. Sororities also promote professional and academic success through elaborate alumni networking programs, directory services, scholarships, and graduate fellowships. At their best, sororities are "feminist" organizations that assist college women in self-expression and autonomy within the confines of patriarchal institutions of higher education. In this way, sororities allow members to create meaningful personal relationships that support satisfaction with college life, academic achievement, graduation, and alumni loyalty.

At their worst, sororities undermine democratic values, distract members from academics, and promote superficial standards of beauty. Although some campus pan-Hellenic organizations are sponsoring recruitment reforms such as philanthropy nights and "no frills" recruitment events devoid of skits, costumes, and fancy refreshments, the painful anecdotes of women feeling "rejected" and transferring or dropping out of school remind critics that sorority recruitment results can disrupt new student orientation and campus-wide efforts to promote inclusion. The fact that individual chapters can easily become stigmatized on a particular campus and fail to thrive despite financial and membership recruitment support from national organizations shows the strong persistence of Greek prestige systems. The Greek hierarchical prestige systems that continually assess women and whole sororities based upon wealth and appearance of members undermine women's self-esteem and further exacerbate health problems such as anorexia. Finally, anecdotes and statistics about hazing and high-risk drinking incidents show that all too often in the name of tradition and sisterhood, sororities have encumbered academic performance and carelessly endangered the lives of their members.

Amy E. Wells

See also Part 6: Black Sororities; Extracurricular Activities

References and further reading

Baird's Manual of American College Fraternities. 1927–1977. Menasha, WI: Collegiate Press, George Banta Publishing Company.

Blair, Karen J. 1980. *The Clubwoman as Feminist: True Womanhood Redefined, 1868–1914.* New York: Holmes and Meier Publishers.

Giddings, Paula. 1988. *In Search of Sisterhood: Delta Sigma Theta and the Challenge of the Black Sorority Movement.* New York: William Morrow.

National Panhellenic Conference website. http://www.npcwomen.org. Cited June 15, 2002.

Nuwer, Hank. 1999. *Wrongs of Passage: Fraternities, Sororities, Hazing, and Binge Drinking.* Bloomington: Indiana University Press.

Ross, Lawrence C. 2000. *The Divine Nine: The History of African American Fraternities and Sororities.* New York: Kensington Publishers.

Wright, Esther. 1996. *Torn Togas: The Dark Side of Campus Greek Life.* Minneapolis: Fairview Press.

Undergraduates and Science

Despite advances in recent decades, women continue to have a minority presence in undergraduate science, mathematics, and engineering (SME) fields. Women's persistent underrepresentation in scientific disciplines is troublesome, given the growing need for scientifically informed, technologically savvy college graduates. If women's perspectives are on the margins of science, we can expect that new technologies will tend to favor men, perhaps ignoring the unique needs of women (and in the case of biased medical research, potentially endangering them). It is critical, then, that we examine women's experiences in science with the goal of understanding factors leading to persistence and attrition. Precollege encounters with science and math contribute to women's decisions to pursue SME majors in college, and classroom experiences, the influence of faculty and peers, and levels of self-confidence during college further shape women's educational and career paths. Recruitment and intervention strategies both before and during the undergraduate years can promote women's commitment to SME fields.

Students performing a scientific experiment (Courtesy of the Association of Women in Science)

The Status of Women in SME Fields During College

Though women are more likely than men to graduate from high school, subsequently enroll in college, and earn a bachelor's degree within five years, they are less visible than men in SME fields. According to the National Science Foundation (2000), in the 1997–1998 academic year, women received only 35 percent of SME bachelor's degrees. These disparities are played out further in the world of work, where women constitute nearly half the workforce but claim only about 12 percent of the science and engineering jobs.

Women are not the minority in all SME fields. In fact, women are overrepresented in the biological and life sciences (55 percent of bachelor's degree earners were women) and have nearly reached parity with men in mathematics, earning 46 percent of the bachelor's degrees in 1997–1998. In agricultural fields and the physical sciences, women are moderately underrepresented (41 percent and 38 percent, respectively), but computer science (27 percent) and engineering (17 percent) severely lack the presence of female students.

The Reasons for Women's Underrepresentation in Some Fields

Girls' precollege educational experiences play a significant role in later decisions to pursue SME majors during college. As early as the seventh grade, girls express less confidence than boys in their math and science abilities, demonstrate more negative attitudes toward these fields, are less likely to aspire to math or science occupations, and have already begun to fall behind in their science preparation. Scores on math and science standardized tests tend to be lower for girls than boys, though girls' achievement in science and math, as measured by course grades, is at least as high (if not higher) than their male peers.

By high school, young women complete fewer math and science courses than do young men, often meeting only the minimum requirements to graduate from high school. At higher levels of math, men tend to outperform women. Women also are less likely to participate in math- and science-related extracurricular activities and have few female role models in these fields.

Socioeconomic status (SES) and racial and ethnic identity contribute to women's math and science aspirations. Women from upper-level SES backgrounds score higher on math and science achievement indicators than those representing the lower SES levels. In addition, young women with more highly educated parents are more likely to enter science fields, as are women with mothers who are employed as college teachers or research scientists. Though women overall are underrepresented among SME degree earners, their underrepresentation is less extreme among racial and ethnic minority groups. That is, nonwhite women tend to earn a more balanced share of SME degrees awarded to all nonwhite students.

At all levels of education (precollege and college), women's socialization acts to discourage their participation in science, mathematics, and engineering. Teachers, parents, and the media may relay messages to girls and young women that science and math are not appropriate pursuits for women, thus steering them into nonscience majors in college. In an effort to fit in with the peer culture and avoid social alienation, women may deemphasize any interest they may have in pursing SME fields. Aside from the overt messages of teachers, parents, peers, and the media, institutional structures may simply fail to support females' pursuit of math and science by withholding the necessary resources to develop talent (e.g., female role models, adequate academic preparation, guidance, etc.). In addition, warm and affirming teacher-learner relationships are found less often in SME fields; this aspect of climate is critical since women tend to base their self-images on the opinions and approval of others.

Another facet of SME that conflicts with female socialization is the perception that such fields are isolating, detached from social contexts, and not conducive to raising a family. Women who need their educational, career, and personal goals to relate holistically may be turned off by science, math, and engineering for these very reasons.

The Science Environment in College

For those who maintain an interest in and commitment to science despite the obstacles, college experiences with SME provide a new set of challenges. In every field except for biology, women will typically find themselves in the minority. The absence of other females, both in terms of peers and faculty, may serve to isolate women.

The lower confidence in math and science exhibited by women in the precollege years is exacerbated during college. Decreases in self-confidence, though, are not matched by decreases in ability or achievement. For example, though degree completion rates in engineering are lower for women than for men, women typically have stronger academic backgrounds and nearly identical college grades.

In the classroom, men have been shown to assert themselves more than do women, often interrupting their classmates. Instructors, in turn, tend to dispense encouragement and praise to men but are not as consistent in the attention they provide female students. Teaching styles often follow the traditional lecture format, with little emphasis on cooperative learning or class participation. Women often describe SME faculty as unapproachable and intimidating and perceive the SME climate as hostile, competitive, and uninviting.

Interventions to Retain and Support Undergraduate Women in SME

The equal representation of women in SME fields will help to transform the way science is practiced. When women's perspectives become more pervasive, the SME culture may become less hierarchical and more cooperative overall. Thus, because of the potential benefits of including women, it is important that measures be taken to balance the gender ratio in these fields.

Programmatic interventions have proven useful in the recruitment and retention of women in SME fields. It is important that strategies to attract women to science, math, and engineering be implemented at crucial points before women enter college. They may take the form of residential mentoring programs in the precollege grades that provide opportunities for hands-on research and mentoring experiences. Dual enrollment programs in which students accumulate both high school and college credit for science and math courses may also be valuable. In general, these interventions strengthen young women's academic preparation in math and science and serve to promote their confidence and commitment to attend college and major in an SME discipline.

At the college level, hands-on research, residential programs, and mentoring experiences also have positive ramifications for women's retention. These investments supply women with the academic and emotional support they need as well as the chance to clarify their professional goals, develop research skills, and foster relationships with key people in the field.

The development of the Internet creates new opportunities for students to interact with their mentors via email. Email mentoring provides an informal and comfortable way for students to ask questions, receive guidance and support, and acquire networking connections.

The example of female mentors who successfully balance their personal and professional lives can contribute to women's understanding of how these roles are integrated. Informal relationships with faculty may enable women to observe the means by which their mentors balance their seemingly conflicting life and work commitments. As more women enter SME fields, there will be expanded opportunities for future generations of women to connect with female role models. In collective groups, female students and faculty can support one another, garner decision-making power in their departments, and validate women's perspectives in their respective disciplines.

Structural mechanisms in college-level SME departments can be used to encourage women's persistence in SME majors. Curricula and textbooks that incorporate women's scholarship may be more welcoming to female students. Additionally, introductory classes can be framed as recruitment efforts instead of as "weed out" courses used to dissuade students from the major. Innovative courses that are interdisciplinary in nature (i.e., combining engineering and liberal arts or science and women's studies) or that connect content to social and political issues have resulted in higher confidence for women, increased participation, and greater interest in SME fields.

Professors who teach SME classes play a key role in encouraging women's persistence. Feminist pedagogical techniques that value diverse learning styles, such as cooperative learning rather than extensive lecturing, may encourage female participation and assertiveness in class. Instructors should use nonsexist language and curtail any harassment directed toward female students. They should also discourage unfriendly competition, support open dialogue about sexism in the classroom and in research, and place course content in its social context.

Linda J. Sax and
Alyssa N. Bryant

See also Part 1: Medical Education; Part 3: Feminist Pedagogy; Curricular and Professional Choices; Graduate Students and Science

References and further reading

Davis, Cinda-Sue, Angela B. Ginorio, Carol S. Hollenshead, Barbara B. Lazarus, and Paula M. Rayman, eds. 1996. *The Equity Equation: Fostering the Advancement of Women in the Sciences, Mathematics, and Engineering.* San Francisco: Jossey-Bass.

Eisenhart, Margaret A., and Elizabeth Finkel. 1998. *Women's Science: Learning and Succeeding from the Margins.* Chicago: University of Chicago Press.

Hanson, Sandra L. 1996. *Lost Talent: Women in the Sciences.* Philadelphia: Temple University Press.

Lederman, Muriel, and Ingrid Bartsch. 2001. *The Gender and Science Reader.* New York: Routledge.

Mappen, Ellen F. 2000. "Exploring Science and Engineering through Mentoring and Research: Enriching Undergraduate Education for Women." *AWIS Magazine* 29, no. 1: 10–13.

National Science Foundation. 2000. *Women, Minorities, and Persons with Disabilities in Science and Engineering.* NSF00–327. Arlington, VA: National Science Foundation.

Seymour, Elaine, and Nancy M. Hewitt. 1994. *Talking about Leaving: Factors Contributing to High Attrition Rates among Science, Mathematics, and Engineering Majors.* Final Report to the Alfred P. Sloan Foundation on an Ethnographic Inquiry at Seven Institutions. Boulder: University of Colorado, Bureau of Sociological Research.

Thom, Mary. 2001. *Balancing the Equation: Where Are Women and Girls in Science, Engineering, and Technology?* New York: National Council for Research on Women.

Wyer, Mary, Mary Barbercheck, Donna Geisman, Hatice Örün Öztürk, and Marta Wayne, eds. 2001. *Women in Science and Technology: A Reader in Feminist Studies.* New York: Routledge.

Women Athletes

The accomplishments of female student-athletes competing at the collegiate level in the United States serve as an example of how women have advanced their status, not only in college classrooms but also on college fields, courts, and tracks. By breaking barriers over the decades, early female student-athlete pioneers paved the way for their contemporaries by having a vision about their place on campus and having the determination to achieve in their sports despite obstacles placed in their path. In the new millennium, female student-athletes continue to achieve success both in their sports and in the college classroom, despite the many challenges that they continue to face on campus and in society, where they are still not viewed as equals to their male peers.

With the growing popularity of women in sports evidenced by the Women's World Cup soccer games of 1999 and the recently formed Women's United Soccer Association (WUSA) and Women's National Basketball Association (WNBA), young women have increased their participation in athletics across the United States at all ages and levels of participation. By 1999, an estimated 2 million girls participated in youth and high school sports. Overall, society is accepting of this increased rate of growth, but most female student-athletes still do not have funding, facilities, programs, coaching and training staffs, and media coverage to equal those of their male peers. In particular, equal opportunity (e.g., opportunities to participate in intercollegiate athletics at a rate proportional to their participation in the student body generally) for female student-athletes on U.S. college campuses is not yet a reality.

Title IX of the Education Amendments of 1972 sparked the growth in college athletic programs and opportunities for female student-athletes in the United States. Title IX requires institutions to provide equitable resources and opportunities for women. According to the legislation, resources and opportunities should be offered in a nondiscriminatory way. Additional legislation, such as the Equity in Athletics Disclosure Act of 1996, requires higher education institutions receiving federal funds to report statistics on the participation of male and female athletes, as well as spending on female and male athletic programs. These data, coupled with scholarly research, reveal information on the demographics and academic achievements of these athletes and present evidence of significant challenges that continue to plague student-athletes on college campuses.

Historically, athletic competition for women, except for sports-related activities and contests organized by physical educators such as intramural and play day events, saw limited development until the passage of Title IX. In 1886, Stanford played against the University of California, Berkeley in basketball, marking the first female intercollegiate athletic contest in the United States. In these early days of female athletics, female student-athletes did not typically participate in sporting events in front of male audiences. The long-held perception that females participating in sports would develop unfeminine characteristics, such as a competitive nature or aggression, and concerns about damage to a young woman's reproductive organs were prevalent in society. Basketball, tennis, softball, and field hockey were the main sports played by women until the 1950s. Prior to the 1970s, athletic activities for American female college students were meant to provide health benefits, not to promote competition.

In 1971 the Association for Intercollegiate Athletics for Women (AIAW) was founded to promote the growth of and provide support for female athletic programs by offering a model different from that of its male counterpart organization, the National Collegiate Athletic Association (NCAA). The AIAW focused on a model that rejected commercialization and similar scholarship-funding principles that were driving male collegiate athletic programs in an attempt to keep female sports focused more on sports rather than money. With the passage of Title IX and some political and legal conflict between the AIAW and NCAA, female athletic programs quickly fell under the auspices of the NCAA. This organizational and operational change marked the beginning of a shift toward more athletic opportunities for female student-athletes. With this assimilation into the male model of college athletics, however, came an increased male influence over the administration of female sports programs and coaching of female student-athletes. Prior to the passage of Title IX, approximately 90 percent of female athletic teams had female coaches; in 1998, females coached only 47 percent of women's sports teams.

Title IX continues to drive the growth of female sports programs on college campuses. Campus administrators employ strategies to comply with Title IX by adding new facilities and purchasing new equipment and uniforms in an attempt to provide equal opportunities and equitable resources for female student-athletes. The popular media, however, typically reports on the occasional loss of male sports programs to accomplish equity under Title IX rather than reporting on the underfunding of women's athletic programs and the achievements of female student-athletes both in the classroom and on the field, court, or track. Some colleges and universities have discovered creative ways to add athletic opportunities for female student-athletes without eliminating male programs. College administrators must create these additional athletic opportunities for females on campus because statistics reveal that female college students make up the majority of the U.S. college and university undergraduate population, yet the majority of U.S. student-athletes are males.

This disparity between the proportion of female undergraduates and the proportion of female student-athletes participating in college sports continues to exist despite Title IX. Gender-equity statistics continue to highlight the underrepresentation of female student-athletes, specifically in Division I schools (the institutions offering the majority of athletic scholarships), compared to the proportion of females in the general student body at these institutions. A 1997–1998 study conducted by the NCAA revealed that at Division I institutions, the majority of students were female, but 63 percent of the student-athletes were male, and men's sports programs received 77 percent of athletic funds. Athletic scholarships awarded to female student-athletes are increasing in numbers at the Division I level, but the gap between male and female scholarship recipients is narrowing at a relatively slow rate. Despite the disproportionate number of female student-athletes across the board, the NCAA reports that female student-athletes graduate in larger numbers than both their female peers who do not participate in Division I athletics and male student-athletes. Female student-athletes participating at the elite collegiate level graduate at a 68 percent rate, compared to the 51 percent rate for their male peers.

The majority of female student-athletes are situated in the colleges and universities classified as Division II and III institutions. A survey conducted in 2000 by the *Chronicle of Higher Education* revealed that females comprised approximately 41 percent of athletes competing at the Division III level, compared to 38 and 32 percent at the Division II and Division I levels, respectively. Additional data revealed that the Division II and III colleges and universities spent a larger proportion of their athletic funding on women's sports programs than did Division I institutions.

Most of the higher education institutions participating in Division III–level sports programs are private liberal arts colleges and universities. These institutions espouse academic standards, educational experiences, and more intimate campus environments that allow for many female student-athletes to play multiple sports for their college and effectively manage their academics.

Key findings from a study of sports at selective institutions (Shulman and Bowen 2001) reveal how female student-athletes and their experiences are beginning to mirror those of male student-athletes as opportunities in college athletics increase for women. This phenomenon is especially true in the recruitment process. Both male and female student-athletes are accepted into colleges and universities with lower entrance exam scores (SAT) than nonparticipating college students. In addition, athletes of both sexes are increasingly underperforming in the college classroom (e.g., earning lower grade point averages)—a phenomenon that causes concern among faculty and administrators. Despite earning lower grades, athletes still graduate at higher rates than their peers. Furthermore, after graduation, female student-athletes are more likely to work full-time and may have an earnings advantage over females who did not participate in college sports.

Additional challenges beyond the percentage of athletic budgets designated for female athletic programs and the number of female student-athletes participating in college sports affect the lives of female student-athletes on campus. Recent media coverage of high-profile lawsuits and results of academic research highlight the unfortunate reality of sexual harassment and a propensity for female student-athletes to develop eating disorders. With the continued increase in males coaching female athletic teams, a need for higher education officials to educate coaches and players on what constitutes inappropriate behavior both on and off the field, court, and track exists. Power issues emerge in coach and player relationships, especially if the student-athlete depends on her athletic scholarship money to attend college. Female student-athletes may not feel equipped to deal with sexual harassment if it means that their scholarship or playing time could be affected by reporting such incidents. In general, this phenomenon is one that female student-athletes experience in greater numbers than male student-athletes.

In addition, studies have illuminated the increasing phenomenon of female athletes with eating disorders. Overall, studies show that female student-athletes are more likely to develop disordered eating patterns than their male peers. Many studies reveal that the risk of a female-athlete developing an eating disorder increases as she competes in higher level sports. Females participating in sports that tend to be more restrictive of weight, such as gymnastics, have an increased risk of showing disordered eating patterns. In addition, studies have shown that the media continues to display stereotypical and distorted images of women in sports, which serves to perpetuate the myth that female athletes should look attractive and feminine. This external societal and cultural pressure increases the likelihood that a female athlete could develop body image issues, eating disorders, and sex-role conflict. Female student-athletes are more likely than male student-athletes to experience intrapersonal conflict as they cope with managing their identity as a female, student, and athlete in the midst of societal stigmas and expectations about each of these social roles.

Janet M. Holdsworth

See also Part 5: Title IX; Part 6: Growth of Women's Athletics

References and further reading

"Gender Equity in College Sports." 2000. *Chronicle of Higher Education* (April 7; April 14; December 1). http://www.chronicle.com/stats/genderequity.htm. Cited June 15, 2002.

Howard, Reet. 1982. *Her Story in Sport: A Historical Anthology of Women in Sports.* West Point, NY: Leisure Press.

Kane, Mary Jo. 1989. "The Post Title IX Female Athlete in the Media: Things Are Changing, but How Much?" *Journal of Physical Education, Recreation, and Dance.* 60: 58–62.

National Collegiate Athletic Association. http://www.ncaa.org. Cited April 30, 2001.

Shulman, James L., and William G. Bowen. 2001. *College Sports and Educational Values: The Game of Life.* Princeton, NJ: Princeton University Press.

Smolak, Linda, Sarah K. Murnen, and Anne E. Ruble. 2000. "Female Athletes and Eating Problems: A Meta-Analysis." *International Journal of Eating Disorders* 27: 371–380.

U.S. Department of Education, Office of Civil Rights, Athletic Equity Resources. http://www.ed.gov/offices/OCR/athleticresources.html. Cited June 10, 2002.

Part 7

WOMEN FACULTY

Overview

The number of women faculty in U.S. colleges and universities has grown substantially since 1900. Partly because of Title VII of the Civil Rights Act of 1964 and the Equal Pay Act, women have made progress in both hiring and promotion decisions, so that between 1970 and 1993, the number of women in faculty positions in colleges and universities doubled. White women have been the primary beneficiaries of these policies, however, the advancement of women in all categories has created an increasingly diverse workforce. Still, these gains have been slow, and women have not reached parity with men. Today, women still hold more part-time positions, more non–tenure track positions, and are clustered in the lower rungs of academic rank. For example, between 1976 and 1993, the number of women in full-time, non–tenure track positions increased by 142 percent (Chronister et al. 1997). Only in private two-year colleges have women reached a majority compared to men.

Although women have made progress in terms of being hired into faculty positions across the country, some reports indicate that almost as many leave the system each year (Blum 1991), many before they reach the tenure threshold. Women faculty are also less likely to obtain promotion and tenure than men. In 1997, over one-quarter of full-time faculty with tenure were women. At the rank of full professor, only one-fifth were women (Integrated Postsecondary Education Data System 1997). Two major issues have been identified regarding tenure and promotion for women: sex differences in access to tenure-track positions and sex differences in outcomes of tenure and promotion decisions. Women not only are less likely to have access to tenure-track positions but may fall behind because of extra demands, such as committee assignments, heavier teaching loads, and student advising. They also have less access to powerful mentors and networks in their field, creating a cumulative disadvantage at the time of promotion and tenure. Thus, although progress for women faculty members has been made in the halls of academe, much work has yet to be accomplished for women to reach parity with men.

Diversity

Although all female faculty suffer from the chilly climate of academe, women of color and lesbian faculty often face greater discrimination and poorer working conditions than heterosexual white women. For the most part, they are underrepresented, especially in research universities. In 1997, women of color constituted only 5.2 percent of all faculty, whereas students of color represented

A woman faculty member at Mount Holyoke helps a student (Courtesy of Mount Holyoke College)

26.8 percent of the student body on campuses across the country. This shortfall leaves students of all ethnicities with few opportunities to encounter minority women faculty and few role models for gay and lesbian students or students of color. The situation is somewhat better for minority women in community colleges. However, their increased numbers at the lower levels of the postsecondary hierarchy only serve to underscore the marginalization these women experience.

Both women faculty of color and lesbian faculty report feelings of isolation and marginalization and are often treated as tokens within their departments and disciplines. These conditions lead to a reduction in their productivity through increased advising loads, demands for more committee work, and a lack of the powerful mentors often available to mainstream faculty. These women face issues of discrimination at four major points: salary, tenure and promotion, work environments, and racial climates.

Latina, African American, Asian American, and American Indian faculty all report the need to address minority concerns. They are often asked to address minority issues in their research, which is then rarely seen as legitimate scholarship. Yet all feel the need to create a body of scholarship that considers these issues. Likewise, lesbian faculty suffer from homophobic as well as racist attitudes and policies that marginalize them from their colleagues and hinder their careers.

Latina faculty, which includes Chicanas, Puerto Ricans, Cubanas, and others, comprise only 1 percent of faculty in academe. Their numbers are lower than for any other racial group except American Indians, whose population is much smaller across the country. They are less likely to be tenured and suffer from disproportionately lower salaries. Salaries for all Latinos are 7 percent lower than for whites, with female faculty in this category receiving 13 percent lower salaries than men. Like other minority groups, they are often forced to make costly choices between their past, language, culture, and identity, all of which contribute to their success or failure as faculty.

African American women continue to be underrepresented in the faculty ranks, despite their numbers in the larger population. The difference is due in part to their poor preparation in the public schools and their alienation from educational systems in general. Although the U.S. teaching workforce is increasingly white, students are becoming increasingly diverse, leaving African American students with few role models and limited access to higher education. Once they enter higher education, unless they enroll in a historically black college or university (HBCU), they are also less likely to graduate, leaving only a small pool of potential candidates for advanced degrees and the professorate. Once they obtain a faculty position, African American women face racial and gender discrimination in the form of stereotyping, disrespect, isolation, hostility, and lack of support networks.

American Indian women comprise only 0.2 percent of faculty across the country. However, it is difficult to know about the conditions for these women faculty because of the aggregated state of statistical data. Often they are relegated to another category or combined with Alaska natives. Their greatest concern is the preservation of their native peoples and communities, which often clashes with the individualistic and competitive nature of academic norms. American Indian women faculty feel the stress of choosing whether to serve their native communities or their academic communities. Those who do reach the level of graduate education are 2.5 times more likely to pursue professional degrees in order to best serve their communities. Those who obtain faculty positions are more likely to be found in two-year public institutions than in four-year colleges and more likely to be clustered at the non–tenure track instructor and lecturer levels.

Lesbian faculty, like women of color, face attitudes and policies that discriminate against them. Despite this marginalization, many have worked to reduce homophobic attitudes and heterosexist policies on their campuses, as well as to create a body of scholarship about lesbian lives. In 1973, the Gay Academic Union was formed in an effort to combat social, medical, and psychological models of deviance and disease that defined scholarly understandings of gay men and women. Many lesbian faculty helped to found and foster women's studies programs and courses on campuses, even as they felt themselves marginalized within the women's studies movement. Likewise, lesbians of color often felt marginalized by white lesbian women, leading them to challenge monolithic definitions and experience. A split between activist and theoretical work has also emerged, as lesbian faculty have made increasing efforts to legitimize lesbian scholarship. Lesbian faculty face continual dilemmas about how and when to "come out": at the point of hire, in their departments, in their classrooms, and so on. Even as lesbian faculty and their scholarship are increasingly visible in the academy, they continue to grapple with issues of tokenism and "ghettoization" by their colleagues and departments.

In summary, women of color and lesbians encounter many of the same issues as all women faculty. However, their experience carries the overlay or increased stress of racist and homophobic attitudes still perpetuated in the larger culture. These same forces are recreated in campus departments and classrooms across the country and are the very forces these women seek to eradicate through their scholarship, teaching, and service efforts.

Institutions of Higher Education and Faculty Women

Both individuals such as those described above and institutions of higher education are inextricably intertwined with the lives and work of women faculty. Colleges and universities influence women faculty through their research and teaching requirements, the hiring process, salary negotiations, and the work of unions on the campuses where they exist. Institutions also influence the work of faculty women through the socialization process, campus climate, and use of evaluation procedures. Finally, campuses around the world, not just here in the United States, influence the work of women faculty in many countries.

Elements of Faculty Work. One of the central criteria used to judge faculty productivity is publication output. Although women generally publish less than men do, the differences have narrowed considerably since the 1980s. The differences are most notable at four-year universities, with no noticeable differences by gender in two-year institutions. Women's family responsibilities are most often cited when explaining this gender difference in publication rates. However, other factors may be of more importance, since the publication rates of married women, unmarried women, and women with children are not that different. These factors may include location at a prestigious research institution and access to influential mentors, collegial networks, and resources. Currently, women hold only 28 percent of the faculty positions at research universities (Sax et al. 1999). Thus the majority of women faculty, who work in institutions other than research universities, are provided fewer opportunities to publish extensively. It takes twenty to thirty years to become a prolific scholar in a particular field. Because women's careers are more likely to be characterized by part-time employment, periods of unemployment, or underemployment, they have fewer opportunities to amass the number of publications required for prolific scholar status.

Women tend to coauthor more often than men and are less likely than men to appear as the first author of a publication. Women and minorities are also more likely than white men to publish on topics that are devalued by mainstream thinkers and that may not be acceptable to top-tier journals. Campuses may want to consider more emphasis on quality rather than quantity of journal articles published and more flexible ways to measure faculty productivity.

Almost all women faculty teach, a factor that unites them, even though they may be working in a wide variety of institutional types and may hold either full- or part-time positions. More women can be found teaching in traditional women's fields, such as education and nursing, where they are likely to be paid less and more likely to teach undergraduate courses than men. Research indicates no significant difference between the student ratings of women and men faculty.

Women do tend to differ according to their disciplinary specialization, a factor that may be even more important than gender in differentiating academics at work. Yet regardless of discipline, women report more pressure to perform service in their roles as faculty and increased pressure to appear nurturing and supportive, requiring what is sometimes known as "smile work."

Where a woman works has major implications for her teaching and research productivity. Faculty in community colleges teach much heavier loads than those in research universities, for example. In addition, a greater number of women are working at more than one institution, as full-time tenure-track jobs shrink in numbers and part-time jobs increase. Thus, the hiring process is a crucial one, setting a woman's career on a particular course for years to come.

Advice for job seekers includes gathering information about all possible jobs, both those outside and inside one's discipline, carefully preparing one's curriculum vita, ensuring the inclusion of all relevant ienformation, and entering the job interview armed with questions potential faculty might be asked, as well as questions candidates need to ask in order to make a thoughtful decision. Women need to gather as accurate a picture as possible of their potential department. Finding the proper match is crucial.

New hires may experience reality shock, or conflicts between what they anticipated and what they actually find. This period of organizational entry is central to the establishment of professional identity and supportive collegial relationships. At this point, women faculty may encounter institutional racism, misogyny, or homophobia or some combination of the three. They must deal with the realities of establishing a viable research agenda and decisions about what to teach in the classroom. Institutions that desire to make new faculty welcome and to ensure their success must be alert to providing adequate mentoring, setting realistic teaching and service requirements, and meeting the greater needs of women with regard to spousal employment and child care.

Once the job offer is made, women are cautioned to negotiate for more than the initial salary offer. The best strategy against pay discrimination is prevention in the form of shrewd negotiating at the time of the job offer. Women still earn only 70–75 percent of what their male counterparts earn in equal jobs, despite the Equal Pay Act of 1963. Pay inequities persist, partly based on the continuing misconception that women are less qualified than their male counterparts. Even after controlling for variables such as seniority, educational level, years of experience, length of appointment, and different pay plans, male faculty are still paid more than female faculty.

Finally, faculty women may encounter the possibility of joining a faculty union at the point of hire. Twenty-five percent of faculty across the country in public institutions of higher education today are unionized. Unions are most prevalent in public two-year colleges, where 70 percent of all collective bargaining agreements exist. Yet more faculty in four-year institutions are covered by bargaining agreements than at two-year institutions since these institutions have larger faculty bases. Issues for women include part-time status and rights, salary gaps, and equity issues.

Around the country, graduate teaching assistants, part-time faculty, and some private institutions are engaged in organizing efforts. Of major concern is the loss of full-time jobs and the subsequent erosion of benefits for faculty. Competition among the three national faculty unions, the American Federation of Teachers, National Education Association, and American Association of University Professors, appears to have impeded the growth of collective bargaining across the country. A more effective approach would be to have a single voice representing faculty interests.

Campus Influences. As mentioned previously, the type of institution a woman finds herself working in is crucial to her experience of higher education. In addition to setting the conditions of faculty work, various campuses affect the lives of faculty women through their socialization processes at both the campus and departmental level, through the overall campus climate, and through their evaluation procedures, including promotion and tenure processes and possibly posttenure review.

Central among campus influences is the socialization process for new faculty.

Although the traditional view of socialization holds that a campus's values, processes, and practices are gender- and color-blind, scholars today recognize that this process is experienced very differently depending on such factors as gender, race, ethnicity, and sexual orientation. Campuses tend to perpetuate institutionalized gender inequities that induce women to act out stereotypical female roles in order to gain acceptance by their predominantly white male senior colleagues.

The two major stages of the faculty socialization process are anticipatory socialization and cultural learning and adaptation. Anticipatory socialization occurs during graduate school, whereas cultural learning and adaptation involves entry into the profession, the gaining of promotion and tenure, and the achievement of milestones throughout the academic career. Although the normative view of socialization is that of a constant linear process, there is growing evidence that socialization is not experienced uniformly by women faculty. An engendered view of socialization reveals that women experience an accumulative disadvantage that begins in graduate school and continues throughout their careers. Possible disadvantages include such factors as failing to attract top advisers in graduate school and disruptions of the career trajectory caused by family obligations. Women also encounter invisible barriers, such as being excluded from powerful social and professional networks that men may enter in the socialization process. Successful socialization for women involves considerations of these factors and includes both the experiences and needs of faculty women throughout their careers.

Socialization takes place at both the campus and departmental levels. A woman's academic discipline has an important impact on her professional values, attitudes, and behaviors. The gender differences in socialization begin with a woman's career choice and shape her behavior over time. The persistent imbalance in gender ratios within certain academic disciplines raises important questions about the origins of these imbalances and the role of socialization. For example, in 1998 women comprised 42 percent of the nation's doctoral pool, yet they earned only 31 percent of the Ph.D.s in chemistry and 14 percent in physics and astronomy and were overrepresented in the social sciences (54 percent) and education (63 percent) (Sanderson et al. 1999).

Institutional socialization and disciplinary socialization interact to form the normative context for a woman's faculty career, establishing the nature and conditions of academic work as well as the professional standards against which her work will be judged. These two interacting subsystems shape her values, norms, attitudes, workload, and career. The experience of socialization is different for women than for men, shaping the structure of opportunities that are available to women faculty. The subtle and overt discrimination accrued over time by women who aspire to academic careers affects their funding opportunities, as well as their opportunities to gain appointments at elite universities. Thus, although some values hold across the institution, such as the importance of being a good teacher and colleague, other discriminatory values serve as a source of fragmentation and divisiveness.

These values, among others, also help to shape both the campus climate and the campus culture. Campus climate is generally considered to be the atmosphere that permeates the moment and is more susceptible to influence and change, whereas campus culture consists of deeply embedded values in the organization that are much more resistant to change. Campus climate is often conceived of as the organization's metaphorical temperature gauge, by which students, faculty, and employees measure a welcoming and receptive versus a cool and alienating learning environment. This metaphor has often been used in describing the "chilly climate" women faculty encounter on campuses across the United States. Various models of person-environment interaction have attempted to describe the experiences of organizational members within a particular college campus. They include considerations of the way in which climate influences behavior, how personal and environmental needs interact, the quality of the person-environment transactions, the degree of fit between individuals and their environments, and the qualities of the campus social climate. The institution's historical legacy, structural diversity, psychological climate, and behavioral climate all shape the organizational climate for women and faculty of color. Women often find that the values embedded in the campus climate include subtle gender-role expectations that affect their teaching, research, salary differentials, and career advancement. If women faculty fail to conform to these expectations, they may find themselves at risk since their department chairs and colleagues may penalize those who do not meet their prescribed notions of correct role behavior. Yet these expectations can be seen as leverage points for change, rather than simply as destructive forces, allowing all members of the academy to achieve their fullest potential.

Inextricably intertwined with the culture and climate of an organization are its elements of evaluation. The norms, values, and expectations embedded in the campus and departmental cultures all come to bear at the various points of evaluation in a woman's career: at the point of contract renewal, during promotion and tenure, and during posttenure review processes. These values may create inequities in the evaluation process that put women at a disadvantage in contrast to their male colleagues. This disadvantage manifests itself in three ways: the type of scholarship a woman pursues may not be as valued, women faculty often carry an unequal teaching load compared to men, and women tend to spend more time on service activities. Faculty rewards are often based on evaluation of the above functions, leaving women at a distinct disadvantage. Two possible solutions are to shift from a "one-size-fits-all" model of evaluation and to be alert to the ways in which women faculty are channeled into "women's work," disadvantaging them in future evaluation processes.

Comparative Issues. The marginalization of women in the academy is not only a national phenomenon but a global one, as well. Although the number of women undergraduate students has increased in many countries, the number of women in graduate school and the professorate remains small. In countries such as Great Britain and New Zealand, women continue to be clustered at the lowest academic ranks, that is, lecturers, junior lecturers, or tutors. Similar patterns of inequity can be found in South Africa, Canada, Norway, and the Netherlands. Although the sociocultural conditions and political particularities of these countries are quite different, the conditions for women faculty remain remarkably the same. Scholars report a systematic pattern of inequitable practices, including issues of pay, workload, promotion and tenure, and sexual harassment.

Disturbing patterns of exclusion involving the intersection of gender, race, and class are also reported by women scholars from South Africa, New Zealand, and the United States. Women of color in the academy find themselves underrepresented not only among their male colleagues but among their female peers, as well. This token status subjects minority women to undue scrutiny of their professional abilities, the need to constantly prove themselves, and the experience of being pigeonholed into restricted roles.

Around the globe, a number of common themes pervade the experiences of women in academe. They include the continued underrepresentation of women at the higher ranks, an increased emphasis on teaching that hampers research and publication activities, promotion criteria that undervalue service (an activity where most women are involved), the application of double standards in evaluation processes, the need for women scholars to prove their abilities relative to their male colleagues, and the influence of race and class in the allocation of academic and professional opportunities.

Joanne E. Cooper

References and further reading

Blum, Debra E. 1991. "Environment Still Hostile to Women in Academe, New Evidence Indicates." *Chronicle of Higher Education* (October 9) A1, A20.

Chronister, Jay L., Bruce M. Gansneder, Elizabeth P. Harper, and Roger G. Baldwin. 1997. "Full-Time Non-Tenure Track Faculty." *NEA Higher Education Research Center Update* 3, no. 5: 1–4.

Glazer-Raymo, Judith. 1999. *Shattering the Myths: Women in Academe.* Baltimore: Johns Hopkins University Press.

Integrated Postsecondary Education Data System. 1997. *Fall Staff Survey.* Washington, DC: National Center for Education Statistics.

Sanderson, Allen R., Bernard Dugoni, Tom Hoffer, and Lance Selfa. 1999. *Doctorate Recipients from United States Universities: Summary Report, 1998.* Chicago: National Opinion Research Center at the University of Chicago.

Sax, Linda J., Alexander W. Astin, William S. Korn, and Shannon K. Gilmartin. 1999. *The American College Teacher: National Norms for the 1998–99 HERI Faculty Survey.* Los Angeles: Higher Education Research Institute, University of California, Los Angeles.

African American Faculty

African American women continue to be underrepresented among the faculty in most institutions of higher education. Although scholarship that examines the impact of race and gender on the experiences of women in higher education is limited, the explanations as to why these circumstances persist typically fall into one of two categories: "either past discriminatory policies or demographic realities that are directly devoid of any racial intent" (Jackson 1991, 136). The end result is the perception that there are few African American scholars causing what some researchers identify as "bidding wars for accomplished minority scholars and teachers" (Solomon and Wingard 1991, 33). Such behavior does not serve to broaden the pool of Ph.D.s, which would increase the numbers of African American faculty.

In 1993–1994, African American students received 7.0 percent of the bachelor's degrees, 5.4 percent of the master's degrees, and 3.1 percent of the doctoral degrees awarded to all students in the United States (Southern Regional Education Board 1996–1997). The reasons for the underrepresentation of African Americans among degree holders are numerous. Leon Botstein (1991) argues that teacher education programs do a poor job of preparing teachers to cope with racially or ethnically diverse student populations. This failure is particularly problematic since the teaching force is "increasingly white while the student population becomes increasingly racially diverse" (Sleeter 1993, 157). Some scholars believe that the cultural differences between teachers and students account for the following problems: the giftedness of African American children goes unrecognized; they are disproportionately disciplined; they drop out at a high rate; and they score significantly lower than their European American cohorts on standardized tests.

Once African Americans enter the academy, scholars cite a multitude of challenges restricting their success. They characterize the experience of these students on predominantly white campuses as isolating, both in terms of the social climate and the manner in which faculty treat these students. In a comparison of the experiences of European American and African American students, Aubert says that "white professors communicated warmth and sincerity toward white students through words, gestures, and attitudes, while using a more rigid and distant approach toward black students" (1997, 142). Similarly, Julian Roebuck and Komanduri Murty's research indicates that the adjustment problems that African American students experience on predominantly white campuses are so severe that they warrant the creation of racially homogenous social worlds (1993, 112). Other scholars characterize these students' experiences at predominantly white universities in a similar manner. Consequently, the experiences of African

Gloria Anderson is chair of the Natural Science Division at Morris Brown College (Courtesy of Morris Brown College)

Americans in postsecondary institutions have been characterized by higher attrition rates, greater states of alienation when compared to their European American cohorts, and less than satisfactory relationships with European American faculty.

Historically black colleges and universities (HBCUs) provide an alternative to predominantly white institutions for African American students. Sandy Aubert (1997) characterized students' experiences with both European and African American faculty at HBCUs as one of caring and concern. Although African American students typically report higher levels of self-esteem and are more likely to graduate from HBCUs when compared to

African American students attending predominantly white institutions, there are only 109 HBCUs. Furthermore, only 12 HBCUs confer doctorate degrees. These institutions produced more than 11.7 percent of all doctorates awarded to African Americans in 1989, even though only approximately 3 percent of the colleges and universities are HBCUs and they account for approximately 2 percent of the total college population in the United States (Patel 1988). African American women received 53 percent of these degrees (Roebuck and Murty 1993, 102). These conditions make it difficult to achieve greater African American representation among degree holders. The climate at predominantly white institutions and the low number of HBCUs offering advanced degrees lessen the likelihood that African American students will pursue advanced degrees, thereby decreasing the possibility that they would consider the academic profession as a viable career option.

The underrepresentation of African Americans among those holding master's and doctoral degrees affects the population's representation among university faculty. Drawing from statistics compiled by the American Council on Education for 1989, Lois Benjamin found that African American women constituted 2.1 percent of full-time faculty and 2.4 percent of part-time faculty (Benjamin 1997, 5). These figures have not increased appreciably since 1990. Although the majority of African American women are employed at HBCUs, they occupy the lower faculty ranks wherever they work. More specifically, at both predominantly white and historically black institutions, African American women are more likely to be assistant professors and instructors rather than full or associate professors. At HBCUs, "the ratio of 73 females for every 100 males at the rank of assistant professor dropped to only 32 females for every 100 males at the rank of professor" (Roebuck and Murty 1993, 105). Thus, in all aspects of higher education, African American women experience racial and gender discrimination in subtle and not so subtle ways that include but are not limited to stereotyping, disrespect, isolation, hostility, and lack of support networks.

Research on the experiences of African American women in the academy highlights a plethora of challenges. The halls of the academy, whether it be at HBCUs or predominantly white institutions, are made hostile because of racist and sexist comments and practices. Many scholars characterize these women's presence as contested space. Their spaces at predominantly white institutions are contested because European American colleagues question whether African Americans' presence in the academy was the result of "affirmative action." When African American women faculty voice their concerns about the racist and sexist oppression they experience at predominantly white colleges and universities, European American women for the most part pose as their allies and attempt to construct a sisterhood. However, as bell hooks has perceptively pointed out, "From our [African American women's] peripheral role in the movement, we saw that the potential radicalism of feminist ideology was being undermined by women, who, while paying lip service to revolutionary goals, were primarily concerned with gaining entrance into the capitalist, patriarchal power structure" (hooks 1981, 502). Consequently, even European women are guilty of "racist verbal expressions" (McKay 1997, 14). Posing as allies, they suggest that black women would be better off if they returned to HBCUs instead of remaining at historically white institutions. This suggestion is made despite the fact that the majority of African Americans who hold doctorates acquired them at predominantly white institutions instead of HBCUs. Although African American women at predominantly white institutions experience both racial and gender discrimination, gender discrimination is pervasive at HBCUs.

Lois Benjamin and others identify the myriad of ways that African American women faculty receive the message, "you don't belong here." To this end, their academic scholarship is invalidated or relegated to research on "black stuff." Furthermore, their accomplishments are either undervalued or begrudgingly recognized. When these women receive acknowledgment, their colleagues are more likely to praise their attractiveness instead of their scholarly achievements (1997, 29).

Despite these challenges, many African American women faculty see their presence in the academy as one that is committed not to assimilation but to the transformation of higher educational institutions. To this end, the scholarship of African American women challenges the Eurocentric hegemony of men and the hegemony of European women in respect to feminist thought. Furthermore, their presence in the academy offers alternative models of success to students from historically disadvantaged populations.

Kimberly Lenease King

See also Part 1: Black Women's Colleges; Historically Black Colleges and Universities; Part 2: Demographics of Gender and Race; Intersection of Gender and Race; Part 3: Black Feminism and Womanism; Part 6: African American Students; Part 7: Women of Color at Predominantly White Institutions; Part 8: African American Administrators

References and further reading

Altbach, Philip., and Kofi Lomotey, eds. 1991. *The Racial Crisis in American Higher Education.* Albany: State University of New York Press.

Aubert, Sandy E. 1997. "Black Students on White Campuses: Overcoming the Isolation." Pp. 141–146 in *Sailing against the Wind: African Americans and Women in U.S. Education,* ed. Kofi Lomotey. Albany: State University of New York Press.

Benjamin, Lois, ed. 1997. *Black Women in the Academy: Promises and Perils.* Gainesville: University Press of Florida.

Botstein, Leon. 1991. "The Undergraduate Curriculum and the Issue of Race: Opportunities and Obligations." Pp. 89–105 in *The Racial Crisis in American Higher Education,* ed. P. Altbach and K. Lomotey. Albany: State University of New York Press.

Feinberg, Walter. 1998. *On Higher Ground: Education and the Case for Affirmative Action.* New York: Teachers College Press.

Gregory, Sheila T. 1995. *Black Women in the Academy: The Secrets to Success and Achievement.* New York: University Press of America.

hooks, bell. 1981. *Ain't I a Woman: Black Women and Feminism.* Boston: South End Press.

Jackson, Kenneth. 1991. "Black Faculty in Academia." Pp. 135–148 in *The Racial Crisis in American Higher Education,* ed. Philip A. Altbach and Kofi Lomotey. Albany: State University of New York Press.

Lomotey, Kofi, ed. 1997. *Sailing against the Wind: African Americans and Women in U.S. Education.* Albany: State University of New York Press.

McKay, Nellie Y. 1997. "A Troubled Peace: Black Women in the Halls of the Academy." Pp. 11–22 in *Black Women in the Academy: Promises and Perils,* ed. Lois Benjamin. Gainesville: University Press of Florida.

Patel, Narendra H. 1988. *Student Transfers from White to Black Colleges.* Washington, DC: NAFEO Research Institute.

Roebuck, Julian R., and Komanduri S. Murty. 1993. *Historically Black Colleges and Universities: Their Place in American Higher Education.* Westport, CT: Praeger.

Sleeter, Christine E. 1993. "How White Teachers Construct Race." Pp. 151–171 in *Race Identity and Representation in Education,* ed. C. McCarthy and W. Crichlow. New York: Routledge.

Solomon, Lewis C., and Tamara L. Wingard. 1991. "The Changing Demographics: Problems and Opportunities." Pp. 19–42 in *The Racial Crisis in American Higher Education,* ed. P. Altbach and K. Lomotey. Albany: State University of New York Press.

Southern Regional Education Board. 1996–1997. *SREB Factbook on Higher Education.* Atlanta, GA: Southern Regional Education Board.

American Indian Faculty

American Indian women faculty comprise only 0.2 percent of the professorate, but this underrepresentation cannot be attributed to one particular factor. However, differences between the cultural and social values of American Indians and the dominant society have been found to negatively affect the representation of American Indian females in the educational pipeline. Additionally, research on American Indian females in the academy is further obscured by the limited data available on the population as a whole.

Research has revealed little about American Indian females in the professorate because the scant research on American Indian faculty is primarily descriptive. Moreover, in these limited studies, American Indian faculty are generally discussed in an ancillary manner with little focus on their particular experiences or discussion of differences across gender. In a related seminal work, the U.S. Department of Education noted the difficulties associated with obtaining data on American Indians. One challenge highlighted by the department's study was that prior to the 1970s, American Indians were not identified in a separate classification but clustered into the "other" category. Another difficulty with research on American Indians is that the terms "American Indian, Alaska Native" are used interchangeably with "Native American," thereby further limiting the data specific to American Indians. According to the National Center for Education Statistics, both terms include individuals with lineage in any of the original peoples of North America who sustain cultural identity through tribal affiliation or community recognition. The small sample size of each group (less than 1 percent total) was frequently listed as a reason the two populations were combined into one category. Hence, separation of the two populations may have compromised the anonymity of the respondents, particularly if analysis was presented by discipline. The many challenges associated with research on American Indian faculty further complicated the process of providing a comprehensive examination of American Indian female faculty.

A preeminent value for many American Indians is total dedication to the preservation of the Indian people. This value clashes with the individualistic and competitive foundation of the dominant society. The dissonance American Indian women encounter when they attempt to reconcile the culture of these two entities—their achievements in the academy and their responsibilities to their respective tribes—hinders their pursuit of an academic career. Further compounding these conflicting values is that a female's social status within the tribe appears to be based, at least to some extent, not on academic or financial success but on compliance with conventional cultural norms or the degree of Indian blood one possesses. In Ardy Bowker's study of American Indian females, she found that college-educated females perceived that they were viewed by their respective tribal society as less traditional. Often, American Indian females who pursue postsecondary educational opportunities are subjected to allegations that they sacrificed part of their heritage in order to succeed in another system. These differing values have affected the educational pursuits of American Indian females across all levels of the pipeline.

The underrepresentation of American Indian women in the educational system can be traced back to the fifteenth century, when the primary purpose of educating American Indians was their assimilation and acculturation into mainstream society. One of the tactics American Indians have used to defy dominant societal values was quitting high school as soon as they were legally able. This rejection of education resulted in the underrepresentation of American Indian females in the educational pipeline, in effect reducing the prospective number of female faculty. Unfortunately, remnants of forced assimilation attempts continue to plague American Indian females, who have the highest high school dropout rate of any group. In a related study, Bowker found that strong ethnic identity (heritage was not important), peer groups, and modeling within families were strong indicators of whether American Indian females would do well in school and subsequently persist through college.

Nonetheless, American Indian women have steadily increased across all categories of the educational pipeline, surpassing Indian males in the number of undergraduate (associate's and bachelor's) and graduate (master's) degrees obtained. If the trend continues, American Indian women will eventually lead Indian men in the number of doctorates awarded. The number of American Indian females pursuing doctorates has risen consistently, with females now accounting for just under 50 percent of doctorates awarded to American Indians annually. Likewise, just over 50 percent of the doctorates earned by American Indian females were in the field of education. However, this preference limits the pool of prospective Indian faculty primarily to the field of education, followed distantly by the field of psychology. Moreover, Wayne J. Stein (1994) reported in a survey of American Indian faculty that few American Indians in higher education envisioned a career in the professorate and came to academe from other careers as diverse as business, government, or secondary education. Further contributing to the underrepresentation of female Indian faculty is the fact that Indian students are two and one-half times more likely to pursue professional degrees, specifically in law and medicine, than a career as a professor. That could be because of the financial rewards the professional degree commands as well as the emphasis placed on professional careers in Indian culture as a strategy for preserving the tribe. The gains made by American Indian women in the educational pipeline correspond with advances women have attained within the professorate.

During the period 1989–1995, the Higher Education Research Institute (HERI) reported that American Indian females increased their representation among American Indian faculty 5 percentage points, to 37 percent. American Indian women faculty were the least likely of all racial and ethnic groups to choose an academic career because of status and prestige but cited the intellectual challenge as their primary reason for joining the professorate. Females account for 41 percent of all tenured American Indian faculty. Additionally, the largest segment of American Indian females (41 percent) are found at the instructor and lecturer levels, which typically are not tenure-track positions, whereas only 12 percent of American Indians with the rank of full professor are females. Relative to institutional type, American Indian women faculty are more likely to be employed in public two-year institutions (41 percent) and public four-year institutions (24 percent), with 8 percent employed at tribal colleges. Consistent with the perceptions of faculty at two-year institutions, American Indian females were the least likely faculty group to hold a doctoral degree, and they spent considerably more time on teaching than their male counterparts. Accordingly, primary sources of stress cited by American Indian female faculty were time pressures, lack of personal time, household responsibilities, and teaching load.

Many of the problems experienced by American Indian female faculty are exacerbated by their status as women and minorities and by the cultural conflicts between American Indians and the dominant society. A qualitative study by Stein found that female American Indian faculty respondents reported they often feel they must work twice as hard as their non-Indian counterparts to prove themselves. Frequently, the institution and tribal communities expect American Indian women faculty to advise and serve as advocates for Indian students. Additionally, faculty may have to contend with expectations for tribal-related public service that is not recognized by the institution. Generally, these service-oriented tasks detract from research and publication efforts.

Often, American Indian faculty may conduct research on tribal-related issues in an attempt to maintain their commitment to the tribe while pursuing an academic career. However, scholarship of this nature may not be viewed by non-Indian faculty members as research and may consequently impede promotion and tenure decisions. Relatedly, the HERI study also found American Indian females were the least likely of all faculty groups to cite engaging in research as a "very important" or an "essential" goal. Thus, American Indian females were less likely than Indian males to have journal articles published, and Indian male faculty were twice as likely as females to have published more than twenty journal articles. The scant research available has revealed the academy may not be designed for the success of American Indian female faculty, given the conflicting cultural values, an obstacle that has resulted in their underrepresentation at all educational levels. Thus, strategies for the recruitment and retention of American Indian women in the professorate should consider the cultural and social values of American Indians.

Barbara J. Johnson

See also Part 2: Demographics of Gender and Race; Part 6: American Indian Students; Part 8: American Indian Administrators

References and further reading

Astin, Helen S., Anthony Lising Antonio, Christine M. Cress, and Alexander W. Astin. 1997. *Race and Ethnicity in the American Professoriat, 1995–96.* Los Angeles: Higher Education Research Institute, University of California.

Bowker, Ardy. 1993. *Sisters in the Blood. The Education of Women in Native America.* Newton, MA: WEEA Publishing Center.

Cook-Lynn, Elizabeth. 1996. *Why I Can't Read Wallace Stegner and Other Essays: A Tribal Voice.* Madison: University of Wisconsin Press.

Cross, William T. 1991. "Pathway to the Professoriat: The American Indian Faculty Pipeline." *Journal of American Indian Education* 30: 13–24.

Pavel, D. Michael, Rebecca Rak Skinner, Elizabeth Farris, Margaret Calahan, John Tipeconnic, and Wayne Stein.

1998. *American Indians and Alaska Natives in Postsecondary Education.* NCES 98–291. Washington, DC: U.S. Department of Education.

Stein, Wayne J. 1994. "The Survival of American Indian Faculty." *Thought and Action: The National Education Association Higher Educational Journal* 10: 101–114.

Asian American Faculty

To develop a broad sense of the experiences of Asian American women faculty, one must sift through the research on Asian Americans, Asian American women, women of color, and faculty of color. However, Asian American women faculty as a distinct group are almost invisible in the research literature. They are outsiders in at least two ways—they are women and people of color. In addition, the stereotype of Asian Americans as a privileged racial group often sets Asian American women faculty apart from other women of color, adding a third level to their outsider status.

As noted in the section on Asian American women students, the recognition of the racial and ethnic group known as Asian Americans, or, more comprehensively, Asian Pacific Americans (APA), is a relatively recent phenomenon, encompassing people whose nations of familial origin are diverse and include any countries on the Asian continent, South Asian subcontinent, and the islands of the Pacific Rim. It is important to note that among these different ancestries are difference in native languages, ethnic heritage, religions, and cultures. APAs become a more cohesive group when examined by the regional proximity of their nations of origin and, it must be acknowledged, by their physical appearance. The APA classification also serves to distinguish between Americans of Asian descent and non-American Asians who live or study in the United States. This distinction becomes particularly important when examining APA women faculty, whose numbers are small at all faculty levels in comparison to Asian internationals, as well as to other women of color and APA men.

The APA population of the United States was 9.6 million (3.6 percent of the population) in 1996 (Hune and Chan 1997), and APA students accounted for 5.6 percent of the undergraduate student population in 1995 (Chang and Kiang 2002). The academic pipeline, from college to graduate school to faculty positions, is marked by the steady decrease in the proportion of APA women earning higher level degrees. APA women earn over 51 percent of all APA bachelor degrees, 46 percent of all APA master's degrees, 45 percent of all APA professional degrees, and 41 percent of all APA doctorates (Hune 1998). This decrease of women as a percentage of overall APA graduates, particularly at the doctoral level, undeniably affects the opportunities for APA women students to become APA women faculty. Further adding to the invisibility of APA women in faculty positions across the campus, APA doctoral graduates are much more likely to earn their advanced degrees in sciences and engineering, which contributes to the lack of APA women serving in faculty roles in other academic areas, such as the liberal arts. This cycle becomes self-perpetuating.

Further clouding the numbers on APA faculty is the combining of APAs and Asian foreign nationals in the counting of Asian faculty. This combination of groups both overinflates the overall numbers of Asian faculty and makes it impossible to

Chien-Shiung Wu, who helped develop the atomic bomb, taught and did research at Columbia University (Bettmann/Corbis)

accurately understand the representation of APAs in faculty positions (Hune 1998). In 1993, there were 6,326 APA and Asian international women serving in faculty positions (from lecturers to full professors), accounting for only 25 percent of all APA faculty, which represents the largest gender gap among all racial groups that year (Hune 1998). APA women also represent a disproportionately high percentage of faculty in foreign languages and the health sciences and are underrepresented in all other areas (Zimbler 1994). The tenure rate of APA and Asian international women faculty declined in the decade from 1983–1993, from 55 percent to 52 percent, as well. With the expected increase in enrollment of multigenerational APA students (Chang and Kiang 2002), however, one might expect to see further expansion of the majors and graduate study pursuits among APA women, with an ideal outcome of greater representation of APA women faculty in fields across higher education.

APA women faculty encounter a myriad of stereotypes that hinder their professional experiences and progress. The "exotic" Asian woman, the "dragon lady," the passive and demure stereotype, and other pejorative caricatures of Asian women have a direct impact on the way APA women faculty are able to do their jobs and interact with students, colleagues, and campus administration. These stereotypes affect how they work with and the respect they get from students, colleagues, administrators, and staff and create barriers to equality and acceptance in many working relationships. APA women faculty often experience difficulties with male faculty and students that are grounded in the perceived vulnerabilities among APA women. The slight stature and youthful appearance of many APA women faculty often contributes to their being treated like they are less mature and deserving of respect than their training or education would indicate.

As with other faculty of color, APA women faculty also often experience the "racialization" of their academic work, regardless of whether their research and teaching areas involve racial issues. Simply by being of their race, they are expected to be intellectual leaders concerning issues of their race (Hune 1997). At the same time, their work in areas unrelated to their race might be discounted or disrespected by other faculty or students who believe their race actually disqualifies APA faculty from studying non-Asian subjects. APA women faculty face both discrimination aimed at women scholars, through which women's scholarship is discounted as less serious than that of men, and the discrimination of being Asian American, through which their scholarship, regardless of discipline, is ascribed a foreignness, irrespective of the fact that APA scholars are by definition American.

In addition, they face a contradictory but equally damaging challenge of dismissive colleagues who do not see Asian Americans as requiring recognition as a separate and affected racial group. The "model minority" stereotype, which holds that since Asian Americans have excelled in the acclimation to the United States, especially in education, they are not affected by the same kinds of discrimination that other minority groups experience, continues to negatively affect efforts to increase awareness of the issues and concerns facing APA faculty, particularly women faculty, on college campuses. The ignorance about existing discrimination can be as equally detrimental as overt racism to the careers and experiences of APA women faculty.

APA women scholars are deserving of research that focuses specifically on their experience as separate from other women of color, other women in general, and APA men. They also deserve to be recognized as separate from Asian international scholars, whose experiences must be distinct and very different from Asian Pacific American scholars. As APA scholars continue to increase in number in graduate schools, as doctoral recipients, and as junior faculty, it ought to be expected that significant and simply more research on APA women and their experience as faculty will follow.

Roberta Malee Bassett

See also Part 6: Asian American Students; Part 8: Asian American Administrators

References and further reading

Chan, Sucheng C., and Liang-Chi Wang. 1991. "Racism and the Model Minority: Asian-Americans in Higher Education." Pp. 43–67 in *The Racial Crisis in American Higher Education,* ed. Philip

G. Altbach and Kofi Lomotey. Albany: State University of New York Press.
Chang, Mitchell, and Peter N. Kiang. 2002. "New Challenges of Representing Asian American Students in U.S. Higher Education." Pp. 137–158 in *The Racial Crisis in American Higher Education,* eds. William A Smith, Philip G. Altbach, and Kofi Lomotey. Albany: State University of New York Press.
Hune, Shirley. 1997. "Higher Education as Gendered Space: Asian American Women and Everyday Inequities." Pp. 181–196 in *Everyday Sexism in the Third Millennium,* ed. Carol Rambo Ronai, Barbara Zsembik, and Joe R. Feagin. New York: Routledge.
———. 1998. *Asian Pacific American Women in Higher Education: Claiming Visibility and Voice.* Washington, DC: Association of American Colleges and Universities.
Hune, Shirley, and Kenyon S. Chan. 1997. "Special Focus: Asian Pacific American Demographic and Educational Trends." Pp. 39–67 in *Minorities in Higher Education,* ed. Deborah J. Carter and Reginald Wilson. Vol. 15. Washington, DC: American Council on Education.
Zimbler, Linda J. 1994. "Faculty and Instructional Staff: Who Are They and What Do They Do?" Washington, DC: American Council on Education Research Briefs 4:1, 6.

Campus Climate

Within the higher education literature, the terms "campus climate" and "campus culture" are often used interchangeably. Although campus culture and climate are at times relatively synchronous, influencing the attitudes and behavioral choices of the participants (e.g., faculty), there are some important distinctions between the two concepts.

Campus culture has been defined as the "collective, mutually shaping patterns of norms, values, practices, beliefs, and assumptions that guide the behavior of individuals and groups in higher education and provide a frame of reference within which to interpret the meaning of events and actions" (Kuh and Whitt 1988, 12–13). Further, campus culture gives meaning to its members by emphasizing the institution's unique characteristics, is deeply embedded, and changes only through repeated and consistent long-term efforts.

Campus climate, however, refers to the current perceptions, attitudes, and expectations that define the institution and its members. The examination of culture entails viewing the organization from a holistic perspective, but climate focuses on interpersonal interactions. According to Marvin Peterson and Melinda Spencer (1990), campus climate (1) encompasses the common attitudes, beliefs, perceptions, behaviors, and observations that can be compared across groups over time; (2) focuses on current patterns of beliefs and behaviors; and (3) is often ephemeral or malleable in character.

To sum up the differences, campus culture consists of the organizational values that are deeply embedded in the organizational structure and fairly resistant to change, whereas, campus climate is the atmosphere or style that permeates the moment and is more susceptible to influence and change. Thus, by attending to campus climate and addressing the issues at hand, an institution is in a greater position for effecting long-term change that eventually reshapes the campus culture. Table 7.1 (which is adapted from Peterson and Spencer 1990) further illustrates the differences between these two concepts.

Campus climate, in other words, is the metaphorical temperature gauge by which we measure a welcoming and receptive versus a cool and alienating learning environment. Indeed, Bernice

Table 7.1 Primary Distinctions of Culture and Climate

Distinction	*Culture*	*Climate*
Basis of Concept	Deeply shared values	Common member perceptions, assumptions, beliefs, or attitudes toward and ideologies of members' feelings about organizational life
Primary Conceptual Source	Anthropology, sociology	Cognitive and social linguistics, and psychology and organizational behavior
Primary Elements or Emphasis	Superordinate meaning	Common views of participants
Major Characteristics	Embedded or enduring	Current patterns or atmosphere
Nature of Change	Cataclysmic or long-term	Various malleable direct and intensive efforts and indirect measures

Source: Adapted from Peterson and Spencer 1990

Sandler and her colleagues were the first to coin the term "chilly climate" to describe the pervasiveness of inhospitable classrooms for women. Thus, campus climate is often a product of cultural assumptions and norms about what are deemed "appropriate" or "inappropriate" behaviors and verbal exchanges within a specific learning or work environment.

One of the challenges of studying and coming to understand a particular institution's campus climate is that the perception of climate is the elusive dimension "where the individual mind, the social group, and the organizational structure meet and interact" (Baird 1988, 45). In 1968, Joseph Rychlak grappled with the issue of whether any environment is best understood as "real" (actually existing independent of observation) or "ideal" (existing only in terms of perceptions).

William Tierney contends that there is no difference between reality and perception: "Reality is not something objective or external to the participants" (1997). Instead, work and learning climates are actively constructed or interpreted by members; thus, one person may evaluate a setting as "friendly," "warm," and "unrestricted," whereas another person may evaluate that same environment as "distant," "cool," and "confining." The importance of this distinction is that such perceptions may affect how individuals respond to a given environment. Negative perceptions and interpretations are likely to contribute to dissatisfaction, instability, and the desire to leave a particular environment; positive perceptions are more likely to be linked with satisfaction, stability, and the desire to remain in an environment.

The idea that people are influenced systematically by their environment is not new; it has, in fact, been discussed in the psychological and sociological literature for years (Huebner 1989). Various models of person-environment interaction have

Campus climate makes a significant difference in the attrition rate of students and in how many students graduate (Courtesy of Mount Holyoke College)

been developed in the last half of the twentieth century, five of which will be briefly reviewed: the behavior setting approach, the need-press model, the transactional approach, the human aggregate model, and the social climate model.

Roger Barker's approach to the study of person-environment relationships is based on the premise that environments select and shape the behavior of people who inhabit them through the operation of "behavior settings." That is, individuals within the same environment may behave in highly similar ways despite their individual differences. In this sense, behavior settings are bounded by "standing patterns of behavior . . . [such as] a basketball game, a worship service, a piano lesson . . . that persist when the participants change" (1968, 18). Such settings also have a "milieu [that is] an intricate complex of times, places, and things" (1968, 19). Other examples of behavior settings might be a monthly faculty meeting or teaching expectations for presenting a classroom lecture.

George Stern's (1964, 1970) need-press model is an extension and elaboration of theories presented by Henry A. Murray (1938) and Kurt Lewin (1936). The key concepts, personal needs and environmental press, are based upon three primary assumptions of the model. First, behavior is a function of the individual and the environment. Second, the person is represented in terms of needs that give direction to a person's behavior and that are inferred from self-reported behavior. Third, the environment is defined in terms of press, which is inferred from the aggregate of self-reported perceptions or interpretations of the environment (Huebner 1989).

Within this framework, behavior is studied as a function of the congruence of need and press or of the congruence between explicit press (stated purposes of an institution) and implicit press (perceived policies and practices as reported by constituents). Stern hypothesizes that a relatively congruent person-environment relationship would result in positive outcomes, such as satisfaction or fulfillment. A dissonant relationship, however, would likely result in negative outcomes, such as discomfort or stress and the desire to flee from the environment.

A third model for studying person-environment "transactions" is set forth by Lawrence Pervin (1968a, 1968b). According to Pervin, for each individual there are both interpersonal and noninterpersonal environments that are suited to, or fit, that individual's personality characteristics. A match between an individual and the environment is viewed as contributing to higher performance, greater satisfaction, and less stress, whereas poor fit is viewed as related to negative outcomes such as decreased performance, greater dissatisfaction, and more stress. However, Pervin further hypothesizes that an ideal environment for any given individual is one in which the congruence of individual and environment is not exact but presents opportunities for change and personal growth.

John Holland (1966, 1973, 1985) puts forth a model in which the influence of the environment is related to the composition of the "human aggregate"—that is, the characteristics of the people inhabiting the environment. In particular, the relationship (congruence) between an individual's characteristics and those of the aggregate determine important outcomes, such as satisfaction and achievement. Holland describes individuals according to their vocational preferences or choices. This perspective rests on Holland's belief that members of a vocational group have similar personalities and histories of development and therefore should respond to given situations in similar ways. Like Pervin, Holland is concerned with the degree of fit or congruence between individuals and their environment. He hypothesizes that a good fit is predictive of vocational satisfaction, stability, and achievement.

Rudolf Moos (1974) initially hypothesized that an environment affects the individuals who inhabit it via the "social climate." Moos's approach is grounded in the theoretical work of Murray (1938) and Lewin (1936) and builds directly from the need-press model of Stern (1964, 1970). Moos and his colleague (Insel and Moos 1974) identified three clusters or broad categories of social climate dimensions: (1) relationship dimensions (how people affiliate together and their involvement and mutual support); (2) personal development or goal orientation dimensions (the available opportunities for personal growth or task performance); and (3) system maintenance and system change dimensions (the extent to which the environment is orderly and clear in its expectations, maintains control, and is responsive to change). Based on their own data and reanalysis of others' climate scales, Insel and Moos concluded that each of these dimensions must be accounted for "in order for an adequate and reasonably complete picture of the environment to emerge" (1974, 186).

Moos (1984) hypothesizes a link between stressful life circumstances and adaptation that is affected by both the environmental system and a personal system as well as by social network resources, appraisal, and coping responses. Furthermore, factors in the environmental and personal systems can interact to produce appraisals that precipitate preventive coping responses that may reduce the possibility of future stressful life events. Much of the empirical work of Moos and his colleagues has involved the description of environments and the study of the impact of various environments and social climate dimensions of the environment on the affect, attitude, and behavior of inhabitants.

More recently, Sylvia Hurtado and her colleagues (1998) have suggested a four-dimensional framework for assessing and describing campus climate. The dimensions of this framework are (1) an institution's historical legacy of inclusion or exclusion of various racial and ethnic groups; (2) its structural diversity with regard to the numerical or proportional representation of various racial and ethnic groups; (3) the psychological climate, which includes perceptions and attitudes between and among groups; and (4) the behavioral climate, which is characterized by the nature of intergroup relations on campus.

Hence, the institutional climate for diversity on a campus is conceptualized as being a product of these four dimensions. Further, Hurtado and colleagues argue that campus climate has been examined almost exclusively from a structural perspective. When structural diversity is increased without consideration of the other dimensions of climate, problems are likely to result. Since perceptions of the institution are inextricably linked with a number of outcomes, such as retention rates of faculty, as well as with students' cognitive and affective development, such as knowledge acquisition and critical thinking skills, enhancing campus climate is directly related to improving the academic culture of the institution. In turn, the campus climate and campus culture both directly affect the academic success of the college or university with respect to student learning outcomes, faculty productivity, and student and faculty retention rates.

A plethora of research demonstrates the relationship between negative (or hostile) campus climates and the likelihood of women and racial and ethnic minorities leaving or being less successful in institutions of higher education. In describing the interplay of campus climate and culture, Hensel (1991) has reported that women are an underrepresented group in tenured faculty positions and suffer from subtle gender discrimination in teaching, research, salary differentials, and promotion. Similarly, Deborah Olsen (1991) revealed that race and gender affect the amount of compensation received, independent of whether personal and professional goals fit within institutional values and norms.

In an investigation of faculty work environments, the Massachusetts Institute of Technology (MIT) acknowledged that female faculty in its school of science earn less salary, have smaller offices, and are less likely to be granted departmental awards and distinctions than their male counterparts (Miller and Wilson 1999). Other studies have indicated that faculty of color and women faculty experience higher levels of stress and lower levels of satisfaction in colleges and universities (Astin and Cress 1998), particularly if their teaching and research interests are incongruent with departmental norms and cultural expectations. Further, the representation of women and faculty of color in significant leadership positions in academe is still quite dismal.

One explanation for these findings is that organizations and social systems tend to replicate themselves. Anthony Giddens's proposed "structuration" theory has at its heart the notion of the duality of structure: "The structural properties of social systems are both medium and outcome of the practices they recursively organize" (Giddens 1984, 25). In other words, individuals "engage in social practices that are the foundation for social structure, yet social structure limits and enables the type of practices that can be engaged in" (Foster 1989, 48).

In this respect, women faculty are often expected by many male colleagues and by the social structure of higher education itself to focus on work that is seen as "metaphoric parenting" (Ferber and Loeb 1997). To perform such "mothering" activities, women are channeled into teaching, advising, and committee work, often without the consent of the female academic herself. For example, she may be assigned to teach large core classes, advise more students, and serve as a representative to more committees by the administration. Since teaching and service are seen as requiring more caretaking capabilities and women are "naturally" able to perform these roles, female faculty dedicate significant time toward these less valued and less rewarded roles. Further complicating this situation, both tenured and nontenured women are at risk if they fail to conform to these gendered roles, since tenure, promotion, and salary increases require review by department heads and colleagues, who may penalize women faculty subtly or explicitly for not meeting their prescribed roles.

Consistent with this perspective, William Tierney and Estela Bensimón (1996) assert that faculty socialization of normative behaviors begins as early as graduate school, continues through the hiring process, and is reinforced in the organizational culture of the academic department. Refusing to heed departmental or college norms can result in being the focus of derogatory or disparaging comments, including unfavorable promotion decisions. Although Tierney and Bensimón reject the notion of a consensual culture that indoctrinates individual faculty members, structures and processes within departments provide faculty with key notions of acceptable teaching and research practices and the associated extrinsic rewards. Within these organizational structures of socialization, individual faculty can interpret their responsibilities on the basis of professional style, intrinsic motivations, and personal values. The effectiveness of individual agency, however, is diminished for some faculty (women, faculty of color, and gay and lesbian faculty) who find that asserting their own teaching and research interests into the academic culture may detrimentally impact tenure and promotion.

In response to data that indicate that academic cultures and climates have in fact inhibited the advancement of women faculty and faculty of color within the academy, educational researchers and administrators continue to search for cultural and climatic leverage points of change that will positively improve academic communities by allowing all members to achieve their fullest potential.

Christine M. Cress

See also Part 7: African American Faculty; American Indian Faculty; Asian American Faculty; Disciplinary Socialization; Hiring; Latina Faculty; Sex Discrimination; Socialization; Tenure and Promotion

References and further reading

Astin, Helene S., and Christine M. Cress. 1998. *A National Profile of Academic Women in Research Universities.* Paper presented at Women in Research Universities conference, Harvard University.

Baird, Leonard L. 1988. "The College Environment Revisited: A Review of Research and Theory." Pp. 1–52 in *Higher Education: Handbook of Theory and Research,* ed. J. C. Smart. New York: Agathon Press.

Barker, Roger G. 1968. *Ecological Psychology: Concepts and Methods for Studying the Environment.* Stanford, CA: Stanford University Press.

Ferber, Marianne A., and Jane W. Loeb, eds. 1997. *Academic Couples: Problems and Promises.* Chicago: University of Illinois Press.

Foster, William. 1989. "Toward a Critical Practice of Leadership." Pp. 39–62 in *Critical Perspectives on Leadership,* ed. J. Smyth. London: Falmer Press.

Giddens, Anthony. 1984. *The Constitution of Society.* Berkeley: University of California Press.

Hensel, Nancy. 1991. *Realizing Gender Equality in Higher Education: The Need to Integrate Work/Family Issues.* ASHE-ERIC Higher Education Report no. 2. Washington, DC: George Washington University.

Holland, John. 1966. *The Psychology of Vocational Choice: A Theory of Personality Types and Model Environments.* Waltham, MA: Blaisdell.

———. 1973. *Making Vocational Choices: A Theory of Careers.* Englewood Cliffs, NJ: Prentice-Hall.

———. 1985. *Making Vocational Choices: A Theory of Vocational Personalities and Work Environments.* Englewood Cliffs, NJ: Prentice-Hall.

Huebner, Lois A. 1989. "Interaction of Student and Campus." Pp. 165–208 in *Student Services: A Handbook for the Profession,* ed. Ursula Delworth and Gary R. Hanson. San Francisco: Jossey-Bass.

Hurtado, Sylvia, Jeffrey F. Milem, A. R. Clayton-Pedersen, and Walter R. Allen. 1998. "Enhancing Campus Climates for Racial/Ethnic Diversity: Educational Policy and Practice." *Review of Higher Education* 21, no. 3: 279–302.

Insel, Paul M., and Rudolf Moos. 1974. "Psychological Environments: Expanding the Scope of Human Ecology." *American Psychologist* 29: 179–186.

Kuh, George D., and Elizabeth J. Whitt. 1988. *The Invisible Tapestry: Cultures in American Colleges and Universities.* ASHE-ERIC Higher Education Report Series, no. 1. Washington, DC: Association for the Study of Higher Education.

Lewin, Kurt. 1936. *Principles of Topological Psychology.* New York: McGraw-Hill.

Miller, D. W., and Robin Wilson. 1999. "MIT Acknowledges Bias against Female Faculty Members." *Chronicle of Higher Education,* April 2, A18.

Moos, Rudolf H. 1974. "Systems for the Assessment and Classification of Human Environments: An Overview." Pp. 5–29 in *Issues in Social Ecology,* ed. Rudolf H. Moos and Paul M. Insel. Palo Alto, CA: National Press Books.

———. 1984. "Context and Coping: Toward a Unifying Conceptual Framework." *American Journal of Community Psychology* 12: 5–23.

Murray, Henry A. 1938. *Exploration in Personality.* New York: Oxford University Press.

Olsen, Deborah. 1991. *Women and Minority Faculty Job Satisfaction: A Structural Model Examining the Effect of Professional Interests.* ASHE Annual Meeting. ERIC Document Reproduction Service No. ED 339 323.

Pervin, L. A. 1968a. "The College as a Social System: Student Perceptions of Students, Faculty, and Administration." *Journal of Educational Research* 61: 281–284.
———. 1968b. "Performance and Satisfaction as a Function of Individual-Environment Fit." *Psychological Bulletin* 69: 56–68.
Peterson, Marvin W., and Melinda G. Spencer. 1990. *Understanding Academic Culture and Climate.* New Directions for Institutional Research, no. 68. San Francisco: Jossey-Bass.
Rychlak, Joseph F. 1968. *A Philosophy of Science for Personality Theory.* Boston: Houghton Mifflin.
Stern, George G. 1964. "B=*f*(P,E)." *Journal of Personality Assessment* 28, no. 2: 161–168.
———. 1970. *People in Context: Measuring Person-Environment Congruence in Education and Industry.* New York: Wiley.
Tierney, William G. 1997. "Organizational Socialization in Higher Education." *Journal of Higher Education* 68, no. 1: 1–16.
Tierney, William G., and Estela M Bensimón. 1996. *Promotion and Tenure: Community and Socialization in Academe.* Albany: State University of New York Press.

Comparative Issues

A review of the literature on women in higher education suggests that the marginalization of women scholars is a global phenomenon. Although women scholars have made notable strides in the academic ranks, albeit with varying degrees of success, there are continuing inequities in the distribution of rank and authority for these scholars. There are common threads that characterize the experiences of women faculty across different political, social, and cultural contexts, but different women in differing national contexts live in unique circumstances. Therefore, the following examples highlight examples of women's gendered experience in the academy worldwide.

Continuing Patterns of Exclusion

The proportion of female students has increased in many countries; for example, in the United States, women have comprised the majority of the undergraduate student body in postsecondary institutions since the 1980s (Bensimón and Marshall 1997). However, their increased presence has not translated into corresponding representation of women in graduate programs and subsequently in faculty and administrator positions across university ranks. Women faculty and administrators are particularly in positions of power and authority. A number of researchers (Harper et al. 2001; Astin et al. 1997) indicate disparities in terms of academic rank, mean income, teaching, and research activities, among other variables. With respect to academic rank, ethnic minorities (with the exception of Asian Americans) and women tend to occupy the lower academic ranks—assistant professor, lecturer, or instructor, whereas at the rank of full professor, men outnumber women at a rate of almost 3 to 1. Further, women also occupy a higher percentage of non–tenure track positions relative to their male counterparts. In cases in which male faculty are in the non–tenure track stream, they are more likely to occupy a higher rank of associate or full professor. Judith Glazer-Raymo (1999) asserts that although institutional efforts such as affirmative action have been in existence since the 1970s, there is continuing resistance and persistence of discriminatory practices that impede the ability of women faculty to participate at their optimal level. Regardless of their rank and institutional prestige, women faculty raised concerns about the need for supportive institutional cultures, equitable salary policies, appointment of women to administrative positions, appointment of women to tenure-stream positions, and implementation of women-friendly policies such as maternity leave (Brooks 1997; Acker and Feuerverger 1997; Martin 2000).

Ann Brooks's (1997) research on academic women in the United Kingdom and New Zealand points to similar patterns of exclusion for female students, faculty, and administrators. Patterns of representation of female undergraduate students in the UK have shifted from complete exclusion at the turn of the twentieth century, to selective admission into academic fields deemed appropriate for women in the 1950s through the 1970s, to a point at which they represented 50 percent of the student population in the 1990s. This increase has been most significant in polytechnics and colleges, as well as among part-time students. The increase in the student population has not translated into a significant change in the representation of female faculty, even in departments in which female students have been heavily recruited. Brooks notes that in 1991, female faculty comprised 4.7 percent of full professors, compared to 95.3 percent of their male counterparts; 10.3 percent of senior lecturers and readers, compared to 89.7 percent for male faculty; and 23.1 percent of lecturers, compared to 76.9 percent for their male colleagues. As in the United States, studies conducted in the UK and New Zealand reveal that a disproportionately high percentage of women are employed as contract workers (non–tenure track) and occupy the lowest academic ranks, that is, lecturers, junior lecturers, or tutors (Brooks 1997).

Similarly in South Africa, in the early 1990s women occupied 32 percent of the total research and teaching positions, compared to 68 percent of males. Further, the majority of women are employed in the lowest academic rank of junior lecturer or lecturer. Research conducted by Reitumetse Mabokela in 1996–1997 indicated that at some historically white South African universities, women comprised 100 percent of the faculty below junior lecturer rank, 89 percent of the junior lecturers, and 45 percent of the lecturers, the three lowest ranks within the academic hierarchy. In contrast, their male counterparts occupied 11 percent of the junior lecturer positions and 54 percent of the lecturer positions. Among the higher academic ranks, women comprised less than 3 percent of professors and about 8 percent of associate professors, compared to 97 percent and 92 percent, respectively, for their male counterparts in these positions (Mabokela 2000).

Patterns of inequity are prevalent in institutions of higher education in other countries, including New Zealand (Brooks 1997), and Canada (Acker and Feuerverger 1997). Although the sociocultural conditions and political particularities in these countries differ significantly from each other, the conditions of female academics are remarkably similar. Research conducted among Canadian women faculty demonstrates similar patterns and further highlights the institutionalization of inequitable practices. That is, the experiences of women faculty are not isolated accounts that affect only a small group but a systematic process through which universities fail to address issues that restrict a significant segment of their population. Sandra Acker's (1994) work revealed similarly disturbing themes of inequity in pay, fewer opportunity for promotion and tenure, imbalance in the workload, sexual harassment, and what Brooks (1997) identifies as "violence" in academic life.

The intersection of race and gender further compounds the position of women scholars. In the case of South Africa, the United States, and New Zealand, race has influenced and continues to influence academic and professional experiences of women of color in the academy. Accounts of women of color in the United States raise a plethora of other issues, the most poignant of which is the impact of race and racial identity. Some scholars (Welch 1990) contend that race continues to affect the professional lives of faculty of color within institutions of higher education, an environment that Turner and Myers (2000) characterize as a "chilly climate." One of the major problems is "tokenism," which Maori scholars (Brooks 1997) identified as prevalent and problematic to their advancement as scholars. That is, because of the small representation of women in predominantly male organizations, they tend to be subjected to treatment that compromises the professional contributions they could make within their organizations. Although the female scholars in the U.S. academic context are not numerically underrepresented at the lower academic ranks, they are underrepresented within the upper ranks of the university structure. For women faculty of color, they are not only underrepresented relative to their male counterparts but are similarly underrepresented among their female peers. Being a minority within a minority group presents a number of challenges for the women, including scrutiny of their professional abilities, the need to constantly prove themselves, and being pigeonholed into restricted roles, among others.

Patterns of representation among black women scholars in the South African context closely mirror those noted among women of color in the United States. A significant proportion of black women faculty are relatively new entrants to the higher education arena, especially at historically white universities, and they tend to be employed on short-term contracts relative to their white female and male counterparts. In the South African context, the race issue was steeped in the apartheid legacy of the country, where educational resources at all levels were apportioned according to one's racial classification. Apartheid ideology, which portrayed blacks as culturally and intellectually deficient, coupled with early missionary educational beliefs, which sought to prepare women to be good wives, mothers, and Christians (Martineau 1997) intensified the perception of black women in particular as intellectually inferior. Since the 1994 change of government, South African institutions of higher education have responded assertively to concerns about racial disparities, but the same cannot be said for gender issues. Although universities have expressed some concerns about gender, these concerns have yet to be translated into positive policies and programs that will affect the academic experiences of female students and the professional development of female faculty and administrators.

Even in countries where women have been somewhat successful in the academy, their experiences mirror and reflect disparities noted in the preceding discussion. For example, Twombly's (2000) study of senior women administrators in Costa Rica revealed the application of a double standard when evaluating scholarly and professional contributions of women and sex stereotyping of women's role. These women administrators believed that they had to be twice as good as their male counterparts to be successful in the university. Because of societal definition of female roles, they were perceived as good secretaries rather than good administrators and thus had to prove themselves. Scholars in Canada, New Zealand (Deem and Ozga 1997), South Africa (Mabokela 2002; Walker 1997), and the United States (Lindsay 1994) echoed this pressure on women faculty and administrators to outwork their male counterparts and prove their worth. Although the administrators in Twombly's study occupied senior positions, some noted that their appointments were in positions "designated for women." These appointments were symbolically important, but they did not necessarily carry power and authority. The Costa Rican scholars attributed their success to individual characteristics. Although they acknowledged the existence of systematic obstacles within the university structures, they also highlighted their knowledge and understanding of "the system" as crucial to their success. It is important to note that these women represent a small proportion of Costa Rican administrators in the higher education sectors, and they recognized their elite status relative to other women scholars.

Suzanne Stiver Lie and Lynda Malik (2000) identified Poland and Turkey as two other countries where women were encouraged in their pursuit of higher education. In Poland, women comprise 31.7 percent of the total faculty and 16.9 percent of full professors, and the figures for Turkey are 25 percent and 20 percent, respectively. In Turkey, the privilege of class provided a small group of elite women the opportunity to pursue advanced degrees and to secure university appointments, primarily as a source of prestige within society. Unlike female academics in other countries who identified family and household responsibilities (particularly their role as primary caregivers) as possible obstacles to their pursuit of scholarly activities, elite Turkish scholars could afford household help. Therefore, although the proportion of female faculty in Turkey is higher than others discussed in this entry, class plays a critical factor in the distribution of educational opportunities. In Poland, the fall of communism introduced major structural and cultural changes, which influenced the status of women within this country. For example, the great shortage of (male) faculty members as a result of World War II created an avenue through which women scholars could enter the ranks of the academy. Therefore, the combination of a shift to more egalitarian societal structure coupled with economic opportunity created an ideal situation for the entry of women scholars into academia in Poland (2000, 448).

Thus, a number of common threads pervade the professional experiences of academic women worldwide:

- More emphasis on teaching, which hampers women's ability to pursue research and publishing activities;
- Promotion criteria that place greater value on research and scholarship but undervalue service activities where women are most actively involved;
- Application of double standards with respect to the evaluation of women's credentials and contributions;
- The need for women scholars to prove their abilities relative to male counterparts;
- Continued underrepresentation of women faculty in academic higher ranks, even in departments with

high enrollment of women students; and
- The impact of race and class in the allocation of academic and professional opportunities.

As they have historically in the United States, academic women continue to experience marginalization and discrimination worldwide. Globally, women in academe challenge cultural, national, and religious norms that limit their education participation.

Reitumetse Obakeng Mabokela

See also Part 7: Hiring; Salaries; Sex Discrimination; Tenure and Promotion

References and further reading

Acker, Sandra. 1994. *Gendered Education.* Buckingham, UK: Open University Press.

Acker, Sandra, and Grace Feuerverger. 1997. "Enough Is Never Enough: Women's Work in Academe." Pp. 122–140 in *Feminist Critical Policy Analysis: A Perspective from Post-Secondary Education,* ed. Catherine Marshall. Washington, DC: Falmer Press.

Altbach, Philip G. 1991. *International Higher Education: An Encyclopedia.* 2 vols. New York: Garland Publishing.

Astin, Helen S., Anthony L. Antonio, Christine M. Cress, and Alexander W. Astin. 1997. *Race and Ethnicity in the American Professoriat, 1995–1996.* Los Angeles: University of California at Los Angeles, Higher Education Research Institute.

Bensimón, Estela M., and Catherine Marshall. 1997. "Policy Analysis for Post-Secondary Education: Feminist and Critical Perspectives." Pp. 143–147 in *Feminist Critical Policy Analysis II: A Perspective from Post-Secondary Education,* ed. Catherine Marshall. Washington, DC: Falmer Press.

Brooks, Ann. 1997. *Academic Women.* Bristol, UK: Society for Research into Higher Education and Open University Press.

Clark, Roger D. 1992. "Multinational Corporate Investment and Women's Participation in Higher Education." *Sociology of Education* 65: 37–47.

Deem, Rosemary, and Jenny Ozga. 1997. "Women Managing for Diversity in a Postmodern World." Pp. 25–40 in *Feminist Critical Policy Analysis: A Perspective from Post-Secondary Education,* vol. 2, ed. Catherine Marshall. Washington, DC: Falmer Press.

Eggins, Heather, ed. 1997. *Women as Leaders and Managers in Higher Education.* Buckingham, UK: Society for Research into Higher Education and Open University Press.

Glazer-Raymo, Judith. 1999. *Shattering the Myths: Women in Academe.* Baltimore: Johns Hopkins University Press.

Habu, Toshi. 2000. "The Irony of Globalization: The Experience of Japanese Women in British Higher Education." *Higher Education* 39, no. 1: 43–66.

Harper, Elizabeth P., Roger G. Baldwin, Bruce G. Gansneder, and Jay L. Chronister. 2001. "Full-Time Women Faculty Off the Tenure Track: Profile and Practice." *Review of Higher Education* 24, no. 3: 237–257.

Kulicha, J. 1991. "Current Trends and Priorities in Canadian Adult Education." *International Journal of Lifelong Education* 10, no. 2: 93–106.

Lie, Suzanne Stiver, and Lynda Malik. 2000. "Trends in the Gender Gap in Higher Education." Pp. 446–452 in *Women in Higher Education: A Feminist Perspective,* ed. Judith Glazer-Raymo, Barbara K. Townsend, and Becky Ropers-Huilman. Boston: Pearson Custom Publishing.

Mabokela, Reitumetse O. 2000. *Voices of Conflict: Desegregating South African Universities.* New York: Routledge.

———. 2002. "The Road Less Traveled: Reflections of Black Women Faculty in South African Universities." *Review of Higher Education* 25, no. 2 (Winter): 185–206.

Mabokela, Reitumetse O., and Kimberly L. King, eds. 2001. *Apartheid No More? Case Studies of Southern African Universities in the Process of Transformation.* Westport, CT: Greenwood Publishing.

Martin, Jane Roland. 2000. *Coming of Age in Academe: Rekindling Women's Hopes and Reforming the Academy.* New York: Routledge.

Martineau, Rowena. 1997. "Women and Education in South Africa: Factors Influencing Women's Educational Progress and their Entry into

Traditionally Male-Dominated Fields." *Journal of Negro Education* 66, no. 4: 383–395.
Nussbaum, Martha. 2000. "Globalization Debate Ignores the Education of Women." *Chronicle of Higher Education,* September 8, B16–B17.
Stromquist, Nellie P. 1991. *Daring to Be Different: The Choice of Nonconventional Fields of Study by International Women Students.* IIE Research Report 22. New York: Institute of International Education.
———. 1998. *Women in the Third World: An Encyclopedia of Contemporary Issues.* New York: Garland.
———, ed. 1992. *Women and Education in Latin America: Knowledge, Power and Change.* Boulder, CO: Lynne Rienner Publishers.
Turner, Carolyn Sotello Viernes, and Samuel L. Myers, Jr. 2000. *Faculty of Color in Academe: Bittersweet Success.* Boston: Allyn and Bacon.
Twombly, Susan B. 2000. "Women Academic Leaders in a Latin American University: Reconciling the Paradoxes of Professional Lives." Pp. 453–471 in *Women in Higher Education: A Feminist Perspective,* eds. J. Glazer-Raymo, Barbara K. Townsend, and Rebecca Ropers-Huilman. Boston: Pearson Custom Publishing.
Walker, Melanie. 1997. "Simply Not Good Chaps: Unraveling Gender Equity in a South African University." Pp. 41–59 in *Feminist Critical Policy Analysis: A Perspective from Post-Secondary Education,* ed. C. Marshall. Washington, DC: Falmer Press.
Welch, Lynn B., ed. 1990. *Women in Higher Education: Changes and Challenges.* New York: Praeger.

Disciplinary Socialization

The disciplinary socialization of college and university faculty is a continuous and often subtle process that begins well before women formally decide to become faculty members. Through developing skills, acquiring appropriate role behaviors, and learning disciplinary norms and values, women are incorporated into the cultures of academic disciplines, especially during their graduate training. This socialization process tends to have a strong and lasting impact on the professional values, attitudes, and behaviors of individuals trained within given disciplines.

However, in considering the effects of disciplinary socialization on the work experiences and behavior of faculty, it is also important to remember that the psychological, behavioral, and social-structural conditions under which women and men experience both their graduate training and their academic work environments differ. These differences hold important implications for successful transition and integration into a given disciplinary field. Changes over time in the gender balance within disciplinary fields also hold important implications for the progressive integration of nontraditional values and behaviors into disciplinary and academic workplace cultures.

Consequently, to understand the role that gender plays in mediating the effects of disciplinary socialization on the perceptions, experiences, and behavior of college and university faculty, it is necessary to understand the role that socialization plays in influencing women's vocational choices and experiences and to be cognizant of the central role that values play in shaping women's behavior. Finally, to more completely comprehend the work lives of women faculty, we must consider the influence of professional socialization and disciplinary values within the context of broader trends in men's and women's degree attainment within different disciplinary fields.

Trends in Degree Attainment by Disciplinary Field

The number of doctorates earned by women in American universities has increased dramatically since the 1950s. For example, in 1958, women earned just

11 percent of awarded doctorates in all fields within the United States. In 1978, women received 27 percent of doctoral degrees. By 1998, they were 42 percent of all U.S. doctoral recipients (Sanderson et al. 1999). Since 1970, there have been notable increases in women's doctoral degree attainment in traditionally "male" disciplines such as the physical sciences. However, women still continue to earn disproportionately fewer of the Ph.D.s awarded in physical science fields (Sanderson et al. 1999, 11–12).

For example, in 1998, women were 42 percent of the overall doctoral pool, yet they earned only 24 percent of doctorates awarded in the physical sciences, including 31 percent of the Ph.D.s awarded in chemistry and just 14 percent in physics and astronomy. Women were also underrepresented in some of the high-demand fields. For example, they earned a mere 27 percent of doctorates in economics; 25 percent in mathematics; 17 percent in computer science; and 13 percent in engineering. However, in 1998, women fared notably better in earned doctorates in the humanities (49 percent); in the social sciences (54 percent); and in education (63 percent) (Sanderson et al. 1999).

The persistent imbalance in gender ratios within certain academic disciplines raises important questions, not only about the origins of these imbalances but also about the resulting implications for the nature of women's graduate school training and academic careers within male-dominated academic disciplines. For example, to what extent do gender differences exist in the values of men and women faculty mentors across academic disciplines? How do men and women graduate students differentially experience their socialization within academic disciplines?

Socialization and the Path to the Professoriat

Socialization fundamentally refers to the process of role taking, which begins early in life as children come to understand and internalize the cultural norms and values of the society in which they live. Through play, family, school, and early work experience, children come to associate certain roles and activities with men and women. Through this process, they also develop expectations about their own adult roles and work activities that are available to them, that they can best perform, and that will best satisfy their career needs (Astin 1984).

Within work-related contexts, socialization reflects the process by which new members of a profession, occupation, or organization become "insiders" who ascribe to broadly agreed upon, culturally specific ways of thinking, working, and interacting (Wanous 1992). Jelyan Mortimer and Roberta Simmons explain that "socialization is a mechanism through which new members learn the values, norms, knowledge, beliefs, and the interpersonal and other skills that facilitate role performance and further group goals" (1978, 422).

For college and university faculty, socialization occurs primarily within disciplinary and institutional contexts. These two interacting subsystems form the normative context of one's professorial career by establishing the nature and conditions of academic work as well as the standards against which professional accomplishments are gauged (Finkelstein 1984). Although men and women share the same basic motivations for work, their work-related expectations, choices, and behavior tend to differ because the structure of opportunity for men and women differs. So too do their socialization experiences. Taken together, these two forces play a central role in shaping people's life choices and behavior (Astin 1984).

In the academic profession, differentials in gender ratios within the disciplines hold potentially important implications for gender differences in the internalization of cultural norms and perceptions of opportunity within the field (Kanter 1977). Furthermore, the experiences of men and women students and faculty within a given disciplinary field can vary tremendously between departments and universities. However, the cumulative effects of disparities in funding for graduate training, mentorship, and access to the disciplinary-based professional networks that are so essential in the work lives of academics may dissuade some women doctorates from pursuing faculty careers. Across fields, only 19 percent of women doctorate recipients (compared with 32 percent of their male counterparts) received primary financial support for their graduate work from research assistantships or traineeships (Sanderson et al. 1999). These differences were most pronounced in the physical sciences and life sciences. Women were comparatively more likely to rely on their own financial resources to fund graduate work. Across fields, 41 percent of women reported that personal resources were their primary source of graduate funding, compared to just 26 percent of men. This disparity was most pronounced in the social sciences (48 percent of women versus 37 percent of men) and the life sciences (23 percent of women versus 14 percent of men).

The subtle and overt discrimination accrued over time by women who aspire to academic careers may also thwart their opportunities to gain academic appointments, particularly at elite institutions. Real and perceived barriers may also negatively impact their long-term career success. To most effectively contend with the causes and consequences of patterned gender differences in disciplinary degree attainment and academic career choice requires the examination of the normative values that characterize different disciplinary cultures and the extent to which gender differences in personal and educational values prevail both within and across disciplines.

Values, Disciplinary Cultures, and Gender

Values can be conceptualized in two main ways. One way to think about values is as a set of core guidelines or beliefs that we rely upon when confronted with situations in which a choice must be made (Gibson, Ivancevich, and Donnelly 1994). Viewed this way, values represent general "modes of conduct" or notions of what we "ought" to do in various contexts and under certain circumstances (Rokeach 1973). Viewed from this perspective, values provide the standards by which we determine whether particular objects (or missions, processes, outcomes, etc.) have "value" or are to be preferred. Inherently judgmental, values essentially "carry" our ideas as to what is good, right, or desirable (Robbins 1998).

Within academic disciplines, the influence that values exert on individual and collective action is subtle yet undeniably powerful. For example, within a given college or university, the prevailing values within disciplinary-based academic units help faculty to determine not only what outcomes should be pursued but also how people should be treated and what kinds of information should be weighed in decisionmaking. As "value-rational" organizations, academic institutions are bound together by their members' broadly shared beliefs about primary roles and responsibilities as well as collectively valued personal traits and behaviors (Satow 1975). Although values can provide a strong, unifying force when people hold them in common, they can also serve as a source of fragmentation when, among a group of individuals, they are highly divergent.

Within academe, there is a core of fundamental values that transcend gender differences and disciplinary boundaries, including the production and communication of knowledge, sustained curiosity, and ongoing intellectual growth and development. Indeed, a recent national survey of college and university faculty shows that over 98 percent of men and women faculty across academic disciplines placed strong emphasis on developing undergraduate students' ability to think clearly. Similarly, regardless of gender or disciplinary background, over 86 percent of faculty placed high value on being a good colleague. Over 96 percent placed high value on being a good teacher (Sax et al. 1999).

Helen S. Astin and
Jennifer Lindholm

See also Part 7: Curricular and Professional Choices; Socialization; Tenure and Promotion

References and further reading

Astin, Helen S. 1984. "The Meaning of Work in Women's Lives: A Sociopsychological Model of Career Choice and Work Behavior." *Counseling Psychologist* 12, no. 4: 117–126.

Becher, Tony. 1987. "The Disciplinary Shaping of the Profession." Pp. 271–303 in *The Academic Profession: National, Disciplinary, and Institutional Settings,* ed. Burton R. Clark. Berkeley: University of California Press.

Finkelstein, Martin J. 1984. *The American Academic Profession: A Synthesis of Social Scientific Inquiry since World War II.* Columbus: Ohio State University.

Gibson, James L., John M. Ivancevich, and James H. Donnelly. 1994. *Organizations: Behavior, Structure, Process.* 8th ed. Burr Ridge, IL: Irwin.

Kanter, Rosabeth Moss. 1977. *Men and Women of the Corporation.* New York: Basic Books.

Kolb, David A. 1981. "Learning Styles and Disciplinary Differences." Pp. 232–255 in *The Modern American College: Responding to the Realities of Diverse Students and a Changing Society,* ed. A. W. Chickering and Associates. San Francisco: Jossey-Bass.

Mortimer, Jelyan T., and Roberta Simmons. 1978. "Adult Socialization." *Annual Review of Sociology* 4: 421–454.

Robbins, Stephen P. 1998. *Organizational Behavior: Concepts, Controversies, Applications.* 8th ed. Upper Saddle River, NJ: Prentice-Hall.

Rokeach, Milton. 1973. *The Nature of Human Values.* New York: Free Press.

Sanderson, Allen R., Bernard Dugoni, Tom Hoffer, and Lance Selfa. 1999. *Doctorate Recipients from United States Universities: Summary Report, 1998.* Chicago: National Opinion Research Center at the University of Chicago.

Satow, Roberta L. 1975. "Value-Rational Authority and Professional Organizations: Weber's Missing Type." *Administrative Science Quarterly* 20: 526–531.

Sax, Linda J., Alexander W. Astin, William S. Korn, and Shannon K. Gilmartin. 1999. *The American College Teacher: National Norms for the 1998–99 HERI Faculty Survey.* Los Angeles: Higher Education Research Institute.

Wanous, John P. 1992. *Organizational Entry: Recruitment, Selection, Orientation, and Socialization of Newcomers.* Reading, MA: Addison-Wesley.

Evaluation

Women in higher education have been regarded as second-class members of the academy. Women strove to gain access to higher education and, once in, struggled to ensure equitable treatment. They still have a long way to go to achieve parity with their male counterparts in areas such as access to and representation across the disciplines, representation in the curriculum and ability to shape it, and equal representation in the professoriat.

The number of women faculty in the academy is far lower than that of male faculty. In 1900, women comprised only 11 percent of the professoriat; today, the ratio has increased to 34 percent. Although the increase does indicate a gain for women, the inequity is still particularly evident as one moves up the professorial ranks toward the most elite level of full professor. Of the more than 500,000 faculty in the United States, 159,333 were full professors, but only 18 percent of that number were women as of 1998. At the rank of associate professor and assistant professor, only 32 percent and 44 percent, respectively, were women (National Center for Education Statistics 2001, table 226).

In the professoriat, women faculty are unequally represented across all ranks, especially in the upper ranks, they are often perceived to be less serious or dedicated than their male counterparts, and senior faculty tend not to spend as much time mentoring women faculty as they do men. Furthermore, collegial environments that are so crucial to maintaining high levels of productivity are often nonexistent for women faculty. Although men generally (and Caucasian men in particular) have access to a "boys' network" that serves as a mentoring and socialization system, women faculty often do not. The absence of such networks for women might hinder the development of important relationships and reduce the range of opportunities available. The result is exclusion from a collegial experience, which can often define the success of a faculty member. Furthermore, influence that usually accompanies top-level positions is wielded mostly by men rather than women. That is critical because those in decisionmaking positions, who tend overwhelmingly to be men, are operating in a system that has been designed to accommodate more closely the needs and experiences of academic men than academic women.

The manner in which faculty move up the professorial ranks is generally through demonstrating excellence in research and scholarship, teaching, and service. What is deemed excellent performance in these three areas differs by institutional type (i.e., research, comprehensive, two-year). For example, even though faculty in research universities engage in research and scholarship, teaching, and service, it is research productivity that takes precedence over other activities. Women faculty tend to be at a disadvantage when it comes to the evaluation of their work, for it often is evaluated less positively than the work produced by their male counterparts. It is the manner in which the work of women faculty is evaluated that brings the particular differences to light.

Faculty evaluation in higher education is a very important process in most institutions. Faculty are evaluated at the time of hire and for tenure and promotion, and some also undergo posttenure evaluation. However, not every evaluation that faculty undergo is for tenure or promotion. Most faculty undergo annual performance evaluations, which is in addition to the other types of evaluation previously mentioned. Oftentimes, one of the outcomes of annual evaluation is to determine salary raises, workloads, and other rewards. The problem for women faculty is not that they are evaluated but that the inequity inherent in the evaluation process puts them at a disadvantage relative to their male counterparts because of the manner in which certain activities are weighted and privileged over others. The disadvantage is problematic for three reasons: (1) the type of scholarship that many women faculty pursue puts them at a disadvantage during the annual evaluation process, (2) women faculty often carry an unequal teaching load, compared to their male colleagues, and (3) women faculty tend to spend more time on service activities.

The type of scholarship that many women faculty pursue puts them at a disadvantage during the annual evaluation process because the scholarship that many women faculty engage in is not always "mainstream." Women faculty may look at issues from a feminist perspective and study topics that are not traditional and that challenge existing power structures. This type of work is often published in feminist or other nonmainstream journals, which tend not to be taken as seriously or evaluated as favorably as the work that appears in more traditional journals. As a result, women faculty who engage in innovative work, although not less productive than their male counterparts, encounter dominant institutional and departmental ideologies that often devalue alternative research perspectives. Faculty committees that are charged with evaluating this scholarship are often composed of men who habitually evaluate the research and scholarship of their female colleagues through the lenses of their own scholarly traditions, many of which have most likely never been challenged.

Studies have shown this milieu to be detrimental to women who engage in nontraditional work because they will find that at evaluation time, their work is devalued and deemed of lesser importance than male-created research and scholarship. Oftentimes, the quality of work is evaluated by committees who are more traditional in their scholarship and do not understand or value work that is different from their own.

Turning now to the area of teaching in the trilogy of faculty responsibilities, women faculty often carry an unequal teaching load at all types of institutions, compared to their male colleagues. In 1998, the average time women faculty were spending on teaching was 61 percent, compared to 43 percent for male faculty. In addition to spending more time in the classroom than their male colleagues, women faculty also spend more time preparing for their classes and more time advising students than their male colleagues. This disparity might be related to the type of courses women are assigned to teach, which tend to be large undergraduate and remedial classes. These types of courses inherently carry greater advising loads and workloads than smaller or advanced courses. A high teaching load is problematic for all faculty because it often comes at the expense of research and scholarship, which is what tends to reap the highest monetary rewards. Therefore, come evaluation time, those who engage in activities that are not rewarded as highly will have lower evaluations and, hence, lower rewards. Unfortunately, this seems to be the case more for women faculty than for male faculty.

Another obligation that women faculty tend to spend more time fulfilling than their male colleagues is service. Women faculty have been found to spend up to 50 percent more time on service activities than their male counterparts. There are two types of service activities: those internal to the institution and those external. The latter includes such activities as serving on a professional or editorial board or holding office in a professional organization. The former are all those activities internal to the institution. More so than their male colleagues, women faculty tend to engage in institutional service activities. A reason for this may be that the numbers of women faculty are low, and therefore in the interest of committee diversity, they are appointed to serve on more committees than their male counterparts. Even within the institution, there are hierarchical service activities, and oftentimes women faculty are relegated to committees that are not as powerful as those to which their male counterparts are appointed. The "choice" committees do have female representation, but often only one or two women among a group of men. This situation may be caused in part by the perpetuation of the "old boys' network" that facilitates access to those who are a part of that network. Furthermore, student and minority groups on campus often request women faculty as advisors or ad hoc members because women faculty are a positive role model for female students. Additionally, women faculty tend to be approached more by students who have personal and academic concerns, probably because of the perception that women are better nurturers and caretakers than men. Or, perhaps because of large teaching loads, by default a large number of students seek out women faculty's guidance and advice.

Service is important in the academy. Much of the work that needs to be done would not be accomplished if it were not for the faculty who serve on these committees. The problem for women faculty is not the act of performing service, but the disparate manner in which service is delegated. Service activities in general are rated lower than research and scholarship and teaching activities. Those who spend a great deal of time on service activities are at a disadvantage. In addition, those who spend their time on institutional service activities are at a greater disadvantage since it tends to be rated lower than external professional service. Unfortunately, women are disproportionately placed in the internal service role. Since annual evaluations are often tied to salary raises and other rewards, spending too much time on service activities can be detrimental. The amount of time faculty spend on service is more consequential at institutions that use annual evaluation as the sole determinant of raises.

In sum, faculty rewards such as salary raises are based on the evaluation of performance in the areas of research and scholarship, teaching, and service. Empirical data indicate that published research is considered to be the most important factor—above teaching and service—in tenure, promotion, and salary increase decisions, regardless of type of institution. Thus, the work that women faculty engage in is often rated lower, which tends to result in lower rewards. It is important to note that not all salary increments are based upon evaluation. Some institutions provide cost-of-living raises or step-salary increases to their faculty. Even these types of increments, however, place those who are at lower salary ranks—including the bulk of female faculty—at a disadvantage, since such increases are often based on a percentage of their smaller base salaries.

The manner in which evaluation is carried out at many institutions puts those who do not fit a traditional profile at a disadvantage relative to those who do. Faculty who undertake activities that are considered to be within the norm in terms of scholarship are privileged over those who do not. Teaching is not rewarded on the same level as research and scholarship, which, again, privileges those who have greater control of the manner in which teaching assignments are distributed. Service is clearly a distant third in the trilogy of faculty work. Unfortunately, women faculty receive the short end of the stick during evaluations because of the manner in which their work is evaluated and how it is distributed by their academic units. A solution to this inequity in the evaluation process is twofold: (1) there must be a shift from tendency for institutions to institute a "one-size-fits-all" approach to annual evaluation that privileges mainstream work; and (2) there must be a conscious effort to ensure that women faculty do not get channeled into "women's work," which is valued less than men's work.

Marta Soto

See also Part 7: Hiring; Socialization; Tenure and Promotion

References and further reading

Aisenberg, Nadya, and Mona Harrington. 1988. *Women of Academe: Outside the Sacred Grove.* Amherst: University of Massachusetts.

Glazer, Judith S., Estela M. Bensimón, and Barbara K. Townsend. 1993. *Women in Higher Education: A Feminist Perspective.* ASHE Reader Series: Needham, MA: Ginn Press.

Glazer-Raymo, Judith. 1999. *Shattering the Myths: Women in Academe.* Baltimore: Johns Hopkins University Press.

National Center for Education Statistics. 2001. *Digest of Education Statistics.* Washington, DC: U.S. Department of Education.

Simeone, Angela. 1987. *Academic Women: Working towards Equality.* South Hadley, MA: Bergin and Garvey.

Statham, Anne, Laurel Richardson, and Judith A. Cook. 1991. *Gender and University Teaching: A Negotiated Difference.* New York: State University of New York.

Hiring

Since 1900 the number of women faculty in American institutions of higher education has grown substantially. However, the proportion of women faculty to men faculty has been slow to change and has suffered a number of setbacks. For example, in 1910 women constituted 20 percent of faculty across the nation. By 1940, that number had reached 28 percent, only to fall back in the postwar years, so that by 1970 women represented only 23 percent of the national professoriat (Busenburg and Smith 1997). In 1992 women held more positions in public two-year institutions (44.6 percent) than in public research institutions (22.8 percent) or in private research institutions (30 percent). The number of women in faculty positions in colleges and universities across the country more than doubled from 1970 to 1993. Despite these gains, in 1993 women held more full-time than part-time positions only in private four-year institutions and were in the majority only in private two-year colleges (Glazer-Raymo 1999, 36–64). The proportion of female to male faculty has grown most at the lower ranks, with most women holding either part-time or non–tenure track positions. Less than two-fifths of all women faculty are on the tenure track. This trend may be changing, however.

Among the ranks of junior faculty (those with less than seven years' experience), women made up 41 percent of the population in 1995 (Glazer-Raymo 1999). By 1997, that number had reached 45 percent at the assistant professor level. However, at the associate professor level, women made up 34 percent of the population and, at the full professor level, just 20 percent (National Center for Education Statistics 2001, table 230).

The number of women faculty in two-year colleges has also grown. In 1997, nearly half the faculty members in U.S. two-year colleges were women. Two-year colleges have increased the size of their faculties to keep pace with full-time-equivalent enrollments, which rose substantially from 1970 to 1995 (National Center for Education Statistics 2001, tables 227 and 173).

As the above statistics indicate, women have made progress in terms of being hired into faculty positions across the country. However, some reports indicate that although the number of women being hired has increased, almost as many leave the system each year. Higher education is simply failing to retain in significant numbers those who have been hired, an issue that speaks to the continuing chilly climate for women and the lack of significant mentoring for both white and minority women. Cutbacks have also affected women faculty unequally in some places across the country. Many colleges and universities have failed to find a way to balance cost cutting with equity, privileging the careers of men over women.

Affirmative action policies have benefited women more than minorities in general. White women, however, have been the central beneficiaries of these policies. In 1997, 83.1 percent of the women who held assistant professor positions in U.S. colleges and universities were white, and 87.2 percent of female associate professors and 87.5 percent of female full professors were white. Of women assistant professors, 7.5 percent were black, constituting the largest percentage of women of color in the fall of 1997. More than 5 percent of female assistant professors were Asian, 3 percent were Hispanic, and 0.5 percent were American Indian (National Center for Education Statistics 2001, table 230). Studies indicate that minority women face the dual burdens of racism and sexism and thus confront special challenges. African American women, for example, report lower satisfaction with their professional lives than men, a greater sense of isolation on campus, and more negative treatment by colleagues (Singh, Robinson, and Williams-Green 1995).

The percentage of women in full-time tenure-track faculty positions also varies widely by discipline. Data from 1995 on junior faculty (those with less than seven years' experience) indicate that the largest increase in new faculty has been in the social sciences, fine arts, education, humanities, and health sciences. The smallest increases were in agriculture and engineering, where only 4 percent of faculty were women.

Despite some gains, new evidence in the 1990s indicated that women still often face a hostile environment in higher education, with minority group women, older women, disabled, and lesbian women facing double discrimination. Another problem for women can be the need to persuade institutions to hire spouses or partners, as more and more academic couples make compromises in their careers to stay together. Couples may take a position where one person has a full-time job and one a part-time job or create a job-sharing position.

The first obstacle a woman faces is getting hired for a tenure-track faculty position. At this point she must convince her prospective colleagues that she is the best candidate for the job; ascertain that the job is one that she wants; and negotiate salary, benefits, and teaching loads. Much advice given to women entering the job market might apply to men as well, but some advice is specific to the particular difficulties women face. Which advice is most helpful depends on the individual woman and her situation.

In beginning the job search, women are advised to consider applying for jobs in other departments, as well as in those identical to their own, to read advertisements in regular publications, to tell everyone they know that they are looking for a job, to attend conferences and enroll in available job placement services, to be alert to last-minute positions in the late spring and early summer, to be explicit about what they want in asking others to write letters of recommendation, and to expect that it might take several years to find the right job. Candidates should consider interim positions, such as postdoctoral work or soft money jobs, as opportunities to make important contacts and to produce work that will aid in the job search. In addition, women who have spent a large part of their careers in part-time or non–tenure track employment may still find permanent full-time employment if they persevere.

An important step in the job search is the preparation of the curriculum vitae. Women should be sure to include all relevant information for the job for which they are currently applying, be aware of the general tendency women have to minimize experiences and achievements, and update their vitae according to the format of their current institution when they are hired. Women should try to enter the job interview armed with a list of questions potential faculty might be asked and questions they need to ask as candidates to fully understand the job. They should try to ascertain what interested the particular institution when it called them for an interview and make sure they understand what the institution is looking for. It is best to rehearse the interview with friends or colleagues before arriving. Even with rehearsals, candidates should be ready for unexpected events and remain flexible; this flexibility may be the one trait departments find most attractive in a candidate.

Before being hired, women need to gather as accurate a picture of their potential department as possible. When interviewed alone, graduate or undergraduate students can give the candidate a clear picture of their experiences and what it feels like to be students in that particular department. Finding the proper match is a central task of new faculty as they proceed through the hiring process.

If offered a job, women should ask in detail about their contracts, talk to the department chair about start-up funds or equipment, teaching load, or other items not spelled out in the contract, ask for the offer in writing, take the time to think carefully before accepting, and ask for feedback if they are not hired. Women are cautioned to negotiate for more than the initial salary offer made. Often they are so grateful to be offered employment that they accept the first salary offer they are given. Many women are then stuck in a lower rung of the salary scale than their male colleagues for years, with no hope of moving up. The best strategy against pay discrimination is prevention in the form of shrewd negotiating at the time of the job offer. The emotional and financial costs of lawsuits to rectify unfair treatment is high.

Once hired, new faculty face many challenges as they begin their academic careers: gaining the acceptance of colleagues, meeting the expectations of their institutions, establishing teaching styles and skills, developing habits of writing productivity, and managing their time well. They are expected to hit the ground running and often experience high levels of stress and low levels of occupational satisfaction. Their level of satisfaction is often based on whether they have found a good match between their interests, expectations, values, and skills and those of their new department or college.

Newcomers are likely to experience reality shock, or conflicts between what they anticipated and what they believe they have found. The period of organizational entry, both during the initial job interview and during a faculty member's first days on the job, is the point at which an individual is most susceptible to organizational socialization efforts. This is the period during which a woman establishes the core of her organizational identity. For women, this period is layered with the gendered expectations of her department members. One of the most common is that women are more nurturing and should therefore take on a greater advising role than the male members of the department. For women of color, there are both gender and racial stereotypes to deal with. For many women, institutional misogyny is a fact of life in the academy. Feminist scholars face questions about whether to pursue a feminist research agenda, what courses to teach, and how to integrate their feminist concerns into those courses at every turn during this initial period. They face real fears about how their research agenda may be devalued, creating additional obstacles to tenure and promotion and whether their teaching evaluations might be more negative if they pursue issues of class, race, and gender in the classroom.

Discrimination can be felt in all three central functions of new faculty: teaching, research, and service, to the point at which some feminist scholars have described faculty work for women as "working in the ivory basement" (Benokraitis 1998). Discrimination can take the form of gatekeeping (keeping women off key committees or out of collaborative research projects), professional diminution, or intellectual intimidation. Benokraitis concludes that "the action of women themselves is critical for major reforms at the individual, organizational, institutional and cultural levels" (1998, 31). However, individual women are not solely responsible for the changes that must take place for faculty women to achieve equity in higher education. The nation's colleges and universities must also take steps to ensure equitable hiring and employment practices.

What can colleges and universities that are committed to hiring women and minorities do to facilitate equity in the hiring process? Institutional commitment means more than simply complying with federally mandated affirmative action requirements. As hiring becomes more competitive, institutions with the best working environments will have a larger pool of candidates from which to choose. Negative attitudes often impede the hiring of women candidates, such as the subconscious belief that no qualified minority or female candidates exist. If departments are hiring women or minorities simply because they are being compelled to by political or social pressures, candidates will be likely to sense it and feel patronized or fear that if they are hired, they will not be truly welcomed into the academic community. To ascertain whether a department holds negative attitudes, hiring, retention, and exit figures must be examined. In addition, colleges and universities must be alert to common arguments for not hiring women, such as the fact that there are simply not enough qualified women in the pool. This argument is no longer true, given that 42 percent of those receiving doctorates in 1997–1998 were women (National Center for Education Statistics 2001, table 248).

Two problems cited by faculty at the point of hire are the lack of faculty mentors and overwhelming service requirements. Women often have greater needs for spousal employment and child care, points that should be attended to in the recruiting process. A recent study indicates that 45 percent of research universities and only 20 percent of liberal arts colleges had such policies (Wolf-Wendel, Twombly, and Rice 2000).

Institutions are best served by developing recruiting networks that are in place when it is time to hire new faculty. Women faculty already at the institution can be a rich source of recommendations and referrals. The use of visiting scholar programs and postdoctoral fellowships are also important tools in the recruiting process. When the search begins, institutions must be alert to inappropriate questions faculty may ask that could skew the interview process and subtle or unconscious attitudes about those that are different from present faculty (Swoboda 1993).

Joanne E. Cooper

See also Part 1: Lesbian, Gay, Bisexual, and Transgender Issues on Campus; Part 7: African American Faculty; American Indian Faculty; Asian American Faculty; Campus Climate; Latina Faculty; Salaries; Sex Discrimination; Tenure and Promotion

References and further reading

Benokraitis, Nijole V. 1998. "Working in the Ivory Basement: Subtle Sex Discrimination in Higher Education." Pp. 3–35 in *Career Strategies for Women in Academe: Arming Athena,* ed. Lynn H. Collins, Joan C. Chrisler, and Kathryn Quina. Thousand Oaks, CA: Sage Publications.

Busenberg, Bonnie E., and Daryl G. Smith. 1997. "Affirmative Action and Beyond: The Woman's Perspective." Pp. 149–180 in *Affirmative Action's Testament of Hope: Strategies for a New Era in Higher Education,* ed. Mildred Garcia. New York: State University of New York Press.

Caplan, Paula. 1993. *Lifting a Ton of Feathers: A Woman's Guide to Surviving in the Academic World.* Toronto: University of Toronto Press.

Chronicle of Higher Education. 2000. Almanac Issue. Volume XLVII, no. 1.

Collins, Lynn H., Joan C. Chrisler, and Kathryn Quina, eds. 1998. *Career Strategies for Women in Academe: Arming Athena.* Thousand Oaks, CA: Sage Publications.

Glazer-Raymo, Judith. 1999. *Shattering the Myths: Women in Academe.* Baltimore: Johns Hopkins University Press.

Lewis, Magda. 1999. "The Backlash Factor: Women, Intellectual Labor and Student Evaluation of Courses and Teaching." Pp. 59–82 in *Everyday Knowledge and Uncommon Truths: Women of Academe,* ed. Linda K. Christian-Smith and Kristine S. Kellor. Boulder, CO: Westview Press.

Menges, Robert. 1999. *Faculty in New Jobs: A Guide to Settling In, Becoming Established, and Building Institutional Support.* San Francisco: Jossey-Bass.

National Center for Education Statistics. 2001. *Digest of Education Statistics.* Washington, DC: U.S. Department of Education.

Singh, K., A. Robinson, and J. Williams-Green. 1995. "Differences in Perceptions of African American Women and Men Faculty and Administrators." *Journal of Negro Education,* 64, no. 4: 401–408.

Swoboda, M. J. 1993. "Hiring Women and Minorities." Pp. 123–136 in *The Art of*

Hiring in America's Colleges and Universities, ed. R. H. Stein and S. J. Trachtenberg. Buffalo, NY: Prometheus Books.

Wolf-Wendel, Lisa, Susan Twombly, and S. Rice. 2000. "Dual-Career Couples: Keeping Them Together." *Journal of Higher Education* 71, no. 3: 291–321.

Latina Faculty

Latina faculty are quite diverse, encompassing Chicanas, Puerto Ricans, and Cubanas, among others, as well as some who also identify themselves as black. At the same time, they share language, culture, religion, and experiences of oppression. In academe, they share experiences of underrepresentation, low rewards, isolation, marginalization, and exploitation.

To begin with more objective indicators, Latinas are both underrepresented and underrewarded. Although they have made gains, they still comprise less than 1 percent of faculty in academe (Rai and Critzer 2000). These numbers are lower than for any racial-ethnic and gender group other than American Indians, whose population is much smaller. Further, Latinas are even more underrepresented at more prestigious four-year institutions. In 1995, Latinas were 1.6 percent of faculty in two-year public colleges, but only 0.6 percent in research universities (Finnegan, Webster, and Gamson 1996). Latinas are less likely to be tenured than any other gender or racial-ethnic group; and the higher the rank, the lower their prevalence as well: in 1995, Latinas accounted for 1.2 percent of assistant professors, 0.8 percent of associate professors, and 0.3 percent of full professors (Ortiz 1998). Only 9 percent of Latinas are full professors, and 16 percent are associates (Medina and Luna 2000). Salaries are also disproportionately low for Latinas.

University professor Carmen Iglesias (Rafael Roa/Corbis)

As a group, Latinos' salaries are 7 percent lower than those whites receive; Latinas are further disadvantaged, receiving 13 percent less than men in their racial-ethnic group (Nettles and Perna 1995). These salary gaps persist even when one takes into account differences in teaching and research activity (Nettles, Perna, and Bradburn 2000).

Latinas experience more discrimination than their male counterparts or their white female peers due to the intersections of both racism and sexism. For instance, their advancement is even more obstructed than is white women's (Aguirre 2000). Although all female faculty face heavier service demands than do men, white woman can more easily turn down some of this work than can Latinas, particularly because many Latinas realize there are so few minority women to represent their group. At the same time, Latinas' careers can be obstructed because they are often encouraged to stay in positions in which they would work primarily with students of color or concentrate only on those issues or programs. Such positions tend to be dead-end (Hernandez and Morales 1999).

Latinas must struggle for authority, both as researchers and as teachers. Their scholarship is often devalued because the "brown-on-brown" research taboo means that Latinos' research on their own group is depicted as "too narrow" and not objective. The double standard, of course, means that such research by whites draws praise and that white-on-white research strikes virtually all peers as "objective" and legitimate (de la Luz Reyes and Halcon 1991). Such devaluation of Latinas' research, built into the social psychology of tokenism, influences tenure and promotion decisions.

In the classroom, Latinos report that students at predominantly white institutions feel that they are "too biased" when they discuss either "women's" or "minority" issues. By contrast, whites who discuss "minority" topics and men who pursue "women's" issues can appear progressive, sensitive, and liberal rather than selfish. As a result, Latinas face persistent challenges to their authority in classrooms.

Latinas experience the academy as alienating in other ways as well. As tokens, they must work harder than dominant-group members to demonstrate that they have not relied upon affirmative action for advancement. Their heightened visibility also means that Latinas are expected to be "model" academic citizens who are very different from the rest of their minority group. At the same time, being recognized for their color first and not for their credentials reminds them that they are outsiders. They end up in a contradictory location: outsiders who must be model citizens.

Token status also means isolation. Latinas lack supportive networks, receive little mentoring, and face exclusion from decisionmaking processes. Many report finding the academy an inhospitable place—in the words of one, a "desert" (Hernandez and Morales 1999). "Barrioization" can occur, in which Latinos assume marginal positions (departments and programs within the university such as Chicano studies or ethnic studies programs, Spanish, or bilingual education), rather than move into mainstream programs in which they have often received their degrees, such as sociology. They are further relegated to university committees that are both limited and deal only with issues such as student recruitment or cultural awareness. Such isolation can strengthen perceptions that Latinos are affirmative action hires or that their work amounts to political advocacy rather than disciplined scholarship.

Latina faculty can thus engage in highly visible activities of value to universities yet remain marginal to institutional power. They are supposed to know everything about and represent all Latinos, and they are asked to facilitate minor changes in such curriculum and recruitment. However, they are not to exercise real power that might influence decisionmaking about academic policy or majors. They are asked to address minority concerns but at the same time are rarely seen by majority faculty as legitimate scholars.

Language and accent biases present important barriers. Latinas report that others laugh at their accents and that colleagues' impatience with less-than-perfect English can enforce a type of silence and also cause others to question their competence. It also reinforces cultural isolation and prejudice.

To be a woman in academia is problematic; the culture of academe is traditionally based on commonalities with little allowance for differences. The dictates of a male professoriat require women to remain distant and objective—traits contradictory to much of female socialization. To be Latina in the academy, however, presents yet another cultural contradiction because so many faculty expectations have been defined on the basis of Anglo society. Such cultural conflict can generate stress for Latinas. For instance, norms of tolerance and cooperation place them at odds with a competitive academic environment. Further, the consequent reluctance to challenge others' ideas may be perceived as incompetence. Variations in norms concerning comfort in relation to closer personal space can be misunderstood, and differences in friendship expectations and meanings can enhance feelings of isolation. Similarly, people assume that Latinas have greater family obligations than do Latinos and that home and family must be their main focus. True or not, this stereotype implies to the dominant group that Latinas are dependent and powerless. Thus, their dedication to their work and consequent mobility are further jeopardized.

Latinas thus face a situation in which they are "others" along multiple, intersecting dimensions and cannot truly be faculty and maintain their identity (Martinez 1995). They must make costly choices among their past, language, culture, and identity and their success within the academy.

Toni Calasanti and
Janice Witt Smith

See also Part 5: Affirmative Action and Employment; Part 6: Tenure and Promotion

References and further reading

Aguirre, Adalberto, Jr. 2000. *Women and Minority Faculty in the Academic Workplace.* San Francisco: Jossey-Bass.

de la Luz Reyes, Maria, and John J. Halcon. 1991. "Practices of the Academy: Barriers to Access for Chicano Academics." Pp. 167–186 in *The Radical Crisis in American Higher Education,* ed. Philip G. Altbach and Kofi Lomotey. Albany: State University of New York Press.

Finnegan, D. E., D. Webster, and Z. F. Gamson. 1996. *Faculty and Faculty Issues in Colleges and Universities.* 2nd ed. Needham Heights, MA: Simon and Schuster Custom Publishing.

Hernandez, Thomas J., and Nestor Enrique Morales. 1999. "Career, Culture, and Compromise: Career Development Experiences of Latinas Working in Higher Education." *Career Development Quarterly* 48, no. 1: 45–58.

Martínez Alemán, Ana M. 1995. "Actuando." Pp. 67–76 in *The Leaning Ivory Tower: Latino Professors in American Universities,* ed. Raymond V. Padilla and Rudolfo Chavez Chavez. Albany: State University of New York Press.

Medina, Catherine, and Gaye Luna. 2000. "Narratives from Latina Professors in Higher Education." *Anthropology and Education Quarterly* 31, no. 1: 47–66.

Nettles, Michael T., Laura W. Perna, and Ellen M. Bradburn. 2000. "Salary, Promotion, and Tenure Status of Minority and Women Faculty in U.S. Colleges and Universities." National Center for Education Statistics, Publication 440 608. Washington, DC: U.S. Department of Education.

Ortiz, Flora Ida. 1998. "Career Patterns of People of Color in Academia." Pp. 120–135 in *The Multicultural Campus: Strategies for Transforming Higher Education,* ed. Leonard A. Valverde and Louis A. Castenell, Jr. Walnut Creek, CA: Alta Mira Press.

Padilla, Raymond V., and Rudolfo Chávez Chávez, eds. 1995. *The Leaning Ivory Tower: Latino Professors in American Universities.* Albany: State University of New York Press.

Rai, Kul B., and John W. Critzer. 2000. *Affirmative Action and the University: Race, Ethnicity, and Gender in Higher Education Employment.* Lincoln: University of Nebraska Press.

Turner, Caroline Sotello Viernes, and Samuel L. Myers, Jr. 2000. *Faculty of*

Color in Academe: Bittersweet Success. Boston: Allyn and Bacon.

Lesbian Faculty

Lesbian faculty are those women who teach and conduct research in postsecondary institutions whose primary sexual and emotional expressions and attachments are with women. Lesbian faculty may or may not conduct scholarship in lesbian studies or about issues pertaining to lesbians and may or may not be "out" in their classrooms, departments, institutions, or fields. The presence of lesbian faculty in U.S. colleges and universities has been documented since the emergence of women's colleges in the late nineteenth century. However, until the last three decades of the twentieth century, there were few social or academic networks for these women to explore the meanings of sexuality in academic life or to create self-consciously lesbian scholarship. Despite the marginalization lesbians have faced in their universities and fields, many have worked to improve their professional lives by challenging homophobic attitudes and heterosexist policies on campuses and creating a body of scholarship about lesbians' lives.

Lesbian faculty first organized in postsecondary institutions after the Stonewall rebellion of 1969 in New York City, which marks the emergence of the modern gay liberation movement. A number of scholars founded the Gay Academic Union (GAU) in New York in 1973, which then formed chapters and hosted conferences in such cities as Philadelphia, Ann Arbor, Boston, and Chicago throughout the decade. Tied to gay liberationist activism, the GAU focused on connecting personal liberation in the form of "coming out" to social change, ending discrimination against gays and lesbians through education, and developing new approaches to "gay studies" in the academy. GAU members sought to combat social, medical, and psychological models of deviance and disease that defined scholarly understandings of gay men and lesbians by creating alternative histories and theories pertaining to gay and lesbian lives. These academics made significant inroads in developing gay and lesbian caucuses in disciplinary professional organizations, such as the Modern Language Association in 1973 and the American Anthropological and American Sociological Associations in 1974. However, sexism in the GAU led to the departure of many women from the organization in 1976. As the GAU declined due to internal political differences, disciplines and disciplinary organizations gained importance as alternative sites for defining and legitimizing gay and lesbian scholarship and scholars.

During the 1970s, the scholarship of lesbian faculty was also enabled by the development and institutionalization of women's studies. However, despite the integral roles lesbians played in inaugurating many women's studies programs and courses, homophobia and fear of the delegitimization of women's studies prevented academic feminists from acknowledging the work of lesbian faculty and the importance of scholarship pertaining to lesbians until the mid-1980s. Thus, the early history of post-Stonewall lesbian faculty is defined by marginalization in both the gay and lesbian and the feminist movements as lesbians sought personal and scholarly legitimization in the academy.

An early project of lesbian faculty was to create a field of lesbian studies. Consonant with activism's basis in identity politics, which seeks to create gay and lesbian voice and visibility and a collective position from which to struggle, the definition of the lesbian, lesbian experience, and lesbian culture was integral to gaining credibility as a field. Just as gay male and feminist scholarship developed around collective identity and experience, which led to projects to recover lost history and literature, lesbians sought to create their own area of study by casting lesbian identity and experience in a positive light. Through archival work, lesbian faculty and independent scholars constructed a visible lesbian history, identified a lesbian literary tradition, and created narrative accounts of oppression and resistance in lesbian lives. This work was predicated on a belief that history and literature can offer role models and heroes, examples of agency and change, and an understanding of the world that can be put to use in the present and future. Moreover, this scholarship demonstrated the existence of viable material and topics of study across disciplines.

However, in the late 1970s and early 1980s in and out of the academy, lesbians of color challenged white lesbians' monolithic definitions of lesbian identity and experience at the same time that "sex radicals" questioned lesbian feminists' normative models of lesbian sexuality, pointing out that they were based on essentialized notions of femininity. Concurrent with these political challenges to singular definitions of lesbians, theories of social construction arose in the academy. Social constructionism argues against essentialist understandings of a fixed, unchanging lesbian identity and holds that identities and experiences are socially, historically, and discursively produced. Aligned with poststructuralism, it understands identity as nonunitary, or constructed relationally and in multiple, often contradictory contexts, and thus as fragmented, indeterminable, and fluid. This theoretical development, in which the coherent identity and history created by activist scholarship are replaced by a focus on ideology, representation, and cultural construction, has led to ongoing academic and political divisions among lesbian faculty. Activist faculty who adhere to identity politics often argue that a poststructural decentering of identity vitiates the definition of lesbian, thus rendering impossible collective politics and scholarship organized around identity and experience. For these faculty, a shift to poststructuralism signals a turn away from the social and political movements that have enabled and given lesbian scholarship its purposes and a turn toward a search for academic legitimacy through the use of "high theory."

The split between activist and theoretical work was exacerbated by the university's rise during the 1980s as a primary site for the generation of knowledge pertaining to gay men and lesbians. Early lesbian scholarship was closely aligned with grassroots and community activism, including the 1973 founding of the Lesbian Herstory Archives in New York City, a community institution located outside universities to ensure ongoing access to all researchers. However, the increasing academic legitimization of lesbian scholarship—the very success of lesbians' efforts—has meant that academia's norms and demands continue to supplant lesbian communities in defining the work of lesbian faculty.

Historically, lesbians have suffered discrimination in hiring procedures and tenure and promotion reviews, exclusion from social and professional networks, harassment, and intimidation. Those whose scholarship centers on gay and lesbian topics have had their work devalued or have lost access to prestigious research grants and peer-reviewed journals. These faculty often face heightened homophobia, as some colleagues accept a colleague who is lesbian more easily than a lesbian whose research or teaching engages lesbian studies. Many lesbian faculty members remain "closeted" until receiving tenure, if not afterward as well, to maintain credibility with colleagues and students and to protect their opportunities for advancement. However, although some lesbians find themselves professionally discredited for declaring their sexuality in academic environments predicated on tacit policies of "don't ask, don't tell," openly lesbian faculty are increasingly common. This openness may vary according to geography, institutional conservatism or religious affiliation, or the field in which a faculty member works.

Some lesbian faculty "come out" to students and colleagues for individual reasons, such as maintaining a sense of personal integrity in their relations; others do so as a political act of resistance in order to work against discriminatory attitudes and policies, believing that invisibility allows homophobia and heterosexism to continue unaddressed. In classrooms, some faculty seek to offer their gay and lesbian students role models and their heterosexual students positive examples of lesbians and new sensitivity to lesbian issues. Following feminism's mantra that "the personal is the political," they use their presence in the classroom as a fulcrum for interrupting homophobia as well as for foregrounding humans' connections to topics of study. Like feminist pedagogy, their actions have emphasized questions about the role of subjectivity, personal history, and experience in classrooms.

Change that has opened up possibilities for lesbian faculty has come in the context of the contributions of the civil rights, women's, and gay and lesbian movements to the growth of courses and programs pertaining to race, gender, and sexuality and the implementation of equitable policies on campus. Particularly since the 1980s, students have worked for the creation of gay-lesbian-bisexual support services and activities, have pushed for the inclusion of gay and lesbian material in their coursework, and at some institutions, have encouraged the development of gay and lesbian studies programs. Lobbying by students, faculty, and staff for nondiscrimination clauses inclusive of sexual orientation and domestic partnership benefits has offered lesbian faculty formal and legal resources and protection on many campuses. As part of a process of social change, the adoption of such programs and policies is contingent on the stances taken by boards of trustees, individual and corporate donors, and legislators, who place significant external pressure on institutions and can shape official responses to gay and lesbian populations on campus.

Although early lesbian work sought recognition and visibility, the 1990s signaled the double-edged nature of that recognition. With institutional and social acknowledgment of the need for "inclusion" and the academic rise of gay and lesbian studies and queer theory in the humanities and social sciences, some lesbian faculty found themselves tokenized as spokespersons for or representatives of "the lesbian community." In such fields as literary and cultural studies, lesbian faculty who engage in scholarship in lesbian or queer studies have found themselves and their work commodified. Although some take commodification as a sign of political progress, others argue that it is a market-oriented form of containing lesbian faculty by locating them in a single arena, or "ghettoizing" scholars and scholarship on the basis of identity. Conversely, some lesbian faculty have deemed the rise of queer theory in the 1990s problematic, arguing that it constitutes a new form of erasure of lesbian specificity. Lesbian feminism, they contend, is specific to lesbians' experiences of oppression and marginalization within feminism, gay and lesbian culture, and mainstream culture. The slide from lesbian studies to queer theory, like poststructuralism, decenters lesbian identity and experience such that sexuality in general overtakes the lesbian as a topic of study.

Stemming from the debates between essentialism and social constructionism and continuing with debates between lesbian and queer studies, two opposing constructs of lesbian faculty have developed. Consonant with identity politics, the first describes authentic lesbians who should be empowered to speak and be seen as lesbian. These lesbian faculty attach lesbian identity and consciousness directly to their scholarly lives and argue for an organic connection between the personal and the academic in the content and methods of their teaching and scholarship. The second represents postmodern lesbian faculty members who eschew the essentialism of identity categories and through their work may or may not speak or act as lesbian. These lesbian faculty argue that despite identity politics' usefulness in changing university policies and enabling their presence in academia, identity politics' uniting of identity and experience can reify lesbian faculty by assuming their responsibility to act on identifications that may not be central to their understandings of self or their scholarly and pedagogical priorities. A discourse of authenticity wrongly traps faculty into defining their scholarly perspectives and university work along the axis of sexuality. For these lesbian faculty, voice and visibility as lesbian constitute less an authentic representation of self than a performance of lesbian that takes on different meanings in different contexts.

Although many lesbian faculty do not participate in these debates and some declare little need to "come out," lesbians are increasingly "out" in their fields and universities, teach courses on or that include sexuality, and produce scholarship in gay and lesbian studies or queer theory. The variety of stances lesbian faculty have taken up in their specific social, academic, and institutional contexts continues to generate dialogue and action essential to fostering intellectual vitality and the viability of multiple positions for all lesbian faculty.

Susan Talburt

See also Part 1: Lesbian, Gay, Bisexual, and Transgender Issues on Campus; Part 6: Sexuality

References and further reading

Garber, Linda, ed. 1994. *Tilting the Tower: Lesbians Teaching Queer Subjects.* New York: Routledge.

McNaron, Toni A. H. 1997. *Poisoned Ivy: Lesbian and Gay Academics Confronting Homophobia.* Philadelphia: Temple University Press.

Mintz, Beth, and Esther D. Rothblum, eds. 1997. *Lesbians in Academia: Degrees of Freedom.* New York: Routledge.

Talburt, Susan. 2000. *Subject to Identity: Knowledge, Sexuality, and Academic Practices in Higher Education.* Albany: State University of New York Press.

Zimmerman, Bonnie, and Toni A. H. McNaron, eds. 1996. *The New Lesbian Studies: Into the Twenty-First Century.* New York: The Feminist Press.

Researchers

Publication output is one of the central criteria used to judge faculty productivity and is a key to advancement in the profession. Generally measured by journal articles, publication output is critical because it is assumed to reflect research productivity. Because of the rigorous process of peer review required for publication in most prestigious journals, publication output provides some measure of credibility among colleagues with comparable expertise. Researchers have identified gender differences in publication output. When comparing all full-time faculty, women publish less than men do. Women are much less likely than men to appear in the list of top publishers in a field when measured by number of publications. This issue is critical to discussions of gender in higher education because the disparity in overall publication rates is often used to justify women's lower status in academe. Women's secondary status is reflected in salaries that are lower on average than men's, as well as lower and slower promotion rates. Thus, stereotypes about the incompatibility of women, work, and the family can have a direct and powerful impact on their treatment in the workplace.

The argument that women publish less than men is grounded in a comparison of faculty working at different types of colleges and universities, including universities that place a strong emphasis on research and four-year colleges, where greater emphasis is placed on teaching than research. For example, when looking at all institutions, men are six times more likely than women to have published fifty or more journal articles (Sax et al. 1999). Faculty women are one and a half times more likely than faculty men to be among the group of nonpublishers.

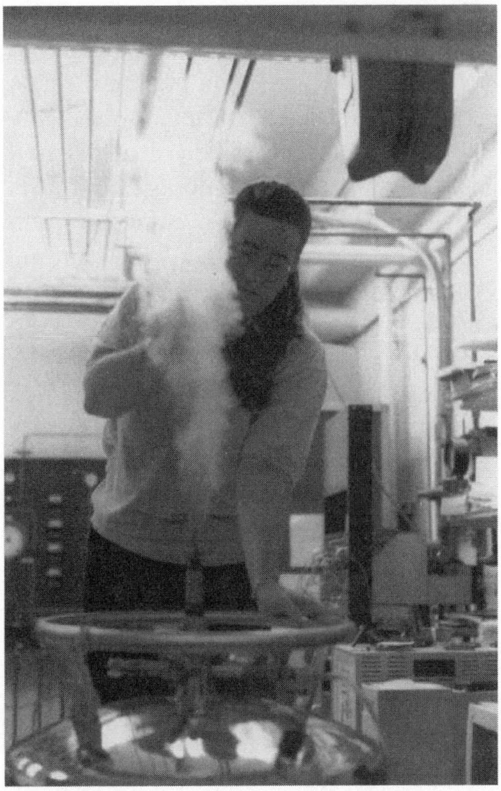

Performing an experiment (Courtesy of the Association of Women in Science)

Gender differences in publication rates narrow substantially in comparisons between men and women who are in the same academic discipline, at the same type of institution, and at the same position and rank. Although women are still underrepresented among the most prolific, the gap between men's and women's publishing rates has narrowed considerably since the 1980s. There are no longer significant differences by gender in most disciplines when comparing two-year publication rates.

Women's family responsibilities are most often singled out as an explanation for the gender gap in publication rates. Research shows quite the contrary. The expected differences between married and single women's publication levels prove insignificant, even among women with children. Although this finding seems contradictory, given the reality that women, including women working full-time, still carry the majority of the responsibility in the household, it is less contradictory when it is understood that a wide range of factors are associated with publication level, including location in a prestigious research institution and access to influential mentors, collegial networks, and resources.

A number of factors explain why, at the aggregate level, women continue to be underrepresented among the most prolific publishers in a field, despite growth in the number of women holding faculty positions in colleges and universities across the United States. A much smaller percentage of women than men occupy positions in the top tier of the higher education system. Women constitute only about 28 percent of the faculty at research universities (Sax et al. 1999). Faculty members holding such senior-level positions are more likely than their colleagues at other institutions to produce a significant number of publications, in part because they are in an environment that supports these activities. The support is reflected not only in the academic reward structure and salary but also in the resources available to encourage faculty research. They include equipment and funds to attend professional conferences to report research findings but also come in the form of research leaves and access to prestigious university presses that can expedite the process of publication.

Another very significant factor that helps to explain the so-called publication gap among men and women is that faculty at research universities generally teach fewer courses each semester than faculty in other types of institutions. Because of their smaller teaching load and the greater degree of autonomy or control over time that generally characterizes this kind of appointment, faculty at research universities are much more likely to be in a position than faculty at other types of institutions to devote time to research and writing on a regular basis. To reach the status of prolific scholar in a field requires a twenty- to thirty-year commitment to activities that contribute to publication. Because women's careers are much more likely than men's to be characterized by periods of unemployment, part-time employment, and underemployment, women are much less likely than men to hold positions that allow them to amass the record required to earn the accolade of prolific publisher.

Affiliation with an influential mentor and access to collegial networks are two additional factors that are consistently found to characterize the experiences of prolific scholars. As with the other factors discussed, there are consistent gender differences on these dimensions as well. Women, particularly unmarried women and women of color, are significantly less likely to report that they had an influential mentor in graduate school. Mentors play many roles for graduate students who aspire to join the ranks of the faculty. Preparing for a career as an academic resembles an apprenticeship. Many young scholars learn "at the elbow" of an older, more senior scholar who teaches them the skills of the trade by working side by side in the laboratory or other research setting and often providing opportunities to coauthor articles, do presentations at professional conferences, and interact with influential people in the field. Such experiences are extremely critical to securing a prestigious position and later advancement in a career. In part because mentor-apprentice relationships are almost always same-sex and same-race and the faculty is still largely white and male, women are much less likely than men to report having had a close working relationship with a mentor. Women are thus less likely than their male counterparts to have had the opportunity to coauthor with a mentor in graduate school and to develop the skills necessary to get an early start on a publishing career.

Although female graduate students are less likely than males to have had a significant relationship with a faculty mentor, female faculty spend more time teaching and advising students than their male counterparts. This situation explains why, at the aggregate level, women faculty are much more likely than men faculty to be among those who have never published an article in a professional journal, a chapter in a book, or a book and is also related to institutional location and the types of positions women most commonly hold. Across all institutional types, women spend more time teaching and advising than do men. Some defend this phenomenon by arguing that women in general show a higher level of interest in teaching than do men, but not all research supports this conclusion. Women are more likely than men are to be in positions that require that they teach undergraduate students, whereas men are more likely to teach smaller, graduate courses that help to support a research agenda. Women, especially minority women, typically carry much heavier responsibility for service activities, such as committee membership, than do men. All these factors influence the amount of time available for research, a factor directly related to research output.

Among those who publish, women are criticized for some patterns of behavior that are often to their detriment in the traditional academic reward structure. They are more likely than men to coauthor articles and less likely than men to appear as the single author or first author of a publication. Single authors and lead authors generally receive the most recognition for a publication because they are assumed to be the intellectual owner of the conceptual orientation or the idea that is its central organizing principle. Women and minorities are also more likely than white men to publish on topics that are devalued as being outside mainstream thinking and paradigms and to have their work appear in specialized journals that are not among the most prestigious in a field. Characteristics such as these are used as a justification for women's lower status in academe, as reflected in their lower rates of earning tenure, ranks, and salaries.

Some people have observed rather caustically that the factors that identify prolific scholars and consequently what is rewarded and granted the most prestige in higher education are actually (white) male traits and career patterns. That is because these factors, although they may seem objective measures, are much more characteristic of the life experiences of men than the life experiences of women.

Inflexibility about the credentials required to gain access to a faculty position at most elite U.S. institutions and rigidity about the way that faculty productivity is measured provide partial explanations for why the diversification of U.S.

faculty has occurred so slowly. Expanding measures of faculty productivity to embrace a broader range of behaviors as a manifestation of scholarly achievement can occur by more reliance on quality and less reliance on quantity of publications. Rewarding many different types of publications, rather than relying primarily on journal articles published in prestigious outlets, is another way to expand the measures of faculty productivity. Finally, as we move into an age when electronic means of publication expand the audience for publications beyond the small group of scholars with a similar, specialized expertise, expanding traditional measures of productivity to reward a variety of forms of scholarly communication, including those that influence practice, will greatly enhance the diversity of people who can achieve success in the field of higher education as faculty.

Elizabeth G. Creamer

See also Part 6: Graduate and Professional Education; Graduate Students and Science; Part 7: Evaluation; Tenure and Promotion

References and further reading

Blackburn, Robert T., and Janet H. Lawrence. 1995. *Faculty at Work.* Baltimore: Johns Hopkins University Press.

Creamer, Elizabeth G. 1998. *Assessing Faculty Publication Productivity: Issues of Equity.* ASHE-ERIC Higher Education Report 26, no. 2. Washington, DC: George Washington University.

Sax, Linda J., Alexander W. Astin, William S. Korn, and Shannon K. Gilmartin. 1999. *The American College Teacher: National Norms for the 1998–99 HERI Faculty Survey.* Los Angeles: Higher Education Research Institute, University of California.

Schneider, Allison. 1998. "Why Don't Women Publish As Much As Men?" *Chronicle of Higher Education,* September 11, A14–A16.

Salaries

Many people believe that the Equal Pay Act of 1963 and other legislation dealt with any wage inequities for women faculty that existed in the past. This act mandated that organizations compensate men and women doing the same job at the same rate of pay, which is known as "equal pay for equal work." It was designed to lessen the difference between male and female pay rates. People believe that between federal law and raised consciousness, any gender inequities with regard to earnings have been addressed. However, although some progress has been made in narrowing the wage gap in the nearly forty years since passage of the act, women still earn roughly 70–75 percent of what their male counterparts earn in equal jobs. Studies have shown that some progress has been made in achieving gender equity in salaries in various labor markets, but women still often earn less than other male employees who have comparable characteristics. Indeed, as recently as 1999, President Bill Clinton proposed that the U.S. government spend $14 million to help end gender discrimination in the labor market.

Academic women have been on the faculty in higher education institutions for more than 100 years yet still earn less salary across all ranks than do men. Such inequities in pay have persisted since the 1970s, when data on pay inequities first started being collected. The existence of gender inequities in such salaries touches on several important issues. Certainly, it is a moral concern about the issue of fairness. At the same time, however, it is a moral issue with roots in potential misperceptions. Some people believe that the wage gap either does not exist or should not be closed because women may be less qualified than their male counterparts.

Research does not support this belief. Also, some argue that other factors could influence earnings. For example, if male faculty members were in the workforce longer than female faculty members were, then such a wage differential might be expected. Yet even after controlling for variables such as seniority, educational level, years of experience, length of appointment, and different pay plans, male faculty are still paid more than female faculty.

Identifying the separate parts that make up the total wage gap between male and female faculty members is not an easy task. For example, if promotion from assistant professor to associate professor causes an increase of $1,000 each year in the salaries of faculty members and a larger percentage of males were then at the rank of associate professor, then the total pay gap could be explained by a difference in rank. What becomes the total pay gap is the difference in pay *after* accounting for unique gender characteristics.

Salaries for men and women differ not only within institutions but also by rank and type of institution. There is greater variance at master's-level institutions than there is at doctoral-level universities. In other words, the gap has narrowed at doctoral-level institutions but has actually increased at master's-level institutions. Women's salaries also indicate that they are disproportionately found in the lower ranks of faculty. In addition, those with tenure are disproportionately found in the ranks of associate professors rather than full professors. The data collected and analyzed by the National Center for Education Statistics for the National Survey of Postsecondary Faculty 1992–1993 indicate that at all academic ranks and in all types of ranked institutions of higher education, women earn on average less than men do. Figure 1 reflects the findings of this data collection.

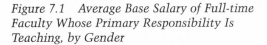

Figure 7.1 Average Base Salary of Full-time Faculty Whose Primary Responsibility Is Teaching, by Gender

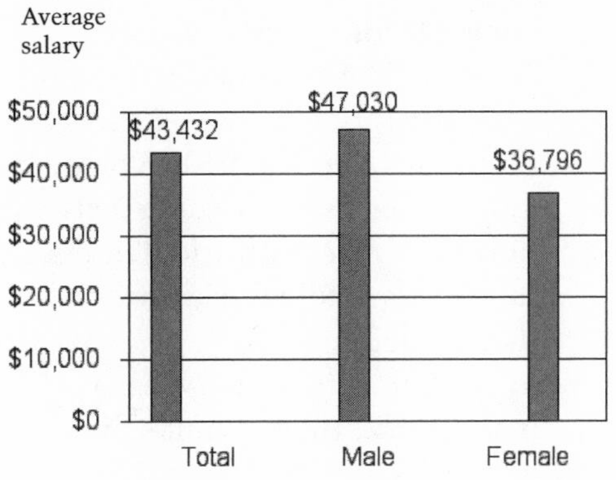

Note: Includes U.S. citizens only. Also excluded are respondents with base salaries greater than $400,000.

Source: Adapted from National Center for Education Statistics. *National Study of Post-secondary Faculty 1992–93.* NSOPF:93. Washington, DC: U.S. Department of Education.

As can be determined from Figure 7.1, the average difference in salary between male and female faculty across all types of institutions and for all ranks was $10,234, or approximately 22 percent. According to the executive summary from a 2000 National Center for Education Statistics report on salary, promotion, and tenure status of women faculty in the United States, "female full-time faculty averaged lower salaries than male faculty by about $10,000 in the fall of 1992." In the same report, 66 percent of full-time female faculty earned base salaries of less than $40,000, compared with 37 percent of men. In contrast, 5 percent of women reported salaries of $60,000 or more, compared to 19 percent of men who did so.

More recent data indicate the following important points:

- Across all institutions and ranks, female faculty members earn between 80.4 percent (lecturer, private institution, two-year institutions with rank) and 104.5 percent (instructor, church-related institution, two-year institution) of male salaries (excluding institutions that do not rank).
- In general, across the types of institutions, the top ranks of female faculty (professor, associate professor, assistant professor) are paid less equitably, in comparison with male faculty salaries, than the lower ranks (instructor, lecturer).
- The biggest discrepancy between male and female faculty salaries is found among the no rank faculty: females at church-related doctoral institutions earn 62.3 percent of male salaries, and females at public undergraduate institutions earn 76.7 percent of male salaries.

In addition to research demonstrating salary inequity, several recent court cases have sought to prove salary inequities through legal means. Currently awaiting a federal district court decision, the case of *Anderson v. State University of New York at New Paltz* (1999), raises the question of whether the Equal Pay Act supersedes states' Eleventh Amendment rights to be immune from lawsuits by individuals for monetary damages (after certain decisions rendered by the Supreme Court in another case). The American Association of University Professors, in addition to other groups, has joined a friend of the court brief because members are concerned that this type of suit will impair the ability of professors to protect themselves from wage discrimination.

In another case, *Smith v. Virginia Commonwealth University* (1994), disparate salaries between men and women professors at Virginia Commonwealth University could not be explained, and the university established a special fund so that women could apply for increases as a means of correcting the disparity. When a group of male faculty members whose salaries were not increased through the special fund sued the university, several courts and appeal processes were involved, and at last note, a trial was pending for a final decision to be rendered.

Dana E. Christman

See also Part 5: Affirmative Action and Employment; Gender Inequality; Part 7: Hiring; Sex Discrimination; Tenure and Promotion

References and further reading

American Association of University Professors. 2002. "The Annual Report on the Economic Status of the Profession, 2001–2002." http://www.aaup.org/research/salary/02salary/2002rep.htm. Cited June 11, 2002.

Anderson v. State University of New York at New Paltz, 169 F. 3d 117 (Second Circuit 1999), remanded by 120 S. Ct. 929 (U.S. 2000).

Evans, Clarice. 2000. "Facts about Female Faculty: 1999–00 AAUP Faculty Compensation Survey." American Association of University Professors. http://www.aaup.org/wsalrep.htm. Cited June 11, 2002.

Glazer-Raymo, J. 1999. *Shattering the Myths: Women in Academe.* Baltimore: Johns Hopkins University Press.

Hampton, M., C. Oyster, L. Pena, and P. Rodgers. 2000. "Gender Inequity in

Faculty Pay." *Compensation and Benefits Review* 32, no. 6: 54–59.
National Center for Education Statistics. 2000. *Statistical Analysis Report: 1993 National Study of Postsecondary Faculty.* NSOPF: 93. Washington, DC: U.S. Department of Education.
Smith v. Virginia Commonwealth University, 856 F. Supp. 1088 (E.D. Va. 1994), rev'd, 62 F. 3d 659 (Fourth Circuit 1995), vacated, 1995 U.S. App. LEXIS 28831 (Fourth Circuit, 13 October 1995) (en banc), rev'd 84 F. 3d 672 (Fourth Circuit 1996).

Sex Discrimination

Freedom from discrimination on the basis of one's sex is an employment right of faculty. Though such rights are protected by an array of state and federal laws and regulations that are generally applicable to employees, both individual and class action gender discrimination cases among faculty fall under the auspices of Title VII of the Civil Rights Act of 1964 and the Equal Pay Act of 1963. These laws and regulations protect faculty who can show that they have been denied some employment benefit to which they were entitled, not because they were unqualified but because of discrimination based upon their gender. Moreover, in some instances, combined claims of gender and race discrimination are filed concurrently, invoking the multiple protections of these statues.

Title VII of the Civil Rights Act of 1964 is the most comprehensive and frequently used of the employment discrimination laws. The law states that it is unlawful for an employer (1) to fail or refuse to hire or to discharge any individual, or otherwise to discriminate against any individual with respect to his or her compensation, terms, conditions, or privileges of employment, because of such individual's race, color, religion, sex, or national origin; or (2) to limit, segregate, or classify his or her employees or applicants for employment in any way that would deprive or tend to deprive any individual of employment opportunities or otherwise adversely affect his or her status as an employee, because of such individual's race, color, religion, sex, or national origin. In 1972, the nation's public and private colleges and universities came under the purview of Title VII, opening up the floodgates of employment discrimination litigation brought by faculty, as individuals, and as groups in class action lawsuits.

There are two basic types of Title VII claims, disparate impact and disparate treatment. In disparate impact claims, plaintiffs argue that some seemingly neutral employment policy has had a discriminatory impact on the plaintiffs or the class of persons they represent. Statistical analysis often forms the backbone of disparate impact cases, with plaintiffs relying on frequencies, percentages, multiple regression, and other quantitative evidence of the defendant institution's discriminatory practices. For instance, in *Lamphere v. Brown University* (1976), the plaintiffs relied almost exclusively on quantitative evidence to demonstrate the discriminatory impact of the university's hiring, promotion, and tenure processes. The plaintiffs prevailed in their class action suit, which led to a consent decree, promotion and tenure for three plaintiffs, and an overhaul of the university's employment procedures.

In a disparate treatment claim of gender discrimination, an individual who has been subjected to an adverse employment decision, such as denial of a job, promotion, or tenure, claims to have been treated differently than otherwise similar individuals because of his or her gender. In disparate treatment cases, statistics can be combined with other forms of evidence. A successful discrimination claim generally depends on a plaintiff's ability to demonstrate unequal treatment of otherwise similar individuals. Discrimination claims are particularly complex for college faculty to prove and for colleges to defend against because of the subjective nature of employment decisions in higher education. Historically, courts have been reluctant to second-guess the appropriateness of academic employment decisions and have focused instead on the procedures for making decisions, not the substance of the decisions themselves. Thus, plaintiffs have prevailed on procedural or jurisdictional grounds far more often than on merit.

Subjective assessments are an integral part of the award system for faculty around the country; as such, the confidentiality of peer review records pertinent to hiring and firing and promotion and tenure decisions has been a subject of debate for Title VII litigants. The Equal Employment Opportunity Commission, an agency that holds oversight and investigative authority for Title VII, fought to make peer review files available to plaintiffs during the discovery phase of litigation. Embracing the idea that the right to a fair trial depends on access to evidence, courts have ordered institutions of higher education to relinquish previously confidential records, without an opportunity to censor individual documents contained in them. Peer review committees, search committees, department heads, and deans may be discouraged from keeping detailed minutes or notes, fearing the disclosure of their identities.

The Equal Pay Act, like Title VII, prohibits sex discrimination in employment compensation, and in many cases, plaintiffs have filed simultaneous Equal Pay Act and Title VII claims. The Equal Pay Act is designed to ensure equal pay for equal work by outlining criteria or conditions under which compensation should be equal. Salaries must be equal when jobs, not individuals, require equal skills, equal effort, and equal responsibilities that are performed under similar working conditions. In *Maitland v. University of Minnesota,* a women's basketball coach sued her university for sex discrimination in compensation under the Equal Pay Act. The university argued that there was insufficient evidence that the plaintiff was equal in skill, effort, and responsibility to her colleague, a male coach. The court decided that there was ample evidence to support the equitability of the positions and ruled in favor of the plaintiff. The statute requires that jobs must be substantially equal but not necessarily identical, thereby giving rise to the legal concept of comparable worth.

Comparable worth attempts to show that two jobs involving different services are of the same worth within an organization and should receive equitable compensation. In higher education, though, comparable worth is complicated by variations in individual talent among faculty, differences in the prestige of disciplines, measurements of scholarly productivity, and the lack of consistent procedures to determine salaries across various academic units within colleges or universities. In *Spaulding v. University of Washington,* a class of female nursing faculty claimed that their jobs were comparable to jobs in other academic departments that had predominantly male faculties. The court ruled that jobs in differing academic departments within a university are not comparable because the academic units placed differing degrees of emphasis on teaching, research, and community service.

The most difficult issue in cases of wage disparity or systematic pay discrimination against women is the attribution of the difference in salaries to gender rather than some other unprotected factor. In one case, a male faculty member charged discrimination when a female faculty member in a comparable job was paid a higher salary. The court found that the higher salary award was not based on gender but resulted from a job offer from another institution; thus, the female faculty member's competitiveness in the job market, not her gender, resulted in the salary differential. In addition to the use of market values to justify differences in salaries, the law provides employers with several justifications for salary differentials across comparable jobs, including (1) a seniority system, (2) a merit system, (3) a system that measures earnings by quantity or quality of production, or (4) a differential based on any factor other than sex.

In settling salary equity cases, some colleges, universities, and state systems for higher education have had to cautiously yet comprehensively implement salary adjustments for both men and women faculty because the Equal Pay Act stipulates that employers may not reduce the wages of either sex in order to equalize differences in men's and women's compensation. For example, when a university implemented a settlement decree that raised the salaries of a class of female employees, while the male faculty's salaries remained the same, a male professor sued the university, alleging sex discrimination in the awarding of salary increases, and won.

Other statutes and case law address issues related to gender discrimination in academe. For instance, the law stipulates that pregnancy, childbirth, and related medical conditions must be treated in the same way as other temporary illnesses or conditions of employees. The Family Medical Leave Act of 1993 requires employers to grant unpaid leave for up to twelve weeks for the care of a sick, newborn, or recently adopted child or seriously ill family member. Also, the law prohibits the use of sex-based mortality tables in retirement plans sponsored by postsecondary employers.

The law is clear regarding gender discrimination in higher education, but courts have yet to develop fully an analytical construct for examining the dual discriminations of race and gender. Title VII champions a singular analysis that favors the experiences of those who are privileged "but for" some one protected characteristic (i.e., sex, race, national origin, religion, or age). Women of color are not privileged "but for" their race or their sex in isolation; rather they experience double jeopardy, or the dual discriminations of racism and sexism. Therefore, in the early 1990s, women of color within the legal academy posited a new genre of contemporary legal thought, called critical race feminism, to cast attention on the legal and social plight of those suffering from double jeopardy.

An outgrowth of critical legal studies and feminist jurisprudence, critical race feminism addresses criticisms of the other two theoretical approaches. Critical race theorists have been criticized for producing genderless accounts of race, and feminist legal scholars' focus on patriarchal domination has been deemed too simplistic, for it negates the fact that patriarchal domination affects women of color differently from how it affects white women. Critical race feminists are interested in multiple discriminations. They espouse the theory of intersectionality, seeking to explore how factors of race, gender, and class interact within a system of racial oppression and white male patriarchy. Critical race feminists argue for recognition of the comembership of women of color in multiple classes of domination and seek redress for harms caused by discrimination based on race and gender.

Women of color have not had a great deal of success, though, with their combined claims of employment discrimination. Courts were slow to accept the theory of the combined claim and instead treated claims of sex and race discrimination as mutually exclusive. *DeGraffenreid v. General Motors* was the first case to explicitly address the question of whether black women should gain combined race and gender relief under Title VII. In the case, the district court rejected the plaintiffs' attempt to bring suit, not on the behalf of blacks or women, but specifically on the behalf of black women. The court ruled that the plaintiffs were entitled to bring a suit for race discrimination or sex discrimination but not a combination of both. It was not until *Jeffries v. Harris County Community Action Association* that the courts allowed a woman of color to sue on the grounds of both race and sex discrimination, rejecting the district court's approach of evaluating the claims separately and embracing "sex-plus" analysis.

Sex-plus analysis is applied when an employer discriminates on the basis of a person's sex and an additional characteristic unrelated to sex. The analysis originated in a case in which a woman sought relief for sex discrimination because she was denied employment by a company that explicitly forbade the hiring of women with preschool-age children while continuing to hire men with preschool-age children. As the first sex discrimination case to reach the Supreme Court, the case characterized the "plus factor" as a modifier of gender, or a neutral category that could apply equally to men and women (e.g., marital or parenting status). The application of the sex-plus doctrine to cases involving combined claims of discrimination has been widely criticized because, in combined claims, sex-plus analysis does not involve a prohibited factor modified by a more neutral characteristic; rather it involves the combination of two prohibited factors—race and gender. Thus, when combined claims of race and sex discrimination have been accepted, courts have privileged sex discrimination claims by assigning race discrimination claims to a cursory level of significance.

Cassandra P. Evans

See also Part 2: Demographics of Gender and Race; Part 5: Gender Inequality; Legal Issues; Part 7: Tenure and Promotion

References and further reading

Hendrickson, Robert M. 1991. "The Colleges, Their Constituencies, and the Courts." Number 43 in the NOLPE Monograph/Book Series. Topeka, KS: National Organization on Legal Problems of Education.

Kaplin, William A., and Barbara A. Lee. 1995. *The Law of Higher Education.* 3rd ed. San Francisco: Jossey-Bass.

LaNoue, George R., and Barbara A. Lee. 1987. *Academics in Court: The Consequences of Faculty Discrimination Litigation.* Ann Arbor: University of Michigan Press.

Leap, Terry L. 1985. *Tenure, Discrimination, and the Courts.* 2nd ed. Ithaca, NY: Cornell University Press.

Wing, Adrien K., ed. 1997. *Critical Race Feminism: A Reader.* New York: New York University Press.

Socialization

Conventional explanations of socialization of new faculty assume that academic structures, processes, and practices are gender- and color-blind. The lack of attention to gender, both as a conceptual category and an analytical lens, means that the different experiences of female and male academics are attributed to individual differences rather than to the consequences of a male-dominated academic world. Normative views of the academic profession attribute the underrepresentation of women in the professoriat in general and their overrepresentation in the lower salary scales, the less selective institutions, and the junior academic ranks to their not having been socialized to be as career-oriented and ambitious as men. Child rearing and other domestic duties also get in the way of women's scholarly work.

The aim of "engendering" socialization is to bring into focus institutionalized forms of sexism embedded in supposedly neutral structures, norms, and policies and to challenge the normative assumption that the opportunity structure of the academy is gender-blind (or color-blind). An "engendered" view of socialization of new faculty acknowledges that the academy is a patriarchal organization and has a patriarchal socialization process. Consequently, it perpetuates cultural practices and processes that not only institutionalize gender inequities but also induce women to act out stereotypical female roles to gain acceptance by their predominantly white male senior colleagues. From an "engendered" view of socialization, research and policy agendas reveal the institutional origins of gender inequities and invisible barriers that contribute to the less successful performance of women faculty members. Engendering socialization provides individuals in positions of power with an alternative set of gender-specific practices that can be used to create more equitable and affirming academic cultures.

Normative Explanations of Socialization

The process of faculty socialization has two major components—anticipatory socialization and cultural learning and adaptation. Anticipatory socialization typically occurs during graduate school as students (i.e., prospective faculty members) learn the necessary behaviors, work habits, and values associated with academic work. Anticipatory socialization occurs in three stages: the selection of a graduate school, graduate school and its accompanying activities (e.g., going to class, writing papers, preparing the dissertation), and the expansion of roles (e.g., presenting papers, conference attendance) that ultimately prepare an individual for a faculty position.

The second component of socialization, cultural learning and adaptation, also has three stages: entry into the profession, validation with the granting of tenure and promotion, and achievement of milestones throughout the academic career. Socialization is most intense during the early years of an academic career, when new roles and expectations must be learned. In this stage, new faculty must learn about and adapt not only to one academic culture but also to many other cultures as well, including the cultures of the discipline, profession, institution, department, and higher education system as a whole. Socialization and acceptance as a faculty member require that one adapt to these cultures in varying degrees, depending on the particular department, institution, and discipline.

Those who successfully negotiate this process are initiated into the culture of higher education through the granting of tenure. Those who are not successfully initiated (i.e., socialized) are denied tenure and terminated from their positions. Central to both components of socialization is the ability to work with others. Successful socialization is facilitated by senior faculty members who act as advisors, mentors, facilitators of networking, and helpful colleagues.

A normative view of academic socialization suggests a linear process that encompasses both anticipatory socialization and cultural learning and adaptation. For example, a successfully socialized individual might attend graduate school for five years, apprenticing as a graduate assistant or lecturer while researching and writing a dissertation under the watchful eye of a principal adviser. Upon defending the dissertation, the student is welcomed by his or her committee into the fraternity of doctors of philosophy (or holders of other terminal degrees). The new Ph.D. then joins the ranks of the professoriat as an assistant professor, learning the culture of a different department and institution with the guidance of an experienced mentor and other colleagues. After a six-year probationary period on the tenure track, during which time he or she continues to learn and assimilate academic culture, the assistant receives tenure and is promoted to the rank of associate professor. For some faculty, this socialization process continues on to the rank of full professor.

Clearly, what has been described thus far is a normative and evolutionary model of socialization that recounts how things typically (and perhaps ideally) proceed for new faculty members. As with all normative constructs, some people conform, and others do not. There is a growing body of research that suggests the process of socialization may not be experienced uniformly on the basis of gender. Examining socialization from the perspective of gender can yield a different view of anticipatory socialization and cultural learning.

An Engendered View of Socialization

An engendered view of socialization accounts for the culture and history of the academic profession and of institutions. Historically, higher education has been and continues to be a male-dominated enterprise. As a result, academic culture and the socialization that accompanies it reflect the experiences of men. The addition of women to the professoriat has called into question much of what the community of scholars has come to know and expect about faculty socialization and the progression of an academic career. An engendered view of socialization notes that although much of the traditional socialization of graduate students and new faculty is assumed to be gender-neutral, in fact, the experiences of new academics differ greatly by gender (as well as by race, ethnicity, sexual orientation, etc.). These gender-based differences appear at each stage along the traditional path of faculty socialization.

The first difference relates to the traditional path itself. The idealized trajectory of a faculty career (i.e., from graduate school to assistant, associate, and full professor, in direct succession) may not describe the actual or expected career of an academic woman. For some women, the balance between work and family or personal life can disrupt the standard timetable for the ideal career trajectory. In the interest of spouses, children, or personal commitments, women may extend or suspend their graduate school careers, wait to join the professoriat, or attempt to stop or slow the tenure clock. Although men are increasing their share of responsibility for family life, surveys show that women still tend to be primary caregivers for young children and aging parents. A faculty member looking to establish her career in the face of conflicting time demands between workplace and home may not be able to follow the traditional trajectory of faculty advancement.

Successful anticipatory socialization is key to gaining access to the professoriat. Graduate school experiences prepare the student for a career as an academic, but not all of these experiences occur in the classroom. Anticipatory socialization includes attracting and working with advisers, mentors, and alumni; networking and establishing connections throughout the institution and the discipline; and finding opportunities to present and publish research. Research indicates that women have more difficulty than men attracting advisers at the top of their fields. Because the majority of senior academics are male, men have more opportunities than women for unofficial socialization (e.g., the "old boys' network," the squash court). Disadvantages that begin in graduate school can continue to affect a woman throughout her career; this concept is known as "accumulative disadvantage." Different experiences in graduate school can lead to different experiences in the profession. Given the time limits of the tenure track, it is of the utmost importance for faculty to start their professional careers with a firm foundation from graduate school.

Socialization does not occur in isolation. Working relationships, networking, and mentoring are crucial to effective socialization in graduate school and as a faculty member. Senior faculty are particularly influential in helping graduate students obtain academic positions. They can also help their protégés achieve tenure and reach other milestones of the profession. One does not get far in academia without the assistance of others through direct mentoring and supportive colleagueship. These working relationships can be quite different for men and women.

Conducting Research on Academic Socialization from an Engendered Perspective

From a conventional perspective, research on socialization focuses on questions such as the following: "How do women and men compare in their level of research productivity?" "Are women faculty different from male faculty?" "Do women faculty have the same expectations as male faculty?" Research based on questions such as these invariably shows that women are less successful than men in obtaining tenure; they publish less; they do not generate as much funded research; and they do not manage their time as effectively or strategically as male academics.

From studies that posit gender as a variable, we have learned that there are several differences between male and female faculty members in areas such as salary, tenure, and rank. Female full-time faculty earn on average about $10,000 less than male full-time faculty. They are also less likely to be tenured (42 percent as opposed to 66 percent) or to be full professors (15 percent as opposed to 39 percent). Male and female faculty also engage in different professional activities. Full-time female faculty spend more time than their male colleagues in teaching or service activities and less in research or administrative activities. For example, about 51 percent of female full-time faculty spend at least three-quarters of their time in teaching activities, as compared to 37 percent of the males. Furthermore, male faculty devote an average of 15 percent of their time to research activities, compared to 10 percent for females.

To be sure, these differences are important in enabling us to understand the multiple disadvantages that affect women academics. When they are examined from a normative perspective of socialization, it might be assumed that these inequities result from the failure of female academics to behave like male academics. However, research questions that put gender at the center will lead to a different interpretation.

Rather than asking why women are less productive than men and fail to become socialized and integrated into the academic culture, the focus shifts to documenting how seemingly neutral structures and policies contribute to the accumulation of advantages by males (usually white) and the accumulation of disadvantages by females. Accordingly, the research questions are these: "How do theories and practices of socialization reproduce gender stratification in the academy?" "Why do salary inequities persist?" "To what extent is gender built into definitions of merit?" "How does gender affect experiences in the academy?" "How do socialization processes perpetuate patriarchal academic cultures?" "What gender-salient experiences have women had in the anticipatory socialization and entry stages of their careers?" "How were sponsorship processes (advising, mentoring, collegiality) experienced by these women?" "How might the criteria for achieving tenure contribute to differential patterns of success for men and women."

These questions reveal the invisible barriers that female academics face as a result of being excluded from the social and professional networks in which male graduate students and beginning faculty learn the unwritten rules for success. As a result of this exclusion, women are deprived of valuable information, such as how to achieve tenure; how to negotiate a salary; or how to obtain travel funds, release time, and equipment. Studies done from an engendered perspective have shown that for women to succeed in departments with strong masculinist cultures, they must engage in gendered practices; otherwise, they are characterized as lacking in collegiality. A practice described as "smile work" is a culturally imposed strategy women use to fit into departments with a tradition of male dominance. Smile work entails the symbolic management of behavior to present oneself as being pleasant and agreeable. Another such practice of accommodation is described as "mom work," which refers to the imposition of nurturing and caregiving roles on women.

Engendering socialization calls for a rethinking of the processes associated with successful socialization, such as the achievement of tenure on a truncated timeline, the need to assimilate to be accepted, and the role senior colleagues and mentors play in supporting junior faculty throughout the process. An engendered view of socialization recognizes that women (and men) can succeed as academics when definitions of socialization are altered to include them, their experiences, and their needs.

Kelly Ward and
Estela M. Bensimón

See also Part 6: Graduate and Professional Education; Part 7: Disciplinary Socialization; Researchers; Teachers; Tenure and Promotion

References and further reading
Bensimón, Estela M., and Catherine Marshall. 1997. "Policy Analysis for Postsecondary Education: Feminist and Critical Perspectives." Pp. 133–147 in *Feminist Critical Policy Analysis II: A Perspective from Post-Secondary Education,* ed. C. Marshall and Associates. London: Falmer Press.
Clark, Shirley M., and Marilyn Corcoran. 1986. "Perspectives on the Professional Socialization of Women Faculty: A Case of Accumulative Disadvantage." *Journal of Higher Education* 57, no. 1: 20–43.
Tierney, William G., and Estela Mara Bensimón. 1996. *Promotion and Tenure: Community and Socialization in Academe.* Albany: State University of New York Press.
Tierney, William G., and Robert A. Rhoads. 1994. *Faculty Socialization as Cultural Process: A Mirror of Institutional Commitment.* ASHE-ERIC Higher Education Report no. 93–6. Washington, DC: George Washington University.

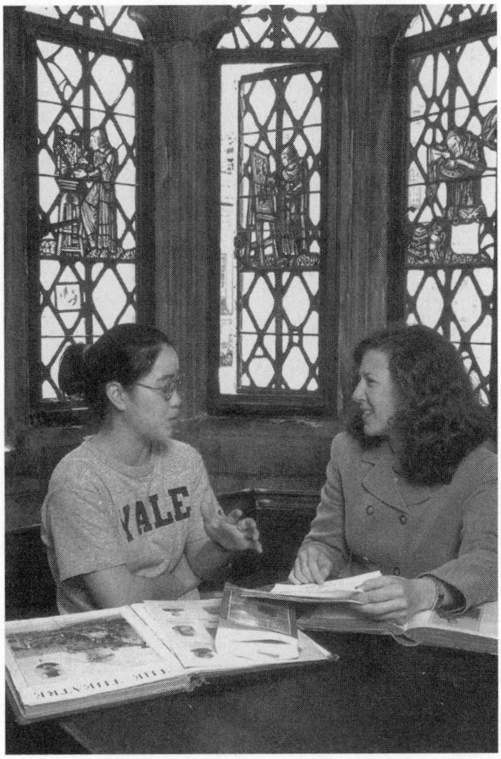

Dean Nicole Parisier advises a student at Branford College (Michael Marsland/Yale University)

Teachers

There are approximately 369,000 faculty women in the United States, which constitutes 40 percent of the of the United States professoriat (National Center for Education Statistics 2001). As a group, it may appear that there are more differences than similarities among women faculty. Women faculty vary, depending on the type of institution in which they are employed, full-time or part-time status, tenure versus non–tenure track positions, and most important, academic disciplines. Yet they are similar in the historical context they inhabit, the values that bind them together, and the fact that they share a tremendously powerful interest in ideas. The role of teaching, which provides a natural extension of one's values and interests, unites women faculty.

Any discussion of women faculty as teachers must be embedded within the demographic profile of the contemporary women professoriat. Overall, women faculty are fewer in numbers in the professoriat, are unequally distributed by type of institution, tend to be in lower ranks, are overly distributed in traditional women's fields such as nursing and education, are paid less than men at the same rank, and are more likely to be in a part-time or non–tenure track position (American Association of University Professors 2002).

Women are more likely to be part-time instructors than men. However, the benefits and barriers related to part-time status must be explored from the perspective of the individual's career goals, needs, and interests. Some women prefer part-time status because it offers greater flexibility. Many part-timers enjoy being less involved in academic maintenance activities, such as student advising, curriculum development, shared governance, and other committee involvements. Yet, for women who aspire to progress up the academic ladder, part-time or non–tenure track status may serve as a barrier to success. William G. Tierney and Estela M. Bensimón (1996) assert that the large number of women faculty who enter academia in non–tenure track instructor or part-time lecturer positions can limit women's potential because they are not part of the professional and social circles in which one learns about important resources, such as funding and negotiating time for research.

A disproportionate number of women work at community colleges, and the gaps in institutional type become even wider among full-time women faculty. At public two-year institutions, 47.5 percent of the full-time professors are women, compared to 32 percent at public four-year institutions (National Center for Education Statistics 2001, table 227).

Where a woman faculty member works has major implications for her teaching and research productivity. In larger institutions with a heavy emphasis placed on research, faculty tend to be autonomous and organize and control their own time, and subcultures of faculty tend to develop (e.g., part-time versus full-time, or camps with differing views on key campus issues). In contrast, community college faculty tend to organize and establish goals for their work based on the institutional mission of teaching large numbers of students with widely divergent goals and backgrounds. As a result, most community college faculty are motivated and rewarded by seeing students learn rather than by personally producing knowledge in their respective discipline.

The nature of women's employment in various institutional types is rapidly changing. One of the major changes is that a significant number of women are working simultaneously at more than one institution. The increasing need for part-time instructors offers opportunities for those who wish to take on additional teaching loads. At present, 13 percent of full-time women faculty state they have taught at more than one institution in the same term during the last two years (Higher Education Research Institute 1999).

The largest proportions of women faculty are in instructor (51 percent) and lecturer (53 percent) positions. Among the American professoriat, women comprise 45 percent of assistant professors, 34 percent of associate professors, and less than 20 percent of the full professor rank. Twenty-two percent of full-time women are not on the tenure track (National Center for Education Statistics 2001, table 244).

Disciplinary specialization tends to separate faculty in terms of their beliefs, commitments, and behavior. As a result, it may seem that faculty are more different than they are alike. Women comprise the highest proportion of faculty (across all types of institutions) in the academic disciplines of education (50 percent), health sciences (50 percent), and humanities (41 percent). The academic disciplines with the lowest proportion of women faculty are engineering (6 percent), occupationally specific programs (15 percent), and the natural sciences (20 percent) (National Center for Education Statistics 2001, table 233).

Some authors suggest that the academic discipline of the faculty member may be even more important than gender in understanding the similarities and differences among women faculty. The array of disciplines and subspecialties differ in their traditions, directions of inquiry, modes of doing work, and career lines. These factors influence all aspects of one's teaching.

Several authors have described clusters of faculty types. One of the first typologies was proposed by Alvin Gouldner (1957), who made the distinction between "cosmopolitan" and "local" faculty. Cosmopolitan faculty are those who principally identify with the discipline, and their department is viewed as the local site of their discipline. In contrast, locals describe themselves in terms of their primary commitment to the home institution.

Dorothy Harnish and Donald Creamer (1985–1986) categorize faculty based on the feelings or emotional responses of faculty members toward the various aspects of their work. They developed a typology of four job-involvement attitude patterns: job-involved, critics, psychic dropouts, and clock punchers. Job-involved faculty and clock punchers tend to report the highest levels of job satisfaction.

A third example of faculty typologies was proposed by Jessie Bernard (1974), who divides faculty into two categories: "teachers and men of knowledge" or women of knowledge. The distinction is related to the way in which faculty members see themselves in relation to the subject matter, students, and other scholars in the field. The teacher sees her role as serving as an instrument of communication. In contrast, the woman of knowledge serves as a collaborator with the original material of her discipline. The person of knowledge faculty member is perceived by himself or herself and others as having the knowledge, authority, and perspective necessary to convey information and resolves controversies in a discipline. According to Bernard's research, women are much more likely to fall into the teacher category rather than the person of knowledge category, and the opposite is true for men.

Although the expectations of faculty vary according to institutional type and academic discipline, the daily life of most faculty revolves around teaching, research, and service activities. One of the primary issues in the life of a faculty member relates to teaching loads: 53 percent of full-time faculty women report being satisfied or very satisfied with their teaching load (Higher Education Research Institute 1999). Although many women faculty report being satisfied, gender differences in teaching loads do exist. For instance, women are more likely than men to teach undergraduate courses. Some suggest this situation must be taken into consideration when comparing the teaching evaluations of women and men because student evaluations tend to be higher for graduate courses.

In *Academic Women* (1974), Jessie Bernard was one of the earliest scholars to discuss a prevailing myth—that women prefer teaching and service over scholarship. She reported the existence of the myth that women are noncompetitive and that part of their inferior status in rank, salary, and working conditions may be related to a lack of interest in status and prestige. Drawing on her own experience, she attests that she may have engaged in behaviors that perpetuated this myth. Although the extent to which current academicians hold this myth is not known, many current women faculty perceive that expectations for women to perform service as part of their duties exceed those for their male counterparts. Some women faculty, who prefer research over teaching, believe they need to hide this preference in order to behave in gender-appropriate ways.

The myth that women prefer teaching and service over scholarship may be perpetuated by some of the data on actual productivity. Based on surveys collected from faculty at 378 colleges and universities, 48 percent of full-time faculty women report they have not had a professional article published or accepted for publication in the past two years (Higher Education Research Institute 1999). In regard to service, women are more likely than men to have excessive committee service responsibilities (Carnegie Foundation for the Advancement of Teaching 1990).

Many faculty express anxiety related to teaching, especially in their first year as a faculty member. Mary Deane Sorcinelli (1994) reports 33 percent of first-year faculty mention stress related to their careers. It has been suggested that teaching can initially provoke anxiety for many women, especially for women who may have been socialized not to be outspoken or speak in front of a class. Others argue there is added pressure for women to appear nurturing and not to appear assertive and intellectually stimulating. Although initially stressful for many faculty, research indicates teaching becomes less of an anxiety-provoking activity for women faculty over time.

Today, many faculty are finding that they need to reconsider their teaching approaches, given the diversity among their students in terms of learning rates and styles. Beginning in the 1960s, the goal of expanding access to higher education became a top priority in the United States. Some say the open access philosophy has led to an influx of many underprepared college students, especially in the community college system. For women, many of whom work in community colleges, this pivotal issue has challenged them to find effective ways to meet the individual needs of an extremely diverse student population.

Teaching offers many women faculty a means for acting on their beliefs relative to the purpose and goals of undergraduate education. According to recent data from the Higher Education Research Institute (1999), one of the strongest beliefs held by full-time faculty (99.6 percent) is that developing students' ability to think clearly is essential or very important in undergraduate education. Among full-time women faculty, the majority believe the primary goals of undergraduate education should be to prepare students for employment after college, develop moral character among students, help students develop personal values, and enhance students' self-understanding. There does appear to be slight gender difference regarding some of the goals of undergraduate education. For example, 68 percent of women faculty believe it is very important to prepare students for responsible citizenship, compared to 60 percent of men faculty. Also, 74 percent of full-time women faculty believe undergraduate education must enhance students' knowledge of and appreciation for other racial and ethnic groups, whereas 58 percent of men view this as essential.

There is a great amount of variability, but overall women self-report high levels of satisfaction in regard to their faculty life (Higher Education Research Institute

1999). In particular, women report being satisfied or very satisfied in the following areas: opportunities for scholarly pursuits, autonomy and independence, opportunity to develop new ideas and new courses, and job security. Among full-time faculty women, over 75 percent report being satisfied or very satisfied with their jobs. Overall job satisfaction was fairly consistent across different types of institutional settings.

Although the majority of women faculty report high amounts of satisfaction, there are periods in the academic life cycle that can produce stress. Occupational stress among faculty typically peaks in the fifth year, as evidenced by the fact that 71 percent of faculty report job-related stress at that time, which for most faculty is the critical year prior to promotion and tenure (Sorcinelli 1994). However, most faculty generally have an increase in occupational satisfaction over their professional career.

Much of the research on teaching performance is based on students' evaluations. The issue of gender of instructor has received a considerable amount of attention, but the results are still mixed (Wachtel 1998). Some report that women tend to have higher student evaluations, and others report that men have higher student evaluations. In a meta-analysis of the existing research on student ratings of male and female faculty, Kenneth Feldman (1993) reports no significance difference between the genders. Feldman also found that students tend to rate same-gender teachers slightly higher than opposite-gender teachers. This finding can be viewed as optimistic for women faculty who have a desire to teach other women and influence their intellectual development.

Gypsy M. Denzine

See also Part 7: Disciplinary Socialization; Socialization; Tenure and Promotion

References and further reading

American Association of University Professors. 2002. "The Annual Report on the Economic Status of the Profession, 2001–2002." http://www.aaup.org/research/salary/02salary/2002rep.htm. Cited June 11, 2002.

Bernard, Jessie. 1964. *Academic Women.* University Park: Pennsylvania State University Press.

Carnegie Foundation for the Advancement of Teaching. 1990. "Women Faculty Excel as Campus Citizens." *Change* 22, no. 5 (September–October): 39–44.

Clark, Burton R. 1987 *The Academic Life: Small Worlds, Different Worlds.* Princeton, NJ: Carnegie Foundation for the Advancement of Teaching,.

Feldman, Kenneth A. 1993. "College Student Views of Male and Female College Teachers. Part II—Evidence from Students' Evaluations of Their Classroom Teachers." *Research in Higher Education* 20: 367–374.

Gouldner, Alvin W. 1957. "Cosmopolitans and Locals: Toward an Analysis of Latent Social Roles." *Administrative Science Quarterly* 2: 281–307.

Harnish, Dorothy, and Donald G. Creamer. 1985–1986. "Faculty Stagnation and Diminished Job Involvement." *Community College Review* 13: 33–39.

Higher Education Research Institute. 1999. *Faculty Survey Executive Summary: The American College Teacher 1998–1999.* Los Angeles: University of California.

National Center for Education Statistics. 2001. *Digest of Educational Statistics.* Washington, DC: U.S. Department of Education.

Rai, K. B., and J. W. Critzer. 2000. *Affirmative Action and the University: Race, Ethnicity, and Gender in Higher Education Employment.* Lincoln: University of Nebraska Press.

Sorcinelli, Mary D. 1994. "Effective Approaches to New Faculty Development." *Journal of Counseling and Development* 72, no. 5: 474–479.

Tierney, William G., and Estela M. Bensimón. 1996. *Promotion and Tenure: Community and Socialization*

in Academe. Albany: State University of New York Press.
Wachtel, H. K. 1998. "Student Evaluation of College Teaching Effectiveness: A Brief Review." *Assessment and Evaluation in Higher Education* 23, no. 2: 191–212.

Tenure and Promotion

Tenure and promotion are among the most visible and valued signs of achievement for college and university faculty. In addition to status- and prestige-related benefits, Howard R. Bowen and Jack H. Schuster (1986) note four other benefits that are associated with tenure. First, because of tenure, faculty have the freedom to engage in teaching and research activities without interference from any source. The job security provided by tenure not only enables faculty to engage in longer-term projects that contribute to the advancement of knowledge but also offsets the lower salaries received by faculty compared to other professionals. In addition, tenure creates a bond between individual faculty members and the institution, thereby committing faculty to work with others in their institution to accomplish shared goals.

Promotion to higher academic rank also has several benefits. In addition to the increased status, prestige, and influence associated with higher rank, higher academic ranks are also associated with higher salaries. Among full-time instructional faculty employed at four-year institutions in 1998–1999, average salaries were substantially higher for full professors ($71,322) than for associate professors ($52,576), assistant professors ($43,348), and instructors ($33,819) (National Center for Education Statistics 2001, table 238).

Observed Sex Differences in Tenure and Rank

A review of the observed distribution of women and men faculty by tenure status and academic rank suggests that women are less likely than men to realize the benefits associated with tenure and promotion. Despite the American Association of University Professors' 1983 statement urging institutions to critically review their "appointment and advancement criteria to ensure that they do not inadvertently foreclose consideration of the best qualified persons by untested presuppositions which operate to exclude women and minorities" (1995, 163), women continue to represent a substantially smaller proportion of tenured faculty than tenure-track and non–tenure track faculty. Analyses of the Integrated Postsecondary Education Data System Fall Staff Survey show that, in 1997, only 28 percent of full-time faculty with tenure were women, compared with 44 percent of full-time faculty who were on a tenure track and 45 percent of full-time faculty who were not on a tenure track. Women also continue to represent a substantially smaller share of the highest ranking faculty than they do of the lowest ranking faculty. Among full-time faculty in 1997, only 20 percent of full professors were women, but women accounted for 34 percent of associate professors, 45 percent of assistant professors, 51 percent of instructors, and 53 percent of lecturers (Integrated Postsecondary Education Data System 1997, 6).

The observed sex differences in tenure and promotion appear to be greater among faculty at four-year colleges and universities than among full-time faculty at public two-year institutions. In 1997 only 25 percent of tenured full-time faculty at four-year institutions were women, compared with 44 percent of tenured full-time faculty at public two-year institutions. Also in that year, only 18 percent of full professors at four-year institutions were women, compared with 41 percent of full professors at public two-year institutions (Integrated Postsecondary Education Data System 1997, 6).

Although the representation of women among the nation's college and university faculty has increased since the mid-1970s, the greatest growth has been among part-time and non–tenure track appointments. Between 1976 and 1993, the number of non–tenure track, full-time faculty increased by 142 percent for women and 54 percent for men (Chronister et al. 1997). As a result, about 48 percent of all full-time, non–tenure track faculty in fall 1992 were women, compared with only 21 percent of all full-time, tenured faculty and 39 percent of all full-time, tenure-track faculty (Gansneder, Harper, and Baldwin 2001).

Theoretical Reasons for Observed Differences

At least part of the observed sex differences in tenure and rank should be attributable to differences between women and men faculty in the characteristics that are expected to be associated with being awarded tenure and promoted to the highest rank. Research suggests that two theoretical approaches are useful for understanding sex differences in the employment experiences of college and university faculty: human capital and structural theories. The economic theory of human capital predicts that observed differences between women and men in tenure and promotion are attributable to differences in their productivity and the investments they have made in their productivity, including the quantity and quality of formal education acquired, amount of experience acquired, geographic mobility, and improvements in emotional and physical health.

Despite the popularity of human capital theory for explaining labor market experiences, some economists and sociologists have noted the theory's limitations. Critics have argued that "focusing on the supply of human skills to explain economic inequality and lack of productivity is a theoretical mistake" (DeYoung 1989, 155) and that "human capital theory has not generated an explanation of occupational sex segregation that fits the evidence" (1989, 358). Among the limitations of human capital theory is its failure to adequately explain the lower returns on educational investments for women and minorities.

Social scientists interested in issues of social inequality and poverty have responded to the inadequacies of human capital theory by developing structural or institutional approaches to labor markets. Structural approaches to academic labor markets focus on the influence of the characteristics of the colleges and universities in which faculty were trained and work, including financial resources, student enrollment, the tenure system, and collective bargaining agreements. According to structural models, sex differences in tenure and rank are attributable to the segregation of women in the types of academic fields, institutions, and work roles that have lower prestige and value.

Research on Sex Differences in Tenure and Rank

Researchers have consistently shown that women faculty hold lower academic ranks than men faculty, even after taking into account differences in the variables suggested by human capital and structural theories, including educational attainment, experience, productivity, institutional characteristics, and academic discipline. Using causal modeling and a sample of full-time faculty employed nationwide in 1984, John C. Smart (1991) found sex was related to academic rank directly and indirectly. In other words, women held lower ranks in part because they were women and in part because they had lower levels of education. Michael R. Ransom and Sharon Berstein Megdal (1993) concluded that women were less likely than men to hold the rank of associate or full professor in 1969, 1973, 1977, and 1984, after controlling for differences in educational attainment, experience, and publications. Using data from the 1993 National Study of Postsecondary Faculty (NSOPF:93) and controlling for educational attainment, experience, career publications, institutional Carnegie classification, and academic field, Robert K. Toutkoushian (1999) found that women full-time faculty at four-year institutions were less likely than men to hold tenured positions and the rank of full professor but were as likely as men to hold the rank of associate professor. Also using the NSOPF:93 but limiting the sample to faculty "eligible" for tenure (i.e., full-time tenured or tenure-track faculty), Laura W. Perna (2001) found that, after controlling for differences in human capital and structural characteristics, women were as likely as men to hold tenured positions at both four-year and public two-year institutions. She also found that, among tenured faculty at four-year institutions, women were less likely than their male counterparts to hold the highest rank of full professor. Controlling for differences in human capital and structural characteristics eliminated the observed sex differences in representation among full professors at public two-year institutions.

Other evidence suggests that the criteria applied in promotion decisions are different for women than for men faculty. Using a sample of criminology faculty in 1989, Karen McElrath (1992) found that the probability of tenure was positively related to experience, publications, service, and continuous employment (i.e., no career interruption) among women but related only to experience among men. Among faculty in 1972, Howard P. Tuckman (1979) found that, on average, men who published books had a higher probability of being promoted to both associate and full professor ranks than men who did not publish books. Among women faculty, publishing books was related only to the probability of promotion to full professor. Public service was related to promotion to full professor for men but not women. Based on their exploration of the degree of bias in academic rank using discriminant analysis, Matt L. Riggs and colleagues (1986) concluded that the academic rank of men faculty is more predictable than the rank of women faculty after controlling for "objective personnel data," including educational attainment, experience, average merit score, and department head status. Moreover, women were more likely to hold lower academic ranks than predicted based on the objective criteria.

In one of the few examinations of the relationship between non–tenure track employment status and sex, Laura Perna (2001) used the NSOPF:93 to show that, after controlling for differences in race, family responsibilities, human capital, and structural characteristics, women junior faculty in fall 1992 were more likely than their male counterparts to hold full-time, non–tenure track positions than full-time, tenure-track positions. She also found that the employment of women in non–tenure track positions is attributable in part to their marital and parental status. Although a smaller share of women than men junior faculty were married (67 percent versus 78 percent), being married increased the odds of holding a part-time, non–tenure track position for women but not for men. Although a smaller share of women than men junior faculty had at least one child (53 percent versus 70 percent), having at least one child reduced the odds of holding a full-time, non–tenure track position for men but was unrelated to employment status for women (2001, 594).

Through interviews with 200 faculty at twelve colleges and universities nationwide, William G. Tierney and Estela M. Bensimón (1996) found that, although the particular aspects of tenure and promotion processes vary across different institutions, the challenges that women faculty face in these processes transcend institutional characteristics. Both women and men junior faculty are typically confused by the haphazard nature of the tenure and promotion process and do not understand the performance or procedural requirements or the time frame. Although few women faculty described encountering overt sexism, Tierney and Bensimón noted that academic structures, policies, and practices that are intended to be gender-neutral often create a working environment that is unsupportive, patronizing, and even hostile. "Gender-blind" policies and practices assume that all individuals interpret institutional life in the same way. But some evidence suggests that academic experiences and the interpretations of these experiences are different for women than for men faculty. Based on an exploratory study of faculty at one university, Linda K. Johnsrud and Christine D. Des Jarlais (1994) found that, compared with men faculty, women faculty perceived a more negative institutional climate and felt both structural and personal discrimination to be barriers to advancement.

Implications for Higher Education

Identifying and eliminating sex differences in tenure and promotion require attention to two issues: (1) sex differences in access to the types of faculty positions that are eligible for tenure and promotion to the highest academic rank and (2) sex differences in the outcomes of tenure and promotion processes among eligible faculty.

Although variable serving as proxies for differences in personal preferences and tastes for non–tenure track employment may have been insufficient, some research suggests that the observed overrepresentation of women among non–tenure track faculty is only partially explained by the variables that are expected to be related to employment status, including measures of human capital and structural characteristics. Although anecdotal evidence suggests that not all faculty who hold positions off the "career ladder" (e.g., non–tenure track positions) are dissatisfied with their status, many tenure-ineligible faculty may be considered to be marginal "in the sense that they hope for full integration into academe" (Bowen and Schuster 1986, 65) because they are at a disadvantage relative to tenured and tenure-track faculty with regard to workload, pay, career development opportunities, job security, and other issues (Baldwin and Chronister

2001) and because they represent a lower rung on the hierarchy of academic labor markets. According to Ted I. K. Youn (1992), the existence of hierarchies within the academic labor market contributes to various forms of segmentation, including segmentation by job status (e.g., full-time or part-time). Movement from one job status segment to another (e.g., from part-time to full-time or from non–tenure track to tenure track), is restricted just as is movement from one academic discipline to another (e.g., from mathematics to English). Competition among faculty in different segments is limited, thereby permitting inequities among faculty across segments.

A review of the research on sex differences in tenure and promotion suggests several areas for colleges and universities to intervene. First, because Roger G. Baldwin and Jay L. Chronister (2001) concluded, based on their national study of non–tenure track faculty, that the use of non–tenure track faculty positions will continue, colleges and universities must work to ensure that faculty who hold part-time and non–tenure track appointments are not treated or viewed as "second-class" citizens. They recommended that colleges and universities should use non–tenure track faculty only to achieve "specific, clearly defined objectives." Colleges and universities should also adopt various strategies to support and integrate these faculty, such as involving them in shared governance; providing access to professional development opportunities (e.g., orientation), instructional and research support, and institutional rewards and recognition; and giving the same protections of academic freedom. Although these strategies will benefit all non–tenure track faculty, they will have a disproportionate impact on women since women are relatively overrepresented in these positions.

Second, individual colleges and universities should use what is known from prior research to examine the extent to which observed sex differences in tenure and promotion can be explained by criteria that are legitimately related to such rewards. Individual colleges and universities should also examine the criteria used in tenure and promotion decisions to ensure that the criteria appropriately reflect the mission and goals of the institution. Voluntarily or involuntarily, women and men have been found to allocate their time differently, with women allocating more time to such nonresearch activities as teaching, service, committee work, and student advising (Bellas and Toutkoushian 1999). Therefore, colleges and universities should review their tenure and promotion policies and practices to ensure not only that such practices are not discriminatory but also that such policies recognize the full range of research, teaching, and services activities in which women engage and that such policies encourage faculty to accomplish institutional objectives.

Individual colleges and universities must also ensure that all faculty have access to the resources necessary to achieve required results. The overrepresentation of women among non–tenure track faculty and the underrepresentation of women among tenured faculty and the highest ranking faculty may be attributable to "accumulative disadvantage," whereby initial disadvantages grow over time, as well as to the "Salieri" phenomenon, whereby relative newcomers to the academy (e.g., women) are evaluated by a dominant network of individuals (e.g., white men) who limit their advancement. Cumulative advantage describes the ways in which productive individuals acquire resources for research and predicts that individuals who are successful early in their career are able to command additional resources, including time, facilities, and support, to conduct more research. A special type of cumulative advantage is the "Matthew" effect, under which researchers who are already eminent become more so. This theory predicts that because women have historically had less access to our nation's most elite graduate programs and most eminent sponsors, they are further disadvantaged over time, particularly with regard to peer recognition, access to resources for research, and scientific productivity. Consequently, women not only assume faculty positions at a relative disadvantage in terms of access to information and professional networks but also fall behind because of extra demands, particularly with regard to committee assignments and student advising.

One reflection of cumulative disadvantage may be inadequate socialization to the faculty role. Many women faculty receive inadequate mentoring, both during graduate school and as new faculty, and have fewer networking opportunities. Researchers have recommended a number of strategies to ensure adequate socialization, including providing ongoing orientation for tenure-track faculty; involving senior faculty in the process of communicating faculty culture and institutional requirements for success; facilitating and funding collaborative work relationships and research opportunities between junior and senior faculty; establishing faculty development plans; providing clear and accurate information about the criteria for tenure and promotion; conducting annual, constructive reviews of new faculty by the dean or department chair; developing faculty mentor programs; allowing faculty to stop the tenure clock or pursue tenure while working part-time; and providing training for department chairs on sexual harassment, affirmative action, work climate, and staff training and development. Research also suggests that individual campuses must not only adopt such policies but also encourage faculty to take advantage of them. Although most faculty agree that faculty should be allowed to stop the tenure clock to care for a newborn child, only a very small percentage of faculty actually use such policies.

Through such actions, individual colleges and universities may correct the continued underrepresentation of women among tenured faculty and faculty with the highest academic ranks and may reduce the relative overrepresentation of women among non–tenure track faculty. Such actions will also help ensure that women are as likely as men to realize the benefits associated with tenure and promotion and reduce the possible marginalization of women within the academy. Such actions may also raise faculty satisfaction and morale since some research suggests that levels of global job satisfaction are higher and stress levels are lower among women faculty with tenure and higher academic ranks than among other women faculty.

Laura Perna

See also Part 5: Gender Inequality; Part 7: Campus Climate; Evaluation; Hiring; Researchers; Salaries; Sex Discrimination; Socialization

References and further reading

American Association of University Professors. 1995. *Policy Documents and*

Reports. Washington, DC: American Association of University Professors.
Baldwin, Roger G., and Jay L. Chronister. 2001. *Teaching without Tenure: Policies and Practices for a New Era.* Baltimore: Johns Hopkins University Press.
Bellas, Marcia L., and Robert K. Toutkoushian. 1999. "Faculty Time Allocations and Research Productivity: Gender, Race, and Family Effects." *Review of Higher Education* 22, no. 4: 367–390.
Bowen, Howard R., and Jack H. Schuster. 1986. *American Professors: A National Resource Imperiled.* New York: Oxford University Press.
Chronister, Jay L., Bruce M. Gansneder, Elizabeth P. Harper, and Roger G. Baldwin. 1997. "Full-Time Non-Tenure-Track Faculty." *NEA Higher Education Research Center Update* 3, no. 5: 1–4.
DeYoung, Alan J. 1989. *Economics and American Education: A Historical and Critical Overview of the Impact of Economic Theories on Schooling in the United States.* White Plains, NY: Longman.
Gansneder, Bruce M., Elizabeth P. Harper, and Roger G. Baldwin. 2001. "Who Are the Full-Time Non-Tenure-Track Faculty?" In *Teaching without Tenure: Policies and Practices for a New Era,* ed. Roger G. Baldwin and Jay L. Chronister. Baltimore: Johns Hopkins University Press.
Integrated Postsecondary Education Data System. 1997. *Fall 1997 Staff Survey.* Washington, DC: National Center for Education Statistics.
Johnsrud, Linda K., and Christine D. Des Jarlais. 1994. "Barriers to Tenure for Women and Minorities." *Review of Higher Education* 17, no. 4: 335–353.
McElrath, Karen. 1992. "Gender, Career Disruption, and Academic Rewards." *Journal of Higher Education* 63, no. 3: 269–81.
National Center for Education Statistics. 2001. *Digest of Education Statistics.* Washington, DC: U.S. Department of Higher Education.
Perna, Laura W. 2001a. "The Relationship between Family Responsibilities and Employment Status and College and University Faculty." *Journal of Higher Education* 72, no. 5: 584–611.
———. 2001. "Sex and Race Differences in Faculty Tenure and Promotion." *Research in Higher Education* 42, no. 5 (October): 541–567.
Ransom, Michael R., and Sharon Bernstein Megdal. 1993. "Sex Differences in the Academic Labor Market in the Affirmative Action Era." *Economics of Education Review* 12, no. 1: 21–43.
Riggs, Matt L., R. G. Downey, P. E. McIntyre, and D. P. Hoyt. 1986. "Using Discriminant Analysis to Predict Faculty Rank." *Research in Higher Education* 25, no. 4: 365–376.
Smart, John C. 1991. "Gender Equity in Academic Rank and Salary." *Review of Higher Education* 14, no. 4: 511–526.
Tierney, William G., and Estela M. Bensimón. 1996. *Promotion and Tenure: Community and Socialization in Academe.* Albany: State University of New York Press.
Toutkoushian, Robert K. 1999. "The Status of Academic Women in the 1990s: No Longer Outsiders, but Not Yet Equals." *Quarterly Review of Economics and Finance* 39 (Special Issue): 679–698.
Tuckman, Howard P. 1979. "The Academic Reward Structure in American Higher Education." Pp. 165–190 in *Academic Rewards in Higher Education,* ed. Darrell R. Lewis and William E. Becker. Cambridge, MA: Ballinger Publishing.
Youn, Ted I. K. 1992. "The Sociology of Academic Careers and Academic Labor Markets." *Research in Labor Economics* 13: 101–130.

Unionization

Faculty unionization involves the purposeful organization of the faculty on campus to bargain collectively with the administration over issues of wages, benefits, working conditions, hiring practices, and other concerns of university governance. Negotiations through collective bargaining, with either an employee negotiating team or designated bargaining agent, represent the mechanism through which unions advance the issues of their members. The bargaining agent represents all employees in the unit on every matter covered by the contract. The agent negotiates for all members, even when only a minority of the members may have formally joined the union. In 1997, 96 percent of higher education unions existed at public institutions, representing 250,716 professors (approximately 25 percent of total faculty). The U.S. Supreme Court's decision in *National Labor Relations Board v. Yeshiva University* in 1979 denied bargaining rights to faculty at private universities and served to slow down the expansion of unionization in higher education.

The bargaining process in higher education remains deeply influenced by its industrial origins. Unionization of higher education institutions followed the pattern established by unions in manufacturing environments, including the presumption of an adversarial relationship between faculty and administration. Another carryover of manufacturing unions is the grievance process. Negotiated contracts invariably provide for formal grievance procedures. Most agreements encourage informal resolution of difficulties, with successive steps of recourse then available. Strikes, often used in the business sector, do not occur frequently in institutions of higher education because of "no strike" provisions in contracts. The recent increase of union activities in higher education, however, has spotlighted strike activity on some campuses.

The History of Unions in Higher Education

The American Federation of Teachers (AFT) and the National Education Association (NEA) began to enter into faculty collective bargaining in the mid-1960s, but the American Association of University Professors (AAUP) came to the process later, not officially promoting unionization until 1971. In 1997 the NEA was the bargaining agent for 46 percent of contract negotiations, the AFT for 31 percent, and the AAUP for 11 percent.

The late 1960s and 1970s were the period of largest growth of unions in higher education. The confluence of a number of factors influenced the high interest in unions on campus:

1. A depressed job market
2. Economic hard times on campus
3. Centralization of state campuses and loss of campus autonomy
4. Lack of faculty governance at former teacher colleges turned state liberal arts colleges
5. Changes in state laws favoring public employee collective bargaining and the National Labor Relations Board's assertion of jurisdiction over most private institutions

Some organizers saw unionization as shared governance. Others were concerned that collective bargaining would threaten the nature of the academic community. The tension between who decided academic policy, the union or the internal governance senates, was a source of controversy. Although some faculty were spurred to organize for higher salaries (statistics support the fact that faculty union membership results in higher wages), faculty rights and working conditions were often behind organizing efforts.

The majority of faculty unions began in public two-year colleges, with Milwaukee Technical Institute unionizing in 1963. Two-year public colleges were ripe for unionization because their roots lay in secondary schools that were unionized. Today, 70 percent of all collective bargaining agreements are in two-year institutions. Yet more faculty in four-year institutions are covered by bargaining agreements than at two-year institutions since the four-year institutions have larger faculty bases. The first four-year institution to unionize was the U.S. Merchant Marine Academy in 1966, and it was organized by the AFT. The marine union, however, was atypical, resulting from the academy's association with federal government employees' union efforts. As a result, Bryant College, a small, private, liberal arts college that organized in 1967, represents the first traditional four-year institution to unionize. A big boon to the organizing effort occurred when unions were voted in at City University of New York (CUNY) in 1969 and State University of New York (SUNY) in 1971. That decision affected all the schools in these systems and brought large numbers of faculty to the bargaining table.

Unions and Women

Issues for women faculty in the early days of organizing centered around maternity leave and salary parity. Early women union members understood that unions worked for the interests of the majority, which at the time in higher education meant men. Women, therefore, also organized informally outside unions to advance their issues.

Concerns for women in unions today center on part-time status and rights, salary gaps, and equity issues. In 1993, women represented 38.7 percent of the professoriat, with the growth in representation occurring mostly in the lower ranks. In proportional terms, women are most highly concentrated in the ranks of part-time faculty (43 percent of part-time faculty are women) and in the lower status institutions (65 percent of two-year faculty are part-time, compared to 40 percent nationwide) and fields that have the highest percent of part-time faculty. The greatest salary stratification between men and women occurs in the "feminized fields" (education, English, nursing, etc.) versus the "masculinized fields" (engineering, physics, and medicine). Recent research on union contracts found that 13 percent of contracts contained an equity clause, but only three of the twenty-six contracts spoke to gender. Most equity provisions do not deal directly with gender or race but rather address equality of salaries with respect to market forces.

A review of the salary gap between men and women in universities finds salaries stratified by gender. The difference is higher than the wage gap in the workforce as a whole but considerably less than the difference for professional women. There is less wage stratification, however, between men and women in union shops.

Current Issues

Unionizing efforts in the 1990s and early twenty-first century centered around organization of graduate student teaching assistants and part-time faculty, the duty to bargain in good faith, workload concerns, and the rights of individual faculty members within unions. Although the *National Labor Relations Board v. Yeshiva University* decision stalled organizing on private campuses, recent organizing efforts at private colleges have encouraged faculty groups to hope for legal gains in the battle to organize and bargain.

A major issue facing unions and their membership is the loss of full-time jobs. Even with a unionized faculty, retrenchment at SUNY and CUNY involved the firing of tenured faculty and elimination of departments and programs. A shift to part-time positions results in deprofessionalization of the faculty. Part-time employees frequently lack job security, have no health benefits, lack retirement plans, and have no say in university governance.

Competition among the three national faculty unions has impeded the growth of collective bargaining in higher education.

The AFT, NEA, and AAUP are often on the same ballot to represent faculty on a campus, which frequently results in the splitting of votes and the campus not succeeding in getting a union. There is no single voice representing faculty interests in higher education, which weakens the efforts and effects of faculty unions.

Pamela L. Eddy

See also Part 9: Unionization

References and further reading

Hurd, Richard, Amy Foerster, and Beth Hillman Johnson. 1997. *Directory of Faculty Contracts and Bargaining Agents in Institutions of Higher Education.* Vol. 23. New York: National Center for the Study of Collective Bargaining in Higher Education and the Professions.

Hutcheson, Philo A. 2000. *A Professional Professoriat: Unionization, Bureaucratization, and the AAUP.* Nashville, TN: Vanderbilt University Press.

National Labor Relations Board v. Yeshiva University, 444 U.S. 672 (1979).

Reuben, Elaine, and Leonore Hoffmann, eds. 1975. *"Unladylike and Unprofessional": Academic Women and Academic Unions.* New York: Modern Language Association of America, Commission on the Status of Women.

Rhoades, Gary. 1998. *Managed Professionals: Unionized Faculty and Restructuring Academic Labor.* Albany: State University of New York Press.

Zoe, Lucinda, and Beth Hillman Johnson. 1998. *Collective Bargaining in Higher Education and the Professions. Bibliography Nos. 23–25, January 1995–1997.* New York: National Center for the Study of Collective Bargaining in Higher Education and the Professions.

Women of Color at Predominantly White Institutions

American colleges and universities have been described as chilly and alienating places for women and faculty of color, although these individuals play important roles within these institutions. The term "chilly climate" was coined in 1982 by Roberta Hall and Bernice Sandler as a negative barometric gender measure of women's classroom experiences and career advancement in postsecondary institutions. This term is as salient two decades later in describing women and faculty of color's conditions in higher education.

Nobel Prize–winning author Toni Morrison is a popular professor at Princeton University, an Ivy League, predominantly white university (Pelletier Micheline/ Corbis Sygma)

Although women represent 51 percent of the total U.S. population, they comprise just under a third (32 percent) of all faculty with the primary activity of teaching in four-year colleges and universities and almost half (47.5 percent) at community colleges. In fact, women spend more time teaching (58 percent) than men do (46 percent) and much less time in research—16 percent for women and 27 percent for men. Furthermore, just over half of women (54.1 percent) hold full-time faculty positions, as compared to nearly two-thirds (63.5 percent) of their male colleagues (National Center for Education Statistics 2001, table 227).

How well faculty women of color are represented on U.S. college campuses is of equally strong interest. In fall 1997, for example, all full-time and part-time faculty from African American, Hispanic and Latino/a, Asian and Pacific islander, and American Indian and Alaska native backgrounds represented just 13.7 percent of total faculty, thus clearly constituting a minority group among white faculty in postsecondary institutions. More to the point, women of color constituted an even smaller group, with a mere 5.2 percent representing them among all faculty (National Center for Education Statistics 2001, table 230). By contrast, students from the same race and ethnic groups represented well over a fourth (26.8 percent) of all students (National Center for Education Statistics 2001, table 208). Moreover, the number of students of color, particularly females of color, has continued to increase annually for the past two decades. Yet both white and minority students interact with female faculty in four-year classrooms approximately one-third of the time and just under half of the time in two-year ones. These facts are all the more salient in the twenty-first century, when one also considers that as recently as 1999, women constituted more than half (56 percent) of all students who attended college and also earned the greater proportion of the associate's (61.2 percent), bachelor's (56.3 percent), and master's (57.8 percent) degrees (National Center for Education Statistics 2001, table 248). But a concern exists that perhaps largely because of fewer female classroom role models and mentors available in all disciplines, most of these women students are continuing to choose traditional majors and staying away from the sciences and mathematics, which are still dominated by both male faculty and students. The academy remains "largely a white male enterprise" at the beginning of the twenty-first century, despite the enactment of affirmative action laws since the 1960s to counteract the chilly climate for women and minorities who attend or teach in two- and four-year colleges.

Research findings further bear out what is known anecdotally about women faculty of color: that they experience more barriers in the professional workplace than white women faculty. The result is that many minority faculty women are marginalized and isolated because of any number of factors.

First, minority women are often the only faculty of color or, even less frequently, just one of two or perhaps three others in their departments or colleges. As such, they quickly find themselves functioning in a somewhat alienating environment, seeing no one like themselves. It is also difficult for them to find senior faculty who will take an active, personal interest in them as well as in their research, who will serve as mentors and role models, and who will aid them in their faculty socialization and career development. White women faculty, however, appear to do better in being welcomed by male faculty, getting acclimated, and learning the ropes of the organization than do female minority faculty.

Second, added to the burden of being the only person or one of a few others of color, women minority faculty find that they fulfill a "twofer" role in the organization, counting once as a woman and again as a minority for institutional affirmative action purposes. As such, they are often seem by other faculty as "tokens"—merely hired for their gender and color and assumed to be lacking stellar credentials such as majority faculty hold. This perception further serves to marginalize minority women faculty in an organization in which status and prestige are highly valued. Perceived as such, female faculty of color find that they have to work at least twice as hard—that is, be overachievers—to be recognized as contributing at an acceptable productive level compared to their white counterparts.

Third, with no one to advise them or protect them, minority women faculty quickly find themselves overburdened with gendered types of activities that symbolically thrust them into "big sister" or "motherly" caretaker roles with needy students. Most students of color gravitate to these faculty members, seeking someone they can relate to culturally, or are sent by other faculty, thus increasing these faculty members' advising loads. Adding to the growing advising load are white students who also want to interact with faculty of color and who learn quickly that these faculty will spend more time with them than most other faculty. Thus, female faculty of color soon find themselves overburdened with students, a situation uncommon with their white male colleagues (Aguirre 2000). Also unacknowledged is the fact that this type of time-consuming commitment counts for little to nothing in the reward structure leading to tenure and promotion.

Fourth, another detraction from their productivity is the call to serve on committees such as those that deal with minority and student affairs issues. Although the issues may be of interest and minority representation important, these activities do not necessarily offer the types of learning experiences or network connections that will advance minority women faculty in their careers. Unless they are guided by the department chair or a faculty mentor as to how many and which committee appointments to accept, women faculty of color can easily find themselves attending too many meetings to their detriment.

Fifth, faculty are hired to teach, especially in comprehensive, liberal arts, and two-year colleges where that is the main component of their role. Thus, added to demands for women faculty of color's time is a full teaching load, often coupled with new preparations, large classes, and office hours. Entry-level and bigger classes typically go to newer faculty, and without any guidance or protection, it is easy for new minority women faculty to get the larger brunt of these. Furthermore, without research funds or faculty development grants to buy out some of their time, the expectation is that they will be in their classrooms performing their teaching duties as scheduled.

Sixth, garnering recognition and respect for scholarship that focuses on race and ethnic issues remains a critical area of concern for faculty women of color. Moreover, it is an area that can exacerbate their isolation. It is not uncommon for minority faculty to publish some of their research in lesser known journals and in other less traditional venues outside the academic mainstream, where their work may be considered intellectually cutting edge, professionally stimulating, and more applicable to influencing policy and practice. An unfortunate consequence can occur, however. Faculty of color may find themselves pressured to conform to values associated with mainstream research—that is if they want their scholarship to be respected and considered worthy of merit for promotion and tenure by their white senior colleagues—or be shunned for deviating from the norms.

The question then arises as to the satisfaction of women faculty of color in two- and four-year colleges and universities, if these burdens exist and the climate is a chilly one for them. Studies indicate that the level of satisfaction varies with race and ethnic groups and with type of institution as much as it does with the unique circumstance of the individual female. Although there are a number of issues that influence women faculty of color's attitudes and perceptions, recent studies have found four common themes: salary, promotion and tenure, work environment, and racial climate.

Salaries are typically used as a career barometer to determine status and equity in the workplace. They also affect morale, as it is not so much the exact amount of pay itself as it is faculty's perceptions of the value the institution places on the individual. Some evidence suggests that faculty of color, particularly women, feel they are underpaid for their services compared to their white colleagues. This sense of being undervalued in turn affects faculty's job satisfaction and self-esteem. American Indian faculty, for example, have reported they are underpaid compared to all other faculty and have voiced dissatisfaction over this inequity. Perhaps because of the influence of collective bargaining in the past two decades in most community colleges, however, female faculty members have fared pretty well compared to their male colleagues. This more equitable distribution is attributed to the early presence of women on the collective bargaining teams as they came into being. Nonetheless, women faculty of color continue to express dissatisfaction that they do not enjoy full salary equity.

Promotion and tenure reflect opportunities to advance through the faculty ranks and as such are considered the prime indictors of career success in higher education, but they also create high levels of stress among faculty. Limited opportunities for advancement through the professorial ranks in four-year institutions are evident for every minority group except Asian Americans, but even within this heterogeneous group, women do less well. By contrast, African Americans, American Indians, and Hispanics are more likely to be concentrated at the lower levels of the professoriat, especially in the lecturer and assistant professor ranks. The exception are community colleges, where excellence in teaching, not research, is rewarded, and no faculty ranks exist once tenure is granted. Nonetheless, women faculty of color have fared less well than their male counterparts in achieving tenure, mainly because of the plethora of commitments thrust upon them that leave them much less time for attending to their scholarship. In sum, four-year colleges and universities remain deeply rooted in a reward system based on research and publications for promoting faculty. This system continues to diminish rather than enhance women of color's opportunities for increasing their numbers as permanent members in higher education—and will remain so as long as their other contributions go unacknowledged.

The work environment for faculty is associated with internal factors such as autonomy and freedom to work, intellectual exchange, student-faculty interaction, teaching and learning opportunities, good working relations, a sense of belonging, and appointment or election to important committees. Small in number as they are at most institutions, minority women faculty report limited opportunities for developing working relationships and enjoying intellectual exchanges with majority faculty. Although female faculty of color, along with all faculty, indicate satisfaction with the autonomy and freedom to do their work, they report less satisfaction with other aspects of their work environment highlighted earlier. Nevertheless, teaching, the opportunity to interact with and influence students, and giving something back to their own or others' ethnic communities are highly valued by minority faculty, render high levels of satisfaction—and form the essence of why many of them became faculty members.

The organizational culture that even covertly supports a climate of racism contributes to an overall chilliness that in turn leads to faculty of color's dissatisfaction and potential departure. In addition to the burdens highlighted earlier, faculty of color express dissatisfaction with the subtle discrimination they experience from majority colleagues and students in a variety of ways. Among these discriminating practices are white students who are not accustomed to faculty of color in the classroom and especially challenge female faculty of color in ways they would not do with white faculty. Another subtle discriminatory practice comes from colleagues who virtually ignore faculty of color, rendering them invisible, or those who make subtly racist comments about such aspects as their appearance or linguistic skills. Male administrators who overload women faculty of color with new courses, students, and busy committee work rather than protect them and guide them toward tenure and promotion continue to be a cause for concern as well.

Women of color as faculty bring a high degree of value to higher education. For instance, they are more likely to place personal importance on engaging in research activities and to spend more time per week engaged in research and writing, despite their other demands. As teaching faculty, they are innovative and more focused on using newer pedagogic strategies, incorporate cooperative learning techniques more frequently, have more class discussions and encourage overall greater student participation, focus on active student-centered presentations, and encourage group and peer-reviewed projects. They are highly motivated to pursue and persist in an academic position because of the perceived connection between the professoriat and the ability to effect social change. In the service area, minority women of color tend to advise more student groups involved in community service, and they are more likely to provide service to the community in their efforts to make a difference. In sum, women of color who hold faculty positions in all types and levels of higher education are significant contributing members who are slowly but surely helping to transform these static, traditional institutions into dynamic places of change.

Berta Vigil Laden

See also Part 7: African American Faculty; American Indian Faculty; Asian American Faculty; Campus Climate; Latina Faculty

References and further reading

Aguirre, Adalberto, Jr. 2000. "Women and Minority Faculty in the Academic Workplace." ASHE-ERIC Higher Education Report no. 6. Washington, DC: George Washington University.

Astin, Helen S., Anthony I. Antonio, Christine M. Cress, and Alexander W. Astin. 1997. *Race and Ethnicity in the American Professoriat, 1995–96.* Los Angeles: Higher Education Research Institute, University of California.

Bower, B. Forthcoming. "Community College Minority Faculty: Their Voices and Views." In *Teaching in the Community Colleges as a Profession,* ed. Charles Outcalt. New Directions in Community Colleges. San Francisco: Jossey-Bass.

Castro, Consuelo R. 2000. "Community College Faculty Satisfaction and the Faculty Union." Pp. 45–55 in *What Contributes to Job Satisfaction among Faculty And Staff,* ed. Linda S. Hagedorn. New Directions for Institutional Research no. 105. San Francisco: Jossey-Bass.

de la Luz Reyes, Maria, and John J. Halcón. 1991. "Practices of the Academy: Barriers to Access for Chicano Academics." Pp. 167–186 in *The Crisis in American Higher Education,* ed. Philip G. Altbach and Kofi Lomotey. Albany: State University of New York.

Hagedorn, Linda S., and Berta V. Laden. Forthcoming. "Feeling a Bit Chilly? Exploring the Climate for Female Community College Faculty." In *Teaching in the Community Colleges as a Profession,* ed. Charles Outcalt. New Directions in Community Colleges. San Francisco: Jossey-Bass.

Hall, Roberta, and Bernice Sandler. 1982. *The Classroom Climate: A Chilly One For Women? Project on the Status and Education of Women.* Washington, DC: Association of American Colleges.

Huber, Mary T. 1998. *Community College Faculty Attitudes and Trends, 1997.* No. R309A60001; NCPI-4-03. Stanford, CA: National Center for Postsecondary Improvement.

Johnsrud, Linda K., and C. D. Des Jarlais. 1994. "Barriers to Tenure for Women and Minorities." *Review of Higher Education* 17: 335–353.

Laden, Berta V., and Linda S. Hagedorn. 2000. "Job Satisfaction among Faculty of Color in Academe: Individual Survivors or Institutional Transformers?" Pp. 57–66 in *What Contributes to Job Satisfaction among Faculty And Staff?* ed. Linda S. Hagedorn. New Directions for Institutional Research n. 105. San Francisco: Jossey-Bass.

Morrison, Ann M., Randall P. White, Ellen Van Velsor, and the Center for Creative Leadership. 1987. *Breaking the Glass Ceiling: Can Women Reach the Top of America's Largest Corporations?* Reading, MA: Addison-Wesley.

National Center for Education Statistics. 2001. *Digest of Education Statistics.* Washington, DC: U.S. Department of Education.

Nieves-Squires, Sarah. 1991. *Hispanic Women: Making Their Presence on Campus Less Tenuous.* Washington, DC: Association of American Colleges. ED 236 261.

Padilla, Raymond V., and Rudolfo Chávez Chávez. 1995. *The Leaning Ivory Tower: Latino Professors in American Universities.* Albany: State University of New York.

Romany, Celina. 1997. "Ain't I a Feminist?" Pp. 19–26 in *Critical Race Feminism: A Reader,* ed. A. K. Wing. Albany: New York State University Press.

Tack, Martha W., and Carol L. Patitu. 1992. *Faculty Job Satisfaction: Women and Minorities in Peril.* ASHE-ERIC Higher Education Report no. 5. Washington, DC: American Association for Higher Education.

Townsend, Barbara K. 1995. "Women Community College Faculty: On the Margins or in the Mainstream?" Pp. 39–46 in *Gender and Power in the Community College,* ed. B. K. Townsend. New Directions for Community Colleges no. 89. San Francisco: Jossey-Bass.

Turner, Caroline Sotello Viernes, and Samuel L. Myers, Jr. 1999. *Faculty of Color in Academe: Bittersweet Success.* Boston, MA: Allyn and Bacon.

Twombly, Susan B. 1995. "Gendered Images of Community College Leadership: What Messages They Send." Pp. 67–77 in *Gender and Power in the Community College,* ed. Barbara K. Townsend. New Directions for Community Colleges no. 89. San Francisco: Jossey-Bass.

Washington, Valora, and William Harvey. 1989. *Affirmative Rhetoric, Negative Action: African-American and Hispanic Faculty at Predominantly White Institutions.* Report no. 2. Washington, DC: School of Education and Human Development, George Washington University.

Part 8

WOMEN ADMINISTRATORS

Overview

The National Center for Education Statistics (2001) reports that in 1997, there were 151,363 individuals holding executive, administrative, and managerial positions in the nation's 4,070 public and private two- and four-year colleges and universities, of which women held approximately 46 percent (2001, table 227). Included in the category of executive, administrative, and managerial positions is a wide range of positions at various levels of authority. To adequately describe women administrators, one must first define what is meant by administrators.

In higher education, there are three dimensions along which administrators can be described. The first dimension is level of responsibility and authority in the organization. Colleges and universities are professional bureaucracies, and as such their structure is complicated. Normally, the category "executive" includes senior-level positions such as president, chancellor, vice presidents, provosts, deans or their equivalents. These are sometimes referred to as top-level administrative positions. The next level in the administrative structure of colleges and universities consists of what are typically labeled midlevel administrative positions. Included in this group are positions such as director and associate director of units and department chairs. Then, there are positions typically known as professional positions that are not designated specifically with administrative authority. Women are more highly represented in this group of positions. In 1997, 60 percent of these positions were held by women (National Center for Education

Nan Keohane, president of Duke University (Courtesy of Duke University)

Statistics 2001, table 227). These positions may actually be entry-level positions. Because the administrative hierarchies of colleges and universities are not as rigid as those of business and public service agencies, the boundaries between entry level and midlevel positions are not always clear. However, such positions as admissions counselor and residence hall area coordinators are examples of typical entry-level, professional staff positions.

A second dimension of administrative structure of colleges and universities is the distinction between the nonacademic and academic administrative hierarchies and the positions each includes. The academic administrative structure includes provost, academic dean, and department chair. This group of administrators has control over and provides resources for the operating core of the organization: the faculty. What most distinguishes this particular group of positions and structure from the nonacademic is the requirement that individuals holding these positions have been faculty members. There are exceptions to this "rule." For example, in community colleges, academic administrators may or may not be hired from the faculty ranks, but in four-year colleges and universities, department chairs, deans, and provosts are almost always faculty members. But colleges and universities also have many units that support the work of the operating core. The "nonacademic" administrative units include positions closely related to the academic heart of the university, such as registrar and academic advising, but they also include a wide range of areas that support the academic mission of the college or university: financial management, alumni affairs, fund-raising, human relations, public relations, and perhaps the largest of all nonacademic areas, student affairs.

The third dimension of administrative positions is closely related to functional identification. Within the overall administrative structure of the college or university, in addition to the academic administrative structure (department chair, dean, provost), there are multiple units, each containing its own ladder of entry-, mid-, and executive-level positions. The area of student affairs provides the best example. Student affairs constitutes its own area within college and university administration. The area has graduate training programs, professional associations, journals, and conferences and is professionalized to the extent that in order to move up the ranks, one typically has to have held a prior position in that area. Within student affairs, there are subfields such as housing, admissions, advising, financial aid, student activities, and so on.

Thus, when we speak of women administrators, we may be speaking of women in executive, midlevel or entry-level positions, of women in academic or nonacademic administrative positions, or of women in one of the various administrative units that supports the academic mission of the institution. Within the nonacademic positions, we include women in any one of the nonacademic areas essential to supporting the academic function and to carrying out the mission of colleges and universities.

Key Topics

Several topics are key to understanding women administrators in higher education, including demographics, or the types and levels of positions women are most likely to be found and the diversity of women holding these positions; leadership, or how women lead and whether they lead differently from men; career mobility, or the paths women take to obtain administrative positions; and campus climate, or the cultural factors that affect women in obtaining and carrying out administrative functions.

Demographics and Diversity

Although it is difficult to obtain up-to-date data on the percentage of administrative positions held by women or the number of women and women of color holding administrative positions in colleges and universities, it is clear that both have increased since the 1970s. Women have made gains both in terms of absolute numbers of women and women of color serving in administrative positions and in terms of the percentage of the total positions held. In 1997, women held 69,432 (46 percent) of the 151,363 total executive, administrative, and managerial positions in higher education, up from 40 percent in 1989 and from 26 percent in 1976, and 284,370 (60 percent) of the 472,016 nonfaculty professional staff positions (National Center for Education Statistics 2001, table 227). The vast majority (83 percent) of the executive, administrative, and managerial positions were held by white women, but 10 percent were held by African American women, 3 percent by Hispanic, 2 percent by Asian American and Pacific Islander, and only 0.5 percent by American Indian and Alaska native women (National Center for Education Statistics 2001, table 226). Comparative data by race and ethnicity were not available for earlier years.

The range of opportunities to create administrative careers has also expanded for women. Historically, student affairs has been more woman-friendly than other administrative units, whereas the presidency and other top-level academic positions have not. However, women have begun to make inroads in those areas as well. Women, including women of color, who attain top-level positions find themselves in the position to influence policy and to exercise *power and influence,* or leadership.

Leadership

Leadership, with its multiple theoretical approaches and applications, remains a powerful phenomenon, and our understanding of leadership within the complexities of academic organizations continues to evolve. In higher education, the focus on leadership takes two paths. One, stemming from the theoretical work on leadership, focuses on how people lead and whether women display different leadership styles from men. This perspective sees leadership as a phenomenon that can be exercised by anyone in any group setting. The second perspective, although not totally separate from the first, equates leadership with people who hold high-level positions, especially the presidency. This perspective examines who holds leadership positions, how they get these positions, and what they do in the position. This perspective assumes that individuals holding top-level positions are leaders and exert leadership.

Much of the theoretical work to date suggests a wide range of definitions and conceptualizations in the way leadership has unfolded over time. Although the notion of leadership in and of itself has often been defined and examined as a broad concept, individuals in leadership positions who represent multiple perspectives that question existing organizational assumptions and past practices provide new and varying points of view. Postmodern and poststructural approaches deconstruct the traditional knowledge base and theory. Rather than focusing on a particular lens for understanding leadership, the implication is that there is no single perspective that is able to capture all aspects of the human experience. From this perspective, understanding leaders' behaviors and motivations would be filtered through lenses of gender and race or ethnicity. In fact, postmodern perspectives call into question the legitimacy of the concept of leadership itself. In contrast, leadership, as understood from a modern perspective, focuses on tasks to be done and the traits needed to effectively lead the organization to accomplish those goals in a rational manner.

There is an emerging body of literature that finds important differences in the leadership styles, qualities, and priorities of women and men as leaders. Many of these studies show that women do not function as leaders in the same way men do and that they behave differently in similar situations. Whether men and women favor gender-specific styles of leadership or not, women leaders often face a set of preconceived norms and attributes by which they are assessed, evaluated, and promoted within academic organizations. The contention is that institutional policies and practices in the social system can perpetuate these differences. What to the untrained eye appears to be choice may actually be the result of socialization or shaping of expectations. That is, women often look at the opportunities within the organizational structure, expect that they are less likely to be promoted or placed in leadership positions, and may not even apply.

Moreover, strongly held cultural beliefs about leaders and leadership continue to be barriers in the fair depiction of academic leaders. A cultural belief or role expectation is the behavior that individuals expect of men and women in a specific position. For example, words such as captain, commander, and battle when used to describe leaders and their roles convey specific beliefs about leaders. Women, in their roles as leaders, can be questioned when these role expectations run counter to accepted norms. Moreover, women may be excluded from leadership positions because cultural beliefs about women and their roles conflict with these images, leading search committees to view women as unsuitable for leadership positions. Women face additional issues as leaders, such as the multiple roles and numerous obligations they encounter as primary care providers, and in the case of women ethnic minorities, as symbolic role models representing their sex as well as their race or ethnicity.

When leadership is equated with positions of influence, the first position that often comes to mind is the one at the top—the college or university presidency. The presidency is considered to be the leadership prize in higher education and the one that measures women's advancement into leadership roles in the academy. There are many data available on the status of women and ethnic minorities holding (or not holding) this position of power and influence. The most recent data provided by the American Council on Education (2000) on women presidents in higher education show that of the 2,380 college and university presidents, approximately 19.3 percent were women, and 80.7 percent were men. Although men still occupy the vast majority of college presidencies, the percentage of women holding these positions has more than doubled since 1986. Of the total number of women presidents, 392 (86 percent) were Caucasian, 38 (8.4 percent) were African American, 18 (4 percent) were Latina, 3 (0.7 percent) were Asian, and 3 (0.7 percent) were Native American. Despite the number of women beginning to enter the pipeline, women and ethnic minorities are still underrepresented in colleges and universities as presidents.

White women and women of color have made notable inroads into the community college leadership ranks. Community colleges have been more open to women administrators than universities. In 1998, 22 percent of community college presidencies were held by women, compared to just 8 percent in 1986 (Shults 2001, 2). The percentage of persons of color in community college presidencies also increased from 9 percent in 1986 to 12 percent by 1998. Likewise, women have advanced into other senior leadership positions, some of which feed into the presidency: chief academic officer, chief business officer, chief student affairs officer, and chief continuing education officer. In 2000, women occupied over 40 percent of the chief academic officer positions in community colleges, compared to less than 20 percent in 1984. Women have always held a greater share of the chief student affairs officer positions, but their share increased from just over 40 percent in 1984 to about 55 percent in 2000 (Shults 2001, 1). These data indicate an enormous shift in the demography of leadership in the nation's community colleges. The 2000 data suggest that the presence of women in top-level positions will continue to increase because the chief academic officer position is one of the main feeders into the presidency.

Persons of color have also made advances into the other top-level positions in community colleges, but not as great as advances made by white women. In fact, data on most administrative positions are not broken down by gender, so we cannot say for sure how many or what percentage of individuals in other top-level positions are women. For example, in 1984 about 6 percent of chief academic officer positions were held by persons of color, but by 2000, 10 percent were. The greatest gains for persons of color have come in the areas of student affairs and continuing education. In 2000, approximately 20 percent of the chief student affairs officer positions and 18 percent of the chief continuing education officer positions were held by people of color (National Center for Education Statistics 2001, table 227).

Career Mobility and Development

Administrative career mobility is central to women attaining executive, administrative, and managerial positions. However, mobility is not as simple as applying for a position. There are many dimensions of career mobility, especially for women administrators. Although mobility has long been a topic of interest for sociologists, it has only been since 1975, as greater numbers of women have sought top-level positions, that researchers have begun to understand the dynamics of career mobility and how they differ for men and women. Professional organizations such as the National Association of Deans of Women can provide important sources of networking and mentoring for women. The American Council on Education's Office of Women in Higher Education has several programs to identify, support, and assist women in attaining senior-level positions in higher education.

The characteristics of the institutions and the various functional units and the institutional environment in which they exist also have an impact on administrator mobility. Some of the most important characteristics are increasing attention to efficiency, the prominence of technology, and the backlash against affirmative action.

To understand fully the number and percentage of women holding top-level positions in higher education, one must understand the pathways from mid- to senior-level administrative positions. Attaining these positions is not merely a matter of holding the appropriate degree and having ability. For example, the traditional pathway to the presidency typically found at four-year and research-intensive universities—most often through the faculty and the office of the provost—requires promotion to full professor. Therefore, the faculty rank of full professor is the pivotal position or access point into paths leading to the college and university presidency. So, the first hurdle for women who seek top-level academic positions is to go through the faculty ranks. That is no easy matter. Recent figures suggest that only 20 percent of full professors in research universities are women. The percentages are higher in comprehensive colleges and universities, liberal arts colleges, and community colleges.

In addition to earning the rank of full professor, the quality of professional socialization and mentoring for women and ethnic minorities is also important to their preparation and movement into senior-level and presidential positions. For example, women who have mentors are likely to be placed in significantly higher administrative positions than those women who have not experienced mentoring. Mentoring does matter, and a positive mentoring experience can provide exemplary professional socialization, visibility, access, and integration into senior-level leadership and thus influence decisionmaking and policy.

Although much research has been carried out on the status of women and people of color in the college and university presidency, little attention has been given to other senior or midlevel administrative positions. For example, with its historical ties to the faculty, the librarianship could be one position that women could readily ascend to in academic organizations, yet they continue to be overlooked. Historically, males have dominated the academic librarianship. Typically, the head librarian was already a faculty member, and "his" status derived from his scholarly and teaching activities, not from his library affiliation. Although women were initially recruited to work in libraries as a relatively cheap source of labor, they now comprise the majority of academic librarian positions at every level except senior administrative positions. Although most of the academic librarians are female, the majority of the senior-level library administrators are male. Similar to other feminized professions, women librarians remain the disadvantaged majority administered by their male colleagues, and they continue to earn less in every capacity.

Multiple perspectives on leadership, strategic placements in the administrative structure, and parity with salary and promotional opportunities have been shown to be important factors affecting the work life and retention of women and people of color in academic organizations. In addition to the unique leadership issues that women and ethnic minorities seem to experience more than their male counterparts, there are climate, collegial, and ethical issues that may also have an impact upon their professional and institutional work life.

Climate

Women in academe may experience what has been called the "chilly climate." This term describes working conditions and collegiality among peers that devalue women. Characteristics of chilly climates include use of male-oriented language and lack of recognition of women's accomplishments. Departmental climate, multiple "role model" responsibilities, and interest in areas of scholarship not valued by a male-oriented academy continue to be barriers to the retention and recruitment of women and ethnic minority faculty members. That is, if the organizational climate is "chilly" to those individuals who bring new ideas, take maternity leaves to have children, or pursue gender-oriented research, then earning tenure, achieving full professor status, moving into the position of provost, and being promoted to the presidency of a college or university becomes especially difficult for women and people of color. And even when one does make it to the "top," a chilly climate can make a woman leader's job more difficult.

In addition to chilliness that women and ethnic minorities experience in academic organizations, the presence and perspectives of women in the academy can also present ethical challenges to higher education as an institution. In this case, the institution can impose certain restraints (subtle or overt) on individuals by defining their identity and influencing behavioral patterns acceptable to the cultural and political activities within the organization. Therefore, from the "institutional" perspective the dominance of a male perspective has shaped women's experiences through behaviors in the academic workplace, approaches to teaching and learning, methods in which to conduct research, and processes of scholarly review.

In the entries that follow, we find that numerous frameworks and lenses have been developed and used to explain the differences in status between men and women within academic organizations. It is, therefore, important to examine how women, through their social interactions and behaviors as leaders and as faculty members, influence those individuals within the units they oversee and participate in. By adding gender to the study of administration and leadership, particularly in higher education, we can draw a much fuller picture of the range of characteristics and multiple perspectives that comprise leadership in complex organizations. Administrative leadership is critical to the future of higher education, and yet our ability to draw effectively from all participants within academic organizations is not well-developed.

Susan B. Twombly and
Vicki J. Rosser

References and further reading

American Council on Education. 2000. *Datasheet on Women Presidents in Higher Education.* http://www.acenet.edu/hena/issues/2000/09_11_00/women.cfm. Cited June 15, 2002.

Moore, Kathryn M. 1990. "Creating Strengths Out of Our Differences: Women and Minority Administrators." Pp. 89–98 in *Administrative Careers and the Marketplace,* ed. K. Moore and Susan B. Twombly. New Directions for Higher Education no. 72. San Francisco: Jossey-Bass.

National Center for Education Statistics. 2001. *Digest of Education Statistics.* Washington, DC: U.S. Department of Education.

Shults, Christopher. 2001. "The Critical Impact of Impending Retirements on Community College Leadership." Pp. 1–12 in *Leadership Series, No. 1.* Washington, DC: American Association of Community Colleges.

African American Administrators

The presence of African American women administrators in higher education has not been widely documented. Data that would inform inquirers about the numbers and percentages by types of positions, institutional characteristics, earnings, academic rank, and years of experience are minimal and are often aggregated within race and ethnicity reports produced by government and other reporting bodies. The contributions and achievements of African American women in higher education administration have received little attention and commentary, largely rendering them as "invisible" in scholarly writings as they are in academic circles beyond the historically black colleges and universities (HBCUs). Women who have risen to the presidency and a few interested scholars have, in large measure, been the message bearers. The vehicles through which they have been heard include higher education publications focused on African American issues, selected research projects, and professional associations that recognize and support eradicating the information deficit. The few high-profile presidential appointments announced in the popular press in recent years are the exception, as evidenced by their newsworthiness.

African American women are prominent in the administration at HBCUs, but despite significant gains since the 1970s, it is still rare to find them at the executive level on a predominantly white campus. The "glass ceiling" for both African American females and males has been hard to break. African American women are at the bottom of the administrative hierarchy and often serve in custodial and service-oriented assignments as the "assistant to," special assistant to the president or provost, director of minority affairs, affirmative action and compliance officer, human resources manager, and student affairs administrator. Roles are often ill defined, budgets are minimal, and authority tends to be limited. These positions frequently do not have an impact on the institution's curricular goals, financial status, cultural norms, and climate in significant ways. In addition, many of these positions are "reserved" for African Americans, carry a temporary status, and are considered to be on the "fringes" of the system. Caucasian males of European descent continue to hold a disproportionate number of the influential and powerful leadership positions at the department chairperson's, dean's, vice presidential, provost, and presidential levels.

African American women hold executive positions in the context of an environment they experience as unwelcoming and unaccepting, unless they are fortunate to have the "right" combination and alignment of credentials, competence, support systems and networks, mentoring relationships, good will, good luck, and timing.

History

African American women administrators have participated in the leadership of postsecondary institutions in the United States since the Civil War. Much of the story about their experience began with Mary McCleod Bethune who, in addition to being an educator, was the first African

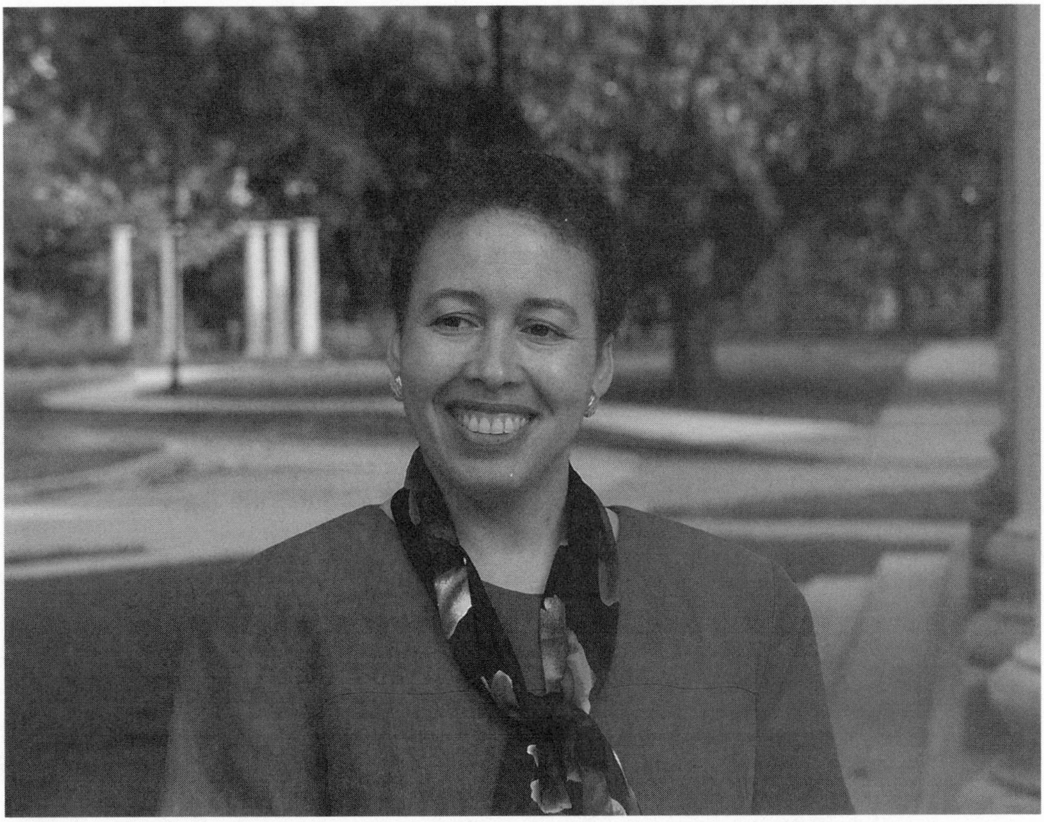

Beverly Daniel Tatum, ninth president of Spelman College (Courtesy of Spelman College)

American woman to become a federal administrator in the District of Columbia. In 1904, Bethune founded an institution for African American women that would later become Bethune-Cookman College in Florida. Most of the early training for African American women beyond primary and secondary school was provided in normal schools established to prepare them for the teaching profession. It was not until later that primarily religious institutions and the Freedman's Bureau established coeducational schools for African Americans. The purpose of these schools was to provide a higher level of education for a newly freed citizenry who had experienced both physical and educational bondage. These four-year colleges and universities located primarily in southern states later became known collectively as HBCUs. Executive-level positions held by African American women were found almost exclusively at HBCUs until the entry of large numbers of African American students into predominantly white colleges and universities at the end of the 1960s and the beginning of the 1970s.

Barriers to Ascending the Hierarchy

African American women face the same obstacles that have generally characterized the plight of African Americans as they strive to make advancements in the mainstream of American culture. Multiple reasons can be cited for the sparse number of African American women in policymaking roles in both two-year and four-year colleges and universities. Social climate, historical institutional barriers, and personal factors have affected career mobility. Racism, sexism, lack of organizational support, lack of tenure and promotional opportunities, and choices about family and personal relationships have created obstacles, even when these administrators' credentials are comparable to or exceed those of their Caucasian colleagues.

Limitations are placed on African American women by the institutions' notion that there is only room for a few minorities, and until recently, gender equity has been a serious concern for all women in the academy. African American women enjoy limited acceptance and credibility in professional areas that form the core of the institution and in which they would have responsibility for ensuring that the central mission of the university—learning and curricular concerns—is accomplished. Predominantly white institutions have not developed a comprehensive plan to recruit, hire, advance, and retain African American administrators, except in isolated cases. The gains made following affirmative action initiatives in the 1970s are in jeopardy of being eroded as a group of African American administrators who entered during that era exit the academy through retirement. Changes are needed in policies that affirm the importance and necessity of their presence in postsecondary institutions. The absence of a long-term plan to facilitate the identification of new talent and to promote and support existing administrators is an omission that causes concern that the numbers will decrease rather than increase in the future.

Racism and sexism, twin barriers whose effects are often hard to distinguish, are inherent in organizations dominated by traditional leaders who are not willing to share power and influence. The combination of racism and sexism creates significant obstacles and serves to impede the progress of African American women who seek to advance in the administration of postsecondary institutions. They often perceive that the climate at predominantly white institutions does not value and embrace them as equals. Consequently, their elevation to positions of power and authority is limited, in part, by the historical path and legacy of racial and gender discrimination. These institutional cultures are not supportive, and the network of "good old boys" and, more recently, the "good old girls" is difficult for many African American women to penetrate. Part of the problem has been the general reluctance of men to recognize and listen to the voices of these women.

Membership in the professoriat is an important qualifying credential in academic administration. In 1997, African American women represented 6.8 percent, or 13,667, of the total full-time faculty in higher education, a 27.2 percent increase from 1989. African American women earned 6.0 percent of all doctoral degrees in 1997 (an increase from 5.3 percent in 1977), but they were unevenly distributed across academic fields. Doctorates in mathematics and computer science, for example, went to a total of four African American women in 1997 (National Science Foundation 2000). These numbers highlight a critical need for support for African American women to obtain the doctorate and graduate with the requisite research and publishing portfolio and a substantial professional network of colleagues.

Even those African American women who are sufficiently armed with the appropriate credentials are not being recruited to join the faculties of the highest-ranking institutions in the country. The environment often proves unresponsive and unsupportive, once entry into the faculty ranks is secured. Women are asked to meet ambiguous standards for tenure and promotion, recruited to serve on committees as "representatives" of their race or gender, and are expected to respond to the needs of African American students who are also faced with similar institutional dynamics. Socialization is difficult, and the professional bureaucracy that characterizes academic institutions rewards individual work. Consequently, the feeling of isolation is commonplace and compounded by the lack of a critical mass of other African Americans who can help create a sense of camaraderie among colleagues.

African American women place self-imposed personal barriers on themselves based on their individual values and preferences. Family and personal relationships can pose challenges when career aspirations and opportunities expand. Like other women in academe, African American women consider the demands of child rearing, their commitment to a spouse or significant other, their community affiliations, and other factors when geographic mobility or additional time commitments are required to advance into higher level positions. Without the professional support and mentoring that most white men receive in higher education, these competing demands pose significant obstacles to African American women's success.

Vernicka K. Tyson

See also Part 3: Black Feminism and Womanism; Part 6: African American Students; Part 7: African American Faculty; Part 8: Mobility

References and further reading

Benjamin, Lois, ed. 1997. *Black Women in the Academy: Promises and Perils.* Gainesville: University Press of Florida.

Harvey, Walter. 2001. "Minorities in Higher Education, 2000–2001: Eighteenth Annual Status Report." Washington, DC: American Council on Education.

———, ed. 1999. *Grass Roots and Glass Ceilings: African American Administrators in Predominantly White Colleges and Universities.* Albany: State University of New York Press.

Lindsay, Beverly, and Manuel Justiz, eds. 2001. *The Quest for Equity in Higher Education: Toward New Paradigms in an Evolving Affirmative Action Era.* Albany: State University of New York Press.

National Science Foundation. 2000. "Division of Science Resource Studies, Survey of Earned Doctorates." http://www.nsf.gov/sbe/srs/nsf00327/append/c4/at04–14.xls. Cited June 10, 2002.

Opp, Ronald, and Penny Gosetti. 2000. *Promoting Equity for Women Administrators of Color.* Paper presented at the annual meeting of the Association for the Study of Higher Education, Sacramento, CA. ERIC Document Reproduction Service no. ED 449 704.

Turner, Caroline, and Samuel L. Myers, Jr. 2000. *Faculty of Color in Academe: Bittersweet Success.* Boston: Allyn and Bacon.

American Indian Administrators

Studies concerning Native American women administrators emphasize their underrepresentation in higher education.

Felicenne Ramey (1995) noted that the lack of research may be due to the small number of these women holding leadership positions in higher education administration. A factor that contributes to the paucity of literature concerning Native American women administrators is that they represent less than 1 percent of the total U.S. population. There are more blacks, Hispanics, and Asians in the United States. Not only are Native Americans few in number, but there is great diversity among them, with approximately 600 different tribes, each with its own cultural identity (Tippeconnic 1998).

In addition, attention to specific racial and ethnic groups and specific institutional characteristics has not found its way consistently into the analyses of national data sets. The lack of comprehensive research or complete databases on women administrators of color in higher education is disturbing and limits the ability to understand the status of all women administrators in higher education.

In 1995 women chief executive officers led 453 postsecondary institutions, constituting 19.3 percent of all administrators (Touchton and Ingram 1995). These women comprised 7 American Indians (2 percent), 2 Asian Americans (less than 1 percent), 39 blacks (9 percent), 24 Hispanics (5 percent), and 381 whites (84 percent) (Opp and Gosetti 2000).

Women administrators of color continue to be disproportionately underrepresented, except at minority-serving institutions. Some of the greatest increases for American Indian (0.11), Asian American (0.21), and Hispanic (0.52) women administrators occurred at two-year institutions (Harvey and Williams 1996). Institutions that had more women administrators of color were minority serving, two-year, or urban or had high percentages of women faculty of color (Opp and Gosetti 2000).

Perceptions of campus climate at minority-serving institutions may provide one explanation for the greater numbers of minority women administrators. Minority-serving institutions have been characterized as having a participatory ethos, an inclusive environment with expectations of success, nonpunitive remediation, positive role models, and a sense of historical affirmation. This climate of participation and inclusivity may be reflected in hiring and promotion policies and practices that are supportive of women administrators and may reduce many barriers (Harvey and Williams 1996).

Tribal Colleges

The studies concerning Native American women who are higher education administrators focus on their leadership and work in two-year, minority-serving institutions—the tribal colleges. Tribal colleges are probably the most successful examples of Indian control of education. Twenty-five thousand students attend thirty two tribal colleges in the United States and Canada (Tippeconnic 1998).

In 1992, Marjane Ambler reported that women presidents led ten of twenty-eight (39 percent) of the American Indian Higher Education Consortium (AIHEC) member colleges; three served in acting capacities; and an eleventh woman president was on leave. That is nearly forty times the 1 percent of American Indian women who head colleges and universities in the United States as a whole, according to the American Council on Education. In addition to the college presidency, women served the tribal colleges in other roles, as vice presidents, deans, vocational education directors, cultural studies teachers, and board members. In 1996, the roster of AIHEC member colleges showed that ten of thirty-one (32 percent) presidents were women.

Leadership

Ambler (1992) interviewed the women serving as tribal college presidents and discussed the current and traditional roles of women in Indian society. The Indian women interviewed did not want to be portrayed as feminists, if that implied they were putting down Indian men. As Carolyn Elgin, president of Southwest Indian Polytechnic Institute, said, "I would not want to be a party to that. I want to see Indian men advance as much as I want to see Indian women advance." Thelma Thomas, president of Nebraska Indian Community College, said, "A lot of the divisions you find in non-Indian societies don't apply in Indian societies, perhaps because there is more respect for the individual in Indian society" (Ambler 1992, 10).

The high-profile leadership of Indian women at tribal colleges does not necessarily reflect the status of women throughout Indian society. Education has always been a more acceptable avenue for female leadership, and as may be expected, the role of women varies among different tribes and cultural groups.

With the exception of the Southwest Indian Polytechnic Institute, all the administrators that Ambler interviewed worked on their home reservations, and all had children living at home. Several mentioned that their extended family members helped take care of their children. That may be one of the reasons that tribal colleges have more women administrators. Women can advance professionally while also living within the family support system.

Bernita Krumm's (1997–1998) study of women tribal college presidents focused on the presidents' leadership roles, their visions for the colleges, the behaviors and strategies they used, and their perceptions and insights to gain an understanding of how they promoted success for their students, faculty, and institutions. One of the presidents, Janine Pease-Pretty on Top, said leadership in education is congruent with the role of woman as caregiver and nurturer. Krumm concluded that tribal college leadership is the embodiment of a lifestyle, an expression of learned patterns of thought and behaviors, values, and beliefs. Culture is the basis of the institution; it formulates the purpose, process, and product. Tribal college leadership is inseparable from tribal culture.

Problems

Women of color in academic and higher education administration experience various degrees of a chilly climate caused by consistent and prevalent gender discrimination and sexual harassment (Blum 1991). The few Native Americans in higher education administration are members of the "A" team—assistants and associates. They are unlikely to become the policymakers (Clever 1983). Women of color are found in positions such as director of affirmative action and equal opportunity employment or as directors of financial aid and student counseling.

Future Research

According to Boyer (1995), there are many avenues available to scholars interested in examining Native American woman higher education administrators. They could explore the difference between traditional leadership and political leadership, who becomes a leader versus who should be a leader, or how a political leader can possess traditional values. A priority should be the development of ethnic knowledge that takes advantage of what is known about the respective groups and employs the best methodologies, instruments, and statistical techniques available to build a knowledge base (Padilla 1994). These issues are worthy of academic investigation.

Marilyn L. Grady

See also Part 1: Tribal Colleges; Part 2: Demographics of Gender and Race; Part 6: American Indian Students; Part 7: American Indian Faculty

References and further reading

Ambler, Marjane. 1992. "Women Leaders in Indian Education." *Tribal College Journal* 3, no. 4: 10–14.

Blum, Debra E. 1991. "Environment Still Hostile to Women in Academia, New Evidence Indicates." *Chronicle of Higher Education,* October 9, A1, A20.

Boyer, Paul. 1995. "Tribal College of the Future." *Tribal College Journal* 3, no. 1: 8–17, 45.

Clever, George. 1983. "The Native American Dean: Two Shirts in Conflict." *NASPA Journal* 21, no. 2: 60–63.

Harvey, William B., and Lea E. Williams. 1996. "Historically Black Colleges: Models for Increasing Minority Representation." Pp. 233–240 in *Racial and Ethnic Diversity in Higher Education,* ed. Caroline Turner, Mildred Garcia, Amaung Nora, and Laura I. Rendon. Needham Heights, MA: Ginn Press.

Krumm, Bernita L. 1997–1998. "Leadership Reflections: Women Tribal College Presidents." *Tribal College Journal* (Winter): 24–28.

Opp, Ronald D., and Penny P. Gosetti. 2000. "Promoting Equity for Women Administrators of Color." Paper presented at the Annual Meeting of the Association for the Study of Higher Education, Sacramento, CA.

Padilla, Amado M. 1994. "Ethnic Minority Scholars, Research, Mentoring." *Educational Researcher* 3, no. 4: 24–27.

Ramey, Felicenne H. 1995. "Obstacles Faced by African American Women Administrators in Higher Education: How They Cope." *Western Journal of Black Studies* 19, no. 2: 113–119.

Tippeconnic, John W., III. 1998. *Attitudes toward the Education of American Indians: A Survey.* Tempe: Center for Indian Education, Arizona State University. ERIC Document ED 312 114.

Touchton, Judith G., and Deborah Ingram. 1995. *Women Presidents in U.S. Colleges and Universities: A 1995 Higher Education Update.* Washington, DC: American Council on Education, Office of Women in Higher Education. ERIC Document Reproduction Service ED 393 325.

Asian American Administrators

Asian women are severely underrepresented in the administration of higher education, although they are well represented as college students. They are less well represented as faculty. Their numbers lessen even more dramatically in the highest realms of academic administration, and as presidents, they are basically nonexistent. In 1996 there were three known Asian women presidents in the entire United States (Hune and Chan 1997). They were located at two-year institutions.

Asian Americans have converged on college campuses in large numbers since the 1970s. This phenomenon can be deceiving. When gender is factored into the analyses of the influx of Asian American college students, the results show that between 1978 and 1998, the proportion of Asian American women undergraduate and graduate students remained the same (Escueta and O'Brien 1991). Asian women lag behind their Asian male counterparts in attaining doctoral degrees, which could correlate with their underrepresentation as faculty members. Asian women faculty also have lower tenure rates than those of Asian male faculty. Although preliminary analyses indicate that Asian Americans are well represented as employees of higher education, when gender is factored in, Asian American women have not reached parity with the overall population (Escueta and O'Brien 1995). This fact may provide evidence that the "glass ceiling" phenomenon is very real and that Asian women are but one group who battle against it. The overall representation of Asians on campuses of higher education, coupled with the "model minority" myth, which is the widely prevalent image that Asians are one of the more successful minority groups, leads to the misconception that Asian Americans do not face discrimination or unfair employment practices (Nakanishi 1993).

Alice Shih-Hou Huang, the dean of science at New York University from 1991 through the present (Courtesy of Alice Huang)

Asian women who do attain administrative posts in higher education tell stories of battling racism, sexism, and stereotypes. They are assumed to be hard working, diligent, highly competent, and eager to please their superiors. These characteristics, whether real or perceived, have a negative impact on Asian women administrators because those around them tend to view them with resentment, allow for others to take advantage of them, and alienate them from their majority colleagues. Characteristics of leadership affirmed and encouraged by the norms of higher education administration are often contrary to those stereotypically assigned to or demonstrated by Asian women. Organizations often reward leaders for displaying behaviors such as heroism, courage, and fortitude (Morgan 1986) while simultaneously frowning upon women for possessing these characteristics because they are considered to be gender-inappropriate.

Asian women face these issues in addition to cultural constraints on their behavior that increase the tension between their roles as women and their tasks as leaders (Ideta and Cooper 1999). They face similar cultural and socioeconomic obstacles to higher education leadership as their male counterparts, but Asian women are socialized into traditional female roles, thus adding another barrier to their progression (Mau 1995). A sense of schizophrenia can easily develop for Asian women while they attempt to negotiate these conflicting constraints and expectations and contemplate or engage in a climb up the administrative ladder. Asian women leaders share that their cultures taught them to be docile, nurturing, and reserved. While at work, they are expected to be aggressive, self-assured, bureaucratic, and decisive. This clash of values between Asian and Western cultures can cause great confusion and pain and tremendous feelings of marginality. Other Asian women, who readily admit that they do not fit into the stereotypes of the submissive, quiet, and reserved female, find that they are confronted with a different battle. When these women display behavior that is contrary to common stereotypes and perceptions, they report that they find themselves labeled as "a Dragon Lady" or "intolerant" and "pushy" (Ideta 1996).

There is a perception held by those in the majority that when Asian Americans are confronted with problems in their employment or promotion, they are more inclined than any other minority group to simply walk away, not confront the issue, and choose the path of least resistance (Nakanishi 1993). This perception is built upon the stereotype that Asians are passive and docile. The attempt to bridge the gulf between the behaviors that are rewarded by Asian cultures and those expected by the world of administration; between being true to who one really is, even if it includes not playing out the stereotypes associated with Asian women and attempting to fit into the world of Western leadership, is a constant battle.

Compounding the multiple and often paradoxical demands of the workplace on Asian women leaders is the Asian cultural expectation that they need to bring honor to their families. To be an Asian woman means to battle the stereotype that one will be less assertive than one's white counterparts. To be Asian also demands that one display the utmost courage in the face of adversity so as to not bring shame to the family name (Ideta and Cooper 1999). Success in the business world or workplace is also essential to Asian culture and is related to the value of honoring one's family. These conflicting and contradictory expectations create a sense of a nonunitary, fractured self for Asian women in higher education, like other women in educational leadership (Bloom and Munro 1995).

Although Asian women can be physically noticeable as both ethnic minorities and as females on campuses of higher education, they are also rendered invisible by those around them in academia. Many Asian women report being perceived as less intelligent, less qualified, or simply invisible because of their childlike stature and youthful appearance (Hune 1998).

Asian women have gained attention because of the model minority myth, along with Asian men, but are notably absent from the literature (Hune 1998). Prior to the 1960s, no research on Asian Americans in higher education had been conducted (Suzuki 1994). In the ensuing forty-plus years, more attention has been given to the topic.

Studies conducted on minorities tend to subsume gender, studying men and women together and only later factoring in gender for statistical reporting. More studies specifically examining Asian women must be conducted if we are to gain a better sense of the multiple paradoxes Asian women struggle with in the workplace.

Lori M. Ideta

See also Part 8: Mobility

References and further reading

Bloom, Leslie, and Petra Munro. 1995. "Conflicts of Selves: Nonunitary Subjectivity in Women's Administrators' Life History Narratives." Pp. 99–112 in *Life History and Narrative,* ed. J. Amos Hatch and Richard Wisnewski. Washington, DC: Falmer Press.

Escueta, Eugenia, and Eileen O'Brien. 1991. "Asian Americans in Higher Education: Trends and Issues." *Research Briefs* 2, no. 4:1–11.

———. 1995. "Asian Americans in Higher Education: Trends and Issues." Pp. 259–272 in *The Asian American Educational Experience,* ed. Don T. Nakanishi and Tina Y. Nishida. New York: Routledge.

Hune, Shirley. 1998. *Asian Pacific American Women in Higher Education: Claiming Visibility and Voice.* Washington, DC: Association of American Colleges and Universities.

Hune, Shirley, and Kenyon S. Chan. 1997. "Asian Pacific American Demographic and Educational Trends." Pp. 39–67 in *Fifteenth Annual Status Report on Minorities in Higher Education,* eds. Debra Carter and Reginald Wilson. Washington, DC: American Council on Education.

Ideta, Lori. 1996. *Asian Women Leaders of Higher Education: Tales of Self-Discovery from the Ivory Tower.* Ann Arbor, MI: UMI.

Ideta, Lori, and Joanne Cooper. 1999. "Asian Women Leaders of Higher Education." Pp. 129–146 in *Everyday Knowledge and Uncommon Truths: Women of the Academy,* ed. L. K. Christian-Smith and K. S. Kellor. Boulder, CO: Westview Press.

Lott, Juanita T. 1997. *Asian Americans: From Racial Category to Multiple Identities.* Walnut Creek, CA: Altamira Press.

Mau, Rosalind Y. 1995. "Barriers to Higher Education for Asian/Pacific-American Females." Pp. 235–245 in *The Asian American Educational Experience,* ed. Don T. Nakanishi and Tina Y. Nishida. New York: Routledge.

Morgan, Gareth. 1986. *Images of Organization.* Newbury Park, CA: Sage.

Nakanishi, Don T. 1993. "Asian Pacific Americans in Higher Education: Faculty and Administrative Representation and Tenure." *New Directions for Teaching and Learning* 53 (Spring): 51–59.

Woo, Deborah. 2000. *Glass Ceilings and Asian Americans: The New Face of Workplace Barriers.* Walnut Creek, CA: Altamira Press.

Wu, Diana Ting Liu. 1997. *Asian Pacific Americans in the Workplace.* Walnut Creek, CA: Altamira Press.

Ethics and Practice

Scholarship on women, ethics, and higher education is notably absent from the professional literature. Since higher education has been shaped and dominated by men and the ethical systems that men have established, it might be suggested that both the presence and perspectives of women present an ethical challenge to higher education as an institution. Ethics, generally, is considered to be a system of values or beliefs to be used in making decisions, guiding the decisionmaker to choose the good over the bad and the fair over the unfair in specific situations.

The gendered nature of ethics rests on the historical and cultural connections between typical male and female differences in defining the good. Modern discussions of gender differences in ethical perspectives have been framed by the works of Lawrence Kohlberg (1971) and Carol Gilligan (1982). Kohlberg, who did most of his research with boys, suggested that higher levels of moral development were characterized by increasing reliance on universal principles. When girls were included in Kohlberg's research, they clustered at a midlevel stage in which the opinions of significant others were more important than adherence to abstract principles in ethical decisionmaking, placing them in a lower stage of development than the highly developed males. Gilligan, in contrast, framed female moral development as different rather than deficient. Women, she asserted, gave far more significance to context than to abstract principles. In addition, female ethical decisionmaking involved an effort to resolve conflicts by addressing the concerns of all parties, rather than trying to decide who was right. Maintenance of relationships while resolving conflicts characterized female moral development.

The ethical framework that governs most areas of university life is quite similar to the structure described by Kohlberg. Reliance on general principles and standard procedures dominates consideration of relationships or contextual concerns, both in the management of the institution and in many disciplines. The search for universal principles that provide consistent explanations regardless of time, space, or context has characterized both Western, male-dominated thinking and the scientific method. Evelyn Fox Keller (1985) described the conflation of masculinity, objectivity, and science as mythic in its power to structure the thinking of modem "man." Parker Palmer (1998) suggested that the dominance of historically male, scientific, and objective ways of teaching and learning undermined the development of compassionate relationships in universities. He characterized higher education as a culture of fear in which collegiality was eroded by these values. The principles that are typically used for decisionmaking in university life are generally related to those that can be measured objectively: limiting costs, increasing financial resources, and achieving gains in areas in which results can be counted, such as publications, ranking in national evaluations, sports, numbers of students and faculty, and so forth. Quantitative standards for measuring the "good" are prototypically masculine and scientific. Although they are not unquestioned, they tend to dominate. Challenges from a female or relational perspective can be dismissed as soft or unrealistic.

The dominance of the masculinist perspective shapes women's experience in higher education. Four areas are of specific concern: (1) ethical behavior in the workplace, (2) ethics in pedagogy, (3) ethics in research, and (4) ethics in editing. Ethical behavior in the workplace has received a great deal of attention. The focus is largely on sexual harassment but also includes hiring of women, unequal assignment of responsibilities for female faculty, and standards of promotion and tenure. Treatment of women revolves around the issue of who holds the power and how that power is used. Sexual harassment occurs when a person with greater power uses that power to intimidate someone with less power. The principle of fundamental fairness is violated when one person harasses another because the target is being treated differently, and unfairly, in comparison to her peers. The same principle is violated when nontenured women faculty receive more committee assignments than their nontenured male peers, a higher student advising load, and inadequate mentoring compared to male peers in establishing a research agenda, acquiring support for their research, and so forth. The courts have been littered with tenure suits brought by female faculty, attesting to the prevalence of perceived discrimination against women in the tenure process.

The ethics of teaching has also been profoundly affected by feminism. Feminist pedagogy rejects masculinist assumptions. It is engaged, personal, constructivist, and contextual. Students and teachers explore topics together, learning from each other and respecting personal as well as academic knowledge. The process emphasizes dialogue, construction of knowledge, and respect for the effect of perspective on understanding. bell hooks (1994) uses the phrases "engaged pedagogy" and "education as the practice of freedom" to describe feminist approaches to teaching. Masculinist ethics would remove the personal perspective and focus on the general, abstract, and universal. A woman does not have to consider herself a feminist to teach in an engaged manner. Engaged pedagogy is a manifestation of connected knowing and is often perceived as a more desirable and comfortable approach by women students and faculty.

Feminist approaches to research tend to take context into account and to be attentive to the specific circumstances of subjects. Feminist research is often concerned with the context in which a problem arises. In contrast to masculine "objective" approaches, feminist scholarship values accuracy and the disclosure of the researcher's perspective in reporting. "Standpoint theory" differentiates between weak objectivity, which occurs when the researcher presumes a universal perspective and therefore distorts perception, and strong objectivity, which reveals the researcher's perspective and minimizes distortion (Harding 1993). A female researcher does not need to define herself as a feminist to frame her approach relationally. Both the ethics of women and feminist ethics emphasize the significance of relationships, complexity, and multiple perspectives.

Editorial ethics also embody distance and supposed objectivity. Papers are written in the third person, presuming that the viewpoint and the data described are universal in their credibility. Reviews are "blind," with the author not knowing who reviewed the work and the reviewer being equally unaware of the author's name. Editorial reviews tend to judge rather than nurture. Articles are returned as either accepted, accepted with requests for revision, or rejected. It is quite unusual for an editorial reviewer to work with an author to help that author improve. Such a face-to-face interaction would be a violation of objectivity, neutrality, and impersonality. This ethic tends to favor a masculine style, which women can learn but may tend to avoid.

Jane Fried

See also Part 2: Sexual Harassment; Part 3: Feminist Epistemology; Feminist Ethics; Feminist Pedagogy; Part 7: Tenure and Promotion

References and further reading

Belenky, Mary Field, Blythe M. Clinchy, Nancy Goldberger, and Jill Tarule. 1986. *Women's Ways of Knowing: The Development of Self, Voice, and Mind.* New York: Basic Books.

Gilligan, Carol. 1982. *In a Different Voice.* Cambridge, MA: Harvard University Press.

Harding, Sandra. 1993. "Rethinking Standpoint Epistemology: What Is Strong Objectivity?" Pp. 49–82 in *Feminist Epistemologies,* ed. Linda Alcoff and Elizabeth Potter. London: Routledge.

hooks, bell. 1994. *Teaching to Transgress.* New York: Routledge.

Keller, Evelyn Fox. 1985. *Reflections on Gender and Science.* New Haven, CT: Yale University Press.

Kohlberg, Lawrence. 1971. "Stages of Moral Development." Pp. 23–92 in *Moral Education,* ed. Clive Beck, Brian Crittenden, and Edmund V. Sullivan. New York: Academic Press.

Palmer, Parker. 1998. *The Courage to Teach.* San Francisco: Jossey-Bass.

Latina Administrators

Three factors pervade the literature on Latina higher education administrators: the paucity of studies on the subject, their invisibility because they have not been *counted,* and the numbers that reflect their underrepresentation. Studies about Latina administrators include those that focus on their work in community colleges, describe the influences on their professional advancement, identify their leadership characteristics, and note the double barriers they experience.

Minerva Gorena (1996) reported that the studies on Latinas in higher education administration are few in number and have been regional or state-specific rather than national. A factor contributing to the paucity of studies relates to the status of ethnic research. Although education and the social and behavioral sciences are the fields in which most minorities obtain their doctorates, scholarship in minority subjects or from a minority or ethnic perspective is often viewed as less than first-rate work (Padilla 1994).

It is difficult to study Latinas in higher education administration because they are not counted. The invisibility of minority women makes the development of an accurate portrait of their presence difficult. The literature on the status of women administrators has been inconsistent in reporting data on women of color and on integrating gender and race ethnicity in the discussion of equity. Specific racial and ethnic groups are not consistently reported in the analyses of national data sets. The lack of comprehensive research or complete databases limits the ability to report the status of Latina administrators in higher education (Opp and Gosetti 2000).

The literature on the status of women in higher education administration frequently references the reports on women presidents by the American Council on Education's Office of Women in Higher Education (OWHE) as a barometer for gauging gender equity among administrators in postsecondary institutions. In 1995, the OWHE reported that women chief executive officers led 453 of 2,341 regionally accredited postsecondary institutions, or 19.3 percent (Touchton and Ingram 1995). The racial and ethnic composition of these women included 7 American Indians (2 percent), 2 Asian Americans (less than 1 percent), 39 blacks (9 percent), 24 Hispanics (5 percent), and 381 whites (84 percent). The study also showed that nearly all Hispanic women presidents led public two-year colleges, of which half were Hispanic-serving institutions (HSIs) (Opp and Gosetti 2000). A 1992 survey of women chief student affairs officers showed that 88.8 percent were white, 5.6 percent were black, 2.5 percent were Hispanic, and 1.9 percent were Asian American (Randall, Daugherty, and Globetti 1995).

Ronald Opp and Penny Gosetti (2000) conducted trend and predictive analyses using both the National Center for Education Statistics Fall Staff Survey and Equal Employment Opportunity Commission data to examine changes in the representation of women by race and ethnicity among higher education administrators. The findings indicated that white women experienced the largest increase in proportional representation, followed by considerably smaller increases for black, Hispanic, Asian American, and American Indian women administrators. Growth occurred in the proportional representation of Hispanic women administrators overall (0.40 percentage points), with the greatest increase in proportional representation at HSIs (3.26 percentage points).

Women administrators of color were disproportionately underrepresented, except at minority-serving institutions. Institutions that had more women administrators of color were minority serving, two-year, or urban or had high percentages of woman faculty of color.

Community Colleges

Many Latina administrators work in two-year or community colleges. For this reason, the limited literature that does exist about Latina higher education administrators focuses on their roles in community colleges. That is understandable since some of the greatest increases for American Indian (0.11), Asian American (0.21), and Hispanic (0.52) women administrators occurred at two-year institutions (Opp and Gosetti 2000).

Elizabeth Cipres (1999) conducted a study to identify and describe the characteristics of Latina presidents of California community colleges that provided the foundation for their ascendancy to the presidency. The findings included their personal life histories, educational experiences, career paths, essential skills, and leadership strategies. The factors that contributed to Latinas attaining presidencies were the following: (1) identifying a significant family member as a role model, (2) having been married and considering their husbands' support an essential factor in their success, (3) having a community service orientation, (4) feeling a strong interest in policy implementation, (5) possessing a drive to achieve and challenge themselves, and (6) defining their leadership style as participatory and shared decisionmaking. Discrimination emerged as an experience that all of the presidents encountered and that provided valuable lessons and motivation. The profile of Latina California community college presidents included the following qualities: (a) probably Catholic, (b) often married to a non-Hispanic male, (c) bilingual and bicultural, and (d) among the first generation in their families to be college-educated (Cipres 1999).

In another community college study, Virginia Hansen (1997) asked, "What do the voices of Latina administrators in higher education identify as salient in their development as successful leaders?" The study examined the bicultural voices of the seventeen Latina presidents and vice presidents of the California community college system in 1996–1997. These administrators expressed enthusiasm, tension, and commitment in their role of supporting the education of students in higher education. Their insights also supported the conceptual framework that persistence, college environment, and bicultural identities influence the leadership style and role of bicultural educational leaders.

Three specific strategies were suggested by this research. First, bicultural administrators adapt their behavior and leadership style to conform to the college community. Second, they develop strategies to work around or with issues of racism, sexism, and classism in the academy. Third, bicultural administrators change their bicultural identity to adapt to the dominant culture of their college—emotionally, cognitively, and physically (Hansen 1997).

Lois Knowlton's (1992) study examined the influence of President Judith Valles's gender and ethnicity on her leadership behavior at Golden West College in Huntington Beach, California, and whether similar influences existed among the other eight Hispanic women presidents of community colleges in the United States. All the presidents were strongly influenced by their close family ties, their cultural identity, and their parents' emphasis on education. They developed their bicultural identity and bilingual ability early in life. The presidents brought new dimensions to leadership because of their lifetimes of experience in blending divergent points of view. Their ability to see the world through two sets of lenses broadened their perspectives and opened their minds to understanding the responses and needs of those whom they led. Their openness to new ideas facilitated their creative problem-solving abilities. Their vision was grounded in personal experiences and has guided them to work for a better society through the institution of the community college.

Advancement Influences

Gorena's 1996 study provided insight into how Latina become higher education administrators. Sixty-eight Hispanic women representing the four major Hispanic subgroups (Central and South American, Cuban, Mexican American, and Puerto Rican) and occupying senior-level administrative positions (president, chancellor, provost, vice president, dean) in higher education institutions in the United States were the subjects of the study. Gorena reported their perceptions of factors that positively influenced or hindered their advancement to leadership positions.

The five major factors seen as positively influencing career advancement included education and training, goal setting, networking, knowledge of the mainstream system, and knowledge of the advancement process. Traditional Hispanic cultural values and ethnicity were seen to hinder advancement. Within the category of family factors, personal economic status, parental economic status, and children were perceived to positively influence advancement, and household duties and other family responsibilities were hindrances. In the support category, family and friends, colleagues and peers, spouse or significant others, and non-Hispanic administrators were identified as positive influences and institutional faculty and staff as hindrances. Other positive influences included non-Hispanic male and female mentors and affirmative action; discrimination was seen by some as a hindrance and by others as nonapplicable. The profile for these women indicated that their first job after completing the bachelor's degree was in a public school system in the southwestern area of the United States (Gorena 1996).

Gloria A. Lopez's (1984) dissertation evaluated the job satisfaction, expectations, and experiences of Mexican American women in higher education administration related to the work environment (work, supervision, pay, promotions, and coworkers). The subjects were 147 Mexican American women in seven states of the Southwest who had been identified by their institutions of higher education or through professional directories as college administrators. Lopez reported that the integration of Mexican American women into higher education administration has been minimal. They primarily hold mid-level positions (directors and coordinators) and are implementers of programs rather than creators or executors of programs.

Leadership

To compile a leadership portrait of Latina administrators, Peery (1998) examined six

Hispanic women leaders' perceptions of the opportunities and barriers they faced in their career progressions. She noted two major difficulties with the current literature on Hispanic women in administration. The first lies in the wide range of ethnic cultures covered by the term "Hispanic," which in research and literature can refer to Puerto Rican, Mexican, Mexican American, Cuban, or Cuban American (Ferdman 1990; Gimenez 1990; Melville 1990). The second is that Hispanic women face the additional difficulties of racial discrimination and cultural influences. Amaro, Russo, and Johnson (1987) noted that Hispanic women face additional areas of stress because of their ethnicity, including more rigid and traditional sex-role norms and expectations.

All the women in Peery's 1998 study followed the expected traditions of early marriage, and all but one became mothers soon after. Trying to balance home and career was difficult for each, but the four women who had married Hispanic men found it impossible. Unable or unwilling to follow the strict traditional roles their Hispanic husbands demanded, they each divorced and remarried non-Hispanic (Caucasian) men. There is documentation in the literature that Hispanic males are not as supportive of their wives' careers as non-Hispanic males (Gonzales 1988).

Double Barriers

Latina administrators face double barriers to advancement. The addition of racial or ethnic minority identification compounds existing barriers for women. Within the higher education context, Hispanic women have faced two overriding factors detrimental to their advancement—gender and race.

Marilyn L. Grady

See also Part 2: Demographics of Gender and Race; Part 6: Latina Students; Part 7: Latina Faculty

References and further reading

Amaro, Hortensia, Nancy F. Russo, and Julie Johnson. 1987. "Family and Work Predictors of Psychological Well-Being among Hispanic Women Professionals." *Psychology of Women's Quarterly* 11, no. 3.

Cipres, Elizabeth L. 1999. "A Case Study of Perceived Characteristics and Life Events that Enabled Latinas to Become California Community College Presidents." *Dissertation Abstracts International* 61, no. 01A: 36.

Ferdman, Bernard M. 1990. "Literacy and Cultural Identity." *Harvard Educational Review* 60, no. 2: 181–204.

Gimenez, Martha E. 1990. "'Latino/Hispanic'—Who Needs a Name? The Case against a Standardized Terminology." *Journal of Health Services* 19, no. 3: 557–571.

Gonzales, Judith T. 1988. "Dilemmas of the High-Achieving Chicana: The Double-Bind Factor in Male/Female Relationships." *Sex Roles: A Journal of Research* 18, nos. 7–8: 367–380.

Gorena, Minerva. 1996. "Hispanic Women in Higher Education Administration: Factors That Positively Influence or Hinder Advancement to Leadership Positions." Paper presented at the Annual Meeting of the American Educational Research Association, New York City.

Hansen, Virginia L. 1997. "Voices of Latina Administrators in Higher Education: Salient Factors in Achieving Success and Implications for a Model of Leadership Development for Latina Women Administrators." *Dissertation Abstracts International* 58, no. 08A: 3036.

Knowlton, Lois M. 1992. "Leadership in a Different Voice: An Ethnographic Study of a Latina Chief Executive Officer in a California Community College." Ph.D. diss., University of California, San Diego.

Lopez, Gloria A. 1984. "Job Satisfaction of Mexican American Women Administrators in Higher Education." Ph.D. diss., University of Texas, Austin. *Dissertation Abstracts International* 45, no. 07A: 1942.

Melville, Margarita. 1990. "Hispanics: Race, Class, or Ethnicity?" *The Journal of Ethnic Studies* 16 (1): 67–83.
Opp, Ronald D., and Penny P. Gosetti. 2000. "Promoting Equity for Women Administrators of Color." Paper presented at the annual meeting of the Association for the Study of Higher Education, Sacramento, CA.
Padilla, Amado M. 1994. "Ethnic Minority Scholars, Research, Mentoring." *Educational Researcher* 3, no. 4: 24–27.
Peery, Kaye L. 1998. "Hispanic Women in Leadership: A Multicase study." Ph.D. diss., University of Nebraska, Lincoln.
Randall, Kathleen P., P. Daugherty, and E. Globetti. 1995. "Women in Higher Education: Characteristics of Female Senior Student Affairs Officers." *College Student Affairs Journal* 14, no. 2: 17–23.
Touchton, Judith G., and D. Ingram. 1995. *Women Presidents in U.S. Colleges and Universities: A 1995 Higher Education Update.* Washington, DC: American Council on Education. ERIC Document Reproduction Service ED 393 325.

Leadership

Discussions of leadership on campus often center on formal positions of authority, generally the college president. There is no singular definition of leadership, but rather numerous and contradictory definitions spanning the spectrum from lists of modernist tasks and traits to postmodern inquiry and deconstruction. Historically, the view of leaders included only men in positions of formal authority within a hierarchical organization. Changes in organizational structures, postmodern epistemology, and an increased percentage of women in positions of higher education administration and leadership pose challenges to traditional notions of who can be a leader and what leadership looks like.

Historical Overview

The first senior women administrators on coeducational campuses were deans of women. Initially, deans of women addressed prevailing concerns regarding coeducation and the supervision and guidance of female students. The role of these deans began to change in the late 1800s, when special dormitories for women were built and faculty members, under pressure to increase research productivity, were reluctant to handle affairs concerning the extracurricular activities of students. The professionalization of the position of dean of women students began with the increase in the number of women deans, particularly in the Midwest, and the creation of a professional literature and association in the early 1900s. In the 1960s, the decline and elimination of positions for deans of women occurred as the services they performed were subsumed by a collection of student affairs professionals.

Women are increasingly entering the office of chief executive officer. However, women presidents are concentrated in two-year institutions, women's colleges, or comprehensive colleges, not the more prestigious research institutions.

Leadership Theories

There are numerous definitions and ways to think about leadership that have clustered into themes over time. Trait theories were among the first scholarly writings on leadership, and their adherents subscribed to notion of the "hero" leader or the "great man," who possessed a host of traits that made him effective. Many of these traits were identified based on studies of men and so corresponded with characteristics generally ascribed to men, such as boldness, strength, vigor, and power. Later analyses showed that traits per se were not essential for success in leadership roles, and the trait theorists gave way to social constructivists.

Social power theory and transformational leadership theory addressed issues of leaders and followers with respect to notions of influence. The various forms of power leaders possess were thought to be constrained by follower expectations and behaviors. Transactional leaders meet follower expectations by exchanging things of value, whereas transformational leaders seek to change follower expectations. Transformational leaders also often are concerned with higher order end goals, such as liberty and equality. These end goals likely correlate with significant organizational change. From this perspective, transforming institutions of higher education is reliant on particular situations, such as periods of crisis or adversity or the size of campuses.

Situational variables are also central to contingency theories of leadership. Contingency theorists argue that leaders adapt their leadership style to match the events at hand. Too many constraints presented by a situation can limit what a leader accomplishes. Similarly, behavioral theories of leadership emphasize what leaders do, rather than traits or sources of power. Described as a series of dichotomies or continua, behaviorists focus on concepts like authoritarian versus democratic and task or structure versus relationship actions. An effective behaviorist leader maintains a balance between perspectives, drawing on certain behaviors over others as the circumstances demand. Alternatively, cultural and symbolic theories rely less on altering situational variables or drawing on particular kinds of interactions and more on the management of meaning and interpretation of the situation for others. The context of an organization and its inherent culture may represent a compilation of multiple organizational frameworks that require leaders to possess adequately complex cognitive ability and the working knowledge of a variety of lenses when viewing the organization. Judging leaders using cognitive theories may give followers' impressions more consideration than the measurable accomplishments of leaders.

More recent theories of leadership emphasize flattening the traditional organizational hierarchy. Common concepts include team leadership and webs of inclusion that place leaders at the center, where they are connected to many others in the organization, as opposed to being located at the apex of the organization. Here, the characterization of leadership is more collective and relational. The leader shares information and power more fully and includes others regularly in decisionmaking. Descriptions of these newer leaders are participatory, flexible, authentic, team-oriented, and collaborative. Current constructions of leadership recognize the complexity of higher education organizations and the need for administrative leaders to think complexly, draw upon an array of leadership tools and paradigms, and be reflective learners. In the current "knowledge-age" learning environment, leaders need to frame issues from multiple perspectives and be willing to question organizational assumptions and past practices.

The designation of women as "generative leaders" often occurs when describing leadership based on gender. Generative leaders encourage participation and empowerment of followers, but this leadership style may be constrained with regard to its actual application because of organizational structure and context. Some research suggests gender-related leadership styles, finding that women tend to adopt more democratic and participative styles, as contrasted with more autocratic or directive styles used by men. As often, research in postsecondary institutions finds that contextual factors, individual beliefs and values, and the role of followers shape leadership as greatly as sex or gender differences.

Issues for Women as Administrative Leaders

As they assume more leadership roles in colleges and universities, women administrators face different constraints than their male counterparts. Foremost is the assessment of leaders based on a singular set of norms and attributes. Strongly held cultural beliefs about leaders and leadership are rampant in colleges and universities, often expressed as metaphors used to depict leaders. Hero, great man, quarterback, superman, or father figure, for example, do not elicit images of women, nor do they readily generate analogous expressions that describe women leaders. Maintaining such limited definitions and images of leaders leaves women with a narrow band of acceptable behavior as leaders. Women administrators report feelings of marginalization, lack of authenticity, and evidence of cumulative disadvantage when confronted with the choice of professional promotion by adhering to traditional norms and expectations or enacting a more personally genuine and therefore perhaps more female construction of leadership.

The idea of impermeable barriers to organizational promotion is another challenge for women. The concept of the glass ceiling, introduced in the literature of the mid-1980s, remains largely unshattered today, in spite of an increased number of women in senior leadership positions. Women remain clustered in midlevel administrative positions (deans and directors), in lower-level positions, or in positions more peripheral to promotion into central administration, such as librarians and student services. Promotion into the college presidency still generally requires a traditional pathway through the academic ranks and the provost's office, particularly at four-year and research-intensive universities. The promotion of women into the full professorship occurs less quickly, but this career position is often a prerequisite for senior administrative positions, again slowing access into formal leadership roles for women.

More differentiated pathways to the presidency occur in community colleges, often heralded as more receptive to the inclusion and promotion of white women and administrators of color. However, even in the diversity of administrative backgrounds found with senior-level community college leaders, women achieve success up to a particular organizational level and then receive promotions more slowly into the presidency than their white male counterparts. In no postsecondary sector does the percentage of women senior leaders compare with the percentage of women in the pipeline, although this gap is smaller at women's colleges. Failure on the part of search committees and organizational followers to recognize the need for and value in changing images of leaders and new forms of leadership slow the demographic diversification of higher education leadership and likely the means of creating necessary organizational change. Truly eliminating the glass ceiling and moving college and university leadership forward in the twenty-first century requires changing current organizational structures that disadvantage and discriminate against women.

Women leaders juggle multiple roles and balance numerous obligations while being held to varying organizational and societal expectations. The image of "Superwoman" has given way to other labels and metaphors, but the facts have changed little. Women still maintain primary responsibility for child rearing and elder care, still take the lead in household management, still report higher percentages of time spent on the job, and deem diminished commitment in any area to be unacceptable. Senior women leaders in higher education who are not members of religious orders are typically in dual-career relationships with partners in equally high-profile positions, adding concerns about mobility and commuter relationships. Even if a woman is single, she is more often a primary care provider than the male leaders in her professional environment. Although more institutions have developed family-friendly policies and more active partner assistance programs, stigma and fear of future retribution attached to taking advantage of these opportunities remain, and they are often underused, particularly by women administrators. Integrating work and life requires a different way of envisioning leadership by women themselves and by the men with whom they work.

Leaders who are women of color have additional constraints. These women have to address issues regarding not only their gender but also their race and ethnicity. Some women of color don a mask of whiteness to replicate acceptable forms of leadership. These women are often few in numbers in an institution of higher education and are frequently called upon to represent all persons of color on committees and in service functions. The risk of burnout is high.

Future Considerations for Women in Administrative Leadership

New ways of structuring postsecondary organizations and the ideal of a flattened hierarchy have resulted in a move to conceptualize leadership as occurring throughout the organization. Such collective leadership relies less on the relative position or status of leaders within an organization and more on the ability of individual campus members to contribute to leading the organization. In a sense, leadership throughout the institution changes the role of followers, elevating the contribution of followers who are not positional leaders and demanding of all members shared responsibility for institutional success. The concept of more holistic leadership roles begins to deconstruct the problems of the glass ceiling inherent in a hierarchy and allows for individuality to be valued.

Juxtaposed against the notion of the hero and great man is the newer model of the servant leader. A servant leader is one who supports others in the organization and their work rather than placing herself or himself at the apex of organizational achievement and goal setting. By serving the needs of others first, the servant leader meets organizational requirements while engendering best efforts and commitment from followers. This approach to leadership also allows for individuality to be accented, as opposed to the case of a positional leader trying to fit a mold of acceptable behavior.

Emergent forms of leadership emphasize a decision to question old norms and not unconditionally accept traditional ways of doing business. Leadership theorists stress that autocratic leadership is counterproductive and espouse instead models of leadership with strong human relations skills and consensus building, just the leadership characteristics often attributed to women leaders. Developing models and images of leadership that integrate the best features of previous theories and allowing for emergent depictions of effective postsecondary leaders will assist in creating opportunities for women administrators. In addition, findings ways to avoid stereotyping that constrains future leaders is essential if organizations are to continually evolve and embrace the leadership needed for change and viability.

Marilyn J. Amey and Pamela L. Eddy

See also Part 3: Community Colleges; Part 5: Affirmative Action and Employment; Part 7: Hiring; Tenure and Promotion; Part 8: Leadership in Catholic Institutions; Mobility; Presidency

References and further reading

Astin, Helen S., and Carol Leland. 1991. *Women of Influence, Women of Vision.* San Francisco: Jossey-Bass.

Chliwniak, Luba. 1997. "Higher Education Leadership: Analyzing the Gender Gap." *ASHE-ERIC Higher Education Report* 25, no. 4: 1–97.

Curry, Barbara K. 2000. *Women in Power: Pathways to Leadership in Education.* New York: Teachers College Press.

Glazer-Raymo, Judith. 1999. *Shattering the Myths: Women in Academe.* Baltimore: Johns Hopkins University Press.

Helgesen, Sally. 1995. *The Web of Inclusion: A New Architecture for Building Great Organizations.* New York: Currency/Doubleday.

Nidiffer, Jana, and Carolyn Terry Bashaw, eds. 2001. *Women Administrators in Higher Education: Historical and Contemporary Perspectives.* Albany: State University of New York Press.

Sagaria, Mary Ann D., ed. 1988. *Empowering Women: Leadership Development Strategies on Campus.* Vol. 44. San Francisco: Jossey-Bass.

Townsend, Barbara K., ed. 1995. *Gender and Power in the Community College.* New Directions for Community Colleges no. 89. San Francisco: Jossey-Bass.

Leadership in Catholic Institutions

The overriding context of Catholic higher education in the United States is the history of the Catholic Church and its traditions. Women's leadership in Catholic higher education must be understood in light of the historical context, culture, and influence of the Catholic Church. As a patriarchal and hierarchical structure, the church has afforded leadership, power roles, and responsibilities to men. Therefore, a persistent reality in the Catholic Church has been the continued controversy over the role of women therein. One of the more vocal critics of the church argues that the history of the Catholic Church "institutionalizes patriarchy to a degree that tests the wiles and perseverance of feminists, not to mention their faith, hope and charity," while offering a legacy "intertwined with authoritarianism and triumphalism" (Boys 1992). Another critic argues that traditionally the church has not accepted women as being equal partners to men or as necessary to men in any activity other than procreation. Yet the present reality of the American Catholic Church reveals a significant dependency on laywomen to serve in a variety of lay ministerial roles. However, laywomen are excluded from ordination and are rejected from leadership roles in the church. Although Pope John Paul II has acknowledged the marginalization of women in the church's history and affirmed women's contributions in his papal teaching, "On the Family," he has in the same document romanticized motherhood and limited the potential of both sexes by reinforcing stereotypic gender expectations (Cahill 1992).

The church's history of ambivalence toward women has had a profound impact on the culture, identity, and leadership of American Catholic higher education. Catholic colleges and universities communicate their religious identity both through what they say and what they do. Structures, policies, curricula, personnel, and institutional culture reflect the way religious identity is both understood and perceived. As the church seeks women out for lay ministerial roles while rejecting them in leadership roles, Catholic institutions of higher education are educating women for professional roles that will lead to lifestyles quite different from those encouraged by the church. Tension within the faith community is a result of a heightened awareness on college campuses of the difference between what the church expects as appropriate for women and what women themselves see as appropriate in professional roles.

This tension is particularly heightened at Catholic institutions founded by male religious. Although women now have equal access to Catholic institutions originally founded by male religious to educate male students and women can now pursue the same degrees as their male counterparts, women students have not necessarily been provided the same educational experience. The imagery and environments still reflect male history and traditions. Leaders and decisionmakers are historically and continue to be mostly white men, both religious and lay. Since men have filled these roles, the cultural images and beliefs on these college campuses associate men with leadership. Yet as membership in founding religious orders diminishes and missions shift, space has been created and doors have begun to open for laywomen to assume leadership positions in traditionally male-dominated institutions of Catholic higher education. Their presence is likely to break down the historically gendered and religious atmosphere characterized by a culture of hierarchy and male dominance. Their presence will also continue a legacy of female leadership in Catholic higher education begun by women religious who founded Catholic women's colleges in the early twentieth century.

The term "woman leader" is an anomaly in itself. Women who assume leadership positions are not able to forget their status as women leaders; gender acts as a filter for assessing and evaluating women's leadership skills and effectiveness. Women experience a sense of tokenism, precariousness, and vulnerability despite their confidence and effectiveness as leaders. Gender interacts with the context or contexts of an organization. Organizational contextual influences include existing social structure, personnel, type of organization, and mission and purpose of the organization. Broader contextual influences may be political, intellectual, social, cultural, religious, and international.

Women's leadership has had a strong presence and influence on the history of Catholic higher education. However, the contributions of women leaders have been only marginally recognized in the research done on the history of Catholic higher education, since much of that literature focuses on institutions founded by male religious, most notably by the Jesuits and the Congregation of Holy Cross. Yet a strong female legacy of leadership exists in the history of Catholic higher education, primarily as a result of the women religious who founded and served in Catholic women's colleges throughout the first half of the twentieth century. The number of colleges alone indicates their strong presence in Catholic higher education. At their peak in the mid-1960s, there were 223 Catholic colleges founded by women religious, almost exclusively female colleges, enrolling approximately one-fourth of the students in Catholic higher education (Morey and Holtschneider 2000). However, most history books on Catholic higher education acknowledge neither the importance of their existence nor the legacy established, let alone give credit to the leadership contributions of many religious women to Catholic higher education.

As early as the 1890s, women religious dared to establish colleges from their existing academies, in spite of the social controversies surrounding the education of women, the ambivalent and sometimes hostile response of male leaders in the church, and limited finances. Although their commitment to the patriarchal church and their immersion in an American culture that had not liberated women imposed limits on educational reform and encouraged traditional roles, the sisters provided models of strength and leadership while offering women students opportunities to participate in leadership as well. Even in the shadows of opposition and male dominance, religious women were able to lead in ways that would improve the conditions and standards of their colleges and provide role models of leadership.

Clearly, what differentiated Catholic women's colleges from their secular counterparts was the dominant presence of nuns. They held most faculty and administrative positions on early Catholic women college campuses. They developed curricula, raised money, and built buildings. It was not unusual, however, to find a faculty of sisters who had not completed an undergraduate degree themselves. The nuns were handicapped by several issues, including the refusal of Catholic universities to admit women except during summer sessions, the unwillingness of bishops to allow sisters to attend secular colleges, and the attitudes of some community members who resented the financial costs and removal of teachers from schools as a result of their pursuit of higher education.

It was not until the 1940s that religious sisters began to promote their own needs for formal education beyond the secondary level. The Sisters Formation Conference (later called the Conference of Major Superiors of Women), operating under the College Department of the National Catholic Educational Association (presently known as the Association of Catholic Colleges and Universities, or ACCU), was formed and committed to providing higher educational opportunities and religious formation to all sisters (Pellegrino 1999). It was in this forum that religious leaders found a place to advocate for their own educational needs while attempting to contribute to the dialogue on Catholic higher education. In chronicling women's leadership in the College Department, however, researchers have suggested that women religious were not particularly welcomed in the College Department proceedings. Although the male leaders of the association created a forum for discussion and discernment of issues relevant to their colleges, women leaders were pushed to the periphery of the organization, and their voices were rarely heard in the larger collective context. It was not until 1947 that the College Department would see its first women president (Mary Molloy, president of St. Teresa's College in Minnesota) and not until 1980 that a woman would take over the directorship of ACCU (Alice Gallin, OSU, noted author and historian).

By the 1960s, however, Catholic colleges all across the United States were redefining themselves in the wake of Vatican II, the subsequent Land O'Lakes gathering, and the changing nature of sponsorship. In particular, Catholic women's colleges struggled with the challenges posed to them as Catholic men's colleges turned coeducational, resulting in a significant decline in enrollments as women decided against single-sex education. Women religious began to leave their communities in significant numbers, and financial problems intensified.

In the late 1970s, a group of sister-presidents from Catholic women's colleges convened to discuss the future of their kind of college, questioning their place among institutions of higher education. Although they believed in the value of Catholic women's colleges, they felt a need to clarify their mission as a response to the growing number of men and women's Catholic colleges shifting to coeducation. Inspired by their coming together as a group, the presidents decided to form an organization whose mission would distinguish the common heritage of this distinctive type of college while promoting the perspectives and issues of these institutions through ACCU. The group decided to take on the name of the Neylan Commission, after Genevieve and Edith Neylan, two sisters who had made a bequest to the Sister Formation Conference (Gallin 1999).

Women's leadership in Catholic higher education must also be understood in the historical and contemporary context of culture and identity. Much of the literature characterizes culture and identity in Catholic higher education as reflected in colleges and universities established by male religious. Historically, the culture and identity of Catholic women's colleges varied significantly, depending upon the tradition of the founding order and the specific women's population the institution chose to serve. It is true today that the identity issues related to Catholic women's colleges are centered around issues related to their founding as Catholic women's colleges and their desire to continue the tradition initiated by the founding religious women, in spite of their changing missions and student populations. Much of the historical literature, however, discloses how the collective Catholic higher education was distinct in its social, institutional, and ideological dimensions. Yet the 1960s and subsequent decades have been marked by an "identity crisis" in Catholic higher education, as Catholic educators and leaders responded to the many internal and external forces that would eventually transform the nature of Catholic higher education. By the end of the century and into the new millennium, leaders in Catholic higher education were still grappling with the identity issue, particularly in light of the *Ex Corde Ecclesiae* document that provoked much dialogue throughout the 1990s.

In response to the identity dialogue, Mary C. Boys (1992) has argued that feminists engage in "perilous opportunity, on the one hand understanding the need to have a vested interest in the rethinking process, on the other hand recognizing powerful people inside and outside the university have reason to control the conversation" (1992, 20). Another feminist has discussed the delicate balance of feminist values and concerns with the identity and values system of the religious institution. Feminists feel a strong need to move women's issues from the margins to the center, but there is also a deep sense of obligation to respect the value system of the institution, despite the fact that those values at times conflict with feminist values. Some feminist scholars have offered their views on the kinds of transformations necessary to reconcile the mission of Catholic colleges with feminist moral visions and social justice perspectives. Judith Wilt (1992) discusses her identity as a Catholic feminist, working at a Catholic university at a time when "government funding, changing ethno-religious demographics, successive and sometimes competing waves of feminism, successive waves of liberation and postliberation theologies, all these entwining heritages, 'private,' 'co-educational,' 'university,' even 'Jesuit,'—all are undergoing constant scrutiny and revision" (1992, 3). Another has argued that feminist values of care and relational and affective virtues have been lost because society, the church, and the academy have gendered these qualities as female. Finally, Lisa S. Cahill has argued that the real challenge in Catholic higher education "is to avoid preconceived limits on the types of leadership we can expect from either sex" and rather "create institutions which respect and encourage intellect, rationality, and leadership as virtues appropriate for women" (Cahill 1992).

In the American higher education context in general, women in administration are beginning to make strides in cracking the wall of a traditionally white male system, although women are still considerably underrepresented in higher and middle administrative positions. Similar to this context, laywomen in Catholic higher education are sorely underrepresented yet making some strides to crack or break the glass ceiling of advancement. However, women in Catholic higher education continue to argue that the "stained" glass ceiling is often perceived to be more shatterproof for women than for men because of the entrenched patriarchal tradition of the Catholic Church. Alice B. Hayes (1993) suggests, "As the number of women in administrative roles increases, we can expect an increase in attention to individuals, a more consultative style of decision making, and less emphasis on hierarchy, confrontation, and dominance" (1993, 17). The continued and increasing presence of laywomen at institutions of Catholic higher education will bring attention to issues of gender, the inclusion of women's views, and the impact of women's leadership.

Mary Lou Jackson

References and further reading

Boys, Mary C. 1992. "Life on the Margins: Feminism and Religious Education." *Initiatives* 54, no. 4: 17–23.

Brabeck, Mary M. 1992. "Feminist and Catholic Values: The View from the Professional Schools." *Initiatives* 54, no. 4: 9–16.

Brewer, Eileen M. 1987. *Nuns and the Education of American Catholic Women, 1860–1920.* Chicago: Loyola University Press.

Brown, Cynthia F. 1992. *Leading Women: Leadership in American Women's Higher Education, 1880–1940.* Ann Arbor: University of Michigan Press.

Cahill, Lisa S. 1992. "Women and Men Working Together in Jesuit Institutions of Higher Learning." *Initiatives* 54, no. 4: 25–33.

Cannon, Kathleen. 1996. "Becoming Catholic Together." Pp. 43–54 in

Labors From the Heart: Mission and Ministry in a Catholic University, ed. M. L. Poorman. Notre Dame, IN: University of Notre Dame Press.
Gallin, Alice. 1999. "Neylan Colleges: Working toward the Twenty-First Century." *ACCU Current Issues in Catholic Higher Education* 19, no. 2: 63–72.
Hayes, Alice B. 1993. "A Women's Place." *Conversation* 4: 9–23.
Hesse-Biber, Sharlene. 1992. "Feminist Faculty at Catholic Institutions: A Women's Studies Director's View." *Initiatives* 54, no. 4: 35–41.
Introcaso, Candace. 2001. "Determination in Leadership: Pioneering Roman Catholic Women Presidents." Pp. 67–83 in *Women Administrators in Higher Education,* ed. J. Nidiffer and C. T. Bashaw. Albany: State University of New York Press.
Kenneally, James K. 1990. *The History of American Catholic Women.* New York: Crossroad Publishing.
Kennelly, Karen. 1989. *American Catholic Women.* New York: Macmillan.
Mahoney, Kathleen A. 1999. "One Hundred Years: The Association of Catholic Colleges and Universities." *ACCU Current Issues in Catholic Higher Education* 19 (Spring): 3–46.
McCarthy, Abigail. 1985. "A Luminous Minority." *ACCU Current Issues in Catholic Higher Education* 5 (Winter): 7–10.
Morey, Melanie, and Dennis Holtschneider. 2000. "Relationship Revisited: Changing Relationships between U.S. Catholic Colleges and Universities and Founding Religious Congregations." *ACCU Current Issues in Catholic Higher Education* 21 (Fall): 62–65.
Nidiffer, Jane. 2001. "New Leadership for a New Century: Women's Contribution to Leadership in Higher Education." Pp. 101–131 in *Women Administrators in Higher Education,* ed. J. Nidiffer and C. T. Bashaw. Albany: State University of New York Press.
Pellegrino, Karen A. 1999. "A Space of Their Own: Women in ACCU." *ACCU Current Issues in Catholic Higher Education* 19 (Spring): 53–62.
"'Stained Glass Ceiling' Challenges Women in Catholic Schools." 1994. *Women in Higher Education* 3, no. 8: 1–2.
Wilt, Judith. 1992. "Ubiquitous, Lost, Found: A Study of Catholic Identities." *Initiatives* 54, no. 4: 1–7.

Librarians

Prior to 1887, there were few women librarians, and none were academic librarians. Only 10 of the 156 attendees of the first meeting of the American Library Association in Philadelphia were women. By opening the first Library School at Columbia University in 1887, Melvil Dewey realized his vision, which he had first revealed in an address before the Association of Collegiate Alumnae titled "Librarianship as a Profession for College-Bred Women." His argument appeared at an opportune time, when universities were expanding after passage of the Morrill Land Grant Act of 1862. Before such expansion, academic library opportunities for women were limited to women's colleges and finishing schools. Few existing universities would employ them. Academic libraries needed technical workers who would accept minimal pay. The genteel atmosphere of the university library offered a respectable occupation for educated women.

By the 1930s, 91 percent of all librarians were women. Those numbers remained static until the 1970s, when men comprised 8 percent of librarian ranks. Although academic librarianship boasts the highest percentage of men because of its prestige, men's influx into librarianship only modestly increased overall salaries. A wide pay gap exists within academic librarianship because of gender, not experience, educational attainment, research, professional activities, or mobility. As with the other feminized professions of teaching, nursing, and social work, women

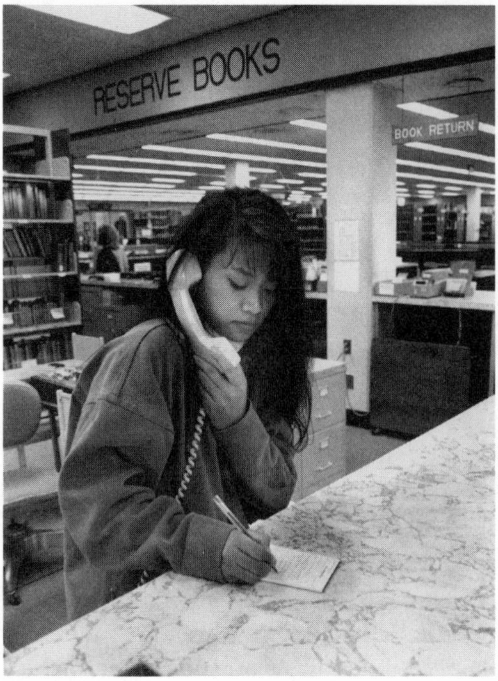

A student librarian at Shippensburg University in Pennsylvania (Strix Pix)

remain the disadvantaged majority administered by the minority. Patterns in academic library administration in the 1930s allowed women to administer small college libraries while men administered large college and university libraries. Men possessed more academic credentials and professional experience and earned larger salaries. A classic study of academic libraries in the 1960s revealed that men comprised 73 percent of administrators and 76 percent of middle management and other categories, but they comprised only 30 percent of the academic librarian populations.

Historically, males dominated academic librarianship. Libraries in the classical college were open few hours, were restricted to select patrons, and were often administered by a member of the faculty. Since the head librarian was already faculty, his status derived from his scholarly and teaching activities, not from his library affiliation. Only later was the librarian's status defined by the academic community as different from and lower than that of the teaching faculty. Early library services were minimal, and most faculty did not require library assistance in locating materials for their research. In the late nineteenth century, the rise in academic scholarship coupled with the availability of materials necessitated guidance in the use of the library.

Requiring an enlarged, well-educated, and relatively cheap source of labor, academic libraries recruited women. Dewey encouraged library administrators to hire women by stating that a competent woman costs less than a comparatively competent man. These early women comprised the bulk of library operations. Filling technical jobs, academic librarians physically processed, cataloged, shelved, circulated, and repaired library materials. Although there was a library administrator as well as departmental supervisors, daily operations and university library funds were controlled by the faculty advisory board.

Development of reference services was one area in which academic librarians could address their growing concerns about faculty attitudes toward undergraduate education and assert their professional philosophy and service ethic. Established by the end of the nineteenth century in many academic libraries, reference services were developed to assist students, not scholars. Most faculty were subject specialists who usually knew enough about library resources to find materials for themselves. In the 1920s, academic librarians expanded their services to teaching faculty, but the reception was minimal; thus the role of the academic librarian was defined by the manner and degree to which she made the collection usable by students.

Academic librarians criticized what they considered outrageous faculty demands on both services and materials budgets. Complaining that faculty members treated them as personal secretaries, librarians longed for equality and professional recognition. Although the faculty controlled book selection and collection development, librarians found it difficult to serve increasing numbers of undergraduate students with materials chosen by faculty. Faculty considered material selection as their domain, a sacred trust. Habitually purchasing obscure monographs relating to their particular research interests, faculty neglected the undergraduate reading collection. Frustrated with the lack of appropriate materials and bolstered by their emerging professionalism, librarians asserted control for book selection responsibilities, which became a primary concern of the profession during the first fifty years of the American Library Association's development. Academic librarians sought autonomy, and this issue put great strains on relations between faculty and academic librarians. Faculty beliefs that salaries for catalogers and other librarians diverted valuable funds from essential materials served to expand the growing divide.

Further dividing librarians and the faculty was control over collections administration. Faculty abuse of generous loan periods and unwillingness to return materials upon conclusion of the academic year left librarians with dismal choices for repossession. Library materials were inconsistently recalled, and fines were charged for missing items, but librarians could not collect replacement funds. Ambivalence continues to characterize faculty-library relations.

Concern over their status is a major obsession of academic librarians, and concern over the image or stereotype of librarians is universally prevalent among librarians in general. During the late nineteenth century, only librarians who were also members of the teaching faculty were given academic titles. By the beginning of the twentieth century, most universities and colleges classified the library director as faculty but did not extend that title to other professional library staff. By the 1920s, it was obvious to librarians that achieving academic equality would be difficult because of the essentially masculine organizational structure of academia.

Initially overlooked for tenure and promotion because they did not teach regular classes and could not be evaluated by that criteria, academic librarians maintained that both group and individual bibliographic instruction constituted teaching. Also in question were the librarian's educational credentials. The master's in library science is considered a terminal degree, and any person with the degree can be employed as an academic librarian, though many academic libraries strongly prefer or sometimes require that the librarian have a second master's degree in a specific subject. A Ph.D. is required for administrative-level positions in prestigious research libraries and most state universities. Educators in library schools also hold the Ph.D. in library science.

By the 1970s, the academic librarian had evolved from a lowly employee of the classical college to a modern researcher. Expansion of library education, library research, and involvement in professional organizations spurred momentum for academic equality via tenure-track positions for academic librarians. Many universities and colleges responded positively and implemented a two-track tenure matrix, wherein the academic librarian holds a position (cataloger) as well as rank (assistant professor), though tenure for academic librarians is not mandated. Though similar to faculty tenure requirements in terms of research, publication, and service, tenure requirements for librarians emphasize their primary assignment in either public or technical services and minimize teaching. Academic librarians find it difficult to find free time for study and research, and access to grants and sabbaticals is fleeting.

Pay scales within academic libraries mimic those of other organizations; employees are well paid at the top and low paid along the base. Fewer than 10 percent of professional academic librarians are in positions in which their average compensation exceeds that of assistant professors in similar institutions. Women comprise the majority of academic librarians at every level except administration, and they earn less in every capacity: 80 percent of academic librarians are female, and 80 percent of library management is male.

Today, women academic librarians are professionally involved and committed to continuing education and enjoy the challenges of academia. Academic librarians support the curriculum, complete original research, and serve the university and broader community. A significant number of women direct major research libraries across the nation. Thirty-nine percent have completed coursework beyond the master's in library science, 40 percent hold a second master's degree, and more than 50 percent belong to two or more professional associations. Numerically dominated by women today, academic librarians find the rigors of their profession satisfying except for the low salaries. The average academic librarian is female, white, professional, married, and middle-aged without children. Although librarians' early and sustained use of technology has raised the profession's status in recent years, the new emphasis on information systems makes librarianship hold more promise for men. However, recent graduates of former library schools, now renamed information schools, bypass library positions in favor of higher-paying jobs outside academia.

Rebecca Tolley-Stokes

See also Part 5: Affirmative Action and Employment; Gender Inequality; Part 7: Tenure and Promotion; Appendix

References and further reading

Altman, Ellen, and Patricia Promis. 1990. "Affirmative Action: Opportunity or Obstacle?" *College and Research Libraries News* 55: 11–24.

Atkins, Stephen E. 1991. *The Academic Library in the American University.* Chicago: American Library Association.

Cravey, Pamela J. 1991. "Occupational Role Identity of Women Academic Librarians." *College and Research Libraries* 52: 150–164.

Hamlin, Arthur T. 1981. *The University Library in the United States: Its Origins and Development.* Philadelphia: University of Pennsylvania Press.

Harris, Roma. 1992. *Librarianship: The Erosion of a Woman's Profession.* Norwood, NJ: Ablex Publishing.

Heim, Kathleen M., ed. 1983. *The Status of Women in Librarianship: Historical, Sociological, and Economic Issues.* New York: Neal-Schuman Publishers.

Irvine, Betty Jo. 1985. *Sex Segregation in Librarianship: Demographic and Career Patterns of Academic Library Administrators.* Westport, CT: Greenwood Press.

Morrison, Perry David. 1961. *The Career of the Academic Librarian: A Study of the Social Origins, Educational Attainments, Vocational Experience, and Personality Characteristics of a Group of American Academic Librarians.* Berkeley: University of California Press.
Shiflett, Orvin Lee. 1981. *Origins of American Academic Librarianship.* Norwood, NJ: Ablex Publishing.

Mobility

Administrative mobility refers to job changes within and between institutions. For many women, mobility in higher education takes place within a single institution, is characterized by different mentoring relationships and networks, and often peaks in lower management. Between 1976 and 1997, women increased their position shares of executive, administrative, and managerial positions from 26 percent, or 26,929 (National Center for Education Statistics 1997–1998) to 45.9 percent, or 69,432 (National Center for Education Statistics 2001). Within this administrative cohort, women increased their leadership role in college and university presidencies. The proportion of college presidents who are women has grown from 9.5 percent (204) in 1986 to 19.3 percent (459) in 1998 (Ross and Green 2000). The encouraging news from these data is that the number of women is increasing and more of them are obtaining senior leadership positions. However, despite these changes, many women are still confined to lower level managerial positions.

The Landscape of Women Administrators' Mobility

Two distinct features mark women administrators' mobility: (1) the core elements of mobility, such as job changes, opportunity structures, networks, and sponsoring and mentoring, and (2) characteristics and dynamics of higher education institutions. The first feature is mobility within the career systems of an organization. University opportunity structures are especially important for women because white women and people of color are more likely than white men to build their careers in one organization (Johnsrud and Rosser 2000). There is little systematic information about opportunity structures because they must be studied within a particular organization. However, relevant generalizations can be drawn. For example, data on the effect of broadbanding, or consolidating salary grades into fewer, wider ranges, and hiring preferences for internal candidates are available on campuses from their women's commissions' reports and offices of human resources. These practices may have the unanticipated consequence of disadvantaging women's career advancement because people tend to hire individuals like themselves. The conditions that counter these tendencies are the presence of diverse individuals within the institution (especially in terms of gender and race and ethnicity) and the willingness of senior administrative leaders' to take risks with hiring decisions (Lively 2000).

Networks, sponsors, and mentors also influence administrative mobility. Contact networks and social and ascribed status contribute to being hired into administrative positions requiring high levels of discretion, such as deanships (Lindsay 1997) and vice presidencies. Networks are also becoming increasingly important as more colleges and universities use private search firms to assist in hiring senior administrators. Before 1985, less than 16 percent of colleges and universities hiring presidents used search firms, but between 1995 and 1998, search firms participated in almost half of the presidential searches reported to the American Council on Education (Ross and Green 2000). These search firms tend to rely upon referrals and informal networks to identify and recommend candidates, rather than firsthand information from administrators and staff in the hiring institution. That may be more of a liability for men and women of color and white women seeking to change jobs than for white men, because white women and people of color are likely to have different networks than the white men who make most administrative hiring decisions (Sagaria forthcoming).

A mentor's tutoring and advocacy can also be an asset for administrative mobility. Women in senior administrative positions, such as chief academic officer, report that university presidents serve as sponsors and provide job skill coaching for subsequent positions. Women in these positions, however, tend not to rely solely on formal institutional leaders' mentoring. Corporate women perceived as having potential for senior leadership roles are more likely than other women to seek out women for instrumental or career-related advice and mentoring. Furthermore, women are more likely than men to have more and a variety of mentors across organizational levels and functional areas.

The second feature of mobility for women administrators encompasses the organizational characteristics and dynamics of higher education, such as the growth of administrative positions or bureaucratic accretion (Gumport and Pusser 1995), the emphasis on efficiency, economic centrality, the development of a midlevel quagmire, and decreased social equality (Fischman and Stromquist 2000). Administrative mobility opportunities increased in tandem with the exponential growth of administrative positions beginning in the mid-1960s (Leslie and Rhoades 1995). For example, institutional support positions in the University of California system increased by 104 percent between 1966 and 1991, nearly two and a half times faster than instructional positions. As a group, administrative and nonteaching professionals have been the fastest-growing job category in higher education; especially in the areas of institutional advancement, technology, and minority student services (Grassmuck 1991).

Technical rationality is driving midlevel managers' mobility. During the 1990s, an increased emphasis on efficiency, economic centrality, and academic capitalism led to the emergence of a new managerial sector. As universities attempted to drive down costs and intensify the return from employees, a feminization of the lower tiers of administration focusing on accountability, external relations, and client services has occurred. Increasingly, women are drawn into subordinate management positions because they previously have been "outsiders," and in these newly created positions, they are being called upon to subvert resistance to management practices and other organizational inefficiencies and to challenge faculty (Prichard and Deem 1999).

The prominence of technology is changing the way higher education functions (Levine 2002). During the 1990s, the greatest area of administrative growth and resources occurred in technology, both in the actual numbers of positions and the importance of the chief information officer. This new and increasingly powerful position is held by a man at three-quarters of colleges and universities (College and University Professional Association 2000). To the extent that women are absent from this technological revolution, women's entry into and possibilities for mobility in higher education are being eclipsed. In 1984 women earned 37 percent of the bachelors' degrees in computer science and computer engineering. However, in 1999 women received less than 20 percent of those degrees (Olsen 2000). Because the B.A. is the typical credential for midlevel administrative positions, with the master's degree becoming increasingly sought, women may have less access and influence in one of the more salient domains of higher education in the future.

Two forces are profoundly diminishing the commitment to diversifying administrative and professorial cohorts. The first is the rollback of affirmative action. The decision by the University of California in 1995 to end the use of sex and race in hiring and admissions marked a watershed that was followed by further legislative attacks on affirmative action. Decisions of this kind and the George W. Bush administration's dismantling of affirmative action have removed legal inducements for colleges and universities to diversify their administrators, staff, or faculty.

The second force is the privileging of economically central and entrepreneurial activities. Without regard for equity issues, university resources are being directed to male-dominated fields such as engineering, computer science, and the physical and natural sciences. Additionally, auxiliary services such as athletics are growing in staff and resources. For example, it is an increasingly common practice to expand these areas and fill appointments such as directors of research or athletics without regard to equity. Instead, units undertake targeted searches with "a license to hunt for a particular person." Paradoxically, the female-dominated areas such as nursing, education, and social work are more likely to be diminishing in importance and therefore receiving declining resources (Slaughter 1993) and reductions in administrative positions. Thus, opportunities may be diminishing for women within those subunits.

Conclusion

The increased representation of women administrators and the growth in opportunities for them have been impressive. In addition, we must look realistically at the meaning of numerical gains by women in administrative positions. In many cases, they are in midlevel managerial positions whose work is becoming more instrumental and that are part of a loosely structured system in which career paths are not defined (Sagaria and Dickens 1990) but are idiosyncratic and confusing (Kanter 1987). The interpersonal dimension of careers—networks, mentoring, and sponsorship—may become increasingly important to offset changing characteristics and dynamics of higher education institutions that may thwart advancement gains and mobility opportunities for women.

Mary Ann Danowitz Sagaria and
Melissa A. Rychener

See also Part 8: Leadership; Presidency

References and further reading

College and University Professional Association. 2000. *2000–01 Administrative Compensation Survey.* Washington, DC: College and University Professional Association–HR.

Fischman, Gusavo, and Nelly Stromquist. 2000. "Globalization and Higher Education in Developing Countries." Pp. 501–521 in *Higher Education:*

Handbook of Theory and Research, ed. John C. Smart. Vol. 15. New York: Agathon Press.
Grassmuck, Karen. 1991. "Throughout '80s, Colleges Hired More Non-Teaching Staff Than Other Employees." *Chronicle of Higher Education* 37: A22.
Gumport, Patricia, and Brian Pusser. 1995. "A Case of Bureaucratic Accretion: Context and Consequences." *Journal of Higher Education* 66, no. 5: 493–520.
Ibarra, Herminia. 1997. "Paving an Alternative Route: Gender Differences in Managerial Networks." *Social Psychology Quarterly* 61, no. 1: 91–102.
Johnsrud, Linda K., and Vicki J. Rosser. 2000. *Understanding the Work and Career Paths of Midlevel Administrators.* San Francisco: Jossey-Bass.
Kanter, Rosabeth Moss. 1977. *Men and Women of the Corporation.* New York: Basic Books.
———. 1987. "The New Managerial Work." *Harvard Business Review* (November–December): 85–90.
Leslie, Larry, and Gary Rhoades. 1995 "Rising Administrative Costs: Seeking Explanations." *Journal of Higher Education* 66, no. 2: 187–212.
Levine, Arthur. 1987. *Higher Education at a Crossroads.* Occasional papers from the Center for Higher Education Policy Analysis. Los Angeles: University of Southern California. http://www.usc.edu/dept/chepa/papers_pastpapers.html. Cited June 11, 2002.
Lindsay, Beverly. 1997. "Surviving the Middle Passage: The Absent Legacy of African American Women Education Deans." Pp. 3–32 in *The Minority Voice in Educational Reform: An Analysis by Minority and Women College of Education Deans,* ed. Louis A. Castenell and Jim M. Tarule. Greenwich, CT: Ablex Publishing.
Lively, Kit. 2000. "Women in Charge." *Chronicle of Higher Education* 14: A33–A35.
National Center for Education Statistics. 1997–1998. *Numbers of Employees in Institutions of Higher Education, Fall 1976.* Washington, DC: U.S. Department of Education.
———. 2001. *Digest of Education Statistics.* Washington, DC: U.S. Department of Education.
Olsen, Florence. 2000. "Institute for Women and Technology Works to Bridge the Other Digital Divide." *Chronicle of Higher Education* 46: A47.
Prichard, Craig, and Rosemary Deem. 1999 "Wo-Managing Further Education; Gender and the Construction of the Manager in the Corporate Colleges of England." *Gender and Education* 11, no. 3: 323–342.
Ross, Marlene, and Madeline F. Green. 2000. *The American College President: 2000 edition.* Washington, DC: American Council on Education.
Sagaria, Mary Ann Danowitz. Forthcoming. "An Exploratory Model of Filtering in Administrative Searches: Toward Counter Hegemonic Discourses." *Journal of Higher Education.*
Sagaria, Mary Ann D., and Cynthia Dickens. 1990 "Thriving at Home: Developing a Career as an Insider." *New Directions for Higher Education* 18, no. 4: 19–28.
Sagaria, Mary Ann D., and Linda K. Johnsrud. 1987. "Many Are Candidates but Few Compete: The Impact of Internal Position Change of Administrative and Professional Staff on White Women and Minorities." Columbus: Ohio State University.
Slaughter, Sheila. 1993. "Retrenchment in the 1980s: The Politics of Prestige and Gender." *Journal of Higher Education* 64, no. 3: 250–282.

Presidency

The college presidency represents the pinnacle of leadership in academic institutions, with men traditionally holding this position of power and influence. Women served as presidents of some of the first women's colleges and now represent almost one in five of all presidencies, with new presidential hires going to women in one of every four cases. However laudable this progress is, women are still more often leading community colleges, women's colleges, or comprehensive colleges, not the more prestigious research institutions.

Investigating the career path to the presidency highlights the historical route by which presidents obtained their positions; starting first in a faculty position and following with steps including department chair, dean, and then provost. Although 70 percent of current college presidents began their career path in a faculty role, the leadership transition occurring as the new millennium progresses shows signs of a breakdown of this traditional career path, especially at the community college level.

Providing the backdrop for women entering the presidency was the entrée of women into higher education; first as students and subsequently in the evolution of the position of deans of women. Two initiatives in the mid- to late 1800s began providing leadership opportunities for women and access to higher education as students: the land grant colleges with their support of coeducation and the establishment of a trio of new women's colleges (Vassar, Smith, and Wellesley). This same period of rapid expansion in higher education witnessed the distinction between faculty and administration because presidents could no longer fulfill both roles.

The first women presidents led the new women's colleges, but men were also at the helm of these institutions. Wellesley was the first college with a woman president, Alice Freeman, who exercised power in more than name only. These early female presidents often required male support, placing these leaders in a much different context than male peers holding the office of president. Even today, the issue of different norms of assessment of women leaders is apparent.

The American system of higher education, after the *Dartmouth College v. Woodward* case (1819), confirmed the right of the governing board of trustees rather than the state to make college operating decisions, vesting control not with the faculty but with an external board. The college president serves at the pleasure of the board of trustees, further reducing ties of allegiance with the faculty. The board of trustees therefore plays a pivotal role in selecting presidents of colleges and universities, with the relationship between the chosen president and the board providing a critical foundation for the fiscal operation and operating climate of the college.

Jewel Plummer Cobb is president emerita of California State University in Fullerton (Courtesy of Jewel Plummer Cobb)

Women slowly began to increase their presence in the office of the president after their inauspicious start leading the first women's colleges in the late 1800s. In 1970, during the second wave of the women's movement, the number of women presidents rose to 6 percent of the total. This number, however, belies extreme progress since 90 percent of these presidents led Roman Catholic women's colleges. By 1986, women were college presidents at one in ten institutions. Although the number holding presidencies by the end of the twentieth century doubled to one in five institutions, only 2 percent of all these women presidents led major research universities, with the remainder leading the less prestigious community colleges, independent colleges, women's colleges, and comprehensive colleges.

Traditionally, the route to a college presidency went through the ranks of faculty, department chair, dean, and the penultimate post of provost. Currently, this career route represents only one of several differentiated pathways to the presidency, particularly at community colleges or independent colleges. However, even in the diversity of administrative backgrounds found with senior–level community college leaders, women achieve success up to a particular organizational level and then receive promotions more slowly into the presidency than their white male counterparts.

Despite the number of women in the pipeline, women are still underrepresented in the higher administrative levels of the organization. The idea of the glass ceiling, first introduced in the literature in the mid-1980s, remains as a barrier of leadership ascension for women. It remains intact for women presidents for two reasons. First, the traditional pathway through academics and the office of the provost typically found at four-year and research-intensive universities requires the promotion of women into the full professorship, which for women occurs less quickly. Second, presidential search committees generally require board of trustees approval for hiring a new president. Leadership teams filling senior positions generally like to hire individuals like themselves, causing a dilemma for aspiring women since most senior administrators and trustees are men. In addition, board members often operate in a different social world than their constituencies, and their loyalties are not always with the faculty, staff, and students of the institutions. Trustees tend to be white males who are older and affluent with strong business connections.

In their ascent to the presidency, women often employ a variety of career strategies. One tactic involves buying into the system and playing by the existing rules that apply to men and were written by men. Others adopt an outsider-within stance that relies on educating and enlightening colleagues and employers on the different ways in which women may work. Still others address the issues of patriarchy head-on.

Some women enter the academy without the purposeful intent of obtaining a college presidency. As a result, in addition to their outsider status as women, many find they have a limited support system, and may lack appropriate mentoring or the sanctioned credentials sought by search teams.

The college president in the new millennium faces a much different world than that faced by the first women presidents. Alternative forms of leadership are often espoused to meet the challenges facing higher education leaders, including team leadership and webs of inclusion that place leadership at the center, where it is connected to many others in the organization, as opposed to being located at the apex of the organization. Leadership throughout the institution addresses the complex issues currently facing higher education as it transitions from a teacher-centered entity to one that is more student-centered. Additional issues of the changing role of faculty, multiculturalism, and outside competition require modern-day presidents to possess a different skill set than their predecessors.

Most presidents develop the college's visions and goals and the operating plans for achieving them for their institutions. Women are often described as generative leaders who encourage participation and empowerment of followers, but limitations between this leadership style may be constrained with regard to its actual application because of organizational structure and context. Leadership style of male and female presidents does not always break cleanly along gender lines. Research in postsecondary institutions finds that contextual factors, individual beliefs and values, and the role of followers shape leadership as greatly as sex or gender differences.

Calls for reconceptualizing the role of the college leader require deconstructing the reigning metaphorical depiction of the president as the hero leader, great man, quarterback, superman, or father figure. When these terms identify the college president, women, and those responsible for hiring new presidents, are unable to picture women in that role.

The constraints faced by women presidents differ from those faced by male leaders. Male norms typically provide the basis for assessment of presidents. Women administrators report feelings of marginalization and lack of authenticity and evidence of cumulative disadvantage when confronted with the choice of professional promotion by adhering to traditional norms and expectations or enacting a more personally genuine, and therefore perhaps more female construction of leadership. Since the board of trustees is often responsible for evaluating the college president, similar issues emanating from male dominance on boards that face women seeking the presidency are also present during periods of evaluation.

When women enter the presidency, they often symbolically represent all women. Presidents who are women of color have additional constraints. These women have to address issues regarding not only their gender but also their race and ethnicity. Again, the measures of assessment are different for women than men.

Women continue to juggle multiple roles and balance numerous obligations outside the workplace. Among current lay presidents, 93 percent of male presidents are married, compared to 48 percent of female presidents. The cultural expectation for these male presidents is that they have a wife at home taking care of the household aspects of life. However, their married women counterparts often still maintain primary responsibility for household management. Even single women leaders are more often primary care providers than male leaders. Women administrators perceive these dual roles as career inhibitors. Given the long ascension to the presidency, these role conflicts can slow down progress for women.

The role of the college president's spouse is conceptualized differently when the president is a woman. A male spouse is often assumed to have a career of his own and does not face the same obligations of his female counterpart. However, the unpaid functions often performed by a female spouse must still be accomplished when a male spouse does not perform them. A woman president must then find a way to get these functions accomplished. Single women presidents are also faced with the delicate question of attending functions with an escort or same-sex partner.

In addition to the changing context of higher education with regard to teaching and learning, multiculturalism, and assessment, there are predictions of a leadership crisis, particularly at the community college level. The expected retirement of many current presidents, who are predominantly men, opens a window of opportunity for women aspiring to the presidency. The demand for qualified applicants allows for expanding the traditional routes to the presidency, giving women more access. For the realization of this potential to occur, underlying organizational structures that disadvantage and discriminate against women must change. They includes search committees, which must recognize the need for and value in changing images of leaders.

Mentoring by current woman presidents of women in the pipeline aids construction of an alternative to the old boys' network and can showcase different routes to the executive office. The number of women in the pipeline is greater than the representation of women in the president's office. Research shows that women who had mentors were in significantly higher administrative positions than women who had not experienced mentoring. Mentoring is one mechanism that can begin to break down and change the current structure of higher education.

A change in the accepted leadership style of the college president helps dismantle stereotypes of what a leader looks like. Emergent forms of leadership emphasize a decision not to unconditionally accept traditional ways of doing business and to question old norms. The autocratic style of leadership is counterproductive. Instead, models of leadership featuring strong human relations skills and consensus building are espoused, just the characteristics often attributed to women leaders. Embracing new definitions of the college president is essential for change to occur.

Pamela L. Eddy

See also Part 8: Leadership

References and further reading

Amey, M. J., and S. B. Twombly. 1992. "Revisioning Leadership in Community Colleges." *Review of Higher Education* 15, no. 2: 125–150.

Curry, Barbara K. 2000. *Women in Power: Pathways to Leadership in Education.* New York: Teachers College Press.

Dartmouth College v. Woodward, 1 N.H. 111 (1819).

Fisher, James L., and James V. Koch. 1996. *Presidential Leadership: Making a Difference.* Washington, DC: American Council on Education and Oryx Press.

Glazer-Raymo, Judith. 1999. *Shattering the Myths: Women in Academe.* Baltimore: Johns Hopkins University Press.

Hoffman, Allan M., and Randal W. Summers. 2000. *Managing Colleges and Universities: Issues for Leadership.* Westport, CT: Bergin and Garvey.

Jablonski, Margaret. 1996. "The Leadership Challenge for Women College Presidents." *Initiatives* 57, no. 4: 1–10.

Nidiffer, Jana, and Carolyn Terry Bashaw, eds. 2001. *Women Administrators in Higher Education: Historical and Contemporary Perspectives.* Albany: State University of New York Press.

Professional Organizations

As the position of dean of women became more common on college campuses in the early 1900s, the need for a professional association for women in higher education administration increased. Several meetings of deans of women took place, with the eventual establishment of the National Association of Deans of Women (NADW) in 1916. This organization went through multiple name changes that mirrored the expanded professional roles women administrators had in higher education, but external circumstances caused it to fold in 2000. Currently, many of the national associations for higher education administrators have offices, committees, or commissions dedicated to the needs of women professionals, and there are several organizations that serve the needs of women administrators in more specific educational settings.

Prior to the founding of the National Association of Deans of Women, there were meetings of deans of women that included discussions about job issues and efforts to secure professional status in the field of higher education. These first meetings were spearheaded by Marion Talbot, the dean of women at the University of Chicago. In 1903 she coordinated the Conference of Deans of Women of the Middle West, which addressed topics such as student housing. Another dean of women, Mary Bidwell Breed from Indiana University, served as president for the group's next meeting in 1905. Prior to the second meeting in 1905, the name changed to the Conference of Deans and Advisers of Women in State Universities, and this organization later evolved into a division of NADW. During the 1905 meeting, the members discussed a wide range of student needs, including admission to institutions, curriculum issues, leadership opportunities, and community on campus. This conference was also seen as an important step in creating a professional identity for deans of women and enabling communication within the field.

NADW was founded in July 1916 during the annual National Education Association convention, and its first president was Kathryn Sisson Phillips. NADW initially focused on serving the needs of deans of women and organizing efforts to legitimize the profession. Other concerns included policies and services that affected women on campus. In 1931 a permanent office for NADW was established in Washington, D.C., and a journal began publishing in 1938. In the early years of NADW, both the membership and leadership of the organization were primarily made up of women administrators from the Midwest and Northeast.

As the roles of women in higher education administration shifted, the organization continually evolved to reflect its membership. A proposal for NADW to merge with the American Personnel and Guidance Association (APGA) was rejected by the membership in a 1951 vote. After World War II, many campuses combined their deans of women and deans of men into a dean of students position, which tended to be filled by men. In 1956, with the position of dean of women less common and more women working in counselor-level positions, NADW changed its name to the National Association of Women Deans and Counselors (NAWDC). It was organized into sections according to the members' institutions: university, four-year college, junior and community college, and continuing education. There was also a small elementary and secondary education section. Another proposal to merge NAWDC with APGA and the National Association of Student Personnel Administration (NASPA) was rejected in a 1971 vote by the NAWDC membership. In 1972 NAWDC changed its name to the National Association of Women Deans, Administrators, and Counselors (NAWDAC) and shifted its organizational structure away from sections to divisions corresponding to members' professional areas: administration, activities and services, continuing education, counseling and individual development, government/agency special programs, and teaching and research. To be inclusive and involve new members, NAWDAC created several new bodies: the graduate student and new professional committee, the national conference for college student leaders, the ethnic women's caucus, the committee of disability issues, and the committee of lesbian and bisexual issues.

The final name change came in 1991, when NAWDAC became the National Association for Women in Education (NAWE). Throughout its history, the organization cooperated with other national professional associations for higher education administrators, such as NASPA and the American College Personnel Association (ACPA). Surveys of the memberships of NAWDC, NAWDAC, and NAWE revealed that most members were midcareer professionals. NAWE's professional development events included annual member conferences, the National Conference for College Women Student Leaders, and the Institute for Emerging Women Leaders in Higher Education, as well as various networking opportunities. It also published the scholarly journal *Initiatives,* a quarterly newsletter, and numerous monographs and reports. As of the year 2000, when NAWE folded, it had thirteen state and regional affiliates and three caucuses that focused on the needs of different populations—graduate students and new professionals, lesbians and bisexuals, and women of color.

Over the years, NAWE's predecessors experienced several challenges to their survival. The Great Depression caused financial hardships for members who could no longer afford dues and conferences costs. The resulting membership decrease placed the future of the organization in jeopardy. During the 1930s, several deans of women from southern institutions who were active members of NADW, Katherine S. Bowersox, Agnes Ellen Harris, Adele H. Stamp, and Sarah Gibson Blanding, worked to include more southern members in the national organization to make the organization more inclusive. There were also efforts to make more connections between the state and regional associations and the national association. Difficulties with membership and finances occurred again in the early 1970s, and the executive board of NAWDC was forced to consider dissolution. As part of efforts to fortify the organization, the name was changed to NAWDAC in 1972, and it expanded its membership base. However, adequate membership levels could not be maintained because many women in higher education administration had more opportunities to became involved in other professional associations. This decline in membership base and conference attendance created further financial difficulties, and the board of directors made the difficult decision to dissolve NAWE in 2000.

Many of the national organizations for higher education administrators have an aspect of their association that is devoted to the concerns of women in the field. NASPA, which originally began as the National Association of Deans and Advisers of Men in 1919, created a women's network in 1971. ACPA has a standing committee on women that works to connect women in the profession. The American Association of Higher Education (AAHE) has a women's caucus, established in 1984, that seeks to enhance professional development, networking, and involvement among women members of AAHE. The Association of American Colleges and Universities (AACU) established the Program on the Status and Education of Women in 1970. This program features a quarterly newsletter, a listserv for administrators, and research projects and publications on issues such as curriculum, campus climate, and women of color in higher education.

The American Council on Education (ACE), an institutionally based association, created the Office of Women in Higher Education (OWHE) in 1973. It works to identify women leaders and provide leadership development and support; their work has also included efforts for women in higher education in South Africa. Another organization, the Higher Education Resources Services (HERS), Mid-America, cosponsors the Summer Institute for Women in Higher Education Administration with Bryn Mawr College. Originally started as HERS, Mid-Atlantic, the Summer Institute was started in 1976 and is a four-week residential program for women faculty and administrators. The Summer Institute's curriculum covers a range of topics in educational administration that are needed for career advancement.

There have also been professional associations for women in more specialized areas of higher education administration. The Association of Deans of Women and Advisers of Girls in Colored Schools took part in a 1954 meeting to create the National Association of Personnel Workers, which later became the National Association of Student Affairs Professionals. The American Association for Women in Community Colleges (AAWCC) was established in 1973 and was originally called the American Association of Women in Community and Junior Colleges. It features a variety of professional development and networking opportunities, publications, advocacy efforts, and leadership training opportunities. The National Association of Collegiate Women Athletic Administrators (NACWAA) was created in 1979 as the Council of Collegiate Women Athletic Administrators. The NACWAA provides conferences, a quarterly publication, and other opportunities for the advancement of women athletes and athletic administrators. The National Association for Women in Higher Catholic Education was founded in 1992, and its membership includes faculty, administrators, staff, and students.

Jennifer Weisman

References and further reading

American Association for Higher Education. http://www.aahe.org. Cited June 11, 2002.

American Association for Women in Community Colleges. http://www.pc.maricopa.edu/aawcc/. Cited June 11, 2002.

American Council on Education. http://www.acenet.edu. Cited June 11, 2002.

Association of American Colleges and Universities. http://www.aacu-edu.org. Cited June 11, 2002.

Bashaw, Carolyn Terry. 1999. *"Stalwart Women:" A Historical Analysis of Deans of Women in the South.* New York: Teachers College Press.

Gangone, Lynn M. 1999. *Navigating Turbulence: A Case Study of a Voluntary Higher Education Association.* Ph.d. diss., Teachers College, Columbia University.

Hanson, Gail Short. 1995. "The Organization of NAWE." *Initiatives* 56, no. 4: 29–36.

Kaplan, Sheila, Cynthia Secor, and Adrian Tinsley. 1984. "Getting the Best: Conclusions, Recommendations, and

Selected Resources." Pp. 85–91 in *Women in Higher Education Administration,* ed. Adrian Tinsley, Cynthia Secor, and Sheila Kaplan. New Directions for Higher Education no. 45. San Francisco: Jossey-Bass.

Martin, Carole. 1979. "Working for Women: Organizations and Services in Education." *College Board Review* 111 (Spring):14–15.

National Association for Women in Catholic Higher Education. http://www.bc.edu/nawche. Cited June 11, 2002.

National Association of Collegiate Women, Athletic Administration. http://www.nacwaa.org/. Cited June 11, 2002.

Nidiffer, Jana. 1995. "From Matron to Maven: A New Role and New Professional Identity for Deans of Women, 1892 to 1916." *Mid-Western Educational Researcher* 8, no. 4: 17–24.

Nuss, Elizabeth M. 1996. "The Development of Student Affairs." Pp. 22–42 in *Student Services: A Handbook for the Profession,* ed. Susan R. Komives, Dudley B. Woodard, Jr., and Associates. San Francisco: Jossey-Bass.

Secor, Cynthia. 1984. "Preparing the Individual for Institutional Leadership: The Summer Institute." In *Women in Higher Education Administration,* ed. Adrian Tinsley, Cynthia Secor, and Sheila Kaplan. New Directions for Higher Education no. 45. San Francisco: Jossey-Bass.

Shavlik, Donna, and Judy Touchton. 1984. "Toward a New Era of Leadership: The National Identification Program." In *Women in Higher Education Administration,* ed. Adrian Tinsley, Cynthia Secor, and Sheila Kaplan. New Directions for Higher Education no. 45. San Francisco: Jossey-Bass.

Speizer, Jeanne J. 1984. "The Administrative Skills Program: What Have We Learned?" In *Women in Higher Education Administration,* ed. Adrian Tinsley, Cynthia Secor, and Sheila Kaplan. New Directions for Higher Education no. 45 San Francisco: Jossey-Bass.

Thrash, Patricia A. 1973. "The State of the Association." *Journal of NAWDAC* 37, no. 1: 43–48.

Tuttle, Kathryn Nemeth. 1996. *What Became of the Dean of Women? Changing Roles for Women Administrators in American Higher Education, 1940–1980.* Ph.D. diss., University of Kansas.

Part 9

WOMEN EMPLOYEES

Overview

Members of the support staff in higher education provide the support functions and day-to-day operations that enable colleges and universities to meet their primary missions of teaching, research, and service. The support staff includes such job titles as secretaries, machinists, groundskeepers, food service workers, fiscal officers, and computer operators. They are employed in nearly 300 different occupations across all units of the institution (e.g., academics, research, student affairs, business, and external affairs). The only employees in most colleges and universities not included in this group are those in executive and managerial positions, the faculty, and instructional and research assistants. There are an estimated 2.5 million individuals employed on the nation's campuses. Support staff represents approximately 60 percent of this workforce, and women hold at least 60 percent of these positions. Although they represent the majority in higher education's workforce, there is little substantive literature or data available regarding the work lives of this group.

Position titles and classification schemes vary by institutions, but specific occupations are commonly aggregated into broad categories such as clerical and secretarial, service and maintenance, skilled crafts, support and service professionals, and technical and paraprofessional. Across all four- and two-year campuses, roughly 34 percent of support staff are in support and service professional positions, 32 percent are in clerical and secretarial, 16 percent are in service and maintenance, 14 percent are in technical and paraprofessional, and 5 percent are in skilled crafts. Although women represent the majority among support staff in general, their presence varies widely within groups. Women tend to be overrepresented in clerical and secretarial positions (roughly 87 percent women and 13 percent men), whereas the opposite is true in the skilled crafts (93 percent men and 7 percent women) and service and maintenance (62 percent men and 38 percent women). Women have a stronger presence in the two other categories, support and service and technical and paraprofessional, in which women hold roughly 60 percent of the positions and men hold 40 percent. Over the years, there have been modest and gradual changes in the representation by sex within these groups. The presence of females increased in the skilled crafts (e.g., an 8 percent increase between 1993 and 1997), and at the same time, the number of males in clerical and secretarial positions increased (e.g., a 16 percent increase between 1993 and 1997).

Salaries vary considerably across the occupational groups, with median salaries in 1997 of $20,300 for service and maintenance staff members and $35,880 for support and service professionals. Salaries also differ markedly by sex. Men consistently earn more than women in every occupational group, including the clerical and secretarial group, in which men are the minority. Salary increases, however, differ marginally by sex. In the most recent data available, women received higher percentage salary increases in two categories: skilled crafts and technical and paraprofessional. Males, in contrast, experienced slightly higher raises in the service and maintenance, clerical and secretarial, and support and service groups.

Although the total number of support staff employees has increased since 1990 by approximately 7 percent, there are differences by occupational groups. According to the most recent data available, the support and service professionals increased their numbers at the same time that the clerical and secretarial and the service and maintenance workers decreased theirs. The number of skilled crafts employees has held steady over the decade. Similarly, the technical and paraprofessional group has held steady, after burgeoning in the early 1990s. The extent of part-time employment has increased in every group of support personnel in higher education. For example, between 1995 and 1997, there was a 9.6 percent increase in the number of part-time employees in the clerical and secretarial group. At the same time, new hiring decreased during the decade, which provides some insight into the priority placed on support personnel by the colleges and universities. Although new hires in support and service increased slightly, new hires decreased for service and maintenance, clerical and secretarial, and technical and paraprofessional.

Limited information exists on specific work life issues of support staff in higher education. One source of information is the unions that represent these workers, but union representation also varies by occupational group. For example, technical and paraprofessional employees have the lowest rate of unionization at 14.8 percent; clerical workers are next at 37.2 percent; and the service and maintenance and skilled crafts workers are highest, with a percentage of 42.8 unionized. Fifty different unions, including both national and independent unions, represent these workers. One study conducted by the National Education Association in 1997 provides some data on how satisfied these employees are, the differences that exist between the groups, and the areas of concern specific to each occupational group. These data were not disaggregated by sex, but nonetheless offer insight into the quality of work life of these workers.

Women represent the majority in the clerical and secretarial and technical and paraprofessional groups, and these groups are generally satisfied with their work lives, particularly with the freedom on the job for those in clerical positions. Primary issues of concern for those in these groups include lack of opportunities for promotion, advancement, and retraining. The increased use of technology on campuses has also had an impact on the work lives of educational support personnel and raises issues such as training, health and safety, position reclassification, and job security.

The support staff in higher education has been called the hidden workforce; their work has been described as essential but not always visible. The quality of the work lives of these employees is rarely a priority for colleges and universities. In times of fiscal constraint, these personnel often bear the brunt of efforts to contain costs. Restructuring, retrenchment, and downsizing often disproportionately affect them. There is often a deinvestment in their training and skill development, and if outsourcing is considered, it is often support staff personnel or positions that are lost. The workload of support staff increases as fewer personnel are challenged to perform the same amount of work.

Support staff members provide critical services to campuses. More substantive research is needed on this important group of individuals who actively support the missions of the higher education enterprise. To improve the quality of their work lives and to retain the services of support staff, the majority of whom are women, personnel practices must be scrutinized to ensure that hiring practices are fair and unbiased, that the loyalty and commitment of these employees is recognized and rewarded, and that they are treated with respect and dignity.

Linda K. Johnsrud and
Lynn T. Inoshita

References and further reading

Firebaugh, Glenn, and Brian Harley. 1995. "Trends in Job Satisfaction in the United States by Race, Gender, and Type of Occupation." *Research in the Sociology of Work* 5: 87–104.

Hurd, Richard W. 1995. *Directory of Staff Bargaining Agents in Institutions of Higher Education.* New York: National Center for the Study of Collective Bargaining in Higher Education and the Professions, School of Public Affairs, Baruch College, City University of New York.

Integrated Postsecondary Education Data System. 1997. *Fall 1997 Staff Survey.* Washington, DC: National Center for Education Statistics.

Johnsrud, Linda K. 1999. "The Worklife Issues of Higher Education Support Personnel." Pp. 111–125 in *NEA 1999 Almanac of Higher Education.* Washington, DC: National Education Association.

———. 2000. "Higher Education Staff: Bearing the Brunt of Cost Containment." Pp. 101–118 in *NEA 2000 Almanac of Higher Education.* Washington, DC: National Education Association.

———. 2001. "Higher Education Support Personnel: Worklife Issues." Pp. 101–116 in *NEA 2001 Almanac of Higher Education.* Washington, DC: National Education Association.

———. Forthcoming. "Higher Education Support Staff: The Impact of Technology." In *NEA 2002 Almanac of Higher Education.* Washington, DC: National Education Association.

Kleeh-Tolley, Karen. 1993. "Women Organizing: Action and Reaction in the Formation of a Clerical Union." *Humanity and Society* 17, no. 4: 447–466.

National Education Association. 1996. *NEA ESP Data Book: A Workforce and Membership Profile of Educational Support Personnel*. Washington, DC: National Education Association.

Rhoades, Gary, and Christine Maitland. 1998. "The Hidden Campus Workforce: (De)Investing in Staff." Pp. 109–118 in *NEA 1998 Almanac of Higher Education.* Washington, DC: National Education Association.

Wichroski, Mary Anne. 1994. "The Secretary: Invisible Labor in the Workworld of Women." *Human Organization* 53, no. 1: 33–41.

Unionization

Unionization of women workers is important for the overall organized labor movement because women's issues are all workers' issues. The organization of women clerical workers since the 1970s has not only increased the percentages of organized labor but has revitalized the labor movement. Unionization campaigns among women workers strive to make all workplaces family-friendly, in that equal employment opportunity, equal pay, child care, health benefits, discriminatory practices, and advancement opportunities are issues that affect all workers. Although women in the twenty-first century comprise 50 percent of the workforce, they still earn seventy-three cents for every dollar earned by men. Unionization bridges the wage gap because union women earn eighty-four cents to the dollar earned by men. The wage gap can lead to working-class families losing up to $3,000 annually. Women's wages are a necessary part of their family's income in a two-parent home, and many women are single parents. During the 1970s, the loss of high-paying union industrial jobs, traditionally held by males, made women's wages even more vital to the family's survival. Because there were few women organized prior to the 1970s, there was a lack of women in union leadership, and the idea that women's issues are workers' issues was not supported.

Most union leaders viewed women as unorganizable, believing that they did not act collectively, identified with management, and were elitist. However, in the 1970s organizers within different unions began challenging this belief and convinced their leaders to support organizing campaigns among teachers, social workers, government workers, and university staff members, who were predominantly women. These organizers recognized the importance of bringing this huge sector into the fold of organized labor, especially at a time when union membership was declining. It was proven that women were indeed organizable, for these union drives yielded the largest gains for the overall labor movement in this era. Women workers had begun to demand respect, were tired of being surrogate wives to their bosses, desired specific job descriptions, and wanted increased wages and benefits and child care programs. They recognized that in order to attain these goals, they would have to join the ranks of organized labor.

Clerical work has been a feminized occupation since the creation of the typewriter in the late nineteenth century. On university and college campuses, the majority of staff were women. Technological innovations changed the job drastically and increased the workload. Before major technological advances in office equipment, secretaries and administrative assistants were assigned to an average of two professors, but with technological modifications, they were assigned to entire departments or even two. Women staff members were more than willing to trade prestige and their surrogate wife position for increased wages and benefits and respect. Clerical workers were beginning to suffer repetitive motion injuries and other word-processing health hazards. They wanted clearly defined rules for job descriptions and a workplace free from sexual harassment. Women staff members wanted a family-friendly work environment with provisions for child care.

Title VII of the 1964 Civil Rights Act provided the basis for equal opportunity in job hiring and promotion, as well as sexual harassment legislation. These legislative measures also served as the basis for the unionization campaigns among university staff members. Some of the traditional blue-collar trade unions launched the initial organizing drives. These unions included United Auto Workers (UAW), United Steel Workers (USW), and the Teamsters. Since plant closures and plant relocations led to shrinking membership among these unions, it is not so surprising that they undertook to organize another sector of the workforce to increase membership. Newer service workers unions, such as the American Federation of State, County, and Municipal Employees (AFSCME) and Service Employees International Union (SEIU) also initiated organizing campaigns for university staff members, since they had already been unionizing government workers, social workers and teachers, and other white-collar workers.

Many of the organizers came from the women's movement, where they had developed increased awareness of gender inequities in the workplace. These women included Karen Nussbaum (SEIU, National Association of Working Women, and 9to5), Jackie Ruff (9to5, SEIU), Barbara Rahke (UAW), and Julie Kushner (AFSCME). John Wilhem of Hotel Employees and Restaurant Employees (HERE) was also a leading organizer of women clerks. The movement began at eastern universities such as Cornell, Boston, Yale, Columbia, and Harvard but spread throughout the nation to the University of Minnesota and the University of California system.

Another important development occurred with the creation of 9to5, which began a drive to organize clerical workers in Boston in 1973. Leaders eventually recognized that they had to affiliate with a union in order to engage in collective bargaining and win enforceable gains for their members. That led to an affiliation with SEIU, the only union willing to support an organizing drive among clerical workers while respecting their request for autonomy and showing sensitivity to women's issues. 9to5 affiliated with SEIU under Local 925, which represented an important step in using independent women's groups as a means to reach women in organizing drives. In 1978, the Working Women's National Association of Office Workers was formed. This organization included twelve local organizations such as 9to5, Women Office Workers, and Women Organized for Employment under the leadership of Karen Nussbaum.

The organizing model developed for clerical workers was built upon the 1930s labor and community models. For example, organizers used strategies that would mobilize and involve members. They included a one-on-one approach, establishing committees throughout the workplace, organizing social events, visiting workers at home, developing leadership training programs, and generally being closely attuned to the workers' needs and issues and involving them in developing strategy and tactics. Other activities included films and discussions on labor history and current labor events, rape crisis forums, and sport and theatrical events. Issues such as sexual harassment, child care, flexible work schedules, and maternity leave were also explored, and viable programs were created. Use of the media was also expanded. This approach was opposed to a business union model or a service or top-down approach. It resulted in an informed and involved membership behind a leadership that was able to win extensive gains for all.

In making use of the above model, the Teamsters organized 1,900 clerical workers at the University of Chicago, and the UAW organized Barnard University, Boston University, and Columbia University. Harvard University's 3,700 clerical workers were organized by AFSCME, despite the fierce opposition of university president Derek Bok, who ironically was a labor scholar who had written extensively on the defense of unions. At Boston University, the clerical and faculty joined together in an organizational strike and won a contract in 1979.

The community model led to many more successful campaigns among university staff members. Organizers emphasized that their goal was to build a community-based social union and not simply win elections and sign up members. This approach was particularly successful when university administrations responded with intensive anti-union campaigns, including legal tactics to challenge these organizing efforts. Because the organizers had mobilized and involved so many workers, they were able to withstand these attacks and win the elections for unionization.

These staff organizing efforts often coincided with organizing faculty. On many campuses, staff unions and faculty unions are affiliated with a larger union. On the California State University campuses, both the California State Employees Association and the California Faculty Association are affiliates of SEIU. In addition, staff unions and faculty unions collaborate on programs through campus labor councils, which also include plant and technical unions.

A recent example of organizing university staff members occurred at the University of Texas (UT), Austin, in the late 1990s. The UT Staff Association, known as USA, fought to secure a living wage for UT's 17,000 nonteaching members, predominantly women. Ninety-four percent of the staff workers were paid 70 percent below the Austin market, which has a relatively high cost of living. Many employees were forced to supplement their incomes with second jobs. Using the community-based model, USA succeeded in involving the majority of staff in their organizing campaign and in enlisting the support of students and faculty, as well as other community, labor, and religious leaders. It was also successful in gaining a public forum through the media and held a march and rally in April 1998 in which 12,000 people marched to the State Capitol under the banner of "I Need a Decent Wage."

In 1993 President Bill Clinton appointed Karen Nussbaum, who had spent over twenty years organizing women clerical workers, including those at universities, as head of the U.S. Women's Bureau, a Department of Labor organization. It is the highest seat in the federal government devoted to women's issues. Nussbaum served for two years as advocate for the nation's 60 million working women. In 1995 she became the first director of the newly created Working Women's Department at the American Federation of Labor–Congress of Industrial Organizations. Nussbaum is currently the advocate for 5.5 million women who are part of organized labor. This new sector of the AFL-CIO was created to ensure that women's issues would be heard throughout organized labor and that these issues would at long last be recognized as workers' issues and vital to the continued viability of the labor movement.

Myrna Cherkoss Donahoe

References and further reading

American Federation of Labor–Congress of Industrial Organizations. http://www.aflcio.org/women. Cited June 10, 2002.

Amott, Teresa, and Julie A. Mattael. 1991. *Race, Gender and Work.* Boston: South End Press.

Baxandall, Rosalyn, Linda Gordon, and Susan Reverby. 1995. *America's*

Working Women. New York: W. W. Norton.
Foner, Philip, S. 1982. *Women and the American Labor Movement.* New York: Free Press.
Koziara, Karen, Michael H. Shallcross, Lucretia Moskow, and Dewey Tanner. 1987. *Working Women: Past Present and Future.* Washington, DC: Bureau of National Affairs.
9to5, National Association of Working Women. http://www.9to5.org/profile.html. Cited June 10, 2002.

Appendix 1: Women's Studies Research Resources

Advocates of women's studies have often had to create their own research resources. When Betty Friedan coined the phrase "the problem that has no name" in 1963, she could have been describing the situation with women's studies research resources at the beginning of the second-wave feminist movement in the late 1960s. The *Oxford English Dictionary* notes that the term "feminism" was first used in 1895. Nonetheless, the Library of Congress did not adopt it as an official subject heading for materials in libraries until 1980. Aside from the medical fields of gynecology and obstetrics or the psychosocial analysis of marriage and family, there were no scholarly journals specializing in women's studies issues. There were no women's studies indexes identifying when and where articles had been published about women or comprehensive directories of archives specializing in women's history materials. There were no for-profit feminist or lesbian publishing companies. There were no directories of scholarships or research grants for women. Although women were attending college and some were university faculty, there was very little mention of women's achievements in the textbooks for any academic discipline. There were no women's studies academic programs in higher education. Much of the development of women's studies research resources is due to grassroots efforts by individuals and small groups volunteering their time and financial support for a goal they deemed worthy of the sacrifice: the formal recognition of women's contributions to history throughout the world.

The Routledge Critical Dictionary of Feminism and Postfeminism (Gamble 2000) is one of several feminist dictionaries published after 1970, as women's studies scholars documented a new tool for their research: women-focused terminology. The feminist-forged words in women's studies classrooms, however, are not necessarily available to assist researchers when they attempt to locate resources in a library's card catalog or online catalog. One of the functions of the Library of Congress in Washington, D.C., is to develop a controlled vocabulary of subject headings to assign to new publications as they are cataloged. In 1901, the Library of Congress began distributing preprinted catalog cards to other libraries. To save staff time, libraries around the world now use Library of Congress subject headings. As a result, these subject headings have had a large role in shaping the language of research. Over time, a growing number of librarians began to complain about the perceived white Christian male bias in the subject headings. Unfortunately, the vast bureaucracy of the Library of Congress, along with its success in worldwide distribution of catalog records, contributed to its slow response in modernizing its subject headings. The use of the term "man" as a subject heading to generically represent all humans, for example, persisted until the Library of Congress replaced it with "human beings" in 1996. It was apparent to many librarians that obsolete and inadequate subject headings were hindering researchers' efforts to find relevant materials in libraries. Sanford ("Sandy") Berman became aware of the racist nature of some official subject headings when he was an assistant librarian at the University of Zambia in 1969. When Berman became principal cataloger for the Hennepin County Library (HCL) in Minnesota, he began a thirty-year crusade to induce the Library of Congress to modernize its subject headings and to discontinue those that were misleading or demeaned minorities. Berman devised an alternative cataloging system, which was based upon contemporary, relevant, and straightforward terminology. These alternative subject headings were shared with other libraries via the bimonthly *HCL Cataloging Bulletin* and Berman's column, "New Subject Headings of Interest to Women" in the *WLW Journal.* With Berman's system, HCL first used the subject heading "feminism in education" in 1974. The Library of Congress did not adopt that subject heading until 1992. Similarly, HCL began using the term "ecofeminism" in 1982, but the Library of Congress did not start using it until 1991. In 1974, the American Library Association's Social Responsibilities Round Table Task Force on Women formed a Committee on Sexism in Subject Headings. The committee emphasized the problems of separate and unequal treatment, the omission of needed headings, and the practice of constructing subject headings in a way that conveyed the white Christian male as the norm. When the Women's Information Services Network was formed in 1975, one of its goals was to assist in developing a consistent, shared vocabulary for research and writing about women. *On Equal Terms: A Thesaurus for Nonsexist Indexing and Cataloging* (Marshall 1977) was published as a tool for circumventing the male bias in Library of Congress subject headings. In 1976, the Women's Education Equity Communications Network produced a basic list of terms about women. This list and contributions from many other groups led to the publication of *A Women's Thesaurus: An Index of Language Used to Describe and Locate Information by and about Women* (Capek 1987). This massive thesaurus did not contain Library of Congress subject headings. Instead, it was designed as a tool to assist scholars using the newly available keyword searching software in the early databases of the 1980s.

Nowhere is the grassroots element in women's studies more apparent than in the emergence of feminist periodicals. When the first edition of *Magazines for Libraries* was published (Katz and Richards 1969), it listed twenty-three women's magazines. Among them were *Harper's Bazaar,* which had begun publication in 1867, and *Ladies Home Journal,* which was first published in 1883. However, the *National NOW Times,* which the National Organization for Women began publishing in 1968, was not included. In 1969, a small group of women activists in Berkeley, California, published *Spazm,* an informal newsletter, which was distributed across the country to share what people were doing to contribute to what later became known as the women's liberation movement. From

1969 to 1974, over 800 small press women's journals and periodicals sprang into print throughout the United States. Laura X, an activist involved with *Spazm,* founded the nonprofit Women's History Research Center in Berkeley in 1968. Its Women's History Library was opened in an effort to preserve the "gray literature" of the women's liberation movement: the grassroots and small press publications, pamphlets, and unpublished manuscript documents. Laura X personally funded the center for two years and coordinated the efforts of international scholars and activists in obtaining current and historical documents about women. When it became obvious that adequate funding would not be available to continue the work of the library, she obtained a grant to underwrite the expense of having the Center's International Women's History Periodical Archive microfilmed. The result was *Herstory 1–3,* a unique, full-text collection of small press periodicals of the women's liberation movement from 1956 to 1974 (*Herstory* 1971–1976). By 1980, over 275 libraries in thirteen countries owned microfilm sets of *Herstory.* When the Women's History Library closed in 1974, Laura X donated its periodical collection to the Special Collections Department of Northwestern University Library, which then had the second-largest women's periodical collection in the world. Other fragments of nonacademic feminist periodicals are available in the microfilm sets of the *Underground Press Collection* and *Radical Periodicals in the United States, 1880–1960.*

Scholarly and for-profit women's studies journals soon followed the grassroots publications. Three women's studies periodicals, which began publication in the United States in 1972, are still active. The Feminist Press, affiliated with the City University of New York and supported by funding from the Ford Foundation, began publication of *Women's Studies Quarterly,* the first U.S. journal devoted to teaching about women. The University of Maryland began publication of the refereed journal, *Feminist Studies.* In the commercial publishing arena, the Ms. Magazine Corporation launched *Ms.* In 1975, the women's studies program at the University of Colorado, Boulder, began publication of *Frontiers: A Journal of Women's Studies.* When the University of Chicago Press began publication of *Signs: Journal of Women in Culture and Society,* it planned for an archives section in each issue to publish women's documents that had been written before 1950 and had been overlooked by past historians. These early journals of second-wave feminism served a critical role in gaining credibility within academe for women's studies as a legitimate academic discipline.

The rapid proliferation of periodicals and other publications by and about women led to growing awareness of the need for more specialized library collections and archives to preserve women's documents for future scholars. The groundwork had been done by an earlier generation of feminists. Mary Ritter Beard, a historian and author, was a visionary pioneer in the area of documenting women's history. In 1935, she formed the planning board for a proposed World Center for Women's Archives, garnering support from Eleanor Roosevelt, Georgia O'Keeffe, and other prominent women with the motto "No documents—no history." After five years of gathering primary resources about women and identifying where other documents were located, Beard realized adequate funding would not be available to establish the world archive. As a compromise, she donated the documents to Radcliffe College and several other colleges. In doing so, she helped foster the idea of collecting and preserving primary women's materials for historical research.

In 1942, the New York Public Library established the Schwimmer-Lloyd Collection, an archive that documents women's role in the international peace movement. In 1943, the Arthur and Elizabeth Schlesinger Library at Radcliffe College began its History of Women in America collection, based upon the earlier donation by Mary Beard. Also during the 1940s, Smith College's library established its archival Sophia Smith Collection. The National Council of Negro Women in Washington, D.C., created the National Archives for Black Women's History. Libraries became consumers of micrographic technology in the 1930s. Microfiche and microfilm were a space-saving solution to preserving many materials printed on poor-quality paper, such as newspapers. The U.S. Department of Education's Educational Resources Information Center (ERIC) has produced full-text microfiche documents about girls' and women's education since 1966. *The Gerritsen Collection of Women's History, 1543–1945* is a mostly western European resource based upon the personal library of Dr. Aletta Jacobs Gerritsen, a feminist activist and the Netherlands' first female doctor (Gerritsen 1975). The landmark *History of Women* microfilm set (1975–1979) from the Schlesinger Library provides full-text publication of primary women's studies resources from the Middle Ages to 1920. In 1977, the Library of Congress microfilmed approximately 60,000 documents about Margaret Sanger's efforts to legalize access to birth control information in the United States. University Publications of America (UPA), a division of Congressional Information Service, is a major supplier of women's studies microfilm sets, including the *Margaret Sanger Papers; Smith College Collections; Papers of Eleanor Roosevelt, 1933–1945; Papers of the League of Women Voters, 1918–1974;* and a series of *Women's Studies Manuscript Collections from the Schlesinger Library, Radcliffe College: Woman's Suffrage; Women in National Politics,* and *Sexuality, Sex Education, and Reproductive Rights.* More recent UPA microfilm projects have addressed the gap in minority women's resources. The *Records of the National Association of Colored Women's Clubs, 1895–1992* became available in 1994. Microfilm sets of the *Mary McLeod Bethune Papers* were released from 1995 to 1999.

In the early stage of the second-wave feminist movement, the federal government and major universities led the way in providing a new infrastructure for resources for and about women. In 1960, Radcliffe College founded the Mary Ingraham Bunting Institute to support research studies by women. In 1964, the University of Michigan established its Center for Continuing Education of Women. In 1970, the Women's Equity Action League filed the first class-action sex discrimination complaint against all universities and colleges in the United States, which resulted in the beginning of systematic gathering of statistics about women's employment in higher education. Also in 1970, the Center for Women and Religion was founded at the Graduate Theological Union in Berkeley. In 1972, Congress approved the Title IX higher education bill, which was designed to eliminate sex discrimination in all programs and activities of educational institutions that received federal grants and contracts, including postsecondary education. Also in 1971, Rutgers University established the Center for American Women and Politics. The nonprofit Center for Women Policy Studies was established in Washington, D.C., in 1972. In 1973, the Carnegie Commission on Higher Education submitted reform recommendations to increase the enrollment and retention of female students, to increase the number of women and minority faculty, and to achieve pay equity in higher education. In 1974, the Women's Educational Equity Act allocated federal funding for grants for women college students. That same year, both Stanford University and Wellesley College established women's studies research centers. The steady growth in scholarly publishing during the 1970s made it apparent that no individual library would be able to subscribe to every journal or purchase every book. The libraries of Columbia University, Harvard University, Yale University, and the Research Libraries of the New York Public Library formed the Research Libraries Group (RLG) consortium in 1974 to explore ways to share the cost of acquiring and preserving research resources. Librarians needed a new tool to evaluate the quality of library collections and to identify gaps or inadequate coverage of specific subjects. Over the next several years, members of RLG created the *RLG Conspectus* as a comprehensive library collection assessment tool (Wood and Strauch 1992). However, it was not until 1990 when RLG published a women's studies component for its *Conspectus* as a guide for assessing the quality of women's studies collections (Pritchard 1990).

When the National Women's Studies Association organized in 1977, 276 women's studies programs were available in U.S. colleges and universities. Also in 1977, the Women's Studies Research Center opened at the University of Wisconsin, Madison. The University of Arizona founded the Southwest Institute for Research on Women in 1979. In 1981, when the National Council for Research on Women was formed, its membership included seventy-five research centers, councils, and projects in twenty-four states and the District of Columbia. Memphis State University launched its Center for Research on Women in 1982. In 1983, librarians active in the American Library Association's (ALA) division of the Association of College and Research Libraries formed a Women's Studies Discussion Group. Several of its members contributed to *Building Women's Studies Collections: A Resource Guide* (Ariel 1987), a tool for librarians as they worked to acquire and organize women's studies resources. The City University of New York founded the Center for Lesbian and Gay Studies in 1986. In the late 1980s, two surveys of U.S. colleges and universities identified academic women's studies programs and the library resources supporting them. The resulting directory was the first national reference for detailed, comprehensive information about women's studies resources for higher education (Stafford 1990).

When *Vice Versa* earned a historical footnote in the 1940s as the first lesbian magazine published in the United States, there was a general climate of sexual repression and denial. Back in the 1890s, Dr. Clelia D. Mosher's survey of forty-five married women revealed that many of them enjoyed sex. This finding was so shocking to her contemporaries that the data were not published in her lifetime. In 1938, the National Office for Decent Literature sued *Life Magazine* because of the illustrations accompanying an article about childbirth. That same year, the Association of Women Students at the University of Indiana petitioned for a class about marital relations. Dr. Alfred C. Kinsey was assigned the task of developing a "marriage" course. When Kinsey realized that almost no scientific data were available about human sexual behavior, he became a pioneer in the field. In 1947, he obtained funding to establish the non-profit Institute for Sex Research at Indiana University. In the 1950s, the *New York Times Index* listed "Homosexuality" under "Sex Perversion." In 1953, the Institute for Sex Research published *Sexual Behavior in the Human Female,* followed by *Pregnancy, Birth, and Abortion* in 1958 (Pomeroy 1972). In 1973, the American Psychiatric Association removed homosexuality from its list of mental disorders. Nonetheless, lesbianism was so controversial that its advocacy led to a rift in the ranks of the National Organization for Women, which had formed in 1966, and the *New York Times* did not allow its reporters to use the word "gay" in their news stories until 1987. The Daughters of Bilitis, a lesbian organization in San Francisco, published *The Ladder* from 1956 to 1972. In 1970, the ALA established a Task Force on Gay Liberation to focus on a neglected area of librarianship. This task force was the first public group of gay professionals in any professional organization. Barbara Gittings coordinated the task force's Gay Book Award, which was launched in 1971 and was the first gay literary award. It became an official ALA award in 1986. In 1972, the Library of Congress established "HQ 76.5" as the classification range for "gay liberation movement" materials in libraries. *LGSN: Lesbian and Gay Studies Newsletter,* is an official publication of the Modern Language Association's Gay and Lesbian Caucus and has been in publication since 1973. Barbara Grier, a book reviewer and staff writer for *The Ladder,* cofounded Naiad Press in Florida in 1973. It has grown to become the world's largest publisher of lesbian books. In addition to fiction, Naiad Press publishes reference resources, including *Black Lesbians: An Annotated Bibliography* and a new edition of *Sex Variant Women in Literature,* which won the ALA Gay Book Award in 1974. *Sinister Wisdom* began publication in 1976 as a scholarly journal specializing in lesbian studies. In 1977, the National Women's Studies Association formed its Lesbian Caucus during the organization's constitutional convention.

In 1975, author Joan Nestle and other lesbian activists founded the Lesbian Herstory Archives. The founders decided not to be affiliated with an academic campus so that the archives would be available to everyone that wanted to use its resources. Its Lesbian Herstory Educational Foundation began publication of the *Lesbian Herstory Archives Newsletter* in 1975. In 1978, the Buffalo Women's Oral History Project undertook the goal of writing a comprehensive history of the lesbian community in Buffalo, New York, from 1940 to 1960 and to create an archive of oral histories and written interviews. The research materials from this project were donated to the Lesbian Herstory Archives. In 1993, the archives moved to its current location in Brooklyn, New York. The *Lambda Book Report* began publication in 1987 and attempts to provide comprehensive reviews of the gay, lesbian, bisexual, and transgendered press. The *Lesbian Review of Books* began publication in 1994, and it focuses upon books by, for, and about lesbians. In 1999, ALA's Gay, Lesbian, and Bisexual

Task Force became the Gay, Lesbian, Bisexual and Transgendered Round Table. New research resources continue to emerge, helping fill a long-standing gap. Among them are the *Gay and Lesbian Biography* (Tyrkus 1997) and the *Lesbian Film Guide* (Darren 2000).

The phenomenal growth in women's studies publishing during the last third of the twentieth century also led to more urgent demands for new indexing tools to simplify the task of finding the interdisciplinary publications being written about women. Long-established print indexes were of some use for women's studies research. Among them were *Biography Index, Dissertation Abstracts International,* and *Public Affairs Information Services Bulletin.* The *Alternative Press Index* and the *Inventory of Marriage and Family Literature* index began publication in 1969 and 1974, respectively. The Institute for Scientific Information (ISI) was the first organization to package computer-generated periodical indexing for use by scholars in academic libraries. Its *Science Citation Index, Social Sciences Citation Index,* and *Arts and Humanities Citation Index* were produced by keyword in context (KWIC) software. The alphabetically arranged subject lists were drawn from words appearing in titles of journal articles. Though the small print was hard on the eyes and the multiple-volume indexes were too expensive for many academic libraries, the ISI citation indexes were a breakthrough for those attempting to find scholarly articles about women. In 1971, *Women's Studies Abstracts* was the first index to focus exclusively on interdisciplinary feminist and women's studies topics. It and the *Alternative Press Index* were among the few resources indexing articles about lesbians. *Feminist Periodicals* is not a true index. However, it was the first table of contents service for over 100 feminist, lesbian, and small print journals. An international indexing resource, *Studies on Women Abstracts,* began publication in 1983. Also in 1983, the Center for Research on Women at Wellesley College began publication of the *Women's Review of Books,* a monthly serial. Naiad Press published *Lesbian Periodicals Index* in 1986. *Women's Studies Index,* an annual compilation, began publication in 1990.

The U.S. government was an early source for computerized federal records relevant to women's studies. The Center for Electronic Records at the National Archives and Records Administration organizes its resources by government agency. Among its holdings are surveys of army nurses and WACS in 1945; data on the pregnancies of 58,000 women from a 1957–1983 study by the National Institutes of Health; and federal employee surveys from 1978 to 1983, which addressed pay equity, sexual harassment, and affirmative action programs (Adams 1990).

Compact disc read-only memory (CD-ROM) technology was patented in 1979. It allows information to be placed on digital laser disks. Several types of CD-ROM products became available for libraries: citation indexes, numeric or statistical resources, full-text publications, and audio recordings. An early CD-ROM was *Women of Influence,* which was an interactive quiz about the achievements of twenty American women from the nineteenth and twentieth centuries. In 1990, the United Nations Statistical Office published its *Handbook for National Statistical Databases on Women and Development.* In 1991, the University of California, Berkeley, began production of the *Chicano Database,* which includes women's studies in its coverage. In 1992, a full-text CD-ROM of *The Clarence Thomas Hearings* was published. In 1993, the U.S. Department of Health and Human Services produced a CD containing two resources, *Health, United States, 1992* and *Healthy People 2000 Review, 1992.* Both databases provide statistics on women's health issues, including abortions, fertility rates, acquired immunodeficiency syndrome (AIDS) by gender, and health care by gender. In 1994, *Women's Studies on Disc* provided the first electronic indexing of women's studies scholarly journals. Two more women's studies CD-ROM databases were released in 1996: *Contemporary Women's Issues,* which was a full-text publication, and *Women's Resources International.* Human Relations Area Files (HRAF), which had been producing full-text anthropological resources on microfiche since 1958, switched to CD-ROM technology in 1996. The HRAF collection has provided generations of scholars with international ethnographic resources about the legal status of women, marriage customs, and human sexuality. In 1997, the full-text, multicultural *Women "R"* CD-ROM became available. When *The Nineteenth Century on CD-ROM* index became available in 1997, it simplified finding primary resources in a full-text microfilm set that includes women authors. In 1998, the Department of Defense released *Women in the U.S. Armed Forces,* an image-based product.

The earliest use of email occurred in the 1960s, when the first time-sharing computers were developed. Email was one of the earliest Internet tools available to university faculty, and it quickly transformed their professional lives. Coauthors or members of professional committees could suddenly communicate with each other despite differences in time zones or geographic separation. In 1992, the first U.S. women's e-conference, or electronic salon, was conducted for two weeks via email to discuss women's communication via the Internet. Specialized listservs, providing discussion forums via email, quickly developed in the early 1990s. Joan Korenman at the Women's Studies Program at the University of Maryland, Baltimore, established the WMST-L women's studies listserv in 1991 as a resource for those involved with teaching women's studies, administrating women's studies programs, or conducting professional women's studies research. Korenman still moderates WMST-L, which had over 4,000 subscribers in forty-seven countries as of February 2001. Other early women's studies listservs were FEMREL-L, focusing on feminist religious topics; CAMPCLIM, which addresses the environment of college campuses, including sexual harassment and physical accessibility issues; and SWIP-L, the forum for the Society of Women in Philosophy. The GAYLIBN-L listserv was launched in 1992 as a forum for gay and lesbian librarians. Korenman maintains a web directory of gender-related electronic forums at http://www.research.umbc.edu/~korenman/wmst/forums.html. In 1999, the Association of College and Research Libraries' (ACRL) Women's Studies Section began its WSS-L listserv as a resource for those involved with all aspects of women's studies librarianship. Many faculty establish listservs for student discussion forums in specific courses. The ACRL publishes a *Directory of Scholarly Electronic Journals and Academic Discussion Lists* to alert faculty and students about subject-specific Internet resources.

Gopher software was first developed in 1991 at the University of Minnesota

Microcomputer and Workstation Networks Center. It is a hierarchical menu-based search program that locates file names and resources on the Internet. As of 1999, there were over 7,000 gopher servers on the Internet. The collective information they make available is called gopherspace. In 1995, the University of Maryland developed the *inforM* women's studies database for access by gopher, telnet, or anonymous ftp. Its files contain specialized women's studies bibliographies, calls for papers at scholarly conferences, and an archive for older logfiles of messages from the WMST-L listserv. The U.S. Labor Department's National Center for the Workplace gopher provides access to the text of the Glass Ceiling Commission's 1995 report. The National Library of Medicine's gopher contains bibliographies about AIDS and women's health care topics. By 1995, many federal agencies were using electronic bulletin board systems to provide full-text information. The various departments and agencies of the federal government produce information about women that is relevant to various aspects of women's studies. The Small Business Administration offers files on women in business. The National Science Foundation provides alerts about research grant opportunities and statistics on the number of women earning bachelor's degrees in science and engineering. By 1996, many federal agencies had migrated to the World Wide Web, an online technology enriched by audio and graphics, which quickly replaced gopher software in popularity.

The first specialized women's online database came into existence as a result of the Women's Educational Equity Act of 1974. The Women's Educational Equity Communications Network offered a compilation of citations from thirteen different databases about gender equity in education. Loss of federal political support led to its demise in 1980. The nonprofit organization Catalyst formed in 1962 to provide resources for women entering the workforce for the first time or returning to it after years of raising a family. In the 1970s, it opened the Catalyst Library and began publishing material about working women. By 1980, Catalyst was specializing in two-career family issues: day care, working mothers, and changing sex roles. With the help of a Mellon Foundation grant, the organization developed the *Catalyst Resources for Women* database and made it available online in 1983 via Bibliographic Retrieval Services (BRS). At that time, its content was unique among online databases. Some resources about women, however, could be found in the *American Men and Women of Science* and *America: History and Life* databases, which became available online via DIALOG in 1983.

FeMiNa was one of the earliest websites created specifically for women. Launched in September 1995 by Cybergrrl, FeMiNa provides a comprehensive directory to women's resources on the Internet. In 1995, no subject category for women existed on the Yahoo! search engine. Two women, Sue Levin and Kathleen McMahon, created a searchable database, WWWomen.com, which became active on the web in February 1996. It offers the "Best of WWWomen Site Award" to encourage quality content on websites. *Contemporary Women's Issues* became available as a full-text online database in 1997. Based on the CD-ROM database of the same name, it specializes in social science coverage and contains some literature not included in other databases. Also in 1997, ISI released an online version of its citation indexes. In

1998, *Studies on Women Abstracts* became available online. It is a comprehensive, interdisciplinary women's studies resource. Also in 1998, the scope of the *Women "R"* database was broadened, and its name was changed to *GenderWatch,* a full-text international resource. Several lesbian studies periodicals are covered by this database, including *The Advocate, Gay and Lesbian Review,* and the *Journal of Lesbian Studies.* Brown University has hosted a Women Writers Project since the late 1980s. Their text-based product, *Women Writers Online,* became available to universities in 1999 via the web. Its focus is English texts by women written before 1830. The *Women's Studies Archives: International Women's Periodicals Online,* an interdisciplinary, full-text selection of journals, magazines, and newspapers, appeared in 1999. *Gay and Lesbian Abstracts* became available online in 2000. It indexes social sciences and humanities topics in popular and scholarly gay, lesbian, bisexual, and transgendered publications. The full-text *Ethnic NewsWatch* database also debuted online in 2000. In early 2001, the Greenwood Publishing Group published the full-text *Pornography and Sexual Representation: A Reference Guide Online,* which covers the fields of cinema, law, literature, marketing, and performance art.

The ninth edition of *Magazines for Libraries* included electronic journals for the first time. In 1997, a scant 4 percent of websites were periodicals. Most of them were digitized versions of print editions. By 1999, there were at least 148 women's ezines on the Internet. In February 2001, Ulrichsweb.com, the online version of *Ulrich's Periodical Directory,* listed 226 active academic feminist, gender, or women's studies journals being published worldwide and 397 active nonacademic women's periodicals being published in the United States.

Internet web technology is blurring traditional concepts within the publishing industry. The web provides a mix of free and fee-based full-text resources, of varying degrees of quality. The Association of College and Research Libraries (ACRL) Women's Studies Section's Collection Development Committee opened its website in 1997 to provide links to various categories of women's studies Internet resources. See http://libraries.mit.edu/humanities/WomensStudies/wscd.html.

Joan Korenman, moderator of the WMST-L listserv, developed the award-winning Women's Studies/Women's Issues Resource Sites as a current resource for all aspects of women's studies involvement. See http://research.umbc.edu/~korenman/wmst/links.html.

Metasites are web versions of print bibliographies, with the added benefit of linking to full text when available. The *Guide to Women's History in Archival Collections* is maintained by the Center for the Study of Women and Gender and the Special Collections and Archives Department at the University of Texas, San Antonio. Go to http://www.lib.utsa.edu/Archives/links.htm. The Office of Women's Studies at the University of Wisconsin, Madison, provides core lists on various women's studies topics, which are maintained by members of the ALA-ACRL Women's Studies Section at http://www.library.wisc.edu/libraries/WomensStudies/. In 2000, the Global Reproductive Health Forum at Harvard made available *Women of Color on the Web* as a resource for the interdisciplinary issues of gender, race, feminism, sexuality, reproductive health, and reproductive rights. It is available at http://

www.hsph.harvard.edu/grhf/woc. The University of Maryland, Baltimore County, established the Center for Women and Information Technology in 1998. One of its goals is to foster research concerning the relationship between gender and information technology. Early in 2001, netLibrary had full-text electronic books available in over 4,000 libraries. It is appropriate that *Betty Friedan and the Making of the Feminine Mystique* (Horowitz 1998) is among the digitized books available via online access. Change is the essence of the Internet. Information technology will continue to transform how information is packaged and the ways in which women's studies research is conducted.

Betty J. Glass

See also Part 3: Feminist Research Methodology; Part 4: Women's Studies

References and further reading

Adams, Margaret O. 1990. "Electronic Records at the National Archives: Resources for Women's Studies." *NWSA Journal* 2: 269–272.

American Library Association. 1992. Association of College and Research Libraries. Women's Studies Section. Collection Development and Bibliography Committee. *Women's Studies Collection Development Policies.* Chicago: American Library Association.

Ariel, Joan, ed. 1987. *Building Women's Studies Collections: A Resource Guide.* Middletown, CT: CHOICE.

Baum, Christina D. 1992. *Feminist Thought in American Librarianship.* Jefferson, NC: McFarland.

Berman, Sanford. 1971. *Prejudices and Antipathies: A Tract on the LC Subject Headings Concerning People.* Metuchen, NJ: Scarecrow.

Boxer, Marilyn Jacoby. 1998. *When Women Ask the Questions: Creating Women's Studies in America.* Baltimore: Johns Hopkins University Press.

Brownmiller, Sara, and Ruth Dickstein. 1996. *An Index to Women's Studies Anthologies: Research across the Disciplines, 1985–1989.* New York: G. K. Hall.

Capek, Mary Ellen, ed. 1987. *A Women's Thesaurus: An Index of Language Used to Describe and Locate Information by and about Women.* New York: Harper and Row.

Cherny, Lynn, and Elizabeth Reba Weise, eds. 1996. *Wired Women: Gender and New Realities in Cyberspace.* Seattle, WA: Seal Press.

Darren, Alison. 2000. *Lesbian Film Guide.* New York: Cassell.

Directory: Curriculum Transformation Projects and Activities in the U. S. 1997. Baltimore: National Center for Curriculum Transformation Resources on Women.

Fialkoff, Francine. 1993. "We've Been 'LC-Centric' Too Long." *Library Journal* 118: 108.

Foster, Jeannette H. 1985. *Sex Variant Women in Literature.* Tallahassee, FL: Naiad Press.

Friedan, Betty. 1963. *The Feminine Mystique.* New York: Norton.

Gamble, Sarah, ed. 2000. *The Routledge Critical Dictionary of Feminism and Postfeminism.* New York: Routledge.

Gerritsen Collection of Women's History 1543–1945. 1975. Glen Rock, NJ: Microfilming Corp. of America, microfiche and microfilm.

Gough, Cal, and Ellen Greenblatt, eds. 1990. *Gay and Lesbian Library Service.* Jefferson, NC: McFarland.

Harcourt, Wendy, ed. 1999. *Women @ Internet: Creating New Cultures in Cyberspace.* New York: Zed Books.

Hawthorne, Susan, and Renate Klein, eds. 1999. *CyberFeminism: Connectivity, Critique and Creativity.* North Melbourne, Victoria, Australia: Spinifex Press.

Herstory: Women's History Collection from the International Women's History Archives, Berkeley, California; 1–3. Women's History Library, Women's History Research Center. Wooster, OH: Bell and Howell, 1971–1976, microfilm.

History of Women. Arthur and Elizabeth Schlesinger Library on the History of Women in America, Radcliffe College, Cambridge, MA. New Haven, CT:

Research Publications, 1975–1979, microfilm.

Horowitz, Daniel. 1998. *Betty Friedan and the Making of the Feminine Mystique.* Amherst: University of Massachusetts Press, netLibrary.

Katz, Bill, and Linda Sternberg Katz, eds. 2000. *Magazines for Libraries.* 10th ed. New Providence, NJ: Bowker.

Katz, William A., and Berry G. Richards, eds. 1969. *Magazines for Libraries.* New York: Bowker.

Korenman, Joan. 1997. *Internet Resources on Women: Using Electronic Media in Curriculum Transformation.* Baltimore: Towson State University, National Center for Curriculum Transformation Resources on Women.

Marshall, Joan K., comp. 1977. *On Equal Terms: A Thesaurus for Nonsexist Indexing and Cataloging.* New York: Neal-Schuman.

Moseley, Eva Steiner, ed. 1995. *Women, Information, and the Future: Collecting and Sharing Resources Worldwide.* Fort Atkinson, WI: Highsmith Press.

Mosher, Clelia Duel. 1980. *The Mosher Survey: Sexual Attitudes of Forty-Five Victorian Women.* New York: Arno Press.

Pomeroy, Wardell B. 1972. *Dr. Kinsey and the Institute for Sex Research.* New York: Harper and Row.

Pritchard, Sarah M. 1990. *RLG Conspectus: Women's Studies.* Mountain View, CA: Research Libraries Group.

Ryan, Barbara. 1996. *The Women's Movement: References and Resources.* New York: G. K. Hall.

Spender, Dale. 1995. *Nattering on the Net: Women, Power and Cyberspace.* North Melbourne, Victoria, Australia: Spinifex Press.

Stafford, Beth, ed. 1990. *Directory of Women's Studies Programs and Library Resources.* Phoenix, AZ: Oryx Press.

Tyrkus, Michael J., ed. 1997. *Gay and Lesbian Biography.* Detroit: St. James Press.

Westbrook, Lynn. 1999. *Interdisciplinary Information Seeking in Women's Studies.* Jefferson, NC: McFarland.

Women Library Workers. *WLW Journal.* 1980–1994.

Women's Information Services and Networks: A Global Source Book. 1999. Amsterdam: Royal Tropical Institute.

Wood, Richard J., and Katina Strauch, eds. 1992. *Collection Assessment: A Look at the RLG Conspectus.* New York: Haworth Press.

Zimmerman, Bonnie, and Toni A. H. McNaron, eds. 1996. *The New Lesbian Studies: Into the Twenty-First Century.* New York: The Feminist Press.

Appendix 2: Colleges Identifying Themselves as Women's Colleges

Agnes Scott College (GA)
Alverno College (WI)
Aquinas College at Milton (MA)
Aquinas College at Newton (MA)
Barnard College (NY)
Bay Path College (MA)
Bennett College (NC)
Blue Mountain College (MS)
Brenau University (GA)
Bryn Mawr College (PA)
Carlow College (PA)
Cedar Crest College (PA)
Chatham College (PA)
Chestnut Hill College (PA)
College of New Rochelle (NY)
College of Saint Benedict (MN)
College of Saint Catherine (MN)
College of Saint Elizabeth (NJ)
College of Saint Mary (NE)
Columbia College (SC)
Converse College (SC)
Cottey College (MO)
Douglass College (NJ)
Georgian Court College (NJ)
Harcum College (PA)
Hartford College for Women (CT)
Hollins University (VA)
Hood College (MD)
Immaculata College (PA)
Judson College (AL)
Lesley College (MA)
Lexington College (IL)
Marian Court Junior College (MA)
Mary Baldwin College (VA)
Marymount College (NY)
Marymount Manhattan College (NY)
Meredith College (NC)
Midway College (KY)
Mills College (CA)
Mississippi University for Women
Moore College of Art and Design (PA)
Mount Holyoke College (MA)
Mount Saint Mary College (WI)
Mount St. Mary's College (CA)
Mount Vernon College (DC)
Newcomb College (LA)
Notre Dame College of Ohio
Peace College (NC)
Pine Manor College (MA)
Radcliffe College (MA)
Randolph-Macon Woman's College (VA)
Regis College (MA)
Rosemont College (PA)
Russell Sage College (NY)
St. Joseph College (CT)
Saint Mary-of-the-Woods College (IN)
Saint Mary's College (IN)
Salem College (NC)
Scripps College (CA)
Seton Hill College (PA)
Simmons College (MA)
Smith College (MA)
Spelman College (GA)
Stephens College (MO)
Stern College (NY)
Sweet Briar College (VA)

Texas Woman's University
Trinity College (DC)
Trinity College of Vermont
Ursuline College (OH)
Wellesley College (MA)
Wells College (NY)
Wesleyan College (GA)
Westhampton College (VA)
William Smith College (NY)
Wilson College (PA)

Bibliography

Abel, Emily. 1987. "Collective Protest and Meritocracy: Faculty Women and Sex Discrimination Lawsuits." Pp. 347–377 in *Women and Symbolic Interaction*, ed. Mary Jo Deegan and Michael R. Hill. Boston: Allyn and Unwin.

The Academic Senate for California Community Colleges. 1986. *Toward a Nonviolent Campus Climate.* ERIC Document Reproduction Service no. ED 304957.

Acker, Sandra. 1994. *Gendered Education: Sociological Reflections on Women, Teaching, and Feminism.* Buckingham, UK: Open University Press.

Acker, Sandra, and Grace Feuerverger. 1997. "Enough Is Never Enough: Women's Work in Academe." Pp. 122–140 in *Feminist Critical Policy Analysis: A Perspective from Post-Secondary Education*, ed. Catherine Marshall. Washington, DC: Falmer Press.

Acosta, Vivian, and Linda J. Carpenter. 2000. "Women in Intercollegiate Sport: A Longitudinal Study—Twenty-Three-Year Update, 1977–2000." Unpublished manuscript, Brooklyn College, Brooklyn, NY.

Adair, Vivyan. 2001. "Poverty and the (Broken) Promise of Higher Education." *Harvard Educational Review* 71, no. 2: 217–239.

Adams, Margaret O. 1990. "Electronic Records at the National Archives: Resources for Women's Studies." *NWSA Journal* 2: 269–272.

Adarand Constructors v. Mineta (*Adarand II*), 534 U.S. 103 (2001).

Adarand Constructors v. Pena, 515 U.S. 200 (1995) (*Adarand I*).

Advancing Women. "Does Society Encourage Girls to Develop Career Goals?" http://www.advancing women.com/grrls4.html. Cited June 12, 2002.

Aguilar-San Juan, Karin, ed. 1994. *The State of Asian American Activism and Resistance in the 1990s.* Boston: South End Press.

Aguirre, Adalberto, Jr. 2000. *Women and Minority Faculty in the Academic Workplace.* San Francisco: Jossey-Bass.

Ainsworth, Dorothy. 1938. *The History of Physical Education in Colleges for Women.* New York: Barnes.

Aisenberg, Nadya, and Mona Harrington. 1988. *Women of Academe: Outside the Sacred Grove.* Amherst: University of Massachusetts.

Allen, Walter R., Edgar G. Epps, and Nesha Z. Haniff. 1991. *College in Black and White: African American Students in Predominantly White and in Historically Black Public Universities.* Albany: State University of New York Press.

Almanac Issue. 1998. *Chronicle of Higher Education* 45, no. 1. http://www.chronicle.com/free/almanac/1998/almanac.htm. Cited June 20, 2002.

———. 1999. *Chronicle of Higher Education* 46, no. 1. http://www.chronicle.com/free/almanac/1999/almanac.htm. Cited June 20, 2002.

———. 2000. *Chronicle of Higher Education* 47, no. 1. http://www.chronicle.com/free/almanac/2000/almanac.htm. Cited June 20, 2002.

———. 2001. *Chronicle of Higher Education* 48, no. 1. http://www.chronicle.com/free/almanac/2001/almanac.htm. Cited June 20, 2002.

Almeida, Deirdre A. 1997. "The Hidden Half: A History of Native American Women's Education." *Harvard Educational Review* 67, no. 4: 757–771.

Alpha Kappa Alpha. www.aka1908.com. Cited June 12, 2002.

Alsgaard, Melissa. 2000. "Digital Feminism: Reaching Women through Web-Based Courses." *Feminist Collections* 22, no. 1: 22–27.

Altbach, Philip G. 1991a. "The Racial Dilemma in American Higher Education." Pp. 3–17 in *The Racial Crisis in American Higher Education,* ed. Philip G. Altbach and Kofi Lomotey. Albany: State University of New York Press.

———. 1991b. *International Higher Education: An Encyclopedia.* 2 vols. New York: Garland Publishing.

Altbach, Philip G., and Kofi Lomotey, eds. 1991. *The Racial Crisis in American Higher Education.* Albany: State University of New York Press.

Altman, Ellen, and Patricia Promis. 1990. "Affirmative Action: Opportunity or Obstacle?" *College and Research Libraries News* 55: 11–24.

Amaro, Hortensia, Nancy F. Russo, and Julie Johnson. 1987. "Family and Work Predictors of Psychological Well-Being among Hispanic Women Professionals." *Psychology of Women Quarterly* 11, no. 3.

Ambler, Marjane. 1992. "Women Leaders in Indian Education." *Tribal College Journal* 3, no. 4: 10–14.

American Association of Higher Education. http://www.aahe.org. Cited June 11, 2002.

American Association for Women in Community Colleges. http://www.pc.maricopa.edu/aawcc. Cited June 11, 2002.

American Association of Community Colleges (AACC). 1997. *National Community College Snapshot.* http://www.aacc.nche.edu/facts/factcc.htm. Cited November 7, 2001.

American Association of Family and Consumer Sciences. www.aafcs.org. Cited December 9, 2001.

American Association of State Colleges and Universities. 1988. *Minorities in Public Higher Education: At a Turning Point.* Washington, DC: American Association of State Colleges and Universities.

American Association of University Professors. 1995. *Policy Documents and Reports.* Washington, DC: American Association of University Professors.

———. 2000. "More Good News, So Why the Blues?" *Academe* 86, no. 2 (March–April): 1–5.

———. 2002. "The Annual Report on the Economic Status of the Profession, 2001–2002." http://www.aaup.org/research/salary/02salary/202rep.htm. Cited June 11, 2002.

American Association of University Women. 1992. *How Schools Shortchange Girls.* Washington, DC: American Association of University Women.

———. 1998. *Gender Gaps: Where Schools Still Fail Our Children.* Washington, DC: American Association of University Women Educational Foundation.

American Association of University Women and the AAUW Educational Foundation. 1999. *Higher Education in Transition: The Politics and Practices of Equity, Symposium Proceedings.* Washington, DC: American Association of University Women and the AAUW Educational Foundation.

American College Personnel Association. 1996. *The Student Learning Imperative.* http://www.acpa.nche.edu/sli/sli.htm. Cited August 30, 2001.

American College Testing Program. 1995. Data compiled from the ACT Institutional Data File for 1994. Iowa City, IA: American College Testing Program.

American Council on Education. 2000. *The American College President: 2000.* Washington, DC: American Council on Education.

———. 2001. *Datasheet on Women Presidents in Higher Education.* Washington, DC: American Council on Education. http://www.acenet.edu/hena/issues/2000/09_11_00/women.cfm. Cited June 15, 2002.

American Indian Higher Education Consortium. 1999. "Tribal Colleges: An Introduction." http://www.aihec.org/intro.pdf. Cited September 26, 2001.

American Institute of Physics. http://www.aip.org. Cited June 10, 2002.

American Library Association. 1992. Association of College and Research Libraries. Women's Studies Section. Collection Development and Bibliography Committee. *Women's Studies Collection Development Policies.* Chicago: American Library Association.

American Psychological Association. 1992. *Survival Guide to Academia for Women and Ethnic Minorities.* Washington, DC: American Psychological Association.

———. 1996. *Sexual Harassment: Myths and Realities.* Washington, DC: American Psychological Association.

———. 2000. *Women in Academe: Two Steps Forward, One Step Back.* Washington, DC: American Psychological Association.

Americans with Disabilities Act of 1990, 42 U.S.C. § 12101 et seq.

Americans United for Affirmative Action. http://www.affirmativeaction.org. Cited June 10, 2002.

Amey, Marilyn J., and Susan B. Twombly. 1992. "Revisioning Leadership in Community Colleges." *Review of Higher Education* 15, no. 2: 125–150.

Amott, Teresa, and Julie A. Mattael. 1991. *Race, Gender and Work.* Boston: South End Press.

Anders, Sarah Frances. 1975. "Woman's Role in the Southern Baptist Convention and Its Churches as Compared with Selected Other Denominations." *Review and Expositor* (Winter): 31–39.

Anderson, Bonnie S. 2000. *Joyous Greetings: The First International Women's Movement, 1830–1860.* New York: Oxford University Press.

Anderson, Bonnie S., and Judith P. Zinsser. 1988a. *A History of Their Own: Women in Europe from Prehistory to the Present.* Vol. 1. New York: Harper and Row.

———. 1988b. *A History of Their Own: Women in Europe from Prehistory to the Present.* Vol. 2. New York: Harper and Row.

———. 2000a. *A History of Their Own: Women in Europe from Prehistory to the Present.* Vol. 1, rev. ed. New York: Oxford University Press.

———. 2000b. *A History of Their Own: Women in Europe from Prehistory to the Present.* Vol. 2, rev. ed. New York: Oxford University Press.

Anderson v. State University of New York at New Paltz, 169 F. 3d 117 (Second

Circuit 1999), remanded by 120 S. Ct. 929 (U.S. 2000).

Anthony v. Syracuse, 224 A.D. 487; 231 N.Y.S. 435 (1928).

Argos, V. P., and Tatiana Shohov. 1999. *Sexual Harassment: Analyses and Bibliography.* Commack, NY: Nova Science Publishers.

Ariel, Joan, ed. 1987. *Building Women's Studies Collections: A Resource Guide.* Middletown, CT: CHOICE.

Association for Women in Science. http://www.awis.org. Cited June 10, 2002.

Association of American Colleges and Universities. http://www.aacu-edu.org. Cited June 11, 2002.

Association of Governing Boards of Universities and Colleges. 1998. *Composition of Governing Boards of Independent Colleges and Universities.* Occasional Paper no. 37. Washington, DC: Association of Governing Boards of Universities and Colleges.

Astin, Alexander W. 1977. *Four Critical Years: Effects of College on Beliefs, Attitudes, and Knowledge.* San Francisco: Jossey-Bass.

———. 1984. "Student Involvement: A Developmental Theory for Higher Education." *Journal of College Student Personnel* 25, no. 4: 297–308.

———. 1993. *What Matters in College: Four Critical Years Revisited.* San Francisco: Jossey-Bass.

———. 1994. *Faculty Socialization as Cultural Process: A Mirror of Institutional Commitment.* ASHE-ERIC Higher Education Report 93, no. 6. Washington, DC: George Washington University.

Astin, Alexander W., and Helen S. Astin. 1993. *Undergraduate Science Education: The Impact of Different College Environments on the Educational Pipeline in the Sciences.* Los Angeles: University of California, Higher Education Research Institute.

Astin, Alexander W., Jesus G. Trevino, and Tamara L. Wingard. 1991. *The UCLA Campus Climate for Diversity: Findings from a Campus Wide Survey Conducted for the Chancellor's Council on Diversity.* Los Angeles: University of California, Higher Education Research Institute.

Astin, Helen S. 1969. *The Woman Doctorate in America: Origins, Career, and Family.* New York: Russell Sage Foundation.

———. 1984. "The Meaning of Work in Women's Lives: A Sociopsychological Model of Career Choice and Work Behavior." *Counseling Psychologist* 12, no. 4: 117–126.

Astin, Helen S., and Carol Leland. 1991. *Women of Influence, Women of Vision.* San Francisco: Jossey-Bass.

Astin, Helen S., and Christine M. Cress. 1998. "A National Profile of Academic Women in Research Universities." Paper presented at Women in Research Universities conference, Harvard University.

Astin, Helen S., Anthony I. Antonio, Christine M. Cress, and Alexander W. Astin. 1997. *Race and Ethnicity in the American Professoriate, 1995–96.* Los Angeles: University of California, Higher Education Research Institute.

Atkins, Stephen E. 1991. *The Academic Library in the American University.* Chicago: American Library Association.

Aubert, Sandy E. 1997. "Black Students on White Campuses: Overcoming the Isolation." Pp. 141–146 in *Sailing against the Wind: African Americans and Women in U.S. Education,* ed. Kofi Lomotey. Albany: State University of New York Press.

Austin, Ann E. 1992. "Faculty Cultures." Pp. 1614–1623 in *The Encyclopedia of Higher Education.* Vol. 3: *Analytical Perspectives,* ed. Burton R. Clark and Guy R. Neave. New York: Pergamon Press.

Bae, Yupin, Susan Choy, Claire Geddes, Jennifer Stable, and Thomas Snyder. 2000. *Educational Equity of Girls and Women.* NCES 2000–030. Washington, DC: U.S. Government Printing Office.

Bailey, Beth. 1999. *Sex in the Heartland.* Cambridge, MA: Harvard University Press.

Bailey, Faith C. 1964. *Two Directions.* Rochester, NY: Baptist Missionary Training School.

Baird, Leonard L. 1988. "The College Environment Revisited: A Review of Research and Theory." Pp. 1–52 in *Higher Education: Handbook of Theory and Research,* ed. John C. Smart. New York: Agathon Press.

Baird's Manual of American College Fraternities. 1927–1977. Menasha, WI: Collegiate Press, George Banta Publishing.

Bakan, David. 1966. *The Duality of Human Existence: An Essay on Psychology and Religion.* Chicago: Rand McNally.

Baldwin, Roger. 1979. "Adult and Career Development: What Are the Implications for Faculty?" *Current Issues in Higher Education* 2: 13–20.

Baldwin, Roger G., and Jay L. Chronister. 2001. *Teaching without Tenure: Policies and Practices for a New Era.* Baltimore: Johns Hopkins University Press.

Bannerji, Himani. 1993. *Returning the Gaze: Essays on Racism, Feminism and Politics.* Toronto: Sister Vision Press.

Barker, Roger G. 1968. *Ecological Psychology: Concepts and Methods for Studying the Environment.* Palo Alto, CA: Stanford University Press.

Barrett, Michele. 1980. *Women's Oppression Today: Problems in Marxist Feminist Analysis.* London: Verso.

Bartky, Sandra Lee. 1990. "Foucault, Femininity, and the Modernization of Patriarchal Power." Pp. 63–82 in *Femininity and Domination: Studies in the Phenomology of Oppression,* ed. Sandra Lee Bartky. New York: Routledge.

Bashaw, Carolyn Terry. 1999. *"Stalwart Women": A Historical Analysis of Deans of Women in the South.* New York: Teachers College Press.

Basow, Susan A. 1994. "Student Ratings of Professors Are Not Gender Blind." Paper presented at the meeting of the Society of Teaching and Learning in Higher Education, Vancouver, British Columbia.

Bassett, Patricia. 1990. "The Minority Female in Postsecondary Administration: Challenges and Strategies." Pp. 238–245 in *Women in Higher Education: Changes and Challenges,* ed. Lynne B. Welch. New York: Praeger.

Baum, Christina D. 1992. *Feminist Thought in American Librarianship.* Jefferson, NC: McFarland.

Baxandall, Rosalyn, Linda Gordon, and Susan Reverby. 1995. *America's Working Women.* New York: W. W. Norton.

Baxter Magolda, Marcia B. 1992. *Knowing and Reasoning in College: Gender-Related Patterns in Students' Intellectual Development.* San Francisco: Jossey-Bass.

———. 1999. *Creating Contexts for Learning and Self-Authorship: Constructive-Developmental Pedagogy.* Nashville, TN: Vanderbilt University Press.

———. 2001. *Making Their Own Way: Narratives for Transforming Higher Education to Promote Self-Development.* Sterling, VA: Stylus Publishing.

———, ed. 2000. *Teaching to Promote Intellectual and Personal Maturity: Incorporating Students' Worldviews and Identities into the Learning Process. New Directions for Teaching and Learning.* Vol. 82. San Francisco: Jossey-Bass.

Beard, Mary Ritter. 1946. *Women as a Force in History: A Study in Traditions and Realities.* New York: Macmillan.

Beauvoir, Simone de. 1949. *The Second Sex.* Trans. and ed. Howard Parshley. New York: Alfred A. Knopf.

Becher, Tony. 1987. "The Disciplinary Shaping of the Profession." Pp. 271–303 in *The Academic Profession: National, Disciplinary, and Institutional Settings,* ed. Burton R. Clark. Berkeley: University of California Press.

Becker, Gary S. 1962. "Investment in Human Capital: A Theoretical Analysis." *Journal of Political Economy* 70, no. 5 (supplement): 9–49.

Belenky, Mary Field, Blythe McVicker Clinchy, Nancy Rule Goldberger, and Jill Mattuck Tarule. 1986. *Women's Ways of Knowing: The Development of Self, Voice, and Mind.* New York: Basic Books.

Belenky, Mary, Lynne A. Bond, and Jacqueline S. Weinstock. 1997. *A Tradition That Has No Name: Nurturing the Development of People, Families, and Communities.* New York: Basic Books.

Bellas, Marcia L. 1993. "Faculty Salaries: Still a Cost of Being Female?" *Social Science Quarterly* 74, no. 1: 62–75.

———. 1997. "The Scholarly Productivity of Academic Couples." Pp. 156–181 in *Academic Couples: Problems and Promises,* ed. Mariane A. Ferber and Jane W. Loeb. Chicago: University of Illinois Press.

———. 1999. "Emotional Labor in Academia: The Case of Professors." *The ANNALS of the American Academy of Political and Social Science* 56, no. 1: 96–110.

Bellas, Marcia L., and Robert K. Toutkoushian. 1999. "Faculty Time Allocations and Research Productivity: Gender, Race, and Family Effects." *Review of Higher Education* 22, no. 4: 367–390.

Benjamin, Lois, ed. 1997. *Black Women in the Academy: Promises and Perils.* Gainesville: University Press of Florida.

Benokraitis, Nijole V. 1998. "Working In the Ivory Basement: Subtle Sex Discrimination in Higher Education." Pp. 3–35 in *Career Strategies for Women in Academe: Arming Athena,* ed. Lynn H. Collins, Joan C. Chrisler, and Kathryn Quina. Thousand Oaks, CA: Sage.

Bensimón, Estela M., and Catherine Marshall. 1997. "Policy Analysis for Post-Secondary Education: Feminist and Critical Perspectives." Pp. 133–147 in *Feminist Critical Policy Analysis II: A Perspective from Post-Secondary Education,* ed. Catherine Marshall. London: Falmer Press.

Benson, Donna J., and Gregg E. Thomson. 1982. "Sexual Harassment on a University Campus: The Confluence of Authority Relation, Sexual Interest, and Gender Stratification." *Social Problems* 29: 236–251.

Berkner, Lutz, Laura Horn, and Michael Clune. 2000. *Descriptive Summary of 1995–96 Beginning Postsecondary Students: Three Years Later.* NCES 2000–154. Washington, DC: U.S. Department of Education.

Berlew, D., and D. T. Hall. 1966. "The Socialization of Managers: Effects of Expectations on Performance." *Administrative Science Quarterly* 11: 207–223.

Berman, Sanford. 1971. *Prejudices and Antipathies: A Tract on the LC Subject Headings Concerning People.* Metuchen, NJ: Scarecrow.

Bernard, Jessie. 1974. *Academic Women.* University Park: Pennsylvania State University Press.

Bernikow, Louise. 1974. *The World Split Open: Four Centuries of Women Poets in England and America.* New York: Vintage Books.

Berstein, Jared, Elizabeth C. McNichol, Lawrence Mishel, and Robert Zahradnik. 2000. *Pulling Apart: A State-by-State Analysis of Income Trends.* Washington, DC: Center on Budget and Policy Priorities.

Bickel, Janet, A. Gaibraith, and R. Quinnie. 1995. *Women in U.S. Academic Medicine: Statistics.* Washington, DC: Association of American Medical Colleges.

Bickel, Robert D., and Peter R. Lake. 1999. *The Rights and Responsibilities of the Modern University: Who Assumes the Risks of College Life?* Durham, NC: Carolina Academic Press.

Blackburn, Robert T., and Janet H. Lawrence. 1995. *Faculty at Work.* Baltimore: Johns Hopkins University Press.

Blair, Karen J. 1980. *The Clubwoman as Feminist: True Womanhood Redefined, 1868–1914.* New York: Holmes and Meier Publishers.

Blau, Francine D. 1998. "Trends in the Well-Being of American Women, 1970–1995." *Journal of American Economic Literature* 36 (March): 112–165.

Bloom, Alan. 1987. *The Closing of the American Mind: How Higher Education Has Failed Democracy and Impoverished the Souls of Today's Students.* New York: Simon and Schuster.

Bloom, Leslie. 1998. *Under the Sign of Hope: Feminist Methodology and Narrative Interpretation.* New York: State University of New York Press.

Bloom, Leslie R., and Petra Munro. 1995. "Conflicts of Selves: Nonunitary Subjectivity in Women's Administrators' Life History Narratives." Pp. 99–112 in *Life History and Narrative,* ed. J. Amos Hatch and Richard Wisnewski. Washington, DC: Falmer Press.

Bluestone, Naomi. 1978. "The Future Impact of Women on American Medicine." *American Journal of Public Health* 68: 760–763.

Blum, Debra E. 1991. "Environment Still Hostile to Women in Academe, New Evidence Indicates." *Chronicle of Higher Education,* October 9, A1, A20.

Blum, Lenore. 1991. "A Brief History of the Association for Women in Mathematics: The Residents' Perspectives." *Notices* 38 (September): 7.

Bohmer, Carol, and Andrea Parrot. 1993. *Sexual Assault on Campus.* New York: Lexington Books.

Boice, Robert. 1992. *The New Faculty Member: Supporting and Fostering Professional Development.* San Francisco: Jossey-Bass.

Bonta, Marcia. 1991. *Women in the Field: America's Pioneering Women Naturalists.* College Station: Texas A & M University Press.

Boris, Eileen, and Nupur Chaudhuri, eds. 1999. *Voices of Women Historians: The Personal, the Political, the Professional.* Bloomington: Indiana University Press.

Botstein, Leon. 1991. "The Undergraduate Curriculum and the Issue of Race: Opportunities and Obligations." Pp. 89–105 in *The Racial Crisis in American Higher Education,* ed. Philip G. Altbach and Kofi Lomotey. Albany: State University of New York Press.

Bouchier, Nancy B. 1998. "Let Us Take Care of Our Field: The National Association for Physical Education of College Women and World War II." *Journal of Sport History* 25, no. 1: 64–85.

Bowen, Howard R., and Jack H. Schuster. 1986. *American Professors: A National Resource Imperiled.* New York: Oxford University Press.

Bower, B. Forthcoming. "Community College Minority Faculty: Their Voices and Views." In *Teaching in the*

Community Colleges as a Profession, ed. Charles Outcalt. New Directions in Community Colleges. San Francisco: Jossey-Bass.

Bowker, Ardy. 1993. *Sisters in the Blood: The Education of Women in Native America.* Newton, MA: WEEA Publishing Center.

Boxer, Marilyn Jacoby. 1998. *When Women Ask the Questions: Creating Women's Studies in America.* Baltimore: Johns Hopkins University Press.

Boyer, Ernest. 1987. *College: The Undergraduate Experience in America.* New York: Harper and Row.

Boyer, Paul. 1995. "Tribal College of the Future." *Tribal College Journal* 3, no. 1: 8–17, 45.

Boys, Mary C. 1992. "Life on the Margins: Feminism and Religious Education." *Initiatives* 54, no. 4: 17–23.

Brabeck, Mary M. 1992. "Feminist and Catholic Values: The View from the Professional Schools." *Initiatives* 54, no. 4: 9–16.

Brady, Kristine L., and Richard M. Eisler. 1995. "Gender Bias in the College Classroom: A Critical Review of the Literature and Implications for Future Research." *Journal of Research and Development in Education* 29, no. 1: 9–19.

Braidotti, Rosi. 1994. *Nomadic Subjects.* New York: Routledge.

Brewer, Eileen M. 1987. *Nuns and the Education of American Catholic Women 1860–1920.* Chicago: Loyola University Press.

Brooks, Ann. 1997. *Academic Women.* Bristol, UK: Society for Research into Higher Education and Open University Press.

Brown, Cynthia F. 1992. *Leading Women: Leadership in American Women's Higher Education, 1880–1940.* Ann Arbor: University of Michigan Press.

Brown, Elaine. 1993. *A Taste of Power: A Black Women's Story.* New York: Anchor Books.

Brown, Lyn Mikel. 1998. *Raising Their Voices: The Politics of Girls' Anger.* Cambridge, MA: Harvard University Press.

Brown, Lyn Mikel, and Carol Gilligan. 1992. *Meeting at the Crossroads: Women's Psychology and Girls' Development.* Cambridge, MA: Harvard University Press.

Brown, M. Christopher, and Kassie Freeman. 2002. "Introduction." *The Review of Higher Education* 25, no.3: 237–240.

Brown, Marjorie M. 1985. *Philosophical Studies of Home Economics in the United States: Our Practical Intellectual Heritage.* Vol. 1. East Lansing: College of Human Ecology, Michigan State University.

Brown, Marjorie M., and Beatrice Paolucci. 1979. *Home Economics: A Definition.* Washington, DC: American Home Economics Association.

Brown, Mark Malloch, and Richard Jolly. 1999. "New Technologies and the Global Race for Knowledge." Pp. 57–76 in *Human Development Report.* New York: United Nations.

Brown v. Board of Education of Topeka, Kansas, 347 U.S. 483 (1954).

Brown v. Boston and Maine Railroad, 19 233 Mass. 502, 124 n.e. 322 (1933).

Brown-Collins, Alice R., and Deborah R. Sussewell. 1986. "The Afro-American Woman's Emerging Selves." *Journal of Black Psychology* 13: 1–11.

Brownmiller, Sara, and Ruth Dickstein. 1996. *An Index to Women's Studies Anthologies: Research across the Disciplines, 1985–1989.* New York: G. K. Hall.

Brubacher, John S., and Rudy Willis. 1976. *Higher Education in Transition: A History of American Colleges and*

Universities, 1636–1976. 3rd ed. New York: Harper and Row.

Buhle, Mary Jo. 2000. "Introduction." Pp. xv–xxvi in *The Politics of Women's Studies: Testimony from 30 Founding Mothers,* ed. Florence Howe. New York: The Feminist Press.

Bunch, Charlotte, and Sandra Pollack, eds. 1983. *Learning Our Way: Essays in Feminist Education.* Trumansburg, NY: Crossing Press.

Burns, Beverly H. 2000. *A Practical Guide to Title IX in Athletics: Law, Principles, and Practices.* Washington, DC: National Association of College and University Attorneys.

Busenberg, Bonnie E., and Daryl G. Smith. 1997. "Affirmative Action and Beyond: The Woman's Perspective." Pp. 149–180 in *Affirmative Action's Testament of Hope: Strategies for a New Era in Higher Education,* ed. Mildred Garcia. New York: State University of New York Press.

Butler, Johnella E., and John C. Walter, eds. 1991. *Transforming the Curriculum: Ethnic Studies and Women's Studies.* Albany: State University of New York Press.

Butler, Judith. 1990. *Gender Trouble: Feminism and the Subversion of Identity.* New York: Routledge.

Butler, Sandra S., and Luisa S. Deprez. Forthcoming. "Something Worth Fighting For: Higher Education for Women on Welfare." *Affilia.*

Cahill, Lisa S. 1992. "Women and Men Working Together in Jesuit Institutions of Higher Learning." *Initiatives* 54, no. 4: 25–33.

Cahn, Steven. 1993. *Affirmative Action and the University: A Philosophical Inquiry.* Philadelphia: Temple University Press.

Campbell, Katy. 1999. "Designs for Computer-Based Learning: Designing for Inclusivity." *Technology and Society: Gender and Computer Technologies* 18, no. 4: 28–34.

Cancian, Francesca. 1986. "The Feminization of Love." *Signs: Journal of Women in Culture and Society* 11: 692–709.

Canes, Brandice J. 1995. "Following in Her Footsteps? Faculty Gender Composition and Women's Choices of College Majors." *Industrial and Labor Relations Review* 48: 486–504.

Cannon, Kathleen. 1996. "Becoming Catholic Together." Pp. 43–54 in *Labors from the Heart: Mission and Ministry in a Catholic University,* ed. Mark L. Poorman. Notre Dame, IN: University of Notre Dame Press.

Capek, Mary Ellen, ed. 1987. *A Women's Thesaurus: An Index of Language Used to Describe and Locate Information by and about Women.* New York: Harper and Row.

Caplan, Paula J. 1994. *Lifting a Ton of Feathers: A Woman's Guide to Surviving in the Academic World.* Toronto: University of Toronto Press.

Carnegie Foundation for the Advancement of Teaching. 1990. "Women Faculty Excel as Campus Citizens." *Change* 22, no. 5 (September–October): 39–44.

Carnevale, Anthony, and Donna Desrochers. 1999. *Getting Down to Business: Matching Welfare Recipient's Skills to Jobs that Train.* Princeton, NJ: Educational Testing Service.

Carnevale, Anthony P., and Kathleen Sylvester. 2000. "As Welfare Rolls Shrink, Colleges Offer the Best Route to Good Jobs." *Chronicle of Higher Education,* February 18, B7.

Carnochan, William B. 1993. *The Battleground of the Curriculum.* Stanford, CA: Stanford University Press.

Carr v. St. John's, 12 N.Y.2d 802; 187 N.E.2d 18 (1962).

Carter, Jane O., ed. 1978. *Second Wind: A Program for Returning Women Students.* U.S. Department of

Education, Women's Educational Equity Act Program. Newton, MA: Education Development Center.

Carter, Patricia. 1992. "Social Status of Women Teachers." Pp. 127–138 in *The Teacher's Voice: A Social History of Teaching in Twentieth Century America,* ed. Richard J. Althenbaugh. London: Falmer Press.

Castro, Consuelo R. 2000. "Community College Faculty Satisfaction and the Faculty Union." Pp. 45–55 in *What Contributes to Job Satisfaction among Faculty and Staff,* ed. Linda S. Hagedorn. New Directions for Institutional Research, no. 105. San Francisco: Jossey-Bass.

Chafe, William. 1972. *The American Woman: Her Changing Social, Economic, and Political Roles, 1920–1970.* London: Oxford University Press.

Chafetz, Janet Saltzman, and Anthony Gary Dworkin. 1986. *Female Revolt: Women's Movements in World Historical Perspective.* Totowa, NJ: Rowman and Allanheld.

Chamberlain, Mariam K. 1988. *Women in Academe: Progress and Prospects.* New York: Russell Sage Foundation.

Chan, Sucheng C., and Ling-chi Wang. 1991. "Racism and the Model Minority: Asian-Americans in Higher Education." Pp. 43–67 in *The Racial Crisis in American Higher Education,* ed. Philip G. Altbach and Kofi Lomotey. Albany: State University of New York Press.

Chang, Mitchell, and Peter N. Kiang. 2002. "New Challenges of Representing Asian American Students in U.S. Higher Education." Pp. 137–158 in *The Racial Crisis in American Higher Education,* ed. William A Smith, Philip G. Altbach, and Kofi Lomotey. Albany: State University of New York Press.

Chávez, Rudolfo Chávez, and Raymond V. Padilla. 1995. "Introduction." Pp. 1–16 in *The Leaning Ivory Tower: Latino Professors in American Universities,* ed. Raymond V. Padilla and Rudolfo Chavez Chavez. Albany: State University of New York Press.

Cheney, Lynne. 1995. *Telling the Truth: Why Our Culture and Our Country Stopped Making Sense and What We Can Do about It.* New York: Simon and Schuster.

Cheng, Lucie, and Philip Q. Yang. 2000. "The 'Model Minority' Deconstructed." Pp. 459–482 in *Contemporary Asian America: A Multidisciplinary Reader,* ed. Min Zhou and James V. Gatewood. New York: New York University Press.

Cherny, Lynn, and Elizabeth Reba Weise, eds. 1996. *Wired Women: Gender and New Realities in Cyberspace.* Seattle, WA: Seal Press.

Chesler, Phyllis. 1973. *Women and Madness.* New York: Avon Books.

Chickering, Arthur W., and Associates, eds. 1981. *The Modern American College: Responding to the New Realities of Diverse Students and a Changing Society.* San Francisco: Jossey-Bass.

Chickering, Arthur W., and Linda Reisser. 1993. *Education and Identity.* 2nd ed. San Francisco: Jossey-Bass.

Children's Defense Fund. 1998. "Welfare to What? Early Findings on Family Hardship and Well-Being." http://publicagenda.org/issues/news.cfm?issue_type=welfare. Cited December 17, 2001.

Childs, Ruth Axman. 1980. "Gender Bias and Fairness." *ERIC Digest.* http://www.ed.gov/databases/ERIC_Digests/ed.328610.html. Cited April 30, 2001.

Chin, Gabriel. 1998. *Judicial Reaction to Affirmative Action, 1989–1997: Things Fall Apart.* Affirmative Action and the Constitution. Vol. 3. New York: Garland Publishers.

Chliwniak, Luba. 1997. *Higher Education Leadership: Analyzing the Gender Gap.*

ASHE-ERIC Higher Education Report 25, no. 4. Washington, DC: George Washington University.

Chodorow, Nancy. 1978. *The Reproduction of Mothering.* Berkeley: University of California Press.

Chronister, Jay L., Bruce M. Gansneder, Elizabeth P. Harper, and Roger G. Baldwin. 1997. "Full-Time Non-Tenure-Track Faculty." *NEA Higher Education Research Center Update* 3, no. 5: 1–4.

Cipres, Elizabeth L. 1999. "A Case Study of Perceived Characteristics and Life Events That Enabled Latinas to Become California Community College Presidents." *Dissertation Abstracts International* 61, no. 01A: 36.

City of Richmond v. J. A. Crosson Co., 488 U.S. 469 (1989).

Civil Rights Restoration Act, 20 U.S.C. § 1687 (1987).

Clark, Burton R. 1987 *The Academic Life: Small Worlds, Different Worlds.* Princeton, NJ: Carnegie Foundation for the Advancement of Teaching.

Clark, Roger D. 1992. "Multinational Corporate Investment and Women's Participation in Higher Education." *Sociology of Education* 65: 37–47.

Clark, Shirley M., and Mary Corcoran. 1986. "Perspectives on the Professional Socialization of Women Faculty: A Case of Accumulative Disadvantage?" *Journal of Higher Education* 57, no. 1: 20–43.

Clever, George. 1983. "The Native American Dean: Two Shirts in Conflict." *NASPA Journal* 21, no. 2: 60–63.

Clifford, Geraldine J. 1989. *Lone Voyagers: Academic Women in Coeducational Universities, 1870–1937.* New York: The Feminist Press.

Code, Lorraine. 1991. *What Can She Know? Feminist Theory and the Construction of Knowledge.* Ithaca, NY: Cornell University Press.

Cohee, Gail, Elizabeth Daumer, Theresa D. Kemp, Paula M. Krebs, Sue A. Lafky, and Sandra Runzo, eds. 1998. *The Feminist Teacher Anthology: Pedagogies and Classroom Strategies.* New York: Teachers College Press.

Cohen, Arthur M., and Florence B. Brawer. 1996. *The American Community College.* San Francisco: Jossey-Bass.

Cohen, Rosetta Marantz. 1998. "Class Consciousness and Its Consequences: The Impact of an Elite Education on Mature, Working-Class Women." *American Educational Research Journal* 35, no. 3: 353–375.

Cohen v. Brown University, 101 F.3d 155, First Circuit (1996).

Cohen v. San Bernadino Valley College, 92 F.3d 968, Ninth Circuit (1996).

Cole, Elsa Kircher, ed. 1997. *Sexual Harassment on Campus: A Legal Compendium.* Washington, DC: National Association of College and University Attorneys.

Cole, Elsa Kircher, and Thomas P. Hustoles. 1997. *How to Conduct a Sexual Harassment Investigation.* Washington, DC: National Association of College and University Attorneys.

College and University Professional Association. 2000. *2000–01 Administrative Compensation Survey.* Washington, DC: CUPA-HR.

Collins, LaVerne Vines. 1997. "Census Facts for Native American Month." http://www.census.gov/Press-Release/fs97-11.html. Cited October 11, 2001.

Collins, Lynn H. 1998. "Competition and Contact: The Dynamics behind Resistance to Affirmative Action in Academe." Pp. 45–74 in *Career Strategies for Women in Academe: Arming Athena,* ed. Lynn H. Collins, Joan C. Chrisler, and Kathryn Quina. Thousand Oaks, CA: Sage.

Collins, Patricia Hill. 1991. *Black Feminist Thought: Knowledge,*

Consciousness, and the Politics of Empowerment. New York: Routledge.
Congressional Committee on the Advancement of Women and Minorities in Science, Engineering, and Technology Development. 2000. *Land of Plenty: Diversity as America's Competitive Edge in Science, Engineering and Technology.* Washington, DC: U.S. Government Printing Office.
Cook, Judith A., and Mary M. Fonow. 1990. "Knowledge and Women's Interests: Issues of Epistemology and Methodology in Feminist Sociological Research." Pp. 69–93 in *Feminist Research Methods: Exemplary Readings in the Social Sciences,* ed. Joyce M. Nielsen. Boulder, CO: Westview Press.
Cook-Lynn, Elizabeth. 1996. *Why I Can't Read Wallace Stegner and Other Essays: A Tribal Voice.* Madison: University of Wisconsin Press.
Council of Graduate Schools. 2001. *Graduate Enrollment and Degrees, 1986 to 1998.* http://www.cgsnet.org/VirtualCenterResearch/graduateenrollment.htm. Cited June 12, 2002.
Cravey, Pamela J. 1991. "Occupational Role Identity of Women Academic Librarians." *College and Research Libraries* 52: 150–164.
Creamer, Elizabeth G. 1998. *Assessing Faculty Publication Productivity: Issues of Equity.* ASHE-ERIC Higher Education Report 26, no. 2. Washington, DC: George Washington University.
Cress, Christine M. 1999. "The Impact of Campus Climate on Students' Cognitive and Affective Development." Ph.D. diss., University of California, Los Angeles.
Cress, Christine, Myra Dinnerstein, Naomi J. Miller, and Jeni Hart. 2001. *The Millennium Project: Summary Report.* Tucson: University of Arizona, Office of the President.
Cronkite, Ruth, Rudolf H. Moos, and John Finney. 1983. "The Context of Adaptation: An Integrated Perspective on Community and Treatment Environments." Pp. 189–215 in *Ecological Models in Clinical and Community Mental Health,* ed. William A. O'Connor and Bernard Lubin. New York: Wiley.
Crosby, Faye J., and Cheryl Van DeVeer. 2000. *Sex, Race and Merit: Debating Affirmative Action in Education and Employment.* Ann Arbor: University of Michigan Press.
Cross, William T. 1991. "Pathway to the Professoriate: The American Indian Faculty Pipeline." *Journal of American Indian Education* 30: 13–24.
Crouse, James, and Dale Trusheim. 1988. *The Case against the SAT.* Chicago: University of Chicago Press.
Crow Dog, Mary, with Richard Erdoes. 1991. *Lakota Woman.* New York: Harper Perennial.
Cruikshank, Margaret, ed. 1982. *Lesbian Studies: Present and Future.* Old Westbury, NY: The Feminist Press.
Culley, Margo, and Catherine Portuges, eds. 1985. *Gendered Subjects: The Dynamics of Feminist Teaching.* London: Routledge and Kegan Paul.
Curry, Barbara K. 2000. *Women in Power: Pathways to Leadership in Education.* New York: Teachers College Press.
Curry, George, ed. 1996. *The Affirmative Action Debate.* Reading, MA: Addison-Wesley.
Dakota Roundtable III. 1996. *Dakota Roundtable III: A Report on the Status of Young Native American Women in the Aberdeen Area.* Aberdeen, SD: Native American Women's Health Education Resource Center.
Daley, Barbara J. 2000. "Learning Human Resource Development through Electronic Discussion." Pp. 25–31 in *Academy of Human Resource Development Conference Proceedings,* ed. K. Peter Kuchinke. Raleigh-Durham,

NC: Academy of Human Resource Development.

Daly, Mary. 1984. *Pure Lust: Elemental Feminist Philosophy.* Boston: Beacon Press.

Darren, Alison. 2000. *Lesbian Film Guide.* New York: Cassell.

D'Augelli, Anthony R. 1989. "Lesbians' and Gay Men's Experiences of Discrimination and Harassment in a University Community." *American Journal of Community Psychology* 17: 317–321.

Davis, Angela Y. 1981. *Women, Race and Class.* New York: Random House.

Davis, Cinda-Sue, Angela B. Ginorio, Carol S. Hollenshead, Barbara B. Lazarus, and Paula M. Rayman, eds. 1996. *The Equity Equation: Fostering the Advancement of Women in the Sciences, Mathematics, and Engineering.* San Francisco: Jossey-Bass.

Davis, Rebecca Harding. 1972. *Life in the Iron Mills.* Old Westbury, NY: The Feminist Press.

Davis v. Monroe County Board of Education, 119 Sup. Ct. 1661 (1999).

de la Luz Reyes, Maria, and John J. Halcon. 1991. "Practices of the Academy: Barriers to Access for Chicano Academics." Pp. 167–186 in *The Racial Crisis in American Higher Education,* ed. Philip G. Altbach and Kofi Lomotey. Albany: State University of New York Press.

DeAngelis, Catherine D., ed. 1999. *The Johns Hopkins University School of Medicine Curriculum for the Twenty-First Century.* Baltimore: Johns Hopkins University Press.

Deaux, Kay. 1985. "Sex and Gender." *Annual Review of Psychology* 36: 49–81.

Deaux, Kay, and Marianne LaFrance. 1998. "Gender." Pp. 788–827 in *The Handbook of Social Psychology,* ed. Daniel T. Gilbert, Susan T. Fiske, and Gardner Lindzey. 4th ed. Vol. 1. Boston: McGraw-Hill.

Deci, Edward, Tim Kasser, and Richard Ryan. 1997. "Self-Determined Teaching: Opportunities and Obstacles." Pp. 57–71 in *Teaching Well and Liking It: Motivating Faculty to Teach Effectively,* ed. James L. Bess. Baltimore: Johns Hopkins University Press.

Deem, Rosemary, and Jenny Ozga. 1997. "Women Managing for Diversity in a Postmodern World." Pp. 25–40 in *Feminist Critical Policy Analysis: A Perspective from Post-Secondary Education,* vol. 2, ed. Catherine Marshall. Washington, DC: Falmer Press.

Dei, George S. 1994. "Afrocentricity: A Cornerstone of Pedagogy." *Anthropology and Education Quarterly* 25: 3–28.

Delgado Bernal, Dolores. 1998. "Using a Chicana Feminist Epistemology in Educational Research." *Harvard Educational Review* 68, no. 4: 555–581.

Delta Sigma Theta, www.deltasigmatheta.org. Cited June 12, 2002.

Democratic Leadership Committees. http://www.senate.gov/~dpc/events/970618/970618.html. Cited December 4, 2001.

DeVane, William C. 1965. *Higher Education in Twentieth-Century America.* Cambridge, MA: Harvard University Press.

Dewey, John. 1956. *The Child and the Curriculum* and *The School and the Society.* 1900 and 1915. Reprint (2 vols. in 1), Chicago: University of Chicago Press.

Deyoung, Alan J. 1989. *Economics and American Education: A Historical and Critical Overview of the Impact of Economic Theories on Schooling in the United States.* White Plains, NY: Longman.

Dickstein, Leah J. 1996. "Overview of Women Physicians in the United

States." Pp. 3–10 in *Women in Medical Education: An Anthology of Experience,* ed. Delese Ware. Albany: State University of New York Press.

Directory of Curriculum Transformation Projects and Activities in the U.S. 1997. Baltimore: National Center for Curriculum Transformation Resources on Women, Towson State University.

Dixon v. Alabama State Board of Education, 294 F.2d 150 (5th Cir. 1961).

Dowd, Alicia C. 1999. "Understanding Women's Career Choices Using Taylor's Concept of Authenticity." Paper presented at the Annual Convention of the American Education Research Association, Montreal, Quebec, Canada. Dialog ERIC, ED434291, April 19–23.

Downey, Gary Lee, and Juan C. Lucena. 1997. "Engineering Selves: Hiring into a Contested Field of Education." Pp. 117–141 in *Cyborgs and Citadels: Anthropological Interventions in Emerging Sciences and Technologies,* ed. Gary Lee Downey and Joseph Dumit. Santa Fe, NM: School of American Research Press.

Drew, Todd L., and Gerald G. Work. 1998. "Gender-Based Differences in Perception of Experiences in Higher Education: Gaining a Broader Perspective." *Journal of Higher Education* 69 (September–October): 542–555.

Drug-Free Schools and Communities Act, 20 U.S.C. § 1102i.

Duin, Ann Hill, Linda L. Baer, and Doreen Starke-Meyerring. 2001. *Partnering in the Learning Marketspace.* EDUCAUSE New Directions for Institutional Research, vol. 4. San Francisco: Jossey-Bass, PricewaterhouseCoopers.

Dziech, Billie Wright, and Linda Weiner. 1990. *The Lecherous Professor: Sexual Harassment on Campus.* 2d ed. Urbana: University of Illinois Press.

Eagly, Alice H. 1987. *Sex Differences in Social Behavior. A Social Role Interpretation.* Hillsdale, NJ: Erlbaum.

———. 1995. "The Science and Politics of Comparing Women and Men." *American Psychologist* 50, no. 3: 145–171.

Eagly, Alice H., and Blair T. Johnson. 1990. "Gender and Leadership Style: A Meta-Analysis." *Psychological Bulletin* 108, no. 2: 233–256.

Eagly, Alice H., and Steven J. Karau. 1991. "Gender and the Emergence of Leaders: A Meta-Analysis." *Journal of Personality and Social Psychology* 60, no. 5: 685–710.

Eagly, Alice H., Steven J. Karau, and Mona G. Makhijani. 1995. "Gender and the Effectiveness of Leaders: A Meta-Analysis." *Psychological Bulletin* 117, no. 1: 125–145.

Eagly, Alice H., Mona G. Makhijani, and Bruce G. Klonsky. 1992. "Gender and the Evaluation of Leaders: A Meta-Analysis." *Psychological Bulletin* 111, no. 1: 3–22.

East, Marjorie. 1982. *Caroline Hunt: Philosopher for Home Economics.* University Park: Division of Occupational and Vocational Studies, Pennsylvania State University.

Economic Policy Institute. "Hourly Wages of Low-Wage Workers by State, 1979–1996," and "Low-Wage Labor Market Indicators by Region, 1979–1996." http:www.epinet.org/datazone. Cited January 27, 2002.

Edwards, Rosalind. 1993. *Mature Women Students: Separating or Connecting Family and Education.* London: Taylor and Francis.

Eggins, Heather, ed. 1997. *Women as Leaders and Managers in Higher Education.* Buckingham, UK: Society for Research into Higher Education and Open University Press.

Eisen, Vitka, and Irene Hall, eds. 1996. "Lesbian, Gay, Bisexual and Transgender

People in Education." *Harvard Educational Review* 66, no. 2 (special issue).

Eisenhart, Margaret A., and Elizabeth Finkel. 1998. *Women's Science: Learning and Succeeding from the Margins.* Chicago: University of Chicago Press.

Elam, Ada M., ed. 1989. *The Status of Blacks in Higher Education.* New York: University Press of America.

Eliason, Michele J. 1996. "A Survey of the Campus Climate for Lesbian, Gay, and Bisexual University Members." *Journal of Psychology and Human Sexuality* 8, no. 4: 39–58.

Ellsworth, Elizabeth. 1989. "Why Doesn't This Feel Empowering? Working through the Repressive Myths of Critical Pedagogy." *Harvard Educational Review* 59, no. 4: 297–324.

Enarson, Cam, and Frederic Burg. 1992. "An Overview of Reform Initiatives in Medical Education: 1906 through 1992." *Journal of the American Medical Association* 268: 1141–1143.

Epstein, Debbie, ed. 1994. *Challenging Lesbian and Gay Inequalities in Education.* Philadelphia: Open University Press.

Epstein, Debbie, Jannette Elwood, Valerie Hey, and Janet Maw, eds. 1998. *Failing Boys? Issues in Gender and Achievement.* Philadelphia: Open University Press.

Erickson, Chris D., and Ester R. Rodriguez. 1999. "Indiana Jane and the Temples of Doom: Recommendations for Enhancing Women and Racial/Ethnic Faculty's Success in Academia." *Innovative Higher Education* 24, no. 2: 149–168.

Erikson, Erik. 1968. *Identity, Youth, and Crisis.* New York: W. W. Norton

Escobedo, Theresa H. 1980. "Are Hispanic Women in Higher Education the Non-existent Minority?" *Educational Researcher* 9 (October): 7–11.

Escueta, Eugenia, and Eileen O'Brien. 1991. "Asian Americans in Higher Education: Trends and Issues." *Research Briefs* 2, no. 4: 1–11.

———. 1995. "Asian Americans in Higher Education: Trends and Issues." Pp. 259–272 in *The Asian American Educational Experience,* ed. Don T. Nakanishi and Tina Y. Nishida. New York: Routledge.

Espinoza, Dionne. 2001. "Revolutionary Sisters": Women's Solidarity and Collective Identification among Chicana Brown Berets in East Los Angeles, 1967–1970." *Aztlán: A Journal of Chicano Studies* 26 no. 1: 17–58.

Evans, Clarice. 2000. "Facts about Female Faculty: 1999–00 AAUP Faculty Compensation Survey." American Association of University Professors. http://www.aaup.org/wsalrep.htm. Cited June 15, 2002.

Evans, Nancy J., Deanna S. Forney, and Florence Guido-Dibrito. 1998. *Student Development in College: Theory, Research, and Practice.* San Francisco: Jossey-Bass.

Eyler, Janet, and Dwight E. Giles, Jr. 1999. *Where's the Learning in Service-Learning?* San Francisco: Jossey-Bass.

Faderman, Lillian. 1991. *Odd Girls and Twilight Lovers: A History of Lesbian Life in Twentieth-Century America.* New York: Penguin Books.

FairTest. "Gender Bias in College Admissions Test." http://www.fairtest.org/examarts/spring1995/nmerit.htm. Cited June 10, 2002.

Falbo, Toni, and Leticia Anne Peplau. 1980. "Power Strategies in Intimate Relationships." *Journal of Personality and Social Psychology* 38: 618–628.

Family Educational Rights and Privacy Act of 1974, 20 U.S.C. § 1232g.

Faragher, John M., and Florence Howe, eds. 1988. *Women and Higher Education in American History.* New York: W. W. Norton.

Fass, Paula S. 1997. "The Female Paradox: Higher Education for Women, 1945–1963." Pp. 699–723 in *The History of Higher Education,* ed. Lester F. Goodchild and Harold Wechsler. Needham Heights, MA: Simon and Schuster.

Feagin, Joe R., Hernan Vera, and Mikitah Imani. 1996. *The Agony of Education: Black Students at White Colleges and Universities.* New York: Routledge.

Feinberg, Walter. 1998. *On Higher Ground: Education and the Case for Affirmative Action.* New York: Teachers College Press.

Feldman, Kenneth A. 1992. "College Student Views of Male and Female College Teachers. Part II—Evidence From Students' Evaluations of Their Classroom Teachers." *Research in Higher Education* 33, no. 4: 415–474.

Ferber, Marianne A., and Jane W. Loeb, eds. 1997. *Academic Couples: Problems and Promises.* Chicago: University of Illinois Press.

Ferdman, Bernard M. 1990. "Literacy and Cultural Identity." *Harvard Educational Review* 60, no. 2: 181–204.

Ferguson, Moira. 1985. *First Feminists: British Women Writers, 1578–1799.* Bloomington: Indiana University Press.

Fialkoff, Francine. 1993. "We've Been 'LC-Centric' Too Long." *Library Journal* 118: 108.

Finkel, Susan Kolker, Steven Olswang, and N. She. 1994. "Childbirth, Tenure, and Promotion for Women Faculty." *Review of Higher Education* 17: 259–270.

Finkelstein, Martin J. 1984. *The American Academic Profession: A Synthesis of Social Scientific Inquiry since World War II.* Columbus: Ohio State University.

Finkelstein, Martin J., Robert K. Seal, and Jack H. Schuster. 1998. *The New Academic Generation: A Profession in Transformation.* Baltimore: Johns Hopkins University Press.

Finnegan, Dorothy E., David Webster, and Zelda F. Gamson. 1996. *Faculty and Faculty Issues in Colleges and Universities.* 2nd ed. Needham Heights, MA: Simon and Schuster Custom Publishing.

Finney, Johanna. 1998. "Welfare Reform and Post-Secondary Education: Research and Policy Update." *IWPR Welfare Reform Network News* 2, no. 1 (April): 2.

Firebaugh, Glenn, and Brian Harley. 1995. "Trends in Job Satisfaction in the United States by Race, Gender, and Type of Occupation." *Research in the Sociology of Work* 5: 87–104.

Fischer, Nancy A., and Sharon D. Peters. 1979. "The Cost for Women in Graduate and Professional Schools: More Than a Question of Money." Paper presented at the Annual Meeting of the Mid-South Sociological Association, Memphis, TN.

Fischman, Gusavo, and Nelly Stromquist. 2000. "Globalization and Higher Education in Developing Countries." Pp. 501–521 in *Higher Education: Handbook of Theory and Research,* ed. John C. Smart. Vol. 15. New York: Agathon Press.

Fisher, Berenice. 2001. *No Angel in the Classroom: Teaching through Feminist Discourse.* New York: Rowman and Littlefield.

Fisher, James L., and James V. Koch. 1996. *Presidential Leadership: Making a Difference.* Washington, DC: American Council on Education and Oryx Press.

Fitzgerald, John. 1997. *Working Hard, Falling Behind: A Report on the Maine Working Parents Survey.* Augusta, ME: Maine Center for Economic Policy.

Fitzgerald, Louise F., Lauren M. Weitzman, Yael Gold, and Mimi Ormerod. 1998. "Academic Harassment: Sex and Denial in Scholarly Garb." *Psychology of Women* 12: 329–340.

Flax, Jane. 1996. "Women Do Theory." Pp. 17–20 in *Multicultural Experiences, Multicultural Theories,* ed. Mary F. Rogers. 1979. Reprint, New York: McGraw-Hill.

Fleming, Jacqueline. 1984. *Blacks in College: A Comparative Study of Students' Success in Black and in White Institutions.* San Francisco: Jossey-Bass.

Flexner, Eleanor. 1975. *Century of Struggle: The Woman's Rights Movement in the United States.* Rev. ed. Cambridge, MA: Harvard University Press.

Flynn, Elizabeth A., J. F. Flynn, Nancy Grimm, and T. Lockhart. 1986. "The Part-Time Problem: Four Voices." *Academe* 72, no. 1: 12–18.

Foner, Philip, S. 1982. *Women and the American Labor Movement.* New York: Free Press.

Fonow, Mary M., and Judith A. Cook. 1991. "Back to the Future: A Look at the Second Wave of Feminist Epistemology and Methodology." Pp. 1–15 in *Beyond Methodology: Feminist Scholarship as Lived Research,* ed. M. M. Fonow and J. A. Cook. Bloomington: Indiana University Press.

Forest, James J. F., and Kevin Kinser, eds. 2002. *Higher Education in the United States: An Encyclopedia.* Santa Barbara, CA: ABC-CLIO.

Foster, Jeannette H. 1985. *Sex Variant Women in Literature.* Naiad Press.

Foster, William. 1989. "Toward a Critical Practice of Leadership." Pp. 39–62 in *Critical Perspectives on Educational Leadership,* ed. J. Smyth. London: Falmer Press.

Foster, William T. 1911. *Administration of the College Curriculum.* New York: Houghton Mifflin.

Fox, Mary Frank. 1983. "Publication Productivity among Scientists: A Critical Review." *Social Studies of Science* 13: 285–305.

———. 1985. "Publication, Performance, and Reward in Science and Scholarship." Pp. 255–282 in *Higher Education: Handbook of Theory and Research,* ed. John C. Smart. New York: Agathon Press.

———. 1996. "Publication, Performance, and Reward in Science and Scholarship." Pp. 408–428 in *Faculty and Faculty Issues in Colleges and Universities,* ed. Dorothy E. Finnegan, David Webster, and Zelda F. Gamson. Needham Heights, MA: Simon and Schuster.

Franklin v. Gwinett County, 112 S. Ct. 1028 (1991)

Freeman, Alan. 1990. "Antidiscrimination Law: The View from 1989." *Tulane University Law Review* 64: 1407.

Freeman, Jo. 1973. "Women on the Move: Roots of Revolt." Pp. 1–32 in *Academic Women on the Move,* ed. Alice S. Rossi and Ann Claderwood. New York: Russell Sage Foundation.

Freire, Paulo. 1993. *Pedagogy of the Oppressed.* 1970. Reprint, New York: Continuum.

"Freshman-Cohort Graduation Rates." 2001. http://www.ncaa.org/grad-rates/2001/d1/aggregate/d1.html. Cited June 23, 2002.

Friedan, Betty. 1963. *The Feminine Mystique.* New York: W. W. Norton.

Friedman, Ellen, Wendy Kolmar, Charley Flint, and Paula Rothenberg. 1996. *Creating an Inclusive College Curriculum: A Teaching Sourcebook from the New Jersey Project.* New York: Teachers College Press.

Fritsche, JoAnn. 1984. *Toward Excellence and Equity: The Scholarship on Women as a Catalyst for Change in the University.* Orono: University of Maine Press.

Frye, John H. 1995. "Women in the Two-Year College, 1900 to 1970." Pp. 5–14 in *Gender and Power in the Community College,* ed. Barbara K. Townsend. New

Directions for Community Colleges no. 89. San Francisco: Jossey-Bass.

Frymer, Tikva S. 2000. "Memories of a 'First Woman.'" Pp. 135–146 in *Wise Women: Reflections of Teachers at Midlife,* ed. Phyllis R. Freeman and Jan Z. Schmidt. New York: Routledge.

Fuhrmann, Barbara S. 1997. "Philosophies and Aims." Pp. 86–99 in *Handbook of the Undergraduate Curriculum,* ed. Jerry G. Gaff and James L. Ratcliff. San Francisco: Jossey-Bass.

"The Future: Women Get More Degrees than Man Except at Doctoral Level." 1997. *About Women on Campus* 6, no. 2 (Spring): 7.

Gallin, Alice. 1999. "Neylan Colleges: Working toward the Twenty-First Century." *ACCU Current Issues in Catholic Higher Education* 19, no. 2: 63–72.

Gamble, Sarah, ed. 2000. *The Routledge Critical Dictionary of Feminism and Postfeminism.* New York: Routledge.

Gandara, Patricia. 1982. "Passing through the Eye of the Needle: High-Achieving Chicanas." *Hispanic Journal of Behavioral Sciences* 4: 167–179.

———. 1995. *Over the Ivy Walls: The Educational Mobility of Low-Income Chicanos.* Albany: State University of New York Press.

Gander, James P. 1999 "Faculty Gender Effects on Academic Research and Teaching." *Research in Higher Education* 40, no. 2: 171–184.

Gangone, Lynn M. 1999. "Navigating Turbulence: A Case Study of a Voluntary Higher Education Association." Ph.D. diss., Teachers College, Columbia University.

Ganguly, Keya. 1992. "Accounting for Others: Feminism and Representation." Pp. 60–79 in *Women Making Meaning: New Feminist Directions in Communication,* ed. Lana F. Rakow. New York: Routledge.

Gansneder, Bruce M., Elizabeth P. Harper, and Roger G. Baldwin. 2001. "Who Are the Full-Time Non-Tenure-Track Faculty?" In *Teaching without Tenure: Policies and Practices for a New Era,* ed. Roger G. Baldwin and Jay L. Chronister. Baltimore: Johns Hopkins University Press.

Garber, Linda, ed. 1994. *Tilting the Tower: Lesbians Teaching Queer Subjects.* New York: Routledge.

Garcia, Mildred, ed. 1997. *Affirmative Action: Testament for Hope: Strategies for a New Era in Higher Education.* Albany: State University of New York Press.

Gardner, Louis E., and Gary K. Leak. 1994. "Characteristics and Correlates of Teaching Anxiety among College Psychology Teachers." *Teaching of Psychology* 21, no. 1: 28–32.

Garza, Hisauro. 1993. "Second-Class Academics: Chicano/Latino Faculty in U.S. Universities." Pp. 33–41 in *Building a Diverse Faculty,* ed. Joanne Gainen and Robert Boice. San Francisco: Jossey-Bass.

Gebser v. Lago Vista Independent School District, 118 Sup. Ct. 1989 (1998).

"Gender Equity in College Sports." *Chronicle of Higher Education.* http://www.chronicle.com/stats/genderequity. Cited June 15, 2002.

Gerald, Debra E., and William J. Hussar. 2000. *Projections for Educational Statistics.* Washington, DC: U.S. Department of Education.

Gerber, Ellen. 1975. "The Controlled Development of Collegiate Sport for Women, 1923–1936." *Journal of Sport History* 2, no. 1: 1–28.

Gerritsen Collection of Women's History. 1975. Glen Rock, NJ: Microfilming Corporation of America, microfiche and microfilm.

Gibson, James L., John M. Ivancevich, and James H. Donnelly. 1994.

Organizations: Behavior, Structure, Process. 8th ed. Burr Ridge, Il: Irwin.

Giddens, Anthony. 1984. *The Constitution of Society.* Berkeley: University of California Press.

Giddings, Paula. 1988. *In Search of Sisterhood: Delta Sigma Theta and the Challenge of the Black Sorority Movement.* New York: William Morrow.

Gilligan, Carol. 1982. *In a Different Voice: Psychological Theory and Women's Development.* Cambridge, MA: Harvard University Press.

Gilligan, Carol, Jane Victoria Ward, and Jill Mclean Taylor, eds. 1988. *Mapping the Moral Domain.* Cambridge, MA: Harvard University Press.

Gimenez, Martha E. 1990. "'Latino/Hispanic'—Who Needs a Name? The Case Against a Standardized Terminology." *Journal of Health Services* 19, no. 3: 557–571.

Ginorio, Angela, and Michelle Huston. 2001. *Sí Se Puede! Yes We Can: Latinas in Education Report.* Washington, DC: American Association of University Women Educational Foundation.

Glaser, Barney, and Anselm Strauss. 1967. *The Discovery of Grounded Theory: Strategies for Qualitative Research.* New York: Aldine de Gruyter.

Glazer, Judith S., Estela M. Bensimón, and Barbara K. Townsend, eds. 1993. *Women in Higher Education: A Feminist Perspective.* Association for the Study of Higher Education Reader Series. Needham Heights, MA: Ginn Press.

Glazer-Raymo, Judith. 1999. *Shattering the Myths: Women in Academe.* Baltimore: Johns Hopkins University Press.

Gleason, Philip. 1995. *Contending with Modernity: Catholic Higher Education in the Twentieth Century.* New York: Oxford University Press.

Gloria, Alberta M. 1997. "Chicana Academic Persistence: Creating a University-Based Community." *Education and Urban Society* 30: 107–121.

Glyn, Andrew, and Wiemer Salverda. 1999. "Employment Inequalities." Working Paper no. 293. Annandale-on-the-Hudson, NY: Levy Economics Institute at Bard College.

Gmelch, Sharon Bohn. 1998. *Gender on Campus: Issues for College Women.* New Brunswick, NJ: Rutgers University Press.

Goldberg, Julie L., and William E. Sedlacek. 1995. *Graduate Women in Engineering.*College Park: University of Maryland, College Park Counseling Center.

Goldberger, Nancy, Jill Tarule, Blythe Clinchy, and Mary Belenky, eds. 1996. *Knowledge, Difference, and Power: Essays Inspired By Women's Ways of Knowing.* New York: Basic Books.

Gonzales, Judith T. 1988. "Dilemmas of the High-Achieving Chicana: The Double-Bind Factor in Male/Female Relationships." *Sex Roles: A Journal of Research* 18, nos. 7–8: 367–380.

Goodlad, John I., Roger Soder, and Kenneth A. Sirotnik, eds. 1990. *Places Where Teachers Are Taught.* San Francisco: Jossey-Bass.

Goodman, Diane J. 1990. "African-American Women's Voices: Expanding Theories of Women's Development." *Sage* 7: 3–14.

Gordon, Edmund T., Edmund W. Gordon, and Jessica G. Nembhard. 1994. "Disproportionate Involvement of Black Males in Violence and Violent Behaviors: Social Science Literature Concerning African American Men." *Journal of Negro Education* 63, no. 4: 508–531.

Gordon, Linda. 1976. *Woman's Body, Woman's Right: A Social History of Birth Control in America.* New York: Grossman.

Gordon, Lynn D. 1990. *Gender and Higher Education in the Progressive Era.* New Haven, CT: Yale University Press.

———. 1997. "From Seminary to University: An Overview of Women's Higher Education, 1870–1920." Pp. 481–482 in *The History of Higher Education,* ed. Lester F. Goodchild and Harold Wechsler. Needham Heights, MA: Simon and Schuster.

Gorena, Minerva. 1996. "Hispanic Women in Higher Education Administration: Factors That Positively Influence or Hinder Advancement to Leadership Positions." Paper presented at the Annual Meeting of the American Educational Research Association, New York, NY.

Gott v. Berea College, 156 Ky. 376, 161 S.W. 204 (1913).

Gough, Cal, and Ellen Greenblatt, eds. 1990. *Gay and Lesbian Library Service.* Jefferson, NC: McFarland.

Gouldner, Alvin W. 1957 "Cosmopolitans and Locals: Toward an Analysis of Latent Social Roles," *Administrative Science Quarterly* 2: 281–307.

Graduate Women in Science. http://www.gwis.org. Cited June 14, 2002.

Graham, Patricia Albjerg. 1993. "Expansion and Exclusion: A History of Women in American Higher Education." Pp. 218–232 in *History of Women in the United States.* Vol. 12, *Education,* ed. Nancy F. Cott. Munich: K. G. Saur.

Grant, Judith. 1993. *Fundamental Feminism: Contesting the Core Concepts of Feminist Theory.* New York: Routledge.

Grassmuck, Karen. 1991. "Colleges Hired More Non-Teaching Staff than Other Employees throughout the 80s." *Chronicle of Higher Education,* August 14, A22.

Grayson, Paul A., and Kate Cauley, eds. 1989. *College Psychotherapy.* New York: Guilford Press.

Green, Madeleine F., ed. 1989. *Minorities on Campus: A Handbook for Enhancing Diversity.* Washington, DC: American Council on Education.

Greenberg, Mark, Julie Strawn, and Lisa Plimpton. 2000. "State Opportunities to Provide Access to Postsecondary Education Under TANF." Washington, DC: Center for Law and Social Policy.

Greenberg, Michael, and Seymour Zenchelsky. 1993. "Private Bias and Public Responsibility: Anti-Semitism at Rutgers in the 1920s and 1930s." *History of Education Quarterly* 33 (Fall): 295–319.

Gregory, Sheila T. 1995. *Black Women in the Academy: The Secrets to Success and Achievement.* New York: University Press of America.

Grimké, Sarah. 1988 [1837]. "Letters on the Equality of the Sexes and the Condition of Women." Pp. 31–103 in *Letters on the Equality of the Sexes and Other Essays,* edited and with an introduction by Elizabeth Ann Bartlett. New Haven, CT: Yale University Press.

Grinstein, Louise, and Paul Campbell. 1987. *Women of Mathematics: A Biobibliographic Sourcebook.* New York: Greenwood Press.

Grove City College v. Bell, 465 U.S. 555 (1984).

Guido-DiBrito, Florence, and Alicia F. Chávez. 2002. "Student Development Theory." Pp. 596–603 in *Higher Education in the United States: An Encyclopedia,* ed. James F. Forest and Kevin Kinser. Santa Barbara, CA: ABC-CLIO.

Gumport, Patricia, and Brian Pusser. 1995. "A Case of Bureaucratic Accretion: Context and Consequences." *Journal of Higher Education* 66, no. 5: 493–520.

Gurock, Jeffrey S. 1988. *The Men and Women of Yeshiva: Higher Education, Orthodoxy, and American Judaism.* New York: Columbia University Press.

Habu, Toshi. 2000. "The Irony of Globalization: The Experience of Japanese Women in British Higher Education." *Higher Education* 39, no. 1: 43–66.

Haffer v. Temple University, 678 F. Supp. 517, E.D. Pa. (1987).

Hagedorn, Linda S. 1996. "Wage Equity and Female Faculty Job Satisfaction: The Role of Wage Differentials in a Job Satisfaction Causal Model." *Research in Higher Education* 37, no. 5: 569–598.

Hagedorn, Linda S., and Berta V. Laden. Forthcoming. "Feeling a Bit Chilly? Exploring the Climate for Female Community College Faculty." In *Teaching in the Community Colleges as a Profession,* ed. Charles Outcalt. New Directions in Community Colleges. San Francisco: Jossey-Bass.

Hall, Christine I. I. 1980. "The Ethnic Identity of Racially Mixed People: A Study of Black-Japanese." Ph.D. diss., University of California, Los Angeles.

Hall, Roberta M., and Bernice Resnick Sandler. 1982. *The Classroom Climate: A Chilly One for Women?* Washington, DC: Project on the Status and Education of Women, Association of American Colleges.

———. 1984. *Out of the Classroom: A Chilly Campus Climate for Women?* Project on the Status and Education of Women. Washington, DC: Association of American Colleges.

Hamilton, Frances D., and Elizabeth C. Wells. 1989 *Daughters of the Dream: Judson College 1838–1988.* Marion, AL: Judson College.

Hamlin, Arthur T. 1981. *The University Library in the United States: Its Origins and Development.* Philadelphia: University of Pennsylvania Press.

Hampton, Mary, Carol Oyster, Leticia Pena, and Pamela Rodgers. 2000. "Gender Inequity in Faculty Pay." *Compensation and Benefits Review* 32 no. 6: 54–59.

Hamrick, Florence A., and Julie R. Nelson. 1999. "A Singular Position: Women Full Professors and Women's Community." Paper presented at the Annual Meeting of the Association for the Study of Higher Education, San Antonio, TX, ERIC Document ED 437 012.

Hansen, Ellen, Susan Kennedy, Doreen Mattingly, Beth Mitchneck, Kris Monzel, and Cheryl Nairne. 1995. "Facing the Future, Surviving the Present: Strategies for Women Graduate Students in Geography." *Journal of Geography in Higher Education* 19, no. 3 (November): 307–315.

Hansen, Virginia L. 1997. "Voices of Latina Administrators in Higher Education: Salient Factors in Achieving Success and Implications for a Model of Leadership Development for Latina Women Administrators." *Dissertation Abstracts International* 58, no. 08A: 3036.

Hanson, Gail Short. 1995. "The Organization of NAWE." *Initiatives* 56, no. 4: 29–36.

Hanson, Sandra L. 1996. *Lost Talent: Women in the Sciences.* Philadelphia: Temple University Press.

Haraway, Donna. 1991a. "A Cyborg Manifesto: Science, Technology, and Socialist-Feminism in the Late Twentieth Century." Pp. 149–18 in *Simians, Cyborgs and Women: The Reinvention of Nature,* by Donna Haraway. New York: Routledge.

———. 1991b. *Simians, Cyborgs, and Women: The Reinvention of Nature.* New York: Routledge.

Harcourt, Wendy, ed. 1999. *Women @ Internet: Creating New Cultures in Cyberspace.* New York: Zed Books.

Harding, Sandra. 1986. *The Science Question in Feminism.* Ithaca, NY: Cornell University Press.

———. 1987. "Introduction: Is There a Feminist Method?" Pp. 1–14 in *Feminism and Methodology,* ed. Sandra

Harding. Bloomington: Indiana University.
———. 1991. *Whose Science? Whose Knowledge? Thinking from Women's Lives.* Ithaca, NY: Cornell.
———. 1993a. "Rethinking Standpoint Epistemology: What Is Strong Objectivity?" Pp. 49–82 in *Feminist Epistemologies,* ed. L. Alcoff and E. Potter. London: Routledge.
———. 1993b. *The "Racial" Economy of Science: Toward a Democratic Future.* Bloomington: Indiana University Press.
———, ed. 1987. *Feminism and Methodology.* Bloomington: Indiana University Press.
Harnish, Dorothy, and Donald G. Creamer. 1985–1986. "Faculty Stagnation and Diminished Job Involvement." *Community College Review* 13: 33–39.
Harper, Elizabeth P., Roger G. Baldwin, Bruce G. Gansneder, and Jay L. Chronister. 2001. "Full-Time Women Faculty Off the Tenure Track: Profile and Practice." *Review of Higher Education* 24, no. 3: 237–258.
Harris, Kathleen Mullan. 1996. "Life After Welfare: Women, Work, and Repeat Dependency." *American Sociological Review* 61 (June): 407–426.
Harris, Roma. 1992. *Librarianship: The Erosion of a Woman's Profession.* Norwood, NJ: Ablex Publishing.
Harris v. Forklift Systems, 115 Sup. Ct. 367 (1993).
Hartman, Moshe, and Harriet Hartman. 1996. *Gender Equality and American Jews.* Albany: State University of New York Press.
Hartmann, Heidi. 1999. "Women Are Paid Less—They and Their Families Deserve Pay Equity." *Civil Rights Journal* (Fall): 31–33.
Hartsock, Nancy. 1997. "The Feminist Standpoint: Developing the Ground for a Specifically Feminist Historical Materialism." Pp. 216–240 in *Feminist Social Thought: A Reader,* ed. Diana T. Meyers. New York: Routledge.
Harvey, William B. 1999. *Grass Roots and Glass Ceilings: African American Administrators in Predominantly White Colleges and Universities.* Albany: State University of New York Press.
———. 2001. "Minorities in Higher Education 2000–2001: Eighteenth Annual Status Report." Washington, DC: American Council on Education.
Harvey, William B., and Lea E. Williams. 1996. "Historically Black Colleges: Models for Increasing Minority Representation." Pp. 233–240 in *Racial and Ethnic Diversity in Higher Education,* ed. Caroline Turner, Mildred Garcia, Amaury Nora, and Laura I. Rendon. Needham Heights, MA: Simon and Schuster.
Harwarth, Irene, ed. 1999. *A Closer Look at Women's Colleges.* Washington, DC: U.S. Department of Education.
Harwarth, Irene, Mindi Maline, and Elizabeth DeBra. 1997. *Women's Colleges in the United States: History, Issues, and Challenges.* Washington, DC: U.S. Government Printing Office.
Hawkins, B. Denise. 1993. "Socio-Economic Family Background Still a Significant Influence on SAT Scores." *Black Issues in Higher Education* (September): 14–16.
Haworth, Jennifer G., and Clifton F. Conrad. 1990. "Curricular Transformations: Traditional and Emerging Voices in the Academy." Pp. 191–204 in *Curriculum in Transition: Perspectives on the Undergraduate Experience,* ed. Conrad and Haworth. Needham Heights, MA: Ginn Press.
Hawthorne, Susan, and Renate Klein, eds. 1999. *CyberFeminism: Connectivity, Critique and Creativity.* North Melbourne, Victoria, Australia: Spinifex Press.
Hayes, Alice B. 1993. "A Women's Place." *Conversation* 4: 9–23.

Hazan, Cindy, and Phillip Shaver. 1987. "Romantic Love Conceptualized as an Attachment Process." *Journal of Personality and Social Psychology* 52: 511–524.

Healy, Patrick. 2001. "Faculty Shortage: Women in Sciences Colleges Talk Perks, New Tenure Rules." *Boston Globe,* January 31, A2.

Healy v. James, 408 U.S. 169; 92 S. Ct. 2338 (1972).

Hebel, Sara. 2000a. "Education Department Report Notes a Quarter-Century of Strides by Women in Academe." *Chronicle of Higher Education,* April 26, 1.

———. 2000b. "In a Shift, Most Americans Say They Value College Education." *Chronicle of Higher Education,* May 3, 1.

Heim, Kathleen M., ed. 1983. *The Status of Women in Librarianship: Historical, Sociological, and Economic Issues.* New York: Neal-Schuman Publishers.

Heintz, James, and Nancy Folbre. 2000. *Field Guide to the U.S. Economy.* New York: New Press.

Helgesen, Sally. 1990. *The Female Advantage: Women's Ways of Leadership.* New York: Doubleday.

———. 1995. "The Web of Inclusion: A New Architecture for Building Great Organizations." New York: Currency/Doubleday.

Henderson, Cathy. 1999. *1999 College Freshmen with Disabilities: A Biennial Statistical Profile.* HEATH Resource Center and American Council on Education.

———. 2001. *2001 College Freshmen with Disabilities: A Biennial Statistical Profile.* HEATH Resource Center and American Council on Education.

Hendrickson, Robert M. 1991. "The Colleges, Their Constituencies, and the Courts." Number 43 in the NOLPE Monograph/Book Series. Topeka, KS: National Organization on Legal Problems of Education.

Hennig, Margaret, and Anne Jardim. 1976. *The Managerial Woman.* New York: Pocket Books.

Hensel, Nancy. 1991. *Realizing Gender Equality in Higher Education: The Need to Integrate Work/Family Issues.* ASHE-ERIC Higher Education Report no. 2. Washington, DC: George Washington University.

Herbst, Jurgen C. 1989. *And Sadly Teach: Teacher Education and Professionalization in American Culture.* Madison: University of Wisconsin Press.

Hernandez, Thomas J., and Nestor Enrique Morales. 1999. "Career, Culture, and Compromise: Career Development Experiences of Latinas Working in Higher Education." *Career Development Quarterly* 48, no. 1: 45–58.

Hernstein, Richard J., and Charles Murray. 1994. *The Bell Curve: Intelligence and Class Structure in American Life.* New York: Free Press.

Herr, Kathryn. 1999. "Private Power and Privileged Education: De/constructing Institutionalized Racism." *International Journal of Inclusive Education* 3, no. 2: 111–129.

Herring, Susan C. 1996. "Gender and Democracy in Computer-Mediated Communication." Pp. 476–489 in *Computerization and Controversy: Value Conflicts and Social Choices,* ed. R. Kling. 2nd ed. San Diego, CA: Academic Press.

Herstory: Women's History Collection from the International Women's History Archives, Berkeley, California; 1–3. Women's History Library, Women's History Research Center. Wooster, OH: Bell and Howell, 1971–1976, microfilm.

Hesse-Biber, Sharlene. 1992. "Feminist Faculty at Catholic Institutions: A

Women's Studies Director's View." *Initiatives* 54, no. 4: 35–41.
Higginbotham, Elizabeth. 2001. *Too Much to Ask: Black Women in the Era of Integration.* Chapel Hill: University of North Carolina Press.
Higginbotham, Evelyn B. 1993. *Righteous Discontent: The Woman's Movement in the Black Baptist Church, 1880–1920.* Cambridge, MA: Harvard University Press.
Higher Education Act of 1965. 1998 "Amendments." http://www.ed.gov/legislation/HE/sec501.html. Cited August 8, 2001.
Higher Education Research Institute. 1999. *Faculty Survey Executive Summary: The American College Teacher 1998–1999.* Los Angeles: University of California.
Hispanic Association of Colleges and Universities. 2001. http://www.hacu.org. Cited February 27, 2001.
History of Women. Arthur and Elizabeth Schlesinger Library on the History of Women in America, Radcliffe College, Cambridge, MA. New Haven, CT: Research Publications, 1975–1979, microfilm.
Hochschild, Arlie Russell. 1989. *The Second Shift: Working Parents and the Revolution at Home.* New York: Viking.
Hoffman, Allan M., and Randal W. Summers. 2000. *Managing Colleges and Universities: Issues for Leadership.* Westport, CT: Bergin and Garvey.
Hoffman, Frances, and Jayne Stake. 1998. "Feminist Pedagogy in Theory and Practice: An Empirical Investigation." *National Women's Studies Journal* 10, no. 1: 79–97.
Hoffman, Nancy. 1981. *Woman's "True" Profession: Voices from the History of Teaching.* New York: The Feminist Press.
Hoffman, Nancy, Cynthia Secor, and Adrian Tinsley, eds. 1972. *Female Studies 6: Closer to the Ground: Women's Classes, Criticism, Programs, 1972.* New York: The Feminist Press.
Hofstadter, Richard, and Wilson Smith, eds. 1961. *American Higher Education: A Documentary History.* Chicago: University of Chicago Press.
Holland, Dorothy C., and Margaret A. Eisenhart. 1990. *Educated in Romance: Women, Achievement and College Culture.* Chicago: University of Chicago Press.
Holland, John. 1966. *The Psychology of Vocational Choice: A Theory of Personality Types and Model Environments.* Waltham, MA: Blaisdell.
———. 1973. *Making Vocational Choices: A Theory of Careers.* Englewood Cliffs, NJ: Prentice-Hall.
———. 1985. *Making Vocational Choices: A Theory of Vocational Personalities and Work Environments.* Englewood Cliffs, NJ: Prentice-Hall.
Hollenbeck, Kevin. 1992. "Postsecondary Education as Triage: Returns to Academic and Technical Programs." Upjohn Institute Staff Working Paper 92-10. Kalamazoo, MI: W.E. Upjohn Institute for Employment Research, April.
Hollenshead, Carol, Patricia Soellner Younce, and Stacy A. Wenzel. 1994. "Women Graduate Students in Mathematics and Physics: Reflections on Success." *Journal of Women and Minorities in Science and Engineering* 1, no. 1 (January–March): 63–88.
Holm, Jeanne. 1982. *Women in the Military: An Unfinished Revolution.* Novato, CA: Presidio Press.
hooks, bell. 1981. *Ain't I a Woman: Black Women and Feminism.* Boston: South End Press.
———. 1989. *Talking Back: Thinking Feminist, Thinking Black.* New York: Free Press.
———. 1990. "From Skepticism to Feminism." *Women's Review of Books* 7 (February): 29.

———. 1994. *Teaching to Transgress.* New York: Routledge.
———. 2000. "Black and Female: Reflections on Graduate School." Pp. 386–390 in *Women in Higher Education,* ed. Judith Glazer-Raymo, Barbara K. Townsend, and Becky Ropers-Huilman. 2nd ed. Boston: Pearson Custom Publishing.
Hopwood v. University of Texas, 518 U.S. 1033 (1996) (*cert. denied*), 78 F 3d 932 (1996, Fifth Circuit).
Horn, Laura J., and Lisa Zahn. 2001. "From Bachelor's Degree to Work: Major Field of Study and Employment Outcomes of 1992–1993 Bachelor's Degree Recipients Who Did Not Enroll in Graduate Education by 1997." *Educational Statistics Quarterly: Postsecondary Education.* http://nces.gov/pubs2001/quarterly/sping/q5_2.html. Cited June 10, 2002.
Horowitz, Daniel. 1998. *Betty Friedan and the Making of* The Feminine Mystique. Amherst: University of Massachusetts Press.
Horowitz, Helen L. 1984. *Alma Mater: Design and Experience in the Women's Colleges from their Nineteenth Century Beginnings to the 1950s.* New York: Alfred A. Knopf.
———. 1987. *Campus Life: Undergraduate Cultures from the End of the Eighteenth Century to the Present.* New York: Alfred A. Knopf.
Howard, Reet. 1982. *Her Story in Sport: A Historical Anthology of Women in Sports.* West Point, NY: Leisure Press.
Huber, Mary T. 1998. *Community College Faculty Attitudes and Trends, 1997.* No. R309A60001; NCPI-4–03. Stanford, CA: National Center for Postsecondary Improvement.
Huebner, Lois A. 1989. "Interaction of Student and Campus." Pp. 165–208 in *Student Services: A Handbook for the Profession,* ed. Ursula Delworth and Gary R. Hanson. San Francisco: Jossey-Bass.
Hull, Gloria R., Patricia Bell Scott, and Barbara Smith. 1982. *All the Women Are White, All the Blacks Are Men, but Some of Us Are Brave.* New York: The Feminist Press.
Hult, Joan. 1985. The Governance of Athletics for Girls and Women: Leadership by Women Physical Educators." *Research Quarterly for Exercise and Sport* Centennial Issue (April).
Hune, Shirley. 1997. "Higher Education as Gendered Space: Asian American Women and Everyday Inequities." Pp. 181–196 in *Everyday Sexism in the Third Millennium,* ed. Carol Rambo Ronai, Barbara Zsembik, and Joe R. Feagin. New York: Routledge.
———. 1998. *Asian Pacific American Women in Higher Education: Claiming Visibility and Voice.* Washington, DC: Association of American Colleges and Universities.
———. 2000. "Doing Gender with a Feminist Gaze: Toward a Historical Reconstruction of Asian America." Pp. 413–430 in *Contemporary Asian America: A Multidisciplinary Reader,* ed. Min Zhou and James V. Gatewood. New York: New York University Press.
Hune, Shirley, and Kenyon S. Chan. 1997. "Special Focus: Asian Pacific American Demographic and Educational Trends." Pp. 39–67 in *Minorities in Higher Education,* ed. Deborah J. Carter and Reginald Wilson. Vol. 15. Washington, DC: American Council on Education.
Hunt, Caroline. 1980 [1912]. *The Life of Ellen H. Richards.* Reprinted with a new preface and foreword, Washington, DC: American Home Economics Association.
Hurd, Richard W. 1995. *Directory of Staff Bargaining Agents in Institutions of Higher Education.* New York: National Center for the Study of Collective

Bargaining in Higher Education and the Professions, School of Public Affairs, Baruch College, City University of New York.

Hurd, Richard, Amy Foerster, and Beth Hillman Johnson. 1997. *Directory of Faculty Contracts and Bargaining Agents in Institutions of Higher Education.* Vol. 23. New York: National Center for the Study of Collective Bargaining in Higher Education and the Professions.

Hurtado, Sylvia, and Deborah Faye Carter. 1997. "Effects of College Transition and Perceptions of the Campus Racial Climate on Latino College Students' Sense of Belonging." *Sociology of Education* 70: 324–346.

Hurtado, Sylvia, Jeffrey F. Milem, Alma R. Clayton-Pedersen, and Walter R. Allen. 1998. "Enhancing Campus Climates for Racial/Ethnic Diversity: Educational Policy and Practice." *Review of Higher Education* 21, no. 3: 279–302.

Hutcheson, Philo A. 2000. *A Professional Professoriate: Unionization, Bureaucratization, and the AAUP.* Nashville, TN: Vanderbilt University Press.

Hutchings, Pat. 1992. "The Assessment Movement and Feminism: Connection or Collision?" Pp. 17–28 in *Students at the Center: Feminist Assessment,* ed. Caryn M. Musil. Washington, DC: Association of American Colleges.

Hyde, Janet Shibley, and Laurie A. Frost. 1993. "Meta-Analysis in the Psychology of Women." Pp. 67–103 in *Psychology of Women: A Handbook of Issues and Theories,* ed. Florence L. Denmark and Michele A. Paludi. Westport, CT: Greenwood Press.

Hyde, Janet Shibley, and Marcia C. Linn, eds. 1986. *The Psychology of Gender. Advances through Meta-Analysis.* Baltimore: Johns Hopkins University Press.

Hyde, Michelle Smoot, and Julie Gess Newsome. 2000. "Factors That Increase Persistence of Female Undergraduate Science Students." Pp. 115–137 in *Women Succeeding in the Sciences: Theories and Practices across Disciplines,* ed. Jody Bart. West Lafayette, IN: Purdue University Press.

Ibarra, Herminia. 1997. "Paving an Alternative Route: Gender Differences in Managerial Networks." *Social Psychology Quarterly* 61, no. 1: 91–102.

Ideta, Lori. 1996. *Asian Women Leaders of Higher Education: Tales of Self-Discovery from the Ivory Tower.* Ann Arbor, MI: UMI.

Ideta, Lori, and Joanne Cooper. 1999. "Asian Women Leaders of Higher Education." Pp. 129–146 in *Everyday Knowledge and Uncommon Truths: Women of the Academy,* ed. Linda K. Christian-Smith and Kristine S. Kellor. Boulder, CO: Westview Press.

Ihle, Elizabeth L. 1992. *Black Women in Higher Education: An Anthology of Essays, Studies, and Documents, Educated Women.* New York: Garland.

Insel, Paul M., and Rudolf H. Moos. 1974. "Psychological Environments: Expanding the Scope of Human Ecology." *American Psychologist* 29: 179–186.

Institute of Electrical and Electronics Engineers. http://www.ieee.org. Cited June 14, 2002.

Integrated Postsecondary Education Data System. 1997. *Fall 1997 Staff Survey.* Washington, DC: National Center for Education Statistics.

Introcaso, Candace. 2001. "Determination in Leadership: Pioneering Roman Catholic Women Presidents." Pp. 67–83 in *Women Administrators in Higher Education,* ed. Jana Nidiffer and Carolyn T. Bashaw. Albany: State University of New York Press.

Irigaray, Luce. 1981. "And the One Doesn't Stir without the Other." Trans. Helene Vivienne Wenzel. *Signs* 7: 60–67.

———. 1985. *This Sex Which Is Not One.* Trans. Catherine Porter. Ithaca, NY: Cornell University Press.

Irvine, Betty Jo. 1985. *Sex Segregation in Librarianship: Demographic and Career Patterns of Academic Library Administrators.* Westport, CT: Greenwood Press.

Jablonski, Margaret. 1996. "The Leadership Challenge for Women College Presidents." *Initiatives* 57, no. 4: 1–10.

Jackson, Kenneth. 1991. "Black Faculty in Academia." Pp. 135–148 in *The Racial Crisis in American Higher Education,* ed. Philip G. Altbach and Kofi Lomotey. Albany: State University of New York Press.

Jackson, Lisa R. 1998. "The Influence of Both Race and Gender on the Experiences of African American College Women." *Review of Higher Education* 21, no. 4: 359–375.

Jacobs, Jerry A. 1996. "Gender, Race, and Ethnic Segregation between and within Colleges." Philadelphia: Draft report to the Mellon Foundation. Available at http://www.ssc.upenn.edu/~jacobs/mellon.html. Cited June 17, 2002.

———. 1999. "Gender and Stratification of Colleges."*Journal of Higher Education* 70, no. 2: 161–187.

Jacobs, Judith, ed. 1978. *Perspectives on Women in Mathematics.* Columbus, OH: Educational Resources Information Center.

Jaggar, Alison M., and Paula S. Rothenberg, eds. 1993. *Feminist Frameworks: Alternative Theoretical Accounts of the Relations between Women and Men.* 3rd ed. New York: McGraw-Hill.

Jeanne Clery Disclosure of Campus Security Policy and Campus Crime Statistics Act, 20 U.S.C. § 1092f.

Jeris, Laurel. 2001. "Comparison of Power Relations within Electronic and Face-to-Face Classroom Discussions: A Case Study." Paper presented at the Annual Meeting of the Adult Education Research Conference, Lansing, MI, June 1–3.

Johnson, Charles D. 1955. *Higher Education of Southern Baptists: An Institutional History, 1826–1954.* Waco, TX: Baylor University Press.

Johnson, Mary L. 1956. *A History of Meredith College.* Raleigh, NC: Meredith College.

Johnson, Stuart. 1997. "Ethnic/Cultural Centers on Predominantly White Campuses: Are They Necessary?" Pp. 155–162 in *Sailing against the Wind: African Americans and Women in U.S. Education,* ed. Kofi Lomotey. Albany: State University of New York Press.

Johnsrud, Linda K. 1991. "Administrative Promotion: The Power of Gender." *Journal of Higher Education* 62, no. 2: 119–149.

———. 1993. "Women and Minority Faculty Experiences: Defining and Responding to Diverse Realities." Pp. 3–16 in *Building a Diverse Faculty,* ed. Joanne Gainen and Robert Boice. New Directions for Higher Education no. 53. San Francisco: Jossey-Bass.

———. 1995. "Women in Graduate Education: Reviewing the Past, Looking to the Future." Pp. 69–80 in *Student Services for the Changing Graduate Student Population,* ed. Anne S. Pruitt-Logan and Paul D. Isaac. San Francisco: Jossey-Bass.

———. 1999. "The Worklife Issues of Higher Education Support Personnel." Pp. 111–124 in *NEA 1999 Almanac of Higher Education.* Washington, DC: National Education Association.

———. 2000. "Higher Education Staff: Bearing the Brunt of Cost Containment." Pp. 101–118 in *NEA 2000 Almanac of Higher Education.*

Washington, DC: National Education Association.

———. 2001. "Higher Education Support Personnel: Worklife Issues." Pp. 101–116 in *NEA 2001 Almanac of Higher Education.* Washington, DC: National Education Association.

———. Forthcoming. "Higher Education Support Staff: The Impact of Technology." In *NEA 2002 Almanac of Higher Education.* Washington, DC: National Education Association.

Johnsrud, Linda K., and Christine D. Des Jarlais. 1994. "Barriers to Tenure for Women and Minorities." *Review of Higher Education* 17: 335–353.

Johnsrud, Linda K., and Vicki J. Rosser. 2000. *Understanding the Work and Career Paths of Midlevel Administrators.* San Francisco: Jossey-Bass.

Jones, Susan Robb. 1997. "Voices of Identity and Difference: A Qualitative Exploration of the Multiple Dimensions of Identity Development in Women College Students." *Journal of College Student Development* 38: 376–385.

Jones, Susan Robb, and Marylu K. McEwen. 2000. "A Conceptual Model of Multiple Dimensions of Identity." *Journal of College Student Development* (July–August): 405–413.

Jordan, I. King. 2001. "Colleges Can Do Even More for People with Disabilities." *Chronicle of Higher Education,* June 15, B14.

Jordan, Judith V., ed. 1997. *Women's Growth in Diversity: More Writings from the Stone Center.* New York: Guilford Press.

Jordan, Judith V., Alexandra G. Kaplan, Jean B. Miller, Irene P. Stiver, and Janet L. Surrey. 1991. *Women's Growth in Connection: Writings from the Stone Center.* New York: Guilford Press.

Josselson, Ruthellen. 1987. *Finding Herself: Pathways to Identity Development in Women.* San Francisco: Jossey-Bass.

———. 1996. *Revising Herself: The Story of Women's Identity from College to Midlife.* New York: Oxford University Press.

Judy, Richard W., and Carol D'Amico. 1998. *Workforce 2020: Work and Workers in the Twenty-first Century.* Indianapolis: Hudson Institute.

Jungreis, Jeremy N. 1996. "Holding the Line at VMI: The Preservation of a State's Right to Offer a Single-Gender Military Education." *Florida State University Law Review* 23, no. 3: 795–839.

Justus, Bennett J., Sandra Freitig, and Leann L. Parker. 1987. *The University of California in the Twenty-First Century: Successful Approaches to Faculty Diversity.* Berkeley: University of California Press.

Kane, Mary Jo. 1989. "The Post Title IX Female Athlete in the Media: Things Are Changing, but How Much?" *Journal of Physical Education, Recreation, and Dance* 60: 58–62.

Kanin, Eugene J. 1957. "Male Aggression in Dating-Courtship Relations." *American Journal of Sociology* 63: 197–204.

Kanter, Rosabeth Moss. 1977. *Men and Women of the Corporation.* New York: Basic Books.

Kaplan, Sheila, Cynthia Secor, and Adrian Tinsley. 1984. "Getting the Best: Conclusions, Recommendations, and Selected Resources." Pp. 81–85 in *Women in Higher Education Administration,* ed. Adrian Tinsley, Cynthia Secor, and Sheila Kaplan. New Directions for Higher Education no. 45. San Francisco: Jossey-Bass.

Kaplin, William A., and Barbara A. Lee. 1995. *The Law of Higher Education: A Comprehensive Guide to Legal Implications of Administrative*

Decision Making. 3rd ed. San Francisco: Jossey-Bass.

———. 2000. *Year 2000 Cumulative Supplement to the Law of Higher Education.* 3rd ed. Washington, DC: National Association of College and University Attorneys.

Kates, Erika. 1993. *Access to Higher Education Project.* Project on Women and Social Change; Final Report. Northampton, MA: Smith College.

Kates, Susan. 2001. *Activist Rhetorics and American Higher Education 1885–1937.* Carbondale: Southern Illinois University Press.

Katz, Bill, and Linda Sternberg Katz, eds. 2000. *Magazines for Libraries.* 10th ed. New Providence, NJ: Bowker.

Katz, J. 1991. "White Faculty Struggling with the Effects of Racism." Pp. 187–198 in *The Racial Crisis in American Higher Education,* ed. Philip G. Altbach and Kofi Lomotey. Albany: State University of New York Press.

Katz, Richard N., and Julia A. Rudy. 1999. *Information Technology in Higher Education: Assessing its Impact and Planning for the Future* no. 102. EDUCAUSE Leadership Strategies. San Francisco: Jossey-Bass.

Katz, William A., and Berry G. Richards, eds. 1969. *Magazines for Libraries.* New York: Bowker.

Kawewe, Saliwe M. 1997. "Black Women in Diverse Academic Settings: Gender and Racial Crimes of Commission and Omission in Academia." Pp. 263–269 in *Black Women in the Academy: Promises and Perils,* ed. L. Benjamin. Gainesville: University Press of Florida.

Keating, Anne B. 1999. *The Wired Professor: A Guide to Incorporating the World Wide Web in College Instruction.* New York: New York University Press.

Kegan, Robert. 1994. *In Over Our Heads: The Mental Demands of Modern Life.* Cambridge, MA: Harvard University Press.

Keim, Jeanmarie, and Chris Erickson. 1998. "Women in Academia: Work-Related Stressors." *Equity and Excellence in Education* (September): 61–67.

Keller, Evelyn Fox. 1983. *A Feeling for the Organism: The Life and Work of Barbara McClintock.* New York: W. H. Freeman.

———. 1985. *Reflections on Gender and Science.* New Haven, CT: Yale University Press.

———. 1997. *Modest Witness: Feminism and Technoscience.* New York: Routledge.

Kelly, Joan. 1977. "Did Women Have a Renaissance?" In *Becoming Visible: Women in European History,* ed. Renate Bridenthal and Claudia Koonz. Boston: Houghton Mifflin.

Kendall, Elaine. 1976. *Peculiar Institutions: An Informal History of the Seven Sister Colleges.* New York: G. P. Putnam's Sons.

Kenneally, James K. 1990. *The History of American Catholic Women.* New York: Crossroad Publishing.

Kennedy, Helen L., and Joe Parks. 2000. "Society Cannot Continue to Exclude Women from the Fields of Science and Mathematics." *Education* 120: 529.

Kennelly, Karen. 1989. *American Catholic Women.* New York: Macmillan.

Kennickell, Arthur B., Martha Starr-McCluer, and Brian J. Surette. "Recent Changes in U.S. Family Finances: Results from the 1998 Survey of Consumer Finances." http://www.federalreserve.gov/pubs/bulletin/2000/0100lead.pdf. Cited March 3, 2001.

Kerber, Linda K. 1998. *No Constitutional Right to Be Ladies: Women and the Obligations of Citizenship.* New York: Hill and Wang.

Kett, Joseph F. 1968. *The Formation of the American Medical Profession: The Role of Institutions, 1780–1860.* New Haven, CT: Yale University Press.

Keyssar, Alexander. 2000. *The Right to Vote: The Contested History of Democracy in the United States.* New York: Basic Books.

Kezar, Adriana, and Deb Moriarty. 2000. "Expanding Our Understanding of Student Leadership Development: A Study Exploring Gender and Ethnic Identity." *Journal of College Student Development* 41, no. 1: 55–69.

Kich, George K. 1992. "The Developmental Process of Asserting a Biracial, Bicultural Identity." Pp. 304–317 in *Racially Mixed People in America,* ed. Maria P. P. Root. Newbury Park, CA: Sage.

Kirkup, Gill. 1992. "The Social Construction of Computers: Hammers or Harpsichords?" Pp. 267–283 in *Inventing Women: Science, Technology and Gender,* ed. Gill Kirkup and Laurie S. Keller. Cambridge, MA: Basil Blackwell.

———. 1995. "The Importance of Gender as a Category in Open and Distance Learning." Paper presented at the conference Putting the Learner First: Learner-Centred Approaches in Open and Distance Learning. Cambridge, UK, July.

Kleeh-Tolley, Karen. 1993. "Women Organizing: Action and Reaction in the Formation of a Clerical Union." *Humanity and Society* 17, no. 4: 447–466.

Knight Foundation. 1993. *Reports of the Knight Foundation Commission on Intercollegiate Athletics, March 1991–March 1993.* Charlotte, NC: Knight Foundation.

Knowlton, Lois M. 1992. "Leadership in a Different Voice: An Ethnographic Study of a Latina Chief Executive Officer in a California Community College." Ph.D. diss., University of San Diego.

Kobliz, Neal. 1990. "Are Student Ratings Unfair to Women?" *Newsletter of the Association for Women in Mathematics* 20: 17–19.

Kohlberg, Lawrence. 1971. "Stages of Moral Development." Pp. 23–92 in *Moral Education,* ed. Clive Beck, Brian Crittenden, and Edmund V. Sullivan. New York: Academic Press.

Kolb, David A. 1981. "Learning Styles and Disciplinary Differences." Pp. 232–255 in *The Modern American College: Responding to the Realities of Diverse Students and a Changing Society,* ed. Arthur. W. Chickering and Associates. San Francisco: Jossey-Bass.

Kolodny, Annette. 1998. *Failing the Future: A Dean Looks at Higher Education in the Twenty-First Century.* Durham, NC: Duke University Press.

Komives, Susan R. 1994. "Women Student Leaders: Self-Perceptions of Empowering Leadership and Achieving Style." *NASPA Journal* 31, no. 2: 102–112.

Korenman, Joan. 1997. *Internet Resources on Women: Using Electronic Media in Curriculum Transformation.* Baltimore: Towson State University, National Center for Curriculum Transformation Resources on Women.

Koziara, Karen, Michael H. Shallcross, Lucretia Moskow, and Dewey Tanner. 1987. *Working Women: Past Present and Future.* Washington, DC: Bureau of National Affairs.

Kramarae, Cheris. 1997. "Technology Policy, Gender, and Cyberspace." *Duke Journal of Gender Law and Policy* 4, no. 1: 149–158.

———. 2000. *The Third Shift: Women Learning Online.* Washington, DC: American Association of University Women Education Foundation.

Kramarae, Cheris, and Dale Spender. 1992. "Exploding Knowledge." Pp. 1–24 in *The Knowledge Explosion: Generations of Feminist Scholarship,* ed. C. Kramarae and D. Spender. New York: Teachers College.

Krumm, Bernita L. 1997–1998. "Leadership Reflections: Women Tribal College Presidents." *Tribal College Journal* (Winter): 24–28.

———. 1998. "Tribal Culture Supports Women in Campus Presidencies." *Women in Higher Education* 7, no. 12: 39.

Kuh, George D., and Elizabeth J. Whitt. 1988. *The Invisible Tapestry: Cultures in American Colleges and Universities.* ASHE-ERIC Higher Education Report Series no. 1. Washington, DC: Association for the Study of Higher Education.

Kuh, George D., John S. Schuh, Elizabeth J. Whitt, and Associates. 1991. *Involving Colleges: Successful Approaches to Fostering Student Learning and Development Outside the Classroom.* San Francisco: Jossey-Bass.

Kuh, George D., Nick Vesper, Mark R. Connolly, and Charles R. Pace. 1997. *College Student Experiences Questionnaire: Revised Norms for the Third Edition.* Bloomington: Center for Postsecondary Research and Planning, School of Education, Indiana University.

Kulicha, J. 1991. "Current Trends and Priorities in Canadian Adult Education." *International Journal of Lifelong Education* 10, no. 2: 93–106.

Kulis, Stephen, and Karen A. Miller. 1988 "Are Minority Women Sociologists in Double Jeopardy?" *American Sociologist* 19: 323–339.

Kunda v. Muehlenburg College, 621 F. 2d 532 (2nd Cir. 1980).

Laden, Berta V., and Linda S. Hagedorn. 2000. "Job Satisfaction among Faculty of Color in Academe: Individual Survivors or Institutional Transformers?" Pp. 57–66 in *What Contributes to Job Satisfaction among Faculty And Staff?* ed. Linda S. Hagedorn. New Directions for Institutional Research no. 105. San Francisco: Jossey-Bass.

Ladson-Billings, Gloria. 1994. *The Dreamkeepers: Successful Teachers of African American Children.* San Francisco: Jossey-Bass.

LaFrance, Arthur B. 1987. *Welfare Law: Structure and Entitlement in a Nutshell.* St. Paul, MN: West Publishing.

LaFromboise, Teresa, Hardin L. K. Coleman, and Jennifer Getron. 1993. "Psychological Impact of Biculturalism: Evidence and Theory." *Psychological Bulletin* 114: 395–412.

Lake Placid Conferences on Home Economics (Proceedings of First through Tenth Conferences). Lake Placid, NY, 1899–1908.

Lambert, Jane L. 1997. "Feminist Assessment: What Does Feminist Theory Contribute to the Assessment Conversation?" Paper presented at the Annual Conference of the Association for the Study of Higher Education, Albuquerque, NM.

LaNoue, George R., and Barbara A. Lee. 1987. *Academics in Court: The Consequences of Faculty Discrimination Litigation.* Ann Arbor: University of Michigan Press.

LaPaglia, Nancy. 1993. *Storytellers: The Image of the Two-Year College in American Fiction and in Women's Journals.* DeKalb, IL: LEPS Press, Northern Illinois University.

Larocca, Michela A., and Jeffrey D. Kromrey. 1999. "The Perception of Sexual Harassment in Higher Education: Impact of Gender and Attractiveness." *Sex Roles: A Journal of Research* 40, nos. 11–12: 921–940.

Lasser, Carol, ed. 1987. *Educating Men and Women Together: Coeducation in a Changing World.* Urbana: University of Illinois Press.

Lather, Patti A. 1990. "Reinscribing Otherwise: The Play of Values in the Practices of the Human Sciences." In

The Paradigm Dialogue, ed. Eson G. Guba. Newbury Park, CA: Sage.

Lawler, Andrew. 1999. "Tenured Women Battle to Make It Less Lonely at the Top." *Science,* November 12, 1272–1278.

Lazere, Edward B. 1996. *Maine Families: Poverty Despite Work.* Washington, DC: Center on Budget and Policy Priorities.

Leap, Terry L. 1985. *Tenure, Discrimination, and the Courts.* 2nd ed. Ithaca, NY: Cornell University Press.

Lederman, Douglas. 1996. "Supreme Court Rejects VMI's Exclusion of Women." *Chronicle of Higher Education,* July 5, A21.

Lederman, Muriel, and Ingrid Bartsch. 2001. *The Gender and Science Reader.* New York: Routledge.

Lee, Mabel. 1983. *A History of Physical Education and Sports in the U.S.A.* New York: John Wiley and Sons.

Leonard, Bill J. 1990. *God's Last and Only Hope: Fragmentation of the Southern Baptist Convention.* Grand Rapids, MI: Eerdmans.

Leonard, Pauline. 1998. "Gendering Change? Management, Masculinity and the Dynamics of Incorporation." *Gender and Education* 10, no. 1: 71–84.

Lerner, Gerda. 1972. *Black Women in White America: A Documentary History.* New York: Pantheon Books.

Leslie, Larry, and Gary Rhoades. 1995 "Rising Administrative Costs: Seeking Explanations." *Journal of Higher Education* 66, no. 2: 187–212.

Levin, Margarita Garcia. 1994. "A Critique of Ecofeminism." Pp. 134–140 in *Environmental Ethics: Readings in Theory and Application,* ed. Lovis P. Pojman. Boston: Jones and Bartlett.

Levine, Arthur. *Higher Education at a Crossroads.* Occasional Papers from the Center for Higher Education Policy Analysis. Los Angeles, CA: University of Southern California. http://www.usc.edu/dept/chepa/papers_pastpapers.html. Cited June 11, 2002.

Levine, Arthur, and Jana Nidiffer. 1996. *Beating the Odds: How the Poor Get to College.* San Francisco: Jossey-Bass.

Levy, Darline Gay, Harriet Branson Applewhite, and Mary Durham Johnson. 1979. *Women in Revolutionary Paris: 1789–1795.* Urbana: University of Illinois Press.

Lewin, Kurt. 1936. *Principles of Topological Psychology.* New York: McGraw-Hill.

Lewis, Magda G. 1993. *Without a Word: Teaching beyond Women's Silence.* New York: Teachers College Press.

———. 1999. "The Backlash Factor: Women, Intellectual Labor, and Student Evaluation of Courses and Teaching." Pp. 59–82 in *Everyday Knowledge and Uncommon Truths: Women of Academe,* ed. Linda K. Christian-Smith and Kristine S. Kellor. Boulder, CO: Westview Press.

Lie, Suzanne Stiver, and Lynda Malik. 2000. "Trends in the Gender Gap in Higher Education." Pp. 446–452 in *Women in Higher Education: A Feminist Perspective,* ed. Judith Glazer-Raymo, Barbara K. Townsend, and Becky Ropers-Huilman. ASHE Reader Series. Needham Heights, MA: Ginn Press.

Lim, Shirley Geo-Lin, Maria Herrera-Sobek, and Genaro Padilla, eds. 2000. *Power, Race, and Gender in Academe: Strangers in the Tower?* New York: Modern Language Association.

Lindsay, Beverly. 1997. "Surviving the Middle Passage: The Absent Legacy of African American Women Education Deans." Pp. 3–32 in *The Minority Voice in Educational Reform: An Analysis by Minority and Women College of Education Deans,* ed. Louis A. Castenell and Jim M. Tarule. Greenwich, CT: Ablex Publishing.

Lindsay, Beverly, and Manuel Justiz, eds. 2001. *The Quest for Equity in Education: Toward a New Paradigm in an Evolving Affirmative Action Era.* Albany: State University of New York Press.

Linton, Simi. 1998. *Claiming Disability: Knowledge and Identity.* New York: New York University Press.

Lively, Kit. 2000. "Women in Charge." *Chronicle of Higher Education,* June 16, A33–A35.

Locke, Edwin A. 1984. "Job Satisfaction." Pp. 93–117 in *Social Psychology and Organizational Behavior,* ed. M. Gruneberg and T. Wall. London: Wiley.

Locke, Mamie E. 1997. "Striking the Delicate Balance: The Future of African American Women in the Academy." Pp. 340–346 in *Black Women in the Academy: Promises and Perils,* ed. Lois Benjamin. Gainesville: University Press of Florida.

Lomotey, Kofi, ed. 1997. *Sailing against the Wind: African Americans and Women in U.S. Education.* Albany: State University of New York Press.

Longmore, Paul K., and Lauri Umansky, eds. 2001. *The New Disability History: American Perspectives.* New York: New York University Press.

Lopez, Gloria Ann. 1984. "Job Satisfaction of Mexican American Women Administrators in Higher Education." Ph.D. diss., University of Texas at Austin. *Dissertation Abstracts International* 45, no. 07A: 1942.

Lott, Bernice, and Mary Ellen Riley, eds. 1996. *Combating Sexual Harassment in Higher Education.* Washington, DC: National Education Association.

Lott, Juanita T. 1997. *Asian Americans: From Racial Category to Multiple Identities.* Walnut Creek, CA: Altamira Press.

Love, Patrick, and Victoria Guthrie. 1999. *Understanding and Applying Cognitive Development Theory.* New Directions for Student Services no. 88. San Francisco: Jossey-Bass.

Lucas, Christopher J. 1994. *American Higher Education: A History.* New York: St. Martin's.

Luke, Carmen. 1992. "Feminist Politics in Radical Pedagogy." Pp. 25–53 in *Feminisms and Critical Pedagogy,* ed. Carmen Luke and Jennifer Gore. New York: Routledge.

Luke, Carmen, and Jennifer Gore, eds. 1992. *Feminisms and Critical Pedagogy.* New York: Routledge.

Luttrell, Wendy. 1997. *Schoolsmart and Motherwise: Working-Class Women's Identity and Schooling.* New York: Basic Books.

Lytton, Hugh, and David M. Romney. 1991. "Parents' Differential Socialization of Boys and Girls: A Meta-Analysis." *Psychological Bulletin* 109, no. 2: 267–296.

Mabokela, Reitumetse O. 2000. *Voices of Conflict: Desegregating South African Universities.* New York: Routledge.

———. 2002. "The Road Less Traveled: Reflections of Black Women Faculty in South African Universities." *Review of Higher Education* 25, no. 2: 185–206.

Mabokela, Reitumetse O., and Kimberly L. King., eds. 2001. *Apartheid No More? Case Studies of Southern African Universities in the Process of Transformation.* Westport, CT: Greenwood Publishing.

Maccoby, Eleanor E., and Carolyn N. Jacklin. 1974. *The Psychology of Sex Differences.* Palo Alto, CA: Stanford University Press.

MacKinnon, Catharine. 1979. *Sexual Harassment of Working Women: A Case of Sex Discrimination.* New Haven, CT: Yale University Press.

———. 1993. *Only Words.* Cambridge, MA: Harvard University Press.

Madsen, Holly. 1997. *Composition of Boards of Public Colleges and Universities.* Occasional Paper no. 36.

Washington, DC: Association of Governing Boards of Universities and Colleges.

———. 1998. *Composition of Governing Boards of Independent Colleges and Universities.* Occasional Paper no. 37. Washington, DC: Association of Governing Boards of Universities and Colleges.

Maher, Frances. 1987. "Toward a Richer Theory of Feminist Pedagogy." *Journal of Education* 169, no. 3: 91–99.

———. 2001. *The Feminist Classroom.* New York: Rowman and Littlefield.

Maher, Frances A., and Mary Kay Thompson Tetreault. 1994. *The Feminist Classroom: An Inside Look at How Professors and Students Are Transforming Higher Education for a Diverse Society.* New York: Basic Books.

———. 1997. "Learning in the Dark: How Assumptions of Whiteness Shape Classroom Knowledge." *Harvard Educational Review* 67 (Summer): 321–349.

———. 2000. "Pedagogy." Pp. 1526–1529 in *Routledge International Encyclopedia of Women,* eds. Cheris Kramarae and Dale Spender. London: Routledge.

Mahoney, Kathleen A. 1999. "One Hundred Years: The Association of Catholic Colleges and Universities." *ACCU Current Issues in Catholic Higher Education* 19 (Spring): 3–46.

Mallory, Sherry L. 1998. "Lesbian, Gay, Bisexual, and Transgender Student Organizations: An Overview." Pp. 321–328 in *Working with Lesbian, Gay, Bisexual, and Transgender College Students: A Handbook for Faculty and Administrators,* ed. Ronni L. Sanlo. Westport, CT: Greenwood Press.

Mappen, Ellen F. 2000. "Exploring Science and Engineering through Mentoring and Research: Enriching Undergraduate Education for Women." *AWIS Magazine* 29, no. 1: 10–13.

Marcia, James E. 1966. "Development and Validation of Ego Identity Status." *Journal of Personality and Social Psychology* 3, no. 5: 551–558.

Marcus, Jacob R. 1981. *The American Jewish Woman: A Documentary History.* New York: KTAV Publishing.

Marshall, Joan K., comp. 1977. *On Equal Terms: A Thesaurus for Nonsexist Indexing and Cataloging.* New York: Neal-Schuman.

Martin, Carole. 1979. "Working for Women: Organizations and Services in Education." *College Board Review* 111 (Spring): 14–15.

Martin, Jane Roland. 2000. *Coming of Age in Academe: Rekindling Women's Hopes and Reforming the Academy.* New York: Routledge.

Martineau, Rowena. 1997. "Women and Education in South Africa: Factors Influencing Women's Educational Progress and Their Entry into Traditionally Male-Dominated Fields." *Journal of Negro Education* 66, no. 4: 383–395.

Martínez Alemán, Ana M. 1995. "Actuando." Pp. 67–76 in *The Leaning Ivory Tower: Latino Professors in American Universities,* ed. Raymond V. Padilla and Rudolfo Chávez Chávez. Albany: State University of New York Press.

Massy, William F., and Robert Zemsky. 1997. "A Utility Model for Teaching Load Decisions in Academic Departments." *Economics of Education Review* 16, no. 4: 349–365.

Mau, Rosalind Y. 1995. "Barriers to Higher Education for Asian/Pacific-American Females." Pp. 235–245 in *The Asian American Educational Experience,* ed. Don T. Nakanishi and Tina Y. Nishida. New York: Routledge.

Mayberry, Katherine, ed. 1996. *Teaching What You're Not: Identity Politics in Higher Education.* New York: New York University Press.

Mayberry, Maralee, and Ellen Rose, eds. 1999. *Innovative Feminist Pedagogies in Action: Meeting the Challenge.* New York: Routledge.

Mayhew, Lewis B., and P. J. Ford. 1971. *Changing the Curriculum.* San Francisco: Jossey-Bass.

McBeth, Leon. 1979. *Women in Baptist Life.* Nashville, TN: Broadman Press.

McCandless, Amy Thompson. 1999. *The Past in the Present: Women's Higher Education in the Twentieth-Century American South.* Tuscaloosa: University of Alabama Press.

McCarthy, Abigail. 1985. "A Luminous Minority." *ACCU Current Issues in Catholic Higher Education* 5 (Winter): 7–10.

McCormick, Naomi B. 1979. "Come-Ons and Put-Offs: Unmarried Students' Strategies for Having and Avoiding Sexual Intercourse." *Psychology of Women Quarterly* 4: 194–211.

McDonough, Patricia M. 1997. *Choosing Colleges: How Social Class and Schools Structure Opportunity.* Albany: State University of New York Press.

McDowell, Linda. 1999. *Gender, Identity and Place: Understanding Feminist Geographies.* Minneapolis: University of Minnesota Press.

McElrath, Karen. 1992. "Gender, Career Disruption, and Academic Rewards." *Journal of Higher Education* 63, no. 3: 269–281.

McEwen, Marylu K., Larry D. Roper, Deborah R. Bryant, and Miriam J. Langa. 1990. "Incorporating the Development of African-American Students into Psychosocial Theories of Student Development." *Journal of College Student Development* 31: 429–436.

McIntosh, Peggy. 1983. *Interactive Phases of Curriculum Re-Vision: A Feminist Perspective.* Working Paper no. 124. Wellesley College Center for Research on Women.

———. 1992. "White Privilege and Male Privilege: A Personal Account of Coming to See Correspondences through Work in Women's Studies." Pp. 70–81 in *Race, Class and Gender: An Anthology,* ed. Margaret L. Andersen and Patricia Hill Collins. Belmont, CA: Wadsworth Publishing.

McKay, Nellie Y. 1997. "A Troubled Peace: Black Women in the Halls of the White Academy." Pp. 11–22 in *Black Women in the Academy: Promises and Perils,* ed. Lois Benjamin. Gainesville: University Press of Florida.

McMillen, Liz. 1991. "Women in Academe Say They Bear Brunt of Cutbacks." *Chronicle of Higher Education,* November 13, A1, A37–A38.

McNaron, Toni A. H. 1997. *Poisoned Ivy: Lesbian and Gay Academics Confronting Homophobia.* Philadelphia: Temple University Press.

Medina, Catherine, and Gaye Luna. 2000. "Narratives from Latina Professors in Higher Education." *Anthropology and Education Quarterly* 31, no. 1: 47–66.

Mednick, Martha T., and Veronica G. Thomas. 1993. "Women and the Psychology of Achievement: A View from the Eighties." Pp. 585–626 in *Psychology of Women: A Handbook of Issues and Theories,* ed. Florence L. Denmark and Michele A. Paludi. Westport, CT: Greenwood Press.

Meece, Judith L., Jacquelynne (Eccles) Parsons, Carolyn M. Kaczala, Susan B. Goff, and Robert Futtennan. 1982. "Sex Differences in Math Achievement: Toward a Model of Academic Choice." *Psychological Bulletin* 91, no. 2: 324–348.

Mellor, Mary. 1997. *Feminism and Ecology.* New York: New York University Press.

Melvill, Margarita B. 1990. "Hispanics: Race, Class, or Ethnicity?" *Journal of Ethnic Studies* 16, no. 1: 67–83.

Menges, Robert J. 1999. *Faculty in New Jobs: A Guide to Settling In, Becoming Established, and Building Institutional Support.* San Francisco: Jossey-Bass.
Menges, Robert J., and William H. Exum. 1983. "Barriers to the Progress of Women and Minority Faculty." *Journal of Higher Education* 54, no. 2: 123–144.
Mercer v. Duke University, 32 F. Supp. 2d 836, M.D. N.C., 1998; *reversed* 190 F.3d 643, Fourth Circuit (1999).
Merchant, Carolyn. 1980. *The Death of Nature: Women, Ecology, and the Scientific Revolution.* San Francisco: Harper and Row.
———. 1989. *Ecological Revolutions: Nature, Gender, and Science in New England.* Chapel Hill: University of North Carolina Press.
———. 1992. *Radical Ecology. The Search for a Livable World.* New York: Routledge.
———. 1995. *Earthcare: Women and the Environment.* New York: Routledge.
Merisotis, Jamie P., and Colleen T. O'Brien, eds. 1998. *Minority-Serving Institutions: Distinct Purposes, Common Goals.* New Directions for Higher Education 102. San Francisco: Jossey-Bass.
Meritor Savings Bank v. Vinson, 477 U.S. 57 (1986).
Merriam, Sharan B., and Rosemary S. Caffarella. 1998. *Learning in Adulthood.* 2nd ed. San Francisco: Jossey-Bass.
Merton, Robert K. 1982. "The Matthew Effect in Science, II: Cumulative Advantage and the Symbolism of Intellectual Property." *Isis* 79, no. 229: 606–623.
Meyer, Katrina A. 1998. *Faculty Workload Studies: Perspectives, Needs and Future Directions.* ASHE-ERIC Higher Education Report 26, no. 1. Washington, DC: George Washington University.
Mezirow, Jack. 1978. *Education for Perspective Transformation: Women's Reentry Programs in Community Colleges.* New York: Columbia University Center for Adult Education.
Mickleson, Rosyln, and Stephen Smith. 1998. "Can Education Eliminate Race, Class and Gender Inequality?" Pp. 328–340 in *Race, Class and Gender: An Anthology,* ed. Margaret Anderson and Patricia Hill Collins. New York: Wadsworth Publishing.
Middaugh, Michael F. 2001. *Understanding Faculty Productivity: Standards and Benchmarks for Colleges and Universities.* San Francisco: Jossey-Bass.
Miller Lite Report on Women in Sports. 1985. Iselin, NJ: New World Decisions.
Miller, D. W., and Robin Wilson. 1999. "MIT Acknowledges Bias against Female Faculty Members." *Chronicle of Higher Education,* April 2, A18.
Miller, Jean Baker. 1976. *Toward a New Psychology of Women.* Boston: Beacon Press.
Miller, John P. 1971. "Graduate Education." Pp. 185–190 in *The Encyclopedia of Education,* ed. Lee C. Deighton. 10 vols. New York: Macmillan.
Miller, Nod. 2001. "The Politics of Access and Communication: Using Distance Learning Technologies." Pp. 187–205 in *Power in Practice: Adult Education and the Struggle for Knowledge and Power in Society,* ed. Ronald M. Cervero and Arthur L. Wilson. San Francisco: Jossey-Bass.
Miller, Patricia H., and Ellin K. Scholnick. 2000. *Toward a Feminist Developmental Psychology.* New York: Routledge.
Miller-Bernal, Leslie. 2001. *Separate by Degree: Women Students' Experiences in Single-Sex and Coeducational Colleges.* New York: Peter Lang.
Mills, Richard. 2001. "Lawsuit Challenges University Housing Policy for Gay Graduate Students." *U. Wire: The Daily*

Californian. http://wwww.uwire.com/content/topnews. Cited May 31, 2002.

Minnich, Elizabeth, Jean O'Barr, and Rachel Rosenfeld, eds. 1988. *Reconstructing the Academy: Women's Education and Women's Studies.* Chicago: University of Chicago Press.

Mintz, Beth, and Esther D. Rothblum, eds. 1997. *Lesbians in Academia: Degrees of Freedom.* New York: Routledge.

Mississippi University for Women v. Hogan, 458 U.S. 718 (1982).

Mitchell, Juliet. 1974. *Psychoanalysis and Feminism.* London: Allen Lane.

Mohanty, Chandra Talpade. 1991. "Under Western Eyes: Feminist Scholarship and Colonial Discourses." Pp. 51–80 in *Third World Women and the Politics of Feminism,* ed. Chandra Mohanty, Ann Russo, and Lourdes Torres. Bloomington: Indiana University Press.

Moore, Katharine M. 1990. "Creating Strengths Out of Our Differences: Women and Minority Administrators." Pp. 89–98 in *Administrative Careers and the Marketplace,* ed. Katharine M. Moore and Susan B. Twombly. New Directions for Higher Education no 72. San Francisco: Jossey-Bass.

Moore, William, and Lonnie H. Wagstaff. 1974. *Black Educators in White Colleges.* San Francisco: Jossey-Bass.

Moos, Rudolf H. 1974. "Systems for the Assessment and Classification of Human Environments: An Overview." Pp. 5–29 in *Issues in Social Ecology,* ed. Rudolf H. Moos and Paul Insel. Palo Alto, CA: National Press Books.

———. 1976. *The Human Context: Environmental Determinants of Behavior.* New York: John Wiley and Sons.

———. 1979. *Evaluating Educational Environments: Procedures, Measures, Findings, and Policy Implications.* San Francisco: Jossey-Bass.

———. 1984. "Context and Coping: Toward a Unifying Conceptual Framework." *American Journal of Community Psychology* 12: 5–23.

Moos, Rudolf H., and Bernice Van Dort. 1979. "Student Physical Symptoms and the Social Climate of College Living Groups." *American Journal of Community Psychology* 7: 31–45.

Moraga, Cherrie, and Gloria Anzaldúa, eds. 1983. *This Bridge Called My Back: Writings by Radical Women of Color.* New York: Kitchen Table Women of Color Press.

Moran, Mary. 1987. "Student Financial Aid and Women." *ERIC Digest.* www.ed.gov/databases/ERIC-Digests/ed284525.html. Cited June 12, 2002.

Morey, Melanie, and Dennis Holtschneider. 2000. "Relationship Revisited: Changing Relationships between U.S. Catholic Colleges and Universities and Founding Religious Congregations." *ACCU Current Issues in Catholic Higher Education* 21 (Fall): 62–65.

Morgan, Frank B., and Susan G. Broyles. 1995. "Degrees and Other Awards Conferred by Institutions of Higher Education, 1992–93." Washington, DC: Office of Educational Research and Improvement, U.S. Department of Education.

Morgan, Gareth. 1986. *Images of Organization.* Newbury Park, CA: Sage.

Morgan, Robin. 1970. *Sisterhood Is Powerful: An Anthology of Writings from the Women's Liberation Movement.* New York: Vintage Books.

Morlock, Laura. 1973. "Discipline Variation in the Status of Academic Women." Pp. 255–312 in *Academic Women on the Move,* eds. Alice S. Rossi and Ann Claderwood. New York: Russell Sage Foundation.

Morrison, Ann M., Randall P. White, Ellen Van Velsor, and the Center for Creative Leadership. 1987. *Breaking the Glass Ceiling: Can Women Reach the Top of America's Largest Corporations?*

Reading, MA: Addison-Wesley Publishing.

Morrison, Perry David. 1961. *The Career of the Academic Librarian: A Study of the Social Origins, Educational Attainments, Vocational Experience, and Personality Characteristics of a Group of American Academic Librarians.* Berkeley: University of California.

Mortimer, Jelyan T., and Roberta Simmons. 1978. "Adult Socialization." *Annual Review of Sociology* 4: 421–454.

Moseley, Eva Steiner, ed. 1995. *Women, Information, and the Future: Collecting and Sharing Resources Worldwide.* Fort Atkinson, WI: Highsmith Press.

Moses, Clair Goldberg, and Leslie Wahl Rabine. 1993. *Feminism, Socialism, and French Romanticism.* Bloomington: Indiana University Press.

Moses, Yolanda. 1997. "Black Women in Academe: Issues and Strategies." Pp. 23–38 in *Black Women in the Academy: Promises and Perils,* ed. Lois Benjamin. Gainesville: University Press of Florida.

Mosher, Clelia Duel. 1980. *The Mosher Survey: Sexual Attitudes of Forty-Five Victorian Women.* New York: Arno Press.

Moss-Kanter, Rosabeth. 1987. "The New Managerial Work." *Harvard Business Review.* November–December: 85–90.

Mulvihill, Thalia M. 2000. "The Extended Influence of Dean M. Eunice Hilton and Katherine Sibley: A Case Study of the Collegial Integration of Programs for Women University Students, 1930s–1950s." *Initiatives* 59 (Fall).

Murray, Henry A. 1938. *Exploration in Personality.* New York: Oxford University Press.

Murrell, Audrey J., and Beth L. Dietz-Uhler. 1993. "Gender Identity and Adversarial Beliefs as Predictors of Attitudes toward Sexual Harassment." *Psychology of Women Quarterly* 17: 169–175.

Musil, Caryn McTighe. 1992. "Relaxing Your Neck Muscles: The History Project." Pp. 3–16 in *Students at the Center: Feminist Assessment,* ed. Caryn McTighe Musil. Washington, DC: Association of American Colleges.

Musil, Caryn McTighe, ed. 1992. *Students at the Center: Feminist Assessment.* Washington, DC: Association of American Colleges and National Women's Studies Association.

Myers, Linda J. 1993. *Understanding an Afrocentric World View: An Introduction to Optimal Psychology.* Dubuque, IA: Kendall/Hunt.

Myers, Linda J., Suzette L. Speight, Pamela S. Highlen, Chikako I. Cox, Amy L. Reynolds, Eve M. Adams, and C. Patricia Hanley. 1991. "Identity Development and Worldview: Toward an Optimal Conceptualization." *Journal of Counseling and Development* 70: 54–63.

Nakanishi, Don T. 1993. "Asian Pacific Americans in Higher Education: Faculty and Administrative Representation and Tenure." *New Directions for Teaching and Learning* 53 (Spring): 51–59.

Namaste, Viviane Ki. 2000. *Invisible Lives: The Erasure of Transsexual and Transgendered People.* Ithaca, NY: Cornell University Press.

Narayan, Uma, and Sandra Harding, eds. 2000. *Decentering the Center: Philosophy for a Multicultural, Postcolonial, and Feminist World.* Bloomington: Indiana University Press.

National Association for Women in Catholic Higher Education. http://www.bc.edu/nawche. Cited June 11, 2002.

National Association of Collegiate Women Athletic Administrators. http://www.nacwaa.org. Cited June 11, 2002.

National Center for Education Statistics. 1995. *Digest of Education Statistics.* Washington, DC: U.S. Department of Education.

———. 1997a. *Characteristics of American Indian and Alaska Native Education.* NCES 97-451. Washington, DC: U.S. Department of Education.

———. 1997b. *Digest of Education Statistics.* Washington, DC: U.S. Department of Education.

———. 1997–1998. *Numbers of Employees in Institutions of Higher Education, Fall 1996.* Washington, DC: U.S. Department of Education.

———. 1999. *Digest of Education Statistics.* Washington, DC: U.S. Department of Education.

———. 2000a. *Statistical Analysis Report: 1993 National Study of Postsecondary Faculty.* NSOPF 93. Washington, DC: U.S. Department of Education.

———. 2000b. *Trends in Educational Equity of Girls and Women.* NCES 2000-030. Washington, DC: U.S. Department of Education.

———. 2001. *Digest of Education Statistics.* Washington, DC: U.S. Department of Education.

National Collegiate Athletic Association. http://www.ncaa.org. Cited April 30, 2001.

———. 1999. "Committee on Women's Athletics Seeks Quicker Solutions for Gender-Equity Issues." *NCAA News,* August 16.

National Consortium of Directors of Lesbian, Gay, Bisexual, and Transgender Resources in Higher Education. www.lgbtcampus.org. Cited June 15, 2002.

National Education Association. 1996. *NEA ESP Data Book: A Workforce and Membership Profile of Educational Support Personnel*. Washington, DC: National Education Association.

———. 1998. *NEA 1998 Almanac of Higher Education.* Washington, DC: National Education Association.

National Labor Relations Board v. Yeshiva University, 444 U.S. 672 (1979).

National Panhellenic Conference. http://www.npcwomen.org. Cited June 15, 2002.

National Science Foundation. 2000a. "Division of Science Resource Studies, Survey of Earned Doctorates." http://www.nsf.gov/sbe/srs/ssed/start/htm. Cited June 20, 2002.

———. 2000b. *Women, Minorities, and Persons With Disabilities in Science and Engineering.* NSF00–327. Arlington, VA: National Science Foundation.

"National Survey of Student Engagement." 2001. http://www.Indiana.edu/%7Ensse/acrobat/overview–2001.pdf. Cited June 12, 2002.

Nettles, Michael T., and Laura W. Perna. 1995. "Sex and Race Differences in Faculty Salaries, Tenure, Rank, and Productivity: Why, on Average, Do Women, African Americans, and Hispanics Have Lower Salaries, Tenure, and Rank?" Paper presented at the Annual Meeting of the Association for the Study of Higher Education, Orlando.

Nettles, Michael, Laura Perna, Ellen Bradburn, and Linda Zimbler. 2000. *Salary, Promotion, and Tenure Status of Minority and Women Faculty in U.S. Colleges and Universities.* Washington, DC: National Center for Educational Statistics, Office of Educational Research and Improvement. http://nces.ed.gov/pubs2000/2000173.pdf. Cited February 14, 2002.

"New Studies Look at Status of Former Welfare Recipients." 1998. *CDF Reports: Newsletter of the Children's Defense Fund* 19, nos. 4–5 (April–May): 4, 12–13.

Newcomer, Mabel. 1959. *A Century of Higher Education for American Women.* New York: Harper and Brothers.

Nichols, Joseph D., William G. Ludwin, and Peter Iadicola. 1999. "A Darker Shade of Gray: A Year-End Analysis of Discipline and Suspension Data."

Equity and Excellence in Education 32, no. 1: 43–55.

Nicklin, Julie. 2001. "Few Women Are Among Presidents with the Largest Compensation Packages." *Chronicle of Higher Education* 48, November 9: A30.

Nidiffer, Jana. 1995. "From Matron to Maven: A New Role and New Professional Identity for Deans of Women, 1892 to 1916." *Mid-Western Educational Researcher* 8, no. 4: 17–24.

———. 2000. *Pioneering Deans of Women: More Than Wise and Pious Matrons.* Athene Series. New York: Teachers College Press.

———. 2001. "New Leadership for a New Century: Women's Contribution to Leadership in Higher Education." Pp. 101–131 in *Women Administrators in Higher Education,* ed. Jana Nidiffer and Carolyn T. Bashaw. Albany: State University of New York Press.

Nidiffer, Jana, and Carolyn Terry Bashaw, eds. 2001. *Women Administrators in Higher Education: Historical and Contemporary Perspectives.* Albany: State University of New York Press.

Nieves-Squires, Sarah. 1993. "Hispanic Women: Making Their Presence on Campus Less Tenuous." Pp. 205–222 in *Women in Higher Education,* ed. Judith S. Glazer, Estela M. Bensimón, and Barbara K. Townsend. Needham Heights, MA: Ginn Press.

Noddings, Nel. 1984. *Caring: A Feminine Approach to Ethics and Moral Education.* Berkeley: University of California Press.

Noel, Lee, Randi Levitz, and Diana Saluri. 1995. *Increasing Student Retention: Effective Programs and Practices for Reducing the Dropout Rate.* San Francisco: Jossey-Bass.

Nora, Amaury, and Alberto F. Cabrera. 1996. "The Role of Perceptions of Prejudice and Discrimination on the Adjustment of Minority Students to College." *Journal of Higher Education* 67, no. 2: 119–148.

North Haven Board of Education v. Bell, 456 U.S. 512 (1982).

NOW Legal Defense and Education Fund, Mid-Atlantic Equity Consortium, and the Network. *An Annotated Summary of the Regulation for Title IX, Education Amendments of 1972.* http://www.maec.org/annotate.html. Cited June 5, 2002.

Nuss, Elizabeth M. 1996. "The Development of Student Affairs." Pp. 22–42 in *Student Services: A Handbook for the Profession,* ed. Susan R. Komives and Dudley B. Woodard, Jr. San Francisco: Jossey-Bass.

Nussbaum, Martha. 1997. *Cultivating Humanity: A Classical Defense of Reform in Liberal Education.* Cambridge, MA: Harvard University Press.

———. 2000. "Globalization Debate Ignores the Education of Women." *Chronicle of Higher Education,* September 8, B16–B17.

Nuwer, Hank. 1999. *Wrongs of Passage: Fraternities, Sororities, Hazing, and Binge Drinking.* Bloomington: Indiana University Press.

O'Brien, David J. 1994. *From the Heart of the American Church: Catholic Higher Education and American Culture.* Maryknoll, NY: Orbis Books.

Office of Civil Rights. "Investigator's Manual." http://www.ed.gov/offices/OCR. Cited April 19, 2001.

———. "Sexual Harassment Guidance: Harassment of Students by School Employees, Other Students, or Third Parties." 62 Fed. Reg, 12034, March 13, 1997. http://www.ed.gov/offices/OCR/docs/sexhar00.html as revised 21 January 2001. Cited February 22, 2001.

Olsen, Deborah. 1991. *Women and Minority Faculty Job Satisfaction: A Structural Model Examining the Effect of Professional Role Interests.* ASHE

Annual Meeting Paper. ERIC Document Reproduction Service no. ED 339 323.
Olsen, Deborah, Sue Maple, and Frances K. Stage. 1995. "Women and Minority Faculty Job Satisfaction: Professional Role Interests, Professional Satisfactions, and Institutional Fit." *Journal of Higher Education* 66, no. 3 (May–June): 267–293.
Olsen, Florence. 2000. "Institute for Women and Technology Works to Bridge the Other Digital Divide." *Chronicle of Higher Education,* February 25, A47.
O'Mara, Kathleen. 1997. "Historicizing Outsiders on Campus: The Re/production of Lesbian and Gay Insiders." *Journal of Gender Studies* 6, no. 1 (March): 17–32.
Ong, Paul. 1999. "Proposition 209 and Its Implications." P. 198 in *Impacts of Affirmative Action: Policies and Consequences in California,* ed. Paul Ong. Thousand Oaks, CA: Sage.
Opp, Ronald D., and Penny P. Gositti. 2000. "Promoting Equity for Women Administrators of Color." Paper presented at the Annual Meeting of the Association for the Study of Higher Education, Sacramento, CA.
Ortiz, Flora Ida. 1998. "Career Patterns of People of Color in Academia." Pp. 120–135 in *The Multicultural Campus: Strategies for Transforming Higher Education,* ed. Leonard A. Valverde and Louis A. Castenell, Jr. Walnut Creek, CA: Alta Mira/Sage.
Osajima, Keith. 2000. "Asian American as the Model Minority: An Analysis of the Popular Press Image in the 1960s and 1980s." Pp. 449–458 in *Contemporary Asian America: A Multidisciplinary Reader,* ed. Min Zhou and James V. Gatewood. New York: New York University Press.
Ost, David H., and Darla J. Twale 1989. "Appointments of Administrators in Higher Education: Reflections of Administrative and Organizational Structures." *Initiatives* 5, no. 2: 23–30.
Packard, Becky Wai-Ling, and E. David Wong. 1999. "Future Images and Women's Career Decisions in Science." Paper presented at the Annual Meeting of the American Education Research Association, Montreal, Canada. Dialog, ERIC, ED430805, April 19–23.
Padilla, Amado M. 1994. "Ethnic Minority Scholars, Research, Mentoring." *Educational Researcher* 3, no. 4: 24–27.
Padilla, Raymond V., and Rudolfo Chávez Chávez. 1995. *The Leaning Ivory Tower: Latino Professors in American Universities.* Albany: State University of New York.
Palloff, Rena M., and Keith Pratt. 1999. *Building Learning Communities in Cyberspace: Effective Strategies for the Online Classroom.* San Francisco: Jossey-Bass.
Palmer, Parker. 1998. *The Courage to Teach.* San Francisco: Jossey-Bass.
Paludi, Michele, and Gertrude A. Steuernagel, eds. 1990. *Foundations for a Feminist Restructuring of the Academic Disciplines.* New York: Hawthorne.
Pankhurst, Richard K. P. 1957. *The Saint Simonians: Mill and Carlyle: A Preface to Modern Thought.* London: Sidgwick and Jackson.
Park, Roberta J., and Joan Hult. 1993. "Women as Leaders in Physical Education and School-Based Sports, 1865 to the 1930's." *Journal of Physical Education, Recreation, and Dance* 64, no. 3: 35–40.
Park, Shelley M. 1994. "Am I Qualified? Gender Bias in University Tenure and Promotion Criteria." *Proceedings of the Seventh Annual International Conference on Women in Higher Education,* 329–332. El Paso: University of Texas at El Paso Press.
———. 1996. "Research, Teaching, and Service: Why Shouldn't Women's Work

Count?" *Journal of Higher Education* 67, no. 1: 46–84.

Parker, Marjorie H. 1990. *Alpha Kappa Alpha: Through the Years 1908–1988.* Chicago: Mobium Press.

Parrot, Andrea. 1991. "Recommendations for College Policies and Procedures to Deal with Acquaintance Rape." Pp. 368–380 in *Acquaintance Rape: The Hidden Crime,* ed. Andrea Parrot and Laurie Bechhofer. New York: Wiley.

Pascarella, Ernest T., and Patrick T. Terenzini. 1991. *How College Affects Students: Findings and Insights from Twenty Years of Research.* San Francisco: Jossey-Bass.

Patai, Daphne, and Noretta Koertge. 1994. *Professing Feminism.* New York: Basic Books.

Patel, Narendra H. 1988. *Student Transfers from White to Black Colleges.* Washington, DC: NAFEO Research Institute.

Pavel, D. Michael, Rebecca Rak Skinner, Elizabeth Farris, Margaret Calahan, John Tipeconnic, and Wayne Stein. 1998. *American Indians and Alaska Natives in Postsecondary Education,* NCES 98–291. Washington, DC: U.S. Department of Education.

Peacock, Thomas D., and Donald R. Day. 1999. "Teaching American Indian and Alaska Native Languages in the Schools: What Has Been Learned." *ERIC Digest* ED 438 155. http://www.ael.org/eric/digests.htm. Cited November 18, 2001.

Pearson, Barbara Z. 1993. "Predictive Validity of the Scholastic Aptitude Test (SAT) for Hispanic Bilingual Students." *Hispanic Journal of Behavioral Sciences* 15, no. 3: 342–356.

Pease, John. 1993. "Professor Mom: Women's Work in a Man's World." *Sociological Forum* 8, no. 1: 133–139.

Peery, Kaye L. 1998. "Hispanic Women in Leadership: A Multicase Study." Ph.D. diss., University of Nebraska, Lincoln.

Pellegrino, Karen A. 1999. "A Space of Their Own: Women in ACCU." *ACCU Current Issues in Catholic Higher Education* 19 (Spring): 53–62.

Peplau, Leticia Anne. 2001. "Rethinking Women's Sexual Orientation: An Interdisciplinary, Relationship-Focused Approach." *Personal Relationships* 8: 1–19.

Perna, Laura W. 2001a. "Sex and Race Differences in Faculty Tenure and Promotion." *Research in Higher Education* 42, no. 5 (October): 541–567.

———. 2001b. "The Relationship between Family Responsibilities and Employment Status and College and University Faculty." *Journal of Higher Education.*

———. 2001c. "Sex Differences in Faculty Salaries: A Cohort Analysis." *Review of Higher Education* 24, no. 3: 283–308.

Perry, William G. 1970. *Forms of Intellectual and Ethical Development in the College Years: A Schema.* Troy, MO: Holt, Rinehart & Winston.

Persell, Caroline Hodges. 1983. "Gender, Rewards and Research in Education." *Psychology of Women Quarterly* 8, no. 1: 33–47.

Pervin, Lawrence A. 1968a. "The College as a Social System: Student Perceptions of Students, Faculty, and Administration." *Journal of Educational Research* 61: 281–284.

———. 1968b. "Performance and Satisfaction as a Function of Individual-Environment Fit." *Psychological Bulletin* 69: 56–68.

Peterson, E. S., A. E. Crowley, J. Rosenthal, and R. Boerner. 1980. "Undergraduate Medical Education." *Journal of the American Medical Association* 244: 2810–2868.

Peterson, Marvin W., and Melinda G. Spencer. 1990. *Understanding Academic Culture and Climate.* New Directions for Institutional Research no. 68. San Francisco: Jossey-Bass.

Pfeffer, Jeffrey. 1977. "Toward an Examination of Stratification in Organizations." *Administrative Science Quarterly* 22: 553–567.

Pharr, Suzanne. 1998. "Homophobia as a Weapon of Sexism." Pp. 565–574 in *Race, Class, and Gender in the United States,* ed. Paula S. Rothenberg. 4th ed. New York: St. Martin's Press.

Phillippe, Kent A., ed. 2000. *National Profile of Community Colleges: Trends and Statistics.* 3rd ed. Washington, DC: Community College Press.

Pinar, William F., ed. 1998. *Queer Theory in Education.* Mataway, NJ: Lawrence Erlbaum.

Pisan, Christine de. 1982. *The Book of the City of Ladies.* Trans. Earl Jeffrey Richards. New York: Persea Books.

Plumwood, Val. 1997. "Androcentrism and Anthropocentrism: Parallels and Politics." Pp. 327–355 in *Ecofeminism: Women, Culture, and Nature,* ed. Karen J. Warren. Bloomington: Indiana University Press.

Poe, Kristen. 1998. "Blinded by the Results: Is Looking to GPA in Addition to Standardized Test Scores Truly a Less Discriminatory Solution to Merit Scholarship Selection?" *Women's Rights Law Reporter* 19 (Winter): 181–196.

Pomeroy, Wardell B. 1972. *Dr. Kinsey and the Institute for Sex Research.* New York: Harper and Row.

Ponce, Theta C. 1988. "Some Basic Considerations on the Role of Women in the Development of Science and Technology." Pp. 158–160 in *The Role of Women in the Development of Science and Technology in the Third World,* ed. Akhtar M. Faruqui, Mohamed H. A. Hassan, and Gabriella Sandri. Teaneck, NJ: World Scientific Publishing.

Posner, Barry Z., and Barbara Brodsky. 1994. "Leadership Practices of Effective Student Leaders: Gender Makes No Difference." *NASPA Journal* 31, no. 2: 113–120.

Poston, William S. C. 1990. "The Biracial Identity Development Model: A Needed Addition." *Journal of Counseling and Development* 69: 152–155.

Pratt v. Wheaton College, 40 Ill. 186 (1866).

Prichard, Craig, and Rosemary Deem. 1999. "Wo-Managing Further Education; Gender and the Construction of the Manager in the Corporate Colleges of England." *Gender and Education* 11, no. 3: 323–342.

Primus, Wendall. 2000. "Success of Welfare Reform Unclear." *News and Issues: Newsletter of the National Center for Children in Poverty* 10, no. 1 (Winter): 5–6.

Pritchard, Sarah M. 1990. *RLG Conspectus: Women's Studies.* Mountain View, CA: Research Libraries Group.

Rai, Kul B., and John W. Critzer. 2000. *Affirmative Action and the University: Race, Ethnicity, and Gender in Higher Education Employment.* Lincoln: University of Nebraska Press.

Ramey, Felicenne H. 1995. "Obstacles Faced by African American Women Administrators in Higher Education: How They Cope." *Western Journal of Black Studies* 19, no. 2: 113–119.

Randall, Kathleen P., Patricia Daugherty, and Elaine Globetti. 1995. "Women in Higher Education: Characteristics of Female Senior Student Affairs Officers." *College Student Affairs Journal* 14, no. 2: 17–23.

Ransom, Michael R., and Sharon Bernstein Megdal. 1993. "Sex Differences in the Academic Labor Market in the Affirmative Action Era." *Economics of Education Review* 12, no. 1: 21–43.

Ransom, Nancy A. 1988. "A Comparative History of Faculty Women at George Peabody College for Teachers and Vanderbilt University, 1875–1970."

Ph.D. diss., George Peabody College for Teachers of Vanderbilt University, Nashville, TN.

Rayman, Paula, and Belle Brett. 1995. "Women Science Majors: What Makes a Difference in Persistence After Graduation." *Journal of Higher Education* 66, no. 4: 388–414.

Raymond, Janice. 1986. *A Passion for Friends: Toward a Philosophy of Female Affection.* Boston: Beacon Press.

Regents of Univ. of California v. Bakke, 98 S. Ct. 2733 (1978).

Reilly, Mary Ellen, Bernice Lott, and Sheila M. Gallogy. 1986. "Sexual Harassment of University Students." *Sex Roles* 15: 333–358.

Reinharz, Shulamit. 1992. *Feminist Methods in Social Research.* New York: Oxford University Press.

Rendon, Laura. 1992. "From the Barrio to the Academy: Revelations of a Mexican American 'Scholarship Girl.'" *New Directions for Community Colleges* 80 (Winter).

Renn, Kristen A. 1998. "Patterns of Situational Identity among Biracial and Multiracial College Students." *Review of Higher Education* 23: 399–420.

Reuben, Elaine, and Leonore Hoffmann, eds. 1975. *"Unladylike and Unprofessional": Academic Women and Academic Unions.* New York: Modern Language Association of America, Commission on the Status of Women.

Reynolds, Amy L., and Raechelle L. Pope. 1991. "The Complexities of Diversity: Exploring Multiple Oppressions." *Journal of Counseling and Development* 70: 174–180.

Rhoades, Gary. 1998. *Managed Professionals: Unionized Faculty and Restructuring Academic Labor.* Albany: State University of New York Press.

Rhoades, Gary, and Christine Maitland. 1998. "The Hidden Campus Workforce: (De)Investing in Staff." Pp. 109–118 in *NEA 1998 Almanac of Higher Education.* Washington, DC: National Education Association.

Rhoads, Robert. 1998. *Freedom's Web: Student Activism in an Age of Cultural Diversity.* Baltimore: Johns Hopkins University Press.

Rhoads, Robert A., and Jeffery P. F. Howard, eds. 1998. *Academic Service Learning: A Pedagogy of Action and Reflection.* New Directions for Teaching and Learning no. 73. San Francisco: Jossey-Bass.

Rich, Adrienne. 1979. "Toward a Woman-Centered University." In *On Lies, Secrets and Silence: Selected Prose 1966–1978,* by Adrienne Rich. New York: W. W. Norton.

———. 1986. "Compulsory Heterosexuality and Lesbian Existence." Pp. 120–141 in *Feminist Frontiers II,* eds. Laurel Richardson and Verta Taylor. New York: McGraw-Hill.

Rifenbary, Deborah C. 1995. "Reentering the Academy: Voices of Returning Women Students." *Initiatives* 56, no. 4: 1–10.

Riger, Stephanie. 1991. "Gender Dilemmas in Sexual Harassment: Policies and Procedures." *American Psychologist* 46: 497–505.

Riger, Stephanie, Joseph P. Stokes, Sheela Raja, and Megan Sullivan. 1997. "Focus on Female Faculty: Measuring Perceptions of the Work Environment for Female Faculty." *The Review of Higher Education* 21, no. 1: 63–78.

Riggs, Matt L., Ronald G. Downey, Patricia E. Mcintyre, and Donald P. Hoyt. 1986. "Using Discriminant Analysis to Predict Faculty Rank." *Research in Higher Education* 25, no. 4: 365–376.

Riordan, Charles. 1994. "The Value of Attending a Women's College: Education, Occupation and Income Benefits." *Journal of Higher Education* 65: 486–510.

Ritterband, Paul, and Harold S. Wechsler. 1994. *Jewish Learning in American Universities: The First Century.* Bloomington: University of Indiana Press.

Robbins, Stephen P. 1998. *Organizational Behavior: Concepts, Controversies, Applications.* 8th ed. Upper Saddle River, NJ: Prentice-Hall.

Roebuck, Julian R., and Komanduri S. Murty. 1993. *Historically Black Colleges and Universities and Their Place in American Higher Education.* Westport, CT: Praeger.

Roiphe, Katie. 1993. *The Morning After: Sex, Fear and Feminism on Campus.* Boston: Little, Brown.

Rokeach, Mitton. 1973. *The Nature of Human Values.* New York: Free Press.

Romano, C. Renee. 1996. "A Qualitative Study of Women Student Leaders." *Journal of College Student Development* 37, no. 6: 676–683.

Romany, Celinda. 1997. "Ain't I a Feminist?" Pp. 19–26 in *Critical Race Feminism: A Reader,* ed. A. K. Wing. Albany: New York State University Press.

Root, Maria P. P. 1990. "Resolving 'Other' Status: Identity Development of Biracial Individuals." *Women and Therapy* 9: 185–205.

Ropers-Huilman, Becky. 1998. *Feminist Teaching in Theory and Practice: Situating Power and Knowledge in Poststructural Classrooms.* New York: Teachers College Press.

Rose, Suzanna. 2000. "Heterosexism and the Study of Women's Romantic and Friend Relationships." *Journal of Social Issues* 56: 315–328.

Rosen, Ruth. 2000. *The World Split Open: How the Modern Women's Movement Changed America.* New York: Viking.

Rosenberg, Rosalyn. 1982. *Beyond Separate Spheres: The Intellectual Roots of Modern Feminism.* New Haven, CT: Yale University Press.

Rosenfeld, Michael. 1991. *Affirmative Action and Justice: A Philosophical and Constitutional Inquiry.* New Haven, CT: Yale University Press.

Rosenfield, A. M. 2001. "The Online University." A lecture presented at the Franke Institute for the Humanities, February 12, 2001. Quoted in "Voices on the Quads." *University of Chicago Magazine* (April). http://www.alumni.uchicago.edu/magazine.

Rosovsky, Nitza. 1986. "The Jewish Experience at Harvard and Radcliffe: An Introduction to an Exhibition Presented by the Harvard Semitic Museum on the Occasion of Harvard's 350th Anniversary, September 1986." Cambridge: Harvard Semitic Museum, distributed by Harvard University Press.

Ross, Lawrence C. 2000. *The Divine Nine: The History of African American Fraternities and Sororities.* New York: Kensington Publishers.

Ross, Marlene, and Madeline F. Green. 2000. *The American College President: 2000 edition.* Washington, DC: American Council on Education.

Rosser, Sue. 1990. *Female-Friendly Science: Applying Women's Studies Methods and Theories to Attract Students.* New York: Pergamon Press.

Rosser, Sue V., and Bonnie Kelly. 1994. *Educating Women for Success in Science and Mathematics.* Columbia: Division of Women's Studies, University of South Carolina.

Rossi, Alice S., ed. 1988. *The Feminist Papers: From Adams to de Beauvoir.* Boston: Northeastern University Press.

Rossiter, Margaret W. 1982a. "Doctorates for American Women, 1868–1907." *History of Education Quarterly* 22, no. 2 (Summer): 159–183.

———. 1982b. *Women Scientists in America: Struggles and Strategies to 1940.* Baltimore: Johns Hopkins University Press.

———. 1997. "The Men Move In: Home Economics in Higher Education, 1950–1970." Pp. 96–117 in *Rethinking Home Economics: Women and the History of a Profession,* ed. Sarah Stage and Virginia B. Vincenti. Ithaca, NY: Cornell University Press.

Rousey, Ann Marie, and E. S. Longie. 2001. "The Tribal College as Family Support System." *American Behavioral Scientist* 44: 1492–1504.

Rowley, Daniel James, Herman D. Lujan, and Michael G. Dolence. 1998. *Strategic Choices for the Academy: How Demand for Lifelong Learning Will Re-Create Higher Education.* San Francisco: Jossey-Bass.

Rubin, Gayle. 1975. "The Traffic of Women: Notes on the Political Economy of Sex." Pp. 157–210 in *Toward an Anthropology of Women,* ed. Rayna R. Reiter. New York: Monthly Review Press.

Rudolph, Frederick. 1962. *The American College and University: A History.* Athens: University of Georgia Press.

———. 1977. *Curriculum: A History of the American Undergraduate Course of Study since 1636.* San Francisco: Jossey-Bass.

Ruscio, Kenneth P. 1987. "Many Sectors, Many Professionals," Pp. 331–368 in *The Academic Profession: National, Disciplinary, and Institutional Settings,* ed. Burton R. Clark. Berkeley: University of California Press.

Rutland, Peter. 1990. "Some Considerations Regarding Teaching Evaluations." *Political Science Teacher* 3: 1–2.

Ryan, Barbara. 1996. *The Women's Movement: References and Resources.* New York: G. K. Hall.

Rychlak, Joseph F. 1968. *A Philosophy of Science for Personality Theory.* Boston: Houghton Mifflin.

Sadker, Myra, and David Sadker. 1994. *Failing at Fairness: How America's Schools Cheat Girls.* New York: Touchstone.

Sagaria, Mary Ann D. 1991. "Administrative Promotion: The Structuring of Opportunity within a University." *Review of Higher Education* 15, no. 2: 191–211.

———. Forthcoming. "An Exploratory Model of Filtering in Administrative Searches: Toward Counter Hegemonic Discourses." *Journal of Higher Education.*

———, ed. 1988. *Empowering Women: Leadership Development Strategies on Campus.* Vol. 44. San Francisco: Jossey-Bass.

Sagaria, Mary Ann D., and Cynthia Dickens. 1990. "Thriving at Home: Developing a Career as an Insider." *New Directions for Higher Education* 18, no. 4: 19–28.

Sagaria, Mary Ann D., and Linda K. Johnsrud. 1987. "Many Are Candidates but Few Compete: The Impact of Internal Position Change of Administrative and Professional Staff on White Women and Minorities." Columbus: Ohio State University.

Sagaria, Mary Ann D., and Kathryn M. Moore. 1983. "Job Change and Age: The Experience of Administrators in Colleges and Universities." *Sociological Spectrum* 3: 353–370.

Sanderson, Allen R., Bernard Dugoni, Thomas Hoffer, and Sharon Myers. 1999. *Doctorate Recipients from United States Universities: Summary Report, 1998.* Chicago: National Opinion Research Center.

Sandler, Bernice R. 1986. *The Campus Climate Revisited: Chilly Climate for Women Faculty, Administrators, and Graduate Students.* Washington, DC: Association of American Colleges.

———. 1991. "Women Faculty at Work in the Classroom, or, Why It Still Hurts to Be a Women in Labor." *Communication Education* 40: 6–15.

———. 2000. "'Too Strong for a Woman'—The Five Words That Created Title IX." *Equality and Excellence in Education* (April): 9–13.

———. 2001. *Eighteen Ways to Warm Up the Chilly Climate.* http://www.Bernicesandler.Com/Id4.htm. Cited June 12, 2002.

Sandler, Bernice R., and Robert J. Shoop, 1997. *Sexual Harassment on Campus: A Guide for Administrators, Faculty, and Students.* Boston: Allyn and Bacon.

Sandler, Bernice R., L. Silverberg, and Roberta M. Hall. 1996. *The Chilly Classroom Climate: A Guide to Improve the Education of Women.* Washington, DC: National Association of Women in Education.

Sanlo, Ronni L. 1998. *Working with Lesbian, Gay, Bisexual, and Transgender College Students: A Handbook for Faculty and Administrators.* Westport, CT: Greenwood Press.

Sanlo, Ronni L., Susan R. Rankin, and Robert Schoenberg. 2002. *A Place of Our Own: LGBT Resource Centers on Campus.* Westport, CT: Greenwood Press.

Sapinsky, Ruth. 1981. "The Jewish Girl at College." Pp. 701–708 in *The American Jewish Woman: A Documentary History,* ed. Jacob R. Marcus. New York: KTAV Publishing House.

Satow, Roberta L. 1975. "Value-Rational Authority and Professional Organizations: Weber's Missing Type." *Administrative Science Quarterly* 20: 526–531.

Sax, Linda J. 1994. *The Dynamics of "Tokenism": How College Students Are Affected by the Proportion of Women in Their Major.* Ph.D. diss., University of California, Los Angeles.

Sax, Linda J., Alexander W. Astin, William S. Korn, and Shannon K. Gilmartin. 1999. *The American College Teacher: National Norms for the 1998–99 HERI Faculty Survey.* Los Angeles: Higher Education Research Institute, University of California.

Sax, Linda J., and M. L. Chun. 1991. "Differential Impacts of Ethnic Studies on Black and White College Students' Racial Attitudes: Evidence from a National Longitudinal Study." Paper presented at the Annual Meeting of the Association for the Study of Higher Education, Boston, MA.

Sayre, Anne. 1975. *Rosalind Franklin and DNA.* New York: W. W. Norton.

Scales, T. Laine. 2000. *All That Fits a Woman: Educating Southern Baptist Women for Charity and Mission, 1907–1926.* Macon, GA: Mercer University Press.

Scarborough, Lee R. 1939. *A Modern School of the Prophets.* Nashville, TN: Broadman Press.

Schiebinger, Linda. 1989. *The Mind Has No Sex: Women in the Origins of Modern Science.* Cambridge, MA: Harvard University Press.

Schier, Tracy, and Cynthia Russett, eds. 2002. *Catholic Colleges for Women in America.* Baltimore: Johns Hopkins University Press.

Schneider, Alison. 1998a. "More Professors are Working Part-time, and More Teach at Two-year Colleges." *Chronicle of Higher Education,* March 13, A14.

———. 1998b. "Why Don't Women Publish as Much as Men?" *Chronicle of Higher Education,* September 11, A14–A16.

———. 2000. "Support for a Rare Breed: Tenured Women Chemists." *Chronicle of Higher Education,* November 10, A12.

Schneider, Susan Weidman. 1985. *Jewish and Female: Choices and Changes in Our Lives Today.* New York: Simon and Schuster.

Schniedewind, Nancy. 1985. "Cooperatively Structured Learning:

Implications for Feminist Pedagogy." *Journal of Thought* 20 (Fall): 74–87.

Schniedewind, Nancy, and Frances Maher, eds. 1987, 1993. *Women's Studies Quarterly* 15, nos. 3–4, special issue on "Feminist Pedagogy." Reissued, with additions, in 1993, vol. 21, nos. 3–4.

Scholnick, Ellin K. 1998. "Paying Athena: Statistics, Statutes, and Strategies." Pp. 81–106 in *Career Strategies for Women in Academe: Arming Athena,* ed. Lynn H. Collins, Joan C. Chrisler, and Kathryn Quina. Thousand Oaks, CA: Sage.

Schultz, Theodore W. 1961. "Investment in Human Capital." *American Economic Review* 51, no. 1: 1–17.

Schuster, Marilyn, and Susan Van Dyne. 1985. *Women's Place in the Academy; Transforming the Liberal Arts Curriculum.* Totowa, NJ: Rowman and Allanheld.

Schwartz, Martin D., and Walter S. DeKeseredy. 1997. *Sexual Assault on the College Campus: The Role of Male Peer Support.* Thousand Oaks, CA: Sage.

Scott, Joan Wallach. 1996. *Only Paradoxes to Offer: French Feminists and the Rights of Man.* Cambridge, MA: Harvard University Press.

Secor, Cynthia. 1984. "Preparing the Individual for Institutional Leadership: The Summer Institute." Pp. 25–34 in *Women in Higher Education Administration,* ed. Adrian Tinsley, Cynthia Secor, and Sheila Kaplan. New Directions for Higher Education no. 45. San Francisco: Jossey-Bass.

Section 504 of the Rehabilitation Act of 1973, 29 U.S.C. § 794.

Selingo, J. 2002. "Bush Budget Will Seek Increases for Historically Black Colleges and Institutions with Many Hispanic Students." *Chronicle of Higher Education,* January 22. http://www.chronicle.com/daily/2002/01/2002012202n.htm. Cited June 20, 2002.

Seymour, Elaine. 1995. "The Loss of Women from Science, Mathematics, and Engineering Undergraduate Majors: An Explanatory Account." *Science Education* 79, no. 4: 437–473.

Seymour, Elaine, and Nancy M. Hewitt. 1994. *Talking about Leaving: Factors Contributing to High Attrition Rates among Science, Mathematics, and Engineering Majors.* Final Report to the Alfred P. Sloan Foundation on an Ethnographic Inquiry at Seven Institutions. Boulder: University of Colorado, Bureau of Sociological Research.

Shakeshaft, Charol. 1987. *Women in Educational Administration.* Newbury Park, CA: Sage.

Shapiro, J. P. 1992. "What is Feminist Assessment?" Pp. 29–37 in *Students at the Center: Feminist Assessment,* ed. Caryn M. Musil. Washington, DC: Association of American Colleges.

Sharif by Salahuddin v. New York State Department of Education, 709 F. Supp. 345, S.D.N.Y. (1989).

Shavlik, Donna, and Judy Touchton. 1984. "Toward a New Era of Leadership: The National Identification Program." Pp. 47–58 in *Women in Higher Education Administration,* ed. Adrian Tinsley, Cynthia Secor, and Sheila Kaplan. New Directions for Higher Education no. 45. San Francisco: Jossey-Bass.

Sherman, Julia. 1978. *Sex-Related Cognitive Differences: An Essay on Theory and Evidence.* Springfield, IL: Thomas.

Sherrill, Jan-Mitchell, and Craig A. Hardesty. 1994. *The Gay, Lesbian, and Bisexual Students' Guide to Colleges, Universities, and Graduate Schools.* New York: New York University Press.

Sherron, Gene T., and Judith V. Boettcher. 1997. *Distance Learning.* Boulder, CO: EDUCAUSE Publishing.

Shiarella, Ann H., Anne M. McCarthy, and Mary L. Tucker. 2000. "Development and Construct Validity of Scores on the Community Service Attitudes Scale." *Educational and Psychological Measurement* 60: 286–300.

Shiflett, Orvin Lee. 1981. *Origins of American Academic Librarianship.* Norwood, NJ: Ablex Publishing.

Shor, Ira. 1996. *When Students Have Power: Negotiating Authority in a Critical Pedagogy.* Chicago: University of Chicago Press.

Showalter, Elaine. 1977. *A Literature of Their Own: British Women Novelists from Bronte to Lessing.* Princeton, NJ: Princeton University Press.

Shryock, Richard H. 1966. "Sylvester Graham and the Popular Health Movement, 1830–1870." Pp. 111–125 in *Medicine in America: Historical Essays,* ed. Richard H. Shryock. Baltimore: Johns Hopkins University Press.

Shulman, James L., and William G. Bowen. 2001. *College Sports and Educational Values: The Game of Life.* Princeton, NJ: Princeton University Press.

Shulman, Shmuel, and Offer Kipnis. 2001. "Adolescent Romantic Relationships: A Look from the Future." *Journal of Adolescence* 24: 337–351.

Shults, Christopher. 2001. "The Critical Impact of Impending Retirements on Community College Leadership." Pp. 1–12 in *Leadership Series, no. 1.* Washington, DC: American Association of Community Colleges.

Sigma Gamma Rho, www.sgr1922.org. Cited June 12, 2002.

Sill, Elizabeth R. 1972. "Shall Women Go to College?" P. 169 in *Early Reform in Higher Education,* ed. David N. Portman. Chicago: Nelson-Hall.

Silva v. University of New Hampshire, 888 F. Supp. 292, D.N.H. (1994).

Simeone, Angela. 1987. *Academic Women: Working towards Equality.* South Hadley, MA: Bergin and Garvey Publishers.

Simon, Robin W., Donna Eder, and Cathy Evans. 1992. "The Development of Feeling Norms Underlying Romantic Love among Adolescent Females." *Social Psychology Quarterly* 55: 29–46.

Simpson, Jacqueline C. 2001. "Segregated by Subject: Racial Differences in the Factors Influencing Academic Major between European Americans, Asian Americans, and African, Hispanic, and Native Americans." *Journal of Higher Education* 72, no.1 (January–February): 63–100.

Singh, Kusum, Adriane Robinson, and Joyce Williams-Green. 1995. "Differences in Perceptions of African American Women and Men Faculty and Administrators." *Journal of Negro Education* 64, no. 4: 401–408.

Slaughter, Sheila. 1993. "Retrenchment in the 1980s: The Politics of Prestige and Gender." *Journal of Higher Education* 64, no. 3: 250–282.

Slaughter, Sheila, and Larry L. Leslie. 1994. "Entreprenurial Science and Intellectual Poverty in Australian Universities." Pp. 112–128 in *Academic Work: The Changing Labor Process in Higher Education,* ed. by John Smyth. Bristol, UK: Society for Research into Higher Education and Open University Press.

Sleeter, Christine E. 1993. "How White Teachers Construct Race." Pp. 157–171 in *Race Identity and Representation in Education,* ed. C. McCarthy and W. Crichlow. New York: Routledge.

Smart, John C. 1991. "Gender Equity in Academic Rank and Salary." *Review of Higher Education* 14, no. 4: 511–526.

Smith v. Virginia Commonwealth University, 856 F. Supp. 1088 (E.D. Va. 1994), rev'd, 62 F. 3d 659 (Fourth Circuit 1995), vacated, 1995 U.S. App. LEXIS 28831 (Fourth Circuit, 13 October 1995) (en banc), rev'd 84 F. 3d 672 (Fourth Circuit 1996).

Smolak, Linda, Sarah K. Murnen, and Anne E. Ruble. 2000. "Female Athletes and Eating Problems: A Meta-Analysis." *International Journal of Eating Disorders* 27: 371–380.

Society for Women Engineers. http://www.swe.org. Cited June 14, 2002.

Solberg, Winton. 1992. "Early Years of the Jewish Presence at the University of Illinois." *Religion and American Culture: A Journal of Interpretation* (Summer): 215–245.

Solomon, Barbara M. 1985. *In the Company of Educated Women: A History of Women and Higher Education in America.* New Haven, CT: Yale University Press.

Solomon, Lewis C., and Tamara L. Wingard. 1991. "The Changing Demographics: Problems and Opportunities." Pp. 19–42 in *The Racial Crisis in American Higher Education,* ed. Philip G. Altbach and Kofi Lomotey. Albany: State University of New York Press.

Solórzano, Daniel. 1995. "The Baccalaureate Origins of Chicana and Chicano Doctorates in the Social Sciences." *Hispanic Journal of Behavioral Sciences* 17: 3–32.

Solórzano, Daniel, and Dolores Delgado Bernal. 2000. "Critical Race Theory, Transformational Resistance, and Social Justice: Chicana and Chicano Students in an Urban Context." *Urban Education* 36, no. 3: 60–73.

Solórzano, Daniel, and Octovio Villalpando. 1998. "Critical Race Theory: Marginality and the Experience of Students of Color in Higher Education." Pp. 211–224 in *Sociology of Education: Emerging Perspectives,* ed. Carlos Torres and Theodore Mitchell. Albany: State University of New York Press.

Solórzano, Daniel, and Tara Yosso. 2001 "Critical Race and Latcrit Theory and Method: Counterstorytelling Chicana and Chicano Graduate School Experiences." *International Journal of Qualitative Studies in Education* 14: 371–395.

Sommers, Christina Hoff. 1994. *Who Stole Feminism?* New York: Simon and Schuster.

———. 2000. *The War against Boys: How Misguided Feminism Is Harming Our Young Men.* New York: Simon and Schuster.

Sorcinelli, Mary Dean. 1994. "Effective Approaches to New Faculty Development." *Journal of Counseling and Development* 72, no. 5: 474–479.

Southern Regional Education Board. 1996–1997. *SREB Factbook on Higher Education.* Atlanta: Southern Regional Education Board.

Spears, Betty. 1986. *Leading the Way: Amy Morris Homans and the Beginnings of Professional Education for Women.* New York: Greenwood Press.

Speizer, Jeanne J. 1984. "The Administrative Skills Program: What Have We Learned?" Pp. 35–46 in *Women in Higher Education Administration,* ed. Adrian Tinsley, Cynthia Secor, and Sheila Kaplan. New Directions for Higher Education no. 45. San Francisco: Jossey-Bass.

Spelman College. http://www.spelman.edu. Cited November 6, 2001.

Spelman, Elizabeth. 1988. *Inessential Woman: Problems of Exclusion in Feminist Thought.* Boston: Beacon Press.

Spender, Dale. 1980. *Man Made Language.* London: Routledge and Kegan Paul.

———. 1983. *Invisible Women: The Schooling Scandal.* London: Writers and Readers.

———. 1995. *Nattering on the Net: Women, Power and Cyberspace.* North Melbourne, Victoria, Australia: Spinifex Press.

Spickard, Paul R. 1997. "What Must I Be? Asian Americans and the Question of

Multiethnic Identity." *Amerasia Journal* 23: 43–60.

Spiro, Rand J., Richard L. Coulson, Paul J. Feltovich, and Daniel K. Anderson. 1988. "Cognitive Flexibility Theory. Advanced Knowledge Acquisition in Ill-Structured Domains." Pp. 375–383 in *Proceedings of the Annual Conference of the Cognitive Science Society.* Hillsdale, NJ: Lawrence Erlbaum.

St. Jean, Yanick, and Joe R. Feagin. 1998. *Double Burden: Black Women and Everyday Racism.* Armonk, NY: M. E. Sharpe.

Stafford, Beth, ed. 1990. *Directory of Women's Studies Programs and Library Resources.* Phoenix: Oryx Press.

Stage, Sarah, and Virginia B. Vincenti, eds. 1997. *Rethinking Home Economics: Women and the History of a Profession.* Ithaca, NY: Cornell University Press.

"'Stained Glass Ceiling' Challenges Women in Catholic Schools." 1994. *Women in Higher Education* 3, no. 8: 1–2.

Stalker, Jacqueline, and Susan Prentice, eds. 1998. *The Illusion of Inclusion: Women in Post-Secondary Education.* Halifax, NS: Fernwood Publishing.

Stanley, Liz, and Sue Wise, eds. 1983. *Breaking Out: Feminist Consciousness and Feminist Research.* Boston: Routledge and Kegan Paul.

Stanton, Elizabeth Cady. 1988. *Selections from* The History of Woman Suffrage. Pp. 415–421 in *The Feminist Papers: From Adams to de Beauvoir,* ed. Alice S. Rossi. Boston: Northeastern University Press.

Stark, Joan S., and Lisa R. Lattuca. 1997. *Shaping the College Curriculum: Academic Plans in Action.* Boston: Allyn and Bacon.

Starr, Paul. 1982. *The Social Transformation of American Medicine.* New York: Basic Books.

Statham, Anne, Laurel Richardson, and Judith A. Cook. 1991. *Gender and University Teaching: A Negotiated Difference.* Albany: State University of New York Press.

Stein, Wayne J. 1994. "The Survival of American Indian Faculty." *Thought and Action: The National Education Association Higher Educational Journal* 10: 101–114.

Stern, George G. 1964. "B=*f*(P,E)." *Journal of Personality Assessment* 28, no. 2: 161–168.

———. 1970. *People in Context: Measuring Person-Environment Congruence in Education and Industry.* New York: Wiley.

Stetson, Dorothy McBride. 1997. *Women's Rights in the U.S.A.: Policy Debates and Gender Roles.* 2nd ed. New York: Garland Publishing.

Stevenson, Richard W. 2000. "Fed Says Economy Increased New Worth of Most Families." *New York Times,* January 19, A1, C6.

Stewart, Kenneth D., Margaret M. Dalton, Geri A. Dino, and Steven P. Wilkinson. 1996. "The Development of Salary Goal Modeling: From Regression Analysis to a Value-Based Prescriptive Approach." *Journal of Higher Education* 67, no. 5: 555–576.

Stewart, Moira, Judith B. Brown, Wayne W. Weston, Ian R. McWhinney, Carol L. McWilliam, and Thomas R. Freeman. 1995. *Patient-Centered Medicine. Transforming the Clinical Method.* Thousand Oaks, CA: Sage.

Stiehm, Judith Hicks. 1981. *Bring Me Men and Women: Mandated Change in the U.S. Airforce Academy.* Berkeley: University of California Press.

Stiver, Suzanne, and Lynda Malik. 2000. "Trends in the Gender Gap in Higher Education." Pp. 446–452 in *Women in Higher Education: A Feminist Perspective,* ed. Judith Glazer-Raymo, Barbara K. Townsend, and Rebecca Ropers-Huilman. Boston: Pearson Custom Publishing.

Stonequist, Everett V. 1937. *The Marginal Man: A Study in Personality and Culture Conflict.* New York: Russell and Russell.

Strange, C. 1994. "Student Development: The Evolution and Status of an Essential Idea." *Journal of College Student Development* 35: 399–412.

Stromquist, Nellie P. 1991. *Daring to Be Different: The Choice of Nonconventional Fields of Study by International Women Students.* IIE Research Report 22. New York: Institute of International Education.

———. 1998. *Women in the Third World: An Encyclopedia of Contemporary Issues.* New York: Garland.

———, ed. 1992. *Women and Education in Latin America: Knowledge, Power and Change.* Boulder, CO: Lynne Rienner Publishers.

Sweeney, Eileen, Liz Schott, Ed Lazere, Shawn Fremstead, Heidi Goldberg, Jocelyn Guyer, David Super, and Clifford Johnsons. 2000. *Windows of Opportunity: Strategies to Support Families Receiving Welfare and Other Low-Income Families in the Next Stage of Welfare Reform.* Washington, DC: Center on Budget and Policy Priorities.

Swoboda, Marian J. 1993. "Hiring Women and Minorities." Pp. 123–136 in *The Art of Hiring in America's Colleges and Universities,* ed. Ronald H. Stein and Stephen J. Trachtenberg. Buffalo, NY: Prometheus Books.

Syverson, Peter D. 2001. "The New Majority CGS/GRE Survey Results Trace Growth of Women in Graduate Education." http://www.cgsnet.org/pdf/cctr706.pdf. Cited October 20, 2001.

Tack, Martha W., and Carol L. Patitu. 1992. *Faculty Job Satisfaction: Women and Minorities in Peril.* ASHE-ERIC Higher Education Report no. 5. Washington, DC: American Association for Higher Education.

Talburt, Susan. 2000. *Subject to Identity: Knowledge, Sexuality, and Academic Practices in Higher Education.* Albany: State University of New York Press.

Tannen, Deborah. 1990. *You Just Don't Understand: Women and Men in Conversation.* New York: William Morrow.

Tatro, Clayton N. 1995. "Gender Effects on Student Evaluations of Faculty." *Journal of Research and Development in Education* 2: 169–173.

Taxman v. Board of Education of Township of Piscataway, 91 F 3d 1547 (1996, Third Circuit).

Taylor, Jenifer. 1997. "Warming a Chilly Classroom." *ASEE Prism,* 29–33.

Thom, Mary. 2001. *Balancing the Equation: Where Are Women and Girls in Science, Engineering, and Technology?* New York: National Council for Research on Women.

Thrash, Patricia A. 1973. "The State of the Association." *Journal of NAWDAC* 37, no. 1: 43–48.

Tidball, Elizabeth, Daryl Smith, Charles Tidball, and Lisa Wolf-Wendel. 1999. *Taking Women Seriously: Lessons and Legacies for Higher Education from Women's Colleges.* Phoenix: AZ: ACE/Oryx Press.

Tierney, William G. 1993. *Building Communities of Difference: Higher Education in the Twenty-First Century.* Westport, CT: Bergin and Garvey.

———. 1997a. *Academic Outlaws: Queer Theory and Cultural Studies in the Academy.* Thousand Oaks, CA: Sage.

———. 1997b. "Organizational Socialization in Higher Education." *Journal of Higher Education* 68, no. 1: 1–16.

Tierney, William G., and Estella Mara Bensimón. 1996. *Promotion and Tenure: Community and Socialization in Academe.* Albany: State University of New York Press.

Tierney, William G., and Robert A. Rhoads. 1993. *Enhancing Promotion, Tenure and Beyond: Faculty Socialization as a Cultural Process.* ASHE-ERIC Higher Education Report no. 6. Washington, DC: George Washington University.

———. 1994. *Faculty Socialization as Cultural Process: A Mirror of Institutional Commitment.* ASHE-ERIC Higher Education Report no. 93-6. Washington, DC: George Washington University, School of Education and Human Development.

Till, Frank J. 1980. *Sexual Harassment: A Report on the Sexual Harassment of Students.* Report on the National Advisory Council on Women's Educational Programs. Washington, DC: U.S. Department of Education.

Tinker v. Des Moines Independent Community School District, 393 U.S. 503; 89 S. Ct. 733 (1969).

Tippeconnic, John W., III. 1998. *Attitudes Toward the Education of American Indians: A Survey.* Tempe: Center for Indian Education, Arizona State University, ERIC Document ED 312 114.

Tisdell, Elizabeth J. 1993. "Interlocking Systems of Power, Privilege, and Oppression in Adult Higher Education Classes." *Adult Education Quarterly* 43: 203–226.

Title VII of the Civil Rights Act of 1964, 42 U.S.C. § 2000d.

Title VIII: Department of Defense Appropriation Authorization Act, P. L. 94-106. 1975.

Title IX of the Educational Amendments of 1972, 20 U.S.C. § 1681 et seq.

Tong, Rosemarie Putnam. 1997. *Feminist Approaches to Bioethics: Theoretical Reflections and Practical Applications.* Boulder, CO: Westview Press.

———. 1998. *Feminist Thought: A More Comprehensive Introduction.* 2nd ed. Boulder, CO: Westview Press.

Toren, Nina. 2000. "The Subtle Ways of Differential Treatment." Pp. 73–76 in *Hurdles in the Halls of Science,* ed. Nina Toren. Lanham, MD: Lexington Books.

Touchton, Judith G., and Deborah Ingram. 1995. *Women Presidents in U.S. Colleges and Universities: A 1995 Higher Education Update.* ERIC Document Reproduction Service No. Ed 393 325. Washington, DC: American Council on Education.

Touchton, Judith G., and Lynne Davis. 1991. *Fact Book on Women in Higher Education.* New York: Macmillan.

Toutkoushian, Robert K. 1999. "The Status of Academic Women in the 1990s: No Longer Outsiders, But Not Yet Equals." *Quarterly Review of Economics and Finance* 39 (Special Issue): 679–698.

Townsend, Barbara K. 1995. "Women Community College Faculty: On the Margins or in the Mainstream?" Pp. 39–46 in *Gender and Power in the Community College,* ed. B. Townsend. New Directions for Community Colleges no. 89. San Francisco: Jossey-Bass.

———, ed. 1995. *Gender and Power in the Community College.* New Directions for Community Colleges no. 89. San Francisco: Jossey-Bass.

Trudeau, Kimberlee J., and Ann S. Devlin. 1996. "College Students and Community Service: Who, with Whom, and Why?" *Journal of Applied Social Psychology* 26: 1867–1888.

Truth, Sojourner. 1998. "Ain't I a Woman." Pp. 520–521 in *Issues in Feminism: An Introduction to Women's Studies,* ed. Sheila Ruth. Mountainview, CA: Mayfield Publishing.

Tuckman, Howard P. 1979. "The Academic Reward Structure in American Higher Education." Pp. 165–190 in *Academic Rewards in Higher Education,* ed. Darrell R. Lewis and William E. Becker. Cambridge, MA: Ballinger Publishing.

Turkle, Sherry. 1995. *Life on the Screen: Identity in the Age of the Internet.* New York: Simon and Schuster.

Turner, Caroline Sotello Viernes, and R. J. Thompson. 1993. "Socializing Women Doctoral Students: Minority and Majority Experiences." *Review of Higher Education* 16, no. 3: 355–370.

Turner, Caroline Sotello Viernes, and Samuel L. Myers, Jr. 2000. *Faculty of Color in Academe: Bittersweet Success.* Boston: Allyn and Bacon.

Turner, Caroline Sotello Viernes, Samuel L. Myers, Jr., and John W. Creswell. 1999. "Exploring Underrepresentation: The Case of Faculty of Color in the Midwest." *Journal of Higher Education* 70, no. 1: 27–59.

Tuttle, Kathryn Nemeth. 1996. "What Became of the Dean of Women? Changing Roles for Women Administrators in American Higher Education, 1940–1980." Ph.D. diss., University of Kansas.

Twale, Darla J., and David M. Shannon. 1996. "Gender Differences among Faculty in Campus Governance: Nature of Involvement, Satisfaction, and Power." *Initiatives* 57, no. 4: 11–19.

Twombly, Susan B. 1993. "What We Know about Women in Community Colleges." *Journal of Higher Education* 64, no. 2: 186–210.

———. 1995. "Gendered Images of Community College Leadership: What Messages They Send." Pp. 67–77 in *Gender and Power in the Community College,* ed. Barbara K. Townsend. New Directions for Community Colleges no. 89. San Francisco: Jossey-Bass.

———. 2000. "Women Academic Leaders in a Latin American University: Reconciling the Paradoxes of Professional Lives." Pp. 453–471 in *Women in Higher Education: A Feminist Perspective,* ed. Judith Glazer-Raymo, Barbara K. Townsend, and Rebecca Ropers-Huilman. Boston: Pearson Custom Publishing.

Twomey Fosnot, Catherine, ed. 1996. *Constructivism: Theory, Perspectives, and Practice.* New York: Teachers College Press.

Tyrkus, Michael J., ed. 1997. *Gay and Lesbian Biography.* Detroit: St. James Press.

"UC Hiring Fewer Professors after Prop. 209." 2001. *Black Issues in Higher Education* (March).

United Nations. 1997. *The World Conferences: Developing Priorities for the Twenty-First Century.* UN Briefing Papers series, New York.

United Nations General Assembly. 1977. *United Nations Declaration of Women's Rights,* Resolution 2263 (XXII), November 7, 1977. Pp. 397–402 in *History of Ideas on Women: A Source Book,* ed. Rosemary Agonito. New York: G. P. Putnam's Sons.

United States v. Commonwealth of Virginia, 116 Sup. Ct. 2264 (1996).

United States v. Fordice, 1125 S. Ct. 2727 (1992).

University of Arizona. 2001. *Millennium Project Enhancing Campus Climate for Academic Excellence: Phase 1, Faculty.* Tucson: University of Arizona Press.

U.S. Bureau of the Census. 1988. *Population Survey: Selected Characteristics of Households.* Washington, DC: U.S. Government Printing Office.

———. 2001. "Census 2000." http://www.census. gov/publications/cen2000. Cited June 11, 2002.

U.S. Department of Education, Office of Civil Rights. 1997. *Title IX: Twenty-five Years of Progress.* http://www.ed.gov/pubs/TitleIX/title.html. Cited June 15, 2002.

———. 1999. *Impact of the Civil Rights Laws.* http://www.ed.gov/offices/OCR/docs/impact.html. Cited June 15, 2002.

———. Athletic Equity Resources. http://www.ed.gov/offices/OCR/athleticresources.html. Cited June 10, 2002.

———. *Case Resolution Manual.* http://www.ed.gov/offices/OCR/docs/ocrcrm.html. Cited June 15, 2002.

———. *How to File a Discrimination Complaint with the Office of Civil Rights.* http://www.ed.gov/offices/OCR/docs/howto.html. Cited June 15, 2002.

———. *Nondiscrimination in Employment Practices in Education.* http://www.ed.gov/offices/OCR/doc/hq53e8.html. Cited June 15, 2002.

———. "Title IX of the Education Amendments of 1972: Policy Interpretation—Title IX Intercollegiate Athletics." 44 Fed. Reg. 71413, December 11, 1979. http://www.ed.gov/offices/OCR/docs/t9interp.html. Cited June 20, 2002.

U.S. Department of Education, Web-Based Education Commission. 2000. *The Power of the Internet for Learning: Moving from Promise to Practice.* http://www.hpcnet.org/webcommission. Cited June 10, 2002.

U.S. Department of Health and Human Services. 1996. *Indicators of Welfare Dependence and Well-Being.* Interim Report to Congress. Washington, DC: Government Printing Office, October, V-2.

U.S. Department of Health, Education and Welfare, Office of Civil Rights. 1975. "Final Title IX Regulation Implementing Educational Amendment of 1972." *Federal Register* 40, no. 108: 901A, June 4.

U.S. Department of Justice. 1990. "Americans with Disabilities Act of 1990." http://www.usdoj.gov/crt/ada/statute.htm. Cited June 12, 2002.

———. 1998. "Title VII Legal Manual." http://www.usdoj.gov/crt/grants_statutes/legalman.htm. Cited June 18, 2002.

U.S. Department of Labor. "Section 504, Rehabilitation Act of 1973." http://www.dol.gov/oasam/regs/statutes/sec504.htm. Cited June 12, 2002.

U.S. Equal Opportunity Commission. 1988. "EEO-6 Higher Education Staff Information Surveys, 1985." Pp. 33–34 in *Minorities in Higher Education: Seventh Annual Status Report.* Washington, DC: American Council on Education.

Urofsky, Melvin I., and Paul Finkerman. 2002. *A March of Liberty: A Constitutional History of the United States.* Vol. 2, *From 1877 to the Present.* 2nd ed. New York: Oxford University Press.

Valian, Virginia. 2000. *Why So Slow?: The Advancement of Women.* Boston: MIT Press.

Van Ast, John. 1999. "Community College Faculty: Making the Paradigm Shift." *Community College Journal of Research and Practice* 23, no. 6: 559–580.

Van Maanen, John. 1976. "Breaking In: Socialization to Work." Pp. 67–130 in *Handbook of Work, Organization, and Society,* ed. Robert Dubin. Chicago: Rand McNally.

Varson, Alex. "The 18–23 Year Old Population." Washington, DC: U.S. Census Bureau. http://www.census.gov/mso/www/pres_lib/dod99/sld022.htm. Cited June 24, 2002.

Verbrugge, Martha H. 1988. *Able-Bodied Womanhood: Personal Health and Social Change in Nineteenth-Century Boston.* New York: Oxford University Press.

Vigil-Laden, Berta. 2001. *Deconstructing Hispanic-Serving Institutions: Is Their Role and Function Unique within Higher Education?* Paper presented at the Annual Meeting of the Association for the Study of Higher Education. Richmond, VA, November.

Wachtel, Howard K. 1998. "Student Evaluation of College Teaching Effectiveness: A Brief Review." *Assessment and Evaluation in Higher Education* 23, no. 2: 191–212.

Waddell, Donna L., Barbara A. Tronsgard, Ann Smith, and Gill Smith. 1999. "An Evaluation of International Nursing Education Using Interactive Desktop Videoconferencing." *Computers in Nursing* 17 (July): 186–192.

Wagoner, Jennings L., and Samuel E. Kellams. 1992. "Professoriate: History and Status." Pp. 1674–1686 in *The Encyclopedia of Higher Education.* Vol. 3, *Analytical Perspectives,* ed. B. R. Clark and G. R. Neave. New York: Pergamon Press.

Walker, Melanie. 1997. "Simply Not Good Chaps: Unraveling Gender Equity in a South African University." Pp. 41–59 in *Feminist Critical Policy Analysis: A Perspective from Post-Secondary Education,* ed. Catherine Marshall. Washington DC: Falmer Press.

Wallace, Kendra R. 2001. *Relative/Outsider: The Art and Politics of Identity among Mixed Heritage Students.* Westport, CT: Ablex Publishing.

Walsh, Mary Roth. 1977. *Doctors Wanted: No Women Need Apply.* New Haven, CT: Yale University Press.

Walsh, W. Bruce. 1978. "Person/ Environment Interaction." Pp. 6–16 in *Campus Ecology: A Perspective for Student Affairs,* ed. J. Banning. Cincinnati: National Association of Student Personnel Administrators.

Wanous, John P. 1992. *Organizational Entry: Recruitment, Selection, Orientation, and Socialization of Newcomers.* Reading, MA: Addison-Wesley.

Warren, Karen. 1994. "The Power and Promise of Ecological Feminism." Pp. 124–134 in *Environmental Ethics: Readings in Theory and Application,* ed. Louis P. Pojman. Boston: Jones and Bartlett.

Warshaw, Robin. 1988. *I Never Called it Rape: The* Ms. *Report on Recognizing, Fighting, and Surviving Date Rape and Acquaintance Rape.* New York: Harper and Row.

Washington, Valora, and William Harvey. 1989. *Affirmative Rhetoric, Negative Action: African-American and Hispanic Faculty at Predominantly White Institutions.* Report no. 2. Washington, DC: School of Education and Human Development, George Washington University.

Waterman, Alan S. 1997. "Student Characteristics in Service-Learning." Pp. 95–106 in *Service-Learning: Applications from the Research,* ed. Alan S. Waterman. Mahwah, NJ: Lawrence Erlbaum.

We Advocate Gender Equity. http://www.wage.org/. Cited March 3, 2002.

Wechsler, Harold S. 1977. *The Qualified Student: A History of Selective College Admissions in America.* New York: John Wiley and Sons.

Weiler, Kathleen. 1991. "Freire and a Feminist Pedagogy of Difference." *Harvard Educational Review* 61 (November): 449–474.

Weiler, William C. 1990. "Integrating Rank Differences into a Model of Male-Female Faculty Salary Discrimination." *Quarterly Review of Economics and Business* 30, no. 1: 3–15.

Weinstein, Michael M. 1999. "When Work Is Not Enough." *New York Times,* August 26, C6.

Welch, Lynn B., ed. 1990. *Women in Higher Education: Changes and Challenges.* New York: Praeger.

Welfare Reform and Higher Education. Fact Sheet. Washington, DC: One Dupont Circle Coalition, 2.

Wenniger, Mary Dee. 1998. *Women in Higher Education, 1998.* Madison, WI: Wenniger.

West, S. Martha. 1995. "Frozen in Time." *Academe* 81: 26–29.

Westbrook, Lynn. 1999. *Interdisciplinary Information Seeking in Women's Studies.* Jefferson, NC: McFarland.

White House Initiative on Historically Black Colleges and Universities. 2002. http://www.ed.gov/OPE/hbcu. Cited June 13, 2002.

Whitley, B. E., Jr., C. M. McHugh, and I. H. Frieze. 1986. "Assessing the Theoretical Models for Sex Differences in Causal Attributions for Success and Failure." Pp. 102–135 in *The Psychology of Gender. Advances through Meta-Analysis,* eds. Janet Shibley Hyde and Marcia C. Linn. Baltimore: Johns Hopkins University Press.

Whitt, Elizabeth J. 1991. "Hit the Ground Running: Experiences of New Faculty in a School of Education." *Review of Higher Education* 14 (Winter): 177–198.

———. 1994. "'I Can Be Anything!': Student Leadership in Three Women's Colleges." *Journal of College Student Development* 35, no 3: 198–207.

Whitt, Elizabeth J., M. I. Edison, Ernest T. Pascarella, Amaury Nora, and Patrick T. Terenzini. 1999. "Women's Perceptions of a 'Chilly Climate' and Cognitive Outcomes in College: Additional Evidence." *Journal of College Student Development* 40, no. 2: 163–177.

Wichroski, Mary Anne. 1994. "The Secretary: Invisible Labor in the Workworld of Women." *Human Organization* 53, no. 1: 33–41.

Wilds, Deborah J. 2000. *Minorities in Higher Education, 1999–2000.* Washington, DC: American Council on Education.

Willdorf, Nina. 2000. "Minority Law Professors Said to Need Mentors." *Chronicle of Higher Education,* January 21, A18.

Williams, Joan. 1999. *Unbending Gender: Why Family and Work Conflict and What to Do About It.* New York: Oxford University Press.

Williams, John B. *Race Discrimination in Public Higher Education: Interpreting Federal Civil Rights Enforcement, 1964–1996.* Westport, CT: Praeger, 1997.

Williams, Patricia J. 1996. "Talking about Race, Talking about Gender, Talking about How We Talk." Pp. 69–94 in *Anti-Feminism in the Academy,* ed. Veve Clark, Shirley Nelson Garner, Margaret Higonnet, and Ketu H. Katrak. New York: Routledge.

Wilson, John Silvanus, Jr. 1993. "The Campus Racial Climate and the Demographic Imperative." Pp. 85–109 in *Opening the American Mind,* ed. Geoffrey M. Sill, Miriam T. Chaplin, Jean Ritzke, and David Wilson. Newark: University of Delaware Press.

Wilson, Robin. 1996. "More Couples in Academe Make Career Sacrifices to Be Together." *Chronicle of Higher Education,* September 20.

———. 1998. "For Some Adjunct Faculty Members, the Tenure Track Holds Little Appeal." *Chronicle of Higher Education* (July): A9–A10.

Wilson, Robin, and Sara E. Melendez. 1988. "Strategies for Developing Minority Leadership." Pp. 118–136 in *Leaders for a New Era: Series for Higher Education,* ed. Madeleine F. Green. New York: Collier Macmillan.

Wilt, Judith. 1992. "Ubiquitous, Lost, Found: A Study of Catholic Identities." *Initiatives* 54, no. 4: 1–7.

Wing, Adrien K., ed. 1997. *Critical Race Feminism: A Reader.* New York: New York University Press.

Wisconsin Commission on the Status of Women. 1999. "Equality for Women in the UW System: A Focus for Action in the Year 2000." Madison: University of Wisconsin Press.

Witt, Allen A., James L. Wattenbarger, James F. Gollattscheck, and Joseph E. Suppiger. 1994. *America's Community*

Colleges: The First Century. Washington, DC: Community College Press.

Wolff, Paula. 2001a. "Part-Time Students in Academe." *Chronicle of Higher Education,* March 16, B20.

———. 2001b. "Very Part Time Students Are Hobbled by Very Little Financial Aid." *Chronicle of Higher Education,* March 16, B20.

Wolf-Wendel, Lisa E. 1998. "Models of Excellence: The Baccalaureate Origins of Successful African American, European American and Hispanic Women." *Journal of Higher Education* 69, no. 2: 144–172.

Wolf-Wendel, Lisa, and Sheila Pedigo. 1999. "Two-Year Women's Colleges: Silenced, Fading, and Almost Forgotten." Pp. 43–112 in *Two-Year Colleges for Women and Minorities,* ed. Barbara K. Townsend. New York: Falmer Press.

Wolf-Wendel, Lisa E., Susan Twombly, and Suzanne Rice. 2000. "Dual-Career Couples: Keeping Them Together." *Journal of Higher Education* 71, no. 3: 291–321.

Wollstonecraft, Mary. 1988. *A Vindication of the Rights of Woman.* Pp. 40–85 in *The Feminist Papers: From Adams to de Beauvoir,* ed. Alice S. Rossi. Boston: Northeastern University Press.

Women in Engineering Programs and Advocates Networks. http://www.wepan.org. Cited June 14, 2002.

Women Library Workers. *WLW Journal,* 1980–1994.

Women's Development Institute. 1995. *Who Gets Welfare in Maine? A Survey of AFDC Families.* Hallowell, ME: Women's Development Institute.

Women's Information Services and Networks: A Global Source Book. 1999. Amsterdam: Royal Tropical Institute.

Women's Voices 2000: The Most Comprehensive Polling and Research Project on Women's Values and Policy Priorities for the Economy. 2000. Washington, DC: Center for Policy Alternative.

Woo, Deborah. 2000. *Glass Ceilings and Asian Americans: The New Face of Workplace Barriers.* Walnut Creek, CA: Altamira Press.

Wood, Richard J., and Katina Strauch, eds. 1992. *Collection Assessment: A Look at the RLG Conspectus.* New York: Haworth Press.

Woods, Rochelle L. 2001. "Invisible Women: The Experiences of Black Female Doctoral Students at the University of Michigan." Pp. 105–115 in *Sisters of the Academy: Emergent Black Women Scholars in Higher Education,* ed. Reitumetse O. Mabokela and Anna L. Green. Sterling, VA: Stylus Publishing.

Woods v. Simpson, 146 Md. 547, 126 A. 882 (1924).

Woody, Thomas. 1929. *A History of Women's Education in the United States.* New York: Science Press.

Woolf, Virginia. 1929. *A Room of One's Own.* New York: Fountain Press.

Wright, Esther. 1996. *Torn Togas: The Dark Side of Campus Greek Life.* Minneapolis: Fairview Press.

Wu, Diana Ting Liu. 1997. *Asian Pacific Americans in the Workplace.* Walnut Creek, CA: Altamira Press.

Wyer, Mary, Mary Barbercheck, Donna Geisman, Hatice Örün Öztürk, and Marta Wayne, eds. 2001. *Women in Science and Technology: A Reader in Feminist Studies.* New York: Routledge.

Yellow Bird, Doreen. 1999. "Turtle Mountain Faculty Helps Build Model Assessment Tool." *Tribal College Journal* 10, no. 2: 10–15.

Youn, Ted I. K. 1992. "The Sociology of Academic Careers and Academic Labor Markets." *Research in Labor Economics* 13: 101–130.

Zemsky, Beth. 1996. "GLBT Program Offices: A Room of Our Own." Pp.

208–214 in *The New Lesbian Studies: Into the Twenty-First Century,* ed. Bonnie Zimmerman and Toni A. H. McNaron. New York: The Feminist Press.

Zeta Phi Beta. www.zpb1920.org. Cited June 12, 2002.

Zimbler, Linda J. 1994. "Faculty and Instructional Staff: Who Are They and What Do They Do?" Washington, DC: American Council on Education Research Briefs 4: 1, 6.

Zimmerman, Bonnie, and Toni A. H. McNaron, eds. 1996. *The New Lesbian Studies: Into the Twenty-First Century.* New York: The Feminist Press.

Zlotkowski, Edward. 1998. *Successful Service-Learning Programs: New Models of Excellence in Higher Education.* Bolton, MA: Anker.

Zoe, Lucinda, and Beth Hillman Johnson. 1998. *Collective Bargaining in Higher Education and the Professions. Bibliography Nos. 23–25, January 1995–1997.* New York: National Center for the Study of Collective Bargaining in Higher Education and the Professions.

Zook, Jim. 1992. "Court Defines How VMI Could Remain All Male." *Chronicle of Higher Education,* October 14, A22.

Zubritsky, Elizabeth. 2000. "Women in Analytical Chemistry Speak." *Analytical Chemistry* 72 (April): 272A–281A.

Index

About the Editors

Ana M. Martínez Alemán is assistant professor of education at the Lynch School of Education at Boston College. Her scholarship includes the theoretical and empirical examination of the impact of gender, race, and ethnicity on U.S. higher education.

Kristen A. Renn is assistant professor of higher, adult, and lifelong education at Michigan State University. Her research activities focus on the construction of identities in higher education in the United States, and on qualitative research methods.